Undeclared Wars with Israel

Undeclared Wars with Israel examines a spectrum of antagonism by the East German government and West German radical leftist organizations, ranging from hostile propaganda and diplomacy to military support for Israel's Arab armed adversaries from 1967 to the end of the Cold War in 1989. This period encompasses the Six Day War (1967), the Yom Kippur War (1973), Israel's invasion of Lebanon in 1982, and an ongoing campaign of terrorism waged by the Palestine Liberation Organization against Israeli civilians. This book provides new insights into the West German radicals who collaborated in "actions" with Palestinian terrorist groups and confirms that East Germany, along with others in the Soviet bloc, had a much greater impact on the conflict in the Middle East than has been generally known. A historian who has written extensively on Nazi Germany and the Holocaust, Jeffrey Herf now offers a new chapter in this long, sad history.

Jeffrey Herf is a Distinguished University Professor in the Department of History at the University of Maryland, College Park. His publications on modern German history include *Reactionary Modernism: Technology, Culture and Politics in Weimar and the Third Reich* (Cambridge University Press, 1984); *Divided Memory: The Nazi Past in the Two Germanys* (1997), winner of the American Historical Association's George Lewis Beer Prize; *The Jewish Enemy: Nazi Propaganda during World War II and the Holocaust* (2006), winner of the National Jewish Book Award; and *Nazi Propaganda for the Arab World* (2009), winner of the biannual Sybil Halpern Milton Prize of the German Studies Association in 2011 for work on Nazi Germany and the Holocaust. He has also published essays and reviews on history and politics in *Partisan Review*, the *New Republic*, the *Times of Israel*, and the *American Interest*.

Undeclared Wars with Israel

East Germany and the West German Far Left, 1967–1989

JEFFREY HERF
University of Maryland, College Park

CAMBRIDGE
UNIVERSITY PRESS

32 Avenue of the Americas, New York NY 10013-2473, USA

Cambridge University Press is part of the University of Cambridge.

It furthers the University's mission by disseminating knowledge in the pursuit of education, learning and research at the highest international levels of excellence.

www.cambridge.org
Information on this title: www.cambridge.org/9781107461628

First published 2016

Printed in the United Kingdom by Clays, St Ives plc

A catalog record for this publication is available from the British Library.

Library of Congress Cataloging in Publication Data
Herf, Jeffrey, author.
Undeclared wars with Israel : East Germany and the West German far left, 1967–1989 / Jeffrey Herf, University of Maryland, College Park.
New York : Cambridge University Press, [2016]
Includes bibliographical references and index.
LCCN 2016010901 | ISBN 9781107089860 (hardback) |
ISBN 9781107461628 (paperback)
Israel – Foreign public opinion, German. | Germany (East) – Politics and government. | Germany (West) – Politics and government – 1945–1990. | New Left – Germany (West) – History. | Public opinion – Germany. | Political culture – Germany – History – 20th century. | Arab-Israeli conflict – Influence.
LCC DS119.8.G4 H47 2016 | DDC 956.04–dc23
LC record available at http://lccn.loc.gov/2016010901

ISBN 978-1-107-08986-0 Hardback
ISBN 978-1-107-46162-8 Paperback

In memory of
Fouad Ajami (1945–2014), Francois Furet (1927–1997)
and Robert Wistrich (1945–2015)

The publication of this book has been supported in part through the generosity of the Division of Research of the University of Maryland, College Park, and by the Virginia Holocaust Museum in Richmond.

Contents

Preface

I began work on this book in spring 2011 in Maryland. Yet it had its actual beginnings in the academic year of 1978–1979 when I lived in Frankfurt/Main, West Germany while doing research for my doctoral dissertation. I heard stories about two members of the Frankfurt leftist scene who had wound up in Entebbe pointing machine guns at unarmed Jews – before Israeli paratroopers arrived to free the hostages and kill the terrorists in a firefight. Why were West German radicals doing that? Why were the East German Communists, who had fought the Nazis and celebrated their anti-fascist traditions, giving aid to Israel's enemies and embracing Yasser Arafat on the front pages of their government controlled press? As I delved more deeply into the project, my interest in why these Germans acted as they did continued but gradually gave way to a historian's desire to establish that these, to my mind, unexpected events actually took place. So this became a book about both political passions as well as a multitude of details about weapons of war and terror and political warfare. It became a book about the anti-Israeli passion in Germany as well as about the resistance to it waged by the government of Israel, Jewish leaders in West Germany, by some political and public figures in West Germany and by the United States government. Historians know that facts do not speak for themselves. They must first be found, selected and interpreted. I hope the reader will agree that the following pages shed light on a subject as heated as any of modern history.

Acknowledgments

With pleasure I acknowledge the people and institutions that supported the research and writing of this book.

My thanks to the Department of History and the Graduate School at the University of Maryland, College Park for a Research and Scholarship Award (RASA) that made it possible to devote my full time to this project in spring semester of 2012. Thanks are due as well to Dr. Sebastian Fohrbeck, director of New York office of the German Academic Exchange Service (DAAD), and to the DAAD in Bonn for their support for a German Academic Exchange Service "Re-invitation" Fellowship for research in Germany in spring 2012. It is fitting that this "re-invitation" was devoted to this project as my interest in some of the issues it raises began in 1978–1979 when I had a DAAD dissertation fellowship in Frankfurt/Main. My thanks to Daniel Pipes and the Middle East Forum, for a Research Fellowship that made it possible to fund a one-course release in the spring semester of 2014 and to Professor Philip Soergel, the chair of our History Department, for facilitating this arrangement.

I am pleased to express my thanks to the following archivists, without whose expertise, knowledge of the files and helpful replies to many questions in person and via email the archival research for this book could not have been done: Christiane Stegemann in the Berlin offices of the Federal Commissioner for the Files of the Security Services of the Former German Democratic Republic; Dr. Johannes Freiherr von Böselager of the Political Archive of the German Foreign Office in Berlin; Susanne Meinicke of the German Federal Archive-Military Archive in Freiburg; Kersten Schenke and Lars Amelung, of the German Federal Archive in Koblenz, and Martina Caspers, of the photo archive of the German

Federal Archive in Koblenz; the staff of the German Federal Archive in Berlin-Lichterfelde; Dr. Reinhart Schwarz, director of the Archive of the Hamburg Institute for Social Research; Dr. Alon Tauber, of the Central Archiv for Research on the History of Jews in Germany in Heidelberg; David Langbart, Textual Archives Services Division of the United States National Archives in College Park; Romain Ledauphin of the United Nations Archive in New York; Dominique Crede in the District Attorney's (Staatsanwaltschaft) Office of the City of Frankfurt/Main; and the staffs of the International Institute for Social History in Amsterdam; the Archiv of Extra Parliamentary Organizations and Social Movements (APO-Archiv) at the Free University of Berlin; and the Military History Museum of the German Armed Forces, Airport, Berlin-Gatow.

It is also a pleasure to acknowledge my debts to fellow scholars: Professor Herman Wentker, the Director of the Institute for Contemporary History in Berlin and a leading expert on the foreign policy of East Germany, offered support for the project in its early stages, invited me to discuss the work in progress at the institute and offered wise counsel about the place of East Germany in the Soviet bloc. Dr. Wolfgang Kraushaar of the Institute for Social Research in Hamburg influenced this work with his important books on the West German Left, terrorism, the Middle East, and anti-Semitism and with his suggestions for research on the leftist organizations of the 1970s and 1980s. In Berlin, Dr. Martin Jander, who has done research with Kraushaar on the West German Left and terrorism, gathered valuable documents from archives in Berlin. Dr. Klaus Storkmann, who has done pioneering research on East German military assistance to third-world countries, offered valuable research suggestions when we met in Freiburg. Dr. Lutz Maeke, whose 2014 doctoral dissertation at the University of Leipzig on East Germany and the PLO will further illuminate issues raised in this book, shared his insights on these matters.

Comments and questions in response to lectures about the work in progress offered much food for thought as the book progressed. Thanks are due to colleagues of the National History Center seminar at the Woodrow Wilson International Center for Scholars, Washington, D.C.; the Program for the Study of Antisemitism, Yale University; the Minda de Gunzberg Center for European Studies, Harvard University; the German Studies Association Annual Meetings in Kansas City, Missouri, in September 2014; the Department of History at the University of Freiburg; the Institut für Zeitgeschichte in Berlin; the Moshe Dayan Center and the Department of History at the University of Tel Aviv; and participants in the conference “International Affairs and the Politics of Memory: German-Jewish-Israeli Affairs after the Holocaust,” January 12–14, 2014, at the University of Haifa, Israel. Thanks as well to Mark Kramer, Editor of the *Journal of Cold War Studies* and to anonymous reviewers for comments on “At War with Israel: East Germany’s Key Role in So “At War with Israel: East Germany’s Key Role in Soviet Policy in the Middle East,” *Journal of Cold War Studies* 16, no. 3 (Summer 2014): 129–163.

The community of scholars encompasses a community of friends. In Germany, my thanks to the hospitality of Anetta Kahane, Matthias and Rose Kuentzel, Ludger and Anöke Kuhnhardt, to Martin Cuppers and to Klaus Faber. I have been fortunate to call Richard Herzinger, one of Germany’s finest and bravest commentators on public affairs, an old and good friend. At Cambridge University Press, thanks are due to probing and helpful comments from readers, to Claudia Bona-Cohen, Joshua Penney and Nisha Vetrivel, who expertly guided the text through production. My special thanks to my editor Lewis Bateman for his strong support for this project and his excellent judgment along the way.

As has been the case for many years, I am blessed with the love and critical judgment of my wife, Sonya Michel. When swimming against the current as this book does, it is invaluable to have a soul mate at one’s side. I have worked with a certain urgency, one that three fine scholars, the historians Francois Furet and Robert Wistrich, and the scholar of Arab political culture, Fouad Ajami gave to their very different scholarly projects. I had the good fortune to be their friend and shared the misfortune and grief when they died too much too soon. Furet died well before I began work on this book, but I am sure he would have taken great interest in this chapter of the history of Communism. I had the great good fortune to get to know Fouad Ajami in the recent years before his terribly premature death in summer 2014. In conversations, in email exchanges, and in his essays, he offered encouragement as I worked on aspects of the Arab predicament he did so much to illuminate. Robert Wistrich, at Hebrew University, did so much to advance scholarship about anti-Semitism both in Nazi Germany and in the Soviet bloc. He too was a valued friend and colleague with whom I discussed this work in progress. His death in 2015 was yet another loss to the community of scholars. All three gave me the huge gift of their friendship and wisdom and the example of their courage. I dedicate this book to their memory.

Abbreviations

CEIRPP	Committee for the Exercise of the Inalienable Rights of the Palestinian Perople
DPFLP	Democratic Popular Front for the Liberation of Palestine
FRG	Federal Republic of Germany or (West Germany)
GDR	German Democratic Republic (East Germany)
GUPA	General Union of Palestinian Workers
GUPS	General Union of Palestinian Students
MFAA	Ministerium für Auswärtige Angelegenheiten (East German Ministry of Foreign Affairs)
MfNV	Ministerium für Nationale Verteidigung (Ministry of National Defense)
MfS	Ministerium für Staatssicherheit (East Germany's Ministry of State Security)
ND	*Neues Deutschland*
PFLP	Popular Front for the Liberation of Palestine
PLO	Palestine Liberation Organization
RAF	Red Army Faction (Rote Armee Fraktion)
RC	*RZ Revolutionäre Zelle* (Revolutionary Cells)
SED	Sozialistische Einheitspartei (Socialist Unity Party), East Germany's governing Communist Party
SSG	Sozialistischen Staatengemeinschaft (Socialist Community of States) (The term generally referred to the Soviet Union and its Warsaw Pact allies in Europe but could also apply to Communist regimes around the world.)
Stasi	Ministerium für Staatssicherheit (East Germany's Ministry of State Security)
ZK	Zentralkomitee (Central Committee of SED)

1

Introduction

If there were an unwritten eleventh commandment of West German history after the Holocaust, it would be that no German government or political group should kill or harm any more Jews or lend assistance to anyone else who was killing or harming Jews. Nor should a German government attack the state of Israel or aid its enemies. It was the moral minimum associated with West Germany's policy of *Vergangenheitsbewältigung*, or "coming to terms with the Nazi past," above all with the crimes of Nazi Germany's mass murder of six million Jews in Europe. It was a tradition more known for financial restitution than timely justice.[1] Yet the basic moral principle of doing no more harm to the Jews animated the decisions of successive West German chancellors, including Konrad Adenauer's determination in 1952 to offer financial restitution to survivors of the Holocaust and to the state of Israel, and Ludwig Erhard's policy of establishing diplomatic relations with Israel in 1965. The tradition persisted after German unification; in 2008, German chancellor Angela Merkel declared in the Israeli parliament, the Knesset, that Israel's survival was a matter of Germany's reason of state.

From its founding in 1949 until its collapse in 1989, the government of the Communist regime in East Germany adopted a very different view, one that entailed hostility to Zionism as an idea and Israel as a reality.

[1] On *Vergangenheitsbewältigung* in West Germany, see Jeffrey Herf, *Divided Memory: The Nazi Past in the Two Germanys* (Cambridge, MA: Harvard University Press, 1997). The tradition led to financial restitution to survivors of the Holocaust, financial payments to the state of Israel, and a mix of judicial reckoning, delay, and integration of former members of the Nazi regime. On the latter see Norbert Frei, *Adenauer's Germany and the Nazi Past* (New York: Columbia University Press, 2002).

Especially beginning in June 1967 during and after the Six-Day War, the West German radical Left also turned against Israel and produced small groups of terrorists who collaborated with Palestinian organizations in the 1970s and 1980s. This book is a history of the anti-Israeli policies and activities of the East German *state* and the West German radical leftist *organizations*. It examines the translation of anti-Zionist, at times anti-Semitic ideology into policies of support for war and terrorism aimed at the state and the citizens of the state of Israel, that is, policies that indeed caused more harm to Jews. It focuses on the years from 1967 to 1989 and especially on the early 1980s. It was then that antagonism reached its most virulent level and when both East Germany and the West German Left supported Arab state and Palestinian organization efforts to destroy the state of Israel by force of arms. The spectrum of antagonism included hostile political warfare at the United Nations and repeated assertions that Israel bore sole responsibility for what was then called "the Middle East conflict." Yet, as the following chapters confirm, the antagonism combined hostile words with providing military training and delivering weapons of war including thousands of Kalashnikov assault rifles, rocket-propelled grenades, land mines, explosives, and on occasion tanks and MiG fighter jets to the Arab states and Palestinian organizations then at war with Israel. In this indirect sense, both the East German government and West German leftist terrorist groups were also at war with Israel. Though the Communist regimes in Europe collapsed in 1989–1990 and though their Arab and Palestinian allies failed in their efforts to destroy Israel by force of arms, the ideas of this era of secular, leftist antagonism toward Israel continue to echo in world politics today.

The terrorism of the West German groups was more famous at the time than the military alliance between the Soviet bloc and the Arab states and Palestinian terror groups. Yet the East German government had far more impact on the course of events in the Middle East than did West German leftist terrorists. The great attention devoted to the latter and the relative neglect of the former reversed the order of their causal impact on events in the Middle East. By drawing attention to the importance of the Soviet bloc and East Germany, this work gives them a causal import often missing in media focus on West German leftist terrorism and connects this history to that of the global Cold War between the Soviet bloc and the Western Alliance. At the time, the United States Central Intelligence Agency estimated that East Germany's arms deliveries to the Arab states constituted about 3 percent of those from the Soviet bloc. As we will see, 3 percent of some very large numbers dwarfed the far better publicized arsenals discovered in the safe houses of West German leftist terrorists. The differences in scale were due to the differences between the resources of a *state* linked to a huge military alliance and those of leftist political *movements and groups*. While the Red Army Faction, June 2nd movement, and Revolutionary Cells captured headlines, it was the East German Communists who could deploy state power – armed forces, embassies, and a diplomatic corps; an effective intelligence service; military training centers; and a controlled press and media – to affect the balance of forces and events in the Middle East. This work presents the most extensive examination to date of the implementation of those instruments of power.

This book is the first work in English to draw on available German archives to examine the history of this period of German antagonism to Israel. It focuses on its causes, but, more than in previous accounts, it also examines the consequences of these policies in the form of political warfare, hostile propaganda, and military support for states and terrorist organizations at war with Israel. It is the first work in any language on this subject that draws not only on the now-open and extensive files of the former East German dictatorship but also on the relevant files of the governments of the United States and West Germany as well as published documents of the Israeli government, especially those produced by its delegation to the United Nations in New York; the views of leaders of West Germany's Jewish community; and the considerable documentation of West German leftist, Arab state, and Palestinian organization statements available in English and German. This is a German story, which had a direct impact on Jews in West Germany as well as on the citizens of Israel. The integration of their voices is a distinguishing feature of this work.

The founders of the Communist regime in East Germany, beginning in 1949, and then the West German radical Left, especially beginning in 1967, did not, however, feel bound by these same above-mentioned moral obligations. In the years from the Six-Day War of 1967 to the Lebanon War and its aftermath in the 1980s, the government of the German Democratic Republic – that is, East Germany – and, with fewer resources but more media attention, the West German leftist terrorist organizations did indeed continue to do more harm to the Jews, especially those living in Israel, and they helped others to harm them as well.

This work is, in part, a sequel to my previous study of the German Communist and radical leftist ideological interpretation of Zionism and the establishment of the state of Israel. The ideological foundations of this antagonism were articulated in the "anti-cosmopolitan purges" of the early 1950s in the Soviet Union and Eastern Europe. It was then that Soviet-bloc support for Zionism and Israel – support that was so important for the establishment of the state and led to assistance for the Jews in the war of 1948 – ended, and that "Zionism" became a term of abuse within Communist discourse. Soviet-bloc Zionism was a product of the exceptional circumstances of World War II and the Holocaust. Soviet-bloc anti-Zionism and hostility to Israel were part of a larger reversion to Marxist-Leninist orthodoxy that accompanied the beginnings of the Cold War. At the most general level, the idea of a Jewish state contradicted both the Communists' claims to universalism and, notwithstanding the secularism of the founding Zionist generation, the Communists' view that religion was the opiate of the people. For orthodox Communists, the Soviet Union, not European Jewry, was the primary victim of Hitler's Germany. During the postwar purges, anti-Zionism, often with anti-Semitic themes about vast Jewish power and its connections to capitalism and imperialism, became standard discourse in the Soviet bloc.

While a minority of German Communists made the case that East Germany[2] should have close and warm relations with the new Jewish state, the orthodox majority rejected the idea that as German Communists they had any particular moral obligation toward the state of Israel. On the contrary, the East German Communists of the 1950s already denounced Israel as an ally of Western and American imperialism and refused to pay any financial restitution to the Jewish state. East Germany was the only member of the Warsaw Pact that never had any diplomatic relations with the state of Israel. As the West German Left in 1967 adopted core elements of leftist anti-imperialism, it too placed Israel on the wrong side of what it regarded as the core global divide between an evil and exploitative imperialism and a virtuous exploited third world. The corollary of this view was support for the Arab states and, in both East Germany and the West German radical Left, especially passionate engagement with the Palestinian groups at war with Israel.

[2] The official name of the East German government was the "German Democratic Republic," abbreviated in English as "GDR." In fact, the regime was a dictatorship and was neither democratic nor a republic. Hence I generally refer to it as "East Germany." The scholarship on East Germany is now extensive. Most recently see Klaus Schroeder, *Der SED-Staat: Geschichte und Strukturen der DDR 1949–1990* (Cologne: Böhlau Verlag, 2013). Other general histories include Mary Fulbrook, *The People's State: East German Society from Hitler to Honecker* (New Haven, CT: Yale University Press, 2005); Hermann Weber, *Die DDR 1945–1990*, 2nd rev. ed. (Munich: R. Oldenbourg, 1993).

The Soviet Union was the driving force and key actor shaping the policy of the Warsaw Pact's hostility to Israel. Contrary to Maoist propaganda and the romanticism of the Western New Left and its successors, the Soviet Union's policy toward third-world revolution was noteworthy for its radicalism and, very importantly, for its material substance. The Soviet Union, not Mao's blustering China, was the primary source of weapons and military training for leftist guerrilla movements around the world. Its military assistance to the Arab states and Palestinian terrorist organizations was part of its global offensive against "U.S. imperialism" as well as of its efforts to gain influence in the strategically important Middle East. Yet small as its contributions were in comparison to the efforts of the Soviet superpower, East Germany was not a reluctant follower. On the contrary, for reasons of mutually reinforcing ideological passions and conventional arguments about national interest, its leaders enthusiastically participated in campaigns against Israel. In the Middle East, the Soviet bloc, including East Germany, supported the forces of radicalism, not moderation and, as we will see, did so both in words and in deeds.

The infamous West German leftist terrorist groups of these years as well the numerically more significant legal organizations of the radical Left voluntarily decided to support the Arab states as well as the various organizations that made up the Executive Committee of the Palestine Liberation Organization, including Al Fatah as well as the Popular Front for the Liberation of Palestine and the Democratic Popular Front for the Liberation of Palestine, two organizations whose leaders dispensed with any pretenses of moderation or the public ambiguity about support for terrorism associated with Arafat's mixture of force and political warfare. One of the issues this work explores is the intensity, voluntarism, and passion with which these Germans turned against Israel and aligned with its enemies. Their antagonism to Israel and willingness to attack not just Israel's policies but its legitimacy and right to exist were hardly unique; both had become common themes of the global Left since the early 1950s. Yet nowhere else did the anti-Israeli passion entail such a striking flight from the burdens of a national past as in Germany. This flight from the past earned East Germany and the West German leftist terrorist organizations many friends around the world.

In one of the bitterest ironies of this era, the Communists and the leftist movements transformed the language of anti-fascism that the world associated with the war against Nazi Germany into a rhetorical arsenal to use against the Jewish state. There were Communists, Jews, and non-Jews who thought that the anti-fascism of World War II should have led to postwar support for Zionism. However, the brief era of Soviet-bloc support for Israel ended in the anti-cosmopolitan purges of the early 1950s. From 1949 to the building of the Berlin Wall in 1961, more than three million persons, about 20 percent of the population, left East Germany for West Germany, among them presumably those most willing to oppose the regime's policies. Hence, by 1967, when East Germany's antagonism to Israel burst most fully into public view, another striking feature of the East German story emerges, namely, the absence of any public protest against its policies. By means of both repression and the safety valve of emigration up to 1961, the GDR had become a polity and society without opposition or at least without an opposition able to express itself publicly. In Poland, rumbles of dissent led to a massive purge of Polish political and intellectual life followed by an exodus of those dissenters able to leave the country. In East Germany there was no such massive purge because by 1967 either the opposition had been repressed or its leaders had fled before the wall was built.[3]

At the time and since, some observers thought that the lingering impact of Nazism in German society was responsible for antagonism to Israel and enthusiasm that may have resonated at the popular level with the anti-Arab states and Palestinian terrorist organizations.[4] Continuities were provided by journalists who had worked in Nazi Germany and who then found employment in East Germany's government propaganda organs. Yet the ideological core of the anti-Israeli turn lay in Marxism-Leninism and the associated leftist third-world anti-imperialism of the 1960s.[5] In East Germany, the passionate embrace of third-world leftist revolution

[3] On Poland during and after the Six-Day War see Dariusz Stola, "Anti-Zionism as a Multipurpose Policy Instrument: The Anti-Zionist Campaign in Poland, 1967–1968," in Jeffrey Herf, ed., *Anti-Semitism and Anti-Zionism in Historical Perspective: Convergence and Divergence* (New York: Routledge, 2007), 157–185.

[4] I have examined those slogans, themes, and images in *The Jewish Enemy: Nazi Propaganda during World War II and the Holocaust* (Cambridge, MA: Harvard University Press, 2006); and in *Nazi Propaganda for the Arab World* (New Haven, CT: Yale University Press, 2009).

[5] On these developments see, among much else, Robert S. Wistrich, *A Lethal Obsession: Anti-Semitism from Antiquity to the Global Jihad* (New York: Random House, 2010); and his *From Ambivalence to Betrayal: The Left, the Jews and Israel* (Lincoln: University of Nebraska Press, 2012); and Herf, *Anti-Semitism and Anti-Zionism*. On journalists in Nazi Germany and East Germany see Simon Wiesenthal, *The Same Language: First for Hitler, Now for Ulbricht: Simon Wiesenthal's Press Conference on September 6th, 1968* (Vienna: Deutschland-berichte, 1968).

found some of its most important partners in the Arab states and in the Palestinian organizations already in a state of war with Israel. The latter developed special relationships with the West German radical Left, both the aboveground Marxist-Leninist and Maoist sects of the 1970s, as well as the ideologically more diffuse residues of New Left thinking and illegal leftist terrorist underground organizations such as the Red Army Faction, the Revolutionary Cells and the June 2nd movement.

In 1980, an authors' collective of researchers and professors working at East Germany's Institute for International Relations of the Academy for Law and Political Science in Berlin published a dictionary of terms for foreign policy and international law. It defined Zionism as "a chauvinistic ideology of the Jewish bourgeoisie featuring a widespread organizational system and expansionist political practice which forms a part of international monopoly capital."[6] Its nineteenth-century roots lay in a "petty-bourgeois reaction to antisemitism" that evolved into a "reactionary conception of the Jewish community, which, in order to divert the Jewish proletariat from the class struggle, ignored the question of class and saw a solution to the so-called Jewish question in the creation of a Jewish national state on the Arab territory of Palestine. From its beginnings, with this conception, Zionism adapted itself to the political, economic, and strategic interests of world imperialism," especially that of "USA imperialism in the Middle East." From the time of its founding in 1948, East German researchers asserted that the state of Israel stood for national chauvinism and anti-communism.[7] It was "directed against the Arab national liberation movement." Its "aggressive politics, supported by the imperialist states, especially the USA, lead to the military conflicts in the Arab region and to the development of the conflict in the Middle East. At the XXX UN General Assembly in 1975 in resolution 3379, Zionism was condemned as a form of racism and racial discrimination."[8] In other words, Zionist ideology and the state it produced had no moral legitimacy. For these authors, the state of Israel was, *from the beginning*, inseparable from American imperialism and its intrusion into "the territory of Palestine."

One of the defining aspects of East German foreign policy was what I will call a "rhetorical fog of seeming moderation" with a vocabulary full

[6] "Zionismus," in Institut für Internationale Beziehungen an der Akademie für Staats- und Rechtswissenschaft der DDR, *Wörterbuch der Aussenpolitik und des Völkerrechts* ([East] Berlin: Dietz Verlag, 1980), 703.

[7] Ibid.

[8] Ibid.

of references to peace, justice, and "political solutions" to the Middle East conflict combined with unflinching support for intransigent Arab governments and radical Palestinian organizations. Soviet and Warsaw Pact policy in these decades of the Cold War combined the language of détente and the rational logic of nuclear deterrence with unambiguous radicalism regarding policy in the Middle East and in the third world more generally. When applied to the conflict between Israel, the Arab states and the Palestinian organizations, this stance held Israel from its beginning to be exclusively responsible for what the East German researchers in 1980 called "a conflict situation brought about by imperialist-Zionist forces ... that is reflected above all in aggressive actions against the Arab peoples and states."[9] East Germany denounced the Camp David Accords of 1978 between Israel and Egypt as a "separate peace" that ignored the rights of the Palestinians to national self-determination and supported a "steadfastness front" composed of Arab states that rejected the agreement along with "peace-loving forces of the whole world" that had emerged.[10] In these years, the East Germans lent support not only to Arafat's Al Fatah forces but also to Palestinian terrorist organizations, such as the Popular Front for the Liberation of Palestine and the Democratic Popular Front for the Liberation of Palestine.

At the time and since, critics of Israel's German antagonists have argued that leftist anti-Zionism was simply anti-Semitism – hatred of the Jews – in another language. In the long history of anti-Semitism, the antagonism to Israel of these years marks a unique chapter. Never before had those who attacked the Jews done so while insisting that their animosity had nothing to do with the fact that its targets were Jews. Yet the questions persisted. In a world of states in which democracies were a minority, why did the leftist anti-Zionists focus on the one functioning democracy in the Middle East? Why were eyes blind to and headlines absent about terrorist attacks on Israelis while Israel's acts of self-defense met with global righteous indignation? Why did Israel's critics assume that its government never told the truth while giving the benefit of the doubt to dictators and terrorist organizations? In the willingness to accuse Israel of horrific crimes, was there not a remnant of the longest hatred's inclination to accuse the Jews of murder of innocents? An important feature of Communist and leftist anti-Zionism and antagonism to Israel

[9] "Nahostkonflikt," Institut für Internationale Beziehungen an der Akademie für Staats- und Rechtswissenschaft der DDR, *Wörterbuch der Aussenpolitik und des Völkerrechts*, 425.

[10] Ibid., 426–427.

was an angry and indignant insistence that even to suggest similarity to the anti-Semitism of the past was an outrageous if clever Zionist trick whose purpose was to deflect criticism by changing the subject. In the court of world public opinion in the United Nations General Assembly, Israel suffered a double defeat in this era. First, only a minority of states agreed with it that the political and military offensive launched against it was a form of anti-Semitism and racism. Second, Israel suffered the ignominy of having its legitimating ideology, Zionism, declared to be a form of racism and even, according to the PLO representatives in the United Nations, itself a form of anti-Semitism directed against the Arab "Semites" of Palestine. Most painful of all was the association of the state of Israel with Nazism. In their important history of Arab responses to the Holocaust, Meir Litvak and Esther Webman concluded that "the equation of Zionism with Nazism ... began shortly after the end of World War II as part of Arab public debate."[11] In this work I do not resolve the issue of whether the Israel-as-Nazi-Germany association began in the Arab countries or in the Soviet propaganda machine after World War II. What is clear is that when the Soviet Union and its allies, including East Germany, accused the Jewish state of replicating the Third Reich, they made an enormous contribution to making this falsehood a ubiquitous slogan of world, not only Arab, political culture.

These issues raise the question of whether the East German Communist regime was the second anti-Semitic dictatorship in Germany's twentieth century, whether parts of the West German radical Left constituted an anti-Semitic movement, and whether both found adherents because hatred of Israel struck familiar chords in Germany. The global and German anti-Israel Left dismissed such questions as Zionist and imperialist propaganda, yet the issues were less easily dismissed in the German context. Here the Israeli-as-Nazi trope played an important role in overcoming what one West German leftist called Germany's "Jewish complex," that is, a supposed reluctance to criticize or oppose Israel due to the memory of German responsibility for the Holocaust. Once the Communists in the East and the radical Left in West Germany identified Israel with Nazi Germany, they managed to define the struggle against Israel as the anti-fascism of the period from the 1960s to 1980s. Israel had become the embodiment of the evils of the Nazi regime that they claimed to despise.

[11] Meir Litvak and Esther Webman, *From Empathy to Denial: Arab Responses to the Holocaust* (London: Hurst, 2009), 215.

Understandably, German historians and historians of anti-Semitism have asked whether anti-Zionism and antagonism to Israel were merely a cover for an atavistic strain of anti-Semitism. Forgotten in some of these discussions was the fact that whether their enemies were motivated by anti-Semitism or "merely" by anti-Zionism made no difference to Israeli soldiers killed and wounded in battles with the armed forces of the Arab states equipped with Soviet-bloc and East German arms, or to Israeli civilians gunned down and blown up on buses and in market squares by the PLO and its various Executive Committee affiliates. For the Israelis, the discussion about whether their enemies were motivated by anti-Semitism or "merely" by a presumably less objectionable anti-Zionism devoted too much attention to the intentions of the killers and too little to the fate of their victims. In the following pages, I give the Arab, Arab Palestinian, East German governmental, and West German leftist voices ample space to present their indictment. However, moreso than in previous accounts, I also draw on what Israelis in their home state and at the United Nations and leaders of the Jewish community in West Germany had to say about events. They pointed out that the people being killed and wounded in the name of the "Palestinian revolution" were not an abstraction called "Zionists." They were flesh-and-blood Jews who were the intended targets of terrorists.

The toll of Jews killed and wounded in the wars and terrorist attacks in the years from 1967 to 1989 was grim, both in absolute numbers and relative to the population that then numbered between two and three million people. According to the Israeli Defense Forces Historical Division, 6,104 Israeli soldiers were killed in the wars of these years.[12] The Israeli government estimates that number of soldiers wounded was between 21,000 and 24,000.[13] During these same years, the Palestinian organizations represented on the PLO's Executive Committee waged terrorist campaigns primarily against the *civilian population* of Israel, occasionally also targeting Israeli soldiers. According to the Israel Ministry of Foreign Affairs, 639 Israelis, mostly civilians, were killed in terrorist attacks from 1967 to

[12] Israel Ministry of Foreign Affairs, "The Arab Israeli Wars," http://www.mfa.gov.il/mfa/aboutisrael/history/pages/the%20arab-israeli%20wars.aspx The specific figures are as follows: Six-Day War, 776; War of Attrition, 1,424; Yom Kippur War, 2,688; First Lebanon War (Peace for Galilee), 1,216.

[13] Based on figures from the Israel Foreign Ministry. On the war of 1948, see Benny Morris, *1948: The First Arab-Israeli War* (New Haven, CT: Yale University Press, 2009); *Righteous Victims: A History of the Zionist-Arab Conflict, 1881–2001* (New York: Vintage 1999); and Anita Shapira, *Israel: A History* (Waltham, MA: Brandeis University Press, 2012), 155–178.

1989.[14] Those figures do not include the 88 people killed in 1974, when TWA Flight 841 was blown up over the Mediterranean by a bomb probably placed by Abu Nadal's Palestinian terrorist organization, nor the 162 Israeli soldiers and officials killed by suicide bombers in Tyre, Lebanon, in 1982 and 1983. Nor do they include 10 persons who were killed and 24 wounded as a result of 21 Palestinian attacks on Israeli embassies around the world during these years.[15]

According to figures available in the Global Terrorism Database (GTD) of the National Consortium for the Study of Terrorism and Responses to Terrorism ("START") at the University of Maryland in College Park, of the 1,723 terrorist attacks perpetrated against Israelis from 1970 to 2013, 958 took place between 1970 and 1990, resulting in injuries to 1,851 people.[16] The GTD database offers the following information about the identity of the attackers: (Unspecified) "Palestinians," 375; "Unknown," 200; "Palestine Liberation Organization" (PLO), 57; "Popular Front for the Liberation of Palestine" (PFLP), 32; "Democratic Front for the Liberation of Palestine" (DFLP), 20; "Al Fatah," 20; "Force 17," 7; "Abu Nidal Group," 6; "Fedayeen," 3; and "Palestine Liberation Front" (PLF), 3. The attacks took place in all of Israel's major cities and in many small towns. Jerusalem, the prime target, was attacked 323 times, Tel Aviv 53. Life was particularly dangerous for Jews in smaller towns near the northern, southern, and western borders that were within reach of raiding parties and rocket and artillery fire from Jordan, Syria, and especially Lebanon.[17]

This work builds on my previous study *Divided Memory: The Nazi Past in the Two Germanys*.[18] In it, I compared the divergent public memory of the Holocaust adopted by East and West Germany. In West Germany, a tradition of "coming to terms with the Nazi past" became embedded in central political traditions. It was expressed in public acknowledgment of the crimes of the Nazi regime against the Jews, in the restitution

[14] Israel Ministry of Foreign Affairs, "Terrorism Deaths in Israel, 1920–1999," http://www.mfa.gov.il/MFA/MFA-Archive/2000/Pages/Terrorism%20deaths%20in%20Israel%20-%201920-1999.aspx

[15] Terrorism against Israel: Attacks against Israeli Representatives Abroad (1969 – Present), archive.today/20121218180852/www.mfa.gov.il/MFA/MFAArchive/2000_2009/2000/1/Terrorism+deaths+in+Israel+-+1920–1999.htm.

[16] "Israel: Search Results: 1723 Incidents," 1967–1990, National Consortium for the Study of Terrorism and Responses to Terrorism (START). (2013). Global Terrorism Database [Data file], www.start.umd.edu/gtd. Print version, pages 28–32 with 100 items per page.

[17] "Israel: Search Results: 1723 Incidents."

[18] Herf, *Divided Memory*.

agreements of the early 1950s that sent funds to Jewish survivors and to the state of Israel, in a modest and then secret program of arms shipments to the state of Israel, and then in diplomatic recognition of the country in 1965. The leaders of the Federal Republic tacitly adopted the eleventh commandment of German history after the Holocaust mentioned previously, namely, to do no more harm to the Jews; to refuse to kill, injure, or terrorize them or to lend assistance to anyone else who intended to do those things. Remembering the crimes of the Nazi past and bringing perpetrators to justice were of varying importance to the founders of the Federal Republic. Konrad Adenauer combined support for the state of Israel and restitution for survivors of the Holocaust with premature reintegration of former officials of the Nazi regime and reluctance to support war crimes trials at the federal level.[19] From center Left to center Right, the leaders of the founding generation of postwar West Germany understood that the Nazi regime's hatred of the Jews had also included opposition to Zionism and to the establishment of a Jewish state in Palestine.[20] While there were important times when West Germany's relationship to Israel was guided by the "normal" diplomatic criteria of national interest, it was also the case that a "special relationship" existed between the two countries. West German diplomats were well aware of the price their country was paying for friendship with Israel in the form of the anger of the Arab states, an awareness that contributed to an official policy of neutrality in the Yom Kippur War of 1973.[21]

In view of the massive Soviet military presence in East Germany during the Cold War and the centrality of East Germany as a bastion for the Soviet empire in Eastern Europe, there has been a tendency to dismiss the East German regime as lacking autonomy and thus historical significance. From 1949 to the late 1960s, the official West German government term for East Germany was not the "German Democratic Republic" but

[19] From a large scholarship on these issues, see Herf, *Divided Memory*; Norbert Frei, *Adenauer's Germany and the Nazi Past*, trans. Joel Golb (New York: Columbia University Press, 2002); and Thomas Schwartz, *America's Germany: John J. McCloy and the Federal Republic of Germany* (Cambridge, MA: Harvard University Press, 1991). On West German restitution, see Constantin Goschler, *Wiedergutmachung: Westdeutschland und die Verfolgten des Nationalsozialismus 1945–1954* (Munich: Oldenbourg, 1992).

[20] On Nazi anti-Zionism, see Herf, *Nazi Propaganda for the Arab World*.

[21] On West German–Israeli relations see *Akten zur Auswärtigen Politik der Bundesrepublik Deutschland* now covering the years from 1949 to 1983. Also see Inge Deutschkron, *Israel und die Deutschen: Das schwierige Verhältnis* (Cologne: Verlag Wissenschaft und Politik, 1983); and Lily Gardner Feldman, *The Special Relationship between West Germany and Israel* (London: Allan and Unwin, 1984).

"the Soviet Zone of Occupation." In 1987, President Ronald Reagan, speaking at the Brandenburg Gate near the Berlin Wall, famously said, "Mr. Gorbachev, tear down this wall!" Notably, he did not appeal to Erich Honecker, the head of the East German regime, to do so. Herman Wentker, the leading historian of East German foreign policy, has demonstrated that though there were occasional differences, policy was indeed conducted within "narrow limits" established by the Soviet Union.[22] At the same time, it was the Soviet Union, not the GDR, that both established the policies and provided the overwhelming proportion of weapons used by the Arab states and Palestinian terrorist organizations against Israel. It is also important to recall that in 1967 other member states in the Warsaw Pact, especially Poland, joined in the anti-Zionist chorus.[23] Yet, as Hope Harrison has demonstrated in her study of Walter Ulbricht's determination to build the Berlin Wall, the East German Communists displayed voluntarism and initiative that pushed the limits of the framework established by the Soviet Union.[24] If, in light of Soviet hegemony, "autonomy" is too strong a word, then passionate and willing agreement is certainly appropriate. The East German regime was not a reluctant participant in the Soviet-bloc assault on Israel.

By 1967, antagonism to Israel had become a longstanding sentiment in the East German leadership. The East German Politburo of June 1967 was firmly united in support for the Arab states. Returning to East Berlin from Moscow in 1945, the East German Communists were convinced that they, not the Jews, had been Nazi Germany's primary enemy.[25] They resented the claims of Jewish "victims" to place their suffering on the same level as Communist "resistance fighters." To them, Zionism was a religious and ethnic anachronism, an atavistic nationalism to be dismissed in favor of Communist internationalism. Even worse, despite the socialist orientation of the founding Israeli leadership, Israeli democracy found affinities with the "American imperialist enemy" in the Cold War.

[22] Herman Wentker, *Aussenpolitik in engen Grenzen: Die DDR im internationalen System, 1949–1989* (Munich: R. Oldenbourg, 2007). Wentker is director of the Institute of Contemporary History in Berlin.

[23] Darius Stola, "Anti-Zionism as a Multipurpose Instrument: The Anti-Zionist Campaign in Poland, 1967–1968," in Herf, *Anti-Semitism and Anti-Zionism*, 159–186; also in the *Journal of Israeli History* 25, no. 1 (2006): 175–201.

[24] Hope Harrison, *Driving the Soviets up the Wall: Soviet-East German Relations, 1953–1961* (Princeton, NJ: Princeton University Press, 2003).

[25] On the veteran Communist leaders and their views see Catherine Epstein, *The Last Revolutionaries: German Communists and Their Century* (Cambridge, MA: Harvard University Press, 2003).

During and after the anti-cosmopolitan purges in the Soviet bloc from 1949 to 1956, hostility to Israel and to Zionism became a defining feature of international Communism. In the Doctors' Plot accusations in Moscow, the Slansky trial in Prague, the Noel Field case in Budapest, and the purges of Paul Merker, Leo Zuckermann, and others sympathetic to Israel in East Berlin in 1952–1953, Communist anti-Zionism was accompanied by a revival of anti-Semitic conspiracy theories that associated the small Jewish communities of Europe and the new state of Israel with the archenemy, the United States. The purge victims in the Communist regimes included Communists, both Jews and non-Jews, who supported Israel in the Middle East conflict because they viewed doing so as continuous with the anti-fascism of World War II from 1941 to 1945. The government officials conducting the prosecutions found these pro-Israeli Communists to be guilty of membership in a vast conspiracy connected to "U.S. imperialism" and "Zionist circles" whose goal was to overthrow the Communist regimes in Eastern Europe. The East German government purged all "pro-Zionist" Communists from positions of political influence and sent still others to prison. Some joined the almost three million East Germans who fled abroad, mostly to West Germany. From the early 1950s on, anti-Zionism infused with conspiracy theories of an anti-Semitic nature remained a feature of Soviet-bloc Communism. In a bitter irony of history, Communist anti-fascism, forged in the decades of opposition to Nazi Germany, now provided language with which to denounce the Jewish state. For the Communists of this period, Israel was now on the wrong side of the global divide between imperialists and anti-imperialists gathered in various "fronts of national liberation." The East German Communists denounced Zionism as a tool of American imperialism, refused to pay any reparations to Jewish survivors, described West German restitution funds as nothing but a cynical effort to purchase respectability, and defined "anti-fascism" to mean antagonism to West Germany.[26]

As noted, the stance of the East German government and of the West German radical Left, including but not limited to leftist terrorist organizations such as the Red Army Faction, June 2nd Movement and Revolutionary Cells, went far beyond simply criticizing Israel.[27] East Germany developed a particularly close relationship with Yasser Arafat

[26] See Herf, *Divided Memory*.

[27] Angelika Timm's early and valuable study speaks of a "destroyed relationship" between East Germany and Israel. See her *Hammer, Zirkel und Davidstern: Das Zerstörte Verhältnis der DDR zu Zionismus und Staat Israel* (Bonn: Bouvier, 1997).

and Al Fatah, the largest organization in the PLO. Hidden from public view while proclaiming its support for "political solutions," East Germany also gave support to the "extremist" organizations of the Palestinian movement such as PFLP and the Marxist-Leninist-oriented PDFLP.[28] Following the Egyptian-Israeli agreements in the Camp David Accords in 1978, both the Warsaw Pact governments and the West German radical Left supported the "rejection front" of Arab states, most importantly the Baathist regime in Syria, as well as the PLO, PFLP and PDFLP. Like its Warsaw Pact allies, East Germany combined support for the "inalienable rights of the Palestinian people" and denunciations of Israeli "aggression" and even "genocide" with calls for a "political solution" to the conflict that would emerge from a Geneva conference on the Middle East proposed by the Soviet Union. This rhetorical fog, with its occasional tones of moderation, was a complement, not an alternative, to a policy that included support for the most intransigent Arab states and the most extreme Palestinian terror organizations.

Political observers at the time and some scholars since have distinguished between moderates and radicals within the Palestinian organizations and examined their disputes.[29] The Israeli government viewed such distinctions as a convenient fiction that allowed Yasser Arafat, the leader of the PLO's Executive Committee, to sustain a shred of plausible deniability for attacks on civilians in Western Europe. Yet the disagreements within the PLO, which at times reached the point of violent conflicts between rival terrorist organizations, did not extend to differences over the long-term goal: the end of Israel. Arafat combined war and terror in the Middle East with political warfare in Western Europe and at the United Nations. He understood that airplane hijackings and terrorist attacks in Western Europe could undermine efforts to isolate Israel in the court of international public opinion. He mastered the art of speaking more moderately when addressing Western audience. Yet, the evidence of both the military battle in the Middle East and the political battle in Europe and at the UN indicates that so long as the Soviet bloc existed and the arms and training continued to flow, the PLO did not abandon or revise the core radicalism embodied in its Charter of 1968. Its goal remained the destruction of the state of Israel by a combination of

[28] See Lutz Maeke, "DDR und PLO. Die Palästinapolitik des SED-Staates," doctoral dissertation, Universität Leipzig, Summer 2014.

[29] On the various armed groups in the PLO see Yezid Sayigh, *Armed Struggle and the Search for a State: The Palestinian National Movement, 1949–1993* (Oxford: Clarendon Press, 1997).

terrorism and political warfare around the world. Thus, in these years, to express solidarity with the PLO, to treat PLO leaders as honored guests in East Berlin and, in West German university towns, to celebrate the heroics of the Palestinian terrorist organizations amounted to support for this goal and approval of using force to achieve it.

Important chapters of the Soviet-bloc attack on Israel took place at the UN headquarters in New York, and East Germany played an active role. These efforts aroused the attention of the Directorate of Intelligence at the US Central Intelligence Agency. In 1984, it reported that the Soviet Union had "made a concerted effort to expand its influence in the UN Secretariat by building an organization within the Secretariat capable of influencing the UN and promoting Soviet objectives." By then, "approximately 1,000 Soviet and East European citizens" were employed at the UN, "a tenfold increase since 1959."[30] The Soviet bloc, including East Germany, used the United Nations effectively to define the agenda of debate, develop connections with countries around the world and protect the regimes of the Soviet bloc from criticism. The famous "Zionism is racism" resolution of November 1975 was only one of many UN General Assembly resolutions designed to isolate Israel that were passed in these decades by an enduring majority of the Soviet bloc, other Communist states, the Arab states and a large number of other third-world member states.

The following chapters draw extensively on the now-open files of the East German Politburo, Council of Ministers, Defense Ministry and Ministry of State Security, which reveal that Soviet-bloc antagonism to Israel led to extensive arms deliveries and military training for the Arab states and the Palestinian terrorist organizations. The East German files lend credence to the reports produced at the time by the United States Central Intelligence Agency on the extent and centrality of Soviet and Soviet-bloc support for the Arab states.[31] When the Arab states went to war with Israel in 1967 and 1973, and when the PLO and its affiliates carried out terrorist attacks from the 1960s to 1989 and acquired a significant arsenal in Lebanon from the mid-1970s to 1982, they did so with Soviet-bloc weaponry and soldiers who had received extensive military training in the countries of the Soviet bloc, including East Germany.

[30] Directorate of Intelligence, CIA, "Soviets in the UN System: A Reference Aid," GI 84-10138, September 1984, 2–3, CREST System, UN National Archives in College Park.

[31] The files are available via the CREST system of declassified files at the US National Archives in College Park.

In accord with Clausewitz's dictum that war is politics by other means, the Soviet-Arab alliance against Israel combined, in the words of Karl Marx, the arm of criticism with the criticism of arms. In the following chapters I pay close attention to the strategic interaction between force and diplomacy, that is, between the clash of arms in the theaters of war in the Middle East and the war of words in Europe and especially at the United Nations in New York. The numerous resolutions against Israel passed by the UN General Assembly majority in these years were an important complement to the war of arms being waged at times by the Arab states and continuously by the PLO. Political warfare was, by definition, a public matter. East Germany's public denunciations of Israel, readily available in UN documents and in the controlled press and media at home, most importantly its official newspaper, *Neues Deutschland*, figure prominently in this work.

The Soviet bloc as a whole waged a persistent and, judged by the number and content of anti-Israeli resolutions that won huge majorities in the UN General Assembly in these decades, overwhelmingly successful campaign of political warfare against Israel at the United Nations. Following its admission to the UN in September 1973, East Germany played a prominent, active and under-examined role in that campaign. As a member state of the UN, East Germany used its position in open debates in the General Assembly to passionately advance the cause of the PLO during the era of the terror war. The country also capitalized on its position to help found the Committee for the Exercise of the Inalienable Rights of the Palestinian People (CEIRPP), the center of the PLO's activities at the UN. CEIRPP and other UN files offer important evidence of East Germany's passionate engagement on behalf of Israel's Arab enemies and of the PLO's own views expressed in New York both in public and in confidential committee meetings.

The East Germans participated in battles over the meaning of words such as "aggression" and "terrorism" at the UN, redefining them in ways that wound up justifying what they purported to condemn. I define terrorism as the use of violence to intentionally attack civilians with the purpose of attaining a political goal. As a violation of internationally accepted laws of war, it was and is a crime and its practitioners criminals. According to this definition, they are neither heroes nor martyrs; they are murderers. To describe the PLO and its affiliates as terrorists is not to "essentialize" its participants, as one scholar has recently argued.[32]

[32] For such assertions see Paul Thomas Chamberlin, *The Global Offensive: The United States, the Palestine Liberation Organization and the Making of the Post-Cold War Order* (New York: Oxford University Press, 2012), 9.

It merely states the obvious, namely that these were organizations that sought to intentionally kill civilians in hopes of thereby achieving a political goal. At the UN, the Soviet Union and its Warsaw Pact allies, the Arab states and the PLO went to great lengths to obscure this reality and present terrorism instead as justified "armed struggle" against colonialism, neo-colonialism, imperialism and foreign occupation–terms that were said to describe Israeli policies toward the Arab states and the Palestinians. Resting on circular logic, such definitions turned the citizens of the state of Israel into legitimate targets of a supposedly justified military campaign.

The files of East Germany's Ministry of State Security, the Stasi, offer abundant examples of refreshing candor regarding such matters. When high-ranking officials of the Stasi met in East Berlin with their counterparts in the PLO's intelligence service, they both dispensed with the euphemisms and evasions Soviet-bloc diplomats offered at the UN. Instead, they were remarkably frank, openly (and precisely) using the terms "terrorism" or "terrorist" or even "extremist" to characterize the persons and activities of organizations gathered on the PLO's Executive Committee. At the UN, however, East German diplomats accused those who referred to the PLO as a terrorist organization as guilty of "slander" and "defamation" of a noble struggle for liberation. Stasi officials in East Berlin, who were not playing to a global audience, knew very well that placing a bomb in a café or a bus, firing Katyusha rockets at villages and machine-gunning civilians in an apartment building were all forms of terrorism. In the following pages, I adopt the same definition of terrorism evident in internal Stasi memos, one that accorded with common sense and the interpretations used by the United States, Israel and the NATO allies in Western Europe.

Ironically, it is in files of the United Nations, bulging with denunciations of Israel, that the historian finds an extensive and detailed record of the terrorist war being waged against it in these years. It comes from the remarkable collection of statements and reports by Israel's ambassadors to the United Nations. Their names and terms were: Gideon Rafael (1967–1968), Yosef Tekoah (1968–1975), Chaim Herzog (1975–1978), and Yehuda Blum (1978–1984). I draw as well on the statements at the UN of Abba Eban, Israel's foreign minister from 1966 to 1974.[33] Israel's voice could be heard in the Security Council and in General Assembly

[33] Abba Eban was Israel's ambassador to the UN from 1949 to 1959. From 1984 to 1988, Benjamin Netanyahu, subsequently Israel's prime minister, occupied the post.

debates as well as in hundreds of letters the Israeli delegation sent to the UN secretary general and president of the Security Council. These previously under-examined reports form an indispensable source for this work and for historians in the future.[34] With state power came the ability of prime ministers to speak for the nation, of a foreign ministry and diplomatic corps to make its case and respond to critics. As a member state of the United Nations, Israel was able to place its case on a record available to all member states. These important documents have been available for many years but have seldom been consulted. They play a valuable role in this work.

Since 1989, research in the files of the former Communist regime in East Germany has revealed its extensive attempts to influence political life in West Germany.[35] Nevertheless, although the agents of the Ministry of State Security infiltrated a variety of West German leftist organizations and funded Communist organizations sympathetic to East Germany, the radicalization of the West German Left and its antagonism to Israel was not due primarily to East Berlin's influence. East Germany did offer escape routes for West German terrorists, but the radicalization of the West German Left regarding Israel had roots in a mixture of indigenous circumstances combined with strong international connections to the Palestinian terror organizations. In Germany, major studies by Stefan Aust, Martin Kloke, Wolfgang Kraushaar and Butz Peters, among others, have examined the path of radicalization from the 1960s New Left in West Germany to the terrorism of the 1970s and 1980s. In so doing, they drew particular attention to the international connections of West German terrorist to Palestinian terrorist organizations.[36]

[34] The integration of Israeli voices, along with those of Germans, Arab and Palestinian voices recalls Saul Friedlander's effort to write an integrated history of the Holocaust. See his *Nazi Germany and the Jews: 1939–1945, The Years of Extermination* (New York: Harper, 2008). On the efforts in the immediate postwar years to save documentation of the Holocaust, see Laura Jockusch, *Collect and Record: Jewish Holocaust Documentation in Early Postwar Europe* (New York: Oxford University Press, 2012).

[35] See for example, Hubertus Knabe, *Die unterwanderte Republik. Stasi im Westen* (Berlin, Propyläen, 1999).

[36] The now-classic study of West German leftist anti-Israeli sentiment remains Martin W. Kloke, *Israel und die deutsche Link: Zur Geschichte eine schwierigen Verhältnisses*, 2nd ed. (Frankfurt/Main: Haag and Herchen, 1994). On the path from antagonism to terror see on West German leftist terrorism see, for example: Stefan Aust, *Der Baader-Meinhof Komplex,* 13th ed. (Hamburg: Hoffmann and Campe, 1999); Butz Peters, *Tödlicher Irrtum: Die Geschichte der RAF* (Frankfurt am Main: Fischer, 2007); Wolfgang Kraushaar, ed., *Die RAF und der Linke Terrorismus* (Hamburg: Hamburger Edition, 2006); Jeremy Varon, *Bringing the War Home: The Weather Underground and the Red Army Faction and Revolutionary Violence in the Sixties and Seventies* (Berkeley: University of California

The collaboration of West German leftist terrorist organizations, especially the Revolutionary Cells but also the Red Army Faction and the June 2nd Movement, with the Popular Front for the Liberation of Palestine (PFLP) was of particular importance. Free of the responsibility of governance and unconcerned about foreign policy complications, the West German leftist terrorists were more willing than the East German government to publicly declare their support for the most extreme of the Palestinian terrorist organizations and to call for Israel's destruction. Like the international Left, the West German organizations championed the cause of the Vietnamese Communists. Yet, for them, the Israeli-Palestinian conflict intersected with German history far more than did the war in Vietnam.

In West Germany the turn against Israel came fifteen years later than in the Soviet bloc. In East Berlin, June 1967 stood for continuity; in West Germany, the months from June to September 1967 constituted a break and a redefinition of the meaning of left-wing anti-fascism. It was in that summer that the leading organization of the West German New Left, the *Sozialistische Deutschen Studentenbund* (Socialist German Student Organization) or SDS, debated and then adopted resolutions denouncing Israel and supporting the Arab states and the Palestinians.[37] Thereafter, the transformation of the meaning of anti-fascism that had occurred in the Soviet bloc in the early 1950s became predominant in the thinking of the West German New Left. In the process, its leaders attacked the traditions of "coming to terms with the past" as actually constituting a form of "philo-semitism," that is, an exaggerated, cynical and insincere public sympathy for the Jews. Following the turn of 1967, as Kloke and Kraushaar have separately pointed out, support for Israel became incompatible with identification with the radical Left. As the American political scientist Andrei Markovits has written insightfully, Israel became a wedge issue demarcating those who were and were not members of the West German and international radical Left.[38] By 1969, Dieter Kunzelmann, a prominent West Berlin leftist, was urging his comrades to overcome what he called "the Jewish complex," that is, a supposedly paralyzing and guilt-inducing memory of the Holocaust that stood in the way of what he regarded as the proper stance toward the Middle East conflict and thus

Press, 2004); and Jeffrey Herf, "The Age of Murder: Ideology and Terror in Germany," *Telos* (Fall 2008), 8–37; and at http://telospress.com/wp-content/uploads/2013/04/Herf_Telos144.pdf.

[37] Kloke, *Israel und die deutsche Link*.

[38] See Andrei S. Markovits, *Uncouth Nation: Why Europe Dislikes America* (Princeton, NJ: Princeton University Press, 2007).

obstructed leftist revolutionary thought and action.[39] The following chapters examine the abundant publications and many unpublished materials of the radical Left in West Germany that are available at the SDS archives at the Free University of Berlin, the files of protest movements at the Institute for Social Research in Hamburg and the International Institute for Social History in Amsterdam.

In West Germany, the existence of a small Jewish community and the formation of the Central Council of Jews in Germany created possibilities for Jews to express views on the events of the day.[40] Their leaders, such as Heinz Galinski (1912–1992) and Hendrik van Dam (1906–1973), paid close attention to the New Left's rhetoric. In their publications, such as the *Jüdische Allgemeine Wochenzeitung* (Jewish General Weekly Newspaper) and the *Jüdischer Presse Dienst* (Jewish Press Service), they chronicled the emergence of what they described as a new anti-Semitism and threat to Israel coming from the anti-Zionist Left. Galinski, the leader of the organized Jewish community in West Berlin and co-editor of the *Jüdische Allgemeine Wochenzeitung*, wrote a stream of editorials and essays about leftist terrorism aimed at Israel and at Jews in West Germany and about East Germany's support for the Arab states and the PLO. His colleagues in the Central Council, Werner Nachman and Alexander Ginsburg, wrote on the same themes, as did van Dam, founder and editor of the *Jüdischer Presse Dienst*. Having survived the Holocaust, these Jewish leaders were focused on the threat of a revival of Nazism. By the late 1960s, they turned increasingly to the threat coming from the Soviet bloc and the far left in West Germany. They left behind a vital documentary record. More than has been the case in the large literature on West German terrorism, I draw on their writings as evidence of what Jews saw and felt about the words and actions of the anti-Israeli Left in West Germany.

The hijacking of an Air France plane to Entebbe in July 1976 occupies an important place in this history because the terrorists held Jews against their will under threat of force, separated Israelis from non-Israelis and in several cases, Jews from non-Jews, collaborated with Idi Amin, an admirer of Hitler, and exchanged fire in combat with Israeli soldiers. The Revolutionary Cells, which had collaborated with the PFLP in the hijacking, also issued communiqués claiming responsibility for bombings of

39 See Kloke, *Israel und die deutsche Link*; and Wolfgang Kraushaar, *Die Bombe im Jüdischen Gemeindehaus* (Hamburg: Hamburger Edition, 2005).

40 On the early years of the Jewish community in postwar West Germany see Jay Howard Geller, *Jews in Post-Holocaust Germany, 1945–1953* (New York: Cambridge University Press, 2005).

Jewish institutions in West Germany. Circumstantial evidence has also emerged connecting West German leftists to an arson attack on a Jewish home for the aged in Munich in 1970 in which seven people were killed, though the case remains unsolved.[41] In 1969, Walter Ulbricht, then in the last years of his leadership of the East Germany dictatorship, suggested to Leonid Brezhnev, General Secretary of the Central Committee of the Communist Party of the Soviet Union, that East German "volunteers" should participate in the war of attrition against Israel following the Six-Day War.[42] East Germany generally limited itself to supplying weapons, military training and diplomatic support. In 1973, for example, the Politburo led by Erich Honecker sent MiG fighter jets to Syria where they were flown by Syrian or perhaps Soviet pilots against the Israelis. The files of the Socialist Unity Party Archives in Berlin and the Defense Ministry in Freiburg offer abundant evidence of the secret details of the SED regime's alliances with Arab states at war with Israel and with the PLO. East Germany backed up its public diplomatic offensive against Israel at the UN and in other international forum with secret delivery of weapons, provision of multi-year military training programs, cooperation by intelligence services, and provision of medical care for wounded Arab and PLO soldiers.

The West German terrorist organizations and the leftist groups of the 1970s, including the Marxist-Leninists, also waged political warfare using German-language leaflets, newspapers and magazines, mostly in the vicinity of West German universities. They did so with fewer resources than those of the East German government, but their views came to dominate the outlook of the West German radical Left and eventually the bulk of the West German Left when it came to the Israeli-Arab-Palestinian conflict. These groups cooperated with organizations of Arab and Palestinian students and workers living in West Germany, most importantly the General Union of Palestinian Students (GUPS) and the General Union of Palestinian Workers (GUPA). Both organizations were controlled by the PLO, had their headquarters in Cairo and existed in order to open a West German "front" in the battle against Israel.[43] Indeed, what we are

[41] On the arson attack on a Jewish home for the aged in Munich in 1970, see Wolfgang Kraushaar, *München 1970: über die antisemitischen Wurzeln des deutschen Terrorismus* (Hamburg: Rowohlt, 2013).

[42] "Schreiben von Walter Ulbricht an Leonid Breschnew vom 27." Oktober 1969, reprinted in Timm, *Hammer, Zirkel und Davidstern*, 535–536.

[43] On West German leftist terrorism see, for example, Aust, *Der Baader-Meinhof Komplex*; Peters, *Tödlicher Irrtum*; Kraushaar, ed., *Die RAF und der Linke Terrorismus* and Herf, "Age of Murder."

accustomed to call the "West German" left of the 1960s to the 1980s reflected the significant impact of the presence of Arabs and Palestinians working and studying in West Germany.[44] In the aftermath of the attack on the Israeli athletes at the Munich Olympics in September 1972, West Germany's interior minister Hans Dietrich Genscher banned both GUPS and GUPA. The following chapters draw as well on extensive and previously under-examined files from investigations into GUPS and GUPA conducted by the West German Federal Ministry of the Interior, and from West German Federal court decisions written in the aftermath of the attack, all of which shed considerable light on the relationship between both organizations and terrorism in West Germany and in the Middle East.

In the years following the collapse of the East German regime, the files of its central decision-making institutions, the Politburo and Central Committee, the Council of Ministers that implemented Politburo decisions, and the Foreign and Defense Ministries as well as the Stasi became accessible. A series of works in German began to document East German foreign and military policy towards Israel, the Arabs and the Palestinians. In 1996, for example, Michael Wolffsohn and a team of researchers began to document the fact and extent of East German arms deliveries to "Israel's enemies" – Gamal Abdel Nasser's Egypt, Hafez al-Assad's Syria, Muamar Khaddafi's Libya, and Yasser Arafat's PLO from the 1960s to 1980s.[45] In 1997, Angelika Timm, a scholar who had formerly worked in the East German Foreign Ministry, published a major study drawing on then available East German archives to examine East Germany's foreign policy towards the Middle East into the context of the international Cold War between the Soviet Union and the West, the competition between West and East Germany, and East Germany's search for diplomatic recognition. Timm also examined the connections between anti-Zionism, Communist marginalization of the memory of the Holocaust, and the resulting intersection of antagonism to Israel with antisemitism in postwar East German society.[46] In 2012, another German historian, Klaus

[44] The annual reports of the West German *Verfassungsschutz,* the Organization to Protect the Constitution, the West German government offer details about the political activities of many groups established by foreign students. Also see Quinn Slobodian, *Foreign Front: Third World Politics in Sixties West Germany* (Durham, NC: Duke University Press, 2012).

[45] Michael Wolffsohn, *Deutschland Akte: Juden und Deutsche in Ost und West, Tatsachen und Legenden* (Munich: edition ferenczy bei Bruckmann, 1996), especially "Feinde Israels als Freunde-die Arabienpolitik der DDR," 249–274.

[46] Timm, *Hammer, Zirkel und Davidstern.*

Storkmann, published a pioneering study of East Germany's military relationships and "secret solidarity" with third-world countries, including Nasser's Egypt.[47] In 2002, the German historian Stefan Meining, revealed still more material about East German weapons deliveries to Israel's Arab enemies, especially to Syria.[48] As the following chapters indicate, since the works of the 1990s and early 2000s, the East and West German archives have opened still more, thus making it possible to offer considerably more evidence about the mix of hard and soft power that the East German government used against the state of Israel.

West German terrorism aroused enormous media attention at the time. A significant German language scholarship now exists. Two excellent works by West German journalists, Stefan Aust and Butz Peters, separately documented connections between West German leftist terrorists and Arab states and Palestinian terror organizations.[49] In 1994, Martin Kloke published what remains a standard work on the turn of the West German Left against Israel and toward the Arab states and the Palestinians.[50] Wolfgang Kraushaar, of the Hamburg Institute for Social Research, has examined these themes but has focused on the turn to terrorism by parts of the West German radical left in the aftermath of the 1960s. In 2006 he edited a two-volume publication of over sixty essays by various authors dealing with the Red Army Faction and leftist terrorism. The essays in those volumes constituted another significant advance in scholarly work on leftist terrorism in West Germany and the issues of leftist anti-Zionism, anti-Semitism, and collaboration with the

[47] Klaus Storkmann, *Geheime Solidarität: Militärbeziehungen und Militärhilfen der DDR in die 'Dritte Welt'*, (Berlin: Ch. Links Verlag, 2012). On East Germany and the PLO, a forthcoming doctoral dissertation at the University of Leipzig promises to offer very important material and interpretation; see Lutz Maeke, "DDR und PLO. Die Palästinapolitik des SED-Staates," doctoral dissertation, Universität Leipzig, Summer 2014.

[48] Stefan Meining, *Kommunistische Judenpolitik: Die DDR, Die Juden und Israel* (Hamburg: LIT Verlag, 2002), "Jom Kippur 1973: Honeckers Krieg gegen Israel," 325–329.

[49] On the connections of the West German terrorist organizations to Palestinian organizations and to the Arab states, see Stefan Aust, *Baader-Meinhof: The Inside Story of the RAF* (New York: Oxford University Press, 2009); Peters, *Tödliche Irrtum: Die Geschichte der RAF* (Frankfurt/Main: Fischer Taschenbuch Verlag, 2007).

[50] Kloke, *Israel und die deutsche Link*. The journalism and essays of the West German author Henryk M. Broker offered an ongoing commentary on these developments. See his *Der ewige Antisemit: über Sinn und Funktion eines beständigen Gefühls* (Frankfurt: Fischer Taschenbuch, 1986; 2nd ed. Berlin: Berliner Taschenbuch, 2006); and *Vergesst Auschwitz: Der deutsche Erinnerungswahn und die Endlösung der Israel-Frage* (Munich: Albrecht Knaus, 2012).

Palestinian terror organizations.[51] One purpose of this work is to bring this still largely untranslated German-language scholarship to the attention of English readers, and to expand on it. The files of the West German government, especially the Foreign Office archives in Berlin and the files of the West German Interior Ministry in Federal Archive in Koblenz offer previously under- and unexamined archival material that sheds important light on these matters.

Seen from the Western side of the forbidding Berlin Wall, East Germany appeared to be an isolated and friendless prison which had locked its citizen inmates behind barbed wire, mine fields and a world-famous barrier. With a population of only seventeen million–less than a third of West Germany's–and an economy that produced little of interest to markets in Western Europe and the United States, the best thing that East Germany had going for it was its deceptive name, the German *Democratic Republic*. From the perspective of the West, it seemed to be enveloped in an isolation of its own making, cut off from the wider world and bereft of friends. Yet behind the Wall, East Germany's antagonism to Israel and its partisanship for the Arab states and the PLO played a major role in breaking out of isolation and making many friends around the globe.[52]

For the Arab governments and the PLO, East Germany was the German government that supported the Arab states and denounced Israel. East Germany's stance was an indispensable causal factor in their decisions to resist West German pressures to refrain from having diplomatic relations with it and instead open grant East Germany the diplomatic recognition it sought. The archives of the East German government confirm what the massive public documentation proclaimed, namely that East German antagonism to Israel was an essential element in the single most

[51] Wolfgang Kraushaar, ed. *Die RAF und der linke Terrorismus* (Hamburg: Hamburger Edition, 2006). See, in particular "Wolfgang Kraushaar, "Antizionismus als Trojanisches Pferd: Zur antisemitischen Dimension in den Kooperation von *Tupamaros West-Berlin*, RAF und RZ mit den Palästinensern," 676–695; Martin Jander, "Differenzen im antiimperialistischen Kampf: Zu den Verbindungen des Ministeriums für Staatssicherheit mit der RAF und dem bundesdeutschen Linksterrorismus," 696–713; and Thomas Skelton Robinson, "Im Netz verheddert: Die Beziehungen des bundesdeutschen Linksterrorismus zur *Volksfront für die Befreiung Palästinas* (1969–1980), 828–904. Also see Martin Jander, "German Leftist Terrorism and Israel: Ethno-Nationalist, Religious-Fundamentalist, or Social-Revolutionary?," *Studies in Conflict & Terrorism*, Vol. 38, No. 6, (June 2015), 456–477.

[52] On the multiple other factors including the domestic politics of the Arab regimes, their relations with West Germany and the efforts of the Soviet Union to gain influence in the Middle East that also played a role in the Arab state's recognition of East Germany, see Wentker, *Aussenpolitik in engen Grenzen*, 278–287.

successful chapter of the foreign policy of East Germany's forty-year history, namely the diplomatic breakthrough it achieved in 1969 by gaining recognition beyond the Warsaw Pact. The anti-Israeli policy was at the center of that achievement and of East Germany's growing popularity in many countries in Asia, Africa and Latin America.[53] The files of the West German Foreign Office confirm that West Germany's support for Israel placed it on the defensive in the Arab world. In its competition with West Germany, East Germany's strongest selling point among the Arab states was that in contrast to West Germany, it despised the state of Israel and supported its enemies. Its most effective criticism of West Germany was that the latter was guilty of being Israel's supporter. In this instance, East German Marxist-Leninist ideological conviction and traditional power politics reinforced one another.

From 1973, when it joined the United Nations, until its collapse in 1989, East Germany won the good will of literally dozens of member states at the United Nations. There, East German diplomats such as Ambassador Peter Florin played the anti-Israeli card with enormous success. At no time did East German political leaders or diplomats express qualms, reservations or even a sense of irony about the fact that a regime that was proud of its anti-fascist credentials had formed an alliance with states and organizations that were trying to destroy the Jewish state by force of arms. They did not discuss possible continuities between their "anti-Zionism" and that of the Nazi regime.[54] They did not criticize or even mention the open expressions of anti-Semitism or the celebrations of terrorist attacks that were broadcast on Arab and Palestinian radio and printed in the Arab press. At the UN the East Germans claimed that accusations that their policy had anything to do with anti-Semitism was a form of "slander."[55] Indeed, some of those celebrations came from groups they were supporting. Those Communists, such as Paul Merker

[53] See Wentker, *Aussenpolitik in engen Grenzen*. On West Germany's efforts to prevent diplomatic recognition of East Germany and the collapse of that policy in 1969, see H. Glenn Gray, *Germany's Cold War: The Global Campaign to Isolate East Germany, 1949–1969* (Chapel Hill: University of North Carolina Press, 2003).

[54] On Nazi Germany's anti-Zionism and its efforts to seek Arab support on that basis, see Herf, *Nazi Propaganda for the Arab World*.

[55] The insistence that the policy of the East German government had nothing to do with anti-Semitism persisted in the years after the end of the regime. On this theme see Anetta Kahane, "Mit Stumpf und Stiel ausgerottet? Antisemitismus in der DDR," in Heike Radvan, ed. "*Das hat's bei uns nicht gegeben!,*": *Antisemitismus in der DDR: Das Buch zur Austellung der Amadeu Antonio Stiftung* (Berlin: Amadeu Antonio Stiftung, 2010), 6–10.

and Leo Zuckermann, who would have objected to the mobilization of anti-Zionism and anti-Semitism for political gain, had long ago been silenced in the anti-cosmopolitan purges of the early 1950s.[56]

The Yom Kippur war of October 1973 – the most acute crisis of Israel's history since 1948 – was also a most revealing moment in the history of both East and West German relations to the Middle East. Despite its famous traditions of *Vergangenheitsbewältigung*, in 1973 when the issue was one of war and peace between Israel and the Arab states, West Germany took an official position of firm and unwavering neutrality. Dependency on Arab oil imports, the softening of support for Israel, especially on the left side of the political spectrum, and the constant pressure from many Arab states meant that the Federal Republic refrained from the kind of solidarity with Israel that one might have expected. At this critical moment, when Israel's survival hung in the balance, West Germany determined that its relationship to Israel was more normal than special. As a result, sharp tensions developed between the United States and its West German ally during the Yom Kippur War over Willy Brandt's policy of neutrality and its reluctance to assist efforts in support of Israel. Although the Communists were disseminating propaganda about a "Bonn-Tel Aviv Axis," such a bond was far removed from the political and military realities of the autumn of 1973. The diplomatic files of the United States and West German governments reveal in great detail the depth of the divide between the United States and West Germany that opened up following President Nixon's decision, supported by Secretary of State Kissinger, to resupply the Israeli armed forces in the midst of the war.

Two years later, however, West Germany was among those states that joined Israel and the United States in opposing the "Zionism is racism" resolution which was eventually passed by the General Assembly on November 10, 1975. The centrality of the American-Israeli alliance was also evident in the public battles at the UN fought by the American UN ambassador, Daniel Patrick Moynihan, together with his Israeli counterpart, Chaim Herzog, against the "Zionism is racism" resolution passed by the General Assembly on November 10, 1975.[57] That resolution was

[56] On the East German purge, see Herf, *Divided Memory*.

[57] See Daniel Patrick Moynihan, *A Dangerous Place* (Boston: Little, Brown, 1978). Also see Gil Troy, *Moynihan's Moment: America's Fight against Zionism as Racism* (New York: Oxford University Press, 2013); and Joshua Muravchik, *Making David into Goliath: How the World Turned against Israel* (New York: Encounter Books, 2014); and Chaim Herzog, *Who Stands Accused: Israel Answers Its Critics* (New York: Random House, 1978).

only one of many passed during those years denouncing Israel. West Germany and the United States often found themselves in the minority while East Germany consistently placed itself in the midst of large anti-Israeli majorities.

The East German Ministry of State Security, (MfS), known as the Stasi, played a central role in the regime's connections with both Palestinian terrorist organizations and the intelligence services of Arab states as they fought against the common enemies, the United States and Israel. This fact is confirmed by the Stasi files in Berlin, which serve as an important source for this work.[58] Stasi officials destroyed many documents in fall 1989 as the regime was collapsing,[59] and it may be that a great deal of material from the late 1960s and early 1970s, an era of numerous airplane hijackings and terrorist attacks by Palestinian organizations inside and outside Israel including the attack on the Munich Olympics, has either not yet been found, was never recorded, or was destroyed in fall 1989. Nevertheless, as the reader will see, significant documents from a variety of departments, such as Department XXII, called (*Terrorabwehr)*, "Counterterrorism" or "Defense against Terror," survived and are in the archives of the Federal Commissioner for the Archives of the State Security Service of the former German Democratic Republic in Berlin.[60] Department XXII was formed in 1975, and by 1980 it had a staff of 140 people. Gerhard Neiber (1929–2008), the deputy minister of the Stasi and second-in-command to the minister, Erich Mielke (1907–2000), oversaw its operations.[61] The files of Department XXII record the Stasi's contacts with, surveillance of, and at times cooperation with terrorist organizations in West Germany and the Middle East including the Red Army Faction (RAF), the Revolutionary Cells, June 2nd Movement, the Italian Red Brigades, the "Carlos" group, the Abu-Nidal group, and the various organizations under the umbrella of the PLO. The files also include material on the Stasi's important and complex relationship with the

[58] The full German title is: *Der Bundesbeauftrage für die Unterlagen des Ministerium des Staatssicherheitsdienstes der ehemaligen Deutschen Demokratischen Republik* hence *(BStU)* or Central Archives in Berlin of the Federal Commissioner for the Records of the State Security Service of the former German Democratic Republic.

[59] Tobias Wunschik, "'Abwehr' und Unterstutzung des internationalen Terrorismus – Die Hauptabteilung XXII," in Hubertus Knabe, ed. *West-Arbeit des MfS: Das Zusammenspiel von 'Aufklärung' und 'Abwehr,"* (Berlin: Ch. Links Verlag, 1999), 263–273.

[60] The BSTU files contain extensive materials on the Stasi's relations with countries and organizations around the world.

[61] Ibid., 264–265.

intelligence service of the Palestine Liberation Organization (PLO) and with the country of South Yemen, where the Popular Front for the Liberation of Palestine (PFLP) had bases.[62]

As we will see, Stasi officials confronted the dilemma of how to reconcile "anti-imperialist solidarity" with the PLO, the PFLP and DPFLP and others on its Executive Committee while trying to defend East Germany from charges that it and the Soviet Union were state sponsors of terrorism and to preserve beneficial financial support from West Germany.[63] Its response was a complex and interesting history of what I am calling East Germany's Eurocentric definition of counter-terrorism. On the one hand, the Stasi and the East German Defense Ministry supported and trained Palestinian terrorist organizations engaged in attacks on Israel and other targets in the third world. On the other hand, the Stasi sought to prevent the same terrorist organizations from carrying out attacks in West Germany and Western Europe that originated in East Germany or elsewhere in the Soviet bloc. It is, of course possible, that the Stasi supported terrorist attacks in West Germany or even carried out acts of terror itself but if so it is unlikely that documentary evidence survived the destruction of files in 1989. On the other hand, its files confirm that well-known Palestinian and Arab terrorists spent time in East Germany and that West German terrorists were able to escape from West to East Germany and thus avoid capture.

This work also includes new archival findings from the East German Ministry of Defense, its Council of Ministers and the Stasi files about East German weapons deliveries and military training to the Arab states before and after the Six-Day War of 1967, the Yom Kippur War of October 1973 and during the two decades of the 1970s and 1980s. In these years, the East Germans signed a series of formal agreements, most importantly with Hafez al-Assad's Baath regime in Syria but also with Iraq and Libya. These files also contain new material on East Germany's role in arming and training the PLO, especially from 1973 to the mid-1980s–that is, before, during and after Israel's invasion of Lebanon of 1982 and the expulsion of the PLO from that country. The GDR's delivery and repair of weapons, officer training and medical care for wounded soldiers offered crucial assistance to the PLO and its military operations. The support of the Soviet bloc more generally encouraged the Arab states and the PLO

[62] Ibid., 265–267.

[63] On West German loans to East Germany and their importance for the East German economy see Jonathan Zatlin *The Currency of Socialism: Money and Political Culture in East Germany* (New York: Cambridge University Press, 2007), esp. chapters 2–3.

in their uncompromising stance toward Israel and nourished their hopes that military victory over Israel was possible.

The East German files indicate that the leaders of the Palestine Liberation Organization were deeply troubled by the impending collapse of the East German regime in fall 1989. In East Berlin, they had been treated as leaders of a state, received official welcomes at airports, had their photos on the front pages of newspapers, dined with national leaders, conferred with high ranking officials, received extensive military training and free medical care, and been celebrated as revolutionary heroes. The collapse of the GDR, along with the other Communist regimes, brought all of this support to an end. So long as the alliance with the Soviet bloc existed, Arafat and Syria's Assad could entertain the hope that a next round of war and terror could eliminate "the Zionist aggressor." When the Soviet-bloc benefactor dissolved, the PLO leaders understood that a near-term military solution was no longer a realistic option. The history of the Soviet-bloc alliance with the Arab states and the PLO illuminates the connection between the revolutions of 1989 in Eastern Europe and the collapse of the Soviet Union in 1991, on the one hand, and the PLO's decision to turn to negotiations in 1993 on the other.

The key figures in this work are persons in East and West Germany who in one way or another took a public position regarding the Arab and Palestinian "armed struggle" against Israel. In East Germany, these people included the veteran Communists in key decision-making positions, among them the first secretaries of the Central Committee of the governing Socialist Unity Party (*Sozialistische Einheitspartei Deutschland*) or "SED" and thus head of the regime. Walter Ulbricht (1893–1973) held that position from 1950 to 1971 and was followed by Erich Honecker (1912–1994), who ruled from 1971 to 1989. Decisions made by the ruling Politburo shaped government policy. Other key East German actors, not as well known outside East Germany, included the following figures. In 1970, Herman Axen (1916–1992), director of the SED Central Committee's department of International Relations since 1966, was elevated into the Politburo.[64] He, along with Gerhard Grüneberg (1921–1981), played prominent roles in shaping foreign policy toward the Middle East. Willi Stoph (1914–1999), another member of the Politburo, was also chair of the government's Council of Ministers, an institution

64 "Axen, Hermann," in Bernd-Rainer Barth et al., eds. *Wer war Wer in der DDR* (Frankfurt/Main: Fischer Taschenbuch Verlag, 1996), 30.

that implemented Politburo decisions. He appointed Gerhard Weiss (1919–1986), the deputy chair of the Council of Ministers, to coordinate East German arms deliveries to a variety of third-world states and guerilla movements around the world. Foreign Minister Otto Winzer (1902–1975) was key to the establishment of diplomatic relations with the Arab states. Peter Florin (1921–2014) was Ambassador to the UN from 1973 to 1982. General Heinz Hoffmann (1910–1985), East Germany's defense minister from 1960 to 1985, was the central figure in the formation and consolidation of East German military alliances with the Arab states and to a lesser extent with the PLO as well. Erich Mielke (1907–2000), head of the Stasi, and Gerhard Neiber (1929–2008), the deputy minister who oversaw the operations of Department XXII, were directly involved in decision-making regarding connections with Arab and Palestinian terrorist organizations, including the PLO's intelligence services. We will have occasion to discuss the role of East Germany's diplomats at the United Nations and at the Embassies in Cairo, Beirut, and Damascus.

Yasser Arafat (1929–2004), chairman of the PLO, left a significant paper trail of public statements about the PLO's policy as did its de facto foreign minister, Farouk Kaddoumi (1931-). The PLO also left a very large record through its representatives at the United Nations and in communiqués of Voice of Palestine radio broadcasts in various Arab capitals that were monitored by the BBC's Summary of World Broadcasts and the United States Foreign Broadcast Information Service. The East Germans carefully recorded their conversations with Arab leaders, including Gamal Abdel Nasser, Hafez al-Assad, and Saddam Hussein. Their public declarations of anti-imperialist solidarity filled many front pages of the East German newspaper *Neues Deutschland*. As will become apparent, Heinz Hoffmann's discussions with Syria's long-serving defense minister, Mustafa Tlass (1932-), were of particular interest. The files do not indicate if Tlass revealed his profound hatred of Jews to the Defense Ministry, but Hoffmann was emphatic in extolling the "community of struggle" between the armed forces of East Germany and Syria. The numerous statements by the UN ambassadors from the Arab states and the PLO are readily available, as are the hundreds of letters that they and the Israelis sent to the office of the UN secretary general and the president of the Security Council.

Antagonism to Israel became a consensus within the radical Left in West Germany during and after the Six-Day War of 1967. In June 1967, Reimut Reiche (1941-) was president of West German SDS and Karl Dietrich Wolff (1943-) was elected to the post in the fall. It was in this four-month period that the organization took its turn against Israel. The turn to much more emphatic support for the PLO's "armed struggle" came in 1969 from the pen of Dieter Kunzelmann (1939-), a leading figure of the West Berlin "Tupamaros." He wrote leaflets and manifestos urging his fellow leftists to overcome "the Jewish complex" and support the Palestinian "Fedayeen." In November 1972, Ulrike Meinhof (1934–1976), by then infamous as a member of the "Baader-Meinhof Gang," celebrated the Black September attack on the Israeli athletes at the Olympics. The two Germans who actually exchanged gunfire with Israeli troops in Entebbe, Wilfried Böse (1949–1976) and Brigitte Kuhlmann (1947–1976), were members of the Revolutionary Cells and veterans of the leftist scene in Frankfurt/Main. A larger number of radical leftists did not take up arms but did join various Marxist-Leninist and Maoist organizations in the 1970s. They offered propaganda support to the PLO and the PFLP.

During and after the Six-Day War, antagonism to Israel and support for the Arab states and the Palestinian armed organizations in both the East German *government* and in the West German radical leftist *organizations* intensified. In the following decades, the lethal instruments of war and terrorism complemented angry words and rhetorical denunciations. The following chapters document and examine the resulting combination of radical leftist ideology with the use of force against the state and the people of Israel.

2

East Germany and the Six-Day War of June 1967

On June 15, 1967, in Leipzig, Walter Ulbricht, the first secretary of the Central Committee of the Socialist Unity Party and leader of the East German regime since 1949, delivered a speech that became one of the canonical texts of East German antagonism to Israel. The summary and the whole text were published in the government's official paper, *Neues Deutschland* (New Germany) (See Ulbricht in Figure 2.1).[1] When he spoke, the hopes for victory over the state of Israel by the Soviet bloc and the Arab states it supported had been dashed. Faced with one of the most devastating setbacks of Soviet policy in the Cold War, Ulbricht laid the entire blame for the war on the Israelis, who were part of what he called a conspiracy organized by the United States, Britain, and West Germany. At the outbreak of the war, the East German Politburo had declared its support for the Arab states and denounced Israeli "aggression." Ulbricht's speech in Leipzig restated what close observers had known for years but came as news to a stunned international public, namely, that the Communist regime in East Germany was an emphatic supporter of the Arab states' efforts to make war on the Jewish state.

Those outside East Germany who were surprised that a self-described anti-fascist regime had taken up sides against the Jewish state may have recalled the Soviet Union's support for the United Nations partition plan

[1] Walter Ulbricht, "Rede des Vorsitzenden des Staatsrates der DDR, Walter Ulbricht, auf einer Wählversammlung in Leipzig zu Frage der Lage im Nahen Osten und zur westdeutschen Expansionspolitik im Rahmen der USA-Globalstrategie" (June 15, 1967), in *Dokumente zur Außenpolitik der Deutschen Demokratischen Republik 1967 Band XV, 1. Halbband* ([East] Berlin: Staatsverlag der Deutschen Demokratischen Republik, 1970), 515–538.

FIGURE 2.1. Walter Ulbricht, fourth from left, secretary of the Central Committee of the SED, after his speech at the Seventh Party Conference of the Socialist Unity Party (SED) in East Berlin, April 17, 1967. From left to right: Yuri Andropov; Erich Honecker, secretary of the Central Committee of the SED; Leonid Breshnev, general secretary of the Communist Party of the Soviet Union; Ulbricht; Kurt Hager and Will Stoph, members of the SED Politburo.
Source: German Federal Archive (Bundesarchiv), Koblenz, Photo Archiv: Bild 183-F0417-0001-054, Allgemeine Deutscher Nachrichtendienst-Zentralbild, (ADN-ZB), Ulrich Kohls.

in 1947. On May 14, 1947, Soviet Foreign Minister Andrei Gromyko made the following statement in the United Nations General Assembly.[2] He took the Western powers to task for failing to ensure "the defence of the elementary rights of the Jewish people, and to safeguard it against the violence of the fascist executioners." That explained "the aspirations of the Jews to establish their own state. It would be unjust not to take this into consideration and to deny the right of the Jewish people to realize this aspiration."[3]

[2] "Mr. [Andrei] Gromyko" (Union of Soviet Socialist Republics), United Nations, General Assembly (May 14, 1947), A/2/PV.77, 6–14.

[3] Ibid., 12.

Gromyko preferred the establishment of "a single Arab-Jewish state with equal rights for Arabs and Jews." However if that was not possible because of conflict between them, then the Soviet Union would support a partition plan for a Jewish and an Arab state. The Soviet foreign minister added that it was "essential to bear in mind the indisputable fact that the population of Palestine consists of two peoples, the Arabs and the Jews. Both have historical roots in Palestine. Palestine has become the homeland of both these peoples, each of which plays an important part in the economy and the cultural life of the country."[4]

Three aspects of Gromyko's statement should be kept in mind as we examine the reversal of Soviet policy in 1949. First, Gromyko connected Soviet support for the Jews' aspiration to establish a state in Palestine to Soviet and Communist anti-fascism. Second, he described this aspiration as just. Third and less frequently noted in subsequent years, he affirmed that the Jews, as well as the Arabs, had "historical roots in Palestine" and that it was their homeland as much as it was that of the Arabs. The emergence of the Soviet and Soviet-bloc alliance with the Arab states and its antagonism to Israel required repudiation of all of these postulates. It also entailed a drastic redefinition of the meaning of anti-fascism as Gromyko understood it in 1947. The reversal of policy transformed the establishment of a Jewish state in Palestine into an injustice, denied that the Jews had historical roots in Palestine, and suppressed mention of the Holocaust.[5]

The repudiation of Soviet and Soviet-bloc support for Israel began in the midst of what were called the "anti-cosmopolitan purges." They were a set of bogus prosecutions of leading Communists, many of them Jews, in which denunciations of Zionism were intertwined with anti-Semitism. The purges began with the Doctors' Plot trial in Moscow in 1949 and continued in fall 1952 with the Slansky trial in Prague and the arrest of Paul Merker and purging of other leading East German Communists in East Berlin.[6] In East Berlin, Merker and other veteran Communists who had supported restitution payments to Jewish survivors of the Holocaust and who favored support for Israel were accused of being agents of a joint American-Zionist conspiracy whose purpose was to overthrow the

4 Ibid., 13.

5 On the shift from support for Israel to opposition see Arnold Krammer, *The Forgotten Friendship: Israel and the Soviet Bloc, 1949–1953* (Urbana: University of Illinois Press, 1974).

6 On the Doctor's Plot see Jonathan Brent and Vladimir Naumov, *Stalin's Last Crime: The Plot against Jewish Doctors, 1949–1953* (New York: Harper Perennial, 2004).

Communist regimes.[7] During and after the purges, the Communist regimes expelled Israel and Zionism from the ranks of praiseworthy anti-fascist efforts and instead vilified Israel as an ally and tool of US and West German "imperialism." By the fall of 1952 at the latest, it was impossible to support Israel publicly and remain active in Communist politics in the Soviet bloc or in Communist parties around the world. The Leninist theory of imperialism and Stalin's decision to seek to expel Western, especially American, power from the strategically vital area of the Middle East led the Communists to regard Israel, which had deep affinities for democracies in Western Europe and the United States, to be a part of the enemy camp in the emerging global Cold War. Communist anti-imperialism of the Cold War was displacing the Communist anti-fascism of 1935–1939 and 1941–1947.[8]

For the Soviet Union as well as the East German Communists, the turn toward the Arabs and against Israel reasserted Marxist-Leninist orthodoxy.[9] East Germany signed its first trade agreement with Egypt in 1953; others with Lebanon, Syria, and Yemen followed in 1955 and 1956. These agreements were accompanied by denunciations of "Israeli aggression" and of Israel's West German supporters.[10] In 1957, Otto Grotewohl, the chairman of the East Germany's Council of Ministers, the powerful body that implemented decisions of the governing Politburo, told Egypt's president, Gamal Abdel Nasser, that the East German struggle against the forces of "fascism and militarism" in West Germany required close relations with Egypt. Grotewohl associated Communist anti-fascism with establishment of close relations with Israel's primary adversary at the time, and in 1959, he visited Nasser in Cairo.[11] In 1958, Gerhard Weiss,

[7] On the East German purges and the Merker case, see Herf, *Divided Memory: The Nazi Past in the Two Germanys* (Cambridge, MA: Harvard University Press, 1997), 106–161.

[8] On Communist anti-fascism during World War II and the Cold War, see Francois Furet, *The Passing of an Illusion: The Idea of Communism in the Twentieth Century*, trans. Deborah Furet (Chicago: University of Chicago Press, 2000); and Anson Rabinbach, *Begriffe aus dem Kalten Krieg: Totalitarismus, Antifaschismus, Genozid* (Göttingen: Wallstein Verlag, 2009).

[9] On the East German Communists see Catherine Epstein, *The Last Revolutionaries;* and Herf, *Divided Memory.* On the Communists, Israel, and Zionism, also see Thomas Haury, *Antisemitismus von Links: Kommunistische Ideologie, Nationalismus und Antizionismus in der frühen DDR* (Hamburg: Hamburger Edition, 2002); Stephen Norwood, *Antisemitism and the American Far Left* (New York: Cambridge University Press, 2013); Robert S. Wistrich, *From Ambivalence to Betrayal: The Left, the Jews and Israel* (Lincoln: University of Nebraska Press, 2012)

[10] Herf, *Divided Memory*, 191.

[11] Otto Grotewohl to Gamel Abdel Nasser (June 24, 1957), Otto Grotewohl NL 90/497, SAPMO-BA, ZPA, 67–75 (now located in the Bundesarchiv Berlin); cited in Herf, *Divided Memory*, 192. Also see Inge Deutschkron, *Israel und die Deutschen*, rev. ed.

who as deputy of the Council of Ministers in the 1970s and 1980s coordinated East German weapons shipments to third-world countries, told a press conference in Baghdad that while East Germany had "no relations of any kind with Israel," West Germany's "so-called reparations payments" were "making an essential contribution to Israel's material and moral strength," which had been repeatedly felt "in the imperialist policy of hostility against the Arabs."[12] Currying favor with the Arab states by denouncing West German support for Israel remained an enduring theme of East German foreign policy.

East Germany's alliance with Nasser's Egypt took a significant step forward when Ulbricht visited Cairo from February 24 to March 2, 1965. There he spoke of a "common struggle" against shared enemies. He denounced Israel as "an imperialist outpost in Arab space," attacked West German military cooperation with Israel, and said that East Germans and Egyptians met on the common terrain of anti-imperialism and socialism. The two governments signed an agreement for expanded exchanges between their universities and in cultural life.[13] It was also then that, on a modest scale, East Germany joined the Soviet-bloc program of arms shipments to Egypt. On March 7, 1965, the Federal Republic of Germany (West Germany) announced its decision to offer formal diplomatic recognition to Israel. On March 14, the Israelis accepted the offer. On March 15 and 16, a majority of the thirteen states of the Arab League voted to break diplomatic relations with West Germany and six – Egypt, Iraq, Yemen, Algeria, Sudan, and Kuwait – indicated a readiness to offer formal diplomatic recognition to East Germany. In so doing they began the erosion of West Germany's "Hallstein doctrine," according to which it refused to have diplomatic relations with any country that established diplomatic relations with East Germany.[14]

(Cologne: Verlag Wissenschaft und Politik, 1991); and Peter Ditmar, "DDR und Israel: Ambivalenz einer Nicht-Beziehung," *Deutschland-Archiv,* pt. 1 (July 1977), 736–754, and pt. 2 (August 1977), 848–861.

[12] Gerhard Weiss (Baghdad, October 27, 1958), in *Dokumente zur Aussenpolitik der Deutschen Demokratischen Republik, 1949–1986* (DADDR), *BD. 6.* 317; cited in Herf, *Divided Memory,* 192.

[13] On Ulbricht in Cairo in 1965, see Herf, *Divided Memory,* 192–195. Also see Walter Ulbricht and Gamal Abdel Nasser, "Gemeinsame Erklärung" (Cairo, March 1, 1965), in DADDR, vol. 13, 855. On the beginnings of arms deliveries see Klaus Storkmann, *Geheime Solidarität: Militärbeziehungen und Militärhilfen der DDR in die "Dritte Welt"* (Berlin: Ch. Links Verlag, 2012).

[14] On West Germany's Hallstein doctrine, see William Glenn Gray, *Germany's Cold War: The Global Campaign to Isolate East Germany, 1949–1969* (Chapel Hill: University of North Carolina Press, 2007), 81–86 and 174–182.

Upon his return to East Berlin from Cairo, Ulbricht spoke of a political battle against "the imperialist military base of Israel" and its supporters in NATO and West Germany. In his view, the issue of Israel was utterly separate from "the suffering and injustice inflicted by the criminal Hitler regime on the Jewish citizens of Germany and other European states."[15] East Germany found common cause with Egypt and other Arab states opposed to imperialism, not with Israel, a state that had established ties to the West. The serene and untroubled confidence with which Ulbricht defended a policy of East German antagonism to Israel remained a striking feature of East German Communism. The Ulbricht visit to Cairo made clear that antagonism to Zionism and to Israel was *both* a matter of deep ideological conviction *and* an effective tool of traditional power politics.[16] As we will see, this *mutually reinforcing* quality of Communist ideology, power politics, and national self-interest was evident in East German diplomatic successes in the 1970s and early 1980s.

As the Soviet Union and its allies, including East Germany, argued that Israel bore sole responsibility for the conflict with the Arabs, they did not acknowledge that Israel faced any threats to its existence in 1967. Hence a brief discussion of events preceding the Six-Day War is in order. By mid-May of that year, Egypt's President Nasser had ordered three Egyptian army divisions across the Suez Canal into the Sinai Desert. Michael Oren, in his history of the war, wrote that each was composed of "15,000 men and close to 100 Soviet T-54 and T-55 tanks, 150 armored personnel carriers and a range of Soviet artillery: howitzers, heavy mortars, Katyusha rockets, SU-100 anti-tank guns," along with vast amounts of ammunition, MiG-17 and -21 fighters, and – IDF intelligence believed – "canisters of poison gas."[17] On May 17, Nasser ordered his navy to blockade the Gulf of Aqaba to Israeli shipping. On May 19, UN Secretary General U Thant acquiesced to Nasser's demand that the United Nations Emergency Force (UNEF) separating Israeli and Egyptian forces be withdrawn from the Sinai.[18] Syria had launched repeated attacks on northern Israel to such an extent that a "miniwar" with Israel broke out in late March. In the last week in May, Syrian army units gathered near

[15] Walter Ulbricht, "Rundfunk- und Fernsehinterview ... mit Gerhart Eisler" (East Berlin, March 7, 1965) in DADDR, vol. 13, 872–873; cited in Herf, *Divided Memory*, 194.

[16] Alexander Troche, *Ulbricht und die Dritte Welt: Ost-Berlins: Kampf gegen die Bonner 'Alleinvertretungsanmaß'* (Erlangen: Palm and Enke, 1996).

[17] Michael Oren, *Six Days of War: June 1967 and the Making of the Modern Middle East* (New York: Oxford University Press, 2002), 63, and 67–75.

[18] Ibid.

the Israeli border and made preparations for an attack. Military units from Iraq in Jordan and from Morocco, Libya, Saudi Arabia, and Tunisia arrived in the Sinai. The Arab states had gathered 900 combat aircraft, more than 5,000 tanks and half a million men, plus funds from the Arab oil producers in preparation for war.[19]

Faced with an imminent attack, the Israeli Air Force launched a preemptive strike on June 5. By the end of that morning, its squadrons, composed primarily of French-made Mirage jets, had destroyed 286 of Egypt's 420 combat aircraft and two-thirds of the Syrian Air Force on the ground. The Israelis also destroyed the Jordanian Air Force. With command of the air, Israeli armored columns won decisive battles against the Egyptian armed forces in the Sinai Desert and against the Jordanian forces in the West Bank following Jordan's decision to enter the war. Fierce fighting continued in the following days in the Sinai Desert and in the battle for Jerusalem. On June 8, faced with a rout of his army in the Sinai, Nasser told his ambassador to the United Nations that Egypt was seeking a cease-fire. After intense fighting with heavy casualties on both sides, Israel's Golani Brigade seized the Golan Heights, from which Syrian forces had bombarded Israel's northern towns. The Syrians accepted a cease-fire on June 10. In six days, faced with the prospect of invasion and destruction by all of its Arab neighbors, Israel had instead won a decisive victory against Soviet supported forces of the Arab states.[20]

As Israel's victory was so overwhelming, the verbal threats that preceded it have faded from history and memory. They should be kept in mind. The British Broadcasting Service (BBC) monitoring service reported them in full. On May 16, "Palestine Service" in Cairo quoted one Fu'ad Yasin as follows:

> Fighting Palestinian masses, Cairo – with you behind it – is moving. It is moving to take the initiative in a confrontation with Israel; moving to wage a life-and-death battle against Israel and all those who stand behind it and act in its behalf .... The menace and challenge of Israel have persisted for too long. The very existence of Israel in our usurped land has endured beyond all expectations. An end must be

[19] Ibid., 162–164.

[20] On the course of the war, see Oren, *Six Days of War,* 170–304. He summarizes the losses in the war as follows: "the Egyptians lost between 10,000 and 15,000 men, among them 1,500 officers and forty pilots; thousands were wounded. An additional 5,000 Egyptians were listed as missing. Seven hundred Jordanian soldiers died, and over 6,000 were wounded or missing. Syria's losses were estimated at 450 dead and roughly four times that number wounded. Israel admitted to 679 dead and 2,653 wounded, though IDF fatality figures were later placed as high as 800 – the equivalent in per capita terms of 80,000 Americans," 305.

put to Israel and to its very existence. So prepare, our rebellious brothers, to rise to your sacred national responsibility for which you have long waited.[21]

Iraqi, Syrian, and Jordanian forces had joined those of Egypt so that by May 30 the encirclement of Israel was complete. On May 19, Cairo government radio asserted, "Today we are ready to begin the most brutal and awful war in order to prevent the imperialists and the UN from protecting Israel. We will fight for the reconquering of Palestine." In another broadcast that day it announced, "We will destroy Israel." On June l, Ahmed Shukeiri, the first leader of the Palestine Liberation Organization, said, "After this war, there were hardly be any Jewish survivors."[22]

On May 19, 1967, the Voice of Palestine in Cairo announced that the Martyr Izz ad Din al Qassam unit "swears by the blood of martyrs that it will make your life hell, you Zionists, before you depart from our country once and for all. Zionists, we shall re-enact the massacres of Dayr Yasin [Deir Yassin] and Nahhlin against you. We will have no mercy on children and women as you had no mercy on ours. We shall make your life on our land impossible."[23] On May 23, 1967, Syrian government radio in Damascus looked forward to a "holy war."[24] It declared, "The time has come for us to throw the usurpers into the sea ... time that we excised the Zionist cancer which is draining the vitality of our people." The United States and the Zionists should "know that we shall hang the last imperialist soldier with the intestines of the last Zionist."[25] On May 23, the Soviet Union's official news agency, TASS, asserted, "Israel's ruling circles have continued to aggravate the atmosphere of military psychosis in that

[21] "Cairo Radio Calls for Preparation for Battle," (a) Cairo 'Palestine Service' in Arabic 13.15 GMT, Excerpts form a broadcast by Fu'ad Yasin (May 16, 1967), BBC, *Summary of World Broadcasts, SWB*. Part 4. *The Middle East and Africa* (May 11, 1967), MR/2468/A/6. For the PLO leader's comments on Chinese Communist military support see "'Palestine Day Rallies'" (a) 'Voice of Palestine' in Arabic 16.30 GMT (May 16, 1967), BBC, *SWB*. Part 4. *The Middle East and Africa*, (May 16, 1967), ME/2469/A/8.

[22] Hendrik van Dam, "Zum Begriff des Angriffskrieges: Arabische Stimmen kommentieren sich selbst." *Jüdischer Presse Dienst*, Nr. 5 (1967), Zentralarchiv zur Erforschung der Geschichte der Juden in Deutschland, Heidelberg, B.1/7.466, Zentralrat der Juden in Deutschland, "Nah Ost Krise 1967, I 466.

[23] "Report on Operations in Israel, Voice of Palestine in Arabic 16:30 GMT, [BBC] *Summary of World Broadcasts*. Part 4. *The Middle East and Africa* (May 19, 1967), ME/2471/A/3.

[24] "Damascus Radio Call for War, Damascus home service in Arabic 11:15 GMY (repeated 18.15 GMT) (May 23, 1967) BBC *SWB, s*. Part 4. *The Middle East and Africa*, ME/2474/A/10. On the support for Syria by East German foreign minister Otto Winzer see "Otto Winzer in Syria," BBC *SWB*. Part 4. *The Middle East and Africa*, EE/2466/A4/3May 11, 1967).

[25] Ibid.

country."[26] President Aref of Iraq stated his war aims: "Our goal is to clear – to wipe Israel off the face of the map."[27] The statements of Arab leaders left no doubt about the slaughter that would befall a defeated Israel.

At the United Nations, Israel's diplomats drew attention to the Arab threats. On May 31, Gideon Rafael, Israel's UN ambassador, told the Security Council that the representatives of Iraq, Jordan, Lebanon, Syria, and Egypt "have threatened Israel and the world with total war ... to destroy the independence of my country and to extinguish the existence of my people." They had portrayed the victim as the aggressor and "pretend[ed] to have no offensive intentions toward Israel. What a mockery." Though the armistice agreements between Israel and its neighbors "prohibited all hostile acts," regular and irregular forces had crossed Israel's borders over the years "thousands of times." The Security Council armistice agreements called for an end to a state of war, but it was "the policy of the Arab states to practice this outlawed belligerence." That was "the crux of the matter" and "the fundamental controversy. The Armistice Agreements envisaged the restoration of total peace, while the Arab states are engaged in preparations for total war."[28]

On June 6, 1967, a day after the Six-Day War began, Israel's foreign minister, Abba Eban, addressed the UN Security Council (Figure 2.2).[29] In the preceding three weeks, he told them, Nasser had massed "an army, greater than any force ever assembled in history in the Sinai." That army was composed of five infantry divisions, two armored divisions, 80,000 men, and 900 tanks. Nasser had dismissed the UN peacekeeping forces. He declared that the city of Eilat did not form part of Israel, a country that he said would soon expire. In addition, Nasser imposed a blockade to shipping to Israel in the Gulf of Aqaba and thus "strangled" its "maritime approaches to the whole eastern half of the world." The UN withdrew its Emergency Force from the Sinai without taking Israel's

[26] "Soviet Government Statement, Moscow home service and Tass in English 20:50 GMT (May 23, 1967), BBC, *SWB*, s. Part 4. *The Middle East and Africa*, SU/2474/A4/1.

[27] Ibid.

[28] Gideon Rafael (Israel), "United Nations Security Council Official Records hereafter UNSCOR], 22nd Year, 1345th Meeting, May 31, 1967, New York, United Nations Official Documents System (UN ODS), S/PV.1345, 11. Also see Abba Eban (Israel), UNSCOR, 22nd Year, 1348th Meeting, June 6, 1967, New York, UN ODS, S/PV.1348, 16–17.

[29] Abba Eban (Israel), UNSCOR, 22nd Year, 1348th Meeting, June 6, 1967, New York, UN ODS, S/PV.1348, 14. Documents of the United Nations are listed in its annual *Yearbooks*. All Security Council documents and many documents of the General Assembly are available at the remarkable UN Official Documents System online.

FIGURE 2.2. Abba Eban (left), foreign minister of Israel, and Gideon Rafael, permanent representative (ambassador) of Israel to the United Nations, United Nations General Assembly debate, June 19, 1967.
Source: United Nations Photo Library, 147670.

interests into account. What, he asked, was the use of a United Nations presence when the umbrella was "taken away as soon as it begins to rain?" Jordan as well joined in the attack, so "every house and street in Jerusalem now came into the range of fire," as "did the crowded and pathetically narrow [twelve miles in 1967] coastal strip in which so much of Israel's fate and population is concentrated." Iraqi troops reinforced Jordanian unity. Expeditionary forces from Algeria and Kuwait had arrived in Egypt. Syrian units, including artillery, overlooked the Jordan valley. "In short, there was peril for Israel wherever it looked.... There was an apocalyptic air of approaching peril. And Israel faced this danger alone." Despite "an unforgettable surge of sympathy across the world ... the dominant theme of our condition was danger and solitude."[30]

Eban pointed out that on May 26 Nasser had said, "We intend to open a general assault against Israel. This will be total war. Our basic aim will be to destroy Israel." It was not idle chatter. "The policy, the arms, the men had all been brought together" for "the murder of a state"

[30] Ibid. 14–15.

that was "the last sanctuary of a people which had seen six million of its sons [*sic*] exterminated by a more powerful dictator two decades before." Hence, "on the morning of 5 June, when Egyptian forces engaged us by air and land, bombarding the villages of Kissufim, Nahal-Oz and Ein Hasheelosha," Israel knew that the "limits of safety had been reached." So "in accordance with its inherent right of self-defence as formulated in Article 51 of the United Nations Charter, Israel responded defensively in full strength." Though Israel hoped to contain the conflict, Jordan "opened artillery attacks across the whole long frontier, including Jerusalem." The Syrian air forces and artillery units joined in as well. From Jordan, the city of Jerusalem itself came under fire.[31]

Nasser's closure of the Strait of Tiran and blockade of the Gulf of Aqaba was an act of war. Eban asked the members of the council to imagine that a foreign power forcibly closed

> New York or Montreal, Boston or Marseille, Toulon or Copenhagen, Rio or Tokyo or Bombay harbor. How would your Governments react? What would you do? How long would you wait? ... These then were the three main elements in the tension: the sabotage movement; the blockade of the port; and perhaps more imminent than anything else, this vast and purposeful encirclement movement, against the background of an authorized presidential statement announcing that the objective of the encirclement was to bring about the destruction and the annihilation of a sovereign State.[32]

After the cease-fire, the first principle for a future peace "must be the acceptance of Israel's statehood and the total elimination of the fiction of its non-existence." It would, Eban added, be "grotesque" if an "international community" of 122 sovereign states could not acknowledge sovereignty of "a people which had given nationhood its deepest significance and its most enduring grace."

Nikolai Fedorenko, the Soviet UN ambassador, had blamed Israel for the war. Eban asked him the following questions:

> Who was it that attempted to destroy a neighboring State in 1948, Israel or its neighbours? Who now closes an international waterway to the port of a neighbouring State, Israel or the United Arab Republic? Does Israel refuse to negotiate a peace settlement with the Arab States, or do they refuse to do so with it? Who disrupted the 1957 pattern of stability [maintained in the Sinai with UN peacekeeping forces, JH], Israel or Egypt? Did troops of Egypt, Syria, Jordan, Iraq, Lebanon, Kuwait and Algeria surround Israel in this menacing confrontation, or

[31] Ibid., 14–15.
[32] Ibid., 16–17.

has any distinguished representative seen some vast Israel colossus surrounding the area between Morocco and Kuwait?[33]

Fedorenko refused to acknowledge any of the threats. The rhetorical attacks on Israel from the Soviet Union, the Warsaw Pact, and the Arab states in 1967 and in the succeeding decades displayed an enduring internal contradiction. On the one hand, the Soviet Union and its allies described Israel in the most pejorative terms possible, comparing it to Nazi Germany or apartheid South Africa and calling it a tool of imperialism and a racist, colonial, settler state. Hence, it was its existence, not just its policies, that was the sole source of war and conflict in the Middle East. Moreover, they called Israel a threat to the "world," not just to Middle East peace. The clear implication of their verbal attacks was that Israel deserved to be destroyed, by force of arms if necessary, and that a war to carry out that goal would be just. Yet at the same time the Soviets and their allies denied or ignored the obvious and undeniable facts that the Arab states and Palestinian guerrilla organizations were, in fact, engaged in precisely such a war. They made a case for Israel's destruction at the same time that they denied that it faced any threats to its existence.

This mixture of denunciation and denial was evident when in the UN Security Council, on June 9, 1967, Fedorenko compared Israel to Nazi Germany and called for Israel's leaders to be put on trial as the Nazi leaders had been in Nuremberg. He said, "Israel's leaders are now repeating the tragic experience of fascist aggression not only in their methods of accusing the victims of aggression and in their attempts to blame them for the crime which has been committed, but also in their 'blitzkrieg' tactics." Israel's leaders "should be put in the dock before an international tribunal such as that which, twenty years ago, condemned the crimes of the main culprits in the war against peace and humanity."[34]

Fedorenko referred to the Warsaw Pact statement of June 10 issued by Bulgaria, Czechoslovakia, the German Democratic Republic, Hungary, Poland, the Soviet Union, and Yugoslavia that denounced "Israel's aggression." Although American military assistance to Israel before 1967 had been quite modest and the United States was preoccupied with the war in Vietnam, Fedorenko claimed that the Six-Day War was "the result of a conspiracy by certain imperialist forces, particularly the United States, against the Arab states." In response, he declared the Soviet bloc's

[33] Ibid., 18.

[34] Nikolai Fedorenko, UNSCOR, 22nd Year, 1353rd Meeting, June 9, 1967, New York, UN ODS, S/PV.1353, 6.

"complete and whole-hearted solidarity with the just struggle of the Arab states" and promised to "assist them in repelling aggression and defending their national independence and territorial integrity."[35] Gideon Rafael in reply denounced Fedorenko's "infamous comparison of Israel with Hitler Germany." Rafael said he had heard "the most infamous threats from the Soviet representative, threats to extinguish Israel." They reminded him "of the language which preceded the events which led up to the trials in Nurnberg."[36] On June 10, Fedorenko said Israel's leaders were "copying the infamous tactics of the Nazi criminals." Did not Israel's policy "bring to mind the grievous memory of the demands made by the leaders of the Reich for so-called *Lebensraum* ... that *Lebensraum* for which they unleashed the Second World War?"[37] Bulgaria's UN ambassador, Milko Tarabanov, added that if Rafael wished to address the Security Council, "He must reply as the party accused of aggression" and should not mention the Soviet Union, "which, at the cost of many lives, helped to save mankind from Hitlerian aggression, to which it nearly fell victim."[38]

Rafael replied, "I am not here as the accused party; I am not here in the dock, and the representative of Bulgaria has not been appointed as a prosecutor." The statements of the Soviet Union and Bulgaria "very much remind us of the very somber chapter of the Moscow trials."[39] Rafael criticized the Soviet and Bulgarian "scrupulous disregard for the facts, which they select and twist to suit their own ulterior motives." The UN Security Council was not a trial but "the highest organ of the United Nations, where representatives of independent Governments represent their countries," as Rafael intended to do. The Soviet Union had reached "a record-low in vilification when he dared to refer in one breath to Israel and to the Nazi monster."[40] Rafael added that Fedorenko "blindly refuses to admit that these same Arab States have for twenty years been threatening to annihilate Israel and to apply to its people the 'final solution' which eluded Hitler." The Soviet Union had "fanned and is continuing to fan, the passions of Arab violence and the flames of hatred and extremism" and thereby "contributed in no small way to the present

35 Ibid., 6.

36 Ibid., 9.

37 Nikolai Fedorenko, UNSCOR, 22nd Year, 1356rd Meeting, June 10/11, 1967, New York, UN ODS, S/PV.1356, 2.

38 Milko Tarabonov, UNSCOR, 22nd Year, 1356rd Meeting, June 10/11, 1967, New York, UN ODS, S/PV.1356, 12.

39 Gideon Rafael (Israel), UNSCOR, 22nd Year, 1356th Meeting, June 10/11, 1967, New York, UN ODS, S/PV.1356, 12.

40 Ibid., 12–13.

calamities of the Arab world."[41] In contrast to the powerlessness of the Jews in the Soviet bloc during the anti-cosmopolitan purges, Rafael as the ambassador of a sovereign state and member of the UN was able to challenge his accusers. As noted previously, the equation of Zionism and Israel with Nazi Germany began in Arab political life soon after World War II. Yet though the association may not have originated in Moscow, its repetition by the Soviet Union and by the Warsaw Pact states spread the idea well beyond the Arabic-speaking world and made it into an element of global Communist and leftist political discourse. Once introduced, it remained an important component of the propaganda offensive waged against Israel in subsequent decades. The East German leaders never publicly rejected the association. On the contrary, their government controlled press and other media repeated variations of the theme.[42]

THE RESPONSE IN EAST BERLIN

During these years, the Communists presented themselves as both supporters of "national liberation struggles" in the third world and sober, practical realists who sought a "political solution" to the Arab-Israeli conflict. Yet as they held Israel – and the United States – solely responsible for the conflict, it was not surprising that in the days preceding the war, their view of a political solution fanned the flames of Arab bellicosity. On June 4, Ulbricht broadcast an expression of solidarity sent to Syria's head of state, Nur ad-Din al-Atasi.[43] He expressed "profound indignation" about the "hostile and aggressive actions of US imperialism and Israel against the Syrian Arab Republic and the other Arab states." Ulbricht denounced support for Israel from the West German government and media. East Germany, on the other hand, "opposed this anti-Arab attitude" of the Federal Republic and "at the present moment considers it its duty to unmask and fight this imperialist conspiracy against the Arab peoples" and to support "with all its strength the measures taken" by Syria, Egypt, and other Arab states to defend "their sovereignty, independence and freedom."[44] Also on June 4, the BBC

41 Ibid., 13.

42 On the equation of Zionism and Israel with Nazi Germany in the Arab states, see the important study by Meir Litvak and Esther Webman, *From Empathy to Denial: Arab Responses to the Holocaust* (London: Hurst, 2009; New York: Oxford University Press, 2011).

43 "Eastern Germany" (Text of Walter Ulbricht's message to Nur ad-Din al-Atasi, the Syrian head of State) ADN in German, 19:45 GMT, 4.6.67, [BBC] *Summary of World Broadcasts*. Part 4. *The Middle East and Africa*, ME/2484/A4/1–2.

44 "Eastern Germany" (Text of Walter Ulbricht's message to Nur ad-Din al-Atasi, the Syrian head of state) ADN in German 19:45 GMT, 4.6.67, BBC *SWB*. Part 4. *The Middle East*

reported on a broadcast in Hebrew from Cairo aimed at Israelis: "The Arab armies are carrying out their duty, destroying your towns and villages.... The Arab armies have decided to destroy your leaders completely."[45] The East German press did not take note of these threats.

The Soviet bloc, including East Germany, fanned Arab radicalism in another way by reinforcing mythical thinking in the Arab capitals. As the war turned into an utter disaster for the Arab states, the Soviet-bloc states reinforced the Arab belief that only American and British intervention had caused such an utter and complete defeat. The extent of Egyptian misperception was evident in a meeting of June 17 in East Berlin between Wolfgang Kiesewetter, East Germany's deputy foreign minister, and Ahmed Fuad, a director of Egypt's State Bank. Fuad claimed that while Egypt was ready to deal "with the problem of Israel by itself," it was not prepared for "a direct confrontation with the United States," which, he claimed, had "given 1,000 planes with volunteer pilots" to Israel that made it possible for Israel to unleash its aerial attack on Egypt.[46] Fuad's claim was a complete fiction. Kiesewetter did not try to correct Fuad's delusions.[47] Syria's government was also unwilling to face facts about defeat. On June 7, with most of its air force decimated and Arab armed forces destroyed on the ground by Israeli land and air forces, Damascus radio broadcast that the enemy was being "defeated in Jerusalem, Janin, Gaza and Sinai. All the enemy's motorized equipment in these areas is being consumed by fire. All its troops in these areas are falling like leaves ... the march on Tel Aviv is thus a question of hours and not of days."[48]

Yet, in these days of Arab defeat, East Germany was a loyal friend. On June 7, the Politburo of the Socialist Unity Party (or SED, for Socialistische

and Africa, ME/2484/A4/1–2. For example, on June 5 Cairo radio informed listeners and the armed forces: "Tel Aviv is your target, the target of your entire nation. Strike the target. Make your way to the target. Batter Tel Aviv for us and destroy for us its gang. Remove the existence of the crime of the Jews, the crime of the Zionists. Strike, our gallant soldiers. Strike the enemy without mercy." "War Reports 5.6.67, 09:23 GMT," BBC, *SWB:* Part 4, *The Middle East and Africa*, ME/2483/A/25.

45 "Cairo Broadcasts to Israel, 5.6.67, Cairo in Hebrew, 09:34-10:00 GMT (June 5, 1967), BBC, *SWB*. Part 4. *The Middle East and Africa*, ME/2483/A/25.

46 "Aktenvermerk über ein Gespräch des ... Dr. Kiesewetter ... mit Herrn Ahmed Fuad," [East] Berlin, June 17, 1967, Bestand Walter Ulbricht, Bundesarchiv Berlin-Lichterfelde (hereafter) BAB NY 4182/1339, 137–138.

47 Gerhard Weis to Walter Ulbricht, Erich Honecker, Willi Stoph, Hermann Axen, and Otto Winzer, "Vermerk über ein Gespräch mit Herrn Ahmd Fouad aus der VAR" [East] Berlin, June 19, 1967, BAB NY 4182/1339, Bestand Walter Ulbricht, 152–154; and "Abschrift des Telegrams 194/67 vom 23.6.67 von Gen. Dr. Scholz, Kairo," 177.

48 "Syrian Broadcasts, Damascus home service in Arabic ... 7.6.67: 10:25 GMT, BBC, *SWB*. Part 4. *The Middle East and Africa*, ME/2486/A/17.

Einheitspartei Deutschland), along with officials from the Foreign and Defense Ministries, met in East Berlin. The Politburo that met in the June days of 1967 was composed of veteran Communists: Walter Ulbricht, Friedrich Ebert, Gerhard Grüneberg, Fritz Hager, Erich Honecker, Herman Matern, Gunter Mittag, Albert Norden, and Willi Stoph.[49] Ulbricht, followed by Axen and Stoph, were the key decision makers in foreign and military policy. Ulbricht had been a founding member of the German Communist Party in 1919. Stoph, a member of the Politburo from 1950 to 1989 and chair of the Council of Ministers from 1976 to 1989, joined the German Communist Party in 1931. Herman Axen joined a Communist youth group in Leipzig in 1932, survived Auschwitz and Buchenwald concentration camps, and rose to the Politburo in 1966. Erich Honecker, Ulbricht's successor, joined the KPD in 1929 and became a member of the SED Politburo in 1958. Gerhard Grüneberg, who joined the Politburo in 1966 and was central to relations with the PLO, joined the KPD and SED in 1946.[50] It was a group that stood for continuity of foreign policy since the establishment of the East German regime in 1949 and the anti-cosmopolitan purge, which, in East Berlin, had been led by Herman Matern in his capacity as head of the Central Party Control Commission.

They assured Nasser and Syria's President Hafez al Assad that "in connection with Israeli aggression, material support will be offered to both states by the GDR [German Democratic Republic]."[51] On June 8, 1967, Willi Stoph, chair of the regime's Council of Ministers, informed Youssef Zoayen, president of the Syrian Council of Ministers, that East Germany was going to deliver the following weapons as a gesture of solidarity, that is, at no cost: ten MiG-17 fighter jets; 40 anti-tank rocket-propelled grenade launchers; 2,400 40 millimeter (hereafter mm) grenades; 80 armored cars; 360 carbines 38/44 caliber; 240 machine guns; 0.4 million 7.62 mm cartridges for the M 43 smooth-bore mortar; 4,000 Soviet machine guns first produced during World War II; 5.6 million 7.62 mm

49 On the East German Communists see Catherine Epstein, *The Last Revolutionaries: German Communists and Their Century* (Cambridge, MA: Harvard University Press, 2003); and Herf, *Divided Memory*.

50 On biographical details of the Politburo members see Bernd-Rainer Barth et al., eds., *Wer war Wer in der DDR: Ein biographisches Handbuch* (Frankfurt/Main: Fischer, 1996).

51 "Anlage Nr. 1 zum Protokoll Nr. 7/67 vom 7.8.1967; Betr.: Maβnahmen im Zusammenhang mit der Situation im Nahen und Mittleren Osten," BAB SAPMO DY 30/J IV 2/2/1117, 7. The Politburo members included Walter Ulbricht, Friedrich Ebert, Gerhard Grüneberg, Fritz Hager, Erich Honecker, Herman Matern, Gunter Mittag, Albert Norden, and Will Stoph.

cartridges used in the Kalashnikov assault rifle; 1,000 98 K carbines produced by the Wehrmacht, captured by the Soviets, and widely distributed as aid in the Cold War; 55 MG 34 (Nazi-era) machine guns; 90,000 7.9 mm cartridges; 2,400 MP 43 (Kalashnikov) assault rifles; 3.7 million 7.9 mm cartridges; 5,000 anti-personnel mines; and 6 Soviet T-34 tanks. East German pilots were to fly the MiG-17s to an airport in Yugoslavia while the rest of the deliveries would arrive by ship at the Syrian port of Latakia. The East Germans covered the transportation costs.[52] On June 21, Stoph ordered additional military goods to be delivered at no cost to Syrian and Egyptian ports and airports. If equipment needed repair, the Ministry of Defense would cover the costs. Medical supplies not covered by the budget of the East German solidarity committee were also to be sent free of charge. The East German government would also bear the cost of experts who were being or had been sent to Egypt and Syria.[53] On June 8, Stoph informed Zoayen that East Germany would also send economic experts, medicines, and medical personnel and was ready to offer medical care for Syrians wounded in the war.[54] All of these deliveries remained secret.

In the month following the Six-Day War, the Soviet Union sent 50,000 tons of arms to Egypt.[55] As the files of the office of Willi Stoph, the president of East Germany's Council of Ministers, indicate, in that same period, East Germany sent arms to the Arab states worth $12.7 million, a small fraction of what the Soviet Union was delivering.[56] In

[52] "Protocole sur la livraison de la technique et equipment militaire de la part de la Republique Allemande a la Republique Arabe Syrienne," BAB Ministerrat der DDR DC20/13002, 6–7.

[53] Willi Stoph, "Vorsitzender des Ministerrat, Verfügung Nr. 89/67 vom 21. Juni 1967, Beschluss des Präsidiums des Ministerrat 15.6.1967 – Maßnahmen im Zusammenhang mit der Situation im Nahen und Mittleren Osten," BAB Ministerrat der DDR DC20/13002, 8–10.

[54] Will Stoph to Yussef Zoayen, "Botschaft des Vorsitzenden des Ministrres der Deutschen Demokratischen Republique, Willi Stop, an den Ministerpräsidenten der Syrischen Arabischen Republik, Dr. Yussef Zoayen" [East] Berlin (June 8, 1967), BAB DC 20/4535, 203–205. In these weeks, East German representatives in Cairo and Damascus sent requests for weapons back to East Berlin. On June 23, Ernst Scholz (1918–1986), head of the East German Consulate in Cairo, reported that Egypt's Assistant Secretary of State El Fekky "urgently" requested 4,000 rockets for the MiG-17, 360 112 mm artillery pieces, and 600 anti-aircraft guns. El Fekky also asked the East Germans to send an officer as a "permanent adviser." Otto Winzer to Walter Ulbricht, [East] Berlin, June 23, 1967, 173, and "Abschrift des Telegramms Nr. 189/67 vom 22.6.67 vn Gen. Dr. Scholz, Kairo," BAB NY 4182/1339, Bestand Walter Ulbricht, 174.

[55] Oren, *Six Days of War*, 286.

[56] General Major Werner Fleißner to Peter Korn, [East] Berlin, July 11, 1967, BAB Ministerrat DC20/13002, 32–38. See "Fleißner, Werner," in Klaus Froh and Rüdiger

July 1967, East German weapons deliveries to Egypt included 30 MiG-17 jet fighters with spare parts and ammunition and 35 T-34/85 tanks with ammunition. Agreements were signed to send 20 MiG-17 jets for delivery in the fourth quarter of 1967 and 29 engines for the MiG-17 for the first quarter of 1968 in June 1967. The East German government sent the following Soviet made weapons to Egypt in June 1967: 6 85 mm Soviet made cannons with 2,160 shells; 12 Soviet made 57 mm anti-tank guns with ammunition; 48 82 mm grenade launchers; 6 120 mm grenade launchers; 5 82 mm recoilless rifles; 13 107 mm recoilless rifles; 60 anti-tank rifles (RPG-20); 3,600 40 mm grenade launchers; 130 sniper rifles; 400 carbines 38/44 caliber; 350 LMG-DP Soviet era Degtyaryov light machine guns; 5,000 MPi-K, the East German version of the Soviet Kalashnikov AK-47 assault rifle; 0.6 million 7.62 mm cartridges for the M-43 assault rifle; 6,000 Mpi-41, Soviet assault rifles used by the East German military; 11 million 7.62 mm cartridges; 1,800 carbine rifles; 80 LMG-34 light machine guns; 3,500 MPi 43/44 Kalashnikov assault rifles; 5 million 7.9 mm cartridges; 100,000 20 mm grenades; and 150,000 land mines.[57] These weapons deliveries also remained secret.

In short, by July 1967, in addition to the modest number of tanks and jet fighters, anti-tank weapons, and anti-personnel mines, East Germany deliveries to Egypt and Syria included 14,500 Kalashnikov submachine guns and 16 million cartridges. The deliveries to Syria, also in addition to tanks, antipersonal mines, and rocket-propelled grenades, included more than 6,200 Kalashnikovs and almost 4 million cartridges.

At its meeting on June 7, 1967, the Politburo also instructed Foreign Minister Otto Winzer to contact the general secretary of the Arab League to convey its condemnation of Israeli aggression and express solidarity with the Arab states. In its controlled press and other media, the government's "Agitation Department" "was ordered to emphasize the legal

Wenzke und Militärgeschichttliches Forschungsamt, *Die Generale und Admirale der NVA: Ein biographisches Handbuch*, (Berlin: Links Verlag, 2000), 93–94. Also see the pioneering research of Klaus Storkmann, *Geheime Solidarität: Militärbeziehungen und Militärhilfen der DDR in die 'Dritte Welt'* (Berlin: Ch. Links Verlag, 2012), "Tabelle 14: Aufstellung der vom MvNV am 14. Juni 1967 gemeldeten Hilfslieferungen an die VAR (Auszüge)," 600. The CIA reports at the time and evidence from the archives confirms an increase in Soviet aid to the Middle East. The Soviet bloc was not "stepping back from the Third World." See Guy Laron, "Stepping Back from the Third World: Soviet Policy toward the UAR, 1965–1967," *Journal of Cold War Studies* 12, no. 4 (Winter 1967): 99–118.

57 General Major Werner Fleißner to Peter Korn, [East] Berlin, July 11, 1967, "Liste I: Vereinigte Arabische Republik," BAB Ministerrat der DDR DC20/13002, 34–36.

position of the Arab states, Israel's aggressive role and its conspiracies with the USA, Great Britain and West Germany" and to explain "the anti-imperialist stance of the GDR."[58] The Politburo agreed that Stoph should tell the Egyptians that East German "weapons and equipment now in the UAR," that is, in Egypt, could be "used according to their own judgment."[59] Stoph was also told to have medical supplies sent to Egypt and Syria, make preparations for accepting their wounded soldiers and children "whose parents were victims of Israeli aggression," and send unspecified specialists from the GDR to support the Arab states. Finally the "German-Arab Society," in collaboration with the Foreign Ministry, was ordered "to organize measures of solidarity with the Arab peoples," that is, to stage mass demonstrations and rallies in East Germany.[60]

The Politburo instructed Albert Norden, director of the National Council of the National Front, to publish "statements by Jewish citizens of the GDR which express indignation about the Israeli aggression and the Israel-Washington-Bonn conspiracy."[61] The effort was one of those rare instances in which the regime met with dissent. A telegram sent on June 7 to Willi Stoph by the executive of the Coordinating Committee of Forty German Societies for Christian-Jewish Cooperation opposed the government's support for the Arabs. Its authors wrote that "a third of Israel's inhabitants are survivors of the fascist attempt to exterminate the Jews. We ask you to oppose the defamation, even the extermination of the victims and fellow citizens in Israel. In these hours all anti-fascist forces must stand together to prevent a new genocide."[62] On June 8, Norden informed Ulbricht about difficulties in obtaining supportive statements from "GDR citizens of Jewish origins on Israeli aggression."[63] Several prominent Jewish writers and leaders in East Germany, including

58 "Anlage Nr. 1 zum Protokoll Nr. 7/67 vom 7.8. 1967; Betr.: Maβnahmen im Zusammenhang mit der Situation im Nahen und Mittleren Osten," 7–8.

59 Ibid., 9.

60 Ibid., 9.

61 Ibid., 8–9. On Jews in East Germany and the role of Albert Norden in East German propaganda campaigns see Herf, *Divided Memory*; Erica Burgauer, *Zwischen Erinnerung und Verdrängung*; Robin Ostow, *Jüdisches Leben in der DDR* (Frankfurt am Main: Jüdischer Athenaum Verlag, 1988); and Mario Kessler, *Die SED und die Juden – zwischen Represion und Toleranz* (Berlin: Akademie Verlag, 1995); and Heike Radvan, ed., *Das hat's bei und nicht gegeben!' Antisemitismus in der DDR: Das Buch zur Austellung der Amadeu Antonio Stiftung* (Berlin: Amadeu Antonio Stiftung, 2010).

62 Willi Stoph to Walter Ulbricht, [East] Berlin, June 8, 1967, and "Abschrift des Telegrammes," Bestand Walter Ulbricht, BAB NY 4182/1339, 11–12.

63 Albert Norden to Walter Ulbricht, [East] Berlin, June 8, 1967, Bestand Walter Ulbricht, BAB NY 4182/1339, 13–14.

the author Arnold Zweig, refused to sign the statement Norden had written. The singer Idn Jaldati referred to the PLO's Ahmed Shukeiri's calls to annihilate the Jews. Helmut Aris, president of the Association of Jewish Communities in East Germany, refused because "in the past our brothers and sisters in Germany were murdered and today their lives are at risk in the Near East." Their refusals led Norden to conclude that "in certain circles the Western propaganda that defamed Nasser as an Egyptian Hitler and presented Israel as a shelter for Jews persecuted by anti-Semitism was not without effect."[64]

Norden did apparently find at least some Jews in East Germany who were willing to sign a "Statement of Jewish Citizens of the GDR." It was published in *Neues Deutschland* on June 9, 1967.[65] "As citizens of Jewish origin of the German Democratic Republic" they condemned "Israel's aggression against its Arab neighbors." They were "justified and obligated" to speak out as "citizens of the GDR, [a state] in which anti-Semitism has been exterminated and in which there is no place for anti-Semitism which we ourselves suffered under the persecution of Hitler-fascism." They had lost many family members "murdered by the German imperialists." Though Israel claimed to speak in the name of the Jews, "the overwhelming majority of Jews live outside Israel and do not regard it as their state. Sympathy in the world for the Jews violated by Hitler-fascism and anti-Semitism should not be misused to camouflage imperialist interests."[66]

The signed statement added that the foundation of Israel rested on "broken words and annexation." It described Israel's establishment as taking place with disregard for UN decisions "in the course of illegal and military actions" that "drove many hundreds of thousands of Arab people out of their homeland, homes and farms by force. Just as USA imperialism built the Federal Republic of Germany as a spearhead against the people of Europe, so Israel was chosen to be a spearhead against the Arab peoples."[67] Israel's "spearhead" role, they claimed, was evident in

[64] Ibid. In addition to Zweig, the others who refused to sign were Heinz Kamnitzer, Peter Edel, the singer Idn Jaldati, and Helmut Aris.

[65] The signers included Carl Heins von Brück, Professor Wolfgang Frankenstein, Kurt Goldstein, Professor Lea Grundig, Professor Dr. Siegbert Kahn, Professor Dr. F. K. Koul, Dr. Habil Franz Loeser, Dr. med. Ernst Reifenberg, Dr. med. Elisabeth Thierfeld, Gerry Wolf, "Erklärung jüdischer Bürger der DDR," *Neues Deutschland*, [East] Berlin (June 9, 1967), 2. Also "Erklärung jüdischer Bürger der DDR," Bestand Walter Ulbricht, BAB NY 4182/1339, 15–17.

[66] Ibid., 2.

[67] Ibid.

the war of 1956 and now again in 1967. Beyond entering "an alliance with imperialism," the Israelis then "went further and openly work[ed] closely with the Nazi murderers of the Jewish people, with the West German imperialists in Bonn," who "helped to build Israel's potential for aggression with large weapons assistance, training military cadres in the camps of Nazi generals and building war production in Israel. The contemptible lack of character of this complicity found expression in the Eichmann trial which, as a result of secret agreements between the government in Bonn and Tel Aviv, the murderer of millions [Hans] Globke and other anti-Semites in positions of influence in the West German state were concealed."[68]

As "GDR citizens of Jewish origin," the signers said that "peace will exist in the near Orient only when the Israeli government abandons its imperialist policy and finally turns to a policy of good neighborliness and respect for the interests of the Arab peoples."[69] The ten signers had been selected by the government. Those who had refused to sign had no outlet in the East German press to express their views. It was fitting that the statement Norden wrote denounced the trial of Adolf Eichmann in Jerusalem, for that trial had the great merit of doing what East Germany and the Soviet-bloc states never did, namely, focusing attention on the centrality of Nazi Germany's policies of murdering the Jews of Europe.[70] The signatures of ten "citizens of Jewish origins" was a political fig leaf intended to protect the regime from the accusation that it was a second German regime practicing anti-Semitism. How could this be so if there were Jews in East Germany who supported the policy? Norden contributed to the comparison of Israel to Nazi Germany. On June 9, 1967, he wrote to Werner Lamberz, director of the Agitation Department of the SED Central Committee, that the East German press, which was furiously denouncing Israel, had not been harsh enough.[71] The press should

[68] Ibid.

[69] Ibid.

[70] See the important chapter on the trial in David Cesarani, *Becoming Eichmann: Rethinking the Life, Crimes and Trial of a "Desk Murderer,"* (Boston: Da Capo Press, 2004), 237–323; and the trial transcript, nizkor.org/hweb/people/eichmann-adolf/transcritps.

[71] The effort at immunization provoked Simon Wiesenthal to probe into the continuities between Nazi propaganda and that of the East German regime. See Simon Wiesenthal, *Die gleiche Sprache: erst für Hitler – jetzt für Ulbricht* (Bonn: Vogel, 1968); and his- *The Same Language: First for Hitler – Now for Ulbricht* (Vienna: Deutschland Berichte, 1968). "Lamberz, Werner," in Barth et al., *Wer war Wer in der DDR: Ein biographisches Handbuch* (Frankfurt/Main: Fischer Taschenbuch1996), 432.

emphasize that Israel's actions in the war were comparable to "Hitler's attack in night and fog on the Soviet Union of June 22, 1941." It must be indicated that the "Israeli imperialists exactly imitated Hitler's illegal tactics and methods of attack."[72]

Telegrams and reports from East German embassies in the Middle East reported Arab enthusiasm for East Germany's policy. On June 15, Horst Grunnert (1928–2005), the head of the East German Consulate in Damascus, reported that the Syrian government would assess relations with all governments "in light of their stance to the current Arab problem."[73] Normalization of relations with East Germany was "at the top of considerations of responsible offices." His Syrian counterpart told him that East Germany's "solidarity measures" were "a good preparation for this step." The Syrians took note that East Germany had "no relations" with Israel.[74] The following day, Grunnert conveyed East Germany's willingness to send immediate assistance to the Syrian military. Syrian Prime Minister Zu'ayyin (Zouayen) "expressed admiration for the stance of the GDR which proved to be a true friend in hard times."[75]

A comparison of events in East Germany with those in Poland in June 1967 underscores a broader theme, namely, the comparative weakness of opposition to the regime in general. Where East Germany never had diplomatic relations at any level with Israel, Poland and Israel upgraded relations to embassy status in 1962. In June 1967, Poland had diplomatic relations with Israel, which were then broken. As Dariusz Stola has pointed out, the Polish Communist leader Wladyslaw Gomulka's speech of June 19 was not only a standard Communist attack on Zionism and British and American imperialism; he also referred to a "fifth column" in Poland. "Israel's aggression in the Arab countries met with applause in Zionist circles – Polish citizens."[76] Gomulka's speech of June 19, 1967,

[72] Albert Norden to Werner Lamberts, [East]Berlin, June 9, 1967, Bestand Walter Ulbricht, BAB NY 4182/1339, 38–39.

[73] Grunnert subsequently served as head of the East German delegation to the United Nations in 1972–1973, deputy foreign minister (1974–1978), and East German ambassador to the United States from 1978 to 1983. See "Grunnert, Horst," in Siegfried Bock, Ingrid Muth, and Hermann Schwiesau, eds., *DDR Außenpolitik: Ein Überblick, Daten, Fakten, Personen (III)* (Münster: LIT Verlag, 2010), 308.

[74] Grunnert, "Abschrift des Telegramms 221/67," Damascus, June 15, 1967, BAB NY 4182/1339, 125–126.

[75] Ibid., 126–127.

[76] Wladyslaw Gomulka cited in Dariusz Stola, "Anti-Zionism as a Multipurpose Policy Instrument: The Anti-Zionist Campaign in Poland, 1967–1968," in Jeffrey Herf, *Anti-Semitism and Anti-Zionism in Historical Perspective: Convergence and Divergence* (New York: Routledge, 2007), 168.

was a signal for the Polish Ministry of Internal Affairs to launch a campaign against the "Zionist threat" within Poland, that is, a purge of Jews suspected of sympathy for Israel working in the Polish government, the universities, the press, and the armed forces. Some 150 Jewish officers were purged from the armed forces in 1967–1968, amounting to almost all of them. The campaign expanded in March 1968, leading to 2,591 arrests. Stola reports that a purge of "Zionists" and "alien elements" affected top government officials, editors in chief, university professors, teachers in elementary schools, and factory foreman. "Between 1968 and 1970, some 13,000 people (i.e. half of the estimated total number of Jews) applied for emigration permits to Israel."[77] The absence of a similar purge in East Germany suggests that after the purges and the refugee flight up to 1961 the opposition to the anti-Israeli policy in East Germany was insignificant and that those very few Jews who remained in positions of prominence, such as Albert Norden and Alexander Abusch, had long since demonstrated their antagonism to Israel and agreement with Communist anti-Zionism. In Poland, June 1967 and the anti-Zionist campaign were turning points away from the diplomatic relations of the 1960s. In East Germany, on the other hand, June 1967 stood for continuity with policies that had been operative since the anti-cosmopolitan purges of 1949 to 1953.

WALTER ULBRICHT'S LEIPZIG SPEECH OF JUNE 15, 1967

Walter Ulbricht's speech in Leipzig on June 15, 1967, was a classic statement of East German Communist anti-Zionism. He began with an expression of "contempt and hatred" for the United States as a result of its "aggression" in Vietnam.[78] While the United States was bombing cities and villages in Vietnam, "the imperialists were carrying out yet another no less criminal military aggression in the Middle East," this one directed against the United Arab Republic, that is, the political union of Egypt and Syria, and other Arab states who had been fighting to overcome "colonial and half-colonial dependency." In his description of "what actually stands

[77] Ibid., 168–177.

[78] Walter Ulbricht, "Rede des Vorsitzenden des Staatsrates der DDR, Walter Ulbricht, auf einer Wählversammlung in Leipzig zu Frage der Lage im Nahen Osten und zur westdeutschen Expansionspolitik im Rahmen der USA-Globalstrategie" (June 15, 1967), in *Dokumente zur Außenpolitik der Deutschen Demokratischen Republik 1967 Band XV, 1. Halbband* ([East] Berlin: Staatsverlag der Deutschen Demokratischen Republik, 1970), 515–538.

behind this Israeli aggression," Ulbricht omitted mention of Arab threats in the weeks before the war. Instead he located the causes of the war in the desire of "imperialist colonial rulers" to prevent the Arab countries from attaining economic independence and to secure "imperialist exploitation" of the riches of the region, that is, access to its oil. The Israeli government had made itself into a "tool of a new, despicable imperialist aggression" and had "brought shame and disgrace on itself by playing the role of an imperialist aggressor against the Arab states."[79] Its "aggression" took place in the context of "the global strategy of USA-imperialism and its NATO military bloc." He claimed that West Germany had contributed to this global strategy by supplying Israel with "heavy American offensive weapons." The turn of Egypt, Syria, Algeria, and other Arab states toward the "non-capitalist path" and toward the Soviet Union threatened "the global strategy of US imperialism. Therefore, Israel was sent [presumably by the United States] to militarily assault the Arab states. The war conspiracy against the Arab states was carefully camouflaged in the framework of the global strategy of the USA imperialists and prepared with enormous material and propagandistic efforts."[80]

Ulbricht denounced West German support for Israel as evidence of imperialism, not, as the West Germans saw it, as an expression of moral obligation and responsibility to aid the Jewish state. He denounced restitution (Wiedergutmachung) payments for "the Jewish citizens of Poland, Czechoslovakia and many other countries murdered by the Nazi regime."[81]

What bloody mockery! Under the Hitler rule, Polish, Dutch, and Hungarian citizens, women, children, the elderly women and men were murdered in Auschwitz and in other extermination camps. As a result, the Bonn government, [which] feels it is the successor to the Hitler regime, does not pay restitution to the states whose citizens were murdered. The Bonn government delivers tanks and other heavy war materiel to Israel. With the help of this "restitution," the thousands of Arab men, women and children are killed, burned by napalm or mutilated in

[79] Walter Ulbricht, "Leipzig" (June 15, 1967), 516–517.

[80] Ibid., 518. "Das Kriegskomplott gegen die arabischen Staaten im Rahmen der Globalstrategie der USA-Imperialisten wurde sorgfältig getarnt und mit enormen materiellen und propagandistischem Aufwand vorbereitet."

[81] Actually, in 1967, the United States had not yet become a major weapons supplier to Israel. None of Israel's major weapon systems were supplied by the United States. Israel's air force fought the Six-Day War primarily with French Mirage jets. It is interesting to note that the East Germans did not describe Israel as a tool of French imperialism. On the weapons of the combatants in the 1967 war, see Oren, *Six Days of War*.

inhuman ways. It is a disgrace that the West German government is capable of such cynicism.[82]

Actually, the West German government did not "feel" it was the successor to Nazi Germany. Instead, it asserted that it carried the burden of the crimes of the Nazi regime and had a moral responsibility to aid the survivors and the new Jewish state. East Germany refused to pay any financial restitution.[83] In the June speech in Leipzig, Ulbricht turned a source of pride in West Germany – the tradition of Vergangenheitsbewältigung, its policies of restitution and support for Israel – into liabilities of shame and windows of opportunity for East German diplomacy in the Arab states.

Ulbricht sarcastically dismissed claims that Nasser "wanted to strangle the poor, innocent Israeli state."[84] Trade with vital goods through the Gulf of Aqaba was of "completely secondary" importance. "The whole moaning and groaning [*gejammer*] about a supposed blockade of Israel was thus only a bluff that was part of the global strategy of USA imperialists" whose purpose was to "give the Israeli military aggression against its Arab neighbors the mantel of a struggle for existence." Actually "it is proven that Israel planned and conducted a war of aggression with a goal that above all was established by the global strategy of the USA imperialists. The decision to go to war was taken before the UAR [Egypt] had control over the Gulf of Aqaba. This was not, as some said, a battle for the so-called survival of the Jews. It was not a matter of racial issues and certainly not about matters related to the Old Testament."[85] He did not present a shred of evidence for any of these assertions.

Israel, he insisted, had not faced any threat at all. Rather than have regard for human rights, "the government and militarists of the state of Israel [then still led by the Labor Party] are apparently struck with blindness, due to chauvinism, racial madness and class rule" (*Klassendunkel)* so that they "believe that they can violate the demands of international law and human rights" of the Arabs. Yet it was not only Israel but also the "men behind the scenes in Washington, London and Bonn" who were responsible for the Arab refugees produced by Israel's past

[82] Ibid., 515.

[83] Ibid. On restitution in West Germany, see Constantin Goschler, *Schuld und Schulden: Die Politik der Wiedergutmachung für NS-Verfolgte seit 1945* (Göttingen: Wallstein Verlag, 2005). On the East German refusal to offer restitution, see Herf, *Divided Memory*., 86–95, and 194–195.

[84] Ibid., 520.

[85] Ibid., 520. Between 1958 and 1961, Egypt and Syria were in a union called the United Arab Republic. Egypt continued to refer to itself with that name until 1971.

and now current "wars of aggression."[86] Despite the widely reported Arab preparations for war, "there was no military threat to the state of Israel."[87] While Israel and the NATO powers had won a military victory, they would not succeed in turning the "political balance of forces in the Middle East" in their favor. To his "friend President Nasser," Ulbricht promised that the GDR did not cultivate a "fair-weather friendship" with Egypt and other Arab states. "We are friends in good as well as in difficult times."[88]

Ulbricht compared Israel, "the Middle East aggressor," to Nazi Germany. "The world cannot accept that a quarter century after the Second World War, the aggressor Israel and its men behind the scenes (*Hintermänner)* create a 'Sinai protectorate' or a 'General government of Jordan' for renewed colonial oppression of the Arab peoples."[89] By using terms such as "men behind the scenes," he drew on the language of Nazi propaganda that referred to Jewish conspiracies operating out of public view. When he referred to a "Sinai protectorate" and the "General Government of Jordan," he was drawing comparisons to Nazi Germany's "protectorate" in Czechoslovakia and to its "General Government" in occupied Poland between 1939 and 1945.[90] The association of Israel with Nazi Germany remained a repeated and important element of Communist, Arab, Palestinian, West German, and West European leftist anti-Zionism. Ulbricht's speech set a pattern in another way as well. The Communists denied that Israel faced threats, whether emanating from the many hostile Arab states that surrounded it or from Palestinian terrorist

86 Ibid.

87 Ibid., 524.

88 Ibid., 526. Walter Ulbricht, "Rede des Vorsitzenden des Staatsrates der DDR, Walter Ulbricht, auf einer Wählversammlung in Leipzig zu Frage der Lage im Nahen Osten und zur westdeutschen Expansionspolitik im Rahmen der USA-Globalstrategie," (June 15, 1967), in *Dokumente zur Außenpolitik der Deutschen Demokratischen Republik 1967 Band XV, 1. Halbband* ([East] Berlin: Staatsverlag der Deutschen Demokratischen Republik, 1970), 515–538.

89 Ibid., 529–530. Ulbricht's German text read as follows: "Die Welt kann und wird sich nicht damit abfinden, daß ein Vierteljahrhundert nach den zweiten Weltkrieg im Nahen Osten von dem Aggressor Israel und dessen Hintermännern ein 'Protektorat Sinai' ode rein 'Generalgouvernement Jordanien' zu erneuter kolonialer Unterdrückung der arabischen Völker gebildet werden."

90 Ibid., 538. In a letter of June 20 sent to the UN General Assembly, which was circulated to member states, Ulbricht repeated these accusations against Israel and West Germany. "Erklärung der Regierung der Deutschen Demokratischen Republik an die Sondertagung der Vollversammlung der Vereinten Nationen vom 20. June1967," *Dokumente zur Außenpolitik der Deutschen Demokratischen Republik, 1967, Band XV, 2. Halbband* ([East] Berlin: Staatsverlag der Deutschen Demokratischen Republik, 1970), 539–544.

organizations. Their press did not report on Arab state preparations for war or on terrorist attacks on Israel. The Soviet-bloc states called Israel a colonial imposition that rested on the expulsion of the native population, thereby offering justification for attacks on it. As they described its existence as the result of an invasion of Arab territory, they presented Arab attacks on Israel as justified acts of "resistance." Thus they merited no condemnation. The corollary of this view was that the Communists described Israel's acts of armed self-defense as unprovoked acts of aggression.[91]

In the weeks following the war, East German officials traveled to Cairo and Damascus to express their solidarity and back up words with agreements to deliver weapons. Stoph sent messages of solidarity to his Arab counterparts while East German diplomats in Cairo and Damascus conducted negotiations about expanded aid. Gerhard Weiss, the deputy chairman of the Council of Ministers, traveled to Cairo and Damascus.[92] There he reaffirmed East German solidarity with the Arab states, assessed what could be done to help them, and broached the subject of establishing formal diplomatic relations. On July 1, 1967, he met with high-ranking officials in the Syrian government and Baath Party in Damascus. He concluded that "there can be no doubt that the majority of the leading forces [in Syria] continue to view the liquidation of Israel as their goal."[93] In view of the militancy of the Baath leadership, encouraged by the Chinese Communists, East Germany joined the Soviet Union in encouraging development of a "more realistic assessment of the balance of forces" with Israel. In the current situation, "the most difficult task may consist in making clear to the Syrian leadership that it must come to terms with the existence of Israel." This was a stance that the East German leaders did not repeat in public. He welcomed Syria's "clear anti-imperialist position" and its support for an "alliance [*Bundnis*] with

91 The themes of Ulbricht's Leipzig speech were repeated in a letter that Otto Winzer sent to the United Nations. "Otto Winzer to Walter Ulbricht, Will Stoph, Erich Honecker and Herman Axen," [East] Berlin, June 19, 1967, 143, and "Erklärung der Regierung der Deutschen Demokratischen Republik an die Sondertagung der UNO-Vollversammlung," [East]Berlin, June 17, 1967, BAB NY 4182/1339, Bestand Walter Ulbricht, 144–151.

92 "Weiss, Gerhard," in Barth et al., *Wer war Wer in der DDR*, 779–780.

93 Gerhard Weiss, "Zwischenberichte über meine Tätigkeit als Sonderbeauftragte des Vorsitzenden des Staatrates der DDR in der Syrischen Arabischen Republik" (Damascus) July 1, 1967, DC 20/ 12188, 35. The German reads: "Es kann aber kein Zweifel bestehen, daß die Mehrzahl der führenden Kräfte weiterhin die Liquidierung des Staats Israel al ihr Ziel betrachtet."

the Soviet Union and other socialist countries."[94] In Syria, Weiss found "a widespread mood in favor of the establishment of diplomatic relations with the GDR. The clear and consequential stance of the GDR on the side of the Arab peoples" had led in Syria to a "considerable rise" in East Germany's reputation, especially in contrast to the "pro-Israeli and anti-Arab [*Araberfeindlich*] role of West German imperialism," that is, West Germany.[95]

On July 9, Weiss met with Nasser in Cairo. He was accompanied by Paul Markowski (1929–1978), director of the Department of International Relations of the Communist's Party Central Committee; Wolfgang Kiesewetter (1924–1991), East Germany's deputy minister of foreign affairs; and Ernst Scholz (1913–1986), East Germany's representative in Cairo.[96] He gave him Arabic and English translations of Ulbricht's Leipzig speech and asked him how "the GDR could better support the UAR [United Arab Republic, that is, Egypt] to quickly overcome the consequences of Israeli aggression," that is, the defeat in the Six-Day War.[97] Nasser called for more aid from the "socialist countries," that is, the Soviet bloc.[98] Weiss raised the issue of establishing diplomatic relations with East Germany, reminding Nasser that the West Germans had "taken a clear stance against the UAR, against progress and the progressive Arab states," whereas the GDR had "taken a stance clearly in favor of the UAR and against imperialism." While Nasser "fully agreed" with Weiss that diplomatic relations should be established, now was not the time to give the Americans a pretext to intervene, when the military and morale in Egypt were "so weak." In his report to the Politburo, Weiss wrote that Nasser "conveyed a defeated impression. It was clear that he had placed his whole hopes on a direct military intervention of the Soviet Union." Yet, Weiss saw no indication that Nasser "intended to mobilize the [Egyptian] people for decisive resistance against a possible extension of aggression."[99] It was essential to convince the UAR leadership

[94] Ibid., 36. The German reads: "In diesem Zusammenhang, dürfte die schwerigste Aufgabe darin bestehen, der syrischen Führung, klarzumachen, daß sie sich mit der Existenz Israels abfinden muß."

[95] Ibid., 38.

[96] Ernst Scholz, "Vermerk über das Gespräche des Sonderbeauftagten des Vorsitzenden des Staatsrates der DDR, Walter Ulbricht, und Stellvertreter des Vorsitzenden des Ministerrat, Dr. Gerhard Weiss, mit dem Präsidenten der VAR, Gamal Abdel Nasser, am 9. Juli 1967, von 12.00 bis 13.25 Uhr in dessen Residenz," Ministerrat der DDR BAB DC 20/ 12188, 19.

[97] Ibid., 20.

[98] Ibid., 21–23.

[99] Ibid., 25–32.

of the "absolute necessity of mobilizing and activating the masses of the people."[100] He did not specify what the content of a mobilization of mass opinion in Egypt against Israel should be.

Weiss, Markowski, and Kiesewetter then traveled to Damascus, where, on July 13, 1967, along with the East Germany's general counsel in Damascus, Horst Grunnert (1928–2005), they met with Habib Haddad and Malik Amin, leaders of the Baath Party. Haddad welcomed the deepening of ties between Syria and East Germany, expressed appreciation for Ulbricht's "clear stance," and asserted that "the crimes of the Israeli aggressors exceeded those of the Nazis." Weiss said that the GDR sought good relations with the Baath Party while Haddad called East German–Syrian relations "a model for relations with the socialist countries."[101] On July 18, Weiss, Markowski, Kiesewetter, and Grunnert met with Youssef Zouayen, minister president of Syria. Zouayen stressed the need for rapid delivery of weapons. Syria also expected its allies to "send volunteers," including pilots; Zouayen asked whether the GDR would be sending volunteer pilots. Weiss demurred but said that establishment of an East German embassy in Damascus would be very important. Zouayen disagreed, saying that the East German Consulate in Damascus "already functioned as an embassy" and that "Syria regards it basically as an embassy."[102] Weiss again raised the issue of establishing diplomatic relations with East Germany, and Zouayen replied that doing so would depend "on the struggle against American imperialism. The sooner the weapons came, the sooner could American imperialism be defeated."[103]

100 Gerhard Weiss, "Erster Bericht über meine Tätigkeit als Sonderbeauftragte des Vorsitzenden des Staatsrates in der VAR vom 6.11.7. 1967," Cairo (July 11, 1967), DC 20/12188, 43, 49, 55.

101 Horst Grunnert to Walter Ulbricht, Erich Honecker, Willi Stoph, Hermann Axen, Gerhard Weiss, Otto Winzer, Paul Markowski and GK (Generalkonsulat) Damaskus, "Vermerk über eine Unterredung zwischen Dr. Gerhard Weiss ... und den Mitgliedern der Baath-Leitung Dr. Habib Haddad und Malik Amin am 17.7.1967," BAB NY 4182/1339, Bestand Walter Ulbricht, 236–237. The German reads: "Die Verbrechen der israelischen Aggressoren würden die Verbrechen der Nazis übertreffen."

102 Otto Winzer to Walter Ulbricht, [East] Berlin, July 14, 1967, and Horst Grunnert, "Aktennotiz über ein Gespräch zwischen ... Gerhard Weiss ... und dem Minister-Präsident der Syrischen Arabischen Republik, Dr. Youssef Zouayen," July 18, 1967, Damascus, BAB NY 4182/1339, Bestand Walter Ulbricht, 241–249.

103 Horst Grunnert, "Aktennotiz über ein Gespräch zwischen ... Gerhard Weiss ... und dem Minister-Präsident der Syrischen Arabischen Republik, Dr. Youssef Zouayen," July 18, 1967, Damascus, BAB NY 4182/1339, Bestand Walter Ulbricht, 250. The German reads: "daß dies vom Kampf gegen den amerikanischen Imperialismus abhänge. Je schneller Waffen kämen, je schneller könne man den amerikanischen Imperialismus beseitigen."

For the Syrians, delivery of weapons was a prerequisite for diplomatic recognition. Though volunteers to fight in the Arab armies and air forces did not arrive, various East German advisers did. According to material in Ulbricht's files, as of September 20, 1967, there were 295 East German experts in Egypt, Syria, Algeria, and Iraq. Ninety-seven were in Syria, where they worked in the universities, television and radio, theater and music, agriculture, as geologists, in transport, and in veterinary medicine; seven served as "advisers to the government." Thirty-five East Germans were working in Iraq and 44 were in Algeria.[104]

Following the Six-Day War, the Soviet Union decided on a program of rearmament and intensified training of the armed forces of the Arab states and of the Palestine Liberation Organization. Soviet and East German military leaders had no illusions regarding the shortcomings of the Arab states' military abilities. In several remarkably frank reports issued in September 1967 about "Israeli Aggression against the Arab States," leaders of the East German Ministry of Defense echoed Soviet assessments that Israel's victory was due to three factors: the achievement of tactical surprise, insufficient preparation by the Arab armed forces, and a higher level of mobilization and readiness for combat by the Israel troops compared to those of the Arab states.[105] The Communists did not think that defeat was due to either the quantitative or qualitative inferiority of Soviet and Warsaw Pact weapons. It was training and leadership that needed to be improved. East Germany's National People's Army (Nationale Volksarmmee) would contribute the rearmament and training effort intended to defeat "American global strategy" in the Middle East.[106] The authors of one postwar assessment concurred with an Israeli officer who said, "The Arabs had the better weapons but our people shoot better."[107] Although the East German report repeated the regime's propaganda claims about the importance of American and West German military supplies to Israel, it candidly acknowledged that "the French aviation industry was the primary supplier of the Israeli Air Force." Further, despite the rhetoric about American "global strategy,"

[104] "Information zum Stand der Expertensendung der DDR in die arabischen Länder, vor allem SAR, Algerian, Irak," BAB NY 4182/1339, Bestand Walter Ulbricht, 253–258.

[105] Ministerium für Nationale Verteidigung, Verwaltung Aufklärung, "Die israelische Aggression gegen die arabischen Staaten 05. bis 13.061967" VVS-Nr.: A7328, *Bundesarchiv Militärarchiv Freiburg*, DWW1-25741j, 79.

[106] "Lesematerial zum Thema 'Die israelische Aggression gegen die arabischen Staaten. Schlußfolgerungen für die Landesverteidigung der Deutsche Demokratischen Republik,'" VS-Nr.: A 12673, *Bundesarchiv Militärarchiv Freiburg*, DVW1-25750.

[107] Ibid., 26.

the authors admitted that "none" of the Western countries including the United States and Britain "openly sided with Israel," noting that the United States had called for stopping military supplies to the warring states.[108] The contrast between this confidential military assessment and Ulbricht's and Winzer's public assertions was stark, but the policy conclusion was identical: it called for expansion of the Soviet and Warsaw Pact alliance with major Arab states as well as with the Palestine Liberation Organization and its various factions.[109]

The East Germans played a prominent role in this chapter of Soviet-bloc foreign and military policy. Their Afro-Asian Solidarity Committee (AASK) worked with the Afro-Asian People's Solidarity Organization (AAPSO), both of which were Soviet-bloc front organizations and played a key role in political warfare and propaganda. The AAPSO met in Cairo, July 1–3, 1967, to "support the struggle of the Arab peoples against the aggression of the state of Israel and its imperialist helpers in Washington, Bonn and London." The East German participants reported that the conference was "a complete success."[110] Part of that success lay in the agreement of the participants that it was necessary "to correct the false image of Israel and above all of Zionism (which should be described as a racist movement related to Nazism and the South African apartheid regime), to explain the true goals of the Arab peoples and to gain allies for the struggle of the Arab peoples and the national liberation movements above all in the revolutionary working class."[111] At the July 1967 Cairo conference, the East German participants cooperated closely with the PLO's Ahmed Schukeiri, who, they reported, gave a "passionate denunciation against West German imperialism in which, in addition to his own experience, he drew above all on our material about facts and numbers about the cooperation of the USA–West Germany–Israel." The East Germans noted that Schukeiri warned of the danger to the Arab countries and to Africa from the "neo-colonialist methods of this triple alliance."[112]

108 Ibid., 11.

109 On the institutional background, decision making processes, key actors, and many details of East German military assistance to many third-world countries, including Nasser's Egypt, see Storkmann's pioneering study on the decisions regarding Africa in 1967, 106–116.

110 "Bericht über die Teilnahme ... des ... AASK ... an der Außerordentlichen Konferenz der ... AASPSO vom 1.bis 3. Juli 1967 in Kairo zur Unterstützung des Kampfes der arabischen Völker gegen die Aggression des Staates Israel und seiner imperialistischen Helfer in Washington, Bonn und London," BAB NY 4182/1339, Bestand Walter Ulbricht, 183–196.

111 Ibid., 187.

112 Ibid.

DEFENSE MINISTER HEINZ HOFFMANN'S ASSESSMENT OF THE SIX-DAY WAR

General Heinz Hoffmann was East Germany's defense minister for a remarkable twenty-five years, from 1960 until he died in office in 1985. He was the central military leader during the emergence and blossoming of the GDR's alliances with the Arab states and the Palestinian Liberation Organization. A veteran Communist, he had joined the German Communist Party in 1930 and was active in its underground from 1933 to 1935. He then fled to the Soviet Union, where he studied in its Lenin School from 1935 to 1937. He was in the Communists' International Brigade in Spain in 1937–1938 and spent the war years of 1939 to 1945 in the Soviet Union. After the war, he returned to East Berlin and served as an aid to Wilhelm Pieck and then Walter Ulbricht. After serving in the Interior Ministry in the early 1950s, he studied at the General Staff Academy in the Soviet Union in 1957–1958. He served as the East German deputy defense minister from 1958 to 1960 before beginning his quarter-century in the top position.[113] Hoffmann became a member of the SED Politburo in 1973. His tenure as defense minister overlapped with the Middle East wars of 1967, 1973, and 1982. Along with Ulbricht, Honecker, Stoph, Axen, and Weiss in the Politburo, and Erich Mielke and Gerhard Neiber in the Stasi, he was one of the key decision makers who shaped the East German alliance with the Arab states and the PLO. The Hoffmann files in the German Federal Archive in Freiburg are crucial for writing the history of the East German–Arab military alliance.

Hoffmann's long and deep roots in the Communist Party and his schooling in the Soviet Union were evident in his speeches to both officers and men of the National People's Army and occasionally to the East German parliament, the Volkskammer. In a presentation to the Politburo in fall 1967, Hoffmann placed "Israeli aggression against the Arab states" into "the framework of the global strategy of the USA" and the "aggressive conceptions of West German imperialism."[114] He presented his views to the East German parliament. They influenced the military academies and "the political education of youth and … their military

[113] "Hoffmann, Heinz," Klaus Froh and Rüdiger Wenzke und Militärgeschichttliches Forschungsamt, *Die Generale und Admirale der NVA: Ein biographisches Handbuch*, (Berlin: Links Verlag, 2000), 113.

[114] Heinz Hoffmann, "Auszug Nr. 376 zum Protokoll 29/67, Betr.: Vorlagen des Nationalen Verteidigungsrates," BAMA DVW 1/114461, "Sekretariat des Ministers: Beschlusse des ZK der SED, 1967," 123–125.

preparation."[115] Hoffmann, like Ulbricht, argued that "the Israeli aggression and the sharper course taken by Bonn's war preparations were not facts isolated from one another." Rather, they were components of "the imperialist global strategy of the USA" and "Bonn's [the West German capital's] preparations for war." Israel's "Blitzkrieg" was not only "a repetition of older conceptions of Blitzkrieg."[116] In his account of the war, Hoffmann found American and West German "imperialists" and their Israeli ally to have sole responsibility for its outbreak. The absence of Arab and Palestinian agency was an enduring irony of Communist and leftist versions of events. The Soviet bloc, including East Germany, celebrated the revolutionary cause of their Arab and Palestinian allies yet simultaneously claimed that their Middle Eastern allies had no responsibility for war and conflict in the region.

On November 20, 1967, Hoffmann presented a report on "Israel's aggression" to the Volkskammer Committee for National Defense.[117] As Ulbricht had in Leipzig in June, Hoffmann placed the Six-Day War into the context of the "global strategy of USA imperialism" and the battle against it.[118] Israel's victory was an example of an American "war on the periphery" and of the consequences of a "slackening of vigilance." That, he said, must not happen in Europe. Hoffmann then referred to the strategic significance of the Middle East. It was on "the south flank" of NATO, which had bases in Cyprus, Turkey, Libya, Malta, Italy, and the Spanish coast. Seventy percent of Western Europe's oil was shipped through the Suez Canal and much else originated in pipelines to Mediterranean ports. The "anti-imperialist movement in the Arab states" threatened American and British oil interests as well as the bases "that were important for an invasion of the Soviet Union and the socialist states in Europe." Egypt and Syria constituted the "most serious threat" to these imperialist interests as they had shifted the orientation of their armed forces to the Soviet Union and fought against foreign capital.[119]

The United States and Britain, together with Israel as their willing tool, were the deep cause of the war.[120] In April and May 1967, the number

[115] Ibid., 123.

[116] Ibid., 124.

[117] Heinz Hoffmann, "Rede des Ministers für Nationale Verteidigung vor dem Volkskammerausschuß für Nationale Verteidigung," [East] Berlin, (November 20, 1967), BAMA DVW 1/114218 Sekretariat des Ministers UA Militärpolitik Referate/Vorträge/Artikel Min. f. NV-AG-Hoffmann, Bd. 18, 15.11-4.12.1967, 43.

[118] Ibid., 1–2.

[119] Ibid., 3–4.

[120] Ibid., 5–6.

of "military incidents created by Israel" on its borders with Jordan and Syria grew. Israel, he claimed, had cleared its plans with the United States and used false plans for negotiations to obscure its intentions.[121] In Hoffmann's version of events, the Arabs did not set events in motion but merely responded to the plans of imperialism.

Yet when he turned to the military details of the war, Hoffmann departed from Communist propaganda. On the Egyptian front, the Arabs had "a clear numerical superiority" in the size of their armies and their air forces. Egypt had a "qualitative superiority" in tanks, planes, and anti-aircraft system. Its superiority was due to its possession of Soviet T-55, T-54, and T-34 tanks; Soviet MiG-15, MiG-17, MiG-19, and MiG-21 fighter jets; Soviet Tupelov-16 medium range bombers and "the most modern fighter-bomber, the SU-7-B." The Israelis had "very maneuverable but lightly armed" French AMX-13 tanks; American medium sized tanks, M-47 and M-48; and the British Centurion tanks. Departing from his rhetoric about the United States and Britain, he observed that Israel's air force was composed of only some American Skyhawk fighters but mostly French Mirage, Mystère, and Super Mystère jets.[122] Yet despite the Arabs' numerical and qualitative superiority in weaponry, the Israelis were superior to the Arabs in the "training of the entire population that was fit for military service." In addition to training in military skills, he mentioned "the intensive ideological preparation not only of the members of the armed forces but of the whole people, especially the youth." He added that "Israel's ruling circles succeeded in educating a youth that gave itself over completely to the state and was determined to make the most extreme sacrifice in the implementation of its goals."[123] The combination of these Arab threats with Israel's "massive ideological work including social demagoguery" meant that "the Israeli imperialists ... possessed a very powerful military instrument."[124] Hoffmann described Arab calls to exterminate the Jews as a tactical blunder that undermined the anti-imperialist cause, not as an immoral or evil endeavor in itself.

He offered a withering criticism of the performance of the Egyptian armed forces. They possessed "considerably less moral fighting value"

[121] Ibid., 6–9.
[122] Ibid., 9–10.
[123] Ibid., 11–12. Hoffmann also noted the impact of slogans painted on Arab tanks: "Tel Aviv-Cairo Express" and "Tel Aviv-Damascus."
[124] Ibid., 12.

(moralische Kampfwert) than did Israel's armed forces. Egypt lacked a "revolutionary vanguard" that could lead it clearly in a "non-capitalist direction." Because the officer corps came from bourgeois circles and the common soldiers from the peasantry, there was "no political-military unity" between officers and soldiers, and thus "a high and intense morale for battle was missing in the UAR's armed forces." Those officers who had been trained in Soviet military academies were unable to exert influence on the use of the very modern Soviet technology or to lead the armed forces. The woeful lack of leadership of the Egyptian officer corps was evident in the fact that the Israeli troops in the Sinai "were able to capture 5 Major Generals, 16 Brigadier Generals and over 3,000 officers of Egypt's armed forces" who had refused to fight on to the bitter end. Lack of political leadership and widespread illiteracy were compounded by outright treason of individual officers. In the Sinai, the Israelis captured or destroyed more than 700 tanks, of which "100 were completely ready for combat with unused battle materials and 200 tanks that had only minor damage" and could still have been used for combat.[125] Egypt's defeat, in short, was not due to lack of support from the Soviet bloc. Although they had been provided with "excellent equipment with modern means of fighting," the Egyptians had shown "little ability to fight" because the country lacked a "mass based revolutionary fighting party" and "the political-moral unity of the people." The masses of the soldiers had weak education and insufficient technical training as well as a "lack of discipline, military order and especially fighting spirit" *(Disziplin, militärischer Ordnung und insbesondere Kampfmoral)*.[126] Ironically, Hoffmann viewed Israel as a model to be emulated because of the ideological engagement of its population. East Germany needed to deepen "unconditional loyalty to the party of the working class and to the military leadership.... Love of homeland and its people, hatred for the enemy, the ability to see him without illusions" also needed to be cultivated. The country needed people whose "entire action was motivated by the value of defending the socialist fatherland."[127] Hoffmann in effect viewed the wartime mobilization of Israel's democracy as a model for the East German dictatorship to emulate.

[125] Ibid., 13–15.
[126] Ibid., 16.
[127] Ibid., 33–36.

THE CIA ESTIMATES OF SOVIET, SOVIET-BLOC, AND EAST GERMAN MILITARY ASSISTANCE TO "THIRD-WORLD" OR "LATE-DEVELOPING COUNTRIES" DURING THE COLD WAR

During the Cold War, the United States Central Intelligence Agency assessed the quantity and purposes of Communist aid to "third-world" or "less developed countries" (LDCs in US government jargon). In recent years many of these reports have been declassified and made available through the CREST system at the US National Archives in College Park. They reveal that East Germany played a modest but valuable role in the Soviet-bloc effort.

From 1955 to 1979, of the $52.77 billion of military agreements signed by Communist states to be delivered to "non-communist LDCS" (less developed countries), $47.34 billion, or about 90 percent, came from the Soviet Union; $4.285 billion, or about 9 percent came, from the states of Eastern Europe; and $1.145 billion, or about 2 percent came, from Communist China. During that same period, $39.67 billion of arms were delivered. Of that figure, $35.34 billion, or 89 percent, was delivered by the Soviet Union; $3.405 billion, or 9 percent, by the states of Eastern Europe; and $940 million, or about 2 percent, by Communist China.[128] During this period, China denounced the Soviet leaders as "social imperialists" and counterrevolutionary "revisionists." The notion of a "moderate" and nonrevolutionary Soviet Union, fanned by Maoists and accepted by much of the Western New Left, was, according to these figures, one of the great myths of the Cold War. It seriously underestimated the Soviet Union's radicalism and the centrality of its military support for Communist movements in the third world.

[128] Central Intelligence Agency, National Foreign Assessment Center, "Table A-1: Communist Countries: Military Aid to Non-Communist LDC's, Million US $," in *Communist Aid Activities in Non-Communist Less Developed Countries 1979 and 1954–79: A Research Paper* (October 1980), NACP, CREST (hereafter CREST). From 1954 to 1979, the Soviet Union sent $18 billion of economic aid to 76 countries; trained 68,000 "LDC nationals" from 100 developing countries at Soviet academic institutions, another 33,000 in technical skills, and about 46,000 in military skills. IV. The files declassified in the CREST system include very extensive quantitative information and interesting analysis about Communist economic aid, technician and military personnel sent to various third-world countries, and numbers of students and military personnel studying and receiving training in the Soviet Union and Eastern Europe. The declassified CIA files in the CREST system are a valuable source for historical research.

The CIA reports included extensive information about weapons deliveries to specific countries and regions. The strategic importance that the Soviet Union placed on the Middle East was apparent in the amounts it sent to that region compared to others. Between 1956 and 1979, the Soviet Union signed agreements with countries in North Africa worth $10.96 billion. The comparable figures for sub-Saharan Africa were $4.635 billion; $8.9 billion for East Asia; $30 million for Europe; $970 million to Latin America; $5.4 billion for South Asia; and $24.445 billion for the Middle East. The figures for Soviet arms delivered from 1956 to 1979 were $7.165 billion to North Africa; $3.53 billion for sub-Saharan Africa; $885 million to East Asia; $675 million to Latin America; $4.410 to South Asia; and $18.675 billion to the Middle East.[129] *That is, from 1955 to 1974 approximately 52 percent of Soviet military agreements and military deliveries to "less developed countries" went to the Arab states in the Middle East.*

Figures for 1974, the year following the Yom Kippur War of October 1973, further illustrate these priorities. In that year, the Soviet Union gave $1.1 billion in military aid to LDCs. Of that sum, $937 million, or 85 percent, went to the countries of the Middle East and the Persian Gulf, and of that amount, $250 million went to Iran, $345 million to Iraq, and $416 million to Syria.[130] Of the $3,829 billion in military agreements signed by the Soviet-bloc countries with Egypt from 1955 to 1974, $3,520 billion came from the Soviet Union, $359 million came from Czechoslovakia, $28 million came from Hungary, $5 million came from Poland, and $6 million came from East Germany.[131] The CIA estimated that from 1956 to 1974, the Soviet-bloc countries signed agreements with Syria worth $2,271 billion. Of that amount $1,862 billion came from the Soviet Union. In May and October of 1973, just before and during the Yom Kippur War, the CIA estimated that East Germany delivered

[129] "Table A-2: Communist Countries: Soviet Military Relations with LDC's," in *Communist Aid Activities in Non-Communist Less Developed Countries 1979 and 1954–79*, 14.

[130] "Table 4: Communist Military Aid Extended to Less Developed Countries, 1974," in *Intelligence Handbook: Communist Aid to Less Developed Countries of the Free World, 1974* (March 1975), NACP, CREST, 12. Also see CIA, National Foreign Assessment Center, *Communist Aid Activities in Non-Communist Less Developed Countries 1978*, ER 79-10412U (September 1979), NACP, CREST and CIA, Directorate of Intelligence *Soviet and East European Aid to the Third World, 1981*, GI 82-10175 (August 1982), NACP, CREST.

[131] "Table 5: Communist Military Agreements with Less Developed Countries by Recipient 1955–74," *Intelligence Handbook: Communist Aid to Less Developed Countries of the Free World, 1974* (March 1975), 4.

weapons to the Arab states worth $12 million. Yet even then its contribution was less than Czechoslovakia's ($111 million).[132] In 1974, for example, the CIA reported that the vast majority of weapons from the Soviet bloc to the Middle East came from the Soviet Union ($937 million), followed in order by Czechoslovakia ($56 million), Bulgaria ($49 million), Romania ($22 million), Hungary ($15 million), and only $4 million from East Germany.[133]

In a 1979 report, the CIA offered evidence of the mutually reinforcing impact of Soviet strategic focus on the Middle East with the significant commercial, hard currency benefits to be gained by arms sales to the Arab states in the aftermath of the OPEC oil price increases after the 1973 war. The analysts divided the $47.34 billion of Soviet military agreements with "non-Communist LDCs" into four periods: $690 million from 1955 to 1959; $3.830 billion from 1960 to 1966 in the years preceding the Six-Day War of 1967; $8.665 billion from 1967 to 1973 while resupplying the Arab states; and $34.155 billion from 1974 to 1979. The report noted a fivefold increase in arms agreements in the period of 1974–1979 over that of 1967 to 1973, an increase that it concluded was due to Arab orders for Soviet arms. "Four major Arab clients [Iraq, Syria, Algeria, and Morocco] accounted for more than 70 per cent of the total sales [around the world, JH] in 1974–1979."[134] The report concluded that rapid growth in Soviet arms sales had been stimulated by "the 1967 and 1973 Middle East wars which triggered unprecedented Soviet supply operations to the Arab belligerents; the opening of Moscow's modern weapons arsenal to LDCs as a reaction to Israel's deep penetration raids of Egypt in 1970; and the emphasis on raising commercial and financial returns from arms sales following the rise in oil prices in 1973/74." Further, in "the lucrative Middle East arms market," the Soviet Union "could no longer be identified as a seller of last resort purveying outmoded, reconditioned equipment. The $750 million arms deal with Egypt in 1970 provided advanced SA-2 and SA-3 surface-to-air missiles (previously deployed only in the USSR and Eastern Europe) and 7,500 soldiers to main them." The participation of Soviet forces supporting the Arab states was the first time

[132] Ibid., 20–21.

[133] These figures suggest that research remains to be done in the archives of the other East European members of the Warsaw Pact concerning their military assistance programs.

[134] Central Intelligence Agency, National Foreign Assessment Center "Table 1: USSR: Military Agreements with Non-Communist LDC's," in *Communist Aid Activities in Non-Communist Less Developed Countries, 1979 and 1954–79: A Research Paper*, ER 80-10318U (October 1980), NACP, CREST, 5.

that the Soviets provided "combat units to operate modern equipment in Third World countries."[135]

The CIA reports also kept track of the people going back and forth between the Soviet bloc and "late-developing" or "third-world countries." This movement of people and ideas was indispensable for the emerging alliances. By 1979, according to one CIA report, the Soviet Union alone had trained 68,000 "LDC nationals from 100 developing countries at Soviet academic institutions, another 33,000 in technical skills, and about 46,000 in military skills. Eastern Europe has supplemented the Soviet effort with $10 billion of economic aid extension and $4 billion of military commitments, supplying large number of economic and military technicians."[136]

The strategic importance that the Soviet Union placed on the Middle East in 1970 was also apparent in the location of its military technicians abroad. The CIA estimated that of the 10,635 Soviet-bloc military technicians in these countries around the world, almost 80 percent, or 7,820, were in the Middle East.[137] In the same year, of the 21,415 students from "non-Communist LDCs" studying in the Soviet bloc, 12,695 were in the Soviet Union and 8,720 were studying in Eastern Europe. Of them, 680 were from North Africa and 2,985 were from the Middle East.[138] The CIA estimated that from 1955 to 1979, 45,585 persons from "late-developing countries" received military training in the Soviet Union, 6,345 in Eastern Europe, and 3,150 in China. The figures for military trainees in the Soviet Union and Eastern Europe in those years from Algeria, Libya, and other North African countries were 3,580 and 555, respectively. The importance of the Middle East in Soviet-bloc policy was also apparent in the following figures: in these years 16,370 people

[135] *Communist Aid Activities in Non-Communist Less Developed Countries, 1979 and 1954–79: A Research Paper*, 4–5. This evidence and the evidence from the East German files regarding increased arms shipments challenges the contentions of Guy Laron that Soviet aid to third-world countries, and to the Middle East in particular, was declining in this period. See Guy Laron, "Stepping Back from the Third World: Soviet Policy toward the UAR, 1965–1967," *Journal of Cold War Studies* 12, no. 4 (Winter 1967): 99–118. Also see Galia Golan, "The Soviet Union and the Outbreak of the June 1967 War," *Journal of Cold War Studies* 8, no. 1 (Winter 2006): 3–19.

[136] Central Intelligence Agency, National Foreign Assessment Center, "Communist Aid Activities in Non-Communist Less Developed Countries 1979 and 1954–79," ER 80-10318U, October 1980, iv.

[137] "Table 2: Communist Countries: Military Technicians in Non-Communist LDC," ibid., 6.

[138] "Table 6: Academic Students from Non-Communist LDCs in Communist Countries," ibid., 11.

from the Middle East received military training in the Soviet Union and 2,505 in Eastern Europe. In East Germany, the numbers included 585 from Egypt, 690 from Iraq, 20 from Yemen, and 1,210 from Syria.[139] As we will see, the East German files contain more detailed information about these programs, which continued to the end of the regime in 1989.

In October 1983, the CIA drew on reports from American embassies, and from the East German and the world press to issue *East Germany: Soviet Partner in the LDCs*. It assessed the importance of East German activities in the context of the overall Communist, and especially Soviet efforts.[140] East Germany's military supply program had begun in 1964. *From then until 1983, its arms sales accounted for less than 3 percent of Warsaw Pact sales to the third world.* Three percent meant that in those two decades it had "signed military sales agreements worth $860 million with about 30 LDCs calling primarily for the supply of vehicles, artillery, small arms and ammunition. Sales exceeded $300 million in 1982 alone, largely reflecting radical Arab states." Since 1955, East Germany had signed economic agreements "totally nearly $3 billion with some 50 LDCs."[141] Although the amount of arms sent abroad by East Germany was less than that by other East European Communist regimes, the CIA concluded that *"of the USSR's Warsaw Pact allies, East Germany plays the most active role in support of Soviet objectives in the Third World."*[142] In addition to its support for Marxist regimes in South Yemen, Mozambique, Ethiopia, and Angola, and to the Sandinistas in Nicaragua, the analysts wrote that "East Germany has provided assistance to the Palestine Liberation Organization (PLO), Syria and Iraq in support of Soviet Middle East policies." From 1964 to 1977, 29.2 percent of its $150 million weapons sales went to the Middle East (70 percent to sub-Saharan Africa), but from 1978 to 1982, fully 78.2 percent of its $710 million in arms sales went to the then-oil-rich Middle East. From 1964 to 1982, East Germany signed arms agreements with Middle Eastern countries worth $600 million and delivered $350 million in weapons. These figures amounted to 70 percent and 60 percent, respectively, of East German arms sales to the LDCs. In 1982, of the 1,000 to 1,500 East German intelligence and military advisers working in the LDCs, between

[139] "Table A-4: Communist Training of LDC Military Personnel in Communist Countries," ibid., 16.

[140] Central Intelligence Agency, *East Germany: Soviet Partner in the LDCs: An Intelligence Assessment* (October 1983), NACP, CREST.

[141] Ibid., IV.

[142] Ibid., 1 (emphasis added).

300 and 550 were in the Middle East.[143] Between 1955 and 1982, East Germany extended $800 million in economic aid to the Middle East, a figure that constituted 26 percent of the $2.976 billion in aid it had extended to LDCs. The largest recipients were Egypt, especially before President Anwar Sadat expelled Soviet advisers in 1972 ($264 million); Iran ($100 million); Iraq ($84 million); and Syria $250 million.[144] The East Germans were also active in training journalists and the national news service and supplied material to foreign media. The CIA estimated that between 1978 and 1982, 18,000 students, many from Africa and the Middle East, had received some academic training in East Germany.[145] By early 1968, East German experts were in Syria offering advice on how to organize a planned economy in industry, agriculture, and foreign trade and how to organize state structures.[146]

The CIA analysts wrote that East Germany was "an active partner in the USSR's drive to increase Communist presence and influence in the Third World." Though its programs were small compared to the Soviet efforts, they had "grown in size and scope to the point where East Germany now provides a number of complementary services that serve Moscow's foreign policy interests." Such services included "developing local security and intelligence services, establishing party and media links, and providing technical training courses" and consolidating pro-Soviet regimes in "Angola, Mozambique, Ethiopia, South Yemen, and Syria."[147] The CIA analysts concluded, "East Germany's investment has paid off well in gains in international recognition and prestige." Where in 1970 it was recognized by only seven non-Communist countries, by 1982, East Germany had "formal relations with over 130 and assistance agreements with 50." It had "gained influence and respect, particularly in Africa and the Middle East where it has established close relations with a number of countries as well as with many of the leading African revolutionary

143 Ibid., 5. Research on East Germans who served in Arab countries and also with Arab students who studied in East Germany should be on the agenda of historians in the future.

144 "Table 3: East Germany: Economic Aid to Non-Communist LDCs, 1955–82," (October 1983), NACP, CREST, 9. For an earlier CIA report on East Germany, see Central Intelligence Agency, Directorate of Intelligence, Office of Research and Reports, "Intelligence Brief: Recent Upsurge in East German Economic Assistance to Les Developed Countries," CIA/R 65-17, March 1965, NACP, CREST, 1–3.

145 Central Intelligence Agency, *East Germany: Soviet Partner in the LDCs*, 3.

146 "Bericht über die Tätigkeit von Regierungsberatern der DDR in der SAR in der Zeit von Februar 1968 bis März 1972," BAB Ministerrat der DDR DC20/ 11658, 86–88.

147 Central Intelligence Agency, *East Germany: Soviet Partner in the LDCs*, iii.

movements and the PLO." It had "signed treaties of friendship and cooperation with Angola, Mozambique, Ethiopia, South Yemen, and Afghanistan and a joint declaration of friendship and cooperation with Syria."[148]

The CIA assessments of East Germany linked its involvement in arms shipments and other forms of assistance to LDCs to growth of its popularity and acceptance around the world. As the material presented in this chapter and the following chapters indicates, the archives of East Germany's Ministry of State Security as well as those of the regime's key decision making and implementing institutions, the SED Politburo, Central Committee, Defense Ministry, and Council of Ministers, offer a wealth of details that confirm and add texture to the picture offered by the CIA analysts. The leaders of the Soviet Union had no desire to risk nuclear war with the West, yet their sanity in that regard was not synonymous with political moderation in the Middle East. They placed great importance on the region and supported the forces of radicalism within it. Though East Germany's contribution to the Soviet-bloc military assistance program was a modest 3 percent of the total, it included, as we have seen and will see again, delivery of tens of thousands of machine guns, land mines, rocket-propelled grenades; millions of cartridges; and even dozens of tanks and jet fighters. It was more than enough to kill and wound many Israelis.

West German leftists who turned against Israel in summer 1967 opposed the West German government's tradition of connecting "coming to terms with the Nazi past" and its related economic, military, and political support for Israel, which led to the establishment of diplomatic relations in 1965. The turn of spring to fall 1967 was not only one against the traditions of Konrad Adenauer and Christian Democracy. It also broke with the pro-Israeli traditions of liberal and left-liberal intellectuals and of the Social Democratic Party in the Federal Republic. We now turn to that conjuncture of domestic and international events in June 1967 in West Germany, one that had a profound and enduring influence on the emergence and persistence of an anti-Israeli Left in West Germany.

[148] Ibid., 6.

3

An anti-Israeli Left Emerges in West Germany: The Conjuncture of June 1967

In the West German New Left, the turn against Israel emerged between June and September 1967. For all of its criticisms of actually existing Communist regimes during the preceding decades, the West German New Left shared much of the criticism of Israel that had been coming from East Berlin. As in the East so now in the West, radical leftist activists transformed the Jewish victims of the past into the Zionist and Israeli aggressors, expellers, exploiters, colonialists, and even racists of the present. It was in these months that leaders of the West German New Left increasingly interpreted Israel through the prism of Marxism or Marxist-Leninism and therefore placed it on the wrong side of the central global divide between "imperialism" and "national liberation." Israel's West German New Left antagonists now placed the language of leftist anti-fascism, which had previously fostered support for the Jewish state and the survivors of the Holocaust, in the service of attacking that very same state and its people. If only, as one prominent leftist wrote, the West German Left could free itself from its "Jewish complex" – that is, supposed guilty feelings about the Holocaust – it would be able to express solidarity with the Palestinians and fight the new fascism in the form of the state of Israel. The attack on and even reversal of the meaning of Vergangenheitsbewältigung, "coming to terms with the past," was a distinctive contribution of the West German radical Left from 1967 to 1969. And for some, this redefinition was important in offering West German leftist support for Palestinian terrorist organizations in the years to come.

From 1949 to 1967, the preeminent stance of non-Communist leftist and left-liberal opinion in West Germany was emphatically pro-Israeli.[1]

[1] On this, see the important now-standard account, Martin Kloke, *Israel und die deutsche Linke: Zur Geschichte eines schwierigen Verhältnis*, 2nd ed. (Frankfurt/Main: Haag

The unspoken eleventh commandment of postwar West German public life – do no more harm to the Jews – was part of the Social Democratic and left-liberal political and moral engagement as well.[2] Though they differed with Adenauer's conservative government of 1949 to 1963 on a range of issues, the Social Democrats shared Adenauer's empathy for Israel. As the German historian Martin Kloke has observed in his standard work on the subject, the predominant view even in young leftist and left-liberal circles before 1967, including within the Sozialistische Deutscher Studentenbund (Socialist German Student Association), or SDS,[3] favored West German diplomatic relations with Israel and support for restitution (Wiedergutmachung) payments to individual Jews and to the state of Israel.[4] In 1957, at the Free University in Berlin, the first "German-Israeli Study Group," Deutsch-Israeli Studiengruppe, or DIS, was established, and in 1962, it opened a campaign to support the establishment of diplomatic relations with Israel.[5] West German liberals and leftists were vocal in their criticisms of the Egyptian government's decision to employ about 500 West German missile engineers and scientists to build missiles to be aimed at Israel. Many of those working on this program had worked on the V2 missile programs for the Nazi regime. When Adenauer's successor, Ludwig Erhard, established diplomatic relations with Israel in 1965, he did so with strong support across the full political consensus of the Federal Republic.[6] Up to the June days of 1967,

+ Herchen, 1990), as well as Jens Benicke, *Von Adorno zu Mao: über die schlechte Aufhebung der antiautoritären Bewegung* (Freiburg: ca ira, 2010). For an excellent study of similar trends in Austria, see Margit Reiter, *Unter Antisemistmus-Verdacht: Die österreichische Linke und Israel nach der Shoah* (Innsbruck: Studien Verlag, 2001).

[2] On Kurt Schumacher and the Social Democratic tradition of coming to terms with the Nazi past, see Jeffrey Herf, *Divided Memory: The Nazi Past in the Two Germanys* (Cambridge, MA: Harvard University Press, 1997). On restitution, that is, Wiedergutmachung, see Constantin Goschler, *Schuld und Schulden: Die Politik der Wiedergutmachung für NS-Verfolgte seit 1945* (Göttingen: Wallstein Verlag, 2005).

[3] The fact that "SDS" in the United States had identical initials to its West German counterpart was simply a coincidence. The former abbreviated "Students for a Democratic Society." On the connections between American and West German SDS, see Martin Klimke, *The Other Alliance: Student Protest in West Germany and the United States in the Global Sixties* (Princeton, NJ: Princeton University Press, 2010).

[4] On the history of restitution, see from an extensive scholarship, Constantin Goschler's excellent history, *Schuld und Schulden: Die Politik der Wiedergutmachung für NS-Verfolgte seit 1945* (Göttingen: Wallstein Verlag, 2005); and Herf, *Divided Memory*.

[5] Kloke, "Oppositioneller Proisraelimsus vor 1967," in *Israel und die deutsche Linke*, 70–105; and Willy Albrecht, *Der Sozialistische Deutsche Studentenbund (SDS): Vom parteikonform Studentenbund zum Repräsentanten der neuen Linken* (Bonn: Friedrich Ebert Stiftung, 1994).

[6] From the extensive scholarship on West German–Israeli relations see Inge Deutschkron, *Israel und die Deutschen: Das schwierige Verhältnis*, rev. ed. (Cologne: Verlag Wissenschaft

the pro-Israeli stance of the West German non-Communist Left remained intact.[7] For liberals and Social Democrats, sympathy for Israel and opposition to anti-Semitism in postwar Germany and Europe were self-evident and logical responses to Nazi Germany's policies of persecution and extermination of the Jews.

A conjuncture, the simultaneity of two causally unrelated episodes of international and local politics in June 1967, war in the Middle East and the shooting death of a student protester by police in West Berlin, reinforced, precipitated, and accelerated a shift of leftist loyalties. In Kloke's view, the actual conflict in the Middle East "played only a subordinate role" in the Left's turn against Israel compared to the impact of local politics.[8] On June 2, a demonstration to protest the visit to West Berlin by the shah of Iran turned into a violent confrontation between police and demonstrators during which a West Berlin policemen, Karl-Heinz Kurras, shot and killed 26-year-old Benno Ohnesorg, a student at the Free University of Berlin. The shooting reinforced a belief in the New Left that the West German government was indeed authoritarian or even fascist in nature and that political opposition needed to be "extra-parliamentary," that is, in the streets and outside the existing political parties. In 2009, research in the files of East Germany's Ministry of State Security (the Stasi) revealed that Kurras had been serving as a Stasi agent since 1955.[9] So far no evidence has emerged that indicates that Kurras was ordered to shoot one of the demonstrators in order to lend credence to East German and Soviet accusations about the "neo-fascist" nature of the West German government and thus radicalize the student Left in the Federal Republic.[10] Nevertheless, that was precisely the result of Kurras's action. Had it been revealed at the time that Kurras was a Stasi agent, the political results

und Politik, 1991); and Lily Gardner Feldman, *The Special Relationship between West Germany and Israel* (London: Allan and Unwin, 1984).

7 Kloke, *Israel und die deutsche Linke*, 70-105.

8 Ibid.

9 "Stasi Archive Surprise: East German Spy Shot West Berlin Martyr," www.spiegel.de/international/germany/stasi-archive-surprise-east-german-spy-shot-west-berlin-martyr-a-626275.html; Nicholas Kulish, "Spy Fired Shot That Changed West Germany," *New York Times* (May 26, 2009), www.nytimes.com/2009/05/27/world/europe/27germany.html?_r=0.

10 "'Die 68er waren betrogene Betrüger': Der Historiker Peter Horvath untersucht die Kontakte der Studentenbewegung zu SED und Stasi: Für ihn handelt es sich um eine "inszenierte Revolte," *Die Welt* (June 12, 2009), www.elt.de/welt_print/article3910491/Die-68er-waren-betrogene-Betrueger.html. Also see Peter Horvarth, *Die inszenierte Revolte: hinter den Kulissen von '68* (Munich: Herbig, 20120).

would likely have been dramatically different, lending credence to warnings about East German Communist efforts to subvert West German democracy by depicting it as a neo-fascist regime.[11] Ironically, a murder carried out by an agent of the East German intelligence services became conclusive evidence for West German leftists that the West German government and the Social Democratic government of West Berlin as well were intolerant of dissent. Indeed, one of the three major leftist terrorist organizations of the 1970s decided to call itself "the June 2nd movement," named for the date when Kurras shot Ohnesorg.

In West Berlin and in West Germany, the newspapers of the conservative Axel Springer press, especially its tabloid *Bild-Zeitung,* took a leading role in denouncing the New Left. Yet the very same papers also were leading voices in support of Israel. Following the principle that "the friend of my enemy is my enemy," the young Left's turn against Israel drew emotional energy from the simultaneity of the Springer press support for Israel and criticism of the New Left. Israel had friends and supporters across the West German political spectrum, but the association of the Jewish state with this tribune of West German conservatism became embedded in the outlook of the radical Left, all the more deeply because the shooting took place just three days before the Six-Day War began. As Reimut Reiche, president of SDS, wrote on June 9, 1967, "We [in SDS] cannot give emphatic support to the state of Israel when the whole [West German] press celebrates this conduct of war with the same concept, 'Blitzkrieg,' with the which Nazis conquered Poland in three days and massacred its Jewish and non-Jewish population."[12] The conjuncture of the shooting in West Berlin and the Six-Day War was apparent on the front page of *Die Welt* on June 10, 1967. Just beneath the banner headline

[11] The leftist attacks of the late 1960s and 1970s on Social Democracy in West Germany recalled the Communist attacks on "social fascism" of the 1920s and 1930s. As the historian Jürgen Kocka pointed out, a major difference lay in the fact that in the second period, the attacks were from East Germany, that is, from another state, and failed to prevent the entry into power of a left-of-center government in the 1970s in the Federal Republic. See Jürgen Kocka, *Geschichte und Aufklärung: Aufsätze* (Göttingen: Vandenhoeck & Ruprecht, 1989). On the comparison of the Communists in Weimar and the radical Left in the 1960s and 1970s, see Heinrich August Winkler, *Der Lange Weg nach Westen*, vol. 2, 5th ed. (Munich: Beck Verlag, 2002).

[12] Cited in Kloke, *Israel und die deutsche Linke*, p. 115; and in Jens Benicke, *Von Adorno zu Mao: Über die schlechte Aufhebung der antiautoritären Bewegung* (Freiburg: ca ira, 2010). Until the end of the Cold War in 1989, the anti-imperialism of the 1960s Left trumped the anti-fascism of the European Left of the 1940s. See Anson Rabinbach, *Begriffe aus dem Kalten Krieg: Totalitarismus, Antifaschismus, Genozid* (Göttingen: Wallstein Verlag, 2009).

announcing Nasser's offer to resign in the face of the Arab defeat was an article about the Ohnesorg funeral in Hannover, noting that 7,000 students marched in that city to remember him and protest the shooting.[13] For the young Left, the conjuncture of the Six-Day War and the Ohnesorg shooting had enduring import.

On June 5, 1967, Reiche issued a statement approved by SDS's National Council about the war that began that day. Compared to subsequent statements it was moderate.[14] The SDS leadership saw "the actual cause of the permanent Israeli-Arab crisis in the different levels of economic-cultural development between Israel and its neighboring countries." The conflict was made worse by "extensive weapons deliveries and direct political and military intervention by the great powers, the USA, France, Great Britain, the Federal Republic and the Soviet Union," who played the countries in the region off against one another and blocked "a progressive solution to the conflict." Israel's "isolationist policies" forced it into dependency on "the imperialist system," while Syria and Egypt were compelled to adopt an anti-capitalist course to overcome underdevelopment. The UN and the great powers should "guarantee the existing borders." A cease-fire agreement "must include the recognition of the inviolability of borders by the participating states [of the Middle East] themselves."[15] By accepting Israel's right to exist in secure borders, the SDS statement of June 1967 was far more moderate than the position it adopted four months later.

SDS leaders also circulated an open letter by Wolfgang Abendroth, a professor of political science at the University of Marburg, whose views carried weight among leaders of SDS. Rejecting solidarity with Israel and urging support for the Arab states, Abendroth wrote that "identification of socialist internationalism in the capitalist states of Europe with Israel's contemporary policy is, despite all sympathy for the Israeli people, impossible." He rejected "the nationalist hysteria of the Arab countries" but argued that it "would grow if the socialist parties in Europe or the official policy of the FRG were to take the side of Israel.... The overall

[13] "Benno Ohnesorg wurde in aller Stille beigesetzt" and "Gamal Abdel Nasser bieten seinen Rücktritt an," *Die Welt* (June 10, 1967), 1; and "Der Abschied von Benno Ohnesorg," *Die Welt* (June 10, 1967), 4.

[14] Bundesvorstand, Sozialistische Deutscher Studentenbund (SDS) (hereafter BV SDS) "Erklärung des SDS zum Nahost-Konflikt" (June 1967), Archiv des Hamburger Instituts für Sozialforschung (Arch HIS) SDS 140, Diskussionspapiere, Organisationsdebatte, Politische Initiativen, Box 01, Blattsammlung, Presse, Flugblätter, Entwicklung des SDS in Jahr 1967.

[15] Ibid.

interests of the colonial revolution, of the socialist countries and also of the revolutionary flank of the international workers' movement in the capitalist countries agrees more with the Arab states (namely Egypt, Syria and Algeria, not the feudal states) than with the interests of Israel."[16] Abendroth was, of course, "against any transformation of war into genocide – as it can all too easily happen with the mobilization of primitive emotions of underdeveloped populations."[17]

Abendroth then took issue with those who referred to the extermination of the Jews in Europe as a reason for West Germany to support the Jewish state in 1967: "Today the people of the Federal Republic are being mobilized with the use of a fundamentally anti-Semitic philo-semitic trauma that serves the interests of the power politics of the USA. However, it does not serve the real interests of the masses of the people in Israel." The "propaganda" of West German print and electronic media fostered such sentiments, "but even understandable stimulation of emotions must not be permitted to move the emotional wave in this direction, for in a crisis or emergency the anti-Semitic club will be revealed behind the philo-Semitic mask."[18] In other words, West German support for Israel was actually a form of anti-Semitism called "philo-semitism," a term defined as a sentimental, uninformed, hypocritical, and undeserved expression of empathy for Jews. The idea that support for Israel was a form of "philo-semitic anti-Semitism" found support from other West German leftists, especially some of those who were in the vanguard of terrorist attacks on Jews in West Germany.[19]

In another statement in June 1967, the SDS National Council responded to public criticism that its turn to neutrality and even criticism of Israel was due to a leftist form of anti-Semitism.[20] The suggestion was

[16] Wolfgang Abendroth, "Offener Brief von Wolfgang Abendroth," 3. Bundesvorstand, Sozialistische Deutscher Studentenbund (SDS) (hereafter BV SDS) "Erklärung des SDS zum Nahost-Konflikt" (June 1967), Archiv des Hamburger Instituts für Sozialforschung (Arch HIS) SDS 140, Diskussionspapiere, Organisationsdebatte, Politische Initiativen, Box 01, Blattsammlung, Presse, Flugblätter, Entwicklung des SDS in Jahr 1967. Also cited in Kloke, *Israel und die deutsche Linke*, 117.

[17] Abendroth, "Offener Brief."

[18] Ibid.

[19] On the leftist turn from "philo-semitism" to antagonism to Israel in summer 1967, also see Aribert Reimann, "Letters from Amman: Dieter Kunzelmann and the Origins of German Anti-Zionism during the Late 1960s," in Ingrid Gilcher-Holtey, ed., *A Revolution of Perception? Consequences and Echoes of 1968* (New York: Berghahn Books, 2014), 69–90.

[20] Bundesvorstand, Sozialistische Deutscher Studentenbund (SDS) (hereafter BV SDS) "Erklärung zum Nahost-Konflikt" (June 1967), Archiv des Hamburger Instituts für Sozialforschung (Arch HIS) SDS 140, Diskussionspapiere, Organisationsdebatte,

"grotesque." It threw "an utterly horrifying light on the function of an underlying anti-Semitism that today begins to produce the philo-semitic mood of [Germany's] bad conscience." In fact, the SDS leaders continued, philo-semitic and hence pro-Israeli sentiment in West Germany was embedded in "the same political structures as political anti-Semitism." The end point of this dialectical reasoning was that support for Israel in the Six-Day War was a form of anti-Semitism, while support for the Arab states or neutrality in the face of their threats to drive the Jews into the sea constituted opposition to anti-Semitism.

Leaders of SDS also presented themselves as voices of reason in contrast to an emotionally burdened West German public opinion. On July 2, 1967, the SDS National Committee noted the refusal of "many professors" to support SDS as it "distanced itself from the wave of Israel support" during the Six-Day War. The Middle East conflict had "split the left."[21] Reiche and fellow SDS National Council member Peter Gäng wrote that "SDS had to immediately oppose the merely emotionally, one-sided and unlimited support of the Israeli government that came from West German public opinion" and express "solidarity with our comrades and political friends in and from Israel and the Arab countries" with whom SDS had long been in contact.[22] In turning against Israel, the SDS leaders presented themselves as voices of reason, in contrast to their fellow West Germans, whose political judgments were presumably clouded by the emotional reactions to the crimes of Nazism against the Jews. Reiche and Lang then turned to the newspapers of the Springer chain, *Die Welt* in particular. In the Federal Republic, they wrote, "the producers of public opinion fall all over themselves, in a roaring, intoxicated (*rauschhaften)* identification with the victors," that is, with Israel. Citizens of the Federal Republic greeted the advance of the Israeli troops with enthusiasm as if the Israelis were "a brother people" (Brudervolkes). SDS, on the other hand, sought "to begin a political discussion," in contrast to "the emotional and even – this time – pro-Jewish racist din of

Politische Initiativen, Box 01, Blattsammlung, Presse, Flugblätter, Entwicklung des SDS in Jahr 1967.

21 "Niederlage oder Erfolg der Protestaktion? Eine Vorlaufige Auswertung (2 Juli 1967), Rundbrief an alle SDS-Mitglieder," Archiv Apo und soziale Bewegungen, Zentralinstitut für sozialwissenschaftliche Forschung der Frei Universität Berlin (FU), Sammlung Bundesvorstand des Sozialistischen Deutschen Studentbundes (SDS), 1967.

22 Reimut Reiche and Peter Gäng, SDS Bundesvorstand 1967, "Einladung zu einem öffentlichen Nahost-Seminar," Frankfurt/Main (n.d., Archiv Apo und soziale Bewegungen, Zentralinstitut für sozialwissenschaftliche Forschung der Frei Universität Berlin (FU), Sammlung Bundesvorstand des Sozialistischen Deutschen Studentbundes (SDS).

the recent varying podium discussions in the universities and the public sphere in the FRG."[23]

From September 4 to 9, 1967, 70 delegates from 48 West German universities met on the campus of Johan Wolfgang Goethe University in Frankfurt/Main for a national SDS meeting. They passed a resolution that signaled the turn of the West German radical Left against Israel.[24] The delegates elected a new National Council and a new president, Karl Dietrich Wolff. Wolff had spent a year as an exchange student in high school in the United States, where he witnessed the growth of the American New Left and the civil rights movement. He contributed a mixture of militancy and political ability to the SDS leadership that accelerated its turn to the left.[25] The other members of the National Council in power as the organization consolidated its anti-Israeli position were Wolff's brother, Frank, and Hans-Jürgen Krahl, a Marxist theorist and student of Theodor Adorno, both from Frankfurt/Main; Herbert Lederer (Cologne); and Bernd Rabehl from West Berlin.[26] Also in attendance at the September meeting were Elmar Altvater, Frank Deppe, Bernhard Blank, and Wolfgang Lefevre, all of whom were prominent figures in SDS who also became professors of history and social science in West German universities. Reiche, who became a psychoanalyst, was also present. Rabehl at times had university teaching positions. Rudi Dutschke, the West German New Left's most famous and charismatic figure, also participated, though in unpublished notes at the time he wrote that "the founding of the state of Israel was the *political emancipation* of Jewry. It must absolutely be preserved."[27] Krahl

[23] Reiche and Gäng, SDS Bundesvorstand, "Einladung zu einem öffentlichen Nahost-Seminar," Frankfurt/Main (n.d.) Archiv Apo FU Berlin, Sammlung BV des SDS 1967, 1–2.

[24] "Deligiertenliste der XXII. ODK (4.–9. September 1967), Archiv Apo FU Berlin, Sammlung BV 1967 SDS, Archiv Apo FU Berlin, Sammlung BV 22.DK 1967 SDS.

[25] Wolff was also the cofounder of the leftist publisher Roter Stern Verlag (Red Star Press). On K. D. Wolff and other connections and interactions between the American and West German New Left see Martin Klimke, *The Other Alliance: Student Protest in West Germany and the United States in the Global Sixties* (Princeton, NJ: Princeton University Press, 2010).

[26] "Sozialistischer Deutscher Studentenbund, 22. Delegiertenkonferenz des SDS, 4.–9 September 1967, Neuwahlen," SDS Bundesvorstand (n.d.) Archiv Apo FU Berlin, Sammlung BV 1967 SDS; and "(Zweite) vorläufige Tagesordnung der 22. Ordentlichen Delegiertenkonferenz des SDS," Frankfurt/Main (September 4–8, 1967), Bundesvorstand, Sozialistische Deutscher Studentenbund (SDS) (hereafter BV SDS), Archiv des Hamburger Instituts für Sozialforschung (Arch HIS) SDS 140, Diskussionspapiere, Organisationsdebatte, Politische Initiativen, Box 01, Blattsammlung, Presse, Flugblätter, Entwicklung des SDS in Jahr 1967.

[27] Rudi Dutschke, "Notizen," Mappe 2, Blatt ½, June 1967, K21/48, Archiv des Hamburger Instituts für Sozialforschung, cited in Wolfgang Kraushaar, "Rudi Dutschke

was regarded as one of Theodor Adorno's leading students and would have likely had an academic career had he not been killed in an automobile accident in 1970. Those who attended the September meeting in Frankfurt/Main and voted in favor of its resolutions were leading and influential, not marginal, members of the West German New Left. They both expressed and helped to shape the anti-Israeli consensus that emerged in the aftermath of the Six-Day War.[28]

On September 7, the SDS delegates approved a resolution offered by members from Frankfurt/Main and Heidelberg.[29] It expressed the mélange of neo-Marxism, Marxism-Leninism, and radical enthusiasm about third-world revolutions that had become a defining feature of the New Left around the world. Like their counterparts elsewhere, the West German SDS leaders were focused on the war in Vietnam. Yet the Nazi past, the geographical proximity of the Middle East, the West German government's "special relationship" and diplomatic relations with Israel, and their own contacts and discussions with Arab students in West Germany made the Middle East a much more salient issue for the New Left in West Germany than in other centers of New Left radicalism in 1967. The Middle East resolution stated that the Six-Day War could "only be analyzed against the background of the anti-imperialist struggle of the Arab peoples against their oppression by Anglo-American imperialism." The nationalization of the region's vast oil reserves was a precondition for social and economic development and for "overcoming the Israeli-Arab conflict in which Arabs and Jews are played off against one another in the effort to oppress the anti-imperialist forces."[30] The "special conditions of Israel's emergence as a Zionist settler state after World War II inevitably led to the political and economic isolation of the immigrants from the

und der bewaffnete Kampf," in Kraushaar, Karin Wieland and Jan Philipp Reemtsma, *Rudi Dutschke, Andreas Baader und die RAF* (Hamburg: Hamburger Edition, 2005), 48, emphasis in the original text. A decade later, Dutschke had rejected terrorism. See Rudi Dutschke, "Toward a Clarifying Criticism of Terrorism," trans. Jeffrey Herf, *New German Critique* (Fall 1977), 9–10.

28 The delegates passed resolutions on the war in Vietnam, black power in the United States, solidarity with American SDS, revolutionary "national liberation movements" in Latin America, and the conflict in the Middle East. See "Inhaltsverzeichnis," Archiv Apo FU Berlin, Sammlung BV 22.DK 1967 SDS.

29 Sozialistischer Deutscher Studentenbund, 22. Delegiertenkonferenz des SDS, 4.–9 September 1967, "V. Dem SDS von der 22. ODk als Material überwiesen: 24. Der Konflikt im Nahen Osten" 48–534 and Volkhart Mosler, "Nahost-Resolution," nd, Archiv Apo FU Berlin, Sammlung BV 22.DK 1967 SDS, 48–54. For the resolution from the Frankfurt/Main SDS group see "Antrag Nr. 16 (Frankfurt)," Frankfurt/Main (September 4–8, 1967), Archiv Apo FU Berlin, Sammlung BV 1967 SDS.

30 Ibid., 48.

Arab economic realm." Though Arabs in fact participated in the Israeli economy from 1948 to 1967, the SDS resolution wrongly claimed that the Jews had hired only Jewish and no Arab workers. It called the Zionist labor union, the Histadrut, part of a system of the "Zionist colonization of Palestine" that entailed the "expulsion and oppression of the Arab population that had been born there by a privileged settler stratum." The "inevitable isolation" from the surrounding Arab economies meant that Israel could "only exist in economic dependency on western, especially American imperialism and Zionist capitalists outside Israel."[31] The resolution called for the "rehabilitation of hundreds of thousands of Arab refugees back to their motherland." The authors of the resolution were confident that doing so would "not mean the new expulsion of the Israeli masses living there, but it would mean the end of the Zionist immigration law (*Einwanderungsgesetze)*, that is, it means repatriation (*Rückführung*) and material restitution (*Entschädigung)* of the Palestinians." That in turn required the socialist transformation in the Arab states "and in Palestine and thus the formation of a socialist unity front in the Middle East."[32] The resolution did not mention the threats and actions by Nasser, Syrian attacks on northern Israel, or military support for the Arab states by the Soviet Union. It ignored the case Israel had made in the United Nations, the efforts of Jews in West Germany to convey that argument, and the by-then widely publicized accounts of the threats the Arab states had made to destroy Israel. With less bombast, it was echoing the themes of East German propaganda, the Arab states, and the Palestinian organizations in West German universities that were becoming a significant factor in student politics. The resolution condemned "the Israeli aggression against the anti-imperialist forces in the Middle East" and supported all of those forces in the Middle East "who defend the accomplishments of anti-imperialism such as the nationalization of the Suez Canal, of foreign capital in Egypt and Syria and the anti-imperialist battles in Yemen." SDS criticized the "petty bourgeois character" of the Baath Party in Syria and Nasserism in Egypt; both had proven themselves "unable to mobilize the anti-imperialist masses" because they were representatives of the national bourgeoisie. Nasserism and the Baath regime in Syria were insufficiently radical for the West German leftists. SDS condemned what it called the "politics of cease-fire adopted by the republican, state-capitalist regimes

[31] "Sozialistischer Deutscher Studentenbund, 22. Delegiertenkonferenz des SDS, 4.–9 September 1967, "BV. Dem SDS von der 22. ODk als Material Überwiesen: 24. Der Konflikt im Nahen Osten," 48–53, and Volkhart Mosler, "Nahost-Resolution," n.d., Archiv Apo FU Berlin, Sammlung BV 1967 SDS, 48–49.

[32] Ibid., 49–50.

with the feudal forces in Saudi Arabia and the oil kingdoms of the Persian Gulf."[33] The resolution acknowledged [Ahmed] "Schukeiri [*sic*] racist outbursts" and the existence of an undefined Arab "chauvinism," but it did not identify them as anti-Semitic in content. It criticized them not because such threats to the Jews were inherently reprehensible, but rather because they "decisively weakened the anti-imperialist forces in the Middle East. The racist propaganda of the national-feudal Arab front became an instrument in the hands of the Israeli leadership to justify its own plans of aggression."[34] It was a tactical blunder, not a moral stain.

The resolution supported Arab nonrecognition of the state of Israel, which "in its current form is not viable without the support of imperialism." Peace was possible only through solving "structural conflict between an Israel supported by imperialism and the Arab peoples who are exploited by imperialism." However, the authors opposed the "chauvinism of the national-feudal Arab front" because "as long as the conflict with Israel is conducted with chauvinist assumptions it will necessarily lead to a further strengthening of the imperialist forces in Israel and in the Arab countries. The recognition of the right of existence of the Jews living in Palestine by the revolutionary movement in the Arab countries must not be identical with the recognition of Israel as a bridge of imperialism and as a Zionist state form."[35] The resolution thus reassured Jews that they had a right to exist "in Palestine" but not to have a state of their own, that is, Israel. The problem would be resolved by a "revolutionary socialist movement" that would "overcome[s] imperialism" and create unity between socialists in the Arab countries and "socialist Israel."[36]

The September resolution at least mentioned and criticized Arab "chauvinist assumptions," something that the radical Left would cease to do in the coming years. SDS's adoption of the Middle East resolution in September 1967 was the moment at which the leftist anti-imperialism of the 1960s New Left displaced and redefined the meaning of West German Vergangenheitbewältigung and its associated focus on the memory of the Holocaust and preoccupation with the past and present of anti-Semitism. In fall 1967, SDS did not mention the alliance between Nazi Germany and some Arab leaders in World War II.[37] The resolution criticized

[33] Ibid., 50–51.

[34] Ibid., 52.

[35] Ibid.

[36] Ibid., 53.

[37] The scholarship is extensive. In recent years see Jeffrey Herf, *Nazi Propaganda for the Arab World* (New Haven, CT: Yale University Press, 2009); Barry Rubin and Wolfgang Schwanitz, *Nazis, Islamists and the Making of the Modern Middle East* (New Haven,

"Anglo-American imperialism" but said nothing about the important role of the Soviet bloc. This silence was all the more striking because the core descriptions of Israel as dependent on "imperialism" were similar to those accounts emerging from Moscow and East Berlin and, for that matter, from Beijing as well.[38]

The following month, SDS organized a "tribunal" of the Springer press. Its slogan was "Expropriate Springer." It found the publisher guilty of committing the sins of anti-communism, erosion of West German democracy, and manipulation of mass consciousness.[39] The tribunal described the Springer press support for Israel as "philo-semitism," which it described as a form of anti-Semitism.

> The philo-semitism of the Springer press that has appeared in the context of the Arab-Israeli conflict represents a refinement of the anti-Semitic psychosis. The depiction of the military capability of Israel's war machinery in a kind of fascist war reportage confirms the historical persecution of the Jews. The persecuted appear as the students who have learned from the persecutor, the persecution itself as the successfully completed education. Protected by the philo-semitic pose, the Springer press turns the stereotypes of historic anti-Semitism against the Arabs. The Springer press serves to revive racist instincts and psychological preparations for war.[40]

In fact, *Die Welt*'s coverage of the Six-Day War, while sympathetic to Israel, bore no resemblance to "fascist war reportage" that had been common, for example, in Nazi Germany's government newspaper, the *Völkischer Beobachter*. There were no depictions of vast international conspiracies; nor did its coverage include racist generalizations about Arabs. Indeed, Nazi propaganda during World War II was noteworthy

CT: Yale University Press, 2012); and David Motadel, *Islam and Nazi Germany's War* (Cambridge, MA: Harvard University Press, 2014).

[38] On East German efforts to influence West German politics, see Hubertus Knabe, *Die Unterwanderte Republik*, 2nd ed. (Munich: Ullstein Verlag, 2001).

[39] "Konzeption des Springer Tribunals: Vorläufiger Entwurf (Oktober 1967)," Archiv des Hamburger Institute für Sozialforschung, SDS 140, Diskussionspapiers, Organisationsdebatten, Politische Initiativen, Box 1, "Blattsammlung, Presse, Flugblätter, Entwicklung des SDS in Jahr 1967." Despite its self-description as an "anti-authoritarian" Left, the New Left on both sides of the Atlantic entertained the idea that tolerance of conservative viewpoints was "repressive." The influential contemporary expression of the need to suppress such speech was offered by Herbert Marcuse in his 1965 essay "Repressive Tolerance," in Robert Paul Wolff, Barrington Moore Jr., and Herbert Marcuse, *A Critique of Pure Tolerance* (Boston: Beacon Press, 1965), 81–118.

[40] "Konzeption des Springer Tribunals: Vorläufiger Entwurf (Oktober 1967)," 6, Archiv des Hamburger Institute für Sozialforschung, SDS 140, Diskussionspapiers, Organisationsdebatten, Politische Initiativen, Box 1, Blattsammlung, Presse, Flugblätter, Entwicklung des SDS in Jahr 1967."

for its enthusiasm for Islam and Arab nationalism.[41] Moreover, the pejorative description of West German government policy toward Israel as a case of "philo-semitism" conveyed the erroneous idea that postwar West Germany suffered from excessive sympathy and concern for the survivors of the Holocaust or the state of Israel. Such sympathy and concern did exist at the level of the West German government and in the center of the political establishment, but it also faced opposition in a society where the legacies of anti-Semitism also persisted.[42] The statement echoed themes of Soviet-bloc and Arab anti-Israeli propaganda campaigns, in another, more sinister form. It was a less bombastic way of calling the Israelis the new Nazis and of demeaning West German support for Israel in the aftermath of the Six-Day War. SDS also pejoratively described West German support for Israel as due to a kind of national narcissism, which saw in Israel in 1967 a mirror of a presumably still admired Nazi Germany in World War II. In so doing, it dismissed the more plausible explanation, namely, that much of the West German political establishment supported Israel because it thought that the German government had a responsibility to prevent further harm to the Jews and thus to support Israel in the face of Arab threats to destroy it by force of arms. The New Left's stance toward Israel comprised a sequence of reaction formations. The West German government supported Israel. As the New Left denounced the Federal Republic as an authoritarian state, it opposed its policies toward Israel. The Springer press criticized the New Left and supported Israel so the New Left turned against Israel. Local circumstances, as much as if not more than those in the Middle East, played a role in the New Left's turn against Israel in 1967.

SDS's turn against Israel led prominent left-leaning West German intellectuals, scholars, and journalists to dissent in a "Common Statement of Twenty Representatives of the German Left on the Middle East Conflict." It was written by a Swiss socialist, Ernst Erdös, and the West Berlin Zionist Michael Landmann. The signers included the following list of prominent liberal and left-leaning writers, scholars, and essayists: Alfred Andersch, Hans-Werner Bartsch, Ernst Bloch, Walter

[41] On the account of World War II that appeared in the *Völkischer Beobachter*, see Jeffrey Herf, *The Jewish Enemy: Nazi Propaganda during World War II and the Holocaust* (Cambridge, MA: Harvard University Press, 2006). On enthusiasm for Islam in the Nazi regime also see David Motadel, *Islam and Nazi Germany's War* (Cambridge, MA: Harvard University Press, 2014).

[42] On the spectrum of support and opposition to the West German official tradition of coming to terms with the Nazi past, see Herf, *Divided Memory*, 267–333.

Dirks, Iring Fetscher, Dietrich Goldschmidt, Helmut Gollwitzer, Günter Grass, Heinz-Joachim Heydorn, Wolfgang Hildesheimer Walter Jens, Uwe Johnson, Rene König, Odo Marquard, Heinz Maus, Alexander Mitscherlich, Helge Pross, Martin Walser, Peter Wapnewski and Ludwig von Friedeburg.[43] They criticized what they described as an ahistorical, abstract, and doctrinaire anti-imperialism that was "an outlet for unacknowledged anti-Judaism.... Simply because the Arabs belong to the third world, they are not *eo ipso* pure angels. The Israelis are those who are endangered. The Arabs, on the other hand, are those who plan attack, expulsion and extermination." The signers dissented from the notion that advocacy of "progressive causes" should lead to "partisanship for Nasser and against Israel."[44] The signers remained embedded in the continuities and burdens of German history. For the New Left in West Germany in 1967 Marxist and Marxist-Leninist ideology transported its advocates out of the specificities – and burdens – of German history after Nazism into common cause with movements around the world. In this sense, hostility to Israel in West and East Germany offered a kind of emotional and intellectual liberation from the German past. The New Leftist view of a world torn between imperialism and anti-imperialist nationalism led to celebration of nationalism in China, Vietnam, Cuba, Egypt, Syria, Iraq, Libya, Yemen, and the PLO while finding Zionism, the movement of national liberation of the Jews, to be unacceptable.

THE WEST GERMAN JEWISH LEADERS DURING AND AFTER THE SIX-DAY WAR

The leaders of West Germany's Jewish communities were appalled at the New Left's turn against Israel. In the days preceding the Six-Day War they viewed Arab threats with great alarm and expressed their solidarity with Israel. *Der Jüdischer Pressedienst* (The Jewish Press Service) of May 1967 published a statement by Nahum Goldmann, president of the World Jewish Congress. "In this fateful hour, in which the existence of Israel is threatened, the Jewish people of the whole world stand firmly shoulder to shoulder with its brothers and sisters in Israel and offer unshakable support for the defense of Israel's freedom and independence."[45] The

[43] "Gemeinsame Erklärung von 20 Vertretern der deutschen Linken zum Nahostkonflikt," cited in Kloke, *Israel und die deutsche Linke*, 120–121.

[44] Ibid.

[45] Nahum Goldmann, "Der Frieden Jerusalems und der Welt, Appell Dr. Goldmanns an das Weltgewissen," *Jüdischer Presse Dienst,* Nr. 4, May 1967, 13. Also "Der Frieden

mood of those days is well captured in the following announcement on the front page of the *Münchener Jüdische Nachrichten* (Munich Jewish News) of a "solidarity meeting" at the main synagogue on Munich's Reichenbachstrasse organized by the "Solidarity committee of Munich's Jewish citizens." "Brothers! Sisters! Israel's Existence is in Danger! The total destruction of the state of Israel and its citizens is the declared goal of Israel's enemies. Today, hundreds of thousands of them surround our country. The extraordinary seriousness of the situation demands extraordinary efforts of every single Jew in the whole world! Our Israeli brothers and sisters sacrifice for Israel's existence!"[46] In the immediate aftermath of the war, the *Münchener Jüdische Nachrichten* declared, "Israel's great success has brought forth the enthusiasm of the free world. The Jewish people are full of pride for Israel."[47] On June 9, 1967, in the midst of the war itself, more than 1,500 people gathered for a solidarity meeting at the Main Synagogue in Munich. "In this fateful hour, the Jews of Munich have come together to publicly express our unshakable bonds with the state of Israel. Scarcely twenty years after the mass murder by the Nazi rulers, the existence of the Jewish people is once again and most seriously threatened." Munich's Jews were "decisively" on Israel's side and were "certain that all people of good will, who stand for justice and peace, will support Israel to preserve and strengthen this bastion of democracy in the Middle East." The resolution's supporters also committed themselves to financial support for Israel.[48] The contrast between the relief and elation over Israel's victory in the Jewish community and the support for the Arabs by the West German radical Left and the East German regime was stark.

In the July issue of the *Jüdischer Presse Dienst (JPD)*, the editor, Hendrik van Dam, expressed the fear and sense of vulnerability that Jews had sensed in the weeks preceding the war. The Arabs' "deadly threat" to Israel had deeply alarmed Jews all over the world, including even those

Jerusalems und der Welt: Appell Dr. Goldmanns an das Weltgewissen," *Münchener Jüdische Nachrichten* (June 2, 1967), 1.

[46] Maxmillian Hellman, Sonderkomitttee der jüdischen Bürger Münchens, "Israels Existenz ist in Gefahr," *Münchener Jüdische Nachrichten* (Munich: June 2, 1967), 1, ZA Heidelberg) Bestand B.8 Frankfurt 7, *Jüdische Nachrichten, 1960–1980*.

[47] "Israel im Kampf um seinen Bestand und seine Freiheit," *Münchener Jüdische Nachrichten* (June 9, 1967), 1, *ZA -Heidelberg*, Bestand B.8 Frankfurt 7, *Jüdische Nachrichten, 1960–1980*.

[48] "Einmütige Solidarität der jüdischen Gemeinschaft Münchens mit Israel," *Münchener Jüdische Nachrichten* (June 9, 1967), 1, ZA -Heidelberg, Bestand B.8 Frankfurt 7, *Jüdische Nachrichten, 1960–1980*.

with loose connections to "Jewish society and values." That accounted for "the passion with which Israel's cause was supported, the strength of moral solidarity and action which should have and which did come to the aid Israel in its isolated situation."[49] Yet in the midst of the outpouring of support for Israel, van Dam asked, "On whom could Israel rely when Western nations such as France agreed with the chorus of enemies in the moment when Israel needed friends?" Israel could still count on some international support, but the ranks of Israel's enemies were impressive. "At the United Nations," he wrote, "despite the exertions of Arab propaganda, criticism of Israel coming above all from the Soviet Union, concerns for West-East détente, Gaullist politics towards Russia, and Islamic sympathies," the Security Council "did not take a decision that reversed the role of aggressor and those attacked in ways that are contrary to the historical facts."[50] Yet "if Israel had been defeated and destroyed and there were no refugees because the ocean would not return them, Arab propaganda ... and those who inspire it would still insist that the Jews were the aggressor and war mongers just as those accused asserted in the concentration camp trials did when they ascribed guilt to those who had been murdered."[51] While the Communist states and the radical Left in the West depicted an Israel embedded in a powerful conspiracy with major Western powers, van Dam saw an Israel that was quite alone, even in its moment of victory.

In the same issue, van Dam examined the reporting about the Six-Day War in the neo-Nazi newspaper, the *Deutsche National-Zeitung und Soldaten-Zeitung*. It featured a photo of Israeli General Moshe Dayan alongside a likeness of Hitler and suggested their comparability, referring to "Israel's Auschwitz in the Desert," "The Mass Murder of Arabs," and "Dayan in Hitler's Tracks." Neo-Nazis, it was clear, were perpetuating the hatred of Zionism and a Jewish state that the original Nazis had voiced. Van Dam noted the similarity of this coverage to Soviet propaganda, which was also comparing Dayan with Hitler.[52] In an article in the

[49] Hendrik van Dam, "Nahost und Öffentliche Meinung," *Jüdischer Presse Dienst*, Nr. 6 (July 1967), 2, ZA -Heidelberg, Bestand B.8 Zentralrat 1, *Jüdischer Presse Dienst, 1965–1974, Sonderinformationen.*

[50] Ibid.

[51] Ibid. Van Dam inserted a cartoon from the cover of a Syrian brochure entitled "Drive them into the sea," which depicted soldiers standing on the territory of Israel with guns pointed at Jews drowning in the Mediterranean.

[52] Hendrik van Dam, "Freiheit der Gedankenlosigkeit," *Jüdischer Presse Dienst*, Nr. 6 (July 1967), 6–8, ZA -Heidelberg, Bestand B.8 Zentralrat 1, *Jüdischer Presse Dienst, 1965–1974, Sonderinformationen.*

same issue, "National Socialist Activists in Arab Service," van Dam asked why, in view of the criticism by the Soviet Union and East European states of former Nazis serving in "important positions in the Federal Republic," they were silent about former members of the Gestapo and SS officers who were then serving in Arab intelligence services or working on anti-Israeli and anti-Jewish propaganda in Cairo. He added sardonically that "the progressive countries and parties may want to address this complex."[53] Neither East Germany nor the West German radical Left did so.[54]

In December 1967, van Dam offered a sobering end-of-the-year assessment. As a result of its engagement in the war in Vietnam, the United States had responded to events in the Middle East with "considerable caution and reservation" while the Soviet Union supported the Arab states in line with "traditional Russian policy of advance" into the region. Faced with Nasser's closing of the Straits of Tiran and the withdrawal of UN troops from the Sinai, the "great powers," that is, the United States, Great Britain and France, had "taken no action" to preserve freedom of navigation. The rearming of the Arab states by "the eastern and western states" did not contribute to peace. Arab propaganda had descended into "medieval ideas" and "anti-Jewish solutions." The language of the Nazi past was evident not only in right-wing radical circles in the Federal Republic. "It was embarrassing that a terminology of the era of National Socialism was now heard from those who claimed the mantle of progressivity."[55] The convergence of old Right and New Left would remain a continuing concern and theme in the writings of the Central Council of Jews in Germany.

THE PLO CHARTER OF 1968

The Palestine Liberation Organization's Charter of July 1968 has not been one of those texts that regularly surface in historical accounts of

53 Hendrik van Dam, "NS-Aktivisten in Arabischen Diensten" *Jüdischer Presse Dienst*, Nr. 6 (July 1967), 8, ZA -Heidelberg, Bestand B.8 Zentralrat 1, *Jüdischer Presse Dienst, 1965–1974, Sonderinformationen.*

54 The issue of former officials of the Nazi regime working in the Arab governments, though neglected by the political Left in those years, has received scholarly attention in recent years. See, for example, Martin Cuppers, *Walter Rauff in deutschen Diensten: Vom Naziverbrecher zum BND-Spion* (Darmstadt: Wissenschaftliche Buchgesellschaft, 2013); Richard Breitman and Norman W. Goda, *Hitler's Shadow: Nazi War Criminals, U.S. Intelligence and the Cold War* (Washington, DC: United States National Archives, 2014); Rubin and Schwanitz, *Nazis, Islamists.*

55 Hendrik van Dam, "Ein Jahr der Härte," *Jüdischer Presse Dienst*, Nr. 11 (December 1967), 3–6, ZA -Heidelberg, Bestand B.8 Zentralrat 1, *Jüdischer Presse Dienst, 1965–1974, Sonderinformationen.*

the global radical Left in 1968. Rather, those histories focus, with good reason, on the Communists' Tet Offensive in Vietnam, the May revolt in France, large anti-war demonstrations at major campuses in the United States, street demonstrations and riots at the Democratic Party's convention in Chicago, Mexican protests during the Olympics and their violent suppression, and the Warsaw Pact invasion of Czechoslovakia in August.[56] Yet as much as any of these iconic events, the PLO's "National Charter," written in July of 1968, superbly conveyed the radicalism of the global Left in that famous year.[57] As it contained all of the PLO's core arguments about Israel, Zionism, and its strategy to destroy them both, arguments that became world famous in the subsequent decades, the text merits our attention. From 1968 to 1993 when the Oslo peace process began, and even into the decades since 1993, this famous and very public document defined the PLO's means and ends. To voice solidarity in these years with the PLO was to affirm support for its charter. Hence it is important to recall its key elements.

First, it designated a geographical area called Palestine, which included all of what was then the state of Israel, as "the homeland of the Arab Palestinian people." Its boundaries were those "it had during the British Mandate," of 1920 to 1948, and it constituted "an indivisible territorial unit." The "Palestinian people" had a "legal right" to this territory. The PLO Charter never referred to the state of Israel but rather, as in Article 4, to "the Zionist occupation." Without mentioning that it was the Arab states and the Palestinians, led by the former Nazi collaborator Haj Amin al-Husseini, who launched the war of 1948 and rejected the UN Partition Plan, Article 4 refers simply to "the dispersal of the Palestinian Arab people, through the disasters which befell them." Nondiscussion of the Arab attack on Israel in 1948 was an essential and enduring aspect of the PLO's story of Palestinian victimization at the hands of imperialism and Zionism.

Article 5 defined Palestinians as "those Arab nationals who, until 1947, normally resided in Palestine regardless of whether they were evicted from it or have stayed there." It also stipulated that a Palestinian was anyone born of a Palestinian father thereafter "whether inside Palestine or outside," thus including those born after 1948. Article 6 stated that

[56] See Carole Fink, Phillip Gassert, Detlef Junker, and Daniel S. Mattern, *1968: A World Transformed* (New York: Cambridge University Press, 1998).

[57] "The Palestinian National Charter: Resolutions of the Palestine National Council July 1–17, 1968," Yale Law School, Avalon Project, Documents in Law, History and Diplomacy, avalon.law.yale.edu/20th_century/plocov.asp.

the Jews who had resided in Palestine "until the beginning of the Zionist invasion will be considered Palestinians." The date of the beginning of that "invasion" was a source of uncertainty. If, as was often the case, the "invasion" was said to have begun in 1917 with the signing of the Balfour Declaration, then only 60,000 of the approximately 2.5 million Jews living in Israel in 1968 would be considered Palestinian. If the "invasion" was dated from 1947, then about 700,000 Jews would be so defined and could thus remain in the Palestinian state to be created. The rest would not be considered "Palestinians" in a new state and would have to leave.

Articles 8 through 10 declared an armed struggle against Israel. Article 8 asserted that the Palestinian people were now in a phase of their history of "national struggle for the liberation of Palestine," one in which those "in the national homeland or in diaspora" constituted "one national front working for the retrieval of Palestine and its liberation through armed struggle." Palestinians living in other Arab countries, or elsewhere, for example, in Western Europe, were part of this national front. Article 9 stated that "armed struggle is the only way to liberate Palestine. This is the overall strategy, not merely a tactical phase." According to Article 10, "commando action constitutes the nucleus of the Palestinian popular liberation war."

The uncompromising radicalism of the charter was also apparent in Article 21, which stated that "the Arab Palestinian people, expressing themselves by the armed Palestinian revolution, reject all solutions which are substitutes for the total liberation of Palestine and reject all proposals aiming at the liquidation of the Palestinian problem, or its internationalization." This article was a rejection of any negotiated settlement that would leave Israel intact or revive the two-state solution envisioned by the UN Partition Plan of 1947. Article 15 underscored the connection between the PLO and support from the Arab states; the latter were obligated to aid "the liberation of Palestine" with military and political support. Article 18 asserted that launching such a liberation war was not an act of aggression; rather, "the liberation of Palestine, from an international point of view, is a defensive action necessitated by the demands of self-defense." Its purpose was to "restore" the Palestinians' "legitimate rights."[58] Article 19 declared that "the partition of Palestine in 1947 and the establishment of the state of Israel are entirely illegal, regardless of the passage of time, because they were contrary to the will of the Palestinian

[58] The Palestinian National Charter, Avalon Project, avalon.law.yale.edu/20th_century/plocov.asp.

people and to their natural right in their homeland, and inconsistent with the principles embodied in the UN Charter, particularly the right to self-determination." The PLO Charter of 1968 declared United Nations Resolution 181 of November 29, 1947, which called for the establishment of two states, one for the Jews and one for the Arabs, to be invalid.[59] The PLO Charter thus denied that Israel had any political, moral, or legal legitimacy.

Articles 20, 22, and 23 contained the PLO's attack on Zionism. Article 20 denied that there was any historical connection between the Jewish people and Palestine or that there even was such a thing as the Jewish people. It read as follows:

> The Balfour Declaration, the Mandate for Palestine, and everything that has been based upon them, are deemed null and void. Claims of historical or religious ties of Jews with Palestine are incompatible with the facts of history and the true conception of what constitutes statehood. Judaism, being a religion, is not an independent nationality. Nor do Jews constitute a single nation with an identity of its own; they are citizens of the states to which they belong.[60]

This stunning denial of the elementary aspects of Jewish history and of the connection of the Jews to the land of Israel, both ancient and modern, became an enduring element of the falsehoods repeated by anti-Zionists, then and since.

Article 22 also obscured the origins of Zionism as a reaction of European Jewry to a long history of anti-Semitism and Jewish vulnerability. It was the opening salvo in a propaganda campaign that reached fruition seven years later when the United Nations General Assembly declared Zionism to be a form of racism. It read as follows:

> Zionism is a political movement organically associated with international imperialism and antagonistic to all action for liberation and to progressive movements in the world. It is racist and fanatic in its nature, aggressive, expansionist, and colonial in its aims, and fascist in its methods. Israel is the instrument of the Zionist movement, and geographical base for world imperialism placed strategically in the midst of the Arab homeland to combat the hopes of the Arab nation for liberation, unity, and progress. Israel is a constant source of threat vis-a-vis peace in the Middle East and the whole world.[61]

[59] See United Nations "Resolution 181 (II), Future Government of Palestine," of November 29, 1947, unispal.un.org/unispal.nsf/0/7F0AF2BD897689B785256C330061D253.

[60] "Article 20, Article 15, The Palestinian National Charter" Avalon Project, avalon.law.yale.edu/20th_century/plocov.asp.

[61] "Article 22, The Palestinian National Charter: Resolutions of the Palestine National Council July 1–17, 1968," Avalon Project, avalon.law.yale.edu/20th_century/plocov.asp.

Article 23 added that "the demand of security and peace, as well as the demand of right and justice, require all states to consider Zionism an illegitimate movement, to outlaw its existence, and to ban its operations, in order that friendly relations among peoples may be preserved, and the loyalty of citizens to their respective homelands safeguarded." Article 29 asserted that "the Palestinian people" would "determine their attitude toward all states and forces on the basis of the stands they adopt vis-a-vis the Palestinian revolution to fulfill the aims of the Palestinian people."[62]

As these articles made clear, the PLO Charter of 1968 was a declaration of a war whose aim was the destruction of the state of Israel by force of arms. It contained all of the key themes of anti-Zionism articulated in the propaganda of the Soviet bloc, including East Germany, and the West European and West German radical Left. It prefigured the anti-Israeli resolutions passed by the UN General Assembly in the 1970s and 1980s and, for that matter, the antagonism to Israel that persisted after the Cold War as well. When the states of the Soviet bloc and Western leftist radicals expressed "solidarity" with the PLO, when the former offered military training and weapons, and when the latter collaborated in various "actions," they were supporting a war whose aims were publicly declared in the 1968 charter. They were thus, more and less directly, also waging war against Israel.

Most famously at the United Nations in 1975, the members of the Executive Committee of the Palestine Liberation Organization were enormously successful in their efforts to gain support for the assertion that Zionism was a form of racism. Of equal but less noted importance was their success in immunizing themselves from any criticism of the racist and anti-Semitic implications of their own charter. As I have pointed out, the PLO's charter meant that victory in its war against Israel would lead to expulsion of the vast majority of Jews living in Israel in 1968, when the Jewish population of Israel was approximately 2.3 million people. Depending on how one read the PLO Charter, Jews who arrived in Palestine after either 1917 or 1947 did not qualify to be Palestinian citizens. Hence, they would have no right to remain in a state of "Palestine." It follows logically that a PLO victory would have then led to the expulsion of at least 2.3 million and at most 2.9 million of the Jews living in Israel in 1968. As Israel's population grew, so, too, would the number of those to be expelled. The number of dead and wounded in the event of

62 The Palestinian National Charter: Resolutions of the Palestine National Council July 1–17, 1968," Avalon Project, avalon.law.yale.edu/20th_century/plocov.asp.

an Israeli defeat would have been considerable. The PLO Charter, which presented itself as an attack on racism, was, in fact, a justification for a mass expulsion or what would later be called "ethnic cleansing" of the Jews from Israel. In light of the Jews' previous expulsion from the Arab states, that would have meant their expulsion from the Middle East as a whole. In that sense, the PLO Charter was an important document in the history of anti-Semitism and racism. To express solidarity with the PLO was to express agreement with these views, these policies, and their clearly foreseeable consequences. One of the PLO's greatest diplomatic successes and Israel's most serious diplomatic and political defeats lay in the fact that the racism of the PLO Charter never became a major theme of international political discussion while the alleged racism of Zionism was asserted by huge majorities at the United Nations. As previous totalitarian movements and states had, the PLO placed the language of human rights, national self-determination, peace, and justice in the service of terror. Though it indignantly rejected assertions that its attacks on Zionism and Israel were also forms of anti-Semitism, in the practice of terror aimed at the Jewish citizens of Israel such distinction became meaningless.

RADICALIZATION OF THE WEST GERMAN NEW LEFT, 1968–1969

In 1970, according to figures of the Central Council of Jews in West Germany, there were 26,799 Jews living in the Federal Republic; in 1980, the number had risen to 28,173.[63] Judging from those figures, the number of Jewish students in West German universities in the 1960s and 1970s would have been modest and probably less of a presence than the approximately 16,000 students from Arab countries, of whom 3,000 were Palestinians.[64] The shift of the New Left's sympathies from Israel to the PLO and its affiliates was in part the result of interaction with Arab, including Palestinian, students at West German universities as well

[63] "Tabelle 2: Mitgliederzahlen der jüdischen Gemeinden," in Erica Burgauer, *Zwischen Erinnerung und Verdrängung – Juden in Deutschland nach 1945* (Reinbek bei Hamburg: Rowohlt Taschenbuch, 1993), 356. The figures for the tiny and declining size of Jewish population in East Germany in 1970, 1976, 1982, and 1987 were 1078, 728, 470, and 370, respectively. See "Tabelle 7: Mitgliederstatistik der DDR-Gemeinden 1955–1990," ibid., 359.

[64] Herbert Freden, "Arabische Terroristen-Umtriebe in der Bundesrepublik," Freier Korrespondenz-Dienst, FKD, Bern (September 6, 1972), BAK B106/ 14650.

as workers from the Middle East in the West German economy.[65] By the 1960s, the combination of the very small numbers of Jewish students at West German universities and the larger number of politically active Arab and Palestinian students had an important impact on the West German Left. The well-organized and well-financed General Union of Palestinian Students, or GUPS, was the key institution for politically active Palestinian students in West Germany and other countries.[66] Insofar as it concerned the conflict in the Middle East, the "West German" Left was more accurately described as a Left composed of Arab, but also Iranian and Arab Palestinian, students and activists working together with West Germans. GUPS was an arm of Al Fatah and the Arab League with headquarters in Cairo.[67] Its purpose was to open up a political front in West Germany in the struggle against Israel. The West German front became the most important of the Arab and Palestinian fronts against Israel in Western Europe.

Jewish students in the West German universities had formed the National Association of Jewish Students in Germany (Bundesverbandes Jüdischer Studenten in Deutschland). In spring 1968, they invited Asher Ban-Natan, the Israeli ambassador to West Germany, to speak about the Middle East conflict at West German universities. That year, he spoke at nineteen campuses to large audiences, mostly without incident. At the University of Munich, however, he faced a banner that read "There will be no peace in Israel until 50 bombs explode in supermarkets."[68] On June 9, 1969, at the Johann Wolfgang Goethe University of Frankfurt-am-Main, members of SDS, together with supporters of Al Fatah in the General Union of Palestinian Students (GUPS) and the anti-Zionist Israel Revolutionary Action Committee Abroad (ISRACA), interrupted Ben Natan's lecture with interjections and chants such as "[West German Chancellor] Nazi Kiesinger and Ben Natan, a clique with [Moshe] Dayan" and "Zionists out of Palestine." The uproar led

[65] On the migration and transnational links in the 1960s Left in West Germany see Klimke, *The Other Alliance*; and Quinn Slobodian, *Foreign Front: Third World Politics in Sixties West Germany* (Durham, NC: Duke University Press, 2012).

[66] On GUPS see the memoir of its leading officer, Abdallah Frangi, *Der Gesandte: Mein Leben für Palästina: Hinter den Kulissen der Nahost-Politik* (Munich: Heyne, 2011).

[67] The annual reports of the Verfassungsschutz documented the role of foreign student political organizations in West Germany.

[68] Asher Ben-Natan, *Die Chutzpe zu Leben: Stationen meines Lebens* (Dusseldorf: Droste, 2003), 172–173, and 177; and Asher Ben-Natan and Niels Hanse, *Israel und Deutschland: Dorniger Weg zur Partnershaft: die Botschafter berichten über vier Jahrzehnte diplomatische Beziehungen (1965–2005)* (Cologne: Böhlau, 2005).

Natan to say, "It would be a historical event if it becomes impossible to hold this discussion. It was 34 years ago," that is, in 1935, when the Nuremberg race laws were passed and Jews were expelled from German universities, "that something like this happened in Germany." Natan left the session after two hours because he could not be heard over the tumult. He stated publicly that leftist anti-Zionism was "hidden anti-Semitism."[69]

The SDS-GUPS demonstration in Frankfurt/Main that day damaged the reputation of the West German Left in the eyes of the liberals as well as conservatives. The liberal *Süddeutsche Zeitung* asked whether "this Germany was going to develop a sad reputation as a swamp of bottomless irrationalism." The moderate conservative *Frankfurter Allgemeine Zeitung* referred to the "anti-Semitic New Left" and recalled the warnings of the left-liberal theorist Jürgen Habermas regarding "left-wing fascism."[70] Ten days later, Theodor Adorno, along with Max Horkheimer, the leading figure of the left-leaning Frankfurt Institute for Social Research, wrote to his old friend and fellow Frankfurt School luminary Herbert Marcuse, who at this point was teaching in the United States. Adorno was Horkheimer's co-author of the classic *Dialectic of Enlightenment* and mentor to prominent figures in the New Left. He informed Marcuse that left-wing students had interrupted his lectures twice in the summer (March to July) semester and that he had to call the police to evict students occupying the Institute for Social Research. He told Marcuse, "The danger that the students will turn toward fascism is one I take more seriously than you do. After people here in Frankfurt screamed at the Israeli Ambassador, I'm no longer convinced of the assurance that this has nothing to do with antisemitism.... You must once look into the manic, cold eyes of those who even when appealing to us [Frankfurt School theorists] turn their rage against us."[71]

In summer 1969, about fifty members of West German SDS accepted invitations from Al Fatah and the Democratic Front for the Liberation of Palestine (DFLP) to spend time during July and August at an "Al Fatah

[69] Ibid.

[70] See Kloke, *Israel und die deutsche Linke*, 127–128.

[71] Theodor Adorno, "Nr. 338 Brief an Herbert Marcuse, 19. Juni 1969," in Wolfgang Kraushaar, *Frankfurter Schule und Studentenbewegung: Von der Flaschenpost zum Molotowcocktail 1946–1995*, vol. 2, *Dokumente* (Hamburg: Rogner and Bernhard bei Zweitausendeins, 1998), 651–652. On July 11, 1969, an anti-Israeli meeting sponsored by the University of Frankfurt student government was violently attacked by pro-Zionist activists. The print media gave those events little notice, a gap that embittered the SDS activists.

Summer Camp" in Jordan.[72] Martin Kloke has written that the trip "deepened the anti-Zionist and romantic revolutionary stance of SDS." The SDS travelers now viewed Al Fatah as "the avant-garde subject of a social revolutionary transformation of the third world," the Middle Eastern analog to the Vietnamese peoples' war and a "source of hope for anti-imperialist yearnings of New Left students."[73] The West Germans, along with radical leftists from other European countries and probably from the United States as well, visited Palestinian refugee camps, received military training in the use of Kalashnikov assault weapons, attended the Fifth Congress of the General Union of Palestinian Students, and met members of the PLO. On his return to West Germany, Hans-Jürgen Krahl was asked whether the travelers had considered going to Israel in order to examine the situation there. He replied with a striking lack of interest in visiting Israel, then still governed by the Labor Party. "What should we do in Israel? We'll go there when it's become socialist."[74]

In a public letter said to be written from Amman, Jordan, on August 15, 1969, West German SDS travelers denied press reports that they had visited a military camp or received military training. The authors claimed that it was "ridiculous to talk of forming a guerrilla auxiliary, international brigade or foreign legion for Al-Fatah" because Fatah had more Arab volunteers than it needed.[75] They insisted that "the Palestinian people themselves are more than ready to fight in their national liberation struggle against Zionism and imperialism." The people they met, "whether political militants of Al-Fatah or other organizations ... are all aware of the difference between Zionists and Jews, and make it clear that their fight is against Zionism and imperialism and not against the Jews. Indeed, the point was made to us more than once that the Palestinian revolution seeks to 'liberate the Jews from Zionism.' "[76] The travelers expressed support for the "the Palestinian revolutionary struggle," which

[72] Wolfgang Kraushaar, "17.Juli.1969," *Frankfurter Schule und Studentenbewegung: Von der Flaschenpost zum Molotowcocktail, 1946–1995, Band I: Chronik* (Hamburg: Rogner and Bernhard bei Zweitausendeins, 1998), 445–447.

[73] Kloke, *Israel und die deutsche Linke*, 129.

[74] Hans-Jürgen Krahl, cited by Hans-Joachim Noack, "Ferienlager bei El Fatah – Der Sozialistische Deutsche Studentenbund auf Erkundungsfahrt bei den arabischen Guerillas," *Die Zeit* (August 15,1969), 7. Cited in Kraushaar, *Frankfurter Schule und Studentenbewegung: Band I*, 447.

[75] "Statement by participants in the Al Fatah Summer Camp, Jordan, July to August 1969," Archiv Apo FU Berlin, Leitz-Ordner R80, Internationalismus, Palästina, L Amerika, Afrika, Asien.

[76] Ibid.

was fighting against "the same enemy" as were the members of the West German SDS. "The guerrillas and other Palestinians we met insisted that their revolution was part of the world revolution against imperialism," and hence was part of the same fight that SDS was waging.[77] They also adopted the PLO's version of history. In "Palestine a whole people was thrown out of their homeland by Zionism supported by British and American imperialism." Zionism was "racialist and imperialist." Israel was "a colonial state." The Palestinians were "therefore right to fight for the creation of a democratic state in Palestine, and to pursue the method of armed struggle and peoples' war to achieve this end." The SDS travelers expressed unconditional "support" for "the Palestinian revolutionary struggle" and returned to their countries – that is, they had traveled from other countries as well – "knowing more than ever that we are fighting the same enemy."[78]

The SDS chapter from the university town of Heidelberg had particular fondness for the Popular Front for the Liberation of Palestine (PFLP) and the Democratic Popular Front for the Liberation of Palestine (DPFLP), both of which had become infamous for their terrorist attacks on civil aviation and on Jewish and Israeli institutions in Europe. In Jordan, the Heidelbergers visited a PFLP camp. In March 1969, a year and a half after SDS had adopted its anti-Israeli course, the Heidelberg chapter took other members of SDS to task for their deficient radicalism and opportunism born "out of fear to stand up against the fascist anti-Arabic witch hunt in the FRG."[79] As if to counter that claim, on February 18, 1970, SDS in Frankfurt/Main along with GUPS, ISRACA/D (Israeli Revolutionary Action Committee Abroad), Trikont,[80] and the Association of Arab, Iranians and Afghani students distributed a leaflet for a teach-in to oppose the visit of Israel's foreign minister, Abba Eban. It described him as the representative of a "racist" and "parasitical state" that fulfilled an "imperialist function in the Middle East." Support was due "only to the Palestinian people and their resistance and to anti-Zionist socialists in Israel." The Palestinian struggle was "part of a struggle of

[77] Ibid.

[78] Ibid.

[79] "Bericht des SDS Heidelberg und der FPDLP über die demokratische Volksbefreiungsfront für Palästina," in SDS-INFO, Nr. 9 (March 20, 1969), 36, cited by Kloke, *Israel und die deutsche Linke*, 126.

[80] Trikont (Tricontinenal) was an offshoot of SDS that focused on what it regarded as the exploitation of the three continents of Africa, Asia, and Latin America by the advanced capitalist economies and called for support of radical leftist movements in the third world.

all oppressed peoples of the third world against imperialism.... Down with the chauvinist and racist Israeli state!"[81] At this early point, that is, by 1970, the juxtaposition of a racist, hence evil, Israel to the virtuous "Palestinian revolution" had found a prominent place within SDS. From 1967 to 1970, the support for Israel that had been an important component of significant parts of the non-Communist Left before 1967 had drastically diminished in the radical leftist organizations that emerged in the wake of the collapse of SDS. These organizations were then able to dominate views of Israel and the Middle East in what the German historian Gerd Koenen has aptly termed "the red decade" from 1967 to 1977.[82]

In late 1969, alarmed at the emergence of leftist antagonism to Israel, the World Jewish Congress asked Dan Diner, then a 23-year-old student at the University of Frankfurt/Main, later a prominent historian of German and Jewish history, to write a "survey on Arab and pro-Arab propaganda in Germany."[83] He drew attention to the interaction of Arab and Palestinian students with the native born West German Left in and around West German universities.[84] He stressed the importance of the GUPS and its chairman at the University of Frankfurt/Main, "al-Hindi," that is, Amin al-Hindi, who later became a leading figure in the PLO's intelligence services. According to Diner, Al Fatah was focusing efforts on the West German universities. It was the GUPS in Frankfurt that had helped to organize the SDS "summer camp" trip to Jordan.[85] Arab activists in Frankfurt/Main presented "the struggle of the Arabs against Israel as a liberation struggle of the third world against imperialism and colonialism" and connected it to protest against the American war in Vietnam

81 "Teach in zum Besuch des israelischen Aussenministers Eban," Frankfurt/Main (February 18, 1970), cited by Kloke, *Israel und die deutsche Linke*, 130. What was this? A flyer?

82 Gerd Koenen, *Das Rote Jahrzehnt: Unsere kleine deutsche Kulturrevolution, 1967–1977* (Frankfurt/Main: Suhrkamp, 2002).

83 Diner became a prolific historian and essayist as well as the founding director of the Simon Dubnow Institute for Jewish History at the University of Leipzig and professor of history at the Hebrew University of Jerusalem. Among his numerous publications, see *Beyond the Conceivable: Studies on Germany, Nazism and the Holocaust* (Berkeley and Los Angeles: University of California Press, 2000).

84 Stella Bornstein, Institute of Jewish Affairs, London, to H. G. van Dam, Zentralrat der Juden in Deutschland, Dusseldorf (December 18, 1969); and Dan Diner, "Bericht über die arabische Propaganda und ihre Auswirkungen in der Bundesrepublik Deutschland," December 1969, *ZA -Heidelberg*, Bestand B.1/7 468, Nah Ost Krise, 1969–1973.

85 Dan Diner, "Bericht über die arabische Propaganda und ihre Auswirkungen in der Bundesrepublik Deutschland," December 1969, ZA -Heidelberg, Bestand B.1/7 468, Nah Ost Krise, 1969–1973, 2.

and thus as part of a "worldwide struggle against oppression."[86] One consequence of such arguments was "financial, organizational and practical support for the Arab students by the militant left of SDS" and other leftist organizations among university students. "For the revolutionaries, the geographical proximity of the conflict zone" combined with a desire at last to "move beyond theory" and to become "Arabic Viet-Cong" led to an "irrational revolutionary pathos and a dangerous heightened emotionalism."[87]

By 1969, according to Diner, Arab propaganda in the Federal Republic was focusing its attack on Zionism, which it described as "a degeneration of the peaceful and persecuted Jewish soul." It equated Zionism with the ideology of racial apartheid in South Africa and white minority rule in Rhodesia. "For months," Diner wrote, "Arabic propaganda spoke of 'National Zionism,'" thus evoking "National Socialism" and associating it with various crimes. The West German New Left had joined in the attack on what it was calling the "'Zionist' fascist State of Israel." Diner warned that these currents would become "dangerous" in West Germany. He anticipated that "verbal anti-Zionism" would be moving "toward physical action" that "would affect the majority of Jews in the diaspora whose identity is thought to be Zionist."[88] It was, he concluded, not yet clear "if a new, psychologically conditioned anti-Semitism will emerge in the New Left. There exists a danger for the Jews of the diaspora that should not be underestimated for Arabic propaganda has established itself [in West Germany]. The issue of 'the legitimation of Jews as Jews' is already up for debate. The conflict in the Middle East serves as a trigger,"[89] that is, presumably a trigger for also unleashing leftist anti-Semitism against Jews living in West Germany.

Diner's fears were realized on November 9, 1969, the thirtieth anniversary of the Nazi pogrom of November 1939. On that day, a bomb that failed to explode was found in the Jewish Community Center in Berlin.[90] Four days later, unnamed members of a radical leftist group that

[86] Ibid., 3–4.

[87] Ibid., 4. Diner noted the impact of GUPS's publication *Resistentia*, and the Democratic Popular Front for the Liberation of Palestine's *Die Front*. He noticed that the pro-Israeli view of the left-leaning *Frankfurter Rundschau* was being challenged by younger, more pro-Palestinian staff members. He attributed the Springer press support for Israel to "certain ideas about the German Volk-soul which must be regarded as suppressed wishes that are projected onto Israel," 6.

[88] Ibid., 10.

[89] Ibid., 11.

[90] Wolfgang Kraushaar, *Die Bombe im jüdischen Gemeindehaus* (Hamburg: Hamburger Edition, 2005).

called itself the "Black Rats, Tupamaros West Berlin" (Schwarze Ratten TW) accepted responsibility for placing the bomb. They did so in a statement entitled "Shalom and Napalm" published in a publication of the West Berlin leftist scene entitled *Agit 883*.[91] They supported the "armed struggle" of the Palestinians who were striking "the Zionists in their own country," that is, in Israel. At the same time they called on German "anti-imperialists" to play an active role in the battle against supporters of Israel in West Germany.[92] In other words, "Shalom and Napalm" supported attacks on Jews in West Germany, especially those who publicly supported Israel. At the time, *Agit 883* had a circulation of about 20,000 readers, primarily in West Berlin.[93]

"Shalom and Napalm" echoed arguments Walter Ulbricht offered in the Leipzig speech of June 1967. European and American capitalism supported "the Zionists in their aggressive military operations" in the Arab world. West German restitution payments (Wiedergutmachung) and development aid contributed to the Zionist defense budget. "Under the guilt-laden pretext of coming to terms with the fascist atrocities against the Jews, they [West German government and industry] make a decisive contribution to Israel's fascist atrocities against Palestinian Arabs."[94] In the following sentences, the leaflet's authors both coyly accepted responsibility for placing a bomb in the Jewish Community Center and declared war on the government of West Germany.

[91] The noun "Tupamaros" was adopted from the name of a terrorist group in Uruguay composed of students inspired by the Brazilian legislator and Communist Carlos Marighella. See Marighella, *Urban Guerilla Minimanual* (Vancouver, CA: Pulp Press, 1974); and on the Web at www.marxists.org/archive/marighella-carlos/1969/06/minimanual-urban-guerrilla/index.htm. In 1971, the German publisher Rowohlt published *Handbuch der Stadtguerillo*. In 110 pages Marighella made the case for a shift from Che Guevara's adventures in the countryside to formation of small groups of cells of four to five persons within cities who would engage in political murders, kidnappings, robbery, and attacks on political institutions with the intent of shattering the ability of the ruling powers to maintain law and order. These actions would, he predicted, spark a mass revolt. Marighella was shot by Brazilian police in São Paolo in November 1969, five months after he published the original edition of the *Minimanual*. The first sentence captured its key message: "The urban guerrilla's reason for existence, the basic condition in which he acts and survives, is to shoot."

[92] "Schalom + Napalm," *Agit 883*, November 13, 1969, 1. Jg., Nr. 40, 9, cited in Kraushaar, *Die Bombe im jüdischen Gemeindehaus*, 46–49; Kloke, *Israel und die deutsche Linke*, 163–164. The original is available at www.agit883.infopartisan.net/. Translated and reprinted in Bommi Baumann, *Wie Alles Anfing, How it all Began: The Personal Account of a West German Urban Guerrilla*, trans. Helene Ellenbogen and Wayne Parker (Vancouver, CA: Pulp Press, 1977), 57–58.

[93] Kloke, *Israel und die deutsche Linke*, 163.

[94] "Schalom + Napalm," in Kraushaar, *Die Bombe im jüdischen Gemeindehaus*, 46–48.

In West Berlin, on the 31st anniversary of the fascist Kristallnacht "Shalom and napalm" and "Al-Fatah" were painted on several Jewish memorials. A bomb was placed in the Jewish Community Center. No longer are both actions to be defamed as an outgrowth of right-wing radicals. Rather, these actions are a decisive link of international socialist solidarity. The previous silence and theoretical paralysis of the left regarding the conflict in the Middle East is a result of the German guilty conscience *(Schuldbewußtsein)*. "We gassed the Jews and must protect the Jews from a new genocide." The neurotic-historicist examination of the historical lack of legitimacy of an Israeli state does not overcome this helpless anti-fascism. True anti-fascism is the clear and simple expression of solidarity with the fighting fedayeen. No longer will our solidarity remain only with verbal-abstract methods of enlightenment as [with opposition to the American war] in Vietnam. Rather, in concrete actions, we will mercilessly fight [*schonungslos bekämpfen*] against the close intertwining of Zionist Israel with the fascist Federal Republic of Germany. Every hour of memory in West Berlin and in the FRG suppresses the fact that Kristallnacht of 1938 is today repeated every day by the Zionists in the occupied territories, in the refugee camps and in Israeli prisons. The Jews who were expelled by fascism have themselves become fascists who, in collaboration with American capital, want to eradicate the Palestinian people. By striking the direct support for Israel by German industry and the government of the Federal Republic, we are aiding the victory of the Palestinian revolution and serve to bring about the renewed defeat of world imperialism. At the same time, we expand our battle against the fascists in democratic clothes and begin to build a revolutionary liberation front in the metropole. BRING THE BATTLE FROM THE VILLAGES INTO THE CITIES! ALL POLITICAL POWER COMES FROM THE BARREL OF A GUN. Black Rats, TW Schwarze Ratten, TW [Tupamoros West Berlin][95]

In contrast to their "guilt-ridden" contemporaries, whose political judgment was supposedly clouded by emotion and sentimentality, the West Berlin Tupamaros, as had the leaders of SDS in 1967, presented themselves as the voice of reason and political clarity. Having overcome unjustified guilt complexes, these West German radical leftists could attack the "fascist" Israelis with a clear conscience. The Zionists, along with a tradition of West German memory of the Holocaust that they declared to be a form of neurosis, had victimized the West Germans with accusations and bad memories. With "Shalom and Napalm" the moment of liberation from those burdens had arrived. The Federal Republic, far from responding to the demands of morality, was complicit in supporting an evil state, Israel. Thus it was time to aim guns at "the fascists in democratic clothes" in the Federal Republic.

[95] Ibid., 48.

Several days later, the West Berlin Tupamaros sent a taped confession and justification for the attempted bombing of the Jewish Community Center. A woman's voice declared that

> [Axel] Springer, the West Berlin Senate and [Heinz] Galinski [the leader of the organized West Berlin Jewish Community and chairman of the Central Council of Jews in Germany] want to sell us their *Judenknacks* [Jewish complex]. We won't join that business.... [West German restitution payments to Israel] finance a new fascist genocide.... Learn from the one who placed the bomb in the Jewish Community Center, learn from the Tupamaros, Che lives! Vietnam is not here. Vietnam is in America. But listen: Palestine is here, we are fedayeen. This afternoon we fight for the revolutionary Palestinian liberation front, Al-Fatah. Strike now.[96]

On November 27, 1969, Dieter Kunzelmann, the leader of the West Berlin Tupamaros and a key figure in the West German Left's turn to support for Palestinian guerrilla organizations, published a "Letter from Amman" in *Agit 883*. Actually, at the time, he was avoiding arrest in West Berlin.[97] He wrote that for the West German Left

> Palestine is what Vietnam is for the Amis [slang for Americans]. The left has not yet understood that. Why? [Because of] the Jewish complex (*Judenknax*). "We gassed 6 million Jews. The Jews today are called Israelis. Whoever fights fascism is for Israel." It's as simple as that but that's all wrong. When we finally learn to understand the fascist ideology of Zionism, we will no longer hesitate to replace our simple philo-semitism with an unambiguous and clear solidarity with AL FATAH. In the Middle East, it has taken up the battle against the Third Reich. What is the meaning of solidarity? It means taking up our battle.[98]

Kunzelmann regretted that a local Palestine committee had failed to "use the opportunity of the bomb [placed at the Jewish Community Center] to start a campaign." The reluctance of his fellow West German leftist radicals to engage in similar terrorist attacks against Jews in West Germany indicated that they had "only theoretical relationship to political work and that the Jewish complex continues to dominate all questions and discussions."[99] In the fall of 1969, Dieter Kunzelmann and the West Berlin

96 "Kopie des fingierten Schreibens bei den Akten zum Prozess gegen Dieter Kunzelmann," cited in Kraushaar, *Die Bombe im jüdischen Gemeindehaus*, 62–64.

97 See Reimann, "Letters from Amman. For a summary of Kunzelmann's political activities see "Dieter Kunzelmann," in Wolfgang Kraushaar, *München 1970: Über die antisemitischen Wurzeln des deutschen Terrorismus* (Hamburg: Rowohlt, 2013), 785–786. Also see Aribert Reimann, *Dieter Kunzelmann – Avantgarde, Protest und Radikalismus nach 1945* (Göttingen: Vandenhoeck and Ruprecht, 2009).

98 Dieter Kunzelmann, "Brief aus Amman (I), *Agit 883*, Nr. 42 (November 27, 1969), 5; cited in Kloke, *Israel und die Deutsche Linke*, 166.

99 Ibid.

FIGURE 3.1. Heinz Galinski, in 1973, Galinski raised alarms about the opening of the PLO office in East Berlin.
Source: Ullstein bild/ Granger, NYC-All rights reserved.

Tupamaros redefined the meaning of leftist anti-fascism to mean support for terrorist attacks against Israelis as well as against their Jewish and non-Jewish supporters in West Germany (Figure 3.1).

In September 1969, the Central Council of Jews in Germany responded to reports of the SDS members' trip to Jordan and to the spread of leftist anti-Israeli political activity in the universities. It criticized "a one-sided extremism that, under the pretext of anti-Zionism or criticism of Israel, has a coarse anti-Semitic impact that affects the Jewish community as a whole. Here different extremisms meet in a highly destructive manner. Instincts are aroused which National Socialism used for its own ends. Les extremes se touchent." The anti-Semitism of the radical Right was finding a common vocabulary with that of the radical Left.[100] The attempted bombing of the Jewish Community Center in West Berlin should not be

[100] "Zentralrat warnt vor Extremismus," *Jüdischer Presse Dienst: Informationen des Zentralrats der Juden in Deutschland*, Nr. 8, September 1969, 3, *ZA -Heidelberg* Heidelberg, B.8. Zentral 1.

dismissed as the work of a lone madman. Rather it was the action of certain fanatical groups. It was "the most serious attack on the Jews in Germany after 1945."[101]

In February 1970, Palestinian terrorists carried out a wave of terrorist attacks against civil aviation to and from Israel and on Jews in West Germany. On February 10, the Action Organization for the Liberation of Palestine (AOLP) used hand grenades and automatic weapons to attack passengers waiting for an El Al flight in Munich's Reim airport. Facing unexpected resistance from several passengers, the terrorists failed to hijack the plane but killed one passenger and wounded twelve. On February 13, 1970, the most deadly attack on Jews in Germany since the Holocaust took place. An arsonist set fire to a home for the aged located in a Jewish community center in Munich. Seven residents died, six in the flames and smoke and one from injuries suffered after jumping from an upper-story window. Six more suffered serious injuries. Damage to the building was estimated at 730,000 deutschmarks. No one claimed responsibility and the case remains unsolved, though circumstantial evidence pointed to involvement of West German leftist and/or Palestinian terrorists. On February 21, a bomb on an Austrian Airlines flight departing from Frankfurt/Main exploded in mid-air, but the damaged plane was able to return safely to the airport shortly after take-off. Later that day, another bomb was placed on Swiss Air Flight 330, departing from Zurich for Tel Aviv. It also exploded in mid-air, causing the plane to crash. All 38 passengers and nine crew members were killed.[102] A representative of the Popular Front for the Liberation of Palestine-General Command (PFLP-GC) led by Ahmed Jibril claimed responsibility. George Habash, leader of the PFLP, announced his support for such actions while Yasser Arafat denounced them. At that time, Arafat was the head of the PLO's "Unified Command" of its Executive Committee, one that included many Palestinian guerrilla organizations such as the PFLP and PFLP-GC. The proliferation of such groups conveyed the impression that they acted

[101] Heinz Galinski, cited in "Bestürzung und Empörung: Stimmen zum Bombenanschlag auf das Jüdische Gemeindehaus in Berlin," *Jüdischer Presse Dienst*, Nr. 10 (November/December, 1969), 3, *ZA -Heidelberg*, Bestand B.8 Zentralrat 1, *Jüdischer Presse Dienst, 1965–1974, Sonderinformationen.*

[102] For a detailed account of the attacks on the planes and the investigations into them, see the important work by Wolfgang Kraushaar, *"Wann endlich beginnt bei Euch der Kampf gegen die Heilige Kuh Israel?" München 1970: Über die antisemitischen Würzeln des deutschen Terrorismus* (Hamburg: Rowohlt Verlag, 2012), 37–81 and 169–250. On the attack on the Jewish home for the aged in Munich, see 86–162.

independently of Arafat, thus giving the most public face of the PLO a frequently used fig leaf of plausible deniability.[103]

On April 3, 1970, Kunzelmann sent another statement "from Amman" that implicitly addressed the attacks on El Al and other airlines flying to Israel as well as on the Jewish home for the aged in Munich. In it he expressed impatience with his leftist "comrades on the home front."

> When are you finally going to begin the battle against the holy cow, Israel? When will we relieve the fighting Palestinian people with practical internationalism? The grenades at the [Munich, JH] Riem airport permit only this criticism: to replace the desperate death commandos with better organized, more clearly focused commandos that we, ourselves will carry out and therefore can be better organized and arranged. Liberation of the imprisoned Palestinians, agitation among German Jews, struggle against the emigration to Israel, prevention of any support [for Israel] (weapons, goods, capital). We have never had such an opportunity to advance the revolution in our own country by direct support of a peoples' liberation war [in Palestine.][104]

His statement clearly implied that it was indeed Palestinians, the "desperate death commandos," who were the perpetrators of the February terrorist attacks. He was urging his fellow West German leftists to engage in similar attacks in West Germany, which could be "better organized and arranged." Though Kunzelmann welcomed a Communist victory in Vietnam, such a victory did not have the same connection to German history and to overcoming "the Jewish complex" as did the Palestinian's "people's war" against Israel.

HEINZ GALINSKI AND THE CENTRAL COUNCIL OF JEWS IN GERMANY RESPOND

Among the leaders of the organized Jewish community in West Germany and West Berlin in the postwar decades, Heinz Galinski (1912–1992) assumed a prominent role as a critic of leftist antagonism to Israel. He did so in editorials in the *Jüdische Allgemeine* and in public statements, and in communications with political figures in West Berlin and West Germany. He was twice elected chair of the Central Council of Jews in Germany, first from 1954 to 1963 and again from 1988 to 1992. He was also the leader of the Jewish community in West Berlin from 1949 to 1992. Galinski's biography illustrates the importance of the Holocaust

103 See Wolfgang Kraushaar, *München 1970*, 184–185.

104 Dieter Kunzelmann, "Brief aus Amman (II) Das palästinensische Volk wird in seinem bewaffneten Kampf siegen," *Agit 883*, Nr. 55 (April 3, 1970), 11.

for his political activity in the Federal Republic.[105] Born in 1912 in West Prussia, he worked in the textile business until the Nazis subjected him, his wife, and his mother to forced labor in 1940. In 1943 his entire family was arrested. His father died in police custody, and he and his wife and mother were deported to Auschwitz-Birkenau, where his wife and mother were murdered and he worked as a forced laborer in the IG Farben plant in the Auschwitz complex. Galinski survived Auschwitz as well as Buchenwald and Bergen-Belsen concentration camps and decided to participate in rebuilding the Jewish community in postwar West Germany. He participated in early efforts to gain restitution for Jewish survivors and members of the anti-Nazi resistance. The primary focus of his activities lay in his work as chairman of the Jewish community in West Berlin. There he concentrated on rebuilding Jewish life, keeping the memory of the Holocaust alive, and fighting anti-Semitism. The construction of the Jewish Community Center in West Berlin played an important role in these efforts, as did his work as co-editor of the *Jüdische Allgemeine*.

Galinski, Alexander Ginsberg, Hendrik van Dam, and the Central Council of Jews in Germany viewed the Federal Republic as a liberal democracy very worth defending, and they were passionate supporters of Israel. Before the late 1960s, they focused on dangers from right-wing extremists.[106] The pages of their local and national publications focused on the dangers of neo-Nazism, the need to bring ex-Nazis to trial, support for restitution to survivors and for Israel.[107] In the aftermath of the Six-Day War their positive view of West German democracy and support for Israel put them at odds with the anti-Israeli Left. By 1969, the gap between the Jewish leadership in West Germany and the West German New Left and its successors had become an unbridgeable abyss. While the Jewish leaders were aware of the shortcomings of judicial reckoning in West Germany, they did not share the New Left's denunciation of the Federal Republic as an authoritarian or "fascist" state. On the contrary, they saw the West German national, regional, and local judicial

105 On Galinski's life and work, see Juliane Berndt, *"Ich weiß, ich bin kein Bequeme..."*: *Heinz Galinski – Mahner, Streiter, Stimme der Überlebenden* ["I know I am not an easy man": Heinz Galinski – A man who warns, debates and is a voice of the survivors] (Berlin: Springer Verlag, 2012). Also see the summary of key events in his life at the Website of the *Stiftung Haus der Geschichte der Bundesrepublik Deutschland*, /hdg.de/lemo/html/biografien/GalinskiHeinz/index.html.

106 See, for example, "Das Vordringen des Rechtsrakalismus," *Jüdischer Presse Dienst*, Nr. 13, Dezember 1966, 5, *ZA -Heidelberg*, Heidelberg, B.8. Zentral 1.

107 On the origins of that tradition in the views of the founding generation of political leaders in West Germany, see Herf, *Divided Memory*, 201–333.

and police authorities and the stability of the country's liberal democratic institutions as indispensable sources of support for and protection of the small Jewish community and its synagogues, schools, and community institutions.

For the radical Left, Adenauer and his successors were enemies, the architect of the alliance with American imperialism, of capitalist restoration at home, premature amnesty for Nazi crimes, and an anti-Communism that it found abhorrent. For these leaders of the organized Jewish community, on the other hand, Adenauer and his successors were the architects of the restitution agreements for Jewish survivors, friends to the state of Israel, and protectors against anti-Semitic violence from neo-Nazis. When Adenauer died in 1967, Ginsburg, the coeditor of the *Jüdische Allgemeine,* wrote that good relations with the Jewish community and with Israel had been "essential" for him. "His death has caused consternation and grief amongst us," that is, among Jews in West Germany.[108] When the radical Left in the 1960s attacked the Federal Republic as an authoritarian state or denounced mainstream Social Democrats for insufficient revolutionary zeal, the Jewish leaders feared yet another attack on the still-young democracy in West Germany. When the New Left turned against Israel, the Jewish leaders dismissed efforts to distinguish between anti-Zionism and anti-Semitism. In post-Nazi Germany, they believed that antagonism to Israel invariably aroused old anti-Jewish sentiments.

After the attack on the El Al passengers at the Munich airport in February 1970, the Central Council stated that "the propaganda wave of unlimited hatred taking place in the Federal Republic has now turned into a violent crime." It was not enough to condemn such actions or place Jewish institutions under police protection. "In addition, finally, there must be consequences taken against the organizers and the organizations that sponsor these kinds of crimes and, as in the case of the attack at the Munich-Riem airport, glorify this assassination."[109] In a Rosh Hashonah message sent to members of the Jewish community in West Berlin in September 1970, Galinski repeated his concern about the anti-Zionism that issued "from circles that regard themselves as progressive," that is,

[108] Alexander Ginsburg, "Zum Tode von Konrad Adenauer," *Jüdischer Presse Dienst*, Nr. 3/67, 5, *ZA -Heidelberg*, Heidelberg, B.8. Zentral 1. Alexander Ginsburg, "Zentralrat gegen Antizionismus, Antisemtismus und Extremismus," *Allgemeine jüdische Wochenzeitung*, Dusseldorf (November 30, 1975), 1.

[109] "Erklärung des Zentralrats" *Jüdischer Presse Dienst,* Nr. 2–3 (February/March, 1970), 2, ZA -Heidelberg, Bestand B.8 Zentralrat 1, *Jüdischer Presse Dienst, 1965–1974, Sonderinformationen.*

from the student Left. He was neither convinced nor reassured by those who made distinctions between anti-Semitism and anti-Zionism.

Whether or not those who spread and advocate this anti-Zionism understand it or intend to do so, it has the function of awakening anti-Semitic prejudices. Anti-Zionism shares with anti-Semitism that we know from earlier times the discrimination against Jews in contrast to all other people because it denies to the Jewish state – and only the Jewish state – the right to exist. Anti-Zionism and anti-Semitism are distinguished from one another only in that one attacks the individual by attacking the Jews as a whole while the other attacks the Jews as a whole in order to attack the individual. We view such differences as completely unimportant.[110]

Galinski's concerns extended beyond the radical Left and arguments about whether anti-Zionism was a form of anti-Semitism. He was just as worried about a policy of neutrality toward the Middle East conflict that he saw emerging in the government of Willy Brandt. Without mentioning the chancellor by name, he called on the Federal Republic "to be conscious of the limits of its policy of neutrality toward the Middle East conflict." Those limits were reached when the Arab states publicly declared that their aim was to "destroy" a member state of the United Nations, that is, Israel. Further, West Germany had "definite obligations" in light of Germany's past regarding the Middle East, obligations that were all the more pressing in light of the recent airplane hijackings in West Germany that had led to deaths and injuries.[111]

In January 1970, the radio and television commentator Matthias Walden (1927–1984) addressed the issue of those obligations in the essay "Antisemitism and Anti-Zionism" in the pages of *Die Welt*. Van Dam reprinted it the *Jüdischer Presse Dienst*.[112] Walden noted that Israeli Ambassador Asher Ben-Natan saw "hatred" in some of the faces of students at the University of Munich who prevented him from completing his lecture. "Haven't the sons learned from the guilt of the fathers? Have the fathers failed to educate their sons differently as they were raised?" In less than a generation has the

110 Heinz Galinski, "Zu Rosch Haschanah 5731," *Für unsere Mitglieder, Vorstand der Jüdischen Gemeinde zu Berlin* West Berlin (September 1970), *ZA -Heidelberg*, German: "Antizionismus und Antisemitismus unsterschieden sich allein dadurch voneinander, daß der eine über die jüdische Gesamtheit den enzelnen und der andere über den einzelnen die jüdische Gesamtheit treffen will."

111 Ibid.

112 "Antisemitismus und Antizionismus," Matthias Wald, *Die Welt*, reprinted in *Jüdischer Presse Dienst*, Nr. 1 (January 1970), 11–12. *ZA -Heidelberg*, Bestand B.8 Zentralrat 1, *Jüdischer Presse Dienst, 1965–1974, Sonderinformationen.*

> cut-off stump of anti-Semitism found new, wild impulses in our fatherland? That appears to be the case. This is too serious to leave things at the level of appearances. We need to know as precisely as possible what is going on and who is advocating such ideas. For the quality of Germany after the war [World War II] is judged by many things but first and last by its relationship to the state of the Jews. The crudest form of betrayal to the fate of the Jews that exists in today's Germany comes from the SED State [East Germany]. It was its hostility to Israel that purchased its international recognition from Israel's enemies, the "progressive" Arab states. It is cynical to deny that this was the price of [East German] friendship that opened the door in Damascus, Baghdad, Khartoum and Cairo, an opening that East Berlin confuses with prestige. The SED regime, whose favor Bonn seeks, rebuffs it and gains fame with the friendship of these states which have sworn to destroy Israel. It cannot be determined how much this comes from ideological antisemitism of a Bolshevik sort or from unprincipled opportunism. The proportion of these motivations is not the decisive issue. The effect [of the policy] is anti-Jewish in its ultimate consequence.[113]

Walden continued that in the Federal Republic until the late 1960s, anti-Semitism had been limited to right-wing radicals. Since the Six-Day War, however, they

> have received company from the extremist left. The etiquette of their denunciation is called "anti-Zionism." It is old and has brown spots. "Anti-Zionism" was always the chalk that the wolf ate to deceive naïve political lambs. He who stands against Israel today must know that he threatens the land of the Jews, their only homeland, with an exodus. It would simply be of academic interest, whether it was anti-semitism or anti-Zionism that led to extermination if Israel were annihilated. Moreover, the extreme left plays games when it falsely describes Zionism as an imperialist movement, something it never was and is not today. Zionism is the opposite of imperialism: it is the effort to create a homeland for the Jews. Whoever wants to take it away from them is both anti-Zionist and anti-Semitic.
>
> There is no area in which the extremes of the right and left meet so closely as on their shared hatred of hostility to Israel. Whoever the perpetrator was who placed a bomb in the Jewish Community Center in Berlin, the act was celebrated in leaflets using the jargon of the radical left. An unfortunately typical example for this jargon was present in a leaflet distributed in the University of Kiel: "Strike the Zionists dead, make the Middle East red!"[114]

Although, he continued, there was not a "broad stream of new anti-Semitism" in West Germany, it was also not the case that "the Federal Republic was firmly on Israel's side in ways that the guilt of the past and justice in the present demands." Walden found echoes in the mainstream of the views that Kunzelmann expressed. "Critical stands

[113] Ibid.
[114] Ibid.

towards Israeli policy in the occupied territories could be evidence of the beginning of a German feeling that the burden of the past is itself in the past (*Unbefangenheit*). In many circles, things have gone so far that whoever does not point the finger at Israel is said to be caught up in the burdens of the past."[115] Walden regretted that West German Chancellor Willy Brandt did not include "a word of encouragement to Israel" in his annual government statement to the parliament. The absence was part of a "rapprochement with the Arab states" associated with a UN resolution that called for Israel to leave the occupied territories. "It would have done the Federal Republic honor" if Brandt had "publicly stated that Israel would be lost if it gave up these territories in exchange for an Arab guarantee of its existence." Distancing oneself from Israel at this moment also failed to oppose "a wind that blows from Moscow."[116] The Communists and the Western Left spoke of Israel's powerful friends and alliances. Walden saw matters quite differently. "Today, Israel ... stands almost all alone. The Federal Republic of Germany has declared itself to be neutral [in the Middle East conflict]. Insofar as this concerns military aspects, there may be grounds for that stance. But in his departing lecture Asher Ben-Natan asked if there can be a neutrality of the heart. Up to this point, his question remains unanswered."[117] The Communist states and the Western Left depicted a powerful Israel linked to a still more powerful conspiracy of imperialist powers. Walden, Galinski, and van Dam, on the other hand, saw Israel very much on its own. In their attacks on "philo-semitism," Kunzelmann and the radical Left attacked a straw man because, as Walden argued, West German foreign policy was less and less guided by supposed burdens of excessive guilt.

THE ORTHODOX AND UNORTHODOX RADICAL LEFT IN WEST GERMANY IN 1972

The annual report for 1972 of the Office for the Protection of the Constitution (Verfassungsschutz), published in September 1973, documented a remarkable persistence and even growth of the radical Left in West Germany following the dissolution of SDS in 1970.[118] It counted 365 left-wing radical organizations with 103,100 members, an increase from

[115] Ibid.

[116] Ibid.

[117] Wald, "Antisemitismus und Antizionismus."

[118] *Verfassungsschutz '72; 17 Öffentlichkeitsarbeit des Bundesministeriums* (Bonn: Der Bundesminister des Innern, September 1973).

88,550 in 1971. Though the New Left received a great deal of publicity, its 7,000 people belonging to organizations described as New Leftist were only 14 percent of this total. According to the Verfassungsschutz report, 88,500 or 86 percent, were members of "orthodox-communist and pro-communist" organizations and 8,300 were in Maoist organizations. From 1970 to 1972, the number of left-wing radical periodicals in West Germany increased from 421 in 1970 to 1183 in 1972. In 1972, 910 of them were "orthodox-communist and pro-communist" publications with a weekly distribution of 333,000 copies. Another 273 had a "New Left" orientation with a weekly circulation of 150,000 copies.[119] Also by 1972, leftist student groups had won 67.5 percent of the positions in the student governments (ASTA) at 34 universities and technical universities, positions that provided access to funds and resources to stress political issues, including but not limited to the Middle East conflict.[120]

In the wake of the dissolution of SDS, the East German–oriented, orthodox Marxist-Leninist Deutsche Kommunistische Partei (DKP), with 36,000 members in 1972, was the single largest of the organizations of the radical Left.[121] The persistence and in many cases the re-emergence of Marxist-Leninist orthodoxy in so-called K-Gruppen, that is, Communist groups, was one of the most striking features of West German leftist fringe politics after the 1960s. The Verfassungsschutz report of 1972 mentioned fourteen organizations with significant membership numbers and another thirty that were local versions of the national organizations. In addition to the DKP, the larger groups included the 12,000 members of the German Socialist Worker Youths (Sozialistische Deutsche Arbeiterjugend, SDAJ) and the 11,000 members of the Union of Those Persecuted by the Nazi Regime – Organization of Anti-Fascists Vereinigung der Verfolgten des Naziregimes – Bund der Antifaschisten (VVN). This network of organizations, along with their many local versions, mobilized activists, who wrote and distributed leaflets and brochures and attended demonstrations and rallies.[122] Some of the Marxist-Leninist Communist groups

[119] Ibid., 54–55.

[120] Ibid., 56–57.

[121] Ibid., 83.

[122] *Verfassungsschutzbericht* '72, 83–93. Others included: *Marxistischer Studenbund Spartakus (MSB)* 2,000; *SHB Sozialdemokratischer Hochschulbund* 3,000; *Deutsche Friedens-Union (DFU)*, 400, *Kommunistische Partei Deutschland (KPD)*, 300; *Kommunistische Partei Deutschland/Marxist-Leninist (KPD/ML)*, 600; *Kommunistische Gruppe (Neues Rotes Forum (KG/NRF) Mannheim-Heidelberg* 500.

rejected terrorism as a tactic; most repeated the ideological assault on Zionism and Israel.[123]

ARAB TERRORIST ATTACKS, 1968–1972

The attack on the Israeli athletes at the Munich Olympics in 1972 captured world attention (see Table 3.1, pp. 116–18). In January 1973, the Jewish Press Service published the following list of acts of Arab terrorism aimed at Israelis in Israel as well as at Jewish institutions in Europe, most of which took place in the four years *before* that event. The attacks received extensive coverage in the West German and world media, especially after the formation and actions of West German terrorist organizations such as the Red Army Faction in 1970.

As we will see in the coming chapters, these attacks meant that in addition to adopting a position regarding the conflict in the Middle East, both the East German government and West German leftist radicals had to adopt a position regarding the use of terrorism against the citizens of Israel and against Jewish and Israeli related targets in Europe. We turn now to the emergence of a formal alliance of East Germany, the Arab states, and the PLO.

[123] Several examples of the 30 local organizations are die Proletarische Linke (PL) in Berlin; die Roten Zellen Kiel (ML); die Kommunistische Hochschulgruppe (KHG) Göttingen; die Kommunistische Initiative (KI) in Cologne; die Kommunistischen Gruppen (KG) Frankfurt/Offenbach; die Arbeiter-Basis-Gruppen (ABG) in Munich; ibid., 93–94. A study in 1990 found that between 1970 and 1975, there were more than 60 organizations in West Germany with the word *Kommunist* in the title. See Jürgen Schröder, *Ideologischer Kampf vs. Regionale Hegemonie: Ein Beitrag zur Untersuchung der "K-Gruppen"* (Berlin: Berliner Arbeitshefte und Berichte zur Sozialwissenschaftlichen Forschung, Nr. 40, 1990), Institut für Sozialforschung, Hamburg.

TABLE 3.1. *Jewish Press Service, Dusseldorf, "Documentation of Arab Terrorist Attacks, 1968–1972"*

July 23, 1968	El-Al flight from Rome to Lod forced to land in Algiers
December 26, 1968	Attack on El-Al flight at Athens airport. An Israeli passenger killed and stewardess wounded.
February 18, 1969	Attack on El-Al plane at Zurich airport; member of the crew killed and a passenger wounded.
May 22, 1969	Attempt to murder David Ben-Gurion thwarted.
August 17, 1969	Arson in London's Marks and Spencer.
August 18, 1969	Sabotage against a Jewish school in Tehran.
August 29, 1969	TWA flight from Los Angeles to Lod forced to land in Damascus. Seven Israeli passengers imprisoned "for a long time."
September 8, 1969	Bomb attacks on Israeli Embassy in Bonn and the Hague and El Al office in Brussels. Hand grenades thrown at Israeli Embassy in Bonn.
November 27, 1969	Bombing of El Al office in Athens. Greek child killed and two civilians wounded.
December 12, 1969	Bomb in El Al office in Berlin found.
December 21, 1969	Attempt to hijack TWA plane in Athens thwarted.
February 10, 1970	Attack at Munich-Riem airport on El Al passengers with hand grenades and other explosives. One dead, twelve wounded.
February 21, 1970	Forty-seven passengers and crew (Israelis, Germans, Swiss) killed by midair explosion on Swissair flight soon after take-off from Zurich airport. Popular Front for the Liberation of Palestine took responsibility.
February 21, 1970	Explosion in Air Austria flight shortly after take-off from Frankfurt. Plane returned safely.
February 22, 1970	Lufthansa jumbo jet forced to land in Aden.
April 25, 1970	Explosion in El Al office in Istanbul.
May 4, 1970	Wife of Israeli diplomat in Israeli Embassy in Paraguay (Asuncion) shot and wounded. Popular Front for the Liberation of Palestine claimed responsibility.
June 9, 1970	Explosion in El-Al office in Tehran.
September 6, 1970	Popular Front for Liberation of Palestine hijacked three planes of Pan Am, TWA, and BOAC with 400 passengers. The Pan-Am flight lands in Cairo and is blown up after passengers are taken off. Two other planes land in Jordan and are also blown up.
September 6, 1970	Effort to hijack El-Al flight from Amsterdam to New York thwarted.

TABLE 3.1 (*continued*)

September 9, 1970	BOAC flight form Bahrain to London forced to land in Zerqa.
October 6, 1970	Two packages with explosives mailed to the Israeli Embassy in London and to the El-AL office found in the London BOAC office.
April 19, 1971	Five terrorists (French husband and wife, two sisters from Morocco, and a French tourist) arrested on arrival in Israel.
September 5, 1971	Two terrorist attacks on El-Al flights from New York to Israel thwarted. Explosives given to women from Netherlands and Peru by two Arabs.
November 28, 1971	Jordan's minister president is shot and killed by members of Black September in Cairo.
December 15, 1971	Attack on Jordanian ambassador in London.
February 6, 1972	Black September sets oil tanks in Netherlands on fire.
February 6, 1972	Black September murdered five Jordanians in West Germany due to their contact with Israel.
February 8, 1972	Engine factory in Hamburg destroyed.
February 22, 1972	Members of "Organisation of Victims of Zionist Conquest of Palestine" hijacked Lufthansa flight from India to Beirut. Hijackers received $5 million cash and released plane and passengers.
February 22, 1972	Black September claimed responsibility for damaging oil pipeline near Hamburg.
May 8, 1972	Sabena Airlines flight from Brussel-Vienna to Tel Aviv seized by terrorists and landed in Lod airport in Tel Aviv. In course of freeing passengers by Israeli forces, one passenger killed and five wounded. Two terrorists killed and two arrested.
May 30, 1972	Three Japanese terrorists who arrived with Air France flight at Lod airport in Tel Avivtook machine guns and hand grenades from their luggage and murdered 24 and wounded 80 in a massacre in airport luggage area.
August 5, 1972	Members of Black September set fire to oil tanks in Trieste.
August 16, 1972	Explosion in luggage compartment of Boeing 707 of El Al flight from Rome to Tel Aviv. Explosives hidden in a record player given to two English women by Arab terrorists.
September 5, 1972	Members of Black September seized Israeli wrestling team at Munich Olympics. Two athletes killed. Nine Israeli wrestlers seized as hostages. In effort to free the hostages, all nine killed. One German policeman also killed. Five Arab terrorists killed and three arrested.

(*continued*)

TABLE 3.1 (*continued*)

September 10, 1972	Members of Black September shot and wounded a staff member of the Israeli Embassy in Brussels.
September 19, 1972	Letter bombs sent to addresses in Europe and Israel. One killed Dr. Ami Schechori, agricultural attaché of the Israeli Embassy in London.
October 6, 1972	Letter bomb sent to deceased resident of home for the aged in Dusseldorf was defused.
October 29, 1972	Members of Black September seized Lufthansa flight from Beirut to Munich and demanded release of the three Arab terrorists involved in the Munich massacre. They threatened to blow up the plane with crew and passengers on board. German authorities released the three prisoners in Zagreb. Plane and passengers first released when the air pirates were in Tripoli, Libya.
November 3, 1972	Central office of Zionist Youth in Germany received a letter bomb that exploded when police opened it. On the same day, Red Star of David received a letter bomb from Singapore.
December 28, 1972	Four Arab terrorists seized Israeli Embassy in Bangkok and took six hostages. After negotiations, the hostages were released and terrorists flew to Cairo.
January 8, 1973	Bomb attack on Paris office of Jewish Agency for Israel.

Source: "Dokumentation arabischer Terrorakte 1968–1972," ZA Heidelberg, Jüdischer Presse Dienst: Informationen des Zentralrats der Juden in Deutschland, Dusseldorf, Nr. 1 (January 1973), 5–8.

4

Diplomatic Breakthrough to Military Alliance: East Germany, the Arab States, and the PLO: 1969–1973

Playing the anti-Israeli card proved beneficial to the East German regime. In 1954, West German Chancellor Konrad Adenauer adopted a policy named for Walter Hallstein, his state secretary in the Foreign Ministry. According to what was called "the Hallstein doctrine," East Germany had no moral or political legitimacy because it was a dictatorship kept in power by the presence of the Red Army. In the hopes of winning a political battle that would culminate with the collapse of the East German regime, Adenauer and Hallstein insisted that the Federal Republic would refuse to have diplomatic relations with any government that established diplomatic relations with East Germany.[1] Thus a primary goal of East German foreign policy was to shatter the Hallstein doctrine by finding states beyond the Warsaw Pact that would be willing to open diplomatic relations with East Germany and thus risk the anger of the much larger, more economically powerful Federal Republic. East Germany's partisanship for the Arab states and against Israel played a central role in its successful effort to shatter the Hallstein doctrine, break out of global isolation, and establish diplomatic relations with states in the Middle East and elsewhere.[2]

Otto Winzer, East Germany's foreign minister, led the successful diplomatic breakthrough of spring and summer 1969. His political activity began in 1919 when he joined the new German Communist Party

[1] See William Glenn Gray, *Germany's Cold War: The Global Campaign to Isolate East Germany, 1949–1969* (Chapel Hill: University of North Carolina Press, 2003).

[2] See Angelika Timm, *Hammer, Zirkel, Davidstern: Das gestörte Verhältnis der DDR zu Zionismus und Staat Israel* (Bonn: Bouvier Verlag, 1997), chaps. 7–9. See the documents in Wolfgang Bator and Angelika Bator, eds., *Der DDR und die arabischen Staaten: Dokument, 1956–1982*. ([East] Berlin: Staatsverlag der Deutsche Demokratische Republik, 1984).

(KPD).[3] In the 1920s, he worked in Communist-affiliated publishing firms in Berlin and Vienna. He fled from Nazi Germany in 1934 to Paris, where he edited a Communist youth magazine. In 1935 he traveled to Moscow, where he again worked in publishing. From 1941 to 1945, he was editorial director of the Soviet German-language radio broadcast "The Home Front Calls the Front" (*Die Heimat ruft die Front)* and was a member of the National Committee for a Free Germany, the Communists' effort to appeal to German soldiers and POWs. He returned to Berlin in 1945 with the group around Walter Ulbricht and became a member of the KPD Central Committee in 1947. From 1949 to 1956 he was the chief of staff in the office of East German President Wilhelm Pieck. There he joined in the attack on the veteran Communist Leo Zuckermann, who, with Paul Merker, supported restitution payments to Jewish survivors of the Holocaust and warm relations with Israel.[4] In 1956, Winzer began his career in the East German Foreign Ministry as deputy foreign minister and served as state secretary from 1956 to 1965. In 1965 he succeeded Lothar Bolz as the East German foreign minister and served in that position until his death in 1975.[5]

Though Cambodia was the first country outside the Warsaw Pact to recognize East Germany in 1969, the politically most consequential recognition decisions were those of Arab states. Winzer was at the center of this great diplomatic success. On April 30, 1969, Iraq announced its decision to establish diplomatic relations with the GDR. The joint declaration issued by Winzer and Iraqi foreign minister Abdul Karim al-Sheikhly on May 10 in Baghdad bore witness to the importance of East Germany's antagonism to Israel. The two foreign ministers stressed the "commonalities of struggle of both now befriended regimes and peoples against the forces of imperialism, neo-Nazism, colonialism and Zionism" and described Israel as "racist, imperialist, reactionary and aggressive." Israel, they said, was the "spearhead of imperialism in the Arab world and threatened peace and international security. The peoples of the GDR and Iraq will struggle fiercely in a common front against this situation." The two foreign ministers also denounced the military and political support for Israel by the United States and West Germany.

[3] "Winzer, Otto," in Bernd-Rainer Barth et al., *Wer war Wer in der DDR: Ein biographisches Handbuch* (Frankfurt/Main: Fischer Taschenbuch Verlag, 1996), 799–800.

[4] On Winzer's attack on Zuckermann's association of the Jews with democracy, see Jeffrey Herf, *Divided Memory: The Nazi Past in the Two Germanys* (Cambridge, MA: Harvard University Press, 1997), 130–132.

[5] "Winzer, Otto," in Barth et al., *Wer war Wer in der DDR*, 799–800.

Winzer stressed "the sympathy of the regime and the people of the GDR for the just struggle of the Palestinian Arab peoples against Israeli aggression." East Germany recognized the rights of the Palestinians for "self-determination and resistance against Israeli occupation."[6] He embedded the description of Israel as a racist state, an imperialist spearhead, and even a state similar to Nazi Germany into the beginnings of East German–Iraqi diplomatic relations.

In recognizing the Palestinian "right of resistance against Israeli occupation" and leaving the noun "occupation" undefined, the joint declaration also legitimated Palestinian attacks against Israeli forces in the West Bank and Gaza as well as terrorism against civilians in Israel proper. On the one hand, the East Germans paid occasional lip service to the United Nations Resolution 242 of November 22, 1967, which called for "withdrawal of Israel armed forces from territories occupied in the recent conflict" as well as "termination of all claims or states of belligerency and respect for and acknowledgment of the sovereignty, territorial integrity and political independence of every State in the area and their right to live in peace within secure and recognized boundaries free from threats or acts of force."[7] That is, the two-part resolution linked Israel's withdrawal from territories occupied during the war to its right to exist within secure borders. Yet in their public statements, Winzer and his fellow East German diplomats never clearly stated that Israel had such a legitimate right to exist. The overwhelming focus of their public descriptions of Israel was on what they called its imperialist, aggressive, and racist character. They often called for Israel to withdraw from territories gained during the war but separated that demand from the other half of Resolution 242.

[6] "Aus dem Gemeinsamen Kommunique über den Besuch des Ministers für Auswärtige Angelegenheiten der DDR, Otto Winzer, in der Republik Irak vom 6. Bis 11. Mai 1969," Baghdad (May 10, 1969), in Bator and Bator, *Der DDR und die arabische Staaten*, 147. The theme of "common struggle" against "imperialism," "Zionism," and "especially against West German imperialism that together with USA imperialism form the major supports for the aggressive and neo-colonialist forces in Israel" were among East German talking points for the conversation between Willi Stoph and Fayik Makki Ahme Al-Tikriti, Iraq's new ambassador to the GDR on October 1, 1969. See "Antrittsbesuch des Außordentlichen und Bevollmächtingen Botschafters der Republik Irak in der Deutschen Demokratischen Republik, Fayik Makki Ahme Al-Tikriti, beim Vorsitzenden der DDR, Will Stoph," [East] Berlin (October 1, 1969), BAB Ministerrat der DDR DC 20/4610.

[7] United Nations Security Council, Resolution 242 (November 22, 1967), S/RES 242 (1967) unispal.un.org/unispal.nsf/0/7D35E1F729DF491C85256EE700686136

Using identical arguments, Winzer succeeded in opening the door to relations with Sudan (June 3, 1969), Syria (June 5, 1969), and Egypt and South Yemen (July 10, 1969).[8] If East Germany can be said to have had a special relationship with one Arab state in particular, then that state was Syria, Israel's most implacable foe among the Arab states. (See Figure 4.1, p. 133.) Winzer contended that establishment of relations between East Germany and Syria would be "an effective blow against the alliance of the forces of imperialism and Zionism in the Middle East, and especially against the alliance of aggressive West German imperialism with aggressive Israel."[9] "German imperialism," he said in Damascus, was "the primary cause" of the "active support" from West Germany "for the preparation and implementation of Israel's aggression against the Arab states." In contrast to what Winzer called West Germany's "anti-Arab policies," the GDR had been a "reliable friend of the Arab states," as evident in its denunciation of "Israeli aggression" in 1967 and subsequent solidarity with the Arab side. Both the "government and the people" of East Germany "feel most closely bound to the Arab peoples." Winzer said that East Germany was the home of a "centuries old humanistic tradition of German-Arab friendship."[10] Winzer did not mention that for some in the Baath Party in Syria, "German-Arab friendship" stretched back to the years of the Nazi regime.

In the joint communiqué issued on June 6, 1969, Winzer and Syrian Foreign Minister Moustafa al-Sayed condemned Israel's "aggressive provocations against the Arab states, the measures of terror and oppression against the Arab people as well as their expulsion by force from their homes." They also agreed that "Israel's essence is racist, colonial

[8] Ibid., 153–169. As we have seen, the East German relationship with Syria preceded the establishment of formal diplomatic relations in June 1969. At the invitation of the Syrian Interior Ministry, Friedrich Dickel, the East German minister of interior and head of the Deutsche Volkspolizei (National Police), led a delegation to Damascus, March 8–15, 1969. On the visit, see BAB Minisiterrates DC 20/4535, 266–273, esp. Willi Stoph, "Konzeption zur Verhandlungfühurng der Delegation des Ministerium des Innern der Deutschen Demokratischen Republik beim Besuch der Syrisichen Arabischen Republik," [East] Berlin, n.d., 268–273.

[9] "Rede des Ministers für Auswärtige Angelegenheiten der DDR, Otto Winzer, bei der Unterzeichnung der Vereinbarungen zwischen der DDR und der Syrischen Arabischen Republik in Damaskus" (Damascus, June 5, 1967), in Bator and Bator, *Der DDR und die arabische Staaten, Dokument 1956–1982*, 155.

[10] Ibid.

FIGURE 4.1. Otto Winzer (left) and Moustafa al-Sayed (right) sign agreement to establish diplomatic relations with Syria.

and aggressive, that it is imperialism's spearhead aimed at the Arab nation and that it threatens peace and international security." In order to end Israeli "aggression" and force its "unconditional withdrawal of its troops from the occupied Arab territories," the GDR and Syria would "fight firmly and decisively in a common front."[11] They supported "the legitimate Arab resistance against the Israeli occupation and regard[ed] it as an essential means for the liberation of occupied territory." They decided to establish diplomatic relations because they shared a "common struggle" against "imperialism, Zionism and all other imperialist and colonialist doctrines that are based on aggression and the oppression of peoples."[12]

[11] "Aus dem Gemeinsamen Kommunique über den Besuch des Ministers für Auswärtige Angelegenheiten der DDR, Otto Winzer, in der Syrischen Arabischen Republik vom 3. Bis. 6. Juni 1969," June 6, 1969, in Bator and Bator, *Der DDR und die arabische Staaten*, 157–158.

[12] Ibid., 158.

The recognition communiqués redefined the meaning of the term "good Germans." They were the Germans who supported the Arab states and the PLO. The bad Germans were the West Germans who took the side of the Jews, that is, who had recognized and offered support to Israel. For the East German regime, antagonism to Israel was both an expression of ideological conviction as well as an effective tool of foreign policy. As Mathias Walden had pointed out, the anti-Israeli card proved to be a powerful battering ram used to smash the Hallstein doctrine and to open the doors to recognition first in the Arab world and then beyond. Ideological conviction and political utility reinforced one another.[13]

WEST GERMAN DIPLOMATS ON EAST GERMANY'S MIDDLE EAST STRATEGY

Officials in West Germany's Foreign Ministry were fully aware of the diplomatic defeat that the Federal Republic was enduring in spring and early summer 1969. On May 7, following Iraq's decision to recognize East Germany, Walter Gelhoff, an official in the ministry working on Middle East issues, wrote, "The German-Arab relationship at present is ruined (*gestörte*) in the first place by political factors, above all the unsolved Middle East conflict, Soviet influence in the Middle East and our Middle East policy which the Arabs regard as too pro-Israeli."[14] To prevent further Arab recognition of the GDR, West Germany could threaten to abandon its "previous neutral policy in the Middle East" including its refusal to send weapons either to the Arab states or to Israel. In fact, he continued, "delivery of weapons to Israel could be excluded because it conflicts with our whole policy, and on the other hand could force our Arab friends (Jordan, Libya, Tunisia, Morocco) to break diplomatic relations" with the Federal Republic.[15] A few weeks later, following the agreements by Cambodia and Iraq to recognize the GDR, Alfons Böcker, head of the West German legation to the United Nations in New York, wrote to foreign minister Walter Scheel that the "most dangerous breaks" in the German effort to prevent diplomatic

[13] Similar points were made when Haissam Kelani, Syria's ambassador to the GDR, spoke with Willi Stoph on September 18, 1969. See "Antrittsbesuch des Außerordentliche und Bevollmäghtigen Botschafters deer Syrischen Arabischen Republik in der Deutschen Demokratischen Republik, Haissam Kelani, beim Vorsitzenden des Ministerrat der DDR, Willi Stoph," BAB DC20/4610

[14] "Dokument 148, Aufzeichnung des Referats I B 4," May 7, 1969, *Akten zur Auswärtigen Politik der Bundesrepublik Deutschland (AAPBD) 1969, Band I: 1 Januar bis 30. June 1969* (Munich: R. Oldenbourg Verlag, 2000), 562–567.

[15] Ibid., 567.

recognition of East Germany were taking place in "the Arab area and in the Buddhist-Hindu world."[16]

In late July, the director of the Political Department in the Foreign Ministry, Andreas Meyer-Lindenberg, approved a memo that addressed the situation.[17] Using the abbreviation "SBZ," for "Soviet Zone of Occupation" the memo stated that "in the Middle East conflict, the SBZ had clearly taken the side of the Arabs and at the same conducted massive attacks against Israel. With all possible means, it defamed the Federal Republic as a one-sided advocate of Israel. Thanks to its efforts, the SBZ has succeeded in reaching agreements to exchange General Counsels."[18] The authors referred to West German government statements that rejected the "campaign of defamation" that "East Berlin and Moscow" had directed at West Germany. They cited a statement of West German state secretary Klaus Schütz of June 21, 1967, made in response to Ulbricht's Leipzig speech, that assertions that West Germany had delivered weapons to Israel were "nonsense.... I assure you again that these communist assertions are absolutely untrue."[19] It was noteworthy that the Lindenberg memo described East German assertions that West Germany was partisan in favor of Israel as a "campaign of defamation." That is, rather than being a point of pride rooted in the country's traditions of coming to terms with the Nazi past, the use of the term "defamation" suggested that the West German–Israeli relationship was an irritant that was responsible for the diplomatic defeat that West Germany was enduring. The Foreign Ministry in Bonn focused on the disadvantages of support for Israel created in relations with the Arab states.

ARMS FROM THE "PEACE STATE"

As a consequence of suppressing political opponents and a free press, dictatorships such as the one in East Berlin have an easier time attacking their enemies abroad while immunizing themselves from comparable scrutiny at home. In the course of "asymmetric strategic interaction,"

16 Dokument 171, Botschafter Böker, New York (UNO), an das Auswärtige Amt," May 23, 1969, Rainer A. Blasius, Franz Eibl and Hubert Zimmermann, *AAPBD, 1969, Band I: 1 Januar bis 30. June 1969* (Munich: R. Oldenbourg Verlag, 2000), 626–628.

17 "283: Aufzeichnung des Ministerialdirektors Meyer-Lindenberg," Rainer Blasius, ed., *AAPBD, 1967, Band II. 1 April bis 31 August 1967* (Munich: R. Oldenbourg Verlag, 1998), 1138–1141.

18 Ibid., 1138.

19 State Secretary Schütz, cited in ibid., 1140, n. 12.

they can turn the vices of dictatorship into tactical virtues and the political virtues of open societies into tactical disadvantages.[20] East Germany's focus on West Germany's military support for Israel, the anxious efforts of West German diplomats to deny what they called "defamation," and the Communist regime's ability to keep Soviet-bloc and East German military support for the Arab states secret offered a case of such asymmetry. Though the East German regime publicly declared its support for the Arab states and "national liberation movements," including the PLO, and called itself a "peace state" (*Friedenstaat)*, its controlled press and media reported nothing about Soviet-bloc arms deliveries and East Germany's role in that effort. The opening of the records of the East German regime following its collapse in 1989–1990 has made it possible to document a significant part of what the regime had concealed. The key files are those of the Politburo and Central Committee, the Ministry of Defense, the Council of Ministers, and the Ministry of State Security (Stasi). These files document weapons agreements and deliveries, military training of foreign forces, and cooperation with foreign intelligence services.

East German military deliveries to Egypt, Syria, Yemen, Tanzania, Iraq, and Guinea began in 1965.[21] As we saw, its military assistance to the Arab states expanded in the aftermath of the Arab defeat in the Six-Day War.[22] According to Defense Minister Hoffmann, the deliveries that year included one MiG-17 F jet; 40 rocket-propelled grenade launchers (RPG-2) with the necessary munitions; 295 light machine guns with munitions; 6,700 Kalashnikov machine pistols with munitions (MPi-K, MPi-41, and MPi 43/44); 1,360 carbine rifles with munitions; 12 ship anti-aircraft guns with munitions; 5,000 mines; and six World War II-era T-34/T Soviet model tanks. In the same year, East Germany sent 4.4 million marks worth of weaponry to Syria's Saika guerrilla organization, which carried out terrorist attacks on Israel. Those deliveries included 3,000 machine pistols with munitions; 560 LMG-34, German-made World War II-era machine guns with ammunition; 2,000 98K carbines, the standard-issue rifle of the Wehrmacht in World War II; 10,000 Soviet-made time-delayed hand grenades (RGD-5); and 260 binoculars

[20] On asymmetric strategic interaction see Jeffrey Herf, *War by Other Means: Soviet Power, West German Resistance and the Battle of the Euromissiles* (New York: The Free Press, 1991), 7-12.

[21] Heinz Hoffmann to Walter Ulbricht, [East] Berlin (August 5, 1970), "Westdeutsche Pressemeldung über NVA Soldaten im Nahen Osten," BAMA DVW1 114478, 70–71.

[22] "Kostenlose Hilfslieferungen, GVS-Nr.: A 76 938," BAMA DVWI 115671, MfNV Sekr. D. Ministers. Unterlagen zur Vorbereitung d. Militärdelegation in den arabischen Staaten, 6–7.

7 x 40.[23] The cost-free deliveries to the Arab states for the year following the Six-Day War also included 30 MiG-17 F and 20 MiG-17 Soviet fighter jets; 48 jet engines; 6 Soviet-made field artillery guns (D-44/85) with munitions; 12 Swiss-made PAK 57 anti-tank guns; 54 grenade launchers for 82 mm (millimeter) and 120 mm munitions; 30 recoilless rifles of 82 mm and 107 mm; 60 Soviet-made shoulder-fired weapons with munitions (RPG-2); 17,500 Kalashnikov machine pistols, better known as the AK-47 (MPi-K, Mpi-41, MPi-43/44); 430 light machine guns with munitions (LMG-D, LMG-34); 2,200 carbines with cartridges; 18 ship anti-aircraft 20 mm guns and munitions; 150,000 anti-personnel land mines (PMN); 3,500 (F-1) Soviet anti-personnel hand grenades F-1; and Soviet-made helmets, uniforms, backpacks.[24]

In winter and spring 1969 the weapons deliveries complemented the diplomatic push for recognition from the Arab states. On January 16, 1969, at a time when Egypt was waging a war of attrition with Israel, Hoffmann wrote to Winzer in the Foreign Ministry and to Weiss in the Council of Ministers that the Defense Ministry would be able to fulfill the request of Egyptian General Mohammed Fawzi for military assistance.[25] The assistance included training equipment for MiG-15 and MiG-17 jets and equipment for training pilots "to shoot at aerial targets" with optical sights; construction of targets for infantry and armored shooting ranges; replacement parts for MiG-15, MiG-17, and MiG-19 jets; and training devices to improve shooting accuracy.[26]

On April 15, General Heinz Keßler, deputy minister of defense and chief of the General Staff of the Army (NVA), wrote to Winzer and Weiss in response to Iraqi requests for tanks and air defenses.[27] East Germany's arms industry did not produce those items but the government could

[23] "Kostenlose Hilfslieferungen, GVS-Nr.: A 76 950" BAMA DVWI 115671, MfNV Sekr. D. Ministers. Unterlagen zur Vorbereitung d. Militärdelegation in den arabischen Staaten, 30–31.

[24] Ibid., 31.

[25] Heinz Hoffmann to Otto Winzer, and Heinz Hoffmann to Gerhard Weiss, [East] Berlin (January 16, 1969), Bundesarchiv-Militärarchiv (BAMA) "Schriftverkehr mit Staatliche Organen MR, MdI, MfS, MFAA 1969. VAR. SAR. Iraq," MfNV, DVW1 115537, 5–7.

[26] Hoffmann to Weiss, [East] Berlin (January 16, 1969), "Aufstellung über Angebote an die VAR," Bundesarchiv-Militärarchiv (BAMA) Schriftverkehr mit Staatliche Organen MR, MdI, MfS, MFAA 1969. VAR. SAR. Iraq. BAMA, MfNV, DVW1 115537, 8.

[27] Heinz Keßler to Gerhard Weiss, [East] Berlin (April 15, 1969) [copy to Otto Winzer], BAMA, Schriftverkehr mit Staatliche Organen MR, MdI, MfS, MFAA 1969. VAR. SAR. Iraq. BAMA, MfNV, DVW1 115537, 21–23. Also see "Keßler, Heinz" in Barth et al., *Wer war Wer in der DDR*, 365–366.

deliver night-vision binoculars, field telephones and cables, telephone switching equipment, protective clothing against chemical and radioactive materials, navigation technology, mine detection equipment, camouflage nets, water filtration stations, ambulances, as well as replacement parts for MiG-15, -17, -19 jets and for T-34 and T-54 tanks.[28] As he prepared to complete the recognition agreements, Winzer asked Keßler about the possibility of delivering 60 MiG-17 and 30 MiG-15 jets on a commercial basis to Syria. The Defense Ministry was receiving so many additional requests for arms from Syria, Egypt, and Iraq that Keßler argued that the government needed to coordinate the efforts of various ministries involved.[29] He informed Weiss and Winzer that items available for sale included 24 Soviet MiG-17-F, 16 MiG-15 UTI, and 11 MiG-17 PF jets. In the course of 1969, another 7 MiG-15 UTI would become available for sale, with yet another 30 MiG-17 and 10 MiG-15 UTI more in 1970.[30] Military assistance was thus a mixture of politics and income.

WILLI STOPH'S SUPPORT ORDER OF SEPTEMBER 30, 1969 AND THE ROLE OF GERHARD WEISS

Over the summer and early fall of 1969, the East German government created the institutional structure that oversaw weapons deliveries for the next two decades. On June 20, 1969, Hoffmann (see Figure 4.2, p. 134) informed Stoph that he was receiving more requests for weapons deliveries, "especially from states which have diplomatically recognized the GDR."[31] The items and services that East Germany could produce domestically included AK-47 machine pistols and ammunition for them, hand grenades, mines, protective clothing, and cable. East Germany had skilled mechanics able to repair engines of the MiG-21 fighter jet. Hoffmann recommended expansion of existing East German arms production "to meet the growing demand and requests."[32]

A week later, Weiss met with officials from the Ministry of Foreign Trade and the Defense Ministry and presented the following principles

[28] Ibid., 24–25.

[29] Heinz Keßler to Gerhard Weiss, [East] Berlin (April 23, 1969) [copy to Otto Winzer], BAMA, Schriftverkehr mit Staatliche Organen MR, MdI, MfS, MFAA 1969. VAR. SAR. Iraq. BAMA, MfNV, DVW1 115537, 26–28.

[30] Keßler to Weiss (April 23, 1969), "Aufstellung über mögliche Abgaben von Flugzeugen MiG-15 UTI und MiG-17 F," BAMA, MfNV, DVW1 115537, 29.

[31] Heinz Hoffmann to Willi Stoph, [East] Berlin (June 20, 1969), VVS-Nr. A 76 176, BAB DC 20/12897, 195–196.

[32] Ibid., 196.

FIGURE 4.2. General Heinz Hoffmann, member of the Politburo of the Central Committee of the SED and East German minister of defense, December 17, 1982. *Source*: German Federal Archive, Koblenz, Photo Archive: Bild: 183-1982-1 217-023, ADN-ZB, photographer not identified.

to guide the expansion of arms shipments: East Germany's defense preparedness should not be impaired in any way; shipments of arms imported from the Soviet Union were to be carried out only with agreement of the minister of defense; countries that opened diplomatic relations with East Germany would receive priority. The Defense Ministry and the office of "engineering technical foreign trade" of the Ministry for Foreign Trade would coordinate the program in order to select material from East Germany's armed forces and decide to what extent "we are interested in sustaining or expanding our own production" of such weapons and services. Officials of the Foreign Ministry and relevant ambassadors would also be consulted to determine which countries had priority.[33]

33 "Vermerk über die Besprechung beim Stellvertreter des Vorsitzenden des Ministerrates, Genossen Dr. Weiss, am 27.6.1969," [East] Berlin (June 30, 1969), BAB DC 20/12897, 191–193.

On September 30, 1969, Willi Stoph, in his capacity as president of the Council of Ministers, issued an "Order regarding preparation and implementation of exports and assistance (*Hilfessendungen*) of military-technical equipment (*Ausrüstungen*) as well as (*Hilfeleistungen*) assistance in the military area to national states of September 30, 1969."[34] On October 4, fellow Politburo member, chairman of the National Defense Council, and future general secretary of the SED and leader of the regime Erich Honecker approved it. Stoph's order placed his deputy, Gerhard Weiss (1919–1986), in charge of the program's implementation.[35] Weiss had been a soldier in the Wehrmacht on the Eastern Front in World War II and was a prisoner of war in the Soviet Union until 1945. He returned to East Germany and joined the SED in 1948. From 1954 to 1965 he was the deputy minister for foreign and inner-German trade, and from 1965 until his death in 1986, served as deputy minister of the Council of Ministers. Together with leading officials in the Defense Ministry, he was at the center of East German arms shipments around the world.[36] Stoph ordered the Foreign Ministry to forward all requests for arms to Weiss. Requests to the "armed organs," the East German military, the police, and presumably the Stasi as well, were also to be decided in coordination with Weiss.[37] As a result of the decision to make Weiss the coordinator of the arms program, the files of his office are rich with details about weapons requests and deliveries.

For the next two decades, Stoph's order of September 30, 1969 shaped both the personal and organizational structure of East German arms deliveries to third-world states and movements, in the Middle East and elsewhere. Key excerpts follow:

[34] Vorsitzender des Ministerrat (Willi Stoph), "Anordnung über die Vorbereitung und Durchführung von Exporten und Hilfssendungen military-technischer Ausrüstungen sowie von Hilfeleistungen auf militärischem Gebiet in Nationalstaaten vom 30. September 1969," BAB Ministerrat der DDR DC20/ 16653, 54–59; and Willi Stoph to Erich Honecker, [East] Berlin, October 1, 1969, BAB DC20/ 16653, 61. Also see the discussion of the order in Klaus Storkmann, *Geheime Solidarität: Militärbeziehungen und Militärhilfen der DDR in die "Dritte Welt"* (Berlin: Christoph Links Verlag, 2012), 121–137.

[35] Willi Stoph to Erich Honecker, [East] Berlin, October 1, 1969, BAB DC20/ 16653, 61. Also see "Honecker, Erich," in Barth et al., *Wer war Wer in der DDR*, 321–322.

[36] "Weiss, Gerhard," in Barth et al., *Wer war Wer in der DDR*, 779–780. Also reference to the order in Heinz Keßler to Paul Markowski, [East] Berlin (July 27, 1970), BAMA, MfNV, DVW1 115537, 107–108.

[37] Stoph, "Anordnung ... vom 30. September 1969," 56–57.

> Due to the expansion of relations of the GDR to national states and to the continuously expanding desires of these states for arms and military equipment and other actions, the following measures are ordered to facilitate the coordinated preparation and implementation of exports and cost-free aid shipments (*Hilfssendungen)* of military-technical equipment as well as cost-free assistance (*Hilfeleistungen)* in the area of military affairs. Based on the determination to strengthen and deepen cooperation with young national states, deliveries of military-technical equipment and activities in the military area are to be incorporated into the formation and development of relationships with these states.[38]

Stoph's order also established the institutional structure to implement the program. The Ministry for Foreign Economic Policy (*Außenwirtschaft*) and the Defense Ministry were to determine "the possibilities for delivery of military-technical equipment to national states from production as well as form the stocks of the [GDR's] armed institutions." The ministers were to coordinate both short- and long-term possibilities of delivery and were to evaluate them on an annual basis. After agreement from the minister of foreign affairs (Otto Winzer), "the Deputy Chairman of the Council of Ministers, Dr. [Gerhard] Weiss, was to request confirmation of these possibilities from the Chairman of the Council of Ministers [Willi Stoph]." Weiss appointed a working group composed of Deputy Minister of Defense and Chief of Armaments and Technology General Major Werner Fleißner (1922–1985), Dieter Albrecht from the Ministry for Foreign Economic Policy, and Deputy Foreign Minister Wolfgang Kiesewetter.[39]

The program was to be kept secret. Besides members of the Politburo, details about the arms deliveries would be known only to relevant officials in the Defense, Foreign, and Economic Ministries; to the offices of the chair and deputy chair of the Council of Ministers; and to the relevant East Germany's diplomatic representatives abroad. The East German press and other media reported nothing about it. Exports and arms sales were to be handled by the Ministry of Foreign Economic Policy and within it an office for "*Ingenieur-Technischer Außenhandel*" (engineering-technical foreign trade) and an office for "*Spezieller Außenhandel*" (special foreign trade) in the Ministry for Foreign Trade. The officials of the Office of Special Foreign Trade were to observe "the most severe vigilance and secrecy."[40] The result was what Klaus Storkmann called "secret solidarity," that is, public expressions of anti-imperialist solidarity with a host of leftist

[38] Ibid., 54–55.
[39] Ibid., 54–57.
[40] Ibid., 58–59.

regimes and movements in Asia, Africa, Latin America, and the Middle East together with preservation of strict secrecy about East German military assistance programs.[41] While the East Germans did not produce larger weapons systems such as tanks, fighter planes, and missiles, they did produce significant numbers of their own versions of the Kalashnikov (AK-47), assault rifles, and ammunition and hand grenades.[42]

Evidence of the intensity of Walter Ulbricht's support for the Arabs was apparent in a remarkable letter he sent to Soviet Premier Leonid Brezhnev on October 17, 1969. He proposed sending "volunteers" from the Warsaw Pact, presumably including East Germans, to join in the "war of attrition" against Israel. It was, he wrote, "necessary to conduct a comprehensive international political action and a war of attrition against the Israeli troops in the occupied territories."[43] He proposed sending "volunteers from the socialist countries" to serve as "flyers, tank commanders (drivers) and special forces" in fighting the Israelis.[44] Though Soviet "advisers" were working with the Egyptian armed forces, East German involvement appeared limited to training forces in East Germany. The issue of whether East German soldiers were actually engaged in battles against Israel was raised in some press reports in West Germany. In a letter to Ulbricht of August 5, 1970, Heinz Hoffmann dismissed them as efforts to "divert attention from the active intervention and support for reactionary forces in these areas by the West German government and to discredit the German Democratic Republic in world public opinion."[45] Though Ulbricht's support for the idea is now a matter

[41] Storkmann, *Geheime Solidarität*. In January 1970, Stoph ordered further agreements for the Ministry for Foreign Economic Policy and the Ministries of Defense, Interior, and State Security regarding arms shipments. See Willi Stoph, "Verfügung Nr. 27/70 über die 'Grundsätze zur Gestaltung des komplexen Systems der Außenwirtschaftsbeziehungen auf dem Gebiet der speziellen Warenlieferungen und Leistungen vom 29. Jan. 1970," [East] Berlin, BAB Ministerrat der DDR DC20/ 16653, GVS-Nr.: 116012, 61–64.

[42] Heinz Hoffmann to Erich Honecker, GVS-Nr. A 391-302, [East] Berlin (August 12, 1976), BAMA DVW1/114448, 11.

[43] Walter Ulbricht to Leonid Brezhnev, "An den Generalsekretär des ZK der KPdSU Genossen Leonid Iljitische Breshnew," [East] Berlin October 17, 1969, Bundesarchiv Berlin-Lichterfelde, Stiftung Archiv der Parteien und Massenorganisationen (SAPMO), Büro Walter Ulbricht, DY 30/3666, 114–120.

[44] Ibid., 118–120. Also see W. Ulbricht to P. A. Abrassimow, Berlin, February 3, 1970, BAB, SAPMO, Büro Walter Ulbricht, DY 30/3666, 159. Also cited as "Dokument 39: Schreiben von Walter Ulbricht an Leonid Brezhnev vom 27. Oktober 1969," in Timm, *Hammer, Zirkel, Davidstern*, 535–536.

[45] Heinz Hoffmann to Walter Ulbricht, [East] Berlin (August 5, 1970), "Westdeutsche Pressemeldung über NVA Soldaten im Nahen Osten," BAMA DVW1 114478, 70–71.

TABLE 4.1. *Plan for Possibilities of Delivery of Military-Technical Equipment in Friendly National States in 1970 (already completed agreements)*

Number	Description	Amount	Value (TVM)*		Receiving Country
1.	Spare parts for MiG-15–19		1,310	Of that: 1,200	Syria
				60	Egypt (UAR)
				50	Iraq
2.	Repairs on MiG-21	5	2,220		Egypt
3.	Spare parts for T-34 and T-54 tanks		1,200		Syria
4.	Binoculars 7 × 40	15	10		Iraq
		Total Value	4,740		

Note: TVM: East German marks, in thousands.
Source: "Plan der Liefermöglichkeiten von military-technischer Ausrüstung in befreundete Nationalstaaten für das Jahr 1970," Berlin, May 28, 1970, BAB DC 20/ 13069.

of record, the issue of whether East German soldiers ever engaged in combat with the Israeli armed forces remains unresolved.

On May 28, 1970, Stoph approved the following plans indicated in Tables 4.1–4.4 for military deliveries. They had been developed by Weiss, Hoffmann, and Minister for Foreign Trade, Horst Sölle.

At a meeting on August 21, 1970, the Weiss committee decided that 80,000 AK-47s would be produced in East Germany. Negotiations over 4,400 Kalashnikovs to Egypt were to continue.[46] Weapons to be sent free of charge were used materials in working condition from the stocks of the Ministry of the Interior. In 1970, the Weiss committee agreed to send 3,000 AK-47s to Syria along with 2.5 million cartridges, 1,000 hand grenades, 500 German-made light machine guns with cartridges, and 2,000 German-made 98 K carbines with 2.9 million cartridges.[47] Weiss

[46] "Protokoll über die Besprechung der Kommission am 21.8.1970 gemäß Anordnung des Vorsitzenden des Ministerrat vom 30.9.1969," [East] Berlin, September 8, 1970, BAB DC 20/ 13069.

[47] "Protokoll vom 15.1.70 über die Festlegungen in der konstituierenden Sitzung der Kommission gemäß Anordnung des Vorsitzenden des Ministerrates vom 30.09.1969," [East] Berlin, January 19, 1970, BAB DC 20/ 13069.

TABLE 4.2. *Plan for Possibilities of Delivery of Military-Technical Equipment in Friendly National States in 1970 (planned deliveries)*

Number	Description	Amount	Value (TVM)	Receiving Country
1.	Machine pistols (AKM)	3,000	1,200	Syria
2.	Machine pistols (AKM)	5,400	2,160	Iraq
3.	Ammunition M-1, 7.62 mm	2.5 million	750	Syria
4.	1 MG-34 German machine gun	560	168	Syria
5.	German carbine 98 K	2,000	320	Syria
6.	7.92 mm cartridges	2.9 million	1,015	Syria
7.	RGD-5 hand grenades (Soviet anti-personnel fragmentation grenade)	10,000	467	Śyria
8.	Turbo power train TSA 210	22	1,800	Egypt, Syria, Iraq, Sudan
9.	Spare parts for MiG-15–19		3,000	Egypt (UAR), Syria
10.	Camouflage nets	500	1,323	Egypt, Syria, Iraq, Sudan
11.	Parachutes	600	930	Egypt, Syria, Iraq, Sudan
12.	Binoculars	260/300	175/200	Egypt, Syria
13.	Helmets	50,000	650	Egypt
14.	Signal equipment		4,500	Egypt, Syria, Iraq, Sudan
15.	Water filtration station (300 liters, 30 liters)	300	2,355	Egypt, Syria, Iraq, Sudan
16.	(Plastic syringes) 2 million	3,640	n.a.	Egypt, Syria, Iraq, Sudan
17.	Spare parts for T-34 and T-54		5,000	Egypt, Syria
18.	Covering materials	500	1,500	Egypt, Syria, Iraq
19.	Tents	300	285	Egypt, Syria, Iraq
20.	Special suits	15,000	225	Egypt, Syria, Iraq
21.	Flexible rubber containers	200	453	Egypt, Syria, Iraq
22.	Underwater devices	300	336	Egypt, Iraq
23.	OB technology 62/20; 62/40; 62/60 30		2,802	Egypt, Syria, Iraq

TABLE 4.2 (*continued*)

Number	Description	Amount	Value (TVM)	Receiving Country
24.	Radiological devices RR 66; RW 64; RW 640 RW 64S; RDC 64A; RDS 64D	200	20	Egypt, Syria
25.	Cable	1500 km	7,700	Syria, Iraq
26.	MiG-15 UTI	33	n.a.	Egypt, Syria, Iraq
	MiG-17 F	54 n.a.		
	MiG-17 PF	11 n.a.		

Note: Items number 1 through 7 were described as "solidarity" or "gifts" and were thus free of charge.
Source: "Plan der Liefermöglichkeiten von military-technischer Ausrüstung in befreundete Nationalstaaten für das Jahr 1970," [East] Berlin, May 28, 1970, BAB DC 20/ 13069. Also filed in BAB DC 20/12897, 158–170.

TABLE 4.3. *Plan for Possibilities of Delivery of Military-Technical Equipment in Friendly National States in 1970*

(Reserve) Number	Description	Amount	Value (TVM)	Receiving Country
Bullets for M-1, 7.62 mm		5.6 million	1925	Egypt, Syria, Iraq
Machine pistol 38/40 9 mm		550	83	Egypt, Syria, Iraq, Sudan
Machine pistol EMP, 9 mm caliber		200	18	Egypt, Syria, Iraq, Sudan
Machine pistol 35/1, 9 mm caliber		180	16	Egypt, Syria, Iraq, Sudan
Carbines 98 K, 7.92 mm		7,100	1,136	Egypt, Syria, Iraq, Sudan
Cartridges 7. 9 mm		1.8 million	540	Egypt, Syria, Iraq, Sudan
Pistol cartridges 9 mm		66,000	7	Egypt, Syria, Iraq, Sudan
Carbines 38/44, 7.62 mm		1100	132	Egypt, Syria, Iraq, Sudan
Cartridges 7.62 mm		1.5 million	495	Egypt, Syria, Iraq, Sudan
T-34/85 Tanks		25	3,250	Egypt, Syria, Iraq, Sudan

Note: Weiss's plans looking ahead to 1973 included delivery of 50,000 Kalashnikovs "on a commercial basis with special credit" to Syria. See Über die Festlegungen des Genossen Dr. Weiss in der Beratung der Arbeitsgruppe am 18.9.1972 (Anordnung des Vorsitzenden des Ministerrat vom 30.9.1969," [East] Berlin, October 11, 1972, BAB DC 20/ 13069.
Source: "Plan der Liefermöglichkeiten von military-technischer Ausrüstung in befreundete Nationalstaaten für das Jahr 1970," [East] Berlin, May 28, 1970, BAB DC 20/ 13069. Also filed in BAB DC 20/12897, 158–170.

also agreed that in 1973 and 1974, East Germany would send 50,000 AK-47s on terms of "commercial special credit" to Egypt. It would also repair Egypt's MiGs and send 280,000 cartridges for the 98 K World War II-era carbines.[48]

On February 5, 1971, Stoph approved a plan (see Table 4.4) from Weiss and approved by Hoffmann, for military deliveries to "befriended national states for 1971."[49]

TABLE 4.4. *Plan for Possibilities of Delivery of Military-Technical Equipment in Friendly National States in 1971 (completed agreements)*

Number	Description	Amount	Total value VM/T	Receiving Country
1.	Repair MiG-21	9	4,082,000	Egypt
2.	Repair MiG-21	2	1,028,000	Egypt
3.	Repair [MiG] engines	2	269,000	Iraq
4.	Repair [MiG] engines	20	2,666,000	Syria
5.	AK-47 AKM-S (Assault rifle)	25,000	12,096,000	Egypt (Commercial special credit)
6.	AK-47 AKM-K	4,400	1,997,000	Egypt
7.	Spare parts: AK-47 AKM-K		67	Egypt
8.	Soviet Makovov Pistol Ammunition 9.02 mm	105,000	29	Egypt
9.	Protective clothing	85,000	9,200	Egypt (commercial special credit)
		Total value	31,434,000[a]	

[a] "Plan der Liefermöglichkeiten von military-technischer Ausrüstung in befreundete Nationalstaaten für das Jahr 1971," 2, [East] Berlin, February 5, 1971, BAB DC20/ 13069.

[48] "Protokolle über die Festlegungen des Genossen Dr. Weiss in der Beratung der Arbeitsgruppe am 18.9.1972 (Anordnung des Vorsitzenden des Ministerrat vom 30.9.1969," [East] Berlin, November 11, 1972, BAB DC 20/ 13069.

[49] "Plan der Liefermöglichkeiten von military-technischer Ausrüstung in befreundete Nationalstaaten für das Jahr 1971," [East] Berlin, February 5, 1971, BAB DC20/ 13069.

In addition, the Weiss plan for 1971 called for sending 7,900 Kalashnikov assault rifles (MPi-AKM) that were produced in East Germany in a commercial transaction.[50]

On May 19, 1971, General Werner Fleißner sent Weiss a list of the cost-free deliveries *(Hilfeleistungen)* that had been sent to "befriended national states" including North Vietnam, North Yemen, South Yemen, Tanzania, as well as Egypt and Syria.[51] In that year alone, East German deliveries included 50 MiGs, 5,000 Kalashnikov assault rifles, 9,000 Soviet style machine pistols, 3,500 German made machine guns, and 150,000 anti-personnel land mines. Table 4.5 lists arms sent in 1967/68 to the United Arab Republic, that is, Egypt and Syria.

On February 5, 1971, Stoph approved the plan for deliveries for 1971 presented by Weiss, approved by Hoffmann and submitted to Hartmut Sölle, the minister for foreign trade. The plan entailed repair of 11 MiG-21 jet fighters and delivery of 294,000 AK-47 assault weapons and ammunition, a dramatic expansion indicative of indigenous East German production. The GDR also sent 85,000 sets of protective clothing to Egypt. In the same year, the East Germans serviced 2 MiG jet engines for Iraq and 20 for Syria on the basis of "commercial credit."[52] In 1972, the plan called for repairing 10 of Egypt's MiG-21 jet fighters, 26 of Syria's, and 6 of Iraq's MiG jet engines, and for sending 110,000 AK-47 assault weapons to Egypt.[53] On November 27, 1972, Stoph approved the plan presented by Weiss and approved by Hoffmann to repair 20 of Egypt's MiG-21 jet fighters and service 78 engines for the R-11-F2s-300 version of the MiG-21. In the same year, the plan called for repairing 25 Iraqi MiG R-121-F2S-300 jet engines and delivering 1,000 of the East German version of the AK-47 assault rifle to Baghdad. East Germany agreed to repair 20 MiG-21 jet engines and deliver 50,700 AK-47 assault rifles for Syria in 1973.[54] As these memos indicate, by the early 1970s, the East Germans were manufacturing their own version of the AK-47 assault weapon. In

[50] Ibid., 4.

[51] Werner Fleißner to Gerhard Weiss, [East] Berlin, May 19, 1991, BAB DC20/ 13069, 266.

[52] Will Stoph, Gerhard Weiss, Heinz Hoffmann, and Horst Sölle, "Plan der Liefermöglichkeiten von militär-technischer Ausrüstung in befreundeten Nationalstaaten für das Jahr 1971," [East] Berlin (February 5, 1971), BAB DC 20/ 12897, 150–151.

[53] "Plan der Lieferungsmöglichkeiten von militär-technischer Ausrüstung für befreundete Entwicklungsländer im Jahre 1972," BAB DC 20/ 12897, 139.

[54] Willi Stoph, Gerhard Weiss, Heinz Hoffmann and Horst Sölle, "Plan der Liefermöglichkeiten von militär-technischer Ausrüstung in befreundeten Nationalstaaten für das Jahr 1973," [East] Berlin (November 27, 1973), BAB DC 20/ 12897, 125–136.

TABLE 4.5. *II. United Arab Republic, 1967/68, Support in Connection with Israeli Aggression. 44 Items with Total Value of 44 million marks*

1.	30 MiG-17 F fighter jets
2.	20 MiG-17 fighter jets
3.	29 Engine RD-45 for MiG-19 Engine WK-1 AS
4.	6 Soviet D-44/85 mm cannon with 3 packages of ammunition
5.	12 Soviet 57 mm anti-tank guns with 7 packages of ammunition
6.	48 82 mm grenade launchers
7.	6 120 mm grenade launchers
8.	5 B-10, 82 mm recoilless rifles
9.	25 B-11/107 mm recoilless rifles
10.	60 RPG-2 rocket-propelled anti-tank grenade launchers with 3,600 40 mm grenades
11.	5,000 MPi-K Kalashnikov assault rifles
12.	9,000 MPi-41 Soviet machine pistols with ammunition
13.	3,500 German Schmeisser machine guns with ammunition (MPi-43/44
14.	350 Degtyaryov (Soviet) light machine guns with ammunition
15.	80 MG 34, German machine guns with ammunition
16.	2,200 carbines with ammunition
17.	18 20 mm anti-aircraft guns with 100,000 tracer shells
18.	150,000 anti-personnel fragmentation land mines
19.	3,500 Soviet F-1 fragmentation hand grenades
20.	12 GP-60 tractors
21.	12 units of helmets, uniforms, backpacks

Source: "Liste über Hilfeleistungen von Bewaffnung und Ausrüstung, II. Vereinigte Arabische Republik, 1967/68 Unterstützung im Zusammenhang mit der israelischen Aggression insgesamt 44 Positionen mit dem Gesamtwert von 44,0 Mio. M," GVS-Nr.: A 76 752, BAB DC 20/13069.

1973, East Germany shipped 15,000 of them to North Vietnam, 25,000 to Egypt, and another 25,000 to Egypt in 1974. In 1973, 1974, and 1975 East Germany exported 35, 55, and 65 million M-43 cartridges used in the AK-47, respectively.[55] From 1970 to 1974, East Germany delivered approximately 580,000 Kalashnikov assault weapons and machine guns to the armed forces of Egypt and Syria, repaired and serviced about 125 of their MiG fighter jets, and delivered millions of bullets, many thousands of rocket-propelled anti-tank grenades and land mines, and millions of cartridges.

[55] Sekretär ... Gerhard Weiss, "Vermerk über die Ergebnisse der Beratung vom 15. February 1973 (Anordnung des Vorsitzenden des Ministerrat vom 30.9.1969)," BAB DC 20/ 12897, 182–185.

These weapons would be targeted primarily against the soldiers and civilians of the state of Israel. The weapons went to the arsenals of Egypt and Syria but also, given their state support for the Palestinian terror organizations, to the latter as well. When Ulbricht, Honecker, Hoffmann, Stoph, and Weiss approved these weapons shipments and programs of military training, they had to know that the intended targets were the Jews in Israel. The delivery of thousands of Kalashnikovs, RPGs, hand grenades, and dozens and eventually hundreds of artillery pieces and dozens of the most modern Soviet MiG fighter jets constituted an active intervention in an ongoing war on the side of states and terrorist organizations seeking to destroy the state of Israel by force of arms.

By 1970, the Palestinian terror organizations and the militant Arab states viewed East Germany as a likely source for weapons. In May, leaders of the Saika guerrilla organization in Syria sent a detailed request for weapons to the East German military attaché in Damascus, who then sent it to the Defense Ministry.[56] East German officials in both Damascus and East Berlin were receptive.[57] The Saika leaders asked for 8,000 MPi Kalashnikov machine guns; 1,000 (Soviet) Degtyaryov machine guns; 1,000 Soviet shoulder launched rocket-propelled grenade launchers (RPG-7); 900 shoulder launched anti-tank grenade launchers (RPG-2); 300 Grinov machine guns; 200 Fla 12.7 mm or 14.7 mm machine guns; 50 82 mm grenade launchers; 200 60 mm grenade launchers; 12,000 Simonov carbine rifles; radio equipment; 20,000 anti-tank grenades; and unspecified amounts of explosives, anti-tank mines, infrared equipment.[58] In the weeks preceding Iraq's opening of diplomatic relations with East Germany, the then–vice president of Iraq, Saddam Hussein, spoke with Horst Hähnel, first secretary of the East German Embassy in Baghdad.[59] He asked whether East Germany could deliver 20,000 automatic and

[56] Schutz, Leiter der Abteilung für Internationale Verbindung in MfNV to Heinz Keßler, GVS-Nr. A 76486, [East] Berlin (April 17, 1970), "Betr.: Waffenbedarfsliste der palästinensischen Widerstandsorganisation 'Al-Saika,' " Sekretariat des Ministers. Schriftverkehr mit dem Vorsitzenden des Ministerrat u. dem Minister für Staatssicherheit, BAMA, MfNV, DVW1 115538, 1970. Iraq. PLO, 37–38.

[57] Ibid.

[58] Ibid., 31. Presumably the request was filled. When requests were not filled, the files generally contain a letter explaining a negative decision.

[59] Heinz Hoffmann to Gerhard Weiss [East] Berlin (May 23, 1970), GVS-Nr. A 76486, Sekretariat des Ministers. Schriftverkehr mit dem Vorsitzenden des Ministerrat u. dem Minister für Staatssicherheit, DVW1 115538, 1970. Iraq. PLO, 27–28. On Hähnel see ""Hähnel, Horst," in Siegfried Bock, Ingrid Muth, Herman Schwiesau, eds., *DDR-Außenpolitik: Ein Überblick, Daten, Fakten, Personen (III)* (Berlin: LIT Verlag, 2010), 309.

semiautomatic pistols as well as anti-tank rocket-propelled grenade launchers (RPG-7), which were "urgently needed." Iraqi Foreign Minister Sheikhly discussed the arms deliveries with Winzer in talks in May about recognition.[60] Hoffmann's briefing points for a 1971 trip to Syria indicated that in 1969, the GDR had delivered to the Syrians free of cost a German-language laboratory as well as 5,000 machine pistols (43/44) and 12 million cartridges.[61]

THE EAST GERMAN MILITARY LEADERS' TRIP TO THE MIDDLE EAST IN 1971

The expanding alliance of the Soviet bloc with the Arab states entailed weapons shipments as well as travel back and forth by high-ranking officials. In October 1971, Defense Minister Hoffmann led a high-level military delegation to Iraq, Syria, Lebanon, and Egypt.[62] The members of the delegation included Admiral Paul Verner, head of the East German Navy; Deputy Defense Minister General Werner Fleißner; General Fritz Streletz, deputy chief of staff of the National People's Army; and General Horst Strechbarth, in charge of military training in the Defense Ministry.[63] Their task was "to deepen the friendly relations … that exist on the basis of common efforts in the battle against the American global strategy and imperialist policy."[64] According to East Germany's director of its trade

[60] Heinz Hoffmann to Gerhard Weiss [East] Berlin (May 23, 1970), GVS-Nr. A 76486, "Anlage I: Abschrift," 29.

[61] "Kostenlose Hilfslieferung, GVS-Nr.: A 76–948," BAMA DVWI 115671, MfNV Sekr. D. Ministers. Unterlagen zur Vorbereitung d. Militärdelegation in den arabischen Staaten, 25–26.

[62] Heinz Hoffmann to General Hamad Shehab, [East] Berlin (October 1971), BAMA, BVW 1/115671, "MfNV Sekr. D. Ministers. Unterlagen zur Vorbereitung d. Militärdelegation in den arabischen Staaten," 2–3; and BAMA DVW 1/115673; MfNV Sekretariat des Ministers : Militärdelegation der DDR nach Syrien, Ägypten, Irak Okt 1971 ; nach Algerien Juni 1972 ; nach Syrien, Mai 1983, Mai 1987 ; Palästinensischen Befreiungsorganisation (PLO) in der DDR Nov. 1987 ; and Heinz Hoffmann to General Mohamed Ahmed Sadek, [East] Berlin (October 1971), BAMA, "MfNV Sekr. D. Ministers. Unterlagen zur Vorbereitung d. Militärdelegation in den arabischen Staaten," DVWI 115671, 6–7.

[63] "Politische Gespräche und Eindrücke: Bericht über den Aufenthalt einer offiziellen Militärdelegation der Deutschen Demokratischen Republik in der Republik Iraq, der Syrischen Republik und der Arabischen Republik Ägypten in der Zeit vom 13.-31. Oktober 1971."

[64] Ibid., 2. On October 20, 1971 a photo was taken of the meeting of the East German and Syrian military leaders in Damascus. It is available in the German Federal Archive in Koblenz but due to a lack of information about the rights to the photo it is not available for digital and hence also not for print publication. The archive citation is: Bundesarchiv Koblenz, Bildarchiv: Bild 183-K01022-322, ADN-BZ, Pohl.

mission in Beirut, the trip to Lebanon had been a great success. About "sixty reports" with photos regarding the Hoffmann delegation's visit to the Middle East appeared in the Lebanese press, which was read in "many other" Arab states. One could say "without exaggeration" that Hoffmann's trip had "contributed to raising the regard and authority of the GDR in the whole region."[65]

In Egypt, the group laid a wreath at Nasser's grave and at the Egyptian memorial to the unknown soldier. They drove to the front with Israel at the Suez Canal, visited the Egyptian military college in Cairo and a naval base in Alexandria, and met with President Sadat for an hour.[66] Hoffmann described West Germany as the strongest ally of the United States in Europe and one that offered "support for the Israeli aggressors." Sadat replied, "The Germans have always been highly regarded here but the Egyptians find their flirting with Israel incomprehensible."[67] In Cairo as in Damascus and Baghdad, Arab leaders fondly recalled the Politburo's emphatic support during the Six-Day War. Egyptian General Mohammed Ahmed Sadek stressed that the Egyptians would "never forget the GDR's stance toward Israeli aggression in 1967."[68] Since 1967, the Egyptians had learned a great deal about electronic warfare and air defense and would be "glad to offer their experiences of the last three years to our brothers in the GDR," including actions in enemy territory and elimination of enemy artillery. Hoffmann said that the NVA could offer its experience with amphibious tanks, overcoming water barriers, and the use of frogmen *(Kampfschwimmern)* as well as "our extensive experience in political education and the battle against the enemy's ideological diversion."[69] The delegation signed agreements for Sadek to lead a military delegation to the GDR in 1972. The East Germans invited 10 to 15 Egyptian generals to visit East Germany in the remainder of 1971 while others were invited for training in East German military institutions.[70]

[65] Gerhard Herder to Heinz Hoffmann, Beirut (December 13, 1971), "MfNV Sekr. D. Ministers. Unterlagen zur Vorbereitung d. Militärdelegation in den arabischen Staaten," DVWI 115671, 8–9. On Herder see "Herder, Gerhard," in Barth et al., *Wer war Wer in der DDR*, 294.

[66] "Politische Gespräche und Eindrücke: Bericht über den Aufenthalt einer offiziellen Militärdelegation der Deutschen Demokratischen Republik in der Republik Iraq, der Syrischen Republik und der Arabischen Republik Ägypten in der Zeit vom 13.-31. Oktober 1971," 23–24.

[67] Ibid., 23–24.

[68] Ibid., 25.

[69] Ibid., 27.

[70] Ibid., 29–30.

In Iraq from October 14 to 19, the Hoffmann delegation met with President and General Secretary of the Baath Party Ahmad Hassan al-Bakr; Saddam Hussein, then deputy chair of Baath Party and of the Revolutionary Council; and Hammad Shehab, Iraq's minister of defense.[71] In conversations with his Iraqi counterparts, Hoffmann stressed "the commonalities of our struggle against imperialism and Zionism." Al-Bakr said Iraq faced "imperialist encirclement and had a right to more support" owing to "ideological commonalities." Hoffmann reported that "without exception, all of our conversation partners – from the president to individual officers in personal talks – assured [our] delegation of their great sympathy, yes love of the people of Iraq and they themselves felt for the German people and the GDR." They "repeatedly expressed" pride that Iraq was the first non-Communist state that offered diplomatic recognition to the GDR. The Iraqis thus expected more support from the GDR and the "socialist states," that is, the Communist regimes of the Soviet bloc. Hoffmann noted that East Germany itself only produced weapons to a "limited degree," yet it could offer training and send expert delegations. Agreements were signed for visits by Iraqi military leaders to East Germany.[72]

HEINZ HOFFMANN MEETS MUSTAFA TLASS IN DAMASCUS

During the week of October 19–24, 1971, the Hoffmann delegation visited Syria.[73] It was an important step in the early phases of what became East Germany's most important state-to-state relationship in the Middle East. The delegation met with President Hafez al Assad and with General Mustafa Tlass, the deputy commander in chief of armed forces and chief of the General Staff. In 1972, Tlass became Syria's defense minister and remained in that position for a remarkable 32 years, until 2004. Hoffmann stressed the need for a close alliance with Soviet Union and Warsaw Pact states in order to "further change of balance of forces in

[71] Ibid., 3–4.

[72] Ibid., 7.

[73] A photo of the meeting between the East German and Syrian military leaders was taken on October 20, 1971. It shows Heinz Hoffmann, East German Deputy Minister of Defense and his fellow East German officers sitting across a table from Syria's Defense Minister, Muteib Shenan. Because digital rights to the photo are not available, it is also not possible to use it in this print edition. The photo is in the files of the German Federal Archive in Koblenz, Germany. The archive citation number is: Bild 183-K1022-322, Allgemeiner Deutscher Nachrichtendienst, Zentralbild.

favor of forces of progress."[74] Assad praised Soviet help in military and civilian area.

Judging from the reports of their conversations and the effusive toasts they offered to one another, it appears that Hoffmann and Tlass developed a relationship that was at least one of mutual respect and perhaps one of friendship and mutual admiration. At their first visit in Damascus in October 1971, Tlass expressed some views that Hoffmann had heard from other "leading officers of the Arab armed forces." Tlass conveyed his "unlimited admiration of fascist Blitzkrieg strategy and of the actual accomplishments of the bourgeois German military."[75] As we will see, Tlass's admiration for Germany's past military accomplishments went hand in hand with a deep hatred of the Jews.

While in Syria, Hoffmann gave interviews to the Syrian press. He assured one questioner, "We are convinced that you will be victorious in your battle against the enemy. We are fighting against the same enemy! The American imperialists support our enemies in Europe and give Israel money and weapons in order to protect their imperialist interests." Regarding the Syrian Army he added, "I say clearly and openly that I will be engaged in support of your army." After meeting with its officers and men, Hoffmann was convinced that "the Syrian Army can fight the enemy that has occupied your country."[76]

The Hoffmann delegation signed agreements for a return visit by Mustafa Tlass and others to East Germany in 1972. They were the beginning of regular exchanges of working delegations between the two defense

[74] Ibid., 15.

[75] "Bericht über den Aufenthalt einer offiziellen Militärdelegation der Deutschen Demokratischen Republik in der Republik Iraq, der Syrischen Republik und der Arabischen Republik Ägypten in der Zeit vom 13.-31. Oktober 1971, MfNV. Sekretariat des Ministers. Militärdelegation der DDR nach Syrien, Ägypten, Irak, [East] Berlin (n.d.), BAMA, DVW 1/115673/, 17. The German reads: "*die rückhaltlose Bewunderung der faschistischen Blitzkriegsstrategie und der sachlichen Leistungen der bürgerlichen deutschen Militärs*"].

[76] "Herr Verteidigungsminister der DDR spricht zu 'Jaych-Ach-Chaab': Bericht über den Aufenthalt einer offiziellen Militärdelegation der Deutschen Demokratischen Republik in der Republik Iraq, der Syrischen Republik und der Arabischen Republik Ägypten in der Zeit vom 13.-31. Oktober 1971, MfNV. Sekretariat des Ministers. Militärdelegation der DDR nach Syrien, Ägypten, Irak, [East] Berlin (n.d.), BAMA, DVW 1/115673/; also see Heinz Hoffmann, "Anlage: Betr.: Vorschläge und Gedanken zu den Antworten für Abschluß-Interview" in Bericht über den Aufenthalt einer offiziellen Militärdelegation der Deutschen Demokratischen Republik in der Republik Iraq, der Syrischen Republik und der Arabischen Republik Ägypten in der Zeit vom 13.-31. Oktober 1971, MfNV. Sekretariat des Ministers. Militärdelegation der DDR nach Syrien, Ägypten, Irak, [East] Berlin (n.d.), BAMA, DVW 1/115673/.

ministries regarding "political-ideological matters ... combat training and the work of the general staff." The 1971 agreement also included "scientific-technical cooperation" and exchange of experiences about technology and the "repair of military weapons." Tlass, who later started his own publishing company, promised to translate German-language works on "military science" into Arabic.[77] In his report on the trip after returning to East Germany, Hoffmann concluded that his traveling to Egypt, Iraq, and Syria had been "a complete success in a political and military sense for the GDR and its armed forces." It was evidence of "the growth of the international authority of our state and contributed to raising the authority of the National People's Army."[78] In Egypt, Iraq, and Syria, there was "uniform agreement" that "the importance of the trip lay in bringing [East Germany's] military relationships [with these Arab states] to the level of the already intensive economic, scientific-technical and cultural connections."[79]

Hoffmann reported that of the three countries, he found Syria to be the "most advanced in a social and political sense." All three states saw the Soviet Union as "the most important ally of the Arab peoples in their battle against imperialism and Zionism." In general, the delegation had been "met with a broad wave of friendship toward the German Democratic Republic and to its National People's Army."[80] Yet it was Baathist Syria that left "the most positive impression" regarding the character of its officer corps and soldiers. It was also in Syria that the delegation saw "the strongest Soviet influence."[81] In view of the fascist lineages of Baathist ideology, the East German–Syrian alliance was an ironic one.[82] If the East German soldiers and diplomats were uncomfortable

[77] "Vereinbarungen: "Bericht über den Aufenthalt einer offiziellen Militärdelegation der Deutschen Demokratischen Republik in der Republik Iraq, der Syrischen Republik und der Arabischen Republik Ägypten in der Zeit vom 13.-31. Oktober 1971, MfNV. Sekretariat des Ministers. Militärdelegation der DDR nach Syrien, Ägypten, Irak, [East] Berlin (n.d.), BAMA, DVW 1/115673/, 21.

[78] "Schlußfolgerungen: Bericht über den Aufenthalt einer offiziellen Militärdelegation der Deutschen Demokratischen Republik in der Republik Iraq, der Syrischen Republik und der Arabischen Republik Ägypten in der Zeit vom 13.-31. Oktober 1971, MfNV. Sekretariat des Ministers. Militärdelegation der DDR nach Syrien, Ägypten, Irak, [East] Berlin (n.d.), BAMA, DVW 1/115673/, 30.

[79] Ibid.

[80] Ibid., 33.

[81] Ibid., 35–36.

[82] On the Baath, see Fouad Ajami, *The Arab Predicament: Arab Political Thought and Politics since 1967* (New York: Cambridge University Press, 1981), 40–50; the discussion of Michel Aflaq and the Baath's ideological lineages in Kanan Makiya, *The Republic of Fear: The Inside Story of Saddam's Iraq* (Berkeley and Los Angeles: University of

with Syrian expressions of enthusiasm for fascism or anti-Semitism, past or present, they did not leave evidence of such displeasure in the files of the East German Foreign and Defense Ministries.[83] The shared interest in defeating Western influence, that is, imperialism and Zionism, trumped concerns about the legacies of anti-Semitism in the Baath's origins and policies.

WEAPONS DELIVERIES, 1972–1974

Partly as a result of the agreements reached during the Hoffmann trip of 1971, the Weiss committee decided to send 2,200 Kalashnikovs produced in East Germany to Syria and 1,200 to Iraq along with 15 million cartridges to Egypt, 7 million to Syria, and 8 million to Iraq. The 1972 shipments would also include 12,000 anti-tank hand grenades for Egypt, 6,000 for Syria, and 3,000 for Iraq; as well as 15,000 helmets to Egypt, 5,000 to Syria, and 5,000 to Iraq. The Weiss committee's plans for the next years envisaged at least a tenfold expansion in arms deliveries to the Arab states. In 1973, they called for sending 35,000 Kalashnikovs to Egypt and 10,000 to Syria as well as to Iraq. In 1974, in the aftermath of the Yom Kippur War, the plan envisaged sending 60,000 Kalashnikovs to Egypt, 30,000 to Syria, and 10,000 to Iraq. The figures for planned shipments in 1975 were 55,000 to Egypt, 25,000 to Syria, and 15,000 to Iraq.[84] Though East Germany's defense industries produced only a small fraction of what was manufactured in the Soviet arms factories, they were still able to deliver considerable amounts of lethal firepower into the hands of Israel's most fierce and uncompromising enemies. In short, in 1974 and 1975, East Germany sent another 100,000 Kalashnikovs to the Arab states.

In addition to their own versions of the Kalashnikov assault rifle, East German industries produced excellent optical targeting devices, aiming control devices for anti-tank weapons and tanks, instructional manuals for driving tanks, as well as air-conditioning systems for the Soviet T-54. The latter was of obvious importance for tank battles in the deserts of

California Press, 1989), 183–228; and Daniel Pipes, *Greater Syria: The History of an Ambition* (New York: Oxford University Press, 1990).

83 "Schlußfolgerungen: Bericht über den Aufenthalt einer offiziellen Militärdelegation der Deutschen Demokratischen Republik in der Republik Iraq, der Syrischen Republik und der Arabischen Republik Ägypten in der Zeit vom 13.-31. Oktober 1971, 35–36.

84 "A. Mögliche Exportlieferungen 1972, GVS-Nr.: A 76 947," BAMA DVWI 115671, MfNV Sekr. D. Ministers. Unterlagen zur Vorbereitung d. Militärdelegation in den arabischen Staaten, 17.

the Middle East.[85] The East German military also offered to train Syrian officers on the use of the Soviet T-54 tank as well as anti-tank artillery. It also trained Syrian mechanics in repair and reconditioning of Soviet T-54 and T-54a tanks, Soviet anti-aircraft guns (Fla-SFL-57-2), and anti-tank artillery systems.[86] In a 1971 memo, Hoffmann reported that the value of current exports to Egypt was 30 million marks, and that the focus of East German efforts was on the Egyptian Air Force and Navy, especially the "repair of the MiG-21" in factories in Dresden. In 1971, East Germany exported the following items to Egypt: 29,000 Kalashnikov machine pistols; 85,000 pairs of protective clothing; 2,000 repair and replacement kits for the AK-47s; 12 sets of spare parts for the MiG-21, as well as lighting grenades for paratroops and parachutes. The Kalashnikovs were delivered with "special credit" arrangements between East Germany and Egypt, while other materials were paid with letters of credit.[87]

On April 23, 1969, Deputy Defense Minister General Heinz Keßler wrote to Gerhard Weiss that in view of the many countries requesting weapons, it was necessary to establish "political considerations" and priorities for deliveries.[88] By April 1971, Weiss, in discussion with Politburo member Herman Axen, articulated those priorities in a memo prepared for adoption by the Politburo.[89] In view of "very limited" means available for exports and aid, Weiss and Axen divided countries into five groups: those that had political and economic importance for East Germany (Group 1); primarily political importance (2); economic importance (3); minimal political and economic importance (4); and specific importance for the GDR (5). Groups 1 and 2 accounted for more than 70 percent of East

[85] "Ausbildungs- und Wartungsgeräte bzw. –mittel, GVS-Nr.: A 76 947," BAMA DVWI 115671, MfNV Sekr. D. Ministers. Unterlagen zur Vorbereitung d. Militärdelegation in den arabischen Staaten, 20–21.

[86] "Mögliche Unterstützung in Fragen der Ausbildung und Wartung durch die NVA, GVS-Nr.: A 76–947," BAMA DVWI 115671, MfNV Sekr. D. Ministers. Unterlagen zur Vorbereitung d. Militärdelegation in den arabischen Staaten, 22–24.

[87] "Arabische Republik Ägypten (ARÄ): Beziehungen der speziellen Außenwirtschaft zu den militärischen Organen der ARÄ," BAMA DVWI 115671, MfNV Sekr. D. Ministers. Unterlagen zur Vorbereitung d. Militärdelegation in den arabischen Staaten, 37–38.

[88] Heinz Keßler to Gerhard Weiss, April 23, 1969, Schriftverkehr mit Staatliche Organen MR, MdI, MfS, MFAA 1969. VAR, SAR. Iraq, BAMA DVWI 115537, 27–28.

[89] Gerhard Weiss to Willi Stoph, "Bildung von Schwerpunkten in den Beziehungen der DDR z Entwicklungsländern," [East] Berlin, April 15, 1969, BAB DC 20/13006, 1–2; and Gerhard Weiss to Willi Stoph, "Schwerpunktbildung in den Beziehungen der DDR zu Entwicklungsländern für den Zeitraum 1971–1975," [East]Berlin, April 15, 1969, BAB DC 20/13006, 3–27.

Germany's foreign trade and exchange.[90] On the basis of these criteria, Weiss and Axen concluded that the countries in Group 1, that is, those that had both political and economic importance for East Germany, were Egypt, Syria, Iraq, Algeria, Sudan, India, Ceylon, and Chile.[91] The largest amount of foreign trade with any developing country between 1965 and 1970 was with Nasser's Egypt, where it expanded from 235 million marks to 437 million, followed by Syria (16 to 68 million) and Iraq (15 to 49 million). The countries in Group 1 accounted for 845 million marks of foreign trade and exchange, or 71 percent of East Germany's total trade with developing countries.[92] Egypt, Syria, and Iraq were all "progressive anti-imperialist national states" that adopted versions of a "non-capitalist path" in economic policy and advocated "close cooperation" with the Soviet Union.[93] So, of the eight countries in Group 1, the three most important were the three Arab states. Of the 28 countries listed in all five groups, the three with the highest priority were the Arab states. The findings in the East German government files confirm the conclusions of the CIA estimates about the priority given to support for the Arab states in Soviet-bloc and East German military assistance programs.

SPEECH AND SILENCE ABOUT TERROR: ISRAEL AT THE UNITED NATIONS AND THE COMMUNISTS IN EAST BERLIN

The Communist press did not report terrorist attacks by the PLO and its affiliates against Israeli civilians. In the aftermath of the Six-Day War, Egypt, Jordan, and Syria continued to attack Israel with irregular forces and lend support to Palestinian organizations that did so. The attacks of 1967 to 1973 were called a war of attrition. At the United Nations, the Israeli delegation offered regular reports about them. On January 25, 1969, Joel Barommi, Israel's acting UN representative, circulated a

90 Weiss to Stoph, "Schwerpunktbildung in den Beziehungen der DDR zu Entwicklungsländern für den Zeitraum 1971–1975," 3.

91 "Schwerpunktbildung in den Beziehungen der DDR zu Entwicklungsländern für den Zeitraum 1971–1975," 8–9. Countries in Group II were Yemen, Tanzania, Guinea, Congo, Nigeria, and Zambia; Group III: Brazil, Colombia, Mexico, Libya, Lebanon, Kuwait; IV: Burma, Cambodia, Maldives, Central African Republic, Somalia; V: Indonesia, Pakistan, Singapore, and Ghana.

92 "Schwerpunktbildung in den Beziehungen der DDR zu Entwicklungsländern für den Zeitraum 1971–1975," 8–11. But also note that India was a significant trade partner (239 million in 1965 but down to 216 million in 1970).

93 Gerhard Weiss, "Anlage 2: Thesen zur Auswahl von Schwerpunkt – Entwicklungsländern für den Zeitraum 1971–1975," BAB DC 20/13006, 12–13.

statement by Israel's Foreign Minister Abba Eban to the president of the Security Council. His office, in accord with the UN dissemination system, sent the text to the delegations of all UN member states. Eban responded to a speech delivered by Gamal Abdel Nasser in Cairo on January 20, 1969, during which the Egyptian president said the following:

In talking about the forces of the Arab struggle, I must stress the glorious actions carried out by the Palestinian resistance forces. The rise of these resistance organizations, the crystallizing of their objectives and the expansion of their activities are one of the conspicuous features of the period after June 1967. These organizations raised a flaming torch at a time of darkness and despair.... They fulfill a vital task in sapping the enemy's strength and spilling his blood. In your name I express our admiration and appreciation to the four major organizations: El Fatah, the Popular Front, the Liberation Organization and the Arab Sinai Organization.... The Palestinian resolve must be given freedom to express itself without hindrance. It must be given the fullest opportunity to achieve its aspirations, without any guardianship. The UAR [United Arab Republic] has maintained a consistent position in this matter since the heroic task of the Palestinian resistance began. In pursuance of this policy, the UAR places all its resources at the disposal of these organizations, without condition or reservation. In line with the same policy, the UAR appreciates the attitude taken by the Palestinian organization in rejecting the Security Council resolution of 22 November 1967 that was accepted by the UAR. They are entitled to reject this resolution, which may serve the purpose of eliminating the consequences of the aggression carried out in June 1967, but is inadequate for determining the Palestinian fate.[94]

Eban said that Nasser's statement had "far-reaching and deeply disturbing implications" regarding maintenance of the cease-fire under the Security Council resolution of June 6, 1967, and that of November 11, 1967, which called for a just and lasting peace. Though the Arab governments officially accepted the cease-fire, they had "been continuing an armed struggle against Israel through irregular forces and terrorist organizations operating from their territory and with their political and material support."[95] Israel would hold the Arab governments responsible. Nasser

94 Joel Barromi, "Letter from Israeli Minister of Foreign Affairs Abba Eban sent in Letter dated 25 January 1969 from the Acting Permanent Representative of Israel to the United Nations Addressed to the President of the Security Council," UNSC, l (25 January 1969), UN ODS S/8978, 2. Also see Yosef Tekoah, "Letter dated 5 February 1969 from the permanent representative of Israel to the United Nations addressed to the Secretary General," UNSC (February 5, 1969), UN ODS S/8994, 1–2. In it Tekoah referred to a recent speech by Nasser in which he "again promised his unreserved support for the pursuance of terror warfare against Israel in breach of the Security Council's cease-fire resolutions"; and Yosef Tekoah, "Letter dated 7 May 1969 from the Permanent Representative of Israel addressed to the President of the Security Council," UNSC (May 7, 1969) UN ODS S/9194, 1–2.

95 Ibid.

was violating the principles of the UN Charter that rejected "aggression by one State against another." Instead Egypt's leader supported the continuation of "armed struggle for the ultimate liquidation of Israel" and thus regarded it "as logical and warranted for the terrorist organizations to reject the Security Council resolution." Resolution 242 had called for "termination of all claims or states of belligerency and respect for and acknowledgment of the sovereignty, territorial integrity and political independence of every State in the area and their right to live in peace with security and recognized boundaries free from threats or acts of force."[96] Eban argued that Nasser's speech and his policy in 1969 were repudiations of the "letter and spirit" of Resolution 242. Nasser's speech, rather than pointing to a durable peace, offered an "ominous concept of continued warfare."[97] Several weeks later, Israel's UN Ambassador Yosef Tekoah (1925–1991) (Figure 4.3) wrote to the president of the Security Council "concerning the warfare by terror continuously being waged by the United Arab Republic against Israel." He said that material gathered from "recent engagements with saboteurs in the Sinai strengthens the evidence" that they were the creation of the Egyptians, "openly recruited" in Egypt, and "dispatched by intelligence officers" of the UAR armed forces, and that this activity had been going on "sporadically since July 1968."[98] Yet the anti-Israeli majority at the UN succeeded in keeping the issue of Arab and Palestinian terrorism off the agenda.

The Israeli UN delegation sent voluminous documentation about the campaigns of terrorism against Israel through the mechanisms available to them at the UN. They did so in statements to the General Assembly, in emergency sessions of the Security Council, and in the hundreds of letters they sent to the office of the secretary general and to the presidents of the Security Council. On February 28, 1969, for example, Ambassador Yosef Tekoah informed the president of the Security Council – and thus all the UN member delegations who always received such communications – about terror attacks "in the last five weeks" mostly carried out "by a terror organization known as el-Fatah." As a result the Israeli air force had attacked Al-Fatah bases between Damascus and Beirut. The targets were operational headquarters; a logistics, administrative, and supply center;

[96] For the text of Resolution 242 see the UN Official Documents Website, unispal.un.org/unispal.nsf/0/7D35E1F729DF491C85256EE700686136.

[97] Ibid., 2–4.

[98] Yosef Tekoah, "Letter dated 12 February 1969 from the Permanent Representative of Israel to the United Nations addressed to the President of the Security Council," UNSC (February 5, 1969), UN ODS S/9004, 1–2.

FIGURE 4.3. Yosef Tekoah, Israel's UN ambassador, 1968–1975.
Source: Israel National Photo Collection, Government Press Office, D749-130.

sites for induction and instruction of recruits; a "reassignment center for el-Fatah members who return from training in Egypt, Algeria and communist China"; and a prison and interrogation branch. It was from the base at el-Hamma in Syria that "acts of terror and murder against Israeli citizens have been initiated and conducted.... The Government of Syria has for years openly sponsored, organized, supported and directed terror warfare against Israel."[99] Tekoah quoted Syrian Foreign Minister Ibrahim Makhus on December 7, 1968, expressing support for the Fedayeen, that is, Syrians engaged in terror attacks on Israel, as "the pioneers of the popular war of liberation." Syria had rejected the Security Council resolution of November 22, 1967, calling for an end to belligerency.[100] Hence, in reply to Syria's letters to the Security Council in April 1969 protesting the Israeli raids, Tekoah said that it had "no right or grounds for complaint

[99] Yosef Tekoah, "Letter dated 28 February 1969 from the Permanent Representative of Israel to the United Nations addressed to the President of the Security Council," (February 5, 1969), S/9033, 1.

[100] Ibid., 1–2.

over defense measures taken by Israel on its side of the cease-fire line," especially in view of "repeated Syrian attempts to violate the cease-fire by its regular forces and by marauders and saboteurs." Syrian attacks on Israel at the UN were efforts to "divert attention from his Government's persistent policy of aggression," opposition to peacemaking, and waging of terror warfare.[101] It was with this Syrian government that East Germany was consolidating a military and political alliance, a truly "special relationship" of friendship and solidarity, in contrast to West German neutrality in the Middle East conflict.

From March to June 1969, Tekoah sent more than ten reports about terrorist attacks and shelling on Israel towns from Jordanian territory.[102] On May 17, he reported that Jordan's deputy prime minister had said publicly of the terror organizations, "We give them all they want. Any

[101] Yosef Tekoah, "Letter dated 15 April 1969 from the Permanent Representative of Israel to the United Nations addressed to the President of the Security Council," UNS (April 15, 1969), UN ODS S/9158. Also see Yosef Tekoah, "Letter dated 25 April 1969 from the Permanent Representative of Israel to the United Nations addressed to the President of the Security Council," UNSC (April 25, 1969), UN ODS S/9177. "Since the policy of the Syrian Government consistently remains one of war on Israel until it is destroyed, Syria has no moral, legal or logical basis for tendering advice to Israel on how Israel should defend itself against Syria's aggressive aims."

[102] Yosef Tekoah, "Letter dated 10 March 1969 from the Permanent Representative of Israel to the United Nations Addressed to the Secretary General," UNSC UNODS (10 March 1969), S/9065. On Israeli retaliation see Muhammad H. El-Farra, "Letter dated 12 February 1969 from the Permanent Representative of Israel to the United Nations Addressed to the Secretary General," UNSC UN ODS (February 13, 1969), S/9006. Other letters from Tekoah that spring are Yosef Tekoah, "Letter dated 17 March 1969 from the Permanent Representative of Israel to the United Nations Addressed to the Secretary General," UNSC UN ODS (March 17, 1969), S/9089. Also see letters by Tekoah on March 27, 1969 (S/9114); Yosef Tekoah, "Letter dated 8 April 1969 from the Permanent Representative of Israel to the United Nations Addressed to the Secretary General," UNSC UN ODS (March 10, 1969), S/9137; Yosef Tekoah, "Letter dated 20 April 1969 from the Permanent Representative of Israel to the United Nations Addressed to the Secretary General," UNSC UN ODS (April 20, 1969), S/9166; Yosef Tekoah "Letter dated 28 April 1969 from the Permanent Representative of Israel to the United Nations Addressed to the Secretary General," UNSC UN ODS (28 April 1969), S/9180; Yosef Tekoah "Letter dated 21 May 1969 from the Permanent Representative of Israel to the United Nations Addressed to the Secretary General," UNSC UN ODS (21 May 1969), S/9217, 1–2; Yosef Tekoah "Letter dated 21 May 1969 from the Permanent Representative of Israel to the United Nations Addressed to the Secretary General," UNSC UN ODS (May 21, 1969), S/9217, 1–2; Yosef Tekoah "Letter dated 24 May 1969 from the Permanent Representative of Israel to the United Nations Addressed to the Secretary General," UNSCOT UN ODS (May25, 1969), S/9217, 1; Yosef Tekoah "Letter dated 28 May 1969 from the Permanent Representative of Israel to the United Nations Addressed to the Secretary General," UNSCOT UN ODS (20 May 1969), S/9228, 1–2.

support they ask of us is given to them. We meet them regularly."[103] On June 23, 1969, Tekoah informed the secretary general, "Thus far this year there have been 600 acts of aggression [against Israel] committed from Jordanian territory. In the last two months there were 40 attacks by artillery, 107 by mortars, 17 by tanks, 17 by Katyusha rockets and 7 by anti-tank and recoilless guns. In addition there were 48 cases of mining and 24 attempts to cross the cease fire-line."[104] These "incessant acts of aggression from Jordan" constituted an "obstacle to a just and lasting peace in the area."[105] In a separate letter sent on June 23, Tekoah informed Secretary General U Thant that three bombs exploded in rapid succession in a 16-foot-wide street that served as passageway for worshippers on their way to the Western (Wailing) Wall in Jerusalem. The Popular Front for the Liberation of Palestine, which had its headquarters in Amman, Jordan, published a communiqué "admitting responsibility for the attack."[106] It was soon after the spate of terrorist attacks described in Tekoah's letters that the SDS travelers from West Germany visited Palestinian guerrilla bases in Jordan.

Terrorist attacks on Israel also originated in Lebanon, a development that became increasingly serious as Lebanon descended into civil war and the authority of the government in Beirut over southern Lebanon eroded. On August 12, 1969, Tekoah informed the secretary general of the "intensification of armed attacks" against Israel carried out from Lebanon. In the "last month alone, twenty-one attacks by shelling, firing and mining were carried out against inhabited localities in Israel"; four Israeli soldiers and four civilians were wounded. It was "generally known" that Lebanon harbored "concentrations of irregular forces which are engaged in waging terror warfare against Israel." Israel responded with a raid on "terror encampments on slopes of Mount Herman."[107] On August 25, Tekoah informed the UN that "armed terrorists groups

[103] Yosef Tekoah "Letter dated 28 May 1969 from the Permanent Representative of Israel to the United Nations Addressed to the Secretary General," UNSC (May 20, 1969), UN ODS S/9228, 1–2.

[104] Yosef Tekoah "Letter dated 23 June 1969 from the Permanent Representative of Israel to the United Nations Addressed to the Secretary General," UNSC (June 23, 1969), UN ODS S/9274, 1–2.

[105] Ibid., 2.

[106] Yosef Tekoah "Letter dated 23 June 1969 from the Permanent Representative of Israel to the United Nations Addressed to the Secretary General," UUNSC (June 23, 1969), UN ODS S/9277, 1–2.

[107] Yosef Tekoah, "Letter dated 12 August 1969 from the Permanent Representative of Israel addressed to the President of the Security Council," INSCOR (August 12, 1969), UN ODS S/9387, 1. For report of further attacks, also see Yosef Tekoah, "Letter dated

have established bases on Lebanese territory and openly operate across the cease-fire lines, by means of firing on Israel villages, infiltration, mine-laying, sabotage and other acts of armed violence in violation of the cease-fire." Israel held the government of Lebanon responsible for restoring quiet on cease-fire lines.[108] On September 4, 1969 Tekoah reported "eleven instances of aggression from Lebanese territory, in violation of the cease-fire." All of the attacks, including the shelling of the town of Kiryat Shmona, "were directed against civilian targets and their objective was murder [for] murder's sake."[109] On October 10, Tekoah wrote to the president of the Security Council to report that "since 1 August 1969 there had been forty-eight" armed attacks against Israel from Lebanon.[110] Six were carried out with Katyusha rockets, six with mortars, ten involved use of bazookas, six used small arms fire, eight laid mines, two clashed with Israeli patrols, and five assaulted vehicles. "Most of these acts of aggression were directed against Israeli villages and their civilian inhabitants. They resulted in four Israeli citizens killed and nineteen wounded." Their continuation required Israel "to take appropriate measures of self-defense."[111]

On December 4, 1969, Edouard Ghorra, Lebanon's ambassador to the UN, described the Israeli retaliation as one aimed at civilians. On December 15, Tekoah replied that such charges were "false." The IDF had taken action against "a para-military encampment which serves as a base for terror operations against Israel," in the course of which twelve members of the irregular forces were killed and "many others" were wounded. "Large quantities of arms and ammunition were seized. No civilian targets were attacked and there were no civilian casualties." These facts had been "confirmed by the Lebanese Press."[112] Since writing to the secretary general in August, "acts of aggression carried out

15 August 1969 from the Permanent Representative of Israel addressed to the President of the Security Council," UNSCOR (August 12, 1969), UN ODS S/9392.

108 Yosef Tekoah to U Thant, "Note to the Secretary General," UNSC (August 25, 1969), UN ODS S/9393/Add.2., 1.

109 Yosef Tekoah, "Letter dated 4 September 1969 from the Permanent Representative of Israel addressed to the President of the Security Council," UNSC (September 5, 1969), UN ODS S/9431.

110 Yosef Tekoah, "Letter dated 10 October 1969 from the Permanent Representative of Israel addressed to the President of the Security Council," UNSC (October 10, 1969), UN ODS S/9470.

111 Ibid.

112 Yosef Tekoah, "Letter dated 15 December 1969 from the Permanent Representative of Israel addressed to the President of the Security Council," UNSC (December 15, 1969), UN ODS S/9556.

against Israel" from bases in Lebanon had "increased particularly in the wake of the agreement concluded between the Government of Lebanon and terror organizations whereby Lebanon permits these organizations to operate in and from its territory in flagrant violation of the cease-fire and the United Nations Charter." In the past five weeks, there had been six artillery attacks and four mining raids into Israel from Lebanon, and thus Israel was "obliged to take defensive measures for the protection of its territory and its population from armed attack."[113]

Tekoah reported that in the last week of December 1969 alone, there had been more than 120 attacks from Jordan. Thirty included indiscriminate shelling, including a hit on a nursery home for the elderly in Kibbutz Massada. Tekoah called it part of a "campaign of aggression aimed at inflicting casualties and destruction on the Israeli civilian population."[114] On January 22, 1970, he referred to "the intolerable situation created by the intensification of aggression from Jordan against Israel." In "the last four weeks," 23 armed attacks on Israeli villages had taken place. On January 20, a unit of IDF entered the area south of the Dead Sea from which the attacks had originated and encountered a saboteur squad moving toward Israel. In the ensuing clash, five members of the squad were killed. The Israeli unit seized two jeeps with the El Fatah insignia, one with a recoilless machine gun, in addition to Kalashnikov rifles, bazookas, and grenades. Tekoah reiterated "the urgent need for the Government of Jordan to put an immediate end to the acts of aggression coming from its territory against Israel."[115] But the attacks continued. On June 1, 1970, Katyusha rockets struck the residential district of Beit Shea, killing a 10-year-old girl and wounding three of her girlfriends when it hit the entrance to their school. From late April to the end of May 1970, Tekoah reported that there had "been 281 armed attacks from Jordan in which six Israelis were killed and sixteen wounded" due to shelling of eleven villages and the town of Beit Shean. The June 1 deaths were the second time in last ten days that "Israeli children are murdered in this terror war directed against the civilian targets and openly proclaimed and supported by the Arab governments." The attacks were an "Arab

[113] Ibid., 1–2.

[114] Yosef Tekoah, "Letter dated 5 January 1970 from the Permanent Representative of Israel addressed to the President of the Security Council," UNSC (January 5, 1970), UN ODS S/9592.

[115] Yosef Tekoah, "Letter dated 22 January 1970 from the Permanent Representative of Israel addressed to the President of the Security Council," UNSC (January 22, 1970), UN ODS S/9821, 1.

campaign of premeditated murderous aggression which is being conducted against the Israeli civilian population."[116]

On June 3, 1970, Tekoah sent to the Security Council a detailed account of an attack on the Israeli town of Tiberias.

> At 1800 hours the town of Tiberias came under artillery fire from Jordan. The fire was concentrated entirely on the residential and commercial districts at an hour when the streets were crowded with shoppers and inhabitants returning home from work. Some of the 130mm shells of Soviet manufacture fell into the courtyard of the Beit Sefer Makif High School, next to the Hagalil High School, the "Elisheva" theatre and the Central Synagogue of Tiberias, in which a Torah scroll was damaged. A man and a woman were killed. Six civilians were wounded. One of them, a twenty-five year old pregnant woman, is in critical condition. The Israeli Defense Forces, supported by aircraft, returned fire against the sources of the artillery fire in the Irbid areas and of the Katyusha rocket fire in Beit Shean earlier in the day.[117]

These were some of the results of the weapons flowing from the Soviet bloc, including East Germany, to the Arab states and the Palestinian terror organizations and of the translation of anti-imperialist and anti-Zionist rhetoric into military attacks.

ARAFAT AND PLO LEADERS VISIT EAST BERLIN

From October 29 to November 2, 1971, during this period of attacks from Jordan and Lebanon on Israel, Yasser Arafat led a delegation of 10 members of the PLO, including Farouk Kaddoumi (Abu Lutf), on their first official visit to East Berlin.[118] (See figure 4.4.) The invitation was from East Germany's Afro-Asian Solidarity Committee (AASK) and followed the PLO delegation's ten-day trip to the Soviet Union. The delegation met with Politburo member Herman Axen. Arafat told Axen that just as the GDR was "in the front trench of the battle for socialism, so the PLO was in the front trench of the battles of the Arab nation." When the

[116] Yosef Tekoah, "Letter dated 3 June 1970 from the Permanent Representative of Israel addressed to the President of the Security Council," UNSC UN ODS (June 4, 1970), S/9817. The eleven villages were Ashdot-Yaacov, Kiar Rupin, Yavnal, Maoz-Haim, Dagania, Hamadia, Gesher, Tel-Katzir, Menahamiya, Masada and Yardena.

[117] Yosef Tekoah, "Letter Dated 4 June 1970 Addressed to the President of the Security Council from the Permanent Representative of Israel," United Nations Security Council, New York, June 4, 1970, UN OCS, S/9821.

[118] "Information über den Aufenthalt einer Delegation der PLO in der DDR," [East] Berlin (November 11, 1971), PAAA MFAA, C 7678, Abt. Naher- und Mittlereer Osten, "Besuche von Delegationen der PLO in der DDR, 1971, 1973–1979," 63–71.

FIGURE 4.4. Yasser Arafat and PLO delegation at Brandenburg Gate in East Berlin, November 2, 1971.
Source: German Federal Archive, Koblenz, Photo Archive: Bild 183-K1102-032, ADN-ZB, Klaus Franke.

East Germans inquired about differences within the PLO, Arafat replied that "the imperialists played them up." He called airplane hijackings "left-wing child's play" (*linke Kindereien)*. In contrast to public presentation of a divided and faction-ridden organization with rival and independent decision makers, he insisted that in 1971 "99 per cent of the armed forces of the Palestinian movement were unified under the leadership of the PLO."[119] From November 1971 on, the East German Politburo knew what Israeli and West German intelligence agencies also believed to be the case, namely, that the seemingly distinct Palestinian organizations were part of one umbrella organization called the PLO, which controlled "99 percent" of the weapons. Tactical differences existed, but the PLO's goal was to destroy the existing state of Israel and return the several million Palestinians to Israel proper.

119 Ibid., 64. German: "Jetz seien jedoch 99% der bewaffneten Kräfte der Palästinensischen Bewegung unter Führung der PLO vereinigt."

Arafat told the East Germans that though the Arab states had ceased fire after Nasser's death, the PLO would continue the battle. He hoped to open a PLO office in East Germany. Arafat repeatedly criticized West Germany for its financial assistance to Israel, which made it possible for Israel "to commit crimes against the Arabs." His "primary enemy was USA imperialism." Axen concluded that relations with the PLO should be deepened via the Afro-Asian Solidarity Committee and that "political and material support would be strengthened." Though he rejected the proposal to open a PLO office in East Berlin at that point, he directed the Foreign Ministry to examine that possibility.[120] East German relations with both the Arab states and the PLO were expanding as the latter was intensifying its terrorist campaign against Israel.

120 "Information über den Aufenthalt einer Delegation der PLO in der DDR," [East] Berlin (November 11, 1971), PAAA MFAA, C 7678, Abt. Naher- und Mittlereer Osten, "Besuche von Delegationen der PLO in der DDR, 1971, 1973–1979," 65–67.

5

Palestinian Terrorism in 1972: Lod Airport, the Munich Olympics, and Responses

On May 30, 1972, three members of the Japanese Red Army, a terrorist offshoot of the Japanese New Left, arrived at Lod Airport in Tel Aviv on Air France flight 132 on the Paris–Rome–Tel Aviv route. In the airport's baggage claim area, they retrieved Kalashnikov assault rifles and hand grenades concealed in their luggage, opened fire, and threw the hand grenades at passengers in the baggage waiting area. They killed 25 people, most of them tourists from Costa Rica, and wounded 78 people in all. One of the terrorists was captured. Two were killed, one accidentally shot by his colleague, the other after landing on a hand grenade. An Israeli journalist wrote, "The scene here at Lod Airport is like after a pogrom. Broken glass panes, doors riddled with bullet holes and blood patches on every side."[1] The attack was coordinated with the Popular Front for the Liberation of Palestine (PFLP). Aside from the destruction of the Swissair flight in 1970 that claimed 47 lives, the Lod Airport attack was the worst single attack in Israel in the post-1967 terrorist campaign carried out by a member organization of the PLO's Executive Committee.

In her speech to the Knesset about the previous day's "wicked act of murder," Israeli prime minister Golda Meir spoke caustically about "the so-called war of liberation the terrorist organizations are waging.... Woe to any revolution, local or global, which is built on blood and murder, conducted in the name of murder. Immediately after they heard of last night's incident, both Cairo and Beirut hailed a great victory. Scores of people

[1] "The Attack at Lod Airport," BBC, *SWB*. Part 4. *The Middle East and Africa* (June 1, 1972), ME/4003/SA/6.

were killed and wounded. And their joy knows no bounds."[2] Judging from the broadcasts of the PLO following the attack, Meir's comment that "their joy knows no bounds" was on the mark. A political culture that celebrated terrorist attacks on Israel was fully in evidence. On May 31, 1972, the BBC monitoring service recorded the following broadcast on *Voice of Fata*h radio in Arabic in Cairo regarding the Lod massacre:

> (i) The great, humane, revolutionary choice by a group of youths [the members of the Japanese Red Army, JH] who were born thousands of miles from Palestine demonstrates the greatness of these youths, which is equal to the justness of the Palestine cause. It also indicates the position our cause occupies on the world level. Finally, it shows that revolutionaries of the world stand in one rank against Zionism, imperialism and the enemy entity.
>
> (ii) The attack on the enemy at Lod airport, which is considered a bridge for transport between the occupying state and the world and a main station for immigrants, is fatal blow to all Zionist immigrations plans the speedy results of which will appear immediately. This in fact is the most serious and important aspect of the operation at the occupied Palestinian Lod airport.[3]

The *Voice of Fatah* statement – thus of Arafat, leader of Al Fatah and chair of the PLO's Executive Committee of which the PFLP was a member – regarded the attack as justified and praised the murderers as "great" and even "humane." It defined the civilians who were killed and wounded in the attack as "the enemy." The participation of the Japanese was taken as evidence that the Palestinians were part of an international terrorist network. As barbaric and senseless as the attack was from a moral point of view or as a way to resolve the conflict with Israel, the *Voice of Fatah* stressed that it had a clear purpose, namely, to deliver a literally "fatal blow" to Israel's efforts to attract immigrants and tourists by making all of Israel, not only the areas occupied since the 1967 war, a dangerous place for anyone to visit or live. It was part of the strategy to isolate and destroy the state of Israel by force that was enshrined in the PLO Charter.

[2] Prime Minister Golda Meir, "Text of Mrs. Golda Meir's Knesset statement" (broadcast live), BBC, *SWB*. Part 4. *The Middle East and Africa* (June 1, 1972), ME/4003/A/9.

[3] "Fida'I Broadcasts on the Lod Airport Attack: (a) *Voice of Fatah* (Cairo) in Arabic 1630 gmt 31 May 1972," BBC, *SWB*. Part 4. *The Middle East and Africa* (June 3, 1972), ME/4004/A/10. The *Voice of Fatah* described "the spread of revolutionary culture in the world" in a broadcast on the Japanese participation in Lod airport attack in "Excerpts from Commentary," from *Voice of Fatah* (Cairo) in Arabic 1630 gmt June 1, 1972, *SWB*. Part 4. *The Middle East and Africa* (June 3, 1972), ME/4005/A/11.

According to Cairo radio monitored by the BBC, the morning papers of June 1 "depict the operation as the most daring fida'I [short for fida'yin] operation in the heart of the enemy's own territory, in which 27 persons were killed and 80 others were wounded." The papers quoted "eye-witness accounts of this thrilling, daring operation and eye-witness statement about how the fida'yin fired their machine-guns with calm faces expressing no anger, how the operation was carried out in a matter of minutes, and how Israel's soldiers were mesmerized and failed to fire even a single shot."[4]

On June 2, East Germany's *Neues Deutschland* (or *ND)* ran a one-paragraph article on page 7 with the headline "Attack threatened again." Its news was that Lebanon's UN ambassador had written to the Security Council to protest Israel's "new attack on his country." With Prime Minister Meir's speech in the Knesset in mind, it reported that "chief of the cabinet Meir and Foreign Minister [Abba] Eban announced new acts of aggression against neighboring Arab states – above all Lebanon." Of the events at Lod airport, it said: "Israel used the serious incident at the airport in Tel Aviv in which Japanese extremists on Tuesday evening perpetrated a frightful bloodbath, as a pretext for its latest act of aggression."[5] It offered no details about the attack and said nothing about the cooperation between the Japanese Red Army terrorists and the PFLP or about the enthusiasm the attack elicited from Al Fatah and other Arab and Palestinian outlets.

Another consistent pattern of Communist journalism regarding Israel was never to lend credibility to anything said by Israeli government spokesmen or by Jewish groups abroad about events in the Middle East. In spring 1972, anti-Semitic legislation affecting the 4,000 Jews remaining in Syria became a source of concern in Israel and for Jews in Western Europe and the United States. On June 18, *Neues Deutschland* reported that a "Religious Council" presumably connected to the Syrian government described those concerns as a "campaign of defamation organized and directed by Israel." According to this council the criticism of the new legislation was "an unacceptable intervention in our affairs and an effort by Israel to exert authority over us." So faced with Jews in Israel and

[4] "Cairo home service in Arabic 0425 gmt June 1, 1972: Excerpts from morning press review," BBC, *SWB*. Part 4. *The Middle East and Africa* (June 3, 1972), ME/4004/A/10. Also see "Other Arab Comment on the Lod Airport Attack: (b) *Voice of Fatah* (Cairo) in Arabic 1630 gmt June 2, 1972," BBC, *SWB*. Part 4. *The Middle East and Africa* (June 3, 1972), ME/4004/A/10.

[5] "Überfällen erneut bedroht," *Neues Deutschland* [East] Berlin (June 2, 1972), 7.

elsewhere who expressed concern about persecution of Jews in Syria, *ND*, and hence the East German government, took the side of the Baath regime. The issue of anti-Semitism in the Arab states was a non-issue as far as *Neues Deutschland* was concerned.[6]

BLACK SEPTEMBER AND THE ATTACK ON THE ISRAELI ATHLETES AT THE MUNICH OLYMPICS

In September of 1970, the government of Jordan attacked PLO camps in Jordan. In the fall of 1971, Arafat and one of his close associates, Mohammed Daoud Oudeh (a.k.a. Abu Daoud), formed the Black September organization. The name was taken from the month in which the Jordanian army expelled the PLO and its bases from Jordan. By late 1971, Salah Khalaf (a.k.a. Abu Ayad), who later became the chief of the PLO's intelligence agency, became its immediate commander. The attack by Black September terrorists on eleven members of Israel's Olympic team at the Munich Olympics on September 5, 1972 was not the worst terror attack on Israelis by Palestinian terror organizations in this period. But, because of the presence of the world press and other media, it was the most famous. The Black September operatives seized eleven members of the Israeli Olympic team hostage and demanded the release of 236 "political prisoners" held in Israeli jails including Okamoto Kozo, the Japanese Red Army member captured during the Lod airport massacre, as well as Andreas Baader and Ulrike Meinhof of the Red Army Faction in West Germany. On September 6, the hostage drama ended in a shoot-out at the Feldfürstenbruck airport outside Munich. In the course of the failed effort to rescue the hostages, the terrorists murdered all of the Israeli athletes. One West German policeman and five of the terrorists died.[7]

In the aftermath of the Munich attack, the East German government did something that it did not do again: it publicly condemned a terrorist attack whose victims were Israelis. However, as an East German government broadcast on September 5 indicated, it did so without addressing the fact that the victims were Israelis and Jews. Rather it expressed "abhorrence" about what it called "a crime against the Olympic Games," which

[6] On these issues as well as on the expulsion of the Jews from the Arab countries, see George Bensoussan, *Juifs en Pays Arabes: Le grand deracinement, 1850–1975* (Paris: Editions Tallandier, 2012); and Martin Gilbert, *In Ishmael's House: A History of Jews in Muslim Lands* (New Haven, CT: Yale University Press, 2011).

[7] David Clay Large, *Munich 1972: Tragedy, Terror and Triumph at the Olympic Games* (New York: Rowman & Littlefield, 2012), 201–248.

united the world's athletes and thereby were "contributing to the cause of peace."[8] The Black September organization had "gravely harmed not only the Olympic idea but also the Arab cause." The GDR had "never left any doubt that in the struggle against the consequences of Israeli aggression" it stood firmly on the side of the Arab states. "But bloody terror and political murder are not the proper means to reach a just and peaceful solution. They do not advance the world by a single step towards the goal of Israeli evacuation of the occupied Arab territories." The event was "as pointless as it is horrible."[9] The same evening, a radio commentary asserted that "official circles in the GDR capital strictly condemn the abominable crime" and that "we, GDR and its citizens, definitely reject terror as means of achieving political ends." Such attacks were "most harmful to the Arab liberation struggle" and only served those "opposed to a peaceful settlement of the Near East problems."[10] An abundance of evidence in the East German archives indicates that these assertions were half-truths and, in some sense, simply lies. The East German government armed and trained terrorists who were engaging in attacks on Israelis in Israel. As we will see, East Germany opposed terrorist attacks carried out by Arabs and Palestinians in Western Europe whose origins could be traced back to East German territory. Yet *ND* did not report the names of the Israeli athletes who were killed, the names of the terrorists who killed them, their demands to release prisoners in West German and Israeli prisons, or the discussion in the West about the relationship between Arab governments and the PLO and Black September.

Neues Deutschland also had not reported on terrorist attacks on Israel's northern towns carried out by the Palestinian organizations that had gathered in southern Lebanon after they had been expelled from Jordan in September 1970. Rather, on September 10, 1972 it published a page 1 story about "the criminal attack by Israeli air pilots on Palestinian refugee camps in Lebanon and Syria" that caused, so it claimed, 61 deaths and 200 injuries. A second article had the headline "[Moshe] Dayan's air gangsters murder innocent women and children."[11] On September 16, *ND* led with "GDR

[8] "East Germany: 'Abhorrence' (a) Radio GDR home service 2110 gmt Sept. 5, 1972," BBC, *SWB*. Part 4. *The Middle East and Africa* (September 7, 1972), EE/4086/C/1.

[9] Ibid.

[10] "Except from commentary by Karl-Heinz Tesch: (b) Berlin (GDR) home service 1935 gmt 5 Sept. 1972," BBC, *SWB*. Part 4. *The Middle East and Africa* (September 7, 1972), EE/4086/C/2; "Terrorsanschlag im olympischen Dorf unterbrach die Spiele," *Neues Deutschland* [East] Berlin (September 6, 1972), 1; and "Zum terroristischen Überfall auf das olympische Dorf," [East] Berlin, *Neues Deutschland* (September 6, 1972), 2.

[11] "Israelische Luftpiraten morden," and "Dayans Luftgangster ermordeten wehrlose Frauen und Kinder," *ND* [East] Berlin (September 1, 1972), 1 and 4.

denounces Israel's barbaric air attack on Syria and Lebanon: Millions announce their firm solidarity with the just struggle of the Arab peoples." The party and government mobilized mass organizations; in factories and schools in East Germany, citizens "expressed their horror and anger about the crimes of the power holders in Tel Aviv." The SED's organizations of youth and women and its peace council, German-Arab Friendship Society, and the Afro-Asian Solidarity Committee issued statements and organized protests to demand that Israel immediately stop "its acts of aggression and leave the occupied Arab territories."[12] On September 17, *ND* led with "Government and people of the GDR raise enraged protests against Israel's acts of aggression."[13]

Neues Deutschland's response to the Munich attack was an exception to the rules that implicitly governed Communist political warfare against Israel in the next 17 years. Some of those rules were the following: First, if the victims of terror were Israeli, the attack was never to be called terrorism. Rather it was "resistance." Second, unless the attack took place in Western Europe and was widely reported, if the perpetrators were Arab or Palestinian and the victims were Israelis, nothing should be reported about the event at all. Third, if the attack did take place in Western Europe, the media were to write, say, or broadcast as little as possible about the identity of the perpetrators. It should condemn terrorism as a tactic that harmed the Arab/Palestinian cause. Fourth, Israeli and American references to Arab and Palestinian terrorism were to be called forms of "slander" and "defamation" of a justified "struggle for national liberation." Fifth, the focus of coverage and condemnation should be on Israel's acts of self-defense and retaliation. As the attacks to which it was responding were not previously mentioned, every Israeli attack on terrorist bases in Lebanon and Syria could be described as an act of unprovoked aggression rooted in the alleged racist and expansionist essence of Zionist ideology and policy. Sixth, when conflicting factual assertions were made by Arabs, Palestinians, and Israelis about the ongoing war, the press and other media were always to assume that the Arab and Palestinian assertions were true and that those of Israeli and pro-Israeli Jewish organizations were false. The obvious implication was that the government of Israel lied all the time. Seventh, all suggestions that this kind of journalism and propaganda had anything whatsoever

[12] "DDR verurteilt barbarisch Luftangriffe Israels auf Syria und Lebanon," *ND* [East] Berlin (September 16, 1972), 1.

[13] "Regierung und Volk der DDR erheben flammenden Protest gegen Aggressionsakt Israels," *ND* [East] Berlin (September 17, 1972), 1.

to do with anti-Semitism were to be dismissed as slander and defamation and clever tactics to fend off legitimate criticism of imperialism and Zionism. These basic rules of Communist journalism reinforced the previously mentioned paradox of justifying terror waged against Israel and presenting Palestinians as innocent victims of injustice.

In particular in view of the significant document destruction in fall 1989 of East German government files, it is not possible to establish whether or not the East German government had contact with the Black September group before the Munich attack. Yet, as a Stasi report on Black September that drew on the extensive reporting in the West German press indicated, the East Germans knew a lot about the organization.[14] They knew that Black September had connections to the Red Brigades in Italy, the Black Panthers in the United States, the IRA in Northern Ireland, Japanese Maoists, the Baader-Meinhof group in West Germany, and armed groups in Turkey. From Beirut to Algeria, young Palestinians received military training, then spent time in "Bulgaria, Hungary and Yugoslavia," where they became familiar with Europe. They then received forged Syrian, Iraqi, and Jordanian passports to travel to West Germany, where they declared themselves to be students and concentrated in Frankfurt/Main, Hamburg, and Munich. As foreign students, many received monthly stipends of 500 to 700 marks from the West German government, some of which was sent on to the Palestinian organizations in Beirut. Black September recruited among these students at West German universities, especially via the 3,000 members of the General Union of Palestinian Students (GUPS). The Stasi authors apparently found credible an interview given to the West German weekly magazine *Quick* in fall 1972 in which a representative of Black September said, "We were picked up by our German friend Hans. Hans and his friends provided us with knives, pistols, machine guns and hand grenades." He estimated that there were about "2,000 people in Germany that help us and other Arab organizations" and that a contact person existed in all the major cities. Hence, the Stasi report concluded, "The FRG had developed into a center and a focus of the activities of Black September in Western Europe."[15] It

14 "Auskunftsbericht zur Organisation 'Schwarzer September'" (February 1973) Der Bundesbeauftrage für die Unterlagen des Staatssicherheitsdienstes der ehemaligen Deutschen Demokratischen Republik, BStU, Zentralarchiv, MfS-Hauptverwaltung Aufklärung (HVA), Nr. 1038, 1–19. The Stasi found *Quick* magazine of those years to be of particular of interest, but also see *Stern*, *Die Zeit*, *Frankfurter Allgemeine*, *Süddeutsche Zeitung*, *Die Zeit*, and the *Tagesspiegel*.

15 Ibid., 13.

offered a complete list of the terrorist attacks carried out by the group from November 1971 to January 1973.[16] Though the report noted that the PLO had denied any links to Black September, the "vagueness (*Nebelhäftigkeit*) and indefiniteness (*Unbestimmtheit*) was convenient." In any case, the "spectacular 'success' " of the organization contributed to "a certain popularity" and to a leading position among the "Arab resistance organizations."[17] The report included an organization chart that placed Black September as under the control of Al-Fatah and connected to the GUPS, the General Union of Palestinian Workers (GUPW), the PFLP, and Al-Fatah.

Following Israel's raids on camps of the PLO and its affiliates, William Buffum, the American ambassador in Lebanon, sent a cable to the US State Department in Washington with a "poststrike" assessment of casualties at three of Israel's target areas in Lebanon. American diplomats were struck that "fedayeen casualties appear extremely light" but that the toll "in and around an orange grove near Al Barid refugee camp has risen to 10 dead (seven children, one elderly Palestinian and 2 Lebanese adults."[18] He doubted that the strikes would have much deterrent effect. Rather the "Fedayeen seem pleased with themselves for having brought about Israeli retaliation which has so aroused Arab public opinion." He observed that the Arab press and political commentary "completely ignores two Fedayeen initiated incidents along the Lebanese-Israeli border on September 6–7 and seems convinced IAF [Israeli Air Force] raids were motivated entirely by desire to avenge Israel's dead Olympians." Hence most Lebanese hostility was directed at Israel rather than the Fedayeen and provided a "welcome shot in the arm for commando morale." Buffum concluded that "the sequence of events over past week is likely to generate (rather than discourage) increased Fedayeen enthusiasm for further terrorist operations."[19]

Buffum's dispatch captured the Israeli dilemma. The absence of self-defense would make life in Israel intolerably dangerous and lead to an exodus of its citizens and thus to political and military defeat. Yet attacks from the air at terrorist bases, which saved the lives of Israeli

[16] Ibid., 15–17.

[17] Ibid., 17–19.

[18] William Buffum from Embassy Beirut to Secretary of State, Washington, DC, "Confidential Beirut 09696, Israeli Raids on Lebanon and Syria," Beirut (September 12, 1972), United States National Archives and Records Administration, College Park, NACP RG59 General Records of the Department of State, SNF, 1970–73, Political and Defense, Pol 27 From ARAB ISR 7.1.72 to Pol 27 ARAB ISR 1/1/73, Box 2060.

[19] Ibid.

soldiers on the ground, were a relatively blunt instrument that entailed the possibility of civilian casualties, the numbers of which were sure to be inflated by the Arab countries and echoed by the Communist and leftist press. The efforts to destroy the terrorist bases and kill or capture the terrorists would receive more press coverage than the Palestinian attacks that the Israelis were trying to stop. The Communist and Arab press would assert that the attacks on civilians were intentional Israeli policy. The United Nations would function as a global echo chamber of those assertions. Even if accurate figures were later made known, the damage to Israel's standing inflicted by initial impressions regarding Israel's alleged misdeeds was hard to repair.

In the following broadcast from Damascus about the Black September attack in Munich the PLO's *Voice of Palestine* on September 6 offered an example of the political culture to which Prime Minister Meir had referred after the Lod airport attack. "Congratulations to the Arab nation on [*sic* for] its] brave sons who have recorded pages of glory and heroism in Germany."[20] It presented the Munich attack as one that redeemed and restored Arab dignity and self-respect. In place of past defeats the "Palestinian Arab fida'iy that stood his ground at Munich airport and himself detonated the bomb is prepared to detonate hundreds of bombs against the Zionist occupation here in our country.... Congratulations on the revolution and on the new man who is bearing the banner of Arabism on the path to victory. Glory, glory and immortality to our noble martyrs. It is a revolution till victory."[21] The idea that killing unarmed hostages contributed to creating "the new man" recalled fascist and Nazi celebrations of the redemptive power of violence as well as the arguments of the Algerian radical Frantz Fanon regarding the intrinsic value of terror and violence for supposedly overcoming colonial legacies.[22] Though the Black September terrorists had murdered the hostages, the *Voice of Palestine* later that same evening rejected that view. "The real murderer is the arrogance of the Zionist enemy, who insisted on not complying with the fid'iyan's humane demand" to release prisoners from Israeli

[20] "Arab Reaction to the Munich Incident: (a) *Voice of Palestine* (Syria) in Arabic 1200 gmt 6 Sept. 1972," BBC, *SWB*. Part 4. *The Middle East and Africa* (September 8, 1972), ME/4087/A/4–5.

[21] Ibid., A/5.

[22] See Frantz Fanon, *The Wretched of the Earth* (New York: Grove Press, 1963). On notions of the new man emerging from World War I, see discussion of Ernst Juenger in Jeffrey Herf, *Reactionary Modernism: Technology, Culture and Politics in Weimar and the Third Reich* (New York: Cambridge University Press, 1984).

jails including the surviving member of the Lod airport attack group. The "real murderer is the deception of the Federal German authorities" and NATO.[23] The responsibility for murder lay with everyone but those who pulled the triggers on the Kalashnikovs and the pins on the hand grenades.

On September 7, Arafat issued a statement about the Black September attack in the Kuwaiti paper *Al Quabas:* "The Palestine Resistance is one body and fights for one aim: to regain Palestine, the Arab land usurped by Zionism which has also rendered its inhabitants homeless and ill-treated them with the ugliest forms of oppression, coercion and terror."[24] If, as Arafat insisted, the Palestine "resistance" was "one body," the PLO and Black September were part of the same organization, namely, the one directed by Arafat. He shared its purpose of regaining "Palestine," that is, the whole of what was by then all of the state of Israel. In the Arab press, he spoke of "one body," but to the Western press he described the PLO as including some extremist organizations over which he had no control or influence.

Also on September 7, the *Voice of Palestine* in Syria offered a rationale for the recent "operations" of Black September. The recent "revolutionary strikes upset the calculations made and torpedo the plans and settlements which have been arranged after every attack against the Palestinian Revolution. The false peace and the peace imposed by terror of the enemy disappear whenever the Palestine Resistance deals a violent blow." The "main aim" of "the Resistance" was "to thwart any settlements," and that aim could "only be realized by daring and most violent operations, to upset calculations, block the road and torpedo [words indistinct]" efforts at negotiated solutions.[25] The *Voice of Palestine* ascribed a clear purpose to terror, namely, to stand in the way of a negotiated settlement of the conflict between Israel and the Arab states, and between Israel and the

[23] "Arab Reaction to the Munich Incident: (a) *Voice of Palestine* (Syria) in Arabic 1800 gmt 6 Sept. 1972," BBC, *SWB*. Part 4. *The Middle East and Africa* (September 8, 1972), ME/4087/A/6. For a statement by Black September extolling the "heroes" in Munich see "Black September Organization Statements on the Munich Incident," *Voice of Palestine* (Cairo) in Arabic 1707 gmt 7 Sept. 1972," Text of statement on the "Kafr Bar am and Iqrit operation in Munich," BBC, *SWB*. Part 4. *The Middle East and Africa* (September 8, 1972), ME/4088/A/3.

[24] "Yasir Arafat on the Munich Incident: Iraqi News Agency in Arabic, 1025 gmt 7 Sept. 1972," BBC, *SWB*. Part 4. *The Middle East and Africa* (September 8, 1972), ME/4088/A/7.

[25] "Palestinian Radio Comment on Fida'i Operations: *Voice of Palestine* (Syria) in Arabic 1200 gmt 7Sept. 1972," BBC, *SWB*. Part 4. *The Middle East and Africa* (September 8, 1972), ME/4088/A/9–10.

Palestinians that diplomats hoped was emerging. In that sense, the Lod and Munich attacks, like the assassination of the Archduke Ferdinand in Sarajevo in 1914, Robert Kennedy (by the Palestinian terrorist Sirhan Sirhan), and Rev. Martin Luther King, Jr. in 1968, stood in a longer tradition of terrorism that aimed to destroy the possibilities of peaceful resolution of conflicts.[26]

The Munich attack shocked a global audience, but for the Israelis, it was another in a long line of attacks. On September 6, Ezer Weizman, then chair of the Herut Party in Israel, said that while the world's attention was focused on Munich, Israel "had tragedies before." Munich was "one link in a chain" of a campaign against Israel that "originated in Cairo and Damascus," both of which needed to understand "more than they have understood up to now that they are responsible" for the terrorist campaign.[27] In his address at the memorial service for the slain Israeli athletes, Israel's Deputy Prime Minister Yigal Allon also placed the Munich attack in a longer chain of events. "Inhuman creatures" had placed time bombs in a busy market and a student cafeteria and had murdered schoolchildren on the way to school, "massacred Israelis and foreign pilgrims in a crowded terminal," and cynically "exploited naïve girls and turn[ed] them into living bombs in crowded airliners" (bombs were given to unknowing women by their Arab "boyfriends" to carry on planes). These people, he continued, were not freedom fighters but "a detestable gang whose only purpose is genocide" and sowing death in order to undermine prospects for peace. The Arab states that were supporting and harboring them would be held responsible. Allon praised West German federal president Gustav Heinemann, who, at a memorial service in Munich, spoke of the link between the Arab states and the terrorist organizations. The Israelis expected "all states to act in this manner." In contrast to those who said that desperation had driven the Palestinians to terror, Allon said: "All the disasters which the Palestinians have suffered were the result of their extremism and blindness. If they

[26] Christopher Clark has recently drawn attention to this dimension of the assassination of the Archduke Ferdinand and his wife in Sarajevo on 1914 in *Sleepwalkers: How Europe Went to War in 1914* (New York: HarperCollins, 2012), 3–64 and 367–403.

[27] "Israeli Leaders' Reactions to the Munich Incident: Israel in English 1130 gmt 6 Sept. 19 72," "Text of interview with Ezer Weizman, Herut Party Chairman," "Palestinian Radio Comment on Fida'i Operations: Voice of Palestine (Syria) in Arabic 1200 gmt 7 Sept. 19.72," BBC, *SWB*. Part 4. *The Middle East and Africa* (September 8, 1972), ME/4087/A/3–4.

have not learned this lesson, they have learned nothing. Peaceful methods can solve everything, their problem as well."[28]

On September 7, 1972, the Soviet Union's Arabic-language station broadcast "Israeli 'Policy of Genocide' towards Arab Peoples." It asserted that "oppression and genocide have been raised by Tel Aviv to the level of official policy to be carried out against the Arab peoples.... The criminal policy of the Israeli aggressors" continued unabated.[29] Broadcasting this text two days after the Munich massacre sent a message to the Palestinian terrorist organizations that the Soviet Union was an ally that would offer political cover for their attacks on Israelis. In addition, it repeated what had become a standard theme of Soviet anti-Israeli propaganda, namely, that the Israelis were criminals and mass murderers.

On September 9, following what it called "a long series of acts of sabotage and murder," the Israeli air force attacked terrorist bases in Syria and Lebanon including three naval bases maintained by Fatah on the coast of Lebanon. The Israelis claimed that Syria supported an estimated 9,000 armed men while 5,000 "terrorists" were dispersed in southern and eastern Lebanon in refugee camps.[30] On the following day, the *Voice of Palestine* (*VOP*) claimed that the Israelis were attacking "civilian targets with premeditation." The *VOP* broadcast pledged that "the blood of your sons will not be wasted. It is a pledge to you from our fighters who reaped glory in Munich and stood fast at Lod airport. It is a pledge and an oath that the enemy children and settlers will never know sleep after today. It is not only our children who die as a result of murder and treachery."[31] The reference to "enemy children" made clear that the PLO was intentionally targeting Israeli civilians. The Israeli air force was doing its best to avoid striking civilians. *VOP* radio made clear that PLO fighters planned to do exactly the opposite.

[28] "Allon Address at Lod Airport Memorial Service," Israel home service in Hebrew 1210 gmt 7 Sept. 1972," BBC, *SWB*. Part 4. *The Middle East and Africa* (September 9, 1972), ME/4088/A4/1.

[29] "Israeli 'Policy of Genocide' towards Arab Peoples," Moscow in Arabic, 1700 gmt 7 Sept. 1972, BBC, *SWB*. Part 4. *The Middle East and Africa* (September 9, 1972), ME/4088/A/12. Ibid.

[30] "Israeli Air Attacks on Syria and Lebanon, Israel home service in Hebrew 1500–1900 gmt 8 Sept. 1972," BBC, *SWB*. Part 4. *The Middle East and Africa* (September 12, 1972), ME/4089/A/1–2.

[31] "Fida'i Radio Appeals for Action, *Voice of Palestine*, (Syria) in Arabic 0430 and 1200 gmt 9 Sept. 1972," BBC, *SWB*. Part 4. *The Middle East and Africa* (September 12, 1972), ME/4090/A/6.

The political culture of celebration of terrorism was also on full display in Muammar el-Qaddafi's Libya. His government sent a plane to return the bodies of "the five martyrs," that is, the Palestinian terrorists killed in the shoot-out at Feldfürstenbruck airport. On September 12, a "solemn funeral procession for the heroic fida'yin who were martyred in the Munich incident by bullets of treachery and treason" took place in Tripoli. The procession was led by the governor of Tripoli, members of El-Qaddafi's Arab Socialist Union, representatives of Al Fatah in Tripoli, and Arab diplomats. "The mourners carried placards welcoming the martyrs on the soil of the Arab revolution" in Libya. Prayers were said for "the souls of the martyrs" in Tripoli's Martyr's Square and "eulogies glorified the spirit of sacrifice and revolution in the hearts of these young men who had sacrificed their lives cheaply for their just cause."[32] In Tripoli, as well as Damascus and Cairo, public celebration of terror and martyrdom had become embedded in parts of Arab political culture.[33]

One of the most chilling responses to the Munich attack came from Uganda's president, Idi Amin, in a rambling, disjointed letter he sent on September 13, 1972, to United Nations Secretary General Kurt Waldheim. He sent copies to Golda Meir and Yasser Arafat. Amin wrote that the Israelis had "occupied Palestine" for 25 years, killed "many thousands of Palestinians," and had made them "slaves of Israel."[34] In addition to his crude hatred of Israel, Amin openly expressed enthusiasm both for Adolf Hitler and for the Nazis' effort to exterminate European Jewry.

> For the Israelis who were taken to Palestine by Britain, it would be better if they are settled in Britain, instead of Palestine because they were taken there internationally by Britain. The same British tactics were used in Rhodesia by Ian Smith.

[32] "Funeral of Munich Fida'yin, Libyan Radio in Arabic 1715 and 2100 gmt 12 Sept. 1972," BBC, *SWB*. Part 4. *The Middle East and Africa* (September 14, 1972), ME/4092/A/2.

[33] On Arab political culture in those years see Fouad Ajami's now-classic study, *The Arab Predicament: Arab Political Thought and Practice since 1967* (New York: Cambridge University Press, 1981). On September 15, Mohamed Heikal, the editor in chief of *Al-Ahram*, published an extended essay on "the violent storm which broke in Munich." It was, he wrote, "easy for me as an Arab to support what has taken place in Munich." Those who spoke of "Arab terrorism" were engaged in what he called a "hate campaign," in "Haykal on the 'Munich Storm,'" Cairo in Arabic home service 1300 and *Voice of the Arabs* 1745 gmt 15 Sept. 1972," BBC, *SWB*. Part 4. *The Middle East and Africa* (September 14, 1972), ME/4095/A/1.

[34] Embassy Kampala to SecState WashDC, "Subject: Amin's Position on ME," (September 13, 1972), NACP RG 59 General Records of the Department of State, SNF, 1970–73, Political and Defense, From Pol. 27 Arab ISR 7/172 to Pol 27 Arab ISR 1/1/73, NWDPH-2 1997, Box 2060. Also see "Amin Praises Hitler for Killing of Jews," *New York Times* (September 13, 1972), 4.

> After the British had settled Israelis in Palestine, they through their intelligence said that they were overthrown in Palestine by the Israelis and then immediately the Israelis formed the state of Israel in Palestine after which the Americans started arming the Israelis with sophisticated modern weapons which are even more powerful than the weapons which the Arabs have even though the population of Arabs is more than the Israelis. Moreover, the power of the arms which the Israelis have got from the United States is ten times than the weapons which the Arab world have got.
>
> Therefore the problem of Palestine is very important. The Secretary-General and all member states of the United Nations must tell the world where the Palestinians will settle because they have no homes where they can settle.
>
> Now the imperialists including their spies have condemned the Palestinian operations at the Olympic Games last week where the angry Palestinians decided themselves as suicide Palestinian unit to combat the Israelis and were taking part in the Olympic Games because they are homeless while the Israelis are enjoying themselves internationally.
>
> The Israelis are the ones and actually should be condemned and removed completely from the United Nations and Palestine because Palestine is for Palestinians and not for Israelis and had been taken there by Britain, the crooks who made mistakes everywhere in the world in marking the boundaries of the countries they formerly occupied as colonies.
>
> Germany is the right place where when Hitler was the prime minister and supreme commander, he burnt over six million Jews. This is because Hitler and all German people knew that the Israelis are not people who are working in the interest of the people of the world and that is why they burnt the Israelis alive with gas in the soil of Germany. The world should remember that the Palestinians, with the assistance of Germany, made that operation possible in the Olympic village.
>
> Therefore, the people of the world must also consider very seriously the removal of the Israelis from the United Nations and also from the Middle East because the presence of the Israelis in the Middle East will mean no peace at all in the world, especially in that part of the world, the Middle East.[35]

The Palestinians, he continued, should be offered assistance "to remove all the Israelis from the Middle East and take them to Britain which was responsible for taking them to Palestine."[36]

As of September 13, 1972, Amin's deranged understanding of events, his open anti-Semitism, justification of the Holocaust, praise for Hitler and for the terrorists who killed the Israeli athletes in Munich and

[35] Embassy Kampala to SecState WashDC, "Subject: Amin's Position on ME," (September 13, 1972), NACP RG 59 General Records of the Department of State, SNF, 1970–73, Political and Defense, From Pol. 27 Arab ISR 7/172 to Pol 27 Arab ISR 1/1/73, NWDPH-2 1997, Box 2060; also in "Non-Arab Africa: Uganda: Amin's Message to the UN, Mrs. Meir and Yasir Arafat: Kampala home service in English 1700 gmt September 11, 1972," BBC, *SWB*. Part 4. *The Middle East and Africa* (September 13, 1972), ME/4091/B/1.

[36] Ibid.

support for removing "all Israelis" from "Palestine" were public knowledge around the world. The leaders of the PLO, the Soviet bloc including East Germany, the terror organizations of the West German radical Left, and the government of Israel all could read Amin's praise for Hitler and the Holocaust. As we will see in more detail, four years later, in the course of the hijacking of an Air France flight to Entebbe airport in Uganda, the PFLP together with the West German Revolutionary Cell terrorist organization actively cooperated with Amin.

In the weeks following the Munich attack, West Germany's Federal Intelligence Service, the Bundesnachrichtendienst (BND), examined the relationship of the Black September organization to the Palestine Liberation Organization and Al Fatah.[37] Its analysts concluded that

> the form of its communiqués confirm that "Black September" is a camouflage name for terror actions that are carried out by members of Fatah but for which Fatah does not want to take [public, JH] responsibility. Thereby, the Fatah leadership will prevent endangering the sympathy it has gained, its prestige and status yet on the other hand demonstrate its capacity to act in the face of the reduced possibilities for action against Israel.... Fatah's considerable financial resources were at its [Black September's, JH] disposal for these [terrorist, JH] actions. ARAFAT himself gave permission for the actions. According the press reports, the department chief within the Fatah leadership is Faruk al KADDOUMI, who oversaw analysis and planning.[38]

The PFLP was the member of the PLO's Executive Committee responsible for contact with members of the West German and West European New Left and for opening an anti-Israeli front in West Germany. The problem for the leadership of Fatah was "to preserve this cover for Black September." As long as Arafat controlled the PLO apparatus and "was recognized as the international speaker of the PLO in the Arab region and in Moscow, he possessed this fiction of legality."[39]

In other words, the BND believed that Arafat and the PLO leadership were connected to Black September and thus to the planning and implementation of the attack on the Munich Olympics or at least were aware of the preparations and did not stop them. Preserving this "fiction of legality" became a key purpose of PLO media strategy, which

37 Bundesnachrichtendienst an das Auswärtiges Amt, StS-Kost, Betr.: Kurzaufzeichnung der "Schwarze September"; Also see "nr. 1037 vom 6.10.1972, betr.: organisation Black September," Bonn (nd) Politisches Archiv des Auswärtiges Amt (PAAA) B 130 Band 9863A, "Attentat Olympiade München, Flugzeugattentate, Attentatsversurche und Entführungen, Naher Osten vom 1971 bis 1972."

38 Ibid.

39 Ibid.

contrasted a more "moderate" Arafat to the "extremists" and "radicals" in the Palestinian splinter organizations.[40] In February 1973, Abu Daud, alleged to have been the organizer of the Munich attack, was arrested in Jordan. On Jordanian television he confessed to organizing an attempt to seize Jordanian government officials to compel release of imprisoned Palestinians. He also offered an analysis of Black September that confirmed the view of West German intelligence and press reports. "There is," he said, "no such thing as Black September. Fatah announces its operations under this name so that it will not appear as direct executor of operations."[41]

The West German government's view of the organizational structure of the PLO was evident in a chart dating from fall 1972. (See Table 5.1.) It shows the PLO at the top tier, followed by the Palestinian National Council and the Palestinian National Fund. The center of power lay in an Executive Committee. Arafat was the chairman. Its thirteen members included four members of Fatah, two from the Syrian controlled Sa'iqa, one from the PFLP, one from the Democratic Popular Front for the Liberation of Palestine (PDFLP), one from the Arab Liberation Front, one from the "Peoples Union," and three independents. The following organizations were said to be directly subordinate to the Executive Committee: Saika (between 3,000 and 7,000 members), PDFLP (500 to 1,000), PFLP (2,000 to 4,000), Arab Liberation Front (500 to 3,000), and Fatah (6,000 to 15,000). The GUPS and GUPA were shown as directly subordinate to Fatah. Another 16,000 persons were thought to be in the PLA, the Palestine Liberation Army.[42] In other words, the Palestinian armed organizations had between 28,000 and 45,000 persons under arms.

The organization chart presented Arafat and the PLO as in control of the various splinter organizations. Black September was not an organization separate from the PLO. The PFLP and PDFLP, which had become notorious for airplane hijacking and terrorist attacks in the Middle East and in Western Europe, were also members of the Executive Committee chaired by Arafat. Though the tactical differences between Arafat and

40 "Einzelbericht nr 35'72, Organisation black September," Ankara (October 6, 1972), PAAA B 130 Band 9863A, "Attentat Olympiade München, Flugzeugattentate, Attentatsversurche und Entführungen, Naher Osten vom 1971 bis 1972."

41 Abu Daud cited in "1973STATE061020, Subj: Abu Da'ud Confession," Washington (April 31, 1973), NACP Diplomatic Records, RG59, Central Foreign Policy Files, Electronic Telegrams, 1/11974-12/31/1974.

42 "Die Palästinensische Befreiungsorganisation (Vereinfachte Darstellung)," PAAA B 130 Band 9863A, "Attentat Olympiade München, Flugzeugattentate, Attentatsversurche und Entführungen, Naher Osten vom 1971 bis 1972."

TABLE 5.1. *Chart from Office IB4, German Foreign Ministry, 1971–1972*

		PLO	
	Palestine National Council		Palestine National Fund
		Executive Committee	
		Chairman	Yasser Arafat
	13 Members:	4 Fatah	"The Conquest" (*Die Eroberung)*
		2 Saika	"The Lightning" (*Das Blitzstrahl*)
		1 PFLP	"Popular Front for the Liberation of Palestine"
		1 PDFLP	"Democratic Popular Front for the Liberation of Palestine"
		1 ALF	"Arab Liberation Front"
		3	Independent

Saika	PDFLP	PFLP	Fatah	ALF	PLA
	GUPS			GUPA	
General Union of Palestinian Students			General Union of Palestinian Workers		

Note: The chart gives the following figures for membership in the various branches of the PLO: Saika, between 3,000 and 7,000; PDFLP, 500 to 1,000; PFLP, 2,000 to 4,000; Fatah, 6,000 to 15,000, ALF, 500 to 2,000; and the Palestine Liberation Army (PLA), 16,000.
Source: "Die Palästinensische Befreiungsorganisation (Vereinfachte Darstellung)," PAAA B 130 Band 9863A, "Attentat Olympiade München, Flugzeugattentate, Attentatsversurche und Entführungen, Naher Osten vom 1971 bis 1972."

other members of the Executive Committee existed, West German – and probably Israeli and American – intelligence agencies viewed efforts to depict them as differences between "moderates" and "extremists" as useful fictions.

While the Israelis were preoccupied with the links of Black September to the Arab states, the West German judicial, intelligence, and police agencies focused on the possible connections of Black September and the Munich attack to Arabs, including Palestinians, working or studying in the Federal Republic.[43] According to the Verfassungsschutz annual public

[43] Herbert Freden, "Arabische Terroristen-Umtriebe in der Bundesrepublik," Freier Korrespondenz-Dienst, FKD, Bern (September 6, 1972), BAK B106/ 14650.

report of 1972 there were 20,000 Arab guest workers and 16,000 Arab students at West German universities, of whom 3,000 were Palestinians. The 1971 report of the Verfassungsschutz had listed 100 political organizations of foreign students with 50,000 members from abroad. Of particular interest to the West German authorities were the General Union of Palestinian Students (GUPS) and its chapters at 26 West Germany universities, and the General Union of Palestinian Workers (GUPA), with 23 chapters.[44] Both GUPS and GUPA were directed by Al Fatah from its offices in Cairo. GUPA included many members of the PFLP. Each member of Al Fatah in the Federal Republic had a number and alias. He/she was required to uphold secrecy and to offer unconditional obedience and was not able to leave the organization. The leaders of Al Fatah in West Germany were "in constant contact with the leadership in the Middle East."[45]

In the course of the attack on the Olympics in Munich, West German authorities intercepted phone calls from the terrorists in Munich to representatives of the GUPS office in Bonn. On October 3, 1972, West Germany's Interior Minister Hans-Dietrich Genscher (1927–) the leader of the liberal Free Democratic Party and a future long-serving foreign minister, signed an order banning both GUPS and GUPA. (See Figure 5.1.) In 1972, the Interior Ministry estimated that there were about 50,000 persons from Arab states living in West Germany, of whom about 6,000 to 8,000 were Palestinians, and about 3,000 were members of Al Fatah.[46] From September 5 until October 3, 1972, the West German authorities expelled 211 persons, deported 85, and arrested 35 who were awaiting deportation. After the ban order, another 44 people were expelled, 13 deported, and 26 held in custody awaiting resolution of their cases.[47] All were members of GUPS. The West German government authorities seized GUPS property and dissolved the organization. According to West German law, "organizations whose members or leaders are entirely or partly

44 Ibid.

45 Ibid. Also on Communist state support for "Palestinian extremists" see Peter Sager, "Ein Nachwort zum Anschlag auf die Olympiade," *Freier Korrespondenz-Dienst, Nr. 36*, Bern (September 6, 1972), 6, BAK B106/ 14650.

46 "Sicherheitslage in der Bundesrepublik Deutschland – Bedrohung durch arabische Terroristen" (September 19, 1972), Bundesarchiv Koblenz (BAK) Bundesministerium des Innern B106/146540, Terroranschlag auf die Israelische Olympiamannschaft.

47 Referat VII 6, Arbeitskreis II der Innenministerium, Novellerung des Auslandergesetzes (October 5, 1972), Bundesarchiv Koblenz (BAK) Bundesministerium des Innern B106/146543, Terroranschlag auf die Israelische Olympiamannschaftt, 1–3.

FIGURE 5.1. Hans-Dietrich Genscher (right) and Justice Minister, Gerhard Jan (left) in the Bundestag (West German Parliament, November 1972). Taken shortly after Genscher, then West Germany's interior minister, approved banning of two Palestinian organizations, GUPS and GUPA, linked to the PLO.
Source: Darchinger/Archiv der Sozialen Demokratie, Friedrich-Ebert-Stiftung, Bonn, Germany.

foreigners (*Ausländervereine)* can be banned according to the law regarding such associations if they, through political activity damage or endanger the inner security and public order of the Federal Republic of Germany."[48] The GUPS was defined as a "foreign association" *(Ausländervereine)* because its headquarters were in Cairo. In the Federal Republic, it was composed of 26 regional chapters with a total membership of between 600 and 800. The West German authorities insisted that GUPS and GUPA were banned because of their willingness to use and support violence to achieve their political goals, not the goals themselves. Genscher wrote that the "decisive

[48] "Der Bundesminister des Innern an die General Union Palästinensischer Studenten – Konfedoration in der Bundesrepublik Deutschland," Bonn (October 3, 1972), Bundesarchiv Koblenz (BAK) Bundesministerium des Innern B106/14650, Bundesarchiv Koblenz (BAK) Bundesministerium des Innern B106/146540, Terroranschlag auf die Israelische Olympiamannschaftt.

issue for the threat to the Federal Republic's internal security" lay in the fact that the GUPS supported "the methods of guerrilla war" of Palestinian organizations and did so "not only on the territory of Palestine," but in West Germany as well.[49]

Genscher's statement accompanying the ban asserted that "leading functionaries" of the GUPS were activists in organizations or underground branches of such organizations that "were responsible for various acts of terrorism in the Federal Republic of Germany against international aviation and had conspiratorial cells in" the FRG. The Black September terrorists who attacked the Israeli team at the Munich Olympics contacted the director of GUPS, Abdaallah Hasan Al-Frangi, editor of a monthly journal, *Palästinensische Revolution* (Palestinian Revolution). GUPS openly supported Black September. Its magazine *Al-Thaura* (The Revolution) of June 2, 1972, published the "communiqué" of Black September that described and justified the hijacking of a Sabena Airlines plane to Lod airport on May 8, 1972.[50] (See Figure 5.2.) After the Munich attack, Genscher wrote that it "had to be assumed" that terrorists who called themselves Palestinian freedom fighters would turn to GUPS for support in carrying out additional terrorist attacks in West Germany. "This danger is all the greater because the GUPS hides its activities from German authorities and because it advocates violence as a means of politics by its celebration among its members of terrorist actions, prepares the ground for support for more terror actions in the Federal Republic of Germany and if allowed to continue unhindered would prepare still more."[51]

Although members of GUPS after the Munich attack publicly distanced themselves from such terrorist actions, Genscher wrote that "there were reasons to believe that these statements were given in order prevent measures of banning that were under consideration by German authorities." He argued that the decision to ban the GUPS was also in the interest of the approximately 50,000 law-abiding citizens from Arab states living in the Federal Republic. Only by banning and dissolving the organization "would it be possible to prevent the GUPS from making itself into a potential organizational and logistical base at the service of foreign terrorists carrying out announced further terrorist actions."[52] The Federal Republic was also expanding security for West German diplomats abroad, especially in Arab countries; for "endangered persons" in

[49] Ibid., 5.
[50] Ibid., 6.
[51] Ibid.
[52] Ibid., 7–8.

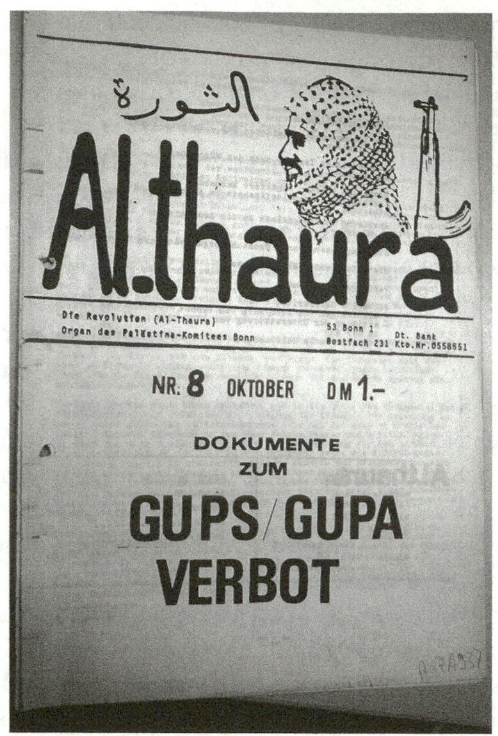

FIGURE 5.2. Cover of *Al-Thaura*, "Dokumente zum GUPS/GUPA Verbot" (Fall 1972). *Al-Thaura*, or "The Revolution," published by the General Union of Palestinian Students attacked collaboration between "Zionists and FRG imperialists."
Source: International Institute for Social History, Amsterdam.

West Germany, including members of the judiciary, the Interior Ministry, their families; as well as for leading national politicians, judges of the constitutional court, Israeli and Arab diplomatic facilities, and persons and offices of air lines and shipping lines.[53]

The Interior Ministry's ban order cited decisions, leaflets, and publications in which the GUPS "declares its support for violence and terror as a means of the politics it advocates." It had called Al Fatah the only organization recognized to speak "in the name of the fighting Palestinian

[53] "Innere Sicherheit: Sicherheitsmaßnahmen der Bundesregierung," Pleanarsitzung – Ständiger Ausschuß Bundestag-Bundesrat, Bonn (October 26, 1972), Bundesarchiv Koblenz (BAK) Bundesministerium des Innern B106/146541, Terroranschlag auf die Israelische Olympiamannschaftt und seine Folgen, 22.9.1972 bis 10.10.1972, 1–3.

people."[54] Its task was to prepare for "the return of our stolen country" and to "prepare Palestinian youth for the battle for return." The student members of GUPS were required to support the goals and methods of Al Fatah and to "undertake military training to support the Palestinian revolution." GUPS collected considerable sums of money for Fatah, including 1 million marks in 1969 alone. All 26 regional branches of GUPS distributed *Palästinensischen Revolution* (Palestinian Revolution), which included articles about the theory and practice of guerrilla warfare and offered "success announcements" (*Erfolgsmeldungen*) about "political terror." The magazine supported "targeted actions against Israeli civilians and lynch justice against so-called traitors was supported in the journal."[55] In issue number 10 of 1970, a writer in *Palästinensischen Revolution* asserted that actions that aimed to "make an impression on the people and in the world" and to speak to the "oppressed peoples of the world, in confronting the enemy, must include attacks in cities, on police in villages and the public execution of agents, conspirators and collaborators."[56] On February 6, 1972, after five Jordanians were murdered in the German city of Brühl, *Al-Thaura (The Revolution)* wrote that "the revolutionary will never be silent about traitors and agents." Regarding the murder of Jordan's ministry president, Wasfi-Tell, in Cairo on November 28, 1971, by Black September agents, *Al-Thaura* referred to "the bullets of our heroic fighters in Cairo [that struck] El-Tell." Essays in GUPS's publications and leaflets celebrated "the armed peoples' revolution" and the "battle against Israel."[57] In issue 14 of 1972 of *Palästinensische Revolution*, the editors published a detailed "Political Program of the Palestinian Revolution,"[58] which called for "organizing all forces of the people for a long lasting peoples' war ... the continuation of political and armed struggle for the liberation of all of Palestine." It attacked compromise and rejected any "plan for a Palestinian state on a part of Palestine. Such plans must be confronted with armed and political struggle."[59]

[54] "Verbotsverfügung," Bundesarchiv Koblenz (BAK) Bundesministerium des Innern B106/146540, Terroranschlag auf die Israelische Olympiamannschaftt, 1–3

[55] Ibid., 3.

[56] "Die Revolution," 6, cited in "Verbotsverfügung," Bundesarchiv Koblenz (BAK) Bundesministerium des Innern B106/146540, Terroranschlag auf die Israelische Olympiamannschaftt, 3.

[57] "Verbotsverfügung," 3. Ibid., 5.

[58] "Das Politische Programm der Palästinensischen Revolution," *Palästinensische Revolution* (Bonn: Resistentia Schriften, 1972), 3–5, Al Thaura, Archiv Institut für Sozialforschung, Hamburg.

[59] Ibid., 3.

By banning GUPS and GUPA, the West German government banned organizations that it believed were using the territory of the Federal Republic to plan or execute terrorist attacks either against Israel or against Jewish and Israeli associated targets in the Federal Republic. The ban was not an effort to suppress speech. The government accepted political agitation against Israel to be a legitimate form of political expression. The West German political and judicial authorities concluded that opening a "front" in West Germany of a terrorist war against Israelis and Jews was criminal activity and would not be tolerated. The ban order found that GUPS's "publications and leaflets contained expressions of support for violence and terror" and thus constituted "a public approval of crime.... Because the goal and activity of GUPS aims with acts of terror and violence to commit legally punishable actions, it is a criminal organization" as defined in German law. As a result of the participation of the GUPS in disrupting the lecture of the Israeli ambassador to the Federal Republic in Frankfurt/Main in October 1969; the occupation of the Jordanian Embassy in Bonn on June 12, 1970; and the attempted occupation of it on September 21, 1970, it committed "criminal trespass" and destroyed property. With the calls for battle against Israel and Jordan that it had made from the territory of the Federal Republic, the GUPS damaged West Germany's reputation abroad and created problems for West German foreign relations.[60]

Those expelled included functionaries of Al Fatah and GUPS. Authorities in Hamburg suspected some were involved in the murders of the five Jordanians and in bomb attacks.[61] The detail in the files about those deported indicated that the police and intelligence services had them under surveillance before the Munich attach. The order for expulsion, however, did not require evidence that the particular individual had engaged in an act of terror or even personally celebrated one. Once the GUPS had been declared to be a criminal organization, playing a leadership role in one of the GUPS chapters was sufficient grounds for deportation. In the case of a GUPS leader in Mainz who objected to the expulsion order, the deciding judges wrote that

> the case concerns a functionary of an organization which, because it glorifies and supports terror – even against innocent and uninvolved persons – has been banned. Such persons should no longer have the possibility, consciously

[60] Ibid., 6–8.

[61] "An das bmi Hern Ministerialdirektor Smoydzin: betr. Ausweisung von Arabern (September 22, 1972)," Bundesarchiv Koblenz (BAK) Bundesministerium des Innern B106/146543, Terroranschlag auf die Israelische Olympiamannschaft.

or unconsciously, to support such acts of terror or persons and organizations which are responsible for them. The public interest demands that these organizations in the Federal Republic not have at their disposal a number of politically like-minded functionaries who could be used as helpers in a corresponding clever manner to assist in the violent implementation of political goals both in the Federal Republic and abroad. The complainant in this case cannot appeal with reference to his right of free speech. As a foreigner he has supported and is active in an organization [GUPS] whose methods are not compatible with the legal foundations of the guest country in which he is living.[62]

As the courts defined GUPS to be a criminal organization, it was not necessary that the individual in this case be shown to have personally been involved in a criminal act. Rather, the court held that an active role in GUPS was sufficient grounds to conclude that "the presence of [this] foreigner objectively endangered the internal security of the Federal Republic."[63] The court reasserted that it was the support for terror and violence, not the expression of certain political views that led to banning the organization. After the Munich attack, the West German Interior Ministry believed the "inner security" of the FRG was "seriously threatened." The massive publicity that the Munich attack created was a motive for yet more acts of terror. The Interior Ministry estimated that because there were about 3,000 members of Al Fatah living in West Germany, "Israeli institutions were especially endangered." Attacking them would affect both the Federal Republic and Israel. German Embassies abroad were also vulnerable.[64]

GUPS activists and their supporters protested the ban and expulsions. On September 19, the GUPS at the University of Munster described the government policy as "measures taken against Arabs" even though "members of GUPS had repeatedly in public decisively opposed the [the practice of] terror by Palestinians on German territory." The ban, they said, was yet another example of the "persecution and banning of progressive organizations which had taken place since the founding of the FRG."[65] The student government (AStA, General Student Council, Allgemeine

[62] "Beschluss in dem Verwaltungsrechtsstreit des Studenten ... der 2.Senat des Oberwaltungsgerichts Rheinland-Pfalz, Mainz (November 9, 1982)," BAK BMI, B106/146543, Terroranschlag auf die Israelische Olympiamannschaftt, 1–5.

[63] Ibid.

[64] "Sicherheitslage in der Bundesrepublik Deutschland – Bedrohung durch arabische Terroristen" (September 19, 1972), Bundesarchiv Koblenz (BAK) Bundesministerium des Innern B106/146540, Terroranschlag auf die Israelische Olympiamannschaft.

[65] "Informationsaustausch zur sicherheitslage, muenster ... flugblaetter der gups," (September 19, 1972), BAK, BMI, 146543, Terroranschlag auf die Israelische Olympiamannschaft.

Studenten Ausschuss) at the University of Bonn denounced the "persecution of foreigners." It described the post-Munich atmosphere as one of "hostility to Arabs" (*Araberfeindlichkeit*).[66] In a statement of October 5, the German National Union of Students asserted that the Interior Ministry "produced no evidence that the GUPS called for the use of violence on the territory of the Federal Republic." It disputed that links had been established between GUPS and Black September and claimed that GUPS's "information activities" in West Germany were being declared illegal. It criticized the Interior Ministry for "dismissing the many statements by GUPS that repeatedly distanced itself from terrorist actions of this or that Palestinian splinter groups as efforts at deception." It disputed that the ban was a counterterrorism measure. Rather it was repression of legitimate political activity. Hence, all of the "innocent arrested foreigners workers and students should be immediately released."[67] The view that the banning of GUPS and GUPA was due to "hostility to Arabs" found echoes both in the Arab states and in East Germany.

The editors of *Al Thaura*, published by the Palestine Committee in Bonn, responded to the ban order.[68] The lead article described "the cooperation between FRG-Imperialism and Zionism." The editors first pointed out that the Central Council of Jews in Germany had said that the activity of foreign terrorist organizations in West Germany was a threat to public security. It then quoted Israel's Foreign Minister Abba Eban about the danger of radical student groups in light of the attack on the Israelis at the Munich Olympics. Thus when Genscher said that the Federal Republic "did not act under pressure from Israel and the Zionists ... that was nothing other than an effort at deception." The statement went on to describe West German governmental support for Israel from Adenauer on as "support for the Israeli government in its battle against the Palestinian people and the other Arab peoples."[69] It attacked what it viewed as the manipulative use of "the deep revulsion of the German people against the anti-Semitic crimes of the German fascists" to justify the "collaboration between Zionists and FRG-imperialists." The effort to impute "Jew-hatred and anti-Semitism to Palestinians and West Germans

[66] AStA (Allgemeine Studenten Ausschuss) Uni Bonn, "Protest gegen Ausländerverfolgung," Bonn (n.d.), BAK, BMI, 146543, Terroranschlag auf die Israelische Olympiamannschaft.

[67] Verband Deutscher Studenten, "Presseinformation Nr. 33: Nach Verbot von GUPS und GUPA: Neue Verfolgungswelle gegen Arabische Studenten und Arbeiter," Bonn (October 5, 1972), BAK, BMI, 146543, Terroranschlag auf die Israelische Olympiamannschaft.

[68] "Dokumente zum GUPS/GUPA Verbot," *Die Revolution (Al Thaura): Organ des Palästina-Komitees Bonn* (Bonn: October 1972).

[69] Ibid., 3.

who supported the liberation struggle in the Middle East is another link in the chain of constant diatribes which are meant to prepare the ground for measures of oppression, which are actually implemented."[70] The editors said nothing about the murders of the Israeli athletes in Munich and did not address the grounds for the ban on the GUPS offered by the Ministry of the Interior. They claimed that the actual purpose of the ban was to strengthen Israel, prevent foreign workers and students from working with German colleagues, and "criminalize the German forces" who supported the Palestinian people against imperialism. In capital letters it declared "FIGHT THE COOPERATION BETWEEN FRG-IMPERIALISM WITH ZIONISM! FREEDOM FOR GUPS AND GUPA."[71] Statements such as this one could be, and as we will see, were read as justification of the attack on the Israelis at the Olympics and of support for war against Israel.[72]

In 1978, two Palestinians appealed to the West German Federal Administrative Court (Bundesverwaltungsgericht) in an effort to overturn the 1972 GUPS ban order. The plaintiffs claimed that the government had not established that there were links between the GUPS and terrorism and that the 1972 order was instead an effort to suppress legitimate political activity. On June 12, 1978, the court issued a 62-page decision, which rejected the complaint and upheld the ban.[73] The judges added important supporting evidence for the claims against GUPS. The court examined GUPS's rules for its members. In 1969, at its Fifth National Congress in Amman, the GUPS discussed the "role of students" regarding "the necessity of the members to strengthen the armed struggle." GUPS members "outside the homeland," such as those studying in Europe, "must arrange their affairs so that they can participate in the summer training camps where then they will be trained in armed struggle." They should connect with "progressive forces" to engage in "all kinds of financial and propaganda support and organize demonstrations to support our revolution," oppose "all Zionist movements," and form

[70] Ibid., 8.

[71] Ibid.

[72] Also see *Al Tahir: Befreiung, Zeitschrift des Komitees zur Unterstützung der Kämpfenden Völker im Nahen und Mittleren Osten*, No. 1 (November 17, 1973) (West) Berlin. The cover declares "Sieg im Volkskrieg" (Victory in Peoples War) and shows a women holding a rifle and ready to throw a grenade, "Zeitschriften, Palästina," Archiv, Institut für Sozialforschung, Hamburg.

[73] "Bundesverwaltungsgericht, Im Namen des Volkes in der Verwaltungsstreitsache der Generalunion Palästinensischen Studenten ... gegen ... die Bundesrepublik Deutschland," (June 12, 1978) in BAK BMI B106/74656, Referat IS 2, Bonn (August 8, 1978); also see Bundesanzeiger, Nr. 122 (June 21, 1978).

alliances with "Arab and international student unions" on the basis of "their standpoint to our armed revolution."[74] The courts cited the GUPS publication *Palästinensische Revolution* of 1970 that asserted that the means of freeing the Palestinian people was "a peoples' war of liberation," which "consisted of political and armed struggle." It had to be "clearly understood that the political and the armed struggle were two connected and complimentary means for attainment of the goal of this revolutionary war and that their separation or one sided neglect represented a great danger for the success of the peoples war."[75]

The court reexamined the response of GUPS publications from 1970 to 1972 to the murder of the Jordanian Minister President Wasfi El Tal (i.e. also Wasfi Tell) on November 28, 1971 in Cairo; the attack on the Jordanian Ambassador Zaid Al Rifa in London on December 15, 1971; the murder of five Jordanians in Brühl on February 6, 1972; the hijacking of Belgian Sabena Airlines to the Israeli Lod airport on May 8, 1972; the attack by members of the Japanese Red Army on the Israeli Lod airport on May 30, 1972; and the attack on the Israeli Olympic team in Munich on September 5, 1972. The court cited internal GUPS memos sent to members and published statements by GUPS that depicted these actions as "effective, worthy of emulation, worthy of support and in every respect justified actions."[76] After the Lod airport massacre, *Al Thaura* of June 1972 published a Black September communiqué that called for "fame and immortality to the fallen heroes of our people and our nation." The judges concluded that the communiqué found the attack at Lod airport to be "effective, worthy of emulation and support and in every respect justified."[77] The GUPS journal *El Ittihad* wrote that the attack had demonstrated "the unity of the power of liberation in the world." It continued that the attack "killed 27 and wounded 76 persons" and referred to "a bitter battle between the three heroes" and the "Zionist army," which led to the deaths of two of the hijackers. The court found that the article was "not just a report but clearly a partisan opinion." The court again found abundant evidence that the GUPS supported, rather than fought against actions such as the terrorist attack at Lod airport.[78]

[74] Cited in ibid., 28–29.

[75] "Der Politische Kampf," *Palestinensische Revolution*, Nr. 11/1970, 3–6. Cited in Bundesverwaltungsgericht, Im Namen des Volkes in der Verwaltungsstretisache der Generalunion Palästinensischen Studenten ... gegen ... die Bundesrepublik Deutschland," 37.

[76] Ibid., 40–53.

[77] Ibid. 46–49.

[78] Ibid., 52.

The 1978 court decision again found that the GUPS posed a threat to the Federal Republic's internal security and that given the opportunity, GUPS members would assist terrorist attacks with financial donations, offer shelter for operatives or fugitives, and transfer messages. The court upheld the 1972 decision that the GUPS supported "violent actions of Palestinian organizations and commandos" within West Germany as well as against Israel. The court did not find the GUPS statements distancing itself from the Munich attack to be credible. After the attack, its focus had been on denouncing a supposed "witch hunt" against Arabs rather than on condemning the Munich attack. Therefore, the court agreed that the 1972 GUPS ban was not an effort to suppress GUPS's political speech. The court upheld the ban on GUPS not only because it was likely to support terrorism within West Germany but also because it sought to use its presence in the Federal Republic to support terrorist attacks elsewhere, primarily against Israel.

During these years, student governments at most major West German universities were governed by a leftist coalition that included young socialists (JUSOS) and an assortment of Marxist-Leninists groups of the radical Left.[79] In view of low student voting participation, it was possible for well-organized minorities to gain control of the student governments and their finances and use them to support political activities. In Heidelberg three months before the Munich attack, student government funds were used to help publish *Palästina Blatt,* "Palestine Paper." Its June 5, 1972, issue supported "the creation of an armed resistance movement."[80] The same issue announced that *'Die Front': Zeitschrift zur Unterstützung des Befreiungskampfes der Völker des Nahen Ostens* (The Front: Journal in Support of the Liberation Struggles of the People of the Middle East), also published by the Palestine Solidarity Committee, would publish an interview with Nayef Hawatmeh, leader of the DPF L P, by then famous for its participation in terrorist activities. It also gave the Palestine Committees' bank account number for donations to support

79 See "The JUSOS and the Popular Front on Campus," and "Table 10. Political Character of Student Government (AStA) at the Twenty-Eight Largest West German Universities and Technical Universities, 1969–1974, Election Results for the Student Elections at West German University, 1968–1983," Jeffrey Herf, *War by Other Means: Soviet Power, West German Resistance and the Battle of the Euromissiles* (New York: Free Press, 1991), 74–82, and 244–245.

80 The June 5, 1972, issue of the *Palästina Blatt* (Palestine Paper) published by the "Socialist-Palestine Committee," in coordination with the Heidelberg university student government and the GUPS, made the case for "the armed struggle, the answer to the imperialist's plan."

the FPDLP, Front of the Popular Democratic Liberation of Palestine. Featured slogans included "Fight the peaceful solution and the [King of Jordan, JH] Hussein plan," "Solidarity with the Palestinian-Jordanian national unity front!" and "Victory to the liberation struggles of the Arab people."[81] As Martin Kloke wrote, by the early 1970s an impressive accumulation of sectarian groups joined West German radical leftists with Arab and Palestinian students in an "anti-Zionist" mobilization that continued to flourish on university campuses and in towns in the 1970s.[82]

On September 22, Heinz Galinski addressed the Munich attacks in the lead article of the *Allgemeine unabhängige jüdische Wochenzeitung* and drew attention to the political situation in the universities.[83] He wrote that the attack "was not the first serious crime committed by Arab terrorists on German territory." The "frightful events in Munich" needed to be placed in "the historical context of the not so distant National Socialist past, whose aftereffects, even when many do not want to see them, are in one way or another still evident in all areas of life." Galinski focused on the

> dangerous circumstances ... in the activity of Arab extremists that have developed in the first place in the colleges and universities. They have distributed anti-Jewish, German language malicious propaganda literature, organized demonstrations, meetings and actions together with radical leftist elements. We [the Central Council] have drawn attention to the fact that when such things happen in Germany they objectively amount to fostering neo-Nazi anti-Semitism.[84]

Galinski expressed understanding for the Federal Republic's desire for good relations with all states, including the Arab states. Limits had been "clearly breached when bands of murderers from Arab states, supplied with finances, weapons and passports by those states are operating on the territory of the Federal Republic to commit their crimes." The celebrations of terrorists as freedom fighters and martyrs from the Arab states were "an affront to the entire civilized world for they seek to establish theft and murder as means for accomplishing political goals."[85] It was

[81] Ibid.

[82] For a summary of these groups and publications, see Martin Kloke, *Israel und die deutsche Linke: Zur geschichte eine schwierigen Verhältnisses* (Frankfurt/Main: Haag and Herchen, 1994), 138–176.

[83] Heinz Galinski, "*Unausweichliche Alternative: Das Verbrechen von München mahnt,*" *Allgemeine unabhängige jüdische Wochenzeitung*, Dusseldorf (September 22, 1972), 1.

[84] Ibid.

[85] Ibid.

"shameful that today Jewish institutions in Germany must be placed under special police protection."[86]

At the same time that the radical Left was denouncing even the Willy Brandt and then the Helmut Schmidt Social Democratic governments as repressive, Galinski, Alexander Ginsburg, Hendrik van Dam, and their colleagues looked to the West German government at the local, state, and national levels for protection of the Jewish community from attacks. On October 25, 1972, van Dam conveyed a resolution of the Central Council to Genscher; to the secretary of state in the Interior Ministry, Bruno Mark; Hans Joachim Vogel, then the mayor of Munich; and Police President Manfred Schreiber. He thanked them for their "courageous stance" during the terrorist attack in Munich when they risked their lives by offering to exchange themselves for the Israeli hostages and thanked "all of the police officials who took part in the operation."[87] For the Jewish leaders, the West Germany that the radical Left was denouncing as fascist and repressive was in reality the government that was protecting Jewish institutions from terrorist attacks. The gap between the Jewish community and the West German radical Left and its successors had become an unbridgeable chasm.

Officials in the Offices for the Protection of the Constitution (Bundesamt für Verfassungsschutz) had been warning of letter bombs sent to Israeli and Jewish addresses since 1967.[88] On October 23, 1972, a letter containing cyanide was sent to "Mr. Moshe Levi Simon" at the Israeli Embassy in Bonn. When opened to the air, it became deadly.[89] On October 6, the Verfassungsschutz sent an internal memo about a letter bomb that had been sent to the Nelly Sachs Jewish Home for the Aged in Dusseldorf.[90] On November 15, officials in the Bundeskriminalamt (BKA), or Federal Criminal Investigation Office, in Bonn described recent

86 Ibid.

87 Hendrik van Damn, "An die Mitglieder des Direktoriums," Dusseldorf (October 25, 1972), *Archiv zur Erforschung der Geschichte der Juden in Deutschland, Heidelberg*, ZA B.1/7 115, Olympiade, München 1972. The Central Council also sent protests to Chancellor Willy Brandt when he decided to release the three surviving members of the Black September organization when faced with terrorist threats to kill hostages on board a hijacked plane in October 1972. See "Zentralrat schreibt an Bundeskanzler Brandt und Ministerpräsident Goppel," *Jüdischer Presse Dienst, Informationen des Zentralrats der Juden in Deutschland*, Dusseldorf (October 31, 1972 and November 2, 1972).

88 "Vermerk," Cologne (June 6, 1972), Bundesarchiv Koblenz (BAK), Bundesamt für Verfassungsschutz, B 443/641.

89 "Gift-Briefe aus Karlsruhe," (October 23, 1972), BAK, B443/641.

90 "Informationsaustausch zur Sicherheitslage – Duesseldorf – Sprengstoffbrief eingegangen beim juedischen altersheim in Duesseldorf," BAK 443/ 641.

"letter bombs to Israeli missions and persons as well as poison letters to the Israeli Embassy in Bonn-Bad Godesberg."[91] On September 18, 1972, the Black September organization sent 46 letter bombs to Israeli missions or persons, to Jewish institutions and persons in London (eight), Brussels (two), Geneva (four), Paris (two), Ottawa (six), Montreal (two), New York (three), Vienna (five), Kinshasa (five), Jerusalem (four), Sydney (two), Canberra (three), Israel (nine), Amman (four), and Phnom Penh (one). In London, the letter bomb exploded and killed Dr. Ami Schechori, the agricultural attaché of the Israeli Embassy.[92] The BKA memos included details of the construction of the bombs, their shape and color, technical details and photos of the letters themselves and destruction they had caused in London.

The terror threat to the Jews in West Germany was apparent in memos sent by the Central Council to its members in the days before and months following the attack on the Munich Olympics. On September 4, 1972, van Dam sent a warning about letter bombs to members of the Central Council; to the Jewish communities in Berlin, Frankfurt, Hamburg, Cologne, and Munich; and to other Jewish organizations in the Federal Republic.[93] On September 29, 1972, the police informed van Dam that "investigations indicated that bomb attacks by terrorist groups" on "Jewish institutions or institutions connected to Israel" using letter bombs and gift packages were "being planned and implemented." The warning included details about the size and appearance of such bombs.[94] On October 6, 1967, a letter bomb mailed from Singapore, Malaysia, was addressed to the Jewish home for the elderly in Dusseldorf. Parcels with bombs and poison were also mailed from Malaysia to the HIAS (Hebrew Immigrant Aid Society) office in Rome while still others had been mailed from Amsterdam. On October 9, van Dam warned the directors of the

[91] Bundeskriminalamt, Abt II Sicherungsgruppe to Bundesamt für Verfassungsschutz, "Sprengstoff an israelische Missionen und Personen sowie Giftbrief an die israelische Botschaft in Bonn-Bad Godesberg," Bonn (November 15, 1972), BAK 443/ 641.

[92] "Bericht: Versand von Sprengstoffbriefen durch arabische Terroristen an israelische Personen," BAK, 443/641; and Bundeskriminalamt Abt. II – Sicherungsgruppe to Bundesamt für Verfassungsschutz, "Versand von Sprengstoff in Briefen an israelische Missionen" (September 26, 1972), BAK 443/ 641.

[93] "Hendrik van Dam an die Mitglieder des Direktoriums Landesverbände und die Gemeinden Berlin, Frankfurt, Hamburg, Köln und München, Jüdischen Organisationen in der Bundesrepublik," Dusseldorf (September 4, 1972), ZA Heidelberg, B.1/7.93, Politisch Divers, 1974–1976.

[94] Der Polizeipräsident – Kriminalhauptstelle/14.K, "Sprengstoffanschlage auf jüdische oder mit Israel in Verbindung stehende Einrichtungen," Dusseldorf (September 29, 1972), ZA, Heidelberg, B.1/7.93, Politisch Divers, 1974–1976.

Central Council to "carefully examine all incoming mail."[95] On October 12, he wrote to the members of the council and to the larger Jewish communities that they should "take special care to ensure security measures to protect Jewish children. With cooperation from the police, all kindergartens, day care centers, schools and school buses should be secured." These added security measures to protect Jewish children were necessary in view of a recent attack on a Jewish school in Belgium, and in the face of "repeated threats of an Arab terrorist organization to use all means, including hostage taking to force the release of the terrorists who were involved in the crime in Munich."[96] On November 4, the *Frankfurter Allgemeine Zeitung* reported that a letter bomb sent from Singapore with 70 grams of explosives was received by the Central Office of Zionist Youth in Germany in Frankfurt/Main. The police were alerted and the police detonated the bomb away from the office.[97] On November 7, van Dam wrote again to the directors, the state associations, and the leaders of the Jewish communities in (West) Berlin, Bremen, Frankfurt/Main, Hamburg, Munich, and Cologne about two package bombs sent by a "Karl Zimmerman" from Singapore. One was sent to the Zionist Youth office and the second to the office of Magen David in Herborn. The letter bomb sent to the Nelly Sachs home for the aged in Dusseldorf had the same return address. Van Dam added that "caution in opening the mail is urgently requested."[98]

ULRIKE MEINHOF CELEBRATES "THE ACTION OF BLACK SEPTEMBER"

In these same weeks, Ulrike Meinhof, then sitting in prison for her activities with the Red Army Faction (RAF) terrorist organization, published "The Action of Black September in Munich, on the Strategy of Anti-Imperialist Struggle" (*Die Aktion des Schwarzen September in München: Zur*

95 Hendrik van Dam an Mitglieder des Direktoriums und an alle Landesverbände, Dusseldorf (October 9, 1967).

96 Ibid.

97 "Sprengstoffbrief an zionistische Organisation," *Frankfurter Allgemeine Zeitung*, Frankfurt/Main, Germany (November 4, 1972). Also see, "Sprengstoffbrief an Jüdische Addresse: Frankfurter Polizei alarmiert," Bonn, Germany (November 4, 1972).

98 Hendrik van Dam, "An die Mitglieder des Direktoriums Landesverbände und die Gemeinden Berlin, Frankfurt, Hamburg, Köln und München, Jüdischen Organisationen in der Bundesrepublik," Dusseldorf (November 7, 1972), Zentralarchiv zur Erforschung der Geschichte der Juden in Deutschland, Heidelberg, B.1/7.93, Politisch Divers, 1974–1976.

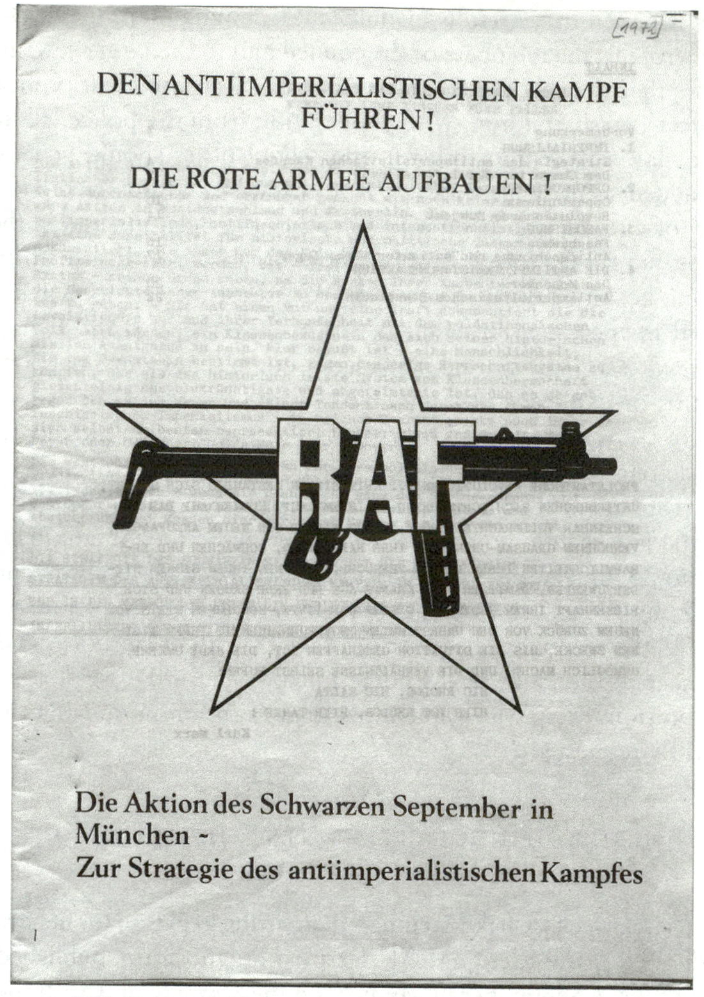
DEN ANTIIMPERIALISTISCHEN KAMPF FÜHREN!

DIE ROTE ARMEE AUFBAUEN!

RAF

Die Aktion des Schwarzen September in München -
Zur Strategie des antiimperialistischen Kampfes

FIGURE 5.3. Title page of Ulrike Meinhof's 1972 essay published by the Red Army Faction, which celebrates the Black September attack on the Israeli Olympic team in Munich. It reads: "Lead the Anti-Imperialist Struggle. Build the Red Army. RAF. The Action of Black September in Munich. On the Strategy of Anti-Imperialist Struggle."
Source: Archive, Institut for Social Research, Hamburg.

Strategie des Antiimperialistischen Kampfes), an essay about the attack on the Israelis at the Munich Olympics.[99] (See Figure 5.3.) It was one of the most important documents in the history of anti-Semitism in Europe

[99] "*Die Aktion des Schwarzen September in München. Zur Strategie des Antiimperialistischen Kampfes,*" *Rote Armee Fraktion: Texte und Materialien*, 151–177.

after the Holocaust. One purpose of the attack on the Munich Olympics was to use hostages to gain release of Meinhof and another leader of the RAF, Andreas Baader, from their West German prison cells. She was grateful for their efforts.

Meinhof celebrated what she called "the action" with great enthusiasm:[100]

> The action of Black September in Munich ... was simultaneously anti-imperialist, anti-fascist and internationalist.... It showed courage and strength that the revolutionaries could only have as a result of their bonds with the Palestinian people, a class consciousness that was aware of its historic mission of being a vanguard – a humanity defined by a consciousness that fought against a system of domination, the historically final system of class domination that is the bloodiest and most cunning that ever existed, against a system whose essence and tendency is thoroughly that of fascist imperialism, no matter in whatever character masks it presents itself: Nixon and Brandt, Moshe Dayan or [Hans Dietrich] Genscher, Golda Meir or [George] McGovern.... The strategy of Black September is the revolutionary strategy of anti-imperialist struggle in the third world and in the metropoles under conditions of the developed imperialism of multi-national concerns.[101]

Meinhof then offered the history of Israel according to the PLO Charter and standard Soviet-bloc propaganda. The Jews from Europe "stole" Palestinian land with the benefit of "restitution capital" and "official weapons" from West Germany. Israel's war of 1967 was a "Blitzkrieg ... an anti-communist orgy" celebrated by the anti-communist Springer press.[102] She thought that "the Arab people were mobilized by the action for anti-imperialist struggle. They celebrated the revolutionaries as heroes. Their will for battle has been enormously strengthened." The Munich "action" against "Israel's Nazi fascism" was an example of "how practice pushes theory forward."[103] "Just as the essence of imperialism is fascist, so anti-fascism is in its tendency anti-imperialist." Thus, the attack on the Israeli athletes was anti-imperialist and hence anti-fascist. She referred to Genscher's decision to ban the GUPS as a "mass deportation of Palestinians" from West Germany. As a result of West Germany's

100 On the early years of the Baader-Meinhof group and Meinhof's arrest, the two most thorough studies are Stefan Aust, *Der Baader-Meinhof Komplex,* rev. ed. (Munich: Goldmann Verlag, 1998); and Butz Peters, *Tödlicher Irrtum: Die Geschichte der RA*, 3rd. ed. (Frankfurt/Main: Fischer Taschenbuch, 2007). Also see Willi Winkler, *Die Geschichte der RAF* (Berlin: Rowholt, 2007).

101 Ibid., 151–152.

102 Ibid., 152.

103 Ibid., 159.

"nationalist policy of extermination" the Palestinians would also be subjected to "Israel's policy of extermination."[104]

Meinhof's essay was also a restatement of the hatred of Social Democracy in the traditions of German Communism. She despised West Germany's left-of-center government. Chancellor Willy Brandt had promised to "dare more democracy" when he assumed office in 1969. Meinhof wrote that more "democracy" had been abolished in the Federal Republic since 1966 when the Social Democrats entered a coalition government in Bonn, "than was the case in the seventeen years before under all CDU [conservative Christian Democratic Union] governments taken together."[105] The Social Liberal coalition stood for a "tasteful or palatable *(schmackhafte)* imperialism."[106] She joined in the by-then familiar equation of the Israelis with the Nazis. The goal of the West German government was "not to be in any way inferior to the Moshe Dayan fascism – Dayan this Himmler of Israel."[107] Since the death of its athletes, "Israel cries crocodile tears. It used its athletes as the Nazis used the Jews–as fuel to be burned for its imperialist policy of extermination."[108]

Meinhof viewed the attack in Munich as a great revolutionary accomplishment. It had "torn away the character masks of the social liberal coalition and their propagandists" by pushing the contradictions of imperialism to their limit. "The Arab peoples have massively understood that in West Germany that face is an imperialist strategy of extermination."[109] She wrote that the deaths of the Israeli athletes were not the fault of the terrorists as it would be "idiotic to believe that the revolutionaries wanted it. They wanted the release of the prisoners."[110] The terrorists of Black September were thus without blame for the deaths of the athletes. "They took hostages from a people that has pursued a policy of extermination against them.... They did not want to kill.... The German police massacred the revolutionaries and their hostages."[111] The statement ended with ringing expressions of "solidarity with the liberation struggle of the Palestinian people!," with the "revolution in Vietnam," and a call for "revolutionaries of all lands"

[104] Ibid., 172.
[105] Ibid., 171.
[106] Ibid., 172.
[107] Ibid., 173.
[108] Ibid. The German reads as follows: "*Israel vergießt Krokodilstränen. Es hat seine Sportler verheizt wie die Nazis die Juden–Brennmaterial für die imperialistische Ausrottungspolitik.*"
[109] Ibid., 175.
[110] Ibid., 176.
[111] Ibid., 177.

to unite.[112] With this essay, Meinhof joined Dieter Kunzelmann as being another prominent, not marginal, member of the radical Left to combine rhetorical solidarity with the Arabs and Palestinians with an even more emphatic celebration of Palestinian terrorist violence aimed at Israelis. It remains one of the canonical statements of leftist anti-Semitism in postwar German and European history.

THE PLO AND EAST GERMANY AFTER THE MUNICH ATTACK

As we have noted, the Stasi was aware from Western sources, and presumably its own as well, that Black September was a part of the PLO and that Arafat's denials of involvement were part of an illusory "fiction of legality." On September 17, 1972 Arafat wrote to Erich Honecker about "the action in Munich." He said that the PLO "was not responsible for the organization Black September." He blamed the West German and Israeli governments for the "bloody end" of the action in Munich. There was "no doubt" the "men of the Black September organization intended to release the Israelis" when Israel freed "Palestinian prisoners" who "endured the worst tortures and oppression in Israeli prisons."[113] He was writing to Honecker because "we [the Executive Committee of the PLO] approve, treasure, are proud of and take hope and strength from the sincere friendship for our cause and your sympathy that you have shown us as well as your recognition of our right in struggle."

Arafat urged "understanding of the action in Munich from the viewpoint of the general problem and its historical events with all of their political, national and human dimensions. If one wants to really distinguish between the deep causes and the peripheral and secondary events, it is futile and useless to view the action apart from the stream of events and from their whole historical framework."[114] In other words, he offered justifications for the Munich attack. Israel, he continued, was using the attack in Munich and the world's ignorance about the Palestinian issue

[112] Ibid., 177. For an analysis of the text by the Bundeskriminalamt, see "Bericht: Illegal Druckschrift der RAF mit dem Titel 'Die Aktion des Schwarzen September in München – Zur Strategie des antiimperialistischen Kampfes,'" BAK B106/83804 Bundeskriminalamt, Bonn (January 15, 1973).

[113] Yasser Arafat to Erich Honecker (September 17, 1972, "Notizen und Schreiben außenpolitischen Charakters zwischen der DDR und der Palästinensischen Befreiungsbewegung zur Unterstützung der PLO durch die DDR, 1972, 1974, 1978–1979," Politisches Archiv des Auswärtiges Amt, Berlin, PAAA, MFAA, Abt. Naher-und Mittlerer Osten, MfAA, C 7.667 (ZR 2040/01), 48–49.

[114] Ibid, 48–49.

not only to label it an act of terror but to "accuse the Arabs of unleashing a war of extermination and thereby turning firm historical realities upside down." It was Israel that by ignoring the rights of the Palestinians sought to justify "murder actions" against them. The American denunciation of the attack in Munich was evidence of antagonism to the Arab countries and had thus given Israel a "green light" to unleash aggression against them.[115] Arafat expressed hope that the East Germans would adopt measures "that guarantee defense against the imperialist and racist attacks [by Israel, JH] whether through diplomatic action or via the United Nations and other international forum, through the press and other methods that you regard as effective." He hoped East Germany would take the side of "right, freedom and human values" against "oppression, aggression and imperialism."[116] Arafat's letter to Honecker of September 17, 1972 contained key elements of the PLO's political warfare against Israel. Black September was not responsible for the loss of life in Munich and in any case the PLO was not connected to Black September. The deaths in Munich were the fault of the West Germans and Israelis. Armed struggle was the only way that the Palestinians could realize their national rights. With the receipt of this confidential letter, Erich Honecker and the East German Politburo understood that in dealing with Arafat they were dealing with a terrorist but one with a Clausewitzian understanding of the interaction of force, diplomacy, and a "political-diplomatic battle" at the United Nations and elsewhere.

On November 27, 1972, Honecker sent a public letter of greetings to the "Arab People's Conference in Support of the Palestinian Revolution" taking place in Beirut. The text was widely distributed by the GDR's press agency.[117] He did not mention the Munich massacre. In the name of the SED's Central Committee and "of the whole people" of the GDR, he sent "warm greetings" to the conference. The gathering was evidence of the "strengthening of the unity and determination of broad strata of the Arab peoples in struggle against imperialism, Zionism and reaction." Honecker referred to "the string of recent Israeli acts of aggression against the Republic of Lebanon and the Syrian Arab Republic," which

[115] Ibid., 51.

[116] Ibid.

[117] Abteilung Internationale Verbindungen, "Entwurf eines Grußschreibens : An die arabische Volkskonferenz zur Unterstützung der palästinensischen Revolution," Berlin (November 24, 1972), 1–2. Also see "*Kongreß zur Unterstutzung des palastinensischen Volkes eröffnet: Delegation der DDR überbracht Grüßdes ZK der SED,*" *Neues Deutschland* (November 28, 1972), BAB ZK der SED, DY 30 9529, 1.

demonstrated "yet again that Israel, with the support of the USA and other imperialist states is not ready to agree to a peaceful settlement of the Middle East conflict."[118] The "history of the world wide confrontation with imperialism" had shown that the unity of the "anti-imperialist front" led by the Soviet Union and the "socialist community of states" lay behind "every success in the struggle for self-determination and social progress." East Germany "in the future as in the past" stood "firmly on the side of the Arabic-Palestinian people." It supported "its resistance movement" and right to self-determination.[119] Honecker's letter demonstrated to Arafat and the PLO Executive Committee that East Germany had a totally different stance toward the PLO and the issue of terrorism than was the case with the West German government, whose position on these matters was clearly expressed in Genscher's decision to ban the GUPS and GUPA. According to Abdallah Frangi, the chair of the GUPS, Honecker accepted Arafat's suggestion that East Germany accept all of the 330 Palestinian students who were deported from West Germany.[120]

West German diplomats were fully aware of the price the Federal Republic was paying in relations with the Arab states for Genscher's crackdown on GUPS and GUPA. Soon after the Munich attack, Gunter von Well, a state secretary in the West German Foreign Ministry, sent a telex about the ban on GUPS and GUPA to all West German embassies in the Arab states as well as to the West German delegation at the UN and in Turkey.[121] The ban "did not imply any position regarding the Palestinian issue as such." But the West German government "could not permit the Middle East conflict to be carried out on the territory of the Federal Republic" and in ways that "endanger the inner security and public order." The government had "found numerous documents that indicate close connections between Black September" and both GUPS and GUPA. It had already informed the Arab embassies in Bonn that Black September agents tried to telephone the already expelled Abdallah Frangi, the unofficial leader of the GUPS.[122] The Foreign Ministry

[118] Ibid., 1–2.

[119] Ibid., 2.

[120] Abdallah Frangi, *Der Gesandte: Mein Leben für Palästina, Hinter den Kulissne der Nahost-Politik* (Munich: Wilhelm Heyne Verlag, 2011), 165.

[121] Gunter van Well, "310-roem 1 b4-82.00'92.sb'3229'72 vs-v," Bonn (nd) PAAA B 130 Band 9863A, "Attentat Olympiade München, Flugzeugattentate, Attentatsversurche und Entführungen, Naher Osten vom 1971 bis 1972," and "An alle Vertretungen in arabischen Staate, UNOgerma, Ankara (f.StS Dr. Frank), SB.3229.72 VS-V," Bonn (nd) PAAA B 130 Band 9863A, "Attentat Olympiade München, Flugzeugattentate, Attentatsversurche und Entführungen, Naher Osten vom 1971 bis 1972."

[122] Ibid.

regretted the "misuse of the guests' rights" by GUPS all the more because the Federal Republic had been "particularly generous especially toward the Palestinians regarding granting permission to live in the country." After the Six-Day War, he wrote, hundreds of these students had received scholarships from the West German government after financial support from their families was cut off. The GUPS ban targeted students whom the government suspected of supporting terrorism. It was not a "mass expulsion of Palestinians."[123]

The West German ambassadors in the Arab states reported sharply negative reactions to the GUPS ban. On October 2, the Cairo Embassy informed the Middle East desk in Bonn that West German–Egyptian relations were under stress because of reports about "a supposed persecution of Arabs in the Federal Republic of Germany" in part from the "apparently communist inspired Palestinian news agency. The Embassy had information that the GDR was responsible for a part of the campaign of defamation."[124] Further, in other Arab countries, there were reports that Arab citizens in West Germany were "treated badly, persecuted and deported without any reason or refused entry."[125] The West German ambassador to Egypt concluded that "with regret that German-Egyptian relations had suffered a great deal of damage in recent weeks."[126]

By mid-November, the West German Foreign Ministry had become aware that Arafat had met with Gerhard Herder, the head of the East German Legation in Beirut.[127] The two discussed a visit by a PLO delegation led by Arafat to East Berlin in winter 1972/73 and the possibility of East German assistance with weapons, provisions, and clothing to Palestinian organizations. Arafat asked for military training of "officers of the Palestine Liberation Army (PLA) and guerrillas in special camps in the GDR" as well as supplies of weapons and fellowships for students

[123] Ibid.

[124] "Aus Kairo, nr. 15076'72, nr. 891 vom 2.10.1972 an bonn: betr.: sicherheitsmassnahmen gegen angehoerige arabischer laender," PAAA B 130 Band 9863A, Attentat Olympiade München.

[125] Ibid.

[126] "Aus Kairo nr. 922 vom 9.10.1972 an bonn: betr.: sicherheitsmassnahmen gegen angehoerige arabischer laender, hier: beschluss der drei konfederiaten staatschefs, gegenmassnahmen gegen die angeblich Araber Verfolgung in der brd zu ergreifen," PAAA B 130 Band 9863A, Attentat Olympiade München.

[127] "Referat 011, Auszug aus dem Kursprotokoll über die 131.Kabinett–: betr.: ddr-plo, Arafat und dr-diplomat verhandeln ueber engere Beziehungen," Beirut (November 16, 1972), PAAA B 130 Band 9863A, Attentat Olympiade München. See "Herder, Gerhard," in Siegfried Bock, Ingrid Muth, Hermann Schwiesau, eds., *DDR-Aussenpolitik: Ein Überblick* (Berlin: LIT Verlag, 2010), 313.

to attend East German universities.[128] In return for expansion of East German support, Herder requested from Arafat that the PLO oppose improved Arab relations with West Germany and "instead call for closer ties to the GDR." Further, the Palestinians' "propaganda media should reveal very close cooperation between the Israelis with the FRG and characterize efforts to prevent and prosecute Palestinian attacks as 'complicity in an anti-Arab policy.' " Further "in the Arab world [the PLO] should fan the flames of hostility against the FRG."[129] East Germany met all of Arafat's requests, while the PLO denounced West Germany both in the Arab world and elsewhere as requested. As Arafat requested more fellowships for Palestinian students to study at East German universities only six weeks after several hundred GUPS members had been expelled from West Germany, it seems plausible that at least some of these German-speaking Palestinian leftists continued their university studies in East Germany, the German state that looked favorably on the PLO and its campaign of "armed struggle" against Israel.

In 1969, East Germany's antagonism to Israel had been indispensable for gaining diplomatic recognition by the Arab states. In the fall of 1972, its enthusiasm for Arafat in the immediate aftermath of the Black September attack on the Israelis in Munich gained it further goodwill among both the Arab states and the PLO. Conversely, West Germany's counterterrorism measures were placing it on the defensive in the Arab states and increased pressures for adopting a policy of neutrality in the Middle East conflict. At the same time a special relationship was in its early stages between East Germany and the PLO.

[128] Ibid.
[129] Ibid.

6

Formalizing the East German Alliance with the PLO and the Arab States: 1973

Soviet and East German support for the Arab states expanded at the high point of détente in Europe. West Germany had opened diplomatic relations with the Communist regimes in Eastern Europe, including with what it now was willing to call publicly the German Democratic Republic. In Vietnam, the United States was withdrawing its troops. What the Communists called the global "correlation of forces" appeared to be shifting in their favor due to the combined impact of the growth of Soviet military power and the success of Communist and leftist armed movements in the third world. The radicalism of 1969, evident in Stoph's "Support Order" and formation of the Weiss Committee to coordinate arms shipments to third-world states and movements, was also apparent in East Germany's deepening support of the Palestine Liberation Organization. In 1973, East Germany became the first country in the Soviet bloc to permit the PLO to open an office in its capital. That decision should be placed in the global context of the Communists' perceptions that the global balance of power was shifting in their favor.

The elevation of the PLO's status in East Berlin took place following two official visits to East Berlin in 1973 by delegations led by Yasser Arafat. The first took place from February 17–22 and the second from July 27 to August 8.[1] The Afro-Asian Solidarity Committee served as

[1] AASK [Afro-Asiastische Solidaritatskomittee] "Programm für den Aufenthält der Delegation der Befreiungsorganisation von Palästina (PLO) unter Leitung ihres Vorsitzenden des Exekutivkomitees Yasser Arafat vom 17.-22. 2.73 in der DDR," BAB ZK der SED, DY 30 9529; and "Program für den Aufenthält der Delegation der Befreiungsorganisation von Palästina (PLO) unter Leitung ihres Vorsitzenden des Exekutivkomitees Yasser Arafat vom 27.Juli bis 8. August 1973." The files of the East

host. In February Arafat and the delegation met a unit of the National People's Army and participated in a press conference with journalists from East German print, radio, and television. Arafat met for several hours with Politburo member Herman Axen. In July and early August, Gerhard Grüneberg greeted Arafat and his delegation at Berlin-Schönefeld airport. Grüneberg's political career traced a path from that of worker skilled in stonemasonry to the top reaches of the Communist Party. He fought in the German army in World War II and spent some of the years between 1941 and 1945 in Soviet captivity. He joined the KPD and then the SED in 1946 upon his return to East Berlin. He rose through the ranks of the latter to become a member of its Central Committee in 1959. He joined the Politburo in 1966. He was a regular presence at the key meetings with the PLO leadership in the formative decade of the relationship in the 1970s.[2]

It was during these meetings in 1973 that the East German leaders agreed to open a PLO office in East Berlin, the first in the Soviet bloc. During the August meeting, Arafat also became a major media attraction in East Germany when he was featured as a star (along with the American Communist Angela Davis) at a "world youth festival" taking place in East Berlin. On August 3, 1973, Erich Honecker (1912–1994), the general secretary of the SED and leader of the East German regime since 1971, met Arafat at the Central Committee headquarters. Their meeting was front page news for *Neues Deutschland*, which featured it with photos showing Arafat, Honecker, and Grüneberg smiling for the cameras. *ND* reported on its front page that Honecker and Arafat underscored their "common struggle against imperialism, colonialism and Zionism" and promised to "deepen" the bonds between the SED and the PLO.[3] The size and personalities of the delegations to these first meetings indicate their importance. Kurt Krüger, the general secretary of the GDR's Solidarity Committee, led the welcoming committee, which also included Wolfgang Krause, the first secretary of the East German Embassy in Beirut.[4]

German photo agency, Allgemeiner Nachricthendienst-Zentralbild (ADN-ZB) archived in the Bundesarchiv Bildarchiv Koblenz (German Federal Archive Picture Archive in Koblenz) hold a photo of Arafat and Grüneberg signing the agreement "for further cooperation between the SED and the PLO" on August 2, 1973. Because digital rights are not available for the photo, it cannot be used in this print edition as well. The Bundesarchiv Bildarchiv archive citation is: Bild 183-M0801-321.

[2] "Grüneberg, Gerhard," in Barth et al., eds., *Wer war Wer in der DDR: Ein biographisches Handbuch* (Frankfurt/Main: Fischer Taschenbuch Verlag, 1996), 252.

[3] "SED und PLO vertiefen ihre weitere Zusammenarbeit: Erich Honecker empfing Yasser Arafat im Hause des Zentralkomitees," *Neues Deutschland* (August 4, 1973), 1.

[4] Abteilung Internationale Verbindungen, "Entwurf: Programm für den Aufenthält der Delegation der Befreiungsorganisation von Palästina (PLO) unter Leitung ihres

These were the first of what became regular visits by Arafat to East Berlin and meetings with Honecker. On the numerous occasions when Arafat visited East Berlin, *Neues Deutschland* published photos of him shaking hands, smiling, and embracing Honecker. The Honecker-Arafat bond became the public face of the East German–PLO alliance. Honecker's roots in the history of German and then East German Communism were long and deep. He joined the German Communist Party in 1929 at the age of 17 and was active in its youth organizations. In 1930–1931, he attended the Lenin School in Moscow and returned to Germany to engage in opposition to the Nazi regime. He was arrested in 1935 and was in the Brandenburg prison from 1937 to 1945. In the postwar years he rose through a series of positions in the KPD and then the SED "youth" organizations and became a member of the ruling Politburo in 1958. In 1971, he succeeded Walter Ulbricht as the general secretary of the Central Committee and thus leader of the government.[5]

The following month, on September 4, 1973, the East German Politburo decided to establish formal relations with the PLO and to open a PLO office in East Berlin.[6] On October 17, 1973, officials in the Ministry of State Security (hereafter MfS or Stasi) Central Office II (Hauptabteilung II) noted that East Germany's support for the Arab states and the PLO had contributed to the decision of the Arab states to offer diplomatic recognition to East Germany and "had great influence on the decision of other states in Africa and in other parts of the world" to do likewise. It also

Vorsitzenden des Exekutivkomitees Yasser Arafat, Vorsitzender des Exekutivkomitees der PLO in der DDR vom 6.-9. August 1974," Berlin (August 2, 1974), Bundesarchiv Berlin Lichterfelde, BAB ZK der SED, DY 30 9529. In addition to Arafat, other members of the PLO delegation included Abou Loft (Farouk Kaddoumi), member of the PLO's Executive Committee and director of Al Fatah's political department; Zouheir Mohsen, PLO Executive Committee member and director of the military department of Al-Saika; Abdel Mohsen Abou Maizar, PLO Executive Committee member and the PLO's official spokesperson; Yasser Abd Rabbo, PLO Executive Committee member and director of its Information Department; Khaled Fahumy, president of the Palestinian National Congress; Abou Ismail, member of the Jordanian Communist Party; Ahmed Azhari, PLO representative for relations with the socialist (i.e., Communist) countries; Abdel Rahman, responsible for PLO propaganda efforts; and Nabil Kuleilat, director of the PLO's office in East Berlin.

[5] "Honecker, Erich," in Barth et al., *Wer war Wer in der DDR*, 321–322. The scholarship on Honecker is extensive. See, for example, Catherine Epstein, *The Last Revolutionaries: German Communists and Their Century* (Cambridge, MA: Harvard University Press, 2003). Among the many volumes of Honecker's essays and speeches, see Erich Honecker, *Unter dem Banner des Internationalismsus: ausgewählte Reden und Aufsätze* ([East] Berlin: Dietz Verlag, 1972).

[6] Leiter, Hauptabteilung II, "1. Stellvertreter des Minister Genossen Generalleutnant Beater," [East] Berlin (October 17, 1973), BStU, Zentralarchiv, MfS HA IX Nr. 270, 4–5.

had "considerable influence" on the decision to admit East Germany to the UN and its various special organizations. East Germany had thereby gained "sympathy and support of the anti-imperialist forces of the Arab region" for its "competition" with "West German imperialism."[7]

The Stasi believed that the opening of the PLO office in East Berlin opened "various new political-operative possibilities for fighting the enemy." First, it could "officially or unofficially" use it in "actions of the MfS in the fight against the common enemy." Second, "special operative actions of the MfS fighting the enemy could be carried out using the legend that these were activities of the PLO."[8] On the other hand, the Stasi was concerned about "possible execution of acts of terror by militant organizations originating from the [East German, JH] base of operations and possible activities of supporters living in the GDR."[9] Nabil Kuleilat, described as a Communist with an "excellent relationship" with Arafat, was to be the office director. Wolfgang Schüßler, the deputy director of the Department of International Relations, was appointed to be his contact person in the SED's Central Committee.[10] Kuleilat intended to develop contacts among the 80 Palestinian and 1,600 Arab students studying in East German universities, including 25 who had been expelled from West Germany after the attack on the Munich Olympics.[11] The officials in Central Office II concluded that the opening of the PLO office required an expansion of its surveillance over it, because it could be the target of attacks "but also because it could itself be the starting point of activities that would do political damage to the GDR."[12] The four Palestinian organizations with members in East Germany that the MfS was observing were "GDR friendly." They included Al Fatah with 60 members; the "left-wing extremist" Popular Front for the Liberation of Palestine with 20 members; 15 members of the Syrian-based Saika; and six members of the Democratic Popular Front for the Liberation of Palestine. The Stasi

7 "Politisch-operative Probleme im Zusammenhang mit der Sicherung und Kontrolle der PLO-Vertretung in der DDR," [East] Berlin (October 17, 1973), BStU, Zentralarchiv, MfS HA IX Nr. 270, 8–41.

8 Ibid.

9 Ibid., 22–23.

10 Ibid., 27. Schüßler had served in the East German Legation in Cairo. He later served as ambassador to India and Nepal, as director of the Near and Middle East Department in the Foreign Ministry, and then as ambassador to Egypt from 1985 to 1990. See "Schüßler, Wolfgang," in Siegfried Bock, Ingrid Muth, and Hermann Schwiesau, eds., *DDR-Außenpolitik: Ein Überblick* (Berlin: LIT Verlag, 2010), 351.

11 "Politisch-operative Probleme im Zusammenhang mit der Sicherung und Kontrolle der PLO-Vertretung in der DDR," [East] Berlin (October 17, 1973), 31 and 40.

12 Ibid., 32.

officials, taking note of the rivalries among the groups and possible "misuse by imperialist secret services," thought that despite their "positive stance" toward the GDR, the groups could be "a factor of uncertainty."[13]

The Stasi memo of October 17, 1973, expressed a fundamental and enduring ambivalence toward the Arabs and Palestinians living and studying in East Germany. On the one hand, the Communist regime welcomed them as part of its contribution to the global struggle against imperialism and Zionism. On the other hand, it viewed them as a source of potential trouble, especially if they carried out terrorist attacks in West Germany and Western Europe that could be traced back to East Germany. Such actions would undermine the GDR's reputation as a "peace state," confirm suspicions that it was rather a state sponsor of terrorism, and thereby undermine détente and the financially lucrative benefits that East Germany was receiving from West Germany. The Stasi had reason to be concerned about the Palestinian terror organizations it had welcomed to its territory.

The reports in *Neues Deutschland* about the establishment of a PLO office in East Berlin drew the attention of the West German press, especially *Die Welt* in West Berlin. Heinz Galinski also took note. On August 15, 1973, both the West Berlin *Taggespiegel* and *Die Welt,* citing reports in the Beirut based Arab information service, published reports that East Germany was increasing its military and political support for Arab-Palestinian guerrillas as a result of the agreements signed with Arafat in East Berlin. Both accurately reported that the agreements called for "civil and also non-civil," that is, military, assistance for the PLO, and the willingness to care for 400 wounded PLO fighters each year in East German hospitals.[14] According to the Beirut report, the agreement made East Germany "the 'godfather' of the whole socialist camp for the Palestinian guerrillas." The Soviet Union had chosen East Germany as a "transit station" for Soviet support of the guerrillas in order to avoid diplomatic involvement in the future that could emerge from Moscow's direct help for the guerillas.[15] *Die Welt* quoted Galinski as describing the agreement as "the greatest scandal in Germany's postwar history."[16] After

[13] Ibid., 41.

[14] "DDR verstärkt Unterstützung palästinensischer Guerillas: Arabisch Nachrichten-Agentur: Arafat schloß in Ost-Berlin Vertrag," *Der Tagesspiegel*, West Berlin (August 15, 1973); "'DDR' verstärkt Hilfe für palästinensische Befreiungsfront," *Die Welt* (August 15, 1973), BStU, Archiv der Zentralstelle, MfS ZAIG, Nr. 11048, 432 and 431.

[15] Ibid.

[16] Cited in "'DDR' verstärkt Hilfe für palästinensische Befreiungsfront."

the "terrible events" in Germany between 1933 and 1945, a German state must not "bring a terror organization to Berlin to continue its work of hatred against people of Jewish faith."[17] *Die Welt* reported that the military assistance amounted to a million dollars a year, a small fraction of what the PLO received from the Soviet Union. East Germany would also provide annual fellowships for students and scholars, medical care for 400 wounded PLO fighters, and education for 50 orphans of PLO members and would engage in a regular exchange of delegations to discuss issues raised by "the common struggle against imperialism and Zionism."[18] A spokesperson for the Israeli Foreign Ministry said that the agreement recalled the cooperation between Hitler and the Grand Mufti, Haj Amin el-Husseini. He added that "East Germany is the actual successor of Nazi Germany. It does not surprise us at all that the 'GDR' is the first European country that gives state support to an organization [the PLO, JH] that officially preaches murder."[19]

On August 17, 1973, Wilfried Ernst-Eichenrode, the editor-in-chief of *Die Welt*, attacked East Germany's decision in a column entitled "East-Berlin in a pact with terror against the Jews."[20] A decision of the West German Supreme Court had asserted that the constitution of the Federal Republic applied to "all of Germany."

> This is not empty theory. It means that we are not only upset about the scandalous agreement that the "GDR" reached with the Palestinian guerillas. It affects us far more as members of the whole German people. From a responsibility to Germany, we cannot be silent about it. The agreement affects us in two ways. All Germans, whether in the Federal Republic or in the "GDR," are burdened before history and before their own conscience with the crimes which the Hitler regime perpetrated against the Jews. Hence, it must burden all Germans, whether on this or that side of the Elbe, in the face of history and their own conscience when now the "GDR" regime carries forward the crimes of the Hitler dictatorship – not by itself murdering Jews but in making a pact with terrorist organizations that murder Jews.
>
> With the delivery of "non-civilian equipment" to Palestinian guerrillas, it is assisting the murder of Jews (*leistet es Beihilfe zum Mord an Juden)* and with the agreement to open a guerrilla-office in East Berlin, it offers Arab terrorists an organizational center in Europe. From now on, Palestinian murder commandos,

[17] Ibid.

[18] "'DDR' verstärkt Hilfe für palästinensische Befreiungsfront," 431.

[19] "DDR wird Operationsbasis für palästinensische Terroristen," *Die Welt* (August 17, 1973), BStU, Archiv der Zentralstelle, MfS ZAIG, Nr. 11048, 429.

[20] W. [Wilfried] Hertz-Eichenrode, "Ost-Berlin im Pakt mit dem Terror gegen die Juden," West Berlin (August 17, 1973), BStU, Archiv der Zentralstelle, MfS ZAIG, Nr. 11048, 428.

such as those who carried out the horrific massacre during the Olympics in Munich, will not have a long way to go to enter the Federal Republic.

The constitution does not free the Federal Republic from the responsibility for all of Germany. Under no circumstances can the Federal Republic retreat when the right of Jews to live is at stake. The "GDR" reminds Israel of Hitler's cooperation with the Grand Mufti. The government of the Federal Republic must speak out to preserve the dignity and respect of the German people. Federal Chancellor Brandt cannot accept in silence that in Germany a red dictatorship [East Germany, JH] continues the crimes of the brown dictatorship [Nazi Germany]. The idea that soon a representative of the Federal Republic of Germany at the United Nations must sit next to a representative of the SED regime is unbearable.[21]

Eichenrode's column of August 17, 1973, illustrated the continuing bond between the Springer press and the leaders of West Germany's Jewish community and disquiet among both that improved relations with the existing Communist regimes, including East Germany, were taking precedence over raising the issue of the GDR's decision to support and open an office of the PLO.

In the August 24, 1973, edition of the *Allgemeine Jüdische Wochenzeitung*, Heinz Galinski wrote the lead editorial "The East Berlin PLO-Office and Its Unfavorable Mission: New Threats for Germany's Jews?"[22] In it he warned of "strengthened activity of Arab guerrillas in the GDR." It was certain that the PLO people in East Berlin would not limit their activities to propaganda within East Germany. He described the prominence given to Arafat at the recently concluded World Youth Festival in East Berlin as the cultivation of a "cult of personality." He asked what purpose was served by giving him such favored prominence if not to assist in building a "terror organization" that had engaged in the murder of innocent people inside and outside Israel. How did association with the PLO serve East Germany's reputation as an advocate of détente and peace? The Jewish community in West Berlin saw "in Arafat and his followers a new embodiment of hatred and a will to extermination that was only comparable to the National Socialist violent rule." Every German state, in the aftermath of the Nazi crimes against the Jews, had a responsibility to the "Jewish community and to the state of Israel."[23] "We," that is, the Jewish community of West Berlin, "find it to be a disgrace that the GDR ... in its demonstrative expression

[21] Ibid.

[22] Heinz Galinski, "Das Ostberliner PLO-Büro und seine zwielichtigen Aufgaben: Neue Bedrohung für Deutschlands Juden?" *Allgemeine Jüdische Wochenzeitung*, Dusseldorf (August 24, 1973), 1–2.

[23] Ibid.

of solidarity with Israel's enemies goes farther than any other East bloc state" in support of the PLO. The opening of a PLO office in East Berlin was "a blow against détente in Europe," violated the spirit of the Allied Four-Power agreements in Berlin, and created further tensions in the city. "We thus expect the Federal Republic and the Allies to take a clear position on these events." The PLO office would certainly produce "a variety of anti-Israeli, anti-Zionist and ultimately anti-Jewish propaganda materials in the whole German-language area." The East German authorities appeared "indifferent that sending such propaganda will assist neo-Nazi elements" in Germany. Galinski cited press reports that the PLO office in East Berlin would be engaged in "still other equally unfavorable tasks," namely, "weapons training of Al Fatah terrorists who then will be infiltrated into the Federal Republic and other West European states." He regretted that rather than posing that issue, too many voices in West Germany were ready to condemn Israel rather than to take measures against terrorism.[24] For the Brandt government, however, improvement of German-German relations had priority over raising the issue of East German support for the PLO.

The following week, Galinski wrote an editorial entitled "Escalation of Hatred: East Berlin Becomes a Terrorist Base."[25] The editors of the *Allgemeine* noted "with regret" that most West German media with several exceptions chose not to comment on the issue. The magazine *Quick* had accurately reported on the details of the GDR-PLO agreement including the financial assistance and delivery of military equipment. Yet most of the press and other media did not follow in discussing the "growing threat" to Europe that the agreement created. Galinski was "astonished" that the German and Allied officials had responded "with silence to the establishment of a terrorist base in East Berlin." Why did "certain circles" appear to believe that protesting the development would endanger their détente policy? If the "resigned acceptance of terrorist planning in East Berlin by responsible politicians and by parts of public opinion became predominant, then the question of the value of such a policy [détente] is appropriate."[26] In other words, Galinski and the leaders of the West Berlin Jewish community argued that Chancellor Brandt was refraining from criticism of East German policy because he believed that doing so would endanger his détente policy. While Israel's enemies spoke of the

[24] Ibid.

[25] Heinz Galinski, "Eskalation des Hasses: Ostberlin wird Terroristenstützpunkt," *Allgemeine Jüdische Wochenzeitung*, Dusseldorf (September 7, 1973), 1.

[26] Ibid.

power of various Jewish lobbies, Galinski's unanswered pleas demonstrated that the small Jewish community in West Germany was not able to influence government policy on this issue.

The primary power that Galinski and his fellow Jewish leaders could muster came from moral and political convictions that Eichenrode expressed regarding the responsibility of a German government after the Holocaust. "As those who were persecuted before," Galinski wrote, "we must speak out when developments take place that lead to an escalation of hatred and that open the doors to violence." He continued that "we" were "deeply upset" to see that hopes that people would learn from the past had been dashed. Instead "new apostles of hatred and extermination have emerged. They have written the extinction of Israel on their banners and are seeking to bring the Middle East conflict to other parts of the world."[27] Galinski again said that "sadly a great part of our political environment fails to react to the phenomenon of terror firmly and with principle." That was especially the case "regarding relations with states that celebrate terrorists as heroes and that actively support them"; the GDR had now "entered that circle of states." Doing so did not seem to harm its efforts to enter the UN, where a vote on the subject was scheduled for the fall session. He argued that "over the long run, détente could not be sustained on the basis of rotten compromises at the expense of human rights."[28] Galinski argued that for the Brandt government, the priority of improving German-German relations was entailing "rotten compromises" and silence about the emergence of a terrorist threat in East Berlin.

An exchange of letters between Galinski and Egon Bahr, the director of the Planning Staff in the Federal Republic's Foreign Ministry and a longtime associate of Chancellor Brandt, revealed the emerging differences between Galinski, other Jewish leaders, and the foreign policy of the Brandt government. On September 4, 1973, Galinski wrote to Bahr to express his concerns about the potential for terrorism emerging from the PLO office in East Berlin. Bahr replied that "a precondition for an [East German] turn away from such a policy, naturally is that the matter not be turned into a question of prestige by its false public treatment," that is, presumably as was the case, in Bahr's view, in Galinski's recent remarks about the PLO office.[29]

[27] Ibid.

[28] Heinz Galinski, "Eskalation des Hasses: Ostberlin wird Terroritenstützpunkt," *Allgemeine Jüdische Wochenzeitung*, Dusseldorf (September 7, 1973), 1.

[29] Egon Bahr to Heinz Galinski, Bonn (September 19, 1973), Archiv Centrum Judaicum, 5 A1, Band 1044, 8–9; cited by Juliane Berndt, "Ich weiß, ich bin kein Bequemer," 158–159.

Bahr was confident that "no use or threat of use of violence" followed from East Germany's decision to open the PLO office.[30] The next day, Galinski received a letter from Franz Josef Strauss, the leader of the conservative Christian Social Union in Bavaria and of the conservative opposition in parliament, in which he expressed his "full agreement" with Galinski. What, Strauss asked, "is the so-called détente worth, if terrorist organizations are not only tolerated but even supported by a government on German soil."[31]

On September 21, 1973, Galinski wrote a remarkable open letter to Erich Honecker to express the "growing concern and anxiety in the Jewish community" about the establishment of the PLO office in East Berlin. On the following day, *Die Welt* published excerpts.[32]

> With astonishment, we see that the stance of the GDR towards Israel is more hostile than other socialist countries.... Now and then we hear from your side the assurance that you have nothing against Jews. Rather it only Zionism that you condemn and fight. We have had negative practical experiences with such theories. There is no doubt that the biased, uninformed and hate-filled reporting about Israel in the press, radio and television in the GDR in recent years again awakens anti-Semitic resentment. In so doing, it accords with the intentions of neo-Nazi elements. People, such as yourself, who belonged to the circle of those persecuted by the Nazi regime, must be especially conscious of such effects. It especially pains us that people [such as yourself] who suffered with us under National Socialism and fought against it, foster such destructive emotions and sentiments.
>
> For over 28 years since the collapse of the National Socialist violent rule, the few survivors [of the Holocaust] who are in our community as well as your political friends emphasized that the solidarity of those persecuted by the National Socialist regime was one of the most important preconditions for the effective fight against the evil spirit of the past. You and your political friends have obviously abandoned this position.[33]

Galinski reminded Honecker that the leaders of the Jewish community in West Germany "had always fought a decisive and uncompromising battle against all forms of neo-Nazism" and "always supported international relaxation of tensions" and improved East-West relations and the agreements signed by the four occupying powers in Berlin. Yet, East Germany's arrangement with the PLO was violating the spirit of the

30 Egon Bahr to Heinz Galinski (October 2, 1973), Archiv Centrum Judaicum, 5 A1, Band 1044, 22–23; cited by Juliane Berndt, "Ich weiß, ich bin kein Bequemer," 159.

31 Franz-Josef Strauss to Heinz Galinski (October 3, 1973), Archiv Centrum Judaicum, 5 A1, Band 1044, 6; cited by Juliane Berndt, "Ich weiß, ich bin kein Bequemer," 160.

32 "Galinski bedauert feindselige Haltung der 'DDR' gegen Israel," West Berlin, *Die Welt* (September 22, 1973), BStU, Archiv der Zentralstelle, MfS ZAIG, Nr. 11048, 398.

33 Ibid.

Four-Power agreement, which was designed to prevent new sources of conflict in Berlin. He urgently appealed to Honecker "to be conscious of the great responsibility that you as well bear for peace and security, and to consider with great concern all of the consequences that could emerge from this stance [with the PLO] of the GDR. It is inconceivable for me that after such fundamental reflections that you would persist in a political course of action that opens the door to racial hatred and murderous violence."[34]

Galinski's effort to appeal to the community of those who had fought against and been persecuted by Nazism fell on deaf ears. Honecker never replied. In effect, Galinski asserted that Communist anti-fascism had become compatible with continuation of hatred of the Jews, dressed up in the form of its anti-Zionist campaign. Moreover, he asserted that Honecker and the East German government had abandoned solidarity with those most persecuted by the Nazi regime. By calling the East German pact with the PLO a violation of the Allied Four-Power agreement in Berlin, he also called into question Honecker's and the SED's understanding of détente and peace. Galinski argued that by opening the PLO office in East Berlin, the East German regime, rather than being a source of peace and understanding, was instead fostering policies of "racial hatred and murderous violence." In the era of Brandt and Bahr's "peace policy in Europe," these were not criticisms voiced by the West German government.

In the November 2, 1973, edition of the *Jüdische Allgemeine*, Galinski described Berlin as becoming a "turnstile of terror."[35] He saw the arrest of "four stateless Arabs" in West Berlin in possession of four and a half kilos of explosives as further evidence that terrorists were taking the path from the Middle East to Berlin-Schönefeld airport and from there to West Berlin. East Germany bore "full responsibility" for this "misuse of the transit routes from East to West Berlin." It "was now obvious that the GDR sympathized with the efforts of Arab terror organizations to include West Berlin and West Germany in their sphere of action. If that were not the case, the GDR would not have allowed the PLO to

[34] Ibid., 398. Also see Juliane Berndt, "Ich weiß, ich bin kein bequemer." Heinz Galinski – Mahner, Streiter, Stimme der Überlebenden (Berlin: be.bra Verlag, 2012), 157–158. Also see "Juden protestieren bei Honecker: Scharfe Kritik an Einrichtung eines Guerillo-Büros in Ostberlin," *Hannoversche Allgemeine* (September 22, 1973), BStU, Archiv der Zentralstelle, MfS ZAIG, Nr. 11048, 397.

[35] Heinz Galinski, "Berlin – Drehscheibe des Terrors," *Allgemeine Jüdische Wochenzeitung*, Dusseldorf (November 2, 1973), 10.

open an office in East Berlin."[36] Galinski sent an "urgent appeal" to the West Berlin Senate, the Federal Republic, and the three Western Allies to use all possibilities to "stop the infiltration of terrorists" from East to West Berlin and thus to prevent Berlin from becoming a "playground for terrorists and a turnstile for terror."[37]

West German newspapers were reporting extensively on the travels of members of the Palestinian terror organizations from East to West Berlin.[38] Arabs, primarily Palestinians and Syrians seeking asylum in West Germany, flew from Damascus and Beirut to Berlin-Schönefeld airport. From there, at times with assistance from the PLO office in East Berlin, they took the subway (*U-Bahn)* or elevated trains (*S-Bahn*) to West Berlin. From there they could travel to West Germany. Many sought asylum as political refugees and were able to drag out their cases for several years. Officials in the West German Interior Ministry suspected that the PLO office in East Berlin was paying the costs of legal representation. They further suspected that refugees who traveled to West Germany for economic reasons served as cover for those who had missions from the PLO to travel to the West. They also thought that the East German government tolerated the process because it meant more business at the airport and because the Arabs affiliated with the PLO were a security risk for West Germany.[39] The stream of Arab refugees from East to West Germany had increased significantly after the Munich massacre, when it became more difficult for Arabs to gain visas to enter West Germany. Arabs, especially from Beirut, claiming to be "politically persecuted," were able to use West Germany's generous asylum policies to enter the country. Soon after the opening of the PLO office in East Berlin in late August, the arriving asylum seekers spent two or three days in East Berlin before formally seeking asylum in the Federal Republic. From West Berlin, it was easy to

[36] Ibid.

[37] Ibid. Galinski made similar points in "Ost-Berlin schleust Terroristen ein: Jüdische Gemeinde warnt vor Zunahme des Antisemitismus," *Berlin Morgenpost* (November 9, 1973), BStU, Archiv der Zentralstelle, MfS ZAIG, Nr. 11048, 386.

[38] "Sicherheitsbehörden besorgt: Monatlich kommen 250 Araber," *Welt am Sonntag* (November 11, 1973); "Terroristen-Asyl am Alexander Platz," *Berliner Morgenpost* (March 26, 1973); Liselotte Müller, "Schönefeld als 'Loch' zu Westen," *Hannoversche Allgemeine* (October 24, 1973); Peter Hornung, "Ein neuer Trick: Über Ost-Berlin kommen arabische Terroristen," *Rheinischer Merkur* (October 5, 1975), BStU, Archiv der Zentralstelle, MfS ZAIG, Nr. 11048, 385–389.

[39] Liselotte Müller, "Schönefeld als 'Loch' zu Westen," *Hannoversche Allgemeine* (October 24, 1973).

circumvent the security precautions that the West European states had built concerning travelers from North Africa and the Middle East.[40]

West German intelligence officials suspected that one goal of the refugee stream was to rebuild organizations similar to the General Union of Palestinian Students (GUPS) and the General Union of Palestinian Workers (GUPA), after their dissolution and banning after the Munich massacre. When Genscher dissolved those groups, the system of financial "donations" to the PLO from some of the more than 50,000 Arabs in the FRG collapsed. Hundreds of thousands of marks had been donated to the PLO, some willingly, some due to extortion. After the GUPS and GUPA were banned, many Arabs in the Federal Republic refused to pay and often called the police when faced with pressures to do so. One purpose of new PLO cadres was to rebuild the system of financial payments. The West German authorities found that those seeking asylum made remarkably similar and in their view dubious claims such as "I left Al Fatah. I can't reconcile terror with my conscience." Or: "I'm fleeing from Al Fatah. I've recognized the senselessness of terror. Now I'm running from their terror commandos." If the flow of asylum seekers with real and bogus claims was to be controlled, it was the four Allied Powers in Berlin that had the responsibility and authority to do so.[41] In fact, the opening of the PLO in East Berlin became a matter of concern to American diplomats in Germany and to policy makers in Washington.

Officials at the American mission in West Berlin, the West Berlin government, the American Embassy in Bonn, and the State Department's European Desk shared Galinski's concern about the opening of the PLO bureau in East Berlin and the refugee stream into West Berlin and West Germany. On August 24, 1973, Lewis Hoffacker, an assistant to the secretary of state and coordinator of counterterrorism in the State Department in Washington, telegraphed the US mission in West Berlin that the State Department was "concerned that opening of PLO office in East Berlin creates possibility of another headquarters or cover for terrorism in Western Europe and possibly Scandinavia."[42] On September 28, Secretary of State

[40] Peter Hornung, "Ein neuer Trick: Über Ost-Berlin kommen arabische Terroristen," *Rheinischer Merkur* (October 5, 1975), BStU, Archiv der Zentralstelle, MfS ZAIG, Nr. 11048, 389.

[41] Ibid.

[42] "1973STATE168894: PLO Office to Open in East Berlin," Washington, DC (August 24, 1973), United States National Archives and Records Administration (NACP), Diplomatic Records, Central Foreign Policy Files, Electronic Telegrams, 1/1/1973–12/31/1973. See Lewis Hoffacker in the "Oral History Interviews done by the Association for Diplomatic Training and Study," adst.org/oral-history/oral-history-interviews/#h.

Henry Kissinger sought French and British support to convey the concerns of the three Western powers in Berlin about the opening of the PLO office in East Berlin. The Western allies had heard that among the activities of the PLO office in East Berlin "will be the training of personnel for acts of terrorism" and that "whatever its function, [a PLO, JH] Berlin office cannot help but introduce a new element of tension into Berlin and work against our mutual efforts to create détente."[43] Kissinger wrote that "it is also in the Soviet interest to do nothing which might encourage terrorism or lead those who are inclined in that direction to believe they have the support – tacit or active – of authorities anywhere in Berlin. It is in this spirit that we ask that the Soviet Embassy [to] use its influence to keep the PLO office from operating. Kissinger."[44] Yet neither Britain nor France nor the Brandt government supported making such a statement to the Soviets.[45]

On December 18, David Klein, the assistant chief of the US mission to West Berlin, sent a long telegram to Washington about "the growing threat of Arab terrorism in Berlin."[46]

A recent large influx of Arabs into West Berlin on pretext of seeking political asylum has compounded existing terrorist threat posed by already large Arab community, processing of Jewish refugees, [from the Soviet Union, JH] presence of PLO office in East Berlin, and forthcoming trial of Arab terrorists now under arrest. [West Berlin, JH] Senate has tried to convince FRG authorities they should take large segment of Arabs, most on dole, off Berlin's hands but thus far without success. There is an additional long-standing problems posed by fact that West Berlin is essentially an open city. We believe in present circumstances it is necessary also to consider means by which Allies and Senate can establish effective controls at points of entry into Western sectors that will not sacrifice single-city

[43] "Confidential: STATE19394: Approach to Soviets on PLO Office," Washington, DC (September 28, 1973), NACP, Diplomatic Records, Central Foreign Policy Files, Electronic Telegrams, 1/1/1973–12/31/1973.

[44] Ibid.

[45] "Confidential Berlin01773: PLO Office in East Berlin," West Berlin (October 15, 1973), NACP, Diplomatic Records, RG59 Central Foreign Policy Files, Electronic Telegrams, 1/1/1973–12/31/1973. Also see memo by Deputy Secretary of State Rush, "ConfidentialS TATE249856: Growing threat of Arab terrorism in Berlin," Washington, DC (December 22, 1973), NACP, Diplomatic Records, RG59 Central Foreign Policy Files, Electronic Telegrams, 1/1/1973–12/31/1973.

[46] David Klein, Head of US Mission in West Berlin, "1973Berlin02155: Subject: Growing Threat of Arab Terrorism in Berlin," West Berlin (December 18, 1973), NACP, Diplomatic Records, RG59 Central Foreign Policy Files, Electronic Telegrams, 1/1/1973–12/31/1973. See "Klein, David," in United States of America, Department of State, *The Biographical Register* (July 1973), 205–206.

concept or important political point made by contrast between openness of West Berlin and East Berlin wall.[47]

Klein reported further that West Berlin Mayor Klaus Schütz told the Allied military commanders in December of the "potential danger posed by the unexpected influx" into the Western sectors of "almost 1,700 Arabs seeking political asylum." Most were Jordanian Palestinians who traveled through Lebanon "and almost all of whom are without work and receiving social aid." West German law required that the country give political asylum to anyone claiming to be politically persecuted. The entire process of deciding whether the claim was legitimate could last up to two years in the event that negative decisions were appealed. During that time the "applicant is looked after by government if he lacks means of support. Word is apparently now out that West Berlin is good place to live and easy place to enter, particularly for individuals with access to Eastern Europe (i.e. Schönefeld Airport in GDR)."[48] "Individuals coming into West Berlin by most major arteries, including U-Bahn and S-Bahn, remain free from any inspection." At least some, unobtrusive controls based on Interpol watch lists should be introduced at Berlin's crossing points "to turn back known terrorists." On December 22, 1973, Assistant Secretary Rush replied that "measures to screen persons at crossing points would be acceptable, if process is unobtrusive and results in no delays."[49]

The idea that security checks, however unobtrusive, would result "in no delays" was indicative of the early days of American and West European counterterrorism policies. In fact, as Klein pointed out, getting from East to West Berlin with a Middle Eastern passport was as easy, even after the Wall was built, as getting on the S-Bahn or U-Bahn. There were, in reality, no effective border controls for screening those seeking asylum coming from the Middle East who wanted to go to the West. In the same years in which the Federal Republic's asylum laws were financing part of the cost of the import of Arab Palestinian – and thus anti-Israeli – politics into West German society, the West German Left and of course East Germany were describing that same West German government as repressive and neo-fascist. The gap between leftist stereotypes and the realities of what was, after all, an era of Social Democratic,

47 Ibid.

48 Ibid.

49 Kenneth Rush, "1973STATE249856: Subject: Growing Threat of Arab Terrorism in Berlin," Washington, DC in (December 22, 1973), NACP, Diplomatic Records, RG59 Central Foreign Policy Files, Electronic Telegrams, 1/1/1973–12/31/1973.

that is, left-of-center, governance widened into a chasm in the years of leftist terror in West Germany. In fact, in 1974, the inclination of the West German government led by Brandt's successor, Helmut Schmidt, to return convicted terrorists to the Middle East to try to prevent future hostage-taking led to very sharp differences with the US officials working on counterterrorism policy.[50]

On August 14, 1974, Klein cabled Washington about the PLO delegation's visit to East Berlin. He noted that in supporting full participation of the PLO in a possible Geneva conference on the Middle East, East Germany had gone further than the Polish government in that regard. Doing so, Klein wrote, "was in line with strong support for PLO evinced by GDR in past." While neither Moscow nor Warsaw had yet decided to permit an official representation of the PLO in their capital cities, "Arafat had no cause to press point in East Berlin, inasmuch as East Berlin PLO office was opened in October, 1973."[51] Klein reminded his colleagues in Washington that East Germany had taken this step before its Soviet patron and Warsaw Pact ally had done so. In September, Kissinger and the European desk in Washington agreed with the US mission in Berlin that it was "useful" to "remind Soviets from time to time that we hold them responsible for impact of what happens in their sector of city on overall security of Berlin." If "as in the past," the British and French did not want to raise the issue, then the US mission should follow "previous unilateral

50 The Americans argued the policy would encourage future terrorist attacks. By the late 1970s, West German policy under Schmidt had changed as the events of fall 1977 made most clear. On the 1973 American–West German disagreements see Kenneth Rush, "1973STATE221190: Subject: Disposition of Arab Terrorists," Washington, DC (November 9, 1973), NACP, Diplomatic Records, RG59 Central Foreign Policy Files, Electronic Telegrams, 1/1/1973–12/31/1973; David Klein, Head of US Mission, West Berlin, "1974BERLIN00623: Subject: Trial of Arab Terrorists – 5th & 6th Sessions, April 1 & 8," [West] Berlin (April 9, 1974)NACP, Diplomatic Records, RG59 Central Foreign Policy Files, Electronic Telegrams, 1/1/1974–12/31/1974; Henry Kissinger, "1974STATE082158: Subject: Arab Terrorist Trial," Washington, DC (April 23, 1974), NACP, Diplomatic Records, RG59 Central Foreign Policy Files, Electronic Telegrams, 1/1/1974–12/31/1974; Deputy Secretary of State Kenneth Rush, "1974STATE100983: Subject: Convicted Arab Terrorist in Berlin," (May 15, 1974), NACP, Diplomatic Records, RG59 Central Foreign Policy Files, Electronic Telegrams, 1/1/1974–12/31/1974; Joseph Sisco, Asst. Secretary of State, "1974STATE122113," Subject: Release of Arabs from Berlin Prison" (June 10, 1974), NACP, Diplomatic Records, RG59 Central Foreign Policy Files, Electronic Telegrams, 1/1/1974–12/31/1974.

51 David Klein, Head, US Mission to West Berlin, "1974BERLIN01375," Subj: Arafat Visit to East Berlin August 6–8 (August 14, 1974), NACP, Diplomatic Records, RG59 Central Foreign Policy Files, Electronic Telegrams, 1/1/1974–12/31/1974.

approaches to Soviets."[52] The British and French again declined. In light of their refusal to act jointly, US ambassador to West Germany Martin Hillenbrand concluded that "we see no alternative other than unilateral follow-up approach to Soviets" by the US Mission in Berlin.[53]

On October 25, 1974, David Klein read the following statement to his Soviet counterpart, Romanovsky: "The United States mission has learned that the local authorities in East Berlin recently cautioned certain Western Embassies accredited to the GDR that they might be the target of terrorist attacks by members of the Palestine Liberation Organization." The United States government regarded terrorism as "an extremely serious problem that all governments were obligated to seek to eliminate by all possible means." He had been instructed to "stress once again that we count on Soviet authorities to take the necessary steps to ensure that the Palestine Liberation Organization office located in East [the text erroneously says "West"] Berlin is not used in any way as a base for activities of terrorism or violence" and that "effective measures" would be taken to counter "threats arising from the presence of other terrorist organizations or individuals." Klein's Soviet counterpart replied that he doubted there was any connection between the PLO office and the GDR's warnings to Western embassies as the GDR "would never permit" organizations that "engaged in or promoted acts of terrorism" to be established on its territory.[54] As of October 25, the United States had informed the Soviet Union that it was going to hold Moscow responsible for any terrorist acts that could be traced back to the PLO office or other terrorists residing in East Germany. The United States was going to assess Moscow's seriousness about sustaining détente in light of its efforts to prevent the use of East Germany as a base from which to launch terrorist attacks on West Berlin, West Germany, and Western Europe. As we examine East Germany's definition of its counterterrorism policies, we will see that it was a warning that the East German and Soviet regimes took seriously.

[52] Henry Kissinger, Secretary of State, "1974STATE213209: Subject: Approach to Soviets on PLO Office in East Berlin," Washington, DC (September 27, 1974), NACP, Diplomatic Records, RG59 Central Foreign Policy Files, Electronic Telegrams, 1/1/1974–12/31/1974.

[53] Martin Hillenbrand, "1974BONN16543, Subject: Approach to Soviets on PLO Office in East Berlin," Bonn (October 21, 1974), NACP, Diplomatic Records, RG59 Central Foreign Policy Files, Electronic Telegrams, 1/1/1974–12/31/1974.

[54] David Klein, "1974USBER01960, Subject: Approach to Soviets on PLO Office in East Berlin," [West] Berlin (October 25, 1974), NACP, Diplomatic Records, RG59 Central Foreign Policy Files, Electronic Telegrams, 1/1/1974–12/31/1974.

THE ADMISSION OF EAST GERMANY AND WEST GERMANY TO THE UNITED NATIONS

On September 18, 1973, the United Nations General Assembly voted overwhelmingly in favor of admitting both East Germany and West Germany to membership in the United Nations. From then until 1989, East Germany's diplomats, along with their Soviet-bloc colleagues, made excellent use of the UN to wage political warfare against Israel. East Germany was an enthusiastic, high-profile, and vigorous member of the huge anti-Israeli majority in the United Nations General Assembly. Its stance gained it many friends and allies around the world, so much so that Peter Florin (1921–2014), East Germany's UN ambassador from 1973 to 1982, was elected president of the General Assembly in 1987–1988. East Germany was a founding member of the Committee for the Exercise of the Inalienable Rights of the Palestinian People (CEIRPP), the political nucleus of the PLO's efforts at the UN. For sixteen years, the East German diplomats heard Israeli representatives offer details of Arab and Palestinian terrorist attacks on the Jewish state. The UN documents offer no examples of any expression of East German sympathy to Israel for any of those Israelis who were killed and wounded. That was not surprising as both the PLO and Arab armed forces personnel had received training and arms in East Germany.

Israel supported the admission of West but not East Germany. As the Soviet bloc succeeded in linking the vote on admission of the two German states in one inseparable resolution, Israeli Ambassador Yosef Tekoah rose to explain Israel's position regarding this "event of profound historical significance."[55] The UN, he observed "was born out of the international struggle in that war against Nazism and the threat it posed to all mankind." He recalled the murder of six million Jews in Europe. "By history, by law and by morality, Germany as a whole has a responsibility for the Holocaust. The Federal Republic of Germany has consistently recognized this heavy responsibility."[56] West Germany had "exerted and is exerting efforts to make amends, if at all possible,

[55] Yosef Tekoah (Israel), United Nations General Assembly, 28th Session, 2117th Plenary Meeting, Tuesday, September 18, 1973, New York, United Nations, Secretary General Kurt Waldheim, German Democratic Republic, January 7, 1972–December 10, 1973, S-0904, Box 62, File 14, Acc 91/5, United Nations Archive, New York, 9–10; and A/PV.2117. Also see Robert Alden, "2 Germanys Join U.N. as Assembly Opens 28th Year," *New York Times* (September 19, 1973), 1 and 5.

[56] Ibid.

for the terrible atrocities perpetrated against the Jewish people by the Nazi regime in the name of the German nation." He then contrasted West Germany with East Germany.

> At the same time, however, Israel notes with regret and repugnance that the other German State has ignored and continues to ignore Germany's historical responsibility for the holocaust and the moral obligations arising from it. It has compounded the gravity of that attitude by giving support and practical assistance to the campaign of violence and murder waged against Israel and the Jewish people by Arab terror organizations. Thus the world stands today before the spectacle of one of the German states being once again associated with the denial to the Jewish people of its fundamental rights.[57]

Though Israel ascribed great importance to "international détente," it could not

> pass in silence over the policy of the German Democratic Republic, which for more than 20 years has been aiming to relegate to oblivion the holocaust wrought upon the Jewish people by Nazi Germany and, in contravention of the United Nations Charter and in particular of its Article 4, has been fanning the flames of hostility and belligerency against Israel, the Jewish State which is inseparable from the Jewish people in its struggle to repel anti-Jewish hatred, to prevent the shedding of Jewish blood and to preserve the right of the Jewish nation to live in freedom, peace and security.

Since the sponsors of the resolution had prevented a separate vote on the admission of East Germany, Tekoah put on the record that had it taken place, Israel would have voted against East Germany's admission.[58] On the other hand, John Scali, the United States ambassador to the UN, expressed pride in the admission of both German states. He hoped that East Germany would "also recognize the just claims of those who suffered as a result of the crimes of the Nazis."[59] The *New York Times* carried a photo of a smiling Walter Scheel, West Germany's foreign minister, speaking to the equally pleased East German foreign minister, Otto Winzer. The day of admission of both German states to the United Nations was a celebration of the spirit of East-West détente and of the priority of improved German-German relations over the moral and political arguments of a small country such as Israel.

57 Ibid.

58 Ibid.

59 John Scali (United States) UNGA, 28th Session, 2117th Plenary Meeting, Tuesday, September 18, 1973, UN ODS A/PV.2117, 16–17. Cited in Robert Alden, "2 Germanys Join U.N. as Assembly Opens 28th Year," *New York Times* (September 19, 1973), 5.

THE TWO GERMANYS, THE UNITED STATES, AND THE YOM KIPPUR WAR

On October 6, 1973, Egypt and Syria attacked Israel on Yom Kippur, the holiest day of the Jewish religious calendar. They caught the Israelis by surprise, crossed the Suez Canal, and inflicted terrible casualties on Israel's first line of defense. Enormous tank battles then raged in the Sinai desert, and fierce fighting took place on the Golan Heights near the Syrian border. The intensity of the battles reminded military observers of major battles of the Second World War. The initial gains made by the Egyptians and Syrians reflected the results of the massive rearmament and training provided by the Soviet Union and its allies in the six years since the Six-Day War. East Germany, along with the Soviet Union, again took the side of the Arab states and launched a furious propaganda barrage that turned facts on their head and presented Israel, the victim of aggression, as the aggressor.

West Germany took a position of firm neutrality. In a speech at the Frankfurt Book Fair early in the war when Israel was reeling from the early Arab successes and was in the early stages of its counteroffensive, Chancellor Willi Brandt stated that "the Federal Republic of Germany is not a party to this conflict" (*Die Bundesrepublik Deutschland ist in diesem Konflikt nicht Partei*). It strove to end the fighting "immediately." It stood with those who "wanted peace on the basis of the United Nations resolution of November 1967." Germany's interest was in a "peaceful resolution," one that acknowledged the right to exist of all the states in the region.[60] In fact, an immediate end to the fighting at that point would have awarded the Arab states the gains of their surprise attack. On October 8, West German foreign minister Walter Scheel told ambassadors from Lebanon, Egypt, Libya, Jordan, Tunisia, Morocco, Sudan, Algeria, and Saudi Arabia that "the Federal Republic has always taken a neutral position toward the conflict in the Middle East."[61] On the same day, Israel's ambassador to West Germany, Eliashiv Ben-Horin, also met with Scheel. He asked for West German support for the Israeli position

[60] Willy Brandt, cited in *Jüdischer Pressedienst*, Informationen des Zentralrats der Juden in Deutschland, October 24, 1973, Zentralarchiv zur Erforschung der Geschichte der Juden in Deutschland, Heidelberg, B.1/7 468, 1–2.

[61] "Dok. 313: Gespräch des Bundesministers Scheel mit den Botschaftern arabischer Staaten," Bonn (October 8, 1973), in Ilse Dorothee Pautsch et al., eds., *Akten zur Auswärtigen Politik der Bundesrepublik Deutschland, 1973: Band III: 1 Oktober bis 31 Dezember 1973* (Munich: R. Oldenbourg Verlag, 2004), 1528–1529.

that the UN should not call for a cease-fire until the aggressors, that is, the Arab states, had withdrawn to their original positions. Scheel rejected the request and insisted that "military action must end immediately," that is, with Arab troops still in positions gained during the initial attack.[62]

On October 26, Werner Nachmann, then chair of the Central Council of Jews in Germany, wrote to Scheel to express his surprise and disappointment about West Germany's neutrality stance. It amounted to a one-sided position in favor of the Arab states even though it was the Arabs who bore responsibility for the war. Israel was in a "battle for its existence." The countries of the Eastern bloc were taking a "clear, unambiguous stance against Israel" and gave the Arabs full military support while "the Western world and especially the Federal Republic of Germany is apparently acting under the pressure of the oil powers." Nachmann and the Central Council then issued a public statement stating that West German policy "favored the Arab side. The fourth Middle East War was minutely planned by the Soviet Union and its Warsaw Pact partners, in crass contradiction to their proclaimed policy of Détente." The recognition of realities that Brandt had called for in Europe had to apply as well to the Middle East.[63] Yet West Germany's neutrality policy persisted.

The United States became Israel's only ally that had both the will and the capability to come to its support in wartime. As the Israeli armed forces were using up enormous amounts of ammunition, successful defense, not to mention a counter-offensive, was impossible without a massive military resupply, especially in the face of an enormous Soviet supply effort flowing to the Arab states. On October 9, 1973, the third day of the war, Israel's ambassador to the United States, Simcha Dinitz, told Secretary of State Kissinger "that in the past three days Israel had lost 14 Phantoms, 28 Skyhawks, 3 Mirages, 4 Supermystères – a total of 49 planes. Tanks – we lost something like 500 tanks," out of its supply of 1,800. Conversely the Arabs were receiving added weapons from the Soviet Union. "So far there are 16 MiG 21's and 32 Sukhoi-7's, all with pilots. ... Egypt has received 18 Mig-21's from Algeria," and there were preparations for more. Libya was "giving hundreds of Strela missiles."

[62] Dok 314: "Gespräch des Bundesministers Scheel mit dem israelischen Botschafter Ben-Horin," Bonn (October 8, 1973), Pautsch et al., *Akten zur Auswärtigen Politik der Bundesrepublik Deutschland, 1973: Band III,* 1530–1532.

[63] "Zentralrat der Juden Fordern Klare Stellungnahme gegenüber Israel," in JPD, Informationen des Zentralrats der Juden in Deutschland, October 24, 1973, *ZA, Heidelberg*, B.1/7 468.

A squadron of Hunters was coming from Iraq along with Me-6 helicopters.[64] The Israeli military attaché in Washington, General Mordechai Gur, stressed the Israelis' urgent need for planes and tanks to replace their losses. Dinitz said that "the Soviets made a supreme effort of supply in the last minute before the war" that included FROG missiles. Thirty Soviet-made SA-6 anti-aircraft batteries were operating in the Egyptian and Syrian fronts.[65] Only two American resupply flights had arrived in six days. The Israelis needed "40 planes, in two to three days."[66] In other words, without a massive American resupply effort, Israel's conventional forces might face defeat.

On October 9, President Richard Nixon met with Kissinger and his aides to discuss the war and Israel's request.[67] Nixon said that "the Israelis must not be allowed to lose" and told his aides to "identify the tanks and planes on a contingency basis – in Europe" that could be sent to Israel.[68] Later that day, Kissinger met again with Dinitz again at the White House and informed him that regarding

> your special requests, the President has approved the entire list of consumables, that is, ordnance, electronic equipment – everything on the list except laser bombs. The President has agreed – and let me repeat this formally – that all your aircraft and tank losses will be replaced. Of the tanks you will be getting, a substantial number will be M-60's, our newest. As for the planes, for immediate delivery, you will be getting 5 F-4s, 2 plus 3.[69]

Dinitz stressed that "it is a question of days, Dr. Kissinger," that is, the weapons were needed immediately. Kissinger added that Secretary of Defense James Schlesinger would work out a schedule for delivery of tanks, anti-tank ammunition, and anti-tank weapons.[70] On October 12–13,

64 Simcha Dinitz, "134. Memorandum of Conversation," Washington, DC (October 9, 1973) in Nina Howland and Craig Daigle, eds., *Foreign Relations of the United States [FRUS] 1969–1976*. Volume XXV. *Arab-Israeli Crisis and War, 1973* (Washington, DC: U.S. Government Printing Office, 2011), 392–393.

65 Ibid., 396.

66 Ibid., 466.

67 "140: Memorandum of Conversation," Washington, DC (October 9, 1973, 4:45 p.m.), Howland and Daigle, eds., *FRUS, 1969–1976*. Volume XXV. *Arab-Israeli Crisis and War, 1973*, 411–413.

68 Ibid., 412–413.

69 Henry Kissinger, "141. Memorandum of Conversation," Washington, DC (October 9, 1973, 6:10–6:35 pm), Howland and Daigle, eds., *FRUS, 1969–1976*. Volume XXV. *Arab-Israeli Crisis and War, 1973*, 413. Also see United States National Archives, College Park, Record Group 59, Central Files, 1970–1973, POL ISR-US. Top Secret; Sensitive; Exclusively Eyes Only.

70 Ibid., 413.

Dinitz told Kissinger about further Israeli losses, Egyptian advances, and Soviet weapon deliveries to Egypt. He then reported that the military deliveries Nixon had ordered had not yet begun. Israel was forced to change its military strategy because "we are depleted." He was "duty bound" to inform Kissinger that "we need twenty planes' [of military supplies] in two to three days or we are subject to an Egyptian attack in Sinai."[71] At a meeting at the White House on October 13, with Secretary of Defense James Schlesinger, Deputy Secretary of State Kenneth Rush, Deputy Secretary of Defense William Clements, Chairman of the Joint Chiefs of Staff Admiral Thomas Moorer, and Director of the Central Intelligence Agency William Colby, Kissinger told the assembled that "the President said that if there were any further delays in carrying out orders [to resupply Israel], we [Nixon and Kissinger] want the resignations of the officials involved."[72]

The irony of the contrast between Nixon's and Brandt's reactions to the war was striking. The West German chancellor who famously kneeled in an act of atonement at the memorial to the Jews killed in the Warsaw Ghetto declared his country to be neutral in the most dire days in Israel's history since 1948. Conversely, the American president, who had received scant support from American Jewish voters, decided to launch "Operation Nickel Grass," the largest American military resupply mission since World War II. He did so because "the Israelis must not be allowed to lose" and because the Soviets must not gain a victory in the Middle East. Nixon's decision of October 9, 1973, was perhaps the most important one any American president had made in Israeli history up to that time since Harry Truman decided to recognize the Jewish state in 1948.[73] Had he decided otherwise, Israel would likely have suffered military defeat or, in order to avoid it, might have used its nuclear weapons. Nixon and Kissinger defended the decision as one needed to restore a military balance that had been upset by the Soviet Union, to make

[71] Simcha Dinitz, "166. Memorandum of Conversation," Washington, DC (October 12–13, 1973, 11:20 pm.–12:33 a.m, Howland and Daigle, eds., *FRUS, 1969–1976*. Volume XXV. *Arab-Israeli Crisis and War, 1973*, 458–466. Also see Library of Congress, Manuscript Division, Kissinger Papers, Box TS 33, Geopolitical File, Middle East, Middle East War Chronological File, 9–15 Oct. 1973. Top Secret. Sensitive; Exclusively Eyes Only.

[72] Henry Kissinger, "173. Memorandum of Conversation," Washington, DC (October 13, 1973, 10:45 a.m., Howland and Daigle, eds., *FRUS, 1969–1976*. Volume XXV. *Arab-Israeli Crisis and War, 1973*, 482.

[73] On Truman's decision, see Ronald Radosh and Allis Radosh, *A Safe Haven: Harry S. Truman and the Founding of Israel* (New York: Harper, 2010).

possible a negotiated settlement after Israel had been able to recover from its initial losses, and to prevent the catastrophe of possible use of nuclear weapons and a direct American-Soviet war in the Middle East. Yet as much as Nixon presented his decision as one embedded in great power politics of the Cold War global competition with the Soviet Union, the fact was that the resupply operation he set in motion made it possible for Israel to defend itself and prevent defeat.

On October 24, Admiral Moorer told Kissinger that 25 Soviet supply ships either had left or were scheduled to go to the Middle East. They had carried 19,000 tons of arms and equipment to the Egyptians and 14,000 tons to Syria with 28,000 tons more en route to destinations unknown, for a total of 61,000 tons. When added to the Soviet airlift, the Soviet Union was sending 70,000 to 75,000 tons of military supplies to the Arab states.[74] At the same meeting, Kissinger said that Israel's casualties had been "enormous. Mrs [Golda] Meir told us they have 1500–2000 dead and 5000–7000 wounded. That's comparable to 500,000 for us. She said there is not a family in Israel that has not been hit directly or indirectly, and that must be true in such a small country."[75] He reminded the assembled that "the President promised the Israelis two weeks ago that we would replace their losses. He also promised that at least 40% of their tank losses would be replaced with M-60 tanks." To prevent a Soviet success in this strategically vital region, to save Israel from defeat, and to create possibilities for a negotiated settlement after the war, it was essential that the resupply effort move ahead with greater speed.[76]

At the end of November and the beginning of December, Nixon administration officials made the case to the US House Foreign Affairs Committee for sending weapons worth $2.2 billion to Israel.[77] Deputy Secretary of State Kenneth Rush reported that since the end of the war in late October "the Soviet Union has been very heavily resupplying the

74 Adm. Thomas Moorer, "259. Minutes of Washington Special Actions Group Meeting," Washington, DC (October 24, 1973), Howland and Daigle, eds., *FRUS, 1969–1976*. Volume XXV. *Arab-Israeli Crisis and War, 1973*, 713.

75 Henry Kissinger, "259. Minutes of Washington Special Actions Group Meeting," Washington, DC (October 24, 1973), Howland and Daigle, eds., *FRUS, 1969–1976*. Volume XXV. *Arab-Israeli Crisis and War, 1973*, 714.

76 "259. Minutes of Washington Special Actions Group Meeting," Washington, DC (October 24, 1973), Howland and Daigle, eds., *FRUS, 1969–1976*. Volume XXV. *Arab-Israeli Crisis and War, 1973*, 716.

77 "Emergence Security Assistance Act of 1973," Hearings before the Committee on Foreign Affairs, House of Representatives, Ninety-Third Congress (November 30 and December 3, 1973) (Washington, DC: U.S. Government Printing Office, 1973).

Arab countries engaged in the conflict." In order to preserve a military balance, "even restoring the Israelis to the condition prevailing before the outbreak of hostilities would not necessarily and, in fact, would not restore the balance because the Arabs have been massively resupplied." He suggested that "in a way they are probably stronger than they were before the outbreak of hostilities." The United States could not "allow the Soviet Union to take over the Middle East by our refusing to assist Israel to have a balance of military power with those countries supplied by the Soviet Union."[78] In the same hearings, Admiral Moorer estimated that the Soviet resupply effort exceeded 100,000 tons.[79]

Operation Nickel Grass led to severe tensions between the United States and its West European allies. American weapons could arrive in Israel in two ways. Some would need to be airlifted to Israel from bases in the United States. In that case planes would need to refuel in Europe. Yet all of the major NATO allies, except Portugal, refused to allow American planes to refuel at their airports. The Portuguese permitted landings at the US Air Force base in the Azores Islands. Or the weapons and ammunition already located at American bases in the Federal Republic of Germany could be flown or sent by ship directly to Israel. The Brandt government's desire to preserve its neutrality and avoid antagonizing the Arab states conflicted with the American policy of rushing supplies to Israel as quickly as possible to prevent a Soviet-backed Arab victory.

On October 16, Scheel and US ambassador to the Federal Republic Martin Hillenbrand had a testy exchange.[80] Hillenbrand stressed the need to restore a military balance upset by Soviet weapons deliveries and warned that "a lack of understanding among some of the allies" could damage bilateral relations with the United States. Scheel spoke of the need for a diplomatic solution and said that the cause of the war "was not only the surprise attack by the Arabs but also the preceding six years. Perhaps the presumed superiority of the Israelis also played a role."[81] The West

[78] Deputy Secretary of State Kenneth Rush, "Emergence Security Assistance Act of 1973," Hearings before the Committee on Foreign Affairs, House of Representatives, Ninety-Third Congress (November 30 and December 3, 1973) (Washington, DC: U.S. Government Printing Office, 1973), 17–18.

[79] Admiral Thomas Moorer, "Emergence Security Assistance Act of 1973," Hearings before the Committee on Foreign Affairs, House of Representatives, Ninety-Third Congress (November 30 and December 3, 1973), 9.

[80] "Dok 322: Gespräch des Bundesministers Scheel mit dem Amerikanischen Botschafter Hillenbrand," Bonn (October 16, 1973), Pautsch et al., *Akten zur Auswärtigen Politik der Bundesrepublik Deutschland, 1973: Band III*), 1557–1563.

[81] Ibid., 1560.

German argument for a "rapid, if possible immediate cease fire," for neutrality, and for a peace agreement based on United Nations Resolution 242 was presented in a Foreign Ministry memo of October 19.[82] It was frank about one source of West German neutrality. It observed that 55.4 percent of Germany's energy was supplied by oil imports, and of them 71 percent were from Arab oil-producing countries who were party to the conflict. Conversely, the United States depended on the Arab states for only 6 percent of its oil imports. Europe and Japan had "much greater need of good relations with the Arabs than the USA." It was essential "to make clear to the Arabs that Europe remained neutral in this conflict." However, the West Germans "had to be prepared for the fact that our relations with the Arab countries will again be burdened" by the fact of American arms deliveries to Israel from depots in West Germany. East Germany "in a massive manner was using false announcements and presentations in an effort to undermine Arab– [West] German relations."[83]

On October 23, Kissinger told his aides that "the Europeans behaved badly. They gave us no support when we needed it."[84] A Soviet victory in the Middle East would have dealt a devastating blow to the Western Alliance, and thus to the security of the West European members of NATO. It would have encouraged those in Moscow who wanted to abandon détente for further aggressive moves against the Western Alliance. On October 24 a cease-fire was declared. On the same day, West Germany's assistant state secretary Paul Frank met with Frank Cash, the deputy chief of mission of the American Embassy in Bonn. Frank said that with the announcement of a cease-fire in the Middle East, American arms deliveries to Israel should cease.[85] The West German government

82 "Dok 329: Runderlaß des Vortragenden Legationsrats I. Klasse Dohms," Bonn (October 19, 1973), Pautsch et al., *Akten zur Auswärtigen Politik der Bundesrepublik Deutschland, 1973: Band III*), 1608–1612.

83 Ibid., 1610–1611.

84 Henry Kissinger, "Secretary's Staff Meeting: Tuesday, October 23, 1973 – 4:35 p.m.," 1, NACP, RG 59, General Records of the Department of State, Subject Numeric Files 1970–1973, Political and Defense, From POL 7 US-Kissinger to POL 7 US-Nixon 7/24–70, Box 2694.

85 "DOK 335: Gespräch des Staatssekretärs Frank mit dem amerikanischen Gesandten Cash," Bonn (October 24, 1973), Pautsch et al., *Akten zur Auswärtigen Politik der Bundesrepublik Deutschland, 1973: Band III: 1 Oktober bis 31 Dezember 1973*, 1638–1643; also the report of the exchange in Martin Hillenbrand to Secretary of State, "Further Concerns Re US Shipments of Military Material to Israel from FRG," (October 24, 1973), Ref Bonn 15408, National Archives and Records Administration (NACP), Diplomatic Records, Central Foreign Policy Files, 1/1/1973–12/31/1973, Electronic Telegrams, 1. Also see "Cash, Frank," Department of State, United States of America, *Biographical Register* (1972).

was "extremely upset" over the continued delivery of weapons from German harbors onto Israeli freighters. Frank asked that the operation be "ended immediately." The West German government "wished that the Israeli ships leave our territory as quickly and quietly as possible." While they could not prevent American ships from being loaded with American weapons, "how could we explain to the Arabs that we have given permission to their enemy at war to do the same in our harbors?... We do not want to be drawn into this military conflict but that is going to happen when the ships of a state at war are permitted to be loaded in the harbors of a neutral country."[86] With the announcement of the cease-fire in the Middle East, the need to establish a military balance at the outset of the conflict no longer applied. He asked that "the whole operation at sea and in the air must be brought to an end."[87] Cash replied that "he [Cash] was not at all sure" that a balance had been restored. Frank repeated that West Germany "wanted to stay entirely out of the military conflict. It did not wish to be involved directly or indirectly."[88]

Hillenbrand informed Kissinger that West German orders that the Israeli ships leave Bremerhaven were "unequivocal" and that it hoped it could "maintain good relations with the Arabs by not permitting further military shipments to Israel from the FRG at this late date."[89] Georg Leber, the Social Democratic minister of defense, told Hillenbrand of "his strong support for our assistance to Israel" but that "many in the Foreign Ministry [were] concerned over the Arab oil leverage on the FRG." Hillenbrand was not optimistic that Leber would be successful in changing the policy in a direction favorable to Israel "since the FRG concern over oil supplies is obviously a matter of serious significance and he may find that the Chancellor [Willy Brandt] would not support him."[90] On October 25, Kissinger told Hillenbrand to inform Frank that the United States "welcomed FRG understanding and cooperation in not interposing

[86] Ibid., 1642–1643.

[87] Ibid., 1641–1642; and Martin Hillenbrand to Secretary of State, "Further Concerns Re US Shipments of Military Material to Israel from FRG," (October 24, 1973), Ref Bonn 15408, NACP), Diplomatic Records, Central Foreign Policy Files, 1/1/1973–12/31/1973, Electronic Telegrams, 1.

[88] Martin Hillenbrand to Secretary of State (October 24, 1973), Bonn 15408, NACP, Diplomatic Records, Central Foreign Policy Files, 1/1/1973–12/31/1973, Electronic Telegrams.

[89] Ibid.

[90] Martin Hillenbrand to Secretary of State, "FRG Concerns Regarding US Weapons Shipments from FRG to Middle East," (October 24, 1973), Secret Bonn 15368, NACP, Diplomatic Records, Central Foreign Policy Files, 1/1/1973–12/31/1973, Electronic Telegrams.

objection our shipping arms to Israel from USG stocks in FRG."[91] "This has been great contribution to stabilizing situation in area and to establishing conditions propitious for ceasefire." However, the Soviet Union was continuing to ship arms to Syria and Egypt. Hillenbrand was to tell Frank that the United States was "extremely concerned at this latest turn in FRG attitudes toward resupply of Israel." However, for the West "to display weakness and disunity in the face of a Soviet-supported military action against Israel could have disastrous consequences." The United States "had no choice but to provide Israel with the military supplies necessary to defend itself" and would continue to do so. American efforts to bring an end to the war had "thus far succeeded, despite the failure of our Western European allies to support those policies. The FRG should know that the USG will not forget the attitudes taken by its allies in this time of crisis."[92]

In a meeting in Bonn on October 25, Hillenbrand conveyed Kissinger's message to Frank. The latter now "remained firm" that "no further US shipments to Israel should occur from FRG territory."[93] The objection was thus to any US shipments, not only those delivered in Israeli ships. Frank said that the Federal Republic was enduring "massive pressures" from Arab governments and "was particularly concerned about an Arab oil boycott." Because of reports of arms shipments from American bases in West Germany, the Arab states were "now charging that German credibility was no longer to be trusted." The latter charge was due to the fact that on October 23 Frank had informed the Egyptian ambassador in Bonn that no further shipments to Israel would take place from the FRG. "The shipping of material in the past few days from Bremerhaven by Israeli ships had made nonsense of this statement to the Egyptian Ambassador."[94] Frank asserted that "at no time" since Hillenbrand's

[91] Secretary of State Henry Kissinger to US Ambassador Martin Hillenbrand, "US Arms Shipments from FRG to ME: FRG Concern," Secret State 210441 (October 25, 1973), NACP, Diplomatic Records, Central Foreign Policy Files, 1/1/1973–12/31/1973, Electronic Telegrams.

[92] Ibid.

[93] Ambassador Martin Hillenbrand to Secretary of State Henry Kissinger, "FRG Unmoving in Opposition to Further US Arms Shipments from FRG to Middle East," Bonn 15456 (October 25, 1973), NACP, Diplomatic Records, Central Foreign Policy Files, 1/1/1973–12/31/1973, Electronic Telegrams.

[94] Ambassador Martin Hillenbrand to Secretary of State Henry Kissinger, "FRG Unmoving in Opposition to Further US Arms Shipments from FRG to Middle East," Bonn 15456 (October 25, 1973), NACP, Diplomatic Records, Central Foreign Policy Files, 1/1/1973–12/31/1973, Electronic Telegrams. For Frank's account of the conversation thatconfirms Hillenbrand's version see "Dok 337: Gespräch des Staatssekretärs Frank

meeting with Foreign Minister Walter Scheel on October 16 "had anyone on the German side conceived it possible that Israeli ships would be used to transport the arms and military goods from Bremerhaven." As soon as it learned that was taking place "it had immediately asked that the ship loading in Bremerhaven to depart ASAP and had made the decision that the ship presently lying in Bremen would not be allowed to load any goods." It did so in order to "restore some degree of credibility with the Arabs," who would not believe that the FRG had no knowledge of what was being shipped from its ports.[95]

Frank closed the discussion with Hillenbrand with the hope that the "present difficult situation" would not "burden US-FRG relations." West Germany had done more than any other West European country to aid the resupply effort. He hoped that "other channels outside Germany" could be found to resupply Israel. Hillenbrand replied that US arms and military goods in Europe "were largely located in Germany" and that some of the specialized ammunition was not readily available in the United States or other European countries. Hillenbrand wrote that "Frank indicated no sympathy for this aspect of the problem." While he would report the German expression in full, he "noted that the US government would be extremely displeased by the seeming unwillingness of the Federal Government to help out in what is obviously still a very difficult and uncertain situation in the Middle East."[96] Hillenbrand concluded that "the prospects for moving the Germans to accept our position are bleak. They obviously perceive their basic interests quite differently from ours.... Only an approach at a high political level," that is, presumably from President Nixon to Chancellor Brandt, "stood any chance of modifying the German stance." At that time, 75,000 rounds of 105 artillery ammunition were still on a special train but not yet loaded onto ships in Bremerhaven.[97]

mit dem amerikanischen Botschafter Hillenbrand," Bonn (October 25, 1973), Pautsch et al., *Akten zur Auswärtigen Politik der Bundesrepublik Deutschland, 1973: Band III*), 1651–1652. For objections to resupply operations in Germany from the ambassador of the Arab League to the West German Embassy in Cairo see "Dok 339: Aufzeichnung des Ministerialdirektors Lahn," Bonn (October 25, 1973), 1655–1658.

95 Ibid.

96 Ambassador Martin Hillenbrand to Secretary of State Henry Kissinger, "FRG Unmoving in Opposition to Further US Arms Shipments from FRG to Middle East," Bonn 15456 (October 25, 1973), NACP, Diplomatic Records, Central Foreign Policy Files, 1/1/1973–12/31/1973, Electronic Telegrams

97 Ambassador Martin Hillenbrand to Secretary of State Henry Kissinger, "FRG Unmoving in Opposition to Further US Arms Shipments from FRG to Middle East," Bonn 15456 (October 25, 1973), NACP, Diplomatic Records, Central Foreign Policy Files, 1/1/1973–12/31/1973, Electronic Telegrams.

On October 26, Kissinger met with Bernd von Staden, West Germany's ambassador to the United States, to discuss the Federal Republic's "attitude toward the military resupply of Israel from US stocks in Germany."[98] Kissinger had been "astonished at the position the FRG had taken on this matter." What had been at issue in the Middle East had been "the possibility of a victory by those aided by the Soviets. If these forces had been allowed to win, there would have been a radicalization of the entire area and a setback for the West." Given what he called "the lack of understanding on this point which our allies have shown, we are asking ourselves fundamental questions about our allies." The United States had sought "understanding in the present situation, but we have been deliberately isolated." Kissinger told von Staden that he could report that he was "speaking on behalf of the President who is prepared to address himself on this point directly to the chancellor [Willy Brandt]."[99] He stressed that US actions in the Middle East "were in defense of Western interests generally." In the first week of the war, the US objective "was to insure that the Israelis were not defeated," and in the second it "was to prevent further Soviet intrusion in the area." What Kissinger called "European capitulation to the Arabs" would not ensure the supply of oil, but it could "have disastrous consequences vis-à-vis the Soviet Union," which "if allowed to succeed in the Near East can be expected to mount ever more aggressive policies elsewhere."[100] Kissinger added that "it was in no one's interest to see the Israelis defeated."[101] The "overall pattern of European behavior" during Operation Nickel Grass would have "disastrous consequences for the alliance."[102]

98 "Secretary's Meeting with FRG Ambassador von Staden, October 26," NACP, RG 59 General Records of the Department of State, Subject Numeric Files 1970–1973, Political and Defense, From POL 7 US-Kissinger to POL 7 US-Nixon 7/24–70, Box 2694. For von Staden's confirming account of the same conversation see "Dok 356: Botschafter von Staden, Washington, an das Auswärtige Amt," Washington, DC (November 2, 1973), Pautsch et al., *Akten zur Auswärtigen Politik der Bundesrepublik Deutschland, 1973: Band III*), 1736–1739.

99 "Secretary's Meeting with FRG Ambassador von Staden, October 26," NACP, RG 59 General Records of the Department of State, Subject Numeric Files 1970–1973, Political and Defense, From POL 7 US-Kissinger to POL 7 US-Nixon 7/24–70, Box 2694, 1–2.

100 Ibid.

101 Ibid., 4.

102 Ibid., 5 and 8. For von Staden's confirming account of the same conversation see "Dok 356: Botschafter von Staden, Washington, an das Auswärtige Amt," Washington (November 2, 1973), Pautsch et al., *Akten zur Auswärtigen Politik der Bundesrepublik Deutschland, 1973: Band III*, 1736–1739.

On October 30, the West German authorities gave permission to allow the train in Kaiserslauten loaded with 75,000 105 millimeter artillery shells to travel to Bremerhaven harbor but stated that "utmost discretion would be observed to prevent any publicity which would only lead to more embarrassment if the press did get on to the story."[103] That same day, Foreign Minister Scheel told Hillenbrand and Assistant Secretary of State Walter Stoessel that the German position was influenced "by two somewhat divergent factors. (A) German sensitivity over the relationship with all Jews everywhere in the world based on the German past. (B) The difficult relationship with the Arabs." The Federal Republic's "wrong decision" to supply Israel secretly with arms in 1965 had led the Arab states to break diplomatic relations with the FRG."[104] On November 2 Hillenbrand reported that an American ship, the *Ranger*, in Bremerhaven "is now loading 105 MM ammunition" and was "due to depart for Israel early next week." He stressed the need for "utmost discretion on part of all concerned ... particularly in view of Libyan threat to cut off oil deliveries to FRG." Any publicity about "the Ranger trip" would have "adverse consequences for the German economy – and for US-German relations."[105]

On October 29, 1973, Chancellor Brandt wrote to President Nixon "to clear up misunderstandings" that had emerged during the war. It would be "a serious error" to assume the Brandt government did not understand the need to preserve a balance of forces in the Middle East and the American role in doing so. That was a matter of "common responsibility of the [Western] Alliance." It was another matter, however, "when American materials located on the territory of the Federal Republic were used for purposes for which the Federal government was not responsible

[103] FM Embassy Bonn to SecState Wash DC, Ambassador Martin Hillenbrand to Secretary of State Henry Kissinger, "Loading of Arms for Israel," Secret Bonn 16715 (October 30, 1973), NACP, Diplomatic Records, Central Foreign Policy Files, 1/1/1973–12/31/1973, Electronic Telegrams.

[104] Ambassador Martin Hillenbrand to Secretary of State Henry Kissinger, "Movement of Supplies to Middle East from FRG," Secret Bonn 15695 (October 30, 1973), NACP, Diplomatic Records, Central Foreign Policy Files, 1/1/1973–12/31/1973, Electronic Telegrams.

[105] Ambassador Martin Hillenbrand to Secretary of State Henry Kissinger, "Arms for Israel – American Ranger," Secret Bonn 15891 (November 2, 1973), NACP, Diplomatic Records, Central Foreign Policy Files, 1/1/1973–12/31/1973, Electronic Telegrams. On Libya's threat to cut off oil deliveries to the Federal Republic see American Embassy, Tripoli to Secretary of State, "Libya Threatens Oil Embargo against FRG," Confidential Tripoli 1386 (October 30, 1973), NACP, Diplomatic Records, Central Foreign Policy Files, 1/1/1973–12/31/1973, Electronic Telegrams.

and about which it was not fully informed not to mention was not informed about beforehand." Brandt thought that the "misunderstandings and tensions" that had emerged would lead to a "better thinking through" of the alliance.[106] It was not a note likely to allay Nixon or Kissinger's concerns.

Three days earlier, Brandt had reasserted his government's position of neutrality in remarks to the Bundestag.[107] The Federal Republic "had always stressed and continues to support an immediate ceasefire" and a "definitive, just and permanent peaceful solution in the Middle East" based on the United Nations Resolution 242 of November 1967.[108] Neutrality was not synonymous with "indifference towards these events." It encompassed "empathy (*Mitgefühl)* for those affected and for suffering people. Our position is, in the first place determined by our great, vital interest in the rapid implementation of peace which can be accepted or even recognized as just by all peoples of the region."[109] He did not refer to a "special relationship" with or particular obligations to Israel. Carl Carstens, the leader of the Christian Democratic Union's parliamentary faction, replied that though there had been "mistakes" on both sides, "it was not Israel that struck first and unleashed this conflict."[110] Rather, the Soviet Union "provided Israel's neighboring states with weapons and war materials." The United States sought to "restore a balance of power in the Middle East after Israel itself had made "extraordinary efforts in service of its own defense.... A word of recognition and acknowledgement from the mouth of the Chancellor to our great ally the United States would be advisable."[111] In the crucial days of October 1973 Brandt maintained his neutrality policy while the mainstream conservatives argued for clearer support for both the United States and Israel.[112]

[106] "Dok 342: Bundeskanzler Brandt an Präsident Nixon," Bonn (October 28, 1973), Pautsch et al., *Akten zur Auswärtigen Politik der Bundesrepublik Deutschland, 1973: Band III*), 1668–1670.

[107] Ibid.

[108] Willy Brandt, October 26, 1973, *Verhandlungen des Deutschen Bundestages*, [hereafter: VDB] 7. *Wahlperiode, Stenographische Berichte, Band 85, 62 Sitzung* (Bonn: 1973), 3630.

[109] Ibid.

[110] Carl Carsten, October 26, 1973, *VDB Stenographische Berichte, Band 85, 62 Sitzung* (Bonn: 1973), 3638.

[111] Ibid., 3639. Also see the defense minister's reaffirmation of the importance of the Western Alliance, George Leber, ibid., 3621.

[112] Egon Bahr, a key adviser to Brandt on foreign policy, was particularly critical of American and Israeli policy. See "Dok 358: Aufzeichnung des Bundesministers Bahr," Bonn (November 5, 1973), Pautsch et al., *Akten zur Auswärtigen Politik der*

The neutrality stance of the Brandt government during the Yom Kippur War is important for this study for several reasons. First, the West German governmental sensitivities about the Nazi past were secondary to fears of antagonizing the Arab states and Arab oil producers. Second, the radical Left claimed that its attacks on Israel smashed taboos of a "philo-semitic" national guilt complex about the Holocaust. Brandt's neutrality policy as the war hung in the balance indicated that such sentiments took a back seat to conventional definitions of national interest. Ironically, despite the West German neutrality policy, the Soviet bloc, including East Germany, as well as the radical Arab states denounced the Federal Republic for following a pro-Israeli policy, which it insisted it was not pursuing. When the outcome of the war hung in the balance, the power of memory of the Holocaust and the traditions of "coming to terms with the Nazi past" mattered less than the political and economic pressures and threats from the Arab states. To be sure, Chancellor Brandt agreed that Israel had a right to exist; yet, as a practical matter, the policy of neutrality evolved into one of opposition to continuation of the American resupply effort. The contrast between the hard-nosed, unsentimental Nixon focused both on Israel's survival and on competition with the Soviet Union in the Middle East, and Brandt, the eloquent inheritor of the West German tradition of "coming to terms with the Nazi past," was another striking irony of the October crisis of 1973. Israel learned that when war broke out, the United States was its only consequential ally.

EAST GERMAN PROPAGANDA DURING THE YOM KIPPUR WAR

By 1973, the word "totalitarianism" had fallen out of favor in Western policy-making and intellectual circles. If applied to the Communist regimes in Europe, it was thought to be an embarrassing relic of a crude "Cold War anti-communism" of the 1950s. Yet in these very same years, the Warsaw Pact's assertion that Israel was the aggressor in October 1973 displayed the same bold falsehoods and reversals of cause and effect that the classic texts about totalitarianism had described as one of its defining features. In East Germany, the anti-Israeli propaganda blitz began the day after Egypt and Syria launched the war with their surprise attack. East German propaganda included three main themes.

Bundesrepublik Deutschland, 1973: Band III: 1 Oktober bis 31 Dezember 1973 (Munich: R. Oldenbourg Verlag, 2004), 1747–1750.

First, Israel was the aggressor; second, East Germany along with the Soviet bloc supported the just cause of the Arab states and the "Arab people of Palestine"; and third, West Germany, regardless of its public talk about neutrality, was, along with the United States, an "accomplice" in Israeli aggression. On October 7, 1973, without mentioning that the Arab states had begun the war the previous day, *Neues Deutschland* ran a page 1 story headlined "Israel's Heavy Attacks on Egypt, Syria and Lebanon."[113] On October 8, 1973, *ND* led on page 1 with "The Soviet Union condemns Israel's continuing policy of conquering."[114] The causes of the war lay in "the expansionist policies of Israel's ruling circles. For years Israel, with the support of imperialist circles has continuously heated up the atmosphere in the Middle East with its lunatic, aggressive (*wahnwitzigen aggressiven*) actions." It had "trampled on the UN Charter and the resolutions of the United Nations as well as the generally recognized norms of human rights."[115] The responsibility for the war lay "completely on Israel and the other reactionary circles which are always lenient towards Israel's aggressive efforts." Peace was "unthinkable without the complete liberation of all of the Arab territories occupied by Israel and without the realization of the legitimate rights of the Arab peoples of Palestine." The Soviet Union therefore supported the "legitimate demands of the Arab states for the liberation of all territories occupied by Israel since 1967." The statement was ambiguous about the meaning of the term "occupied territories." Was all of Israel "occupied territory" that was to be "liberated," or did occupation refer only to territory occupied since 1967? Did the "legitimate rights" of the Palestinians mean a right of return and thus the end of Israel as a Jewish state, or was this a call for a two-state solution? Both interpretations were plausible.[116]

On the same day, *Neues Deutschland* published a statement from the East German Politburo on "the new Israeli aggression." It placed the full blame for tension in the Middle East on "Israel's aggressive policy toward the Arab peoples and states"; its "illegal" occupation of Egyptian, Syrian, and Jordanian territory; as well as its "sabotage" of efforts at the UN by the Arab states and other "peace-loving forces in the world to

113 "Schwere Angriffe Israels auf Ägypten, Syrien und Libanon," *Neues Deutschland*, [East] Berlin (October 7, 1973), 1.

114 "Die Sowjetunion verurteilt Israels fortgesetzte Eroberungspolitik," *ND* (October 8, 1973), 1.

115 Ibid.

116 Ibid.

bring about a political solution in the Middle East."[117] The "Israeli military clique" had "provoked the extraordinarily dangerous situation in the Middle East." Israel had "made the use of force, occupation of foreign territories, oppression and murder its declared state policy."[118] The Arabs, on the other hand, had made "multiple efforts by peaceful means to overcome the consequences of Israeli aggression in the Middle East" through the United Nations. Israel had responded with "a policy of political and military provocation" and pursued a "policy of war and conquest." It needed to withdraw completely "from all of the territories occupied in 1967" and satisfy "the legitimate demands of the Arab people of Palestine."[119] *Neues Deutschland* did not inform its readers that Egypt and Syria had begun the war with a surprise attack. Its assertions and silences amounted to a justification for it. Their partisanship constituted a stark contrast to West German neutrality.

That partisanship and the obliteration of the difference between journalism and propaganda were evident in the headlines in *Neues Deutschland*: October 9, 1973: "The world condemns the aggressor Israel," "International protest against Tel Aviv's violence politics (*Gewaltpolitik*)"; "Israel's war policy decisively condemned";[120] October 10, 1973: "Bitter battles against the aggressor Israel," "Accused: The aggressor Israel: ND documentation, 1967–1973," "June 1967: How Israel stole Arab land," "Chain of provocation and violence," "How Israel torpedoed every peaceful solution in the Middle East" and "Aggressor Israel unleashes pitiless terror," "The way the press celebrates in the FRG";[121] October 11, 1973: "Heavy losses for the Israeli aggressor," "Accomplices of the aggressor Israel: From the USA and FRG, weapons, money and support," "Malik castigates Israel for its war crimes at the UN: Tel Aviv's isolation in the Security Council and General Assembly," "FRG press celebrates the aggressor";[122] October 13, 1973: "Soviet

117 "DDR: Beseitigung des Kriegsherdes zur Friedenssicherung unumgänglich: Erklärung des Politburos des ZK der SED, des Staatrates und des Ministerrat der Deutschen Demokratischen Republik zur neuen Israelischen Aggression," *ND* (October 8, 1973), 1.

118 Ibid.

119 "DDR: Beseitigung des Kriegsherdes zur Friedenssicherung unumgänglich: Erklärung des Politburos des ZK der SED, des Staatrates und des Ministerrat der Deutschen Demokratischen Republik zur neuen Israelischen Aggression," *ND* (October 8, 1973), 1.

120 "Internationale Protest gegen Gewaltpolitik Tel Avivs," and "Die Welt verurteilt Aggressor Israel," *ND* (October 9, 1973), 1.

121 "Angeklagt: Der Aggressor Israel, ND Dokumentation von 1967–1973," "Juni 1967: So raubte Israel arabisches Lande," "Kette der Provokation und Gewalt," "So torpedierte Israel jede friedliche Lösung in Nahost," *ND* (October 10, 1973), 3.

122 "Schwere Verluste für den Israelischen Aggressor," 1"Komplicen des Aggressors Israels: Aus USA und BRD: Waffen, Geld und Rückendeckung," 4, "Malik geißelte

Union decisively denounces Israel's barbaric acts of war";[123] October 14, 1973: "Israel's terror cannot break our (*Kampfmoral)* will to fight: Message of SAR president Hafez al Assad to Willi Stoph";[124] October 16, 1973: "Outrage and repulsion about the aggressor: Broad solidarity movement for the struggle of the Arab peoples," "GDR in solidarity with the Arab peoples";[125] October 17, 1973: "FRG: Propaganda and help for the aggressor: Rabble-rousing reportage stirs war psychosis," "Workers in the GDR protest against the aggressor Israel: Solidarity with the just stuggle of the Arab peoples";[126] October 16, 1973: "Egyptian armed forces defend against counter-attacks of the aggressor";[127] October 18, 1973: "Israel's politics of violence (*Gewaltpolitik*) condemned, citizens of the GDR express solidarity with the Arab peoples, Protest demonstrations and meetings in all parts of the Republic";[128] October 20, 1973: "Weapons for the aggressor in unlimited quantities: Nixon prepares two billion dollars for the war";[129] October 21, 1973: "Weapons delivery from the USA operating 'in full swing': Pentagon charters airplanes to supply the occupier";[130] October 22, 1973: "Egyptian armed forces continue their operations in the Sinai," "Storm of protest deepens Tel Aviv's isolation," "Praise from Israel for the stance of the FRG Government," "Strong dismay in Cairo about Bonn's action";[131] October

israelische Kriegsverbrechen vor UNO: Isolierung Tel Avis in Sicherheitsrat und Vollversammlung," "BRD Presse feirt den Aggresssor," 5 *ND* (October 11, 1973).

123 "Sowjetunion verurteilt entschieden barbarische Kriegsakte Israel," *ND* (October 13, 1973), 7.

124 "Terror Israels kann unsere Kampfmoral nicht antasten: Botschaft des SAR-Präsidenten Hafez al Assad an Willi Stoph," *ND* (October 14, 1973), 2.

125 "Empörung und Abscheu über den Aggressor: Breite Solidaritätsbewegung für den Kampfe der arabischen Völker," "DDR solidarisch mit arabischen Völkern" *ND* (October 17, 1973), 2.

126 "BRD: Propaganda und Hilfe für den Aggressor Israel: Scharmacherische Berichterstattung soll Kriegspsychose schüren," *ND* (October 17, 1973), 1; "Werktätige der DDR protestierien gegen den Aggressor Israel: Solidarisch mit dem gerechten Kampf der arabischen Völker," 2, *ND* (October 17, 1973).

127 "Ägyptische Streitkräfte wehrten Gegenangriffe des Aggressoren ab," *ND* [East] Berlin (October 16, 1973), 1.

128 "Gewaltpolitik Israels entschieden verurteilt, Bürger der DDR solidarisch mit den arabischen Völkern, Protestversammlungen und Meetings in allen Teilen der Republik," *ND* [East] Berlin (October 18, 1973), 2.

129 "Waffen für den aggressor in 'in unbegrenzten Mengen': Nixon will zwei Milliarden Dollar für den Krieg bereitstellen," *ND* [East] Berlin (October 20, 1973), 7.

130 "Waffennachschub der USA läuft 'auf vollen Touren': Pentagon charters Flugzeugen zur Versorgung der Okkupanten," *ND* [East] Berlin (October 21, 1973), 7.

131 "Ägyptische Streitkräfte setzten auf Sinai ihre Operationen fort," "Proteststurm bekräftigt die Isolierung Tel Avivs," "Lob aus Israel für Haltung der BRD-Regierung," "Starke Betroffenheit in Kairo über Verhalten Bonns," *ND* (October 22, 1973), 5.

24, 1973: "Government of the USSR warns Israel about continuation of aggression";[132] October 25, 1973: "GDR: Israel must immediately stop all acts of aggression: Declaration of the Politburo of the Central Committee of the SED, State Council and Council of Ministers of the German Democratic Republic";[133] October 26, 1973: "Soviet Union calls for energetic measures against the aggressor," "Aggressor strikes Suez";[134] October 27, 1973: "First UN units on way to Cairo, Aggressor Israel again violates cease-fire decision, Urgent meeting of Security Council at Egypt's request," "Unambiguous condemnation of the aggressor in Security Council."[135]

EAST GERMAN ARMS DELIVERIES TO SYRIA

While the West German government was urging Israeli ships to get out of Bremerhaven harbor, the East German government *used its own ships* to send weapons to the Arab states. The shipments for what Honecker, in a letter to Hafez al-Assad, called "support for your just freedom struggle" were kept secret. As the German historian Stefan Meining's research revealed, files of the office of Herman Axen in SED Party Archives in Berlin confirmed details of the deliveries.[136] Defense Ministry files of weapons deliveries to Syria in the course of the war of October 1973 offer still more details. About 1,150 East German military personnel participated in sending MiG jet planes and ammunition to Aleppo airport in Syria.[137] The East German Defense Ministry file on support for Syria in fall 1973 contains daily reports to Erich Honecker from Fritz Streletz, deputy chief of staff

[132] "Regierung der UdSSR warnt Israel vor Fortsetzung der Aggression," *ND* (October 24, 1973), 1.

[133] "DDR: Israel muß sofort alle Aggerssionsakte einstellen: Erklärung des Politburos des ZK der SED, des Staatrates und des Ministerrat der Deutschen Demokratischen Republik zur neuen Israelischen Aggression," 1; "Sowjetunion fordert energische Maßnahmen gegen Aggressor," 1, *ND*, [East] Berlin (October 26, 1973),

[134] "Aggressor greift Suez an," 7, *ND*, [East] Berlin (October 26, 1973).

[135] "Erste UNO-Einheiten nach Kairo unterwegs: Aggressor Israel verletzte erneut Feuereinstellungbeschluß, Dringende Sitzung des Sicherheitsrates auf Antrag der ARÄ," 1; "Unzweideutige Verurteilung des Aggressors im Sicherheitsrat," 7, *ND* [East] Berlin (October 27, 1973).

[136] On the extensive weapons deliveries to Syria see Stefan Meining, *Kommunistische Judenpolitik: Die DDR, die Juden und Israel* (Hamburg: LIT Verlag, 2002), "Jom Kippur 1973: Honeckers Krieg gegen Israel," 328.

[137] "Bericht über die Unterstützungsmaβnahmen für die SYRISCHE ARABISCHE REPUBLIK: Stand: 16.10.1973, 04,30 Uhr," BA-MA, VA-01/ 32899, Militärarchiv der Deutschen Demokratischen Republik: Nationale Volksarmee Ministerium für Nationale Verteidigung Stellv. des Chefs des Hauptstabes für operative Fragen Verw. Gefechtsbereictschaft u. op. Ausbildung, 30–35. See "Streletz, Fritz," in Barth et al.,

of the National Peoples' Army (subsequently chief of staff).[138] Honecker personally approved sending a squadron of 12 MiG-21 jet fighters in the East German air force to Syria along with the necessary ammunition and experts. Between October 18 and 23, East German pilots flew the planes first to Budapest, then to an airport in Yugoslavia, and on to Aleppo in Syria. There they flew them fully armed on test flights before handing them over to pilots who spoke Russian, most probably fighter pilots in the Soviet air force, who then flew them in combat against the Israeli air force.[139] Though the East German pilots did not engage in combat with Israelis, the 32 members of the fighter squadron (JG-8) took pride in their efforts. The operation was honored in a poster by the East German air force (see Figure 6.1). The text read: "In fall 1973, the members of JG-8 alongside their Soviet (*Klassen- und Waffenbruder)* class brothers and brothers in arms, fulfilled their international duty in Aleppo (Haleb), a city in the north of Syria. In so doing they contributed to force the Israeli aggressor to stop the war against the Arab peoples."[140]

Streletz gave Honecker daily briefings about an even larger and equally secret operation, the delivery of large weapons carried to Syria by two East German freighters, the *Freyburg* and *Klosterfelde*. The ships departed from Rostock harbor in mid-October and arrived at the Syrian port of Tartus on November 1 and 2, 1973. Their cargo of approximately 2,200 tons of military equipment included 62 Soviet T-54 tanks with the necessary experts and ammunition; 300 anti-tank rifles (RPG-7) with 24,000 shells; 75,000 grenades that were designed to function with the Syrian army's artillery systems; and 30,000 land mines capable of destroying tanks.[141] Defense Minister Hoffmann ordered that all German language markings on the tanks were to be erased and replaced with Russian language markings and accompanying documentation.[142] The

Wer war Wer in der DDR, 722–723. On the Aleppo operation, see Stefan Meining, "Geheimoperation Aleppo: die geheime Beteiligung der DDR am Oktober-Krieg 1973," Report MÜNCHEN, Bayerischer Rundfunk Stand (October 6, 2008).

138 See "Streletz, Fritz," in Barth et al., *Wer war Wer in der DDR*, 722–723.

139 "Bericht über die Unterstützungsmaßnahmen für die SYRISCHE ARABISCHE REPUBLIK: Stand: 16.10.1973, 04,30 Uhr," 34–35. For a careful account of the Aleppo operation also see Stefan Meining, "Geheimoperation Aleppo: die geheim Beteiligung der DDR am Oktober-Krieg 1973," Report MÜNCHEN, Bayerischer Rundfunk Stand (October 6, 2008); and his *Kommunistische Judenpolitik: Die DDR, die Juden und Israel* (Berlin: LIT Verlag, 2002).

140 JG-8 poster on Aleppo mission from collections of Militärisches Museum des Bundeswehr, Flugplatz, Berlin-Gatow.

141 Generalleutnant Fritz Streletz, "VS-Nr.: A 360 179, Informationsbericht Nr. 15 zur Lage im Nahen Osten: Stand: 20.10.1973, 0500 Uhr," BA-MA, VA-01 32899, 65–75.

142 "Heinz Hoffmann to Generallleutnant Stechbarth," Berlin, 14.10.1973, BA-MA, VA-01/ 32899, 265.

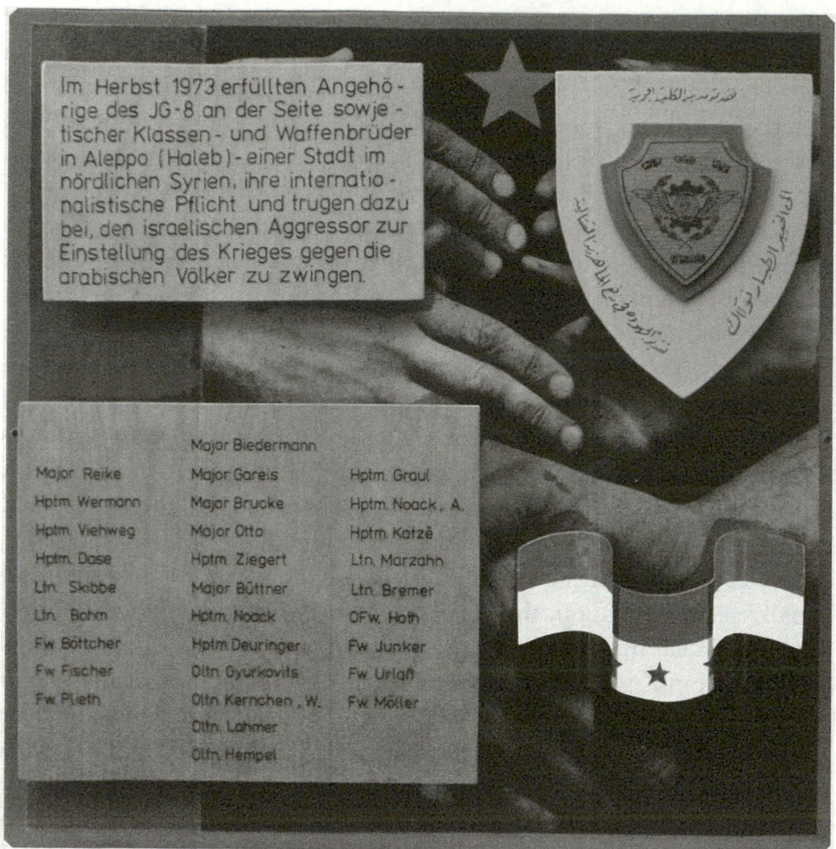

FIGURE 6.1. Plaque honoring 30 members of the JG-8 fighter squadron of the East German air force who flew MiG jets to Aleppo, Syria, during the Yom Kippur War of October 1973. The text reads: "In fall 1973, the members of JG-8 alongside their Soviet class brothers and brothers in arms, fulfilled their international duty in Aleppo (Haleb), a city in the north of Syria. In so doing they contributed to force the Israeli aggressor to stop the war against the Arab peoples."
Source: Collections of Militärhistorisches Museum der Bundeswehr, Flugplatz, Berlin-Gatow.

2,200 tons of military equipment was a small fraction of the 70,000 to 100,000 tons that the Soviet Union and the United States were each sending to the region during the war. Yet it was very important to Honecker. He received 30 daily reports from Streletz on the progress of the *Freyburg* and *Klosterfelde* and the unloading operation in Tartus, Syria.[143] The

[143] "Informationsbericht Nr. 30 zur Lage im Nahen Osten: Stand: 04.11.1973, 05.00 Uhr," BA-MA, VA-01/ 32899, 218–224.

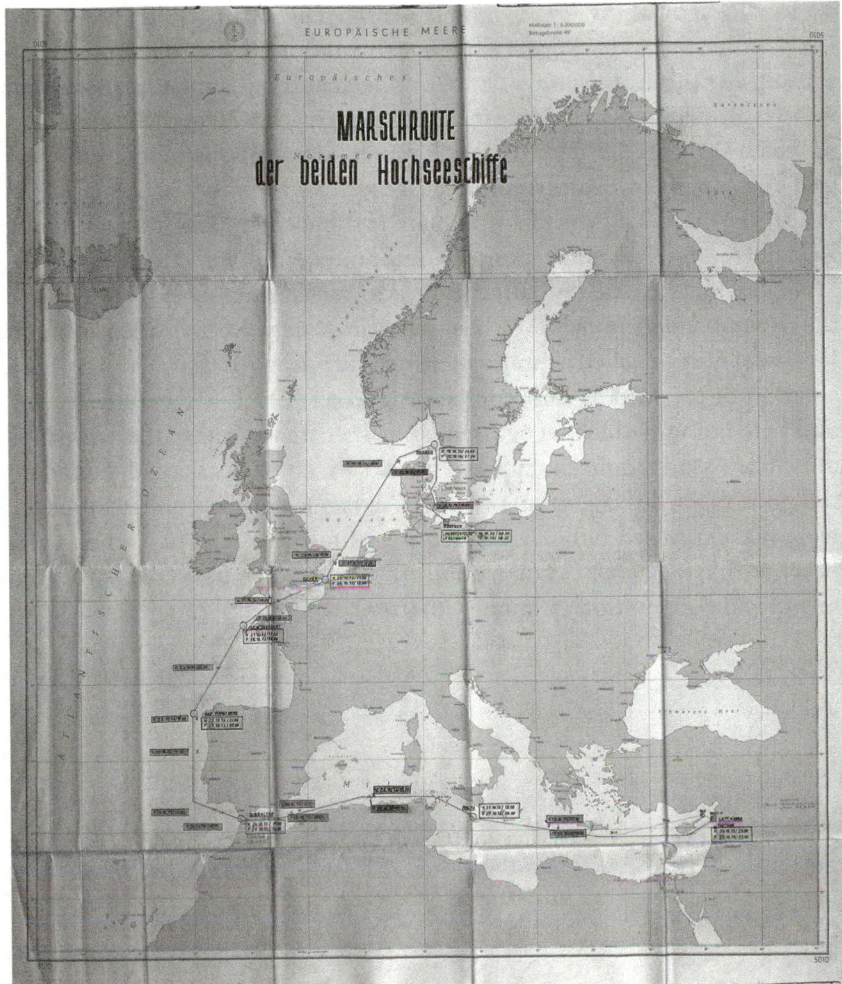

FIGURE 6.2. East German Defense Ministry map showing the voyages of the *Freyburg* (October 19–29, 1973) and *Klosterfelde* (October 18–30, 1973) freighters from Rostock, East Germany, to Tartus, Syria, carrying more than 2,200 tons of heavy military equipment including tanks to the Syrian armed forces.
Source: German Federal Archive-Military Archive, Freiburg, VA 01-3289, 9–440.

Defense Ministry made a large wall map of the voyages to commemorate what the political and military leadership clearly regarded as an important event (see Figure 6.2).

The voyages of the *Freyburg* and *Klosterfelde* dramatically illustrated the contrast between West German neutrality and East German partisanship for the Arab states. The West German government insisted that Israeli ships immediately leave the port of Bremerhaven in the same weeks in which the East German regime was sending weapons in its own ships to Syria. In a memo sent from the East German Embassy in Damascus in January 1974, East German diplomats (probably Ambassador Wolfgang Konschel) saw "the most positive outcome of the war" to be that the "inner stability of the [Syrian] regime was never endangered."[144] Though the Syrians failed to achieve their war aims, they were headed in what Konschel's office called a "more realistic" direction toward a compromise solution of the Middle East conflict in accord with UN Resolutions 242 and 338, both of which recognized Israel's existence within the 1967 borders. The Assad regime, in fact, did not do so. These occasional, confidential nods toward recognition of Israel's existence in the Foreign Ministry were not expressed publicly. As Syria continued to reject a compromise peace with Israel, East German public diplomacy and its secret arms shipments and cooperation in military matters expanded.

[144] Botschaft der DDR in der SAR, "Jahresbericht 1973," Damascus (January 6, 1974), PAAA MFAA, C 998/77, Abt. NMO Sektor Syrien, Libanon, Israel, Jordanien, PLO: Berichte über die syrische Außen- und Innenpolitik sowie über Beziehungen zur DDR und anderen Staaten," 10–29.

7

Political Warfare at the United Nations During the Yom Kippur War of 1973

With its admission to the UN, East Germany joined in the Soviet-bloc propaganda campaign aimed at Israel and in its equally vigorous support for the Arab states and the Palestine Liberation Organization. Two months after East Germany's admission, Peter Florin (1921–2014), its ambassador to the UN from 1973 to 1982, wrote to Secretary General Kurt Waldheim to comment on the 25th anniversary of the UN's "Universal Declaration of Human Rights."[1] East Germany's domestic and foreign policies, Florin stated, were "aimed at preventing that the crimes of German imperialism and fascism perpetrated against the German people and the peoples of the world before and during the Second World War will ever recur." East Germany reaffirmed its "solidarity with peoples struggling for freedom and independence, against [the] imperialist policy of aggression and colonialism" in Vietnam, Chile and South Africa. Further "it condemns the Israeli aggression and practices defying human rights in the illegally occupied Arab territories." Florin recalled World

[1] Peter Florin, "Statement of the Ministry of Foreign Affairs of the German Democratic Republic of the 25th Anniversary of the Universal Declaration of Human Rights" (December 10, 1973), No. 356/73, New York, German Democratic Republic, Permanent Mission to the United Nations, United Nations, Secretary General Kurt Waldheim (hereafter SGKW), German Democratic Republic, Jan. 7, 1972–Dec. 10, 1973, S-0904, Box 62, File 14, Acc 91/5. Born in 1921, Florin fled from Germany with his parents in 1933, lived in the Soviet Union from 1935 to 1945, and returned with the German Communists from Moscow to East Berlin in 1945. By 1949 he was director of the Foreign Policy Office of the SED's Central Committee. See "Florin, Peter," in Siegfried Bock, Ingrid Muth and Hermann Schwiesau, eds., *DDR-Außenpolitik, Ein Überblick: Daten, Fakten, Personen (III)* (Berlin: LIT Verlag, 2012), 304–305.

War II and the crimes of the Nazi regime "against the German people and the peoples of the world."[2] He did not mention the crimes against Europe's Jews. Florin joined the majority in the UN General Assembly that was placing the language of human rights and anti-fascism in the service of a war against Israel.

The rearmament and training of the Egyptian and Syrian armed forces by the Soviet Union and its allies made it possible for Egypt's president, Anwar Sadat, and Syria's president, Hafez al-Assad, to plan a new war that would at least regain the territories won by Israel in 1967.[3] The extent of the Soviet-bloc rearmament effort became apparent in the first hours of the Yom Kippur War. On the afternoon of October 6, close to 100,000 Egyptian soldiers began the successful crossing of the Suez Canal. They overwhelmed Israel's Bar-Lev defense line in the Sinai Peninsula and destroyed 190 of the 300 tanks the Israelis had initially arrayed on that front. That same day, three Syrian infantry divisions supported by 600 Syrian tanks and about 80 artillery batteries attacked Israel's defenses in the Golan Heights. On October 7, two major air operations of the Israel air force failed to destroy Arab anti-aircraft positions in the north, largely because of the effectiveness of Soviet SAM-7 anti-aircraft weapons. Israel's Defense Minister Moshe Dayan feared that Israel might be destroyed.[4]

In the north, the Syrian forces included the equivalent of three reinforced infantry divisions, 930 tanks, around 930 artillery pieces, and more than 30 SAM anti-aircraft batteries. Another two armored divisions, with 460 additional tanks, were positioned in the rear. Facing these five divisions was one undermanned Israeli Defense Force (IDF) division with 177 tanks and 11 artillery batteries on the Golan Heights with 44 guns. As Benny Morris has pointed out, the Israelis were outnumbered by "more than 5 to 1 in armor and 20 to 1 in guns." Just before 2:00 P.M. on October 6 the Syrian attack began with 100 jets and 1,000 artillery pieces attacking the Israeli position. They were followed by infantry and tanks. Morris writes that "what followed during the next four days was the largest tank battle" anywhere in the world "since World War II."[5] On

[2] Ibid.

[3] On planning for the war, see Benny Morris, *Righteous Victims: A History of the Zionist-Arab Conflict, 1881–2001* (New York: Vintage, 2001), 387–398.

[4] Uri Bar-Joseph, "Strategic Surprise or Fundamental Flaws? The Sources of Israel's Military Defeat at the Beginning of the 1973 War," *Journal of Military History* 72 (April 2008), 509–530.

[5] On the early days of the war, see "The October War," in Morris, *Righteous Victims* .

October 8 and 9, Israel launched a successful counteroffensive with armored columns and began to bomb military targets in Syria itself. On October 9, eight Israeli Phantom F-4 jets accurately bombed Syria's General Staff and Air Force Headquarters in Damascus. A number of off-target bombs struck the Damascus government's TV building and the Soviet Cultural Center. Intense battles between Israeli and Syrian infantry and armored forces continued through October 22, ending with the recapture of Mount Herman in the Golan Heights by the IDF's Golani Brigade.[6]

In the south, the Egyptians had the advantage of both surprise and superior numbers, again due to Soviet-bloc rearmament. Their forces outnumbered the Israelis by 5 to 1 in tanks and 20 to 1 in guns. Egypt's achievement of surprise and a delay in mobilizing Israel's reserves exacerbated the imbalance. The Egyptian attack began with an air assault by 150 to 200 planes on IDF forces in the Sinai and an artillery barrage on Israel's defensive lines. According to Morris, Egypt's Field Marshall Mohammed el-Gamasy reported that "during the first minute of the Egyptian offensive, 10,500 artillery and mortar rounds fell on the Bar-Lev Line."[7] Two hours after the attack began, 25,000 Egyptian soldiers had crossed the Suez Canal. By the morning of October 6–7, the Egyptians had moved about 500 tanks, 3,000 artillery pieces, and five divisions loaded with anti-tank guns across the canal. By the evening of October 7, 100,000 men, 1,020 tanks, and 13,500 vehicles had crossed the canal. Two Israeli forts surrendered, five others were abandoned, and 153, or 60 percent, of Israel's Sinai Division's tanks had been put out of commission. "Hundreds of men had been killed or were missing in action."[8] On October 14, in an enormous tank battle, even larger than those on the Syrian front, about 1,000 Egyptian tanks and armored personnel carriers battled about 750 Israeli tanks, this time supported by the Israeli air force. The Egyptians lost hundreds of men and between 200 and 250 tanks; the IDF lost 20 to 25. Both sides regarded the battle as a turning point in the war.[9] With the agreement to UN resolutions calling for a cease-fire, the war formally ended on October 25.

The Yom Kippur War was the most devastating in the history of the Middle East conflict. Israel lost about 2,300 dead, 5,500 wounded, and

[6] Ibid., 402–411.
[7] Ibid., 413.
[8] Ibid., 418.
[9] Ibid., 421–422.

294 prisoners; Egyptian casualties were 12,000 dead, 35,000 wounded, and 8,400 prisoners; Syria lost about 3,000 dead, 5,600 wounded, and 411 captured (including 13 Iraqis and 6 Moroccans). Egypt lost about 1,000 tanks, Syria 1,150, and Israel 400. Israel lost 102 planes, about 30 percent of its combat strength, as well as 5 helicopters. The Egyptians lost 235 airplanes and 42 helicopters and the Syrians, 135 airplanes and 13 helicopters.[10] Morris summarized the impact of Soviet rearmament as follows:

> The [Israeli] Armored Corps was completely unprepared for the massive deployment of Saggers, [Soviet anti-tank guided missiles], recoilless anti-tank guns, and RPGs [rocket-propelled grenades] by the Arab infantry; the IAF had no suitable response to the Egyptian and Syrian interlocking SAM network; and Israel's infantry, equipped with outdated bazooka rocket launchers, FN semiautomatic rifles, and Uzi submachine guns, was no match in firepower for the Egyptian and Syrian infantry, who were equipped with RPG-7s and AK-47 (Kalashnikov) automatic assault rifles. Only in the course of the war did the United States airlift to Israel large quantities of automatic rifles (M-16s), TOW anti-tank guided missiles, and LAW anti-tank rockets.[11]

The Soviet-bloc program of rearmament, training, and supply to the Arab states enabled blows on Israel's armed forces that were so serious that, as we have seen in the preceding chapter, Israel's ability to defend itself and overcome the initial disaster now depended on the supply and resupply by the United States. At the United Nations in New York, the Soviet Union and its allies were waging fierce political warfare on behalf of the Arab states. It mirrored the propaganda campaign evident in the pages of *Neues Deutschland*. On October 7, Israel's foreign minister Abba Eban informed UN secretary general U Thant and thereby all of the UN member nations that Israel, having learned that an attack could be imminent, had informed "a number of friendly governments" that it "would not itself initiate military actions and that the governments of Egypt and Syria could be assured accordingly." Israel was assured that the message was delivered. Eban did not mince words: "This treacherous aggression [by Egypt and Syria] was launched against Israel on the Day of Atonement when, by reason of the special sanctity of the day, the holiest in the Jewish calendar, the everyday routine of life in the country gives way to spiritual reflection and prayer throughout the nation. To the blasphemy and sacrilege involved in the choice of this particular day,"

[10] Ibid., 431.
[11] Ibid., 432.

the Egyptian and Syrian representatives had "added the base and cynical falsehood which alleges that Israel, on the Day of Atonement, with all that this day means for Jews in Israel as elsewhere, began the fighting. The inconceivable mendacity of this allegation" was "fully exposed by the military facts and by reports by the UN military observers." Israel would exercise its right of self-defense "until the aggressors have been thrown back and the cease-fire structure agreed by the parties in 1967 and the 1970s is restored."[12]

At the UN, the Soviet Union and its allies did not deny that Egypt and Syria had, in fact, begun the war. Rather, as the Soviet Union's UN ambassador Yakov Malik put it, the cause of the war was "the expansionist policy of Israel's ruling circles."[13] Israel, he continued, "with the support and protection of the imperialist circles" had been "constantly inflaming the situation in the Middle East by its reckless aggressive acts." It had disregarded "the demands of world public opinion" and trampled on the UN Charter, decisions of the UN, and "the generally recognized rules of international law." Israel's "ruling circles" had "elevated violence and banditry to the level of State policy." Israel's "military clique" had engaged in "ceaseless acts of armed provocation against Egypt, Syria and Lebanon" since 1967. In the days before October 6, he said that Israel "concentrated substantial armed forces on the cease-fire lines with Syria and Egypt," called up reservists, and "after thus inflaming the situation to the utmost ... launched military operations.... Responsibility for the present turn of events in the Middle East and for their consequences rests wholly and entirely with Israel and with those foreign reactionary circles which constantly abet Israel in its aggressive ambitions."[14]

The day after Egypt and Syria had launched an attack on Israel using Soviet weapons, the Soviet UN ambassador placed the entire responsibility for the war on Israel's shoulders. In fact, Israel had not concentrated forces on the cease-fire lines any more than in recent months. Reservists had not been called up before the attack. Israel did not launch any military operations until after it was attacked. Malik ended with the

[12] Abba Eban, "Letter Dated 7 October 1973 from the Minister of Foreign Affairs of Israel to the Secretary General," UNSC, A/9024; S/11011 (October 7, 1973), UN ODS A/9024.

[13] "Letter Dated 7 October 1973 from the Permanent Representative of the Union of Soviet Socialist Republics [hereafter USSR] to the United Nations Addressed to the Secretary General" and "Statement by the Soviet Government," UNSC, A/9295; S/11012 (October 7, 1973) UN ODS, A/9295; S/11012.

[14] Ibid.

following threat. "If, a prisoner of its expansionist ambitions, the Israeli government remains deaf to the voice of reason and continues to pursue a policy of annexation, retaining the occupied Arab lands, ignoring decisions of the Security Council and the General Assembly and defying world public opinion, this may cost the people of Israel dearly. All responsibility for the consequences of such an unreasonable course will rest with the leaders of the state of Israel."[15]

THE EXCHANGES BETWEEN YOSEF TEKOAH AND YAKOV MALIK IN THE SECURITY COUNCIL

On October 9 Malik conveyed to the Security Council what turned out to be a false report that Israel had carried out "the barbaric, bestial and gangster-like bombing of the Soviet Cultural Center" in Damascus.[16] Referring to Agence France Presse and UPI reports that "no less than 10 foreign embassies have been destroyed and 30 staff members of the Soviet embassy have been killed," Malik said that "these bloody crimes are the equal of Hitler's actions as a result of which whole towns and populations centres were removed from the face of the earth.... Just as in their age savage barbarian tribes, in their mad urge for destruction, disrupted, demolished, wiped from the face of the earth towns and the most precious monuments of human culture, so in our civilized age the Zionist barbarians have disrupted and paralyzed the Suez Canal, that work of genius produced by human reason and the science and technology of the last century."[17] As Israel's UN ambassador Yosef Tekoah was replying, Malik left the Security Council chamber accompanied by the applause of the assembled diplomats.[18] Tekoah was repeatedly interrupted by the representative from Sudan as he sought to draw attention to the Soviet Union's role in initiating the war and to "the innocent civilian Jewish men and women who have lost their lives because of the aggression by our two neighboring States." Tekoah informed the Security Council that "for the previous three days Syrian long-range ground-to-ground missiles with warheads of 500 kilos each have rained fire and death on Israeli towns and villages." Yet the Syrians "had the audacity to suggest that in

[15] Ibid.

[16] Yakov Malik, United Nations Security Council Official Records, UNSCOR 1744th Meeting, New York (October 9, 1973), 9, UN ODS S/PV.1744.

[17] Ibid.

[18] Robert Alden, "A Soviet Walkout Marks U.N. Debate," *New York Times* (October 10, 1973), 1.

the face of this aggression that makes no distinction between military and civilian" targets, Israel could not respond with air strikes directed at military headquarters of the Syrian army and air force.[19] Following Tekoah's reply, the ambassadors of the United Kingdom, India, Austria, Kenya, Yugoslavia, Panama, Guinea, and Peru all rose to express varying degrees of shock, anger, grief, condolences, and, in a few cases, indignation at Israel about the alleged loss of life due to a supposed Israeli attack on the Soviet cultural embassy in Damascus. None, including US ambassador John Scali, offered any condolences to Israel for its loss of civilian life.

Two evenings later, as the Security Council met again, Eban and Tekoah responded. Eban attacked Egypt and Syria for "wantonly, unnecessarily, without provocation" deciding to "wage all-out war against Israelis, soldiers and civilians, wherever they could find them," and then, having done so, express the conviction that "they have the right to attack Israelis and yet to seek international protection against any Israeli response. They not only want to make war but they want it to be unilateral." Those who started it were responsible for the Israeli victims and "for the death and disaster suffered by Egyptians and Syrians and by all those who are caught up in the fearful alternation of war. But the doctrine of unilateral war, a war unprovoked to kill Israelis and to be immune from all response, that is what makes these two utterances unusual, even in the history of war."[20] At the UN, the anti-Israeli majority did not criticize attacks on Israel. It reserved criticism for Israel's efforts at self-defense, which it denounced as forms of aggression.

Tekoah responded to Malik's assertions about the supposed Israeli attack on the Soviet Cultural Center in Damascus. He said Israel would "not forget the treachery and mendacity accompanying the renewal of Arab aggression," which reached a climax at the meeting on October 9 in the Security Council. "The orgy of falsehood and abuse, the outbursts of primitive anti-Semitism" at the meeting had "shocked the civilized world, further damaged the Security Council and tarnished the name of the United Nations."[21] According to Tekoah, the charges of the Soviet Union regarding the raids and deaths in Damascus were fictions. "By charging a non-existent raid on the Soviet Embassy in Damascus, and a non-existent

19 Yosef Tekoah, UNCSOR, 1744th Meeting, New York (October 9, 1973), 11, UN ODS, S/PV.1744.

20 Abba Eban, UNSCOR, 1745th Meeting, New York (October 11, 1973), 3, UN ODS, S/PV.1745.

21 Yosef Tekoah, UNSCOR, 1745th Meeting, New York (October 11, 1973), 11, UN ODS, S/PV.1745.

air attack on Cairo, by alleging non-existent casualties among the diplomatic personnel of the Soviet Embassy, the Egyptian and Syrian Foreign Ministers and their supporters created in this Security Council an atmosphere that has been described by eye witnesses, including representatives of international information media, as pogromist."[22] Tekoah reported that the Syrian authorities denied that any Soviet nationals had been killed at the Soviet Embassy or Cultural Center and that the Egyptians said talk of a raid on Cairo was "'downright nonsense.'… Yet under pretext of this nonsense and these falsehoods certain members of the Security Council joined in a demonstration of blind hatred and inveterate one-sidedness." The UN's "known inability" to address the Middle East conflict "in an equitable and responsible manner" had "never been more evident."[23] Tekoah then noted the absence of a UN "resolution condemning the murder of innocent Jewish men, women and children by Arab terrorists" or the expression of "sympathy to the fathers and mothers, to the wives, to the children, of the Israeli athletes killed at the Olympic Games in Munich, or the Jews and Christian pilgrims massacred at Lod Airport?"[24]

Since the East and West German governments had been admitted to the UN several weeks earlier, their delegations were present to hear or read Tekoah's comment about Egypt and Syria's choice of Yom Kippur, the Day of Atonement, to launch their attack.

> The 6th of October, as is known, was the most solemn day of the Jewish calendar – the Day of Atonement, a day of fast and prayer when young and old alike are gathered with their families at worship and at home. This is a time when the entire country is at rest; all work is at a standstill; radio and television stations are silent; transportation immobile. I should like to mention one other aspect of this blasphemous choice for the perpetration of the treacherous attack. It was this day, the Day of Atonement that the Nazis used to select for massacres of Jews. It was on this Day of Judgment in 1941 that the Nazi SS squads brought 90,000 Jewish men, women and children to Babi Yar, in the suburbs of Kiev, made them dig mass graves and then mercilessly mowed them down with machine guns. It was on this day of fast and prayer that they used to surround synagogues and butcher all the worshippers in them. It was on Yom Kippur of 1942 that Nazi military forces attacked and slaughtered the Jewish men, women and children assembled for prayer in the synagogues of Warsaw and Bialystok. In 1943 it was on the Day of Atonement that they did the same in the ghettos of Vilnius and Lublin.

[22] Ibid.

[23] Ibid.

[24] Ibid.

Those who have watched and studied the attitude of the Arab leaders towards the Jewish people and its rights know that it was in a similar spirit of fanatical hatred and bloodlust that Egypt and Syria attacked Israel on the Day of Atonement 1973. Like the Nazis, they too thought we would be caught unaware on such a day, unable to defend ourselves. They were wrong.

The affinity with Nazi thought and the Nazi attitude towards the Jewish people is not new for Egypt's President. Thus, in September 1953, several new agencies reported that Hitler was still alive. On the basis of that report, a Cairo daily, *Al-Moussawar*, asked a number of Egyptian personalities the following question: "If you wish to send Hitler a personal letter, what would you write to him?"[25]

Anwar Sadat was one of those questioned. His answer, published in Cairo's *Al-Moussawar*, number 1510, of 18 September 1953, reads *inter alia:*

"My dear Hitler:

I congratulate you from the bottom of my heart. Even if you appear to have been defeated, in reality you are the victor. You may be proud of having become the immortal leader of Germany. We will not be surprised if you appear again in Germany, or if a new Hitler rises up in your wake."

Well, new Hitlers have risen up: in the Nile Delta and in Damascus."

This is the face of the enemy that Israel confronts today. We know that he feels towards us as the Nazis did. We know that if he could, he would complete the Nazi objective of annihilating the Jewish people and would destroy its state. We shall fight him as the nations' [sic] victims of Nazi aggression fought with all our soul and all our might, until the Jewish people can live like others – in peace and security.[26]

Tekoah's historical references were accurate: The Nazis had chosen Yom Kippur as the date to carry out massacres. Sadat had publicly expressed enthusiasm for Hitler. The Arab governments had repeatedly spoken as if all of Israel were "occupied" territory that was to be "liberated." Yet Tekoah's remarkable statement about the echoes of Nazism had no impact at all on Florin and the East German delegation. Despite their "anti-fascist" ideology, they did not care that some of the Arab states they and their Soviet patrons were celebrating were led by men who had venerated Hitler and Nazism. Such enthusiasm on the part of some Arab nationalists and Islamists, which was well known during and after World War II, never found its way into the pages of *Neues Deutschland* or into the indignant leaflets and essays of West German leftists.[27]

[25] Ibid., 13.

[26] Ibid., 13.

[27] On Arab collaboration with the Nazis, see Jeffrey Herf, *Nazi Propaganda for the Arab World* (New Haven, CT: Yale University Press, 2009); and David Motadel, *Islam and Nazi Germany's War* (Cambridge, MA: Harvard University Press, 2014). On the postwar

Malik, however, turned history upside down as he presented the Yom Kippur War as a replay of World War II on the Eastern Front.

The Soviet people understand the feelings of the Arab peoples very well, for we ourselves experienced Fascist occupation during the Second World War.... We know the feelings of those who are subjected to barbarous attacks by an enemy air force and see the strafing enemy kill their relatives and loved ones before their very eyes. We understand the feelings and the profound righteous indignation, the tremendous feeling of national hatred and anger toward the annexationists and aggressors, and the sacred aspiration to liberate their own soil from foreign occupation. We experienced these feelings to the full during the Second World War.... The Soviet Union supports the just liberation struggle of the Arab people against imperialist aggression and it considers this struggle is legitimate and sacred, as indeed was the struggle of the Soviet people, the people of France, the people of Yugoslavia and the peoples of many other European countries against foreign aggression during the Second World War.[28]

For Malik, the Israelis had become the Nazis of 1973 while the Arabs took the place of the peoples of the Soviet Union suffering under Nazi occupation. Malik did not retract or apologize for the baseless accusations he had made two nights before regarding a supposed attack on the Soviet Embassy and Cultural Center in Damascus. Instead he spoke as if Israel was bombing civilians as the Nazis had. Malik sought an emotional bond with the Arab states based on a shared hatred of fascist aggressors, first in the form of Nazi Germany then in the form of the despised Zionists. He boasted that he was "not intimidated" when the Israelis criticized anti-Semitism, for "whenever Israel is isolated diplomatically, it falls back on the use of that extortion." He knew how to combine familiar anti-Semitic themes of money and murder. In response to the Israelis' comments to the Security Council, he said, "We have the impression that we are not in the Security Council within the framework of the Charter, but at a banquet or $1,000-a-plate dinner organized by the Zionists to buy Phantoms and other weapons to kill our women and children and refugees everywhere in the Middle East."[29]

Tekoah rejected Malik's accusations that Israeli air actions "were not directed against military targets" and cited "official communiqués"

decades in the Arab states see Meir Litvak and Esther Webman, *From Empathy to Denial: Arab Responses to the Holocaust* (London: Hurst, 2009).

[28] Yakov Malik, UNSCOR, 1745th Meeting, New York (October 11, 1973), 15, UN ODS, S/PV.1745.

[29] Ibid.

from the Egyptian and Syrian governments pinpointing their military installations that had been attacked. He cited a Reuters report from Damascus that "official sources ... denied that any Russians at the Soviet Embassy or the Soviet Cultural Center were killed during today's Israeli air attack on Damascus," a report that clearly contradicted Malik's statement to the Security Council of October 9, 1973. "Have you ever expressed any regret, Mr. Malik," Tekoah asked, "over the Jewish blood spilled during these last 25 years?"[30] Malik replied that he was "distressed that 6 million Jews died in Hitler's Germany" but expressed no distress about what Tekoah had in mind, the deaths of Israelis after the Holocaust, for "when Israel became an aggressor, we changed our policy towards it.... Do not speculate about anti-Semitism." Malik actually said, "My best friends are Jews."[31]

Malik's comments demonstrated the connection between Communist anti-Zionism and anti-Semitism. According to Malik, the Israelis were aggressors who committed the crime of intentionally attacking civilians. They behaved as the Nazis had behaved. In short, they were evil. Yet he then asserted that anyone who suggested that such accusations had something to do with the traditions of centuries of anti-Semitism was simply engaging in "extortion," an accusation that had been common in the repertoire of anti-Semitism. Malik said he would not be "intimidated" by Israel's criticisms, as if that tiny country posed a threat to the Soviet superpower. Malik's pose of courage and bravery in the face of the vastly inflated power of the Jews was also characteristic of the paranoia that was a longstanding element of anti-Semitism.

YOSEF TEKOAH'S DETAILED ACCOUNTS OF ATTACKS ON ISRAEL'S NORTHERN TOWNS

On October 12, Ambassador Tekoah sent the secretary general the following list of "recent attacks by Arab terrorists from Lebanese territory against civilian-inhabited localities in Israel, causing casualties and damage to property"[32] (Table 7.1).

[30] Yosef Tekoah, UNSCOR, 1745th Meeting, New York (October 11, 1973), 17, UN ODS, S/PV.1745.

[31] Yakov Malik, UNSCOR, 1745th Meeting, New York (October 11, 1973), 18–19, UN ODS, S/PV.1745.

[32] "Letter Dated 12 October 1973 from the Permanent Representative of Israel to the United Nations Addressed to the Secretary General," UNSC, UN ODS, A/9222; S/11027.

TABLE 7.1. *Tekoah's to Reports to UN on Terrorist Attacks on Northern Israeli Towns, October 1973*

7 October 1973	
0029	Bazooka shells fell on Misgave-Am.
0014	Mortar fire against Margulies.
0030	Katyusha rockets attack on Kiryat Shmona[Shmona].
1041	Small arms fire directed at Her Dove.
2105	Mortar fire against Manor.
8 October 1973	
0040	Mortar fire against Her Miron, Dovev, and Bar Am.
2130	Katyusha rockets fell on Rosh Pinna.
0215	Katyusha rockets fell on Gesher Haziv.
0900	Two mines were discovered near Manara.
1940	Mortar and small arms fire against Har Amiram.
1955	Mortar fire against Zarait.
9 October 1973	
	A squad of armed terrorists discovered in Yir'om.
0207	Mortar fire against Misgav-Am.
0406	Mortar fire against Margaliot, Manara, and Beit Hillel.
1210	Bazooka shells fell on Idmit.
1940	Bazooka shells fell on Margaliot.
2210	Mortar fire against Metulla.
2135	Katyusha rockets fell on Kiryat Shmoneh.
2205	Katyusha rockets fell on Hurshat Tal and Kfar Szold.
10 October 1973	
0015	Mortar fire against Har Avivm.
0016	Katyusha rockets fell on Kiryat Shmonah.
0017	Mortar fire against Manara. Katyusha rockets fell in the Huleh Valley.
0155	Mortar fire against Yir'om.
0215	Mortar fire against Dishon and Ramot Naftali.
0240	Mortar fire against Har Avivim.
0335	Katyusha rockets fell on Gesher Haziv and Sa'ar.
0435	Two explosive charges went off in Yiftech.
0700	Katyusha rockets fell on Nahariya.
0750	Katyusha rockets fell on Meshek Rosh Hanikra.
1358	Mortar fire agains Rosh Hanikra.
2030	Mortar fire against Har Dov.
1610	Mortar fire against Abassiyah and Har Dov.
2320	Mortar fire against Metulla and Kfar Yovel.
2325	Mortar and small arms fire against Zarait.

TABLE 7.1 (*continued*)

11 October 1973	
After midnight	Katyusha rockets fell in or near Dan, Dafna, Ma'ayan, Beit Hilel, Metula, Margalot, Betzet, Gesher Haziv.*
12 October 1973	
2040	Clash with a terrorist squad. One attacker caught. Bazooka shells and hand grenades in their possession seized.
2135	Abassiya attacked by small arms and bazooka fire.
13 October 1973	
0225	Bazooka shells fired at Misgav-Am.
0230	Bazooka shells directed at Idmit.
14 October 1973	
0015	Katyusha rockets fired at Betzet.
0300	Class with terrorist squad in Metulla region. Three terrorists killed. Arms, including bazooka shells, seized.
0110	Small arms fire and bazooka shells directed at Misgav-Am.
2000	Bazooka shells directed at Manara.
2110	Clash with terrorist squad near Abassiyah. Six terrorists killed.
2200	Katyusha rockets directed at Kabri, Gesher Haziv, Shlomi, and Tetzet.
15 October 1973	
1845	Clash with terrorist squad near Biranit.
16 October 1973	
0115	During clash with terrorist unit in Mitzpeh Pe'er three terrorists were killed.
0120	Bazooka shells fired at Zarit.
0335	Small arms fire directed at Misgav-Am.
2120	Bazooka and small arms fire against Malakiya and Metulla.
2215	Katyusha rockets fell on Kiryat Shmoneh.
2245	Katyusha rockets felon Yaara.

Note: *"Annex: Letter Dated 12 October 1973 from the Permanent Representative of Israel to the United Nations Addressed to the Secretary General," UNSC UN ODS, A/9222; S/11027.

Tekoah wrote that the attacks were continuing and that the Lebanese government "must bear full responsibility for them."[33] Either Lebanon was supporting the attacks or it had lost control of the southern part of its

[33] "Annex: Letter Dated 17 October 1973 from the Permanent Representative of Israel to the United Nations Addressed to the Secretary General," UNSC UN ODS, A/9229; S/11032.

country to the armed forces of the Palestine Liberation Organization. On October 19, Tekoah reported attacks since October 6 on the villages and towns of northern Israel by Syrian missiles, artillery, and air attacks "causing heavy civilian casualties in killed (for example no less than 13 in the Druze village of Majda Shams) and wounded and substantial damage."[34] These attacks were carried out with the larger weapons of war – planes, missiles, and artillery – that only states could afford and maintain.

6 October	
1450	Syrian planes attacked Kfar Giladi.
1735	Syrian planes attacked Majdal Shams.
2024	Frog missiles fell on Migdal Haemek.
7 October	
0125	Shelling of Kfar Szold, Horshat Tal, and Shamir.
0700	Artillery bombardment of Shamir and Gadot.
2045	Frog missiles fell on Migdal Haemek.
8 October	
0336	Frog missiles fell on Nahalal and between Afula and Midgal Haemek.
9 October	
0030	Shelling of the Hulta area.
0330	Frog missiles fell on Gevat, hitting nurseries and the kibbutz dining room.
0815	Aerial attack on Ramat Magshimim.
10 October	
0755	Shelling of Lahvot Habashan.
1415	Artillery bombardment of villages in the Golan Heights.
14 October	
2300 to 2400	Long-range artillery bombardment of Hatzor, Ayelet Hashshar, Mahanayim, and the Amiad-Eliffelet areas.
15 October	
0200	Long range artillery bombardment in area of Sed-Eliezer.
1835	Shelling of Kinnereth and Haon.
2345	Long-range bombardment of Tiberias area and missile fire on the Huleh valley.

34 "Letter Dated 19 October 1973 from the Permanent Representative of Israel to the United Nations Addressed to the Secretary General," UNSC UN ODS, A/9245; S/11035.

16 October	
1410	Shelling of Ramat Magshimim.

17 October	
1330	Aerial attack on the Druze village of Majdal Shams.
2115	Artillery bombardment of Gesher Benot Yaakov area.
2200	Shelling of Gadot.

18 October	
0410	Artillery bombardment of Ramat Magshimim.
1445	Artillery bombardment of Mahanayim area.
1535	Artillery bombardment of Hatzor.

19 October	
0500	Artillery bombardment of Ramat Magshimim.*

Note: *Yosef Tekoah, "Letter dated 19 October 1973 from the Permanent Representative of Israel to the United Nations addressed to the Secretary General," UNSC UN ODS A/9245; S/11035.

All of these attacks from Lebanon and Syria were on the civilian towns and villages of northern Israel. None were aimed primarily at military targets. Yet none of the UN resolutions specifically denounced these attacks on Israeli civilians carried out by the Arab states and the Palestinian terrorist organizations. In the following year, the PLO intensified its terrorist campaign against the towns of northern Israel.

8

1974: Palestinian Terrorist Attacks on Kiryat Shmona and Ma'alot and Responses in East Germany, West Germany, Israel, the United States, and the United Nations

After the expulsion from Jordan in 1970, the PLO conducted terrorist attacks on the towns and villages of northern Israel from bases in southern Lebanon. In the aftermath of the Yom Kippur War, Al Fatah, the Popular Front for the Liberation of Palestine (PFLP), the Democratic Popular Front for the Liberation of Palestine (DPFLP), and the Syrian-led Saika organization intensified the campaign. Two of those attacks, one on the town of Kiryat Shmona on April 11, 1974, and another on the town of Ma'alot on May 15, 1974, were particularly noteworthy for their brutality and the revulsion they aroused in Israel, Western Europe and the United States, as well as for the enthusiasm they evoked among the Palestinian terrorist organizations and their supporters in the Middle East.

At the same time that it intensified its campaign of terrorism against Israel, the PLO and its supporters continued a war of words against Israel both in the controlled press and other media of the Soviet bloc as well as in the United Nations General Assembly. While the PLO could not destroy the state of Israel by force of arms, it could consistently win political victories in the UN General Assembly in New York. Using the language of human rights, anti-racism, and desires for a "just and lasting peace" the anti-Israeli majority at the UN served as a political complement to the PLO's terrorist attacks against Israel. In each instance of terrorist attack followed by Israel counterattacks on the bases of the Palestinian armed organizations, UN members were offered contrasting facts and interpretations of events. Without fail, the Soviet-bloc–Arab-state–third-world majority in the General Assembly dismissed Israel's assertions and gave the benefit of the doubt to the PLO and its affiliated groups. East Germany contributed to this large international propaganda assault on Israel.

THE POPULAR FRONT FOR THE LIBERATION OF PALESTINE ATTACK ON KIRYAT SHMONA, APRIL 11, 1974

On April 11, 1974, Israeli ambassador Yosef Tekoah wrote to Secretary General Kurt Waldheim with details of "the barbaric atrocity committed" that day in the northern Israeli town of Kiryat Shmona.[1] "Early this morning," he wrote, "a group of terrorists crossed the Israel-Lebanese frontier, seized an apartment building in the townlet of Kiryat Shmona, situated in the immediate proximity of the border, massacred 18 of its inhabitants including 8 children and 5 women, and wounded 15 other persons. In bestial blood thirst the murderers hurled children to their deaths from windows in the upper floor of the building."[2] The squad first entered the town's school building, but as it was empty because of Passover vacation, it attacked an apartment building. Tekoah reported that on the same day "in a statement in Beirut the terrorist organization known as the Popular Front-General Command [PFLP-GC] announced its responsibility for this savage slaughter." Israeli correspondents confirmed that "while the terrorists were taking control of the apartment building, they threw children out from the third floor of the building" and that "the corpses of women and children shot by the terrorists were found on the staircase." The PFLP-GC squad seized hostages and demanded the release of "some 100 terrorists within six hours, including the Japanese terrorist Kozo Okamoto," the surviving participant in the Japanese Red Army/PFLP joint attack on Lod airport in May 1972.

The BBC monitoring service recorded a PFLP-GC communiqué broadcast on April 16 in Damascus, Beirut, Baghdad and Paris. It claimed that "the terrorists had been ordered to use explosive belts they wore around themselves and kill themselves together with the hostages if the demands were not met or if an attempt to carry out an assault against them was made."[3] Then it blamed the government of Israel for the deaths of the

[1] Yosef Tekoah to Kurt Waldheim, "Letter Dated 11 April 1974 From the Permanent Representative of Israel to the United Nations Addressed to the Secretary General," New York (April 11, 1974), United Nations General Assembly-Security Council, A/9515/S/11259, UN Official Documents System, documents.un.org/, S/11259.

[2] Ibid.

[3] "The Qiryat Shmona Incident in Israel. (a) Excerpts from Israel Home Service reports," BBC, *SWB Summary of World Broadcasts* (April 16, 1974), ME/4575/A/4.

hostages. It also referred to all of those killed in the attack – 16 Israeli civilians, including eight children, and two members of the IDF – as "soldiers," thereby erasing the distinction between soldiers and civilians.[4] The *Voice of Palestine* radio station in Baghdad celebrated "the extraordinarily heroic action of our fighters in the Zionist town of Khalisah [Qiryat Shmona]."[5] On April 11, 1974, the *Voice of Palestine*'s clandestine station broadcast the names of the three "heroes of the Qirat Shmona operation," who were from Syria, Iraq and Palestine.[6] Their "martyrdom" followed "a heroic immortal battle in which Palestinian blood mingled with Syrian and Iraqi blood, thus emphasizing the pan-Arab character of the battle and placing the capitulationists face to face with the attitudes of the masses which reject settlements and negotiations."[7]

In his remarks to the Security Council on April 15, Tekoah listed the names and ages of eight adults, ages 27 to 60; the eight children ranging from 2 to 16; and the two soldiers who had been murdered in Kiryat Shmona.[8] He placed the blame both on the PLO and on the Arab states that supported it. It was, he wrote, "common knowledge" that the Arab states supported "the terror organizations ... politically, militarily and financially." The PLO was able to maintain offices in cities outside the Middle East. Yet the UN had failed to "take firm and concrete measures against it." All of this had "encouraged and given succor to these assassins." The PFLP-GC had its headquarters and training camps and bases in Lebanon, where it was free to publish newspapers and issue communiqués and declarations and "to come and go, appear in public and to carry on their criminal activities without any hindrance. The government of Lebanon must bear full responsibility for this situation, which permits

[4] Ibid., A/4. Ibid., A/6–7.

[5] Ibid., A/7.

[6] "The Qiryat Shmona Incident in Israel. (d) Excerpts from 'military communiqué issued by the general command of the Palestine Liberation Forces,'" BBC, *SWB* April 16, 1974, ME/4575/A/7. The names given were Munir al-Maghribi, or Abu Khalid, "a Palestinian born in 1954," who studied in Baghdad and joined the PFLP-GC in 1971; Ahmad ash-Shaykh Mahmud, or Abu Shakir, born in 1954 near Aleppo in Syria and a PFLP-GC member since early 1972; and Yasin Musa Fazza al-Muzzani, known as Abu Hadi, born in 1947 in Iraq and a PFLP-GC member since early 1972.

[7] Ibid., A/8.

[8] Yosef Tekoah, UNSCOR *1766th Meeting, April 15, 1974*, UN ODS S/PV.1766, UN ODS, documents.un.org/, 5. "Fanny Shitreet, aged 30 and three of her children – Yocheved, 11, Aaron, 8, and Motti, 4; Shimon Bitteon, 33 years old; Avi, 5 and his 2 1/2-year-old sister Miriam; Yacov Guetta and Miraam Guetta, each 30 years old; Hadassah Stern, 27, and her daughter Rachel, 8; Esther Cohen, 49; her son David, 16; and her daughter, Shulamit, 14. Also killed were Esther Yaxada, 60 years old, and Shmuel Ben Abu, 58; and two soldiers, Mordechai Geride and Agahda el Sauhil."

terror attacks to be initiated and carried out from its territory against Israel."[9]

The response of the United Nations General Assembly to the attack on Kiryat Shmona illustrated the connection between political warfare at the UN in New York and the terrorist campaign waged against Israel by the PLO and its affiliated factions. Rather than denouncing the PLO's terrorist campaign, the UN majority rewarded it with resolutions denouncing Israel and an invitation to Arafat to address the General Assembly in fall 1974. Rather than condemn the PFLP, the General Assembly condemned Israel's acts of self-defense and retaliation. Following the attack on Kiryat Shmona, Israeli army units crossed into Lebanon on the night of April 12/13. They struck six villages, seized ten suspected collaborators, and blew up twenty houses in an effort to pressure the Lebanese government to bring the terrorist attacks on Israel to an end.[10] On April 14, Edward Ghorra, Lebanon's UN ambassador, wrote to Secretary General Kurt Waldheim to denounce Israel's "campaign of continued terror and threats against Lebanon."

It was in response to Ghorra's request, not Israel's, that the Security Council met to discuss these events.[11] Because the Soviet Union blocked Israel's efforts to call the council into session to discuss its concerns, the agenda of all such sessions was tailored to the interests of the Arab states, in this case, Lebanon. The minutes of the meetings on April 14 to 24, 1974, illustrate the effective use of the UN machinery by Israel's enemies. Lebanon's foreign minister, Fouad Naffah, deplored acts of violence such as that in Kiryat Shmona but insisted that it had "not in any way been established that those responsible for the Kiryat Shmona attack left from Lebanon." If "isolated elements" managed to escape Lebanese surveillance and Israeli defenses, "well, Israel can blame no one but itself. It is not up to Lebanon to guard the Israeli border." It was Israel's attack on Lebanese villages that was a "premeditated and obvious act of aggression."[12]

[9] Yosef Tekoah to Kurt Waldheim, "Letter Dated 11 April 1974 From the Permanent Representative of Israel to the United Nations Addressed to the Secretary General," New York (April 11, 1974), UNSC, A/9515/S/11259, UN ODS, S/11259. Also see "Questions relating to the Middle East," *United Nations Yearbook 1974*, 189–211.

[10] "Dayan Says Raids against Lebanon Will Be Continued," *New York Times* (April 14, 1974), 1.

[11] Edward Ghorra to Kurt Waldheim, "Letter Dated 11 April 1974 From the Permanent Representative of Lebanon to the United Nations Addressed to the Secretary General," New York, UNSC (April 14, 1974), UN ODS S/11264.

[12] Fouad Naffah, UNSCOR, *1766th Meeting, April 15, 1974*, UN ODS S/PV.1766, 2–3.

Tekoah replied that in recent years Lebanon had become "a principal center for Arab terrorist operations." Beirut was "the seat of its headquarters, information bureau and recruitment offices of terrorist groupings" while training camps and attack bases were established in the countryside. Tekoah referred ironically to a "peaceful Lebanon" from which terrorist attacks had been planned and organized; a "law-abiding Lebanon which has signed formal agreements with the terror organizations granting them freedom to carry on their criminal activities"; a "virtuous Lebanon" that did not call for Security Council sessions "when its sovereignty is violated" by terrorist organizations; a "helpless Lebanon" that did not draw the UN's attention "to the fact that Beirut is being used as a nest for international gangsters and assassination"; and a "pure Lebanon" that turned to the UN Security Council in only one situation, "when Israel, no longer ready to bear the bloody assaults on its citizens launched from Lebanese soil, reacts in self-defence."[13]

Tekoah repeated the details of the Kiryat Shmona attack, adding that "an immediate investigation established that the shoes of the three murderers fully matched the footprints crossing the border" with Lebanon. He noted that the Popular Front-General Command in Beirut claimed responsibility. On April 11 it published photographs of "the three murderers" and their names and then cabled this information to "all international press agencies." Tekoah referred to an interview given in the Beirut English-language newspaper *Daily Star* of April 12 by Zephier Mohsen, a leader of the Syrian-supported Saika terrorist group and a member of the PLO's Executive Committee. Mohsen called the attack on Kiryat Shmona "heroic" and added: "We promise to undertake more such operations as they express the real sacrifice and represent the start of a new stage in the development of commando operations, both in size and level."[14] Tekoah also mentioned a statement to the press by Abu Abbas, a spokesman of the Popular Front, shortly before the Kiryat Shmona massacre in which he asserted, "We refuse to be bound by any agreement preventing crossing into occupied territory for carrying out operations." Tekoah added that "as is well known, all the Arab terrorist organizations consider all of Israel as occupied territory." The Israelis, Tekoah emphasized, had taken action "against the houses of known terrorist collaborators, including homes of villagers in which the murderers had stopped over on their way to Kiryat Shmona."[15]

[13] Yosef Tekoah, UNSCOR, *1766th Meeting, April 15, 1974*, UN ODS S/PV.1766, 4.

[14] Ibid., 5.

[15] Ibid., 5–6.

Tekoah acknowledged that at the UN the Israelis had "no illusions" that they could expect an "equitable attitude based on the merits of the issue before it." They knew that since 1948, the Security Council had "not been able to adopt a single resolution condemning the murder of Israeli citizens in incursions by Arab military forces or by terrorist squads" and that there was an "inherent parliamentary imbalance which prevails in the Council and in other organs of the United Nations in discussions regarding the Middle East situation."[16] The Israelis went to the Security Council rather "to pay tribute to the innocent victims of Arab terrorism" and to assert that "we shall not forget them" and will "see to it that the world does not forget them." Israel pointed "an accusing finger at the Government of Lebanon and all others which harbor, assist and cooperate with Arab terrorist organizations." They could not be absolved of "their obligation to prevent armed attacks against Israel." The UN members should not misjudge Israel's mood "after 25 years of persistent Arab aggression." Events like Kiryat Shmona merely served to unify the people of Israel in purpose and resolve.[17]

Syria's representative replied that Tekoah "expiates on the deeds of a few young Palestinians gnawed by frustration and despair" and referred instead to the Zionists' "terrorist activities."[18] Egypt's foreign minister Fahmy attacked Israel's "vicious and barbaric methods" in its assault on villages in Lebanon and criticized Tekoah for "as usual" having "the audacity to speak about what he calls Arab terrorists." Rather than address the attack on Kiryat Shmona, Fahmy referred to "the tragic saga of 1948" and "the infamous Deir Yassin massacre" in the same year, as if those events justified diverting attention from events in 1974 in Kiryat Shmona.[19] In reply, Tekoah quoted Syrian government radio's comment on the events in Kiryat Shmona to the effect that "the brave and daring Fedayeen operation in Kiryat Shmona is praiseworthy" and its perpetrators were "heroes."[20] East Germany had both diplomatic and military officials in Beirut who, as we will see, were in contact with the full range of the members of the PLO's Executive Committee, including the PFLP and the DFLP. Though they did not send reports back to East Berlin

[16] Ibid.
[17] Ibid., 5–6.
[18] Mr. [Haissam] Kelani (Syrian Arab Republic), UNSCOR, *1766th Meeting, April 15, 1974*, UN ODS S/PV.1766, 7.
[19] Mr. [Nabil] Ahmy (Egypt), UNSCOR, *1766th Meeting, April 15, 1974*, UN ODS S/PV.1766, 8–10.
[20] Yosef Tekoah, UNSCOR, *1766th Meeting, April 15, 1974*, UN ODS S/PV.1766, 11.

about the celebrations of the attack on Kiryat Shmona in the Arab and Palestinian press and other media, they must have been fully informed about them.

The following day, Yakov Malik described Israel's retaliation as a set of "criminal acts" and "terrorism" in support of "intimidation and aggression" and "annexation and appropriation of foreign lands." Israel's policies "call to mind the worst times of the domination of the Hitlerites over the foreign territories which they had temporarily occupied during the Second World War." They were comparable to the Nazis' "scorched earth policy" and "the total destruction of a peaceful population" with "the pretext of 'retaliatory measures' against the activities of patriots."[21] Tekoah took Malik to task for saying "not a word about the right of every State to be free from armed attacks by irregular forces, by murderous gangs, organized and operating from the territory of neighboring states." The Soviet view was to disapprove of international terrorism but assume that "Israel should do nothing at all to protect itself against attacks by terrorists."[22] Yakov Malik's response conveyed the full fury of the Soviet Union's antagonism to Israel:

> The Security Council has condemned your country more than 10 times for similar acts of banditry against Lebanon. Are you deaf? Did you not hear? Are you short-sighted? Did you not see? You spoke about a "tablet." Read the resolutions and decisions of the United Nations – of the General Assembly and Security Council. There in black and white, in the five working languages of the Council and the Assembly, you will find the condemnation of Israel for aggression and the demand that it should liberate the occupied territories and live with its neighbours in accordance with the Charter. Have you not seen this? It must mean you are short-sighted, together with your Government, your Dayan and the other extremists who, in the second half of the twentieth century, are threatening half of the State of Lebanon with destruction. It is monstrous! It is barbarity, cruelty, Hitlerism and fascism in the Zionist version. There is a tablet for you. Read the tablet – it has one inscription: "Get out of the occupied Arab territories." Then everything will be settled, and there will be peace, security and tranquility in the Middle East. You do not see this tablet. That means that you are not merely short-sighted but blind. It is time for you to notice these things, and the sooner you do so, the better it will be.[23]

[21] Mr. [Yakov] Malik (Union of Soviet Socialist Republics), UNSCOR, *1767th Meeting, April 16, 1974*, UN ODS, 1–4.

[22] Yosef Tekoah (Israel) UNSCOR, *1767th Meeting, April 16, 1974*, UN ODS S/PV.1767, 7–8.

[23] Malik (USSR), UNSCOR, *1767th Meeting, April 16, 1974*, UN ODS S/PV.1767, 15.

So in response to the PFLP-GC attack on Kiryat Shmona, the Soviet representative yet again equated Israel with Nazi Germany, offered sarcastic references to the tablet of the Ten Commandments, and offered a not-so-subtle threat. His denunciation also illustrated the way that the Soviet Union used the biased resolutions passed especially by the General Assembly to attack Israel.

At the Security Council meeting of April 24, 1974, Tekoah cited the Popular Front-General Command communiqué published on April 22 in the Beirut newspaper *As-Safa*. The PFLP-GC announced that "it attacked Kiryat Shmona to make it impossible for a peaceful settlement between the Arabs and Israelis." The group's spokesman said there would "be more actions like Kiryat Shmona until all Palestine is liberated." He revealed that the group was also responsible for killing the Israeli military attaché Joseph Allon outside his home in Washington, D.C.; "the explosion aboard a Swissair passenger airliner over Zurich in February 1970, in which 47 people were killed"; and the explosion of an Austrian airlines plane near Vienna, also in February 1970, in which there were no casualties. The PFLP-GC promised that it "would attack Israel wherever it showed itself," both inside and outside the borders of the state of Israel, as the attacks in Europe and the United States indicated.[24] Nevertheless, the Security Council refused to pass a mild American-supported resolution that denounced terrorism in general but did not even mention Kiryat Shmona. Instead, by a vote of 13 to 0, including the United States, it passed Resolution 347 (1974), which condemned "Israel's violation of Lebanon's territorial integrity and sovereignty and calls once more on the Government of Israel to refrain from further military actions and threats against Lebanon."[25]

The refusal to denounce the attack on Kiryat Shmona was a clear victory for the PLO and its PFLP-GC affiliate as well as for the large anti-Israeli majority at the UN. The outcome was so regrettable that the *New York Times* criticized American support for "a shabby and one-sided United Nations Security Council resolution condemning Israel in strident terms but dancing away from any similarly explicit condemnation of wanton Arab terrorists." The danger, the *Times* editors continued, "in what looks like an American cave-in, after years of abstaining from similarly unbalanced U.N. declarations, is that Israel will sense deepening

[24] Yosef Tekoah, UNSCOR, *1769th Meeting, April 24, 1974*, UN ODS S/PV.1769, 3–4.

[25] "Resolution 347" (1974), "Questions Relating to the Middle East," and "Draft Resolution," UNSCOR (April 24, 1974), UN ODS, S/11275.

isolation – not an auspicious condition for responsible negotiations."[26] Actually the greater danger was that the practitioners of Arab terrorism could plausibly conclude that they had been rewarded for engaging in the murder of Israeli civilians. The United Nations anti-Israeli majority again functioned as the diplomatic arm of the PLO's armed struggle.

G. MCMURTRIE GODLEY'S MEMOS ON ARAB REACTION TO THE ATTACK ON KIRYAT SHMONA

On January 18, after "shuttle diplomacy" by secretary of state Henry Kissinger, Egypt and Israel reached an agreement to disengage their forces after the 1973 war. Kissinger then turned to seeking a disengagement agreement between Israel and Syria.[27] The Palestinian terrorist organizations acted to undermine these efforts as a diplomatic solution to Israel's conflict with the Arabs and Palestinians. G. McMurtrie Godley (1917–1999), the United States ambassador to Lebanon from February 13, 1974, to January 13, 1976, sent remarkable memos to the State Department in Washington about the reaction in Beirut to the Palestinian terrorist attacks on Israel in spring 1974. He observed that after the Kiryat Shmona attack, "preliminary local reaction" ranged "from enthusiasm and even gloating among Fedayeen and their sympathizers (including leftist, pro-fedayeen press) to efforts at justification, exoneration and/or rationalization on part of Lebanese officialdom, public and independent press in general. We have yet to see much expression of regret or compassion over fate of civilian victims in local press."[28] The Lebanese government "adhered closely" to the "transparently silly line ... that Israeli accusations re Lebanese involvement are baseless." Privately, Godley noted, Lebanese government officials expressed "sorrow and concern." On the other hand, "Fedayeen spokesmen were quick to voice support for Kiryat Shmona raid, claiming it is a sign that Palestinian movement [was operating, JH] within 'occupied territories.'" The PLO's official WAFA News Agency "praised operation as proof of Fedayeen capabilities to operate [in] their homeland, and [Syrian affiliated] Sa'iqua's

[26] "Dangerous Trifles," *New York Times* (April 27, 1974), 30.

[27] On Kissinger's shuttle diplomacy see U.S. Department of State, Office of the Historian, *Milestones: 1969–1976, Shuttle Diplomacy and the Arab-Israeli Dispute, 1974–1975*, history.state.gov/milestones/1969–1976/shuttle-diplomacy.

[28] G. McMurtrie Godley to SecState, WashDC "Beirut 04343: Lebanese Reaction to Kiryat Shmona Incident," Beirut (April 12, 1974), NACP, Diplomatic Records, RG59 Central Foreign Policy Files, Electronic Telegrams, 1/1/1973–12/31/1973.

Aohary Musen termed it 'beginning of new era' in history of Palestinian struggle." The PPLP-GC and representatives of "other die-hard Fedayeen groups (e.g, PFLP and Iraqi-backed ALF)" were mounting what appeared to be "a concerted propaganda campaign" to present the attack as "proof of popular opposition" to diplomatic efforts to settle the Middle East conflict. The reaction in the "local leftist and pro-Fedayeen press" was "predictably enthusiastic, with fulsome descriptions of 'daring operation' carried out inside Israel by Palestinian 'hero-martyrs' in revenge for last year's IDF raid on Beirut.... Virtually all papers [across the political spectrum] emphasize other past Israeli 'terrorist crimes' in justifying Palestinian resort to use of terror within Israel."[29]

On April 16, Godley reported that "moderates" among the Fedayeen were under "increasing pressure to adopt more negativist attitudes" toward a Middle East peace settlement "in the wake of reaction here and elsewhere in [the] Arab world to Kiryat Shmona operation." There was "a real possibility that Fedayeen organizations such as Fatah and Sa'iqa may feel constrained to engage in terrorist or cross-border operations vs Israel in order to avoid losing prestige to radicals such as PFLP and PFLP/GC."[30] Godley wrote that the

> Kiryat Shmona operation was conceived, planned and executed in order to heat up Arab and Israeli emotions against peaceful settlement, enhance prestige of Fedayeen groups which steadfastly reject it, and serve notice on so-called "moderates" among PLO leadership that their adherence to some kind of Fedayeen role in [a peaceful, negotiated] settlement process will only result in their isolation, repudiation, and eventual downfall. Measured in terms of these objectives (as well as in Israeli casualties) Fedayeen die-hards, Iraq, Libya, etc., can consider Kiryat Shmona operation a distinct success, since it has evoked considerable enthusiasm and praise even from Arab govts, individuals and media who are not sympathetic to the "rejectionist" line (e.g. Amman).[31]

The attack gave the "rejectionist" appeal a "shot in [the] arm in [the] form of enthusiasm generated among Fedayeen rank-and-file by [the] 'successful' Kiryat Shmona operation." Godley expected the PFLP/GC to continue to "mount such operations to capitalize on their demonstrated appeal among Palestinians" and thought the PLO leadership would find

[29] Ibid.

[30] G. McMurtrie Godley to SecState, WashDC "Beirut 04426: Psychological Impact of Kiryat Shmona Incident on Fedayeen Leadership," Beirut (April 16, 1974), NACP, Diplomatic Records, RG59 Central Foreign Policy Files, Electronic Telegrams, 1/1/1973–12/31/1973.

[31] Ibid.

itself "hard pressed to resist extremist pressures" unless there was rapid movement toward a settlement.[32] Terrorist attacks on Israel enhanced rather than detracted from the popularity of its perpetrators in the Arab states and among Palestinian Arabs. In other words, support for terrorist attacks on Israel had become a component of Arab and Palestinian political culture.

In East Berlin, *Neues Deutschland* saw matters rather differently. On April 13, it described the attack on Kiryat Shmona as follows: "A group of partisans who were stationed on Israeli territory occupied two buildings in the settlement of Kiryat Shmona near the Lebanese border." They "seized a group of Israelis as hostages" and demanded the release of 100 Arabs in Israeli prisons.[33] "As a result of an exchange of fire between the partisans and Israeli troops, more than 20 Israelis were killed or wounded" and three of the "partisans" were killed.[34] It was an erroneous report. The PFLP-GC were not "stationed on Israeli territory" but had crossed the Israeli border from Lebanon. The hostages did not die as a result of an exchange of fire; the terrorists killed them with machine guns and grenades. The article failed to mention the murders committed before the building seizure; nor did it refer to the murder of children thrown from upper floors of the seized apartment building. While citing the PFLP-GC communiqué, it did not mention its enthusiasm for the attack or the celebration of the perpetrators as heroic martyrs in the Beirut press.

On April 15, Israel made the front page of *Neues Deutschland* with the headline "Security Council meets as Lebanon accuses Israel."[35] The paper reported on Lebanon's complaints about Israeli attacks on Lebanese villages near the Israeli border: "The Israeli power holders used as a pretext for this new aggression an action of Palestinians in a town occupied by the Israelis in 1948 south of the contemporary Israeli-Lebanese border," thus implying that Israel itself was occupied territory. In obscuring the causal link between the terrorist bases in Lebanon and the series of attacks on northern Israel, including the massacre in Kiryat Shmona,

32 Ibid.

33 "Israel eröffnet erneut Feuer auf Syrischen Stellungen," *Neues Deutschland* [East] Berlin (April 13, 1974), 7.

34 Ibid.

35 "Der Sicherheitsrat tag Libanon klagt an: Kommandotrupps Tel Avivs verübte neue blutige Aggression, UNO Generalsekretär Waldheim verurteilt den schweren Überfall," *ND* (April 15, 1974), 1.

Neues Deutschland again deprived Israeli military actions of legitimate grounds and displayed indifference to the loss of life in Israel.

THE POPULAR DEMOCRATIC FRONT FOR THE LIBERATION OF PALESTINE ATTACKS MA'ALOT, MAY 18, 1974

On May 18, 1974, Jacob Doron, Israel's deputy ambassador to the UN, informed the president of the Security Council of a "massacre in the school-building of Ma'alot on 15 May 1974 as a result of which 21 school boys and girls were murdered and another 70 wounded."[36] On its way to the school in Ma'alot, a Palestinian "murder squad" killed an Arab woman worker in the village of Fassuta, wounded another eight young women who were returning from work in a pickup truck, and "murdered an entire family in its apartment in Ma'alot, consisting of a husband, wife and their four-year-old son," before turning their attention to the school in Ma'alot. Footprints in the area, a map, matches, clothing, shoes, and other personal belongings, all of Lebanese manufacture, that were found on the terrorists "established beyond any doubt" that the squad was from Lebanon. Moreover, Doron added, the Popular Democratic Front for the Liberation of Palestine (PDFLP) put out statements in Beirut taking credit for the attack. On May 15 "the photographs of the three murderers of Ma'alot were supplied in Beirut to news agencies."[37]

On May 16 in Beirut, Nayef Hawatmeh, secretary general of the Democratic Popular Front for the Liberation of Palestine (PDFLP), and Abu Rabbuh, a member of its Politburo, told a press conference that the DPFLP was "determined to escalate" the struggle and "defeat the usurpers in the occupied territory."[38] They claimed that its "Martyr Kamal Nasir unit" had carried out the Ma'alot attack. It "had spared the lives of the hostages until the very last moment when the Israeli command decided to sacrifice the lives of its hostages."[39] At the May 16 press

[36] Jacob Doron, "Letter Dated 18 May 1974 from the Acting Permanent Representative of Israel to the United Nations addressed to the President of the Security Council," New York, UNSCOR, UN ODS, S/11290. For descriptions of the raid, also see "The Ma'alot Raid in Israel, on 15th May," *SWB*. Part 4. *The Middle East and Africa*, May 16, 1974, ME/4601/A/6–8.

[37] Ibid. The PDFLP, was at times called the DPFLP, Democratic Popular Front for the Liberation of Palestine.

[38] On Hawatmeh's role in the PDFLP see Yezid Sayigh, "Guerrilla War in Theory and Practice," in *Armed Struggle and the Search for State: The Palestinian National Movement, 1949–1963* (Oxford: Clarendon Press, 1997), esp. 198–206.

[39] "Palestinian Reports on Ma'alot (a) INA 1345 gmt 16 May 74, Text of reports on DPFLP statement," BBC, *SWB*. Part 4. (May 18, 1974), ME/4603/A/5–6.

conference, Hawatmeh explained that the DPFLP was "struggling to foil Kissinger's mission, because he carries a solution in favor of Zionism, imperialism and reaction." That is, as Godley had pointed out after the attack on Kiryah Shmona, the Ma'alot attack was an effort to undermine efforts to bring about a negotiated settlement of the conflict.[40] In a statement of Orwellian dimensions broadcast on the *Voice of Palestine* radio, Hawatmeh and the DPFLP leaders blamed the Israelis for the deaths of the hostages. "By the massacre that they committed in the village of Tarshihah-Ma'alot, yesterday evening, only a few minutes before the expiration of the ultimatum, the criminal Zionist authorities have once more proved that they are still the same bloodthirsty terrorists who were responsible for the massacre of innocent Palestinians at Dayr Yasin and who do not hesitate to cause the death of large numbers of Jews for the sake of the Zionist cause."[41] The DPFLP also blamed the ambassadors of Romania and France and representatives of the Red Cross for the massacre as they had been involved in negotiations to free the hostages. They referred to the "martyred Fida'iyin" as "heroes of the Palestinian people. They are not terrorists. Terrorists are those who fight in an unjust struggle. Those who fight in a just struggle are humane and revolutionary; hence the Zionist stubbornness and false arrogance are responsible forcing the fida'iyin to resort to killing and throwing bombs." To underscore the honor that the DPFLP bestowed on the terrorists who had been killed in Ma'alot, the DPFLP "Revolution Command" revealed their names on a *Voice of Palestine* broadcast later that day and said they had all participated in past "operations … in the Palestinian lands occupied since 1948," that is, in Israel.[42]

In Beirut, enthusiasm for the Ma'alot raid extended beyond the organization that carried it out. The BBC reported that it overshadowed "all other news in the Lebanese papers." The Beirut press provided details on their front pages and "publish[ed] pictures of its heroes."[43] The editors of *Al Yawm* extolled "the martyrs of Ma'alot today and the martyrs of Khalisah [Kiryat Shmona] yesterday and the martyrs who have been born and those who have not yet been born." The attacks offered

[40] Ibid., A/6.

[41] "Palestinian Reports on Ma'alot (b) *Voice of Palestine* (Clandestine) 0900 gmt 16 May 1974, Text of reports on DPFLP statement," BBC, *SWB*. Part 4. (May 18, 1974), ME/4603/A/6–7.

[42] Ibid., A/7–8. The names given were Ali Ahmad Hasan, Ahmad Salih Nayif, and Iyad Abd ar-Rahim.

[43] "Arab Comment on Ma'alot (b) INA 0830 gmt 16 May 1974," BBC, *SWB*: Part 4 (May 18, 1974), ME/4603/A/3.

"conclusive evidence" that Israel would "remain a place of fear, worry, ruin and destruction."[44] In Damascus, both *Al Thaura* (The Revolution) and *Al Baath*, the papers of the PLO and the Syrian Baath Party, respectively, offered details of the Ma'alot attack on May 15, "the anniversary of the usurpation of Palestine."[45]

On May 15, 1974 Israeli prime minister Golda Meir spoke on radio and television about the events in Ma'alot. It had

> been a bitter day, a day of atrocities which began when terrorists entered a home in Ma'alot, at 0300, murdered the father, the mother and a boy, and wounded an infant six months old. Later, a short while before 0500 they came to the school where children of the 9th, 10th, and 11th grades were on a Gadna [working youth battalions] excursion from Zefat and Hazor. The terrorists entered the school building, placed explosive material on the table and connected it. It was absolutely clear that they were ready to blow up the building.[46]

At that point they held 90 schoolchildren in the building. They demanded the release of 20 terrorists who were imprisoned in Israel. Meir explained that "the Cabinet decided that, as far as the children are concerned, we are not conducting wars [with them, JH] and we decided to accept the terrorists' demand to release 20 terrorists as they requested." However, neither the French nor Romanian ambassadors, who were willing to negotiate with the terrorists, had received the necessary code word from Hawatmeh's PDFLP. The terrorists had set a deadline of 6:00 P.M. By 5:20 P.M., neither the French nor the Romanian ambassador had received the needed codes and the hostage takers would not extend the deadline. For the prime minister and the Israeli cabinet, "not the slightest doubt remained that they [the PDFLP terrorists] indeed intended to blow up the building. Thus, she said, at 5:30 P.M., "the IDF went into action."[47]

The Israeli soldiers wounded the PDFLP terrorists, cut the wires to the explosives, and thereby prevented them from blowing up the building. However, members of the terrorist squad still had "enough strength to shoot into groups of children and to throw grenades." They killed 16

44 Ibid., A/3.

45 Ibid., "Arab Comment on Ma'alot (a) Syrian Arab News Agency 0750 gmt 16 May 1974," BBC, *SWB*. Part 4. (May 18, 1974), ME/4603/A/2. For comment from Baghdad see "Arab Comment on Ma'alot (c) INA 0900 gmt 16 May 1974," BBC, *SWB*. Part 4. (May 18, 1974), ME/4603/A/3.

46 "Golda Meir's Broadcast to the Nation," Israel Home Service 1840 gmt 15 May 1974, BBC, *SWB*. Part 4. (May 17, 1974), ME/4602/A/4. Also see "Israel Chief of Staff on Ma'alot, Israel Home Service 1800 gmt 16 May 1974, Text of reports on DPFLP statement," BBC, *SWB*. Part 4. (May 18, 1974), ME/4603/A/5.

47 Ibid., A/5.

children and wounded 70. After this "bitter and horrible day for every member of the nation" the prime minister acknowledged that she could not "ensure that they will let us live in peace" but she promised that "any Israeli government will do all it can to cut off the hands that want to harm a child, a grown up, a settlement, a town, or a village."[48]

The situation facing Israel's prime minister was the following. The terrorists who murdered Israelis in Kiryat Shmona the previous month had been celebrated in all of the Palestinian and Arab media as heroes and martyrs. The Ma'alot operation terrorists could expect similar praise. Immediately before making their demands, they had just murdered a family before seizing the school. They had wired explosives and refused to extend a deadline. Faced with the credible threat that the Ma'alot squad was, in fact, on a suicide mission that would end with blowing up a building with 90 children in it, the leaders of the government of Israel did what any sovereign government obligated to protect its citizens would do in that situation. It used force to kill the terrorists before they could carry out their plan.

A "military communiqué" in Damascus from the "General Command of the Palestine Revolution Forces" claimed that the Israelis were attempting to deceive "the Martyr Kamal Nasir unit" and that if any harm came to the hostages it would be the fault of the Israeli government.[49] On May 15, the PLO's *Voice of Palestine* (VOP) Baghdad station trumpeted "our fighters' heroic operations" in Ma'alot and referred to Israel's "nazi nature."[50] The PLO again celebrated its fighters as heroes and martyrs yet absolved them of responsibility for the deaths that their attacks caused. On May 17, the *Voice of Palestine* in Baghdad quoted the "leader of the DPFLP" as sending "a thousand greetings to the heroes of Ma'alot because they asserted the will to challenge and to fight ... they have faced the enemy with unswerving courage and resolve.... Blessed be the souls of the Khalisah martyrs. Blessed be the souls of the Ma'alot martyrs. Ours is a revolution until victory."[51] Given the facts of the Ma'alot massacre, the

48 Ibid.

49 "Reports of Statements Issued by the Fida'yin (a) Syrian News Agency 1650 gmt 15 May 1974," BBC, *SWB*. Part 4. (May 17, 1974), ME/4602/A/6. As of May 15, 1974, the "General Command" linked to the PFLP had issued its 118th "communiqué."

50 "Reports of Statements Issued by the Fida'yin (b) *Voice of Palestine* (Baghdad) 1700 gmt 15 May 1974," BBC, *SWB*. Part 4. (May 17, 1974), ME/4602/A/7.

51 "Arab Comment and Reporting on the Raid," (b) Baghdad) 1700 gmt May 1974, "Text of Statements, Including Reference to Leader of DPFLP," BBC, *SWB*. Part 4. (May 17, 1974), ME/4602/A/8 Support for the Ma'alot attack was from Sudan as well.

use of the term "enemy" in the communiqué again erased the distinction between soldiers and civilians in Israel.[52]

Neues Deutschland reported nothing about the Arab and Palestinian celebration of the attacks. On the contrary, it repeated the accusations that Israel had caused the massacre. On May 17, it ran an article about the events in Ma'alot on page 7 with the headline "Tel Aviv's breaking of its word leads to deaths of children and Palestinian partisans."[53] The article asserted that the three Palestinian "partisans" had seized the school building with 90 children inside and demanded the release of their "fellow fighters" held by the Israelis. *ND* misinformed its readers by asserting that the Israelis broke Golda Meir's promise to fulfill the Palestinians' demands. *Neues Deutschland* reported nothing about the terrorists' preparations to blow up the school, their refusal to extend deadlines, or Meir's willingness to exchange prisoners to save the children's lives. It referred to the terrorists as "partisans" who were members of the Palestinian "resistance," even though they used their weapons to kill unarmed civilians. This was the extent of its reporting about the Ma'alot attack.[54]

In Beirut, Godley reported again on Arab and Palestinian enthusiasm about the attacks. "Ma'alot is seen in positive light from tactical viewpoint by many Arabs and likely [will, JH] inspire still more acts of violence inside Israel-occupied territories. As feared following Kiryat Shimona [*sic*], more moderate Fedayeen organizations and leaders seem to be placing increased stress upon violence inside occupied territories (and less on external terrorism)."[55] Godley added that the "successful" attack at Kiryat Shmona had stimulated the PDFLP and "perhaps some Fatah elements" to intensify terrorist and cross-border "operations" in order to "avoid being outbid by die-hards" and retain authority over the rank and file. The attack on the

52 At the UN, Jacob Doron told the Security Council that PFLP and PDFLP had claimed responsibility for "the massacre in Kiryat Shmona and Ma'alot." He observed that in Cairo, the *Voice of the Arabs* broadcast a commentary that extolled the Ma'alot and Kiryat Shmona operations as announcing "a new phase of fida'i action that is assuming an unlimited ability of action inside Palestinian territory and against Israeli targets, individuals and installations." See Jacob Doron, "Letter Dated 18 May 1974 from the Acting Permanent Representative of Israel to the United Nations addressed to the President of the Security Council," UNSC UN ODS, S/11290.

53 "Wortbruch Tel Avivs führte zum Tod von Kindern und Palästinensischen Partisanen," *ND* (May 17, 1974), 7.

54 Ibid. 7. Also see "Libanon appelliert an UNO: Scharfer Protest gegen Israels Terror/ Wirksame Schritte nötig," *ND* (May 19, 1974), 7.

55 "Secret Beirut 05573: Maalot Tragedy and Fedayeen Leadership," G. McMurtrie Godley, Beirut (May 16, 1974), NACP, Diplomatic Records, RG59 Central Foreign Policy Files, Electronic Telegrams, 1/1/1973–12/31/1973.

school in Ma'alot seemed "less upsetting to most Arab govts [governments, JH] and more appealing to Arab public opinion than firing across borders, hijacking, attacking foreign embassies, etc."[56] In short, terrorism against Israelis was popular among significant sections of Arab and Palestinian opinion. Godley had looked with an unflinching gaze at the political culture of terrorism in Lebanon. He pointed to evidence that in 1974 throwing children off roofs, firing point blank with machine guns at defenseless civilians, placing explosives to blow up a school filled with 90 schoolchildren, and wearing suicide belts with explosives all found strong support in an Arab public that celebrated terrorists as blessed martyrs. The source of power and prestige in Palestinian political culture in those years lay in a ruthless willingness to kill, wound, and terrorize Israelis. Though the East German diplomats in the Middle East were in close contact with the various Palestinian terror organizations, they did not send dispatches to the Foreign Ministry in East Berlin about the celebration of terror that had become embedded in these aspects of Arab political culture. Rather, the East Germans remained part of the large anti-Israeli UN majority that denounced Israel's military responses to terrorist attacks but never denounced the attacks that made them necessary. The East German regime had become a supporter of the terrorist organizations carrying out these attacks.

The United States, perhaps aware that its vote in favor of the unbalanced resolution 374/74 following the attack on Kiryat Shmona had delivered a victory to the terrorist organizations, reacted sharply to the Ma'alot attacks. Secretary of State Henry Kissinger wrote to Secretary General Kurt Waldheim that he "was shocked and outraged to learn of the attack by Fedayeen terrorists against a teenage campsite in Ma'alot early this morning and against other innocent civilians in the same area. Our hearts go out to the families and to all of Israel." The United States "strongly condemned this mindless and irrational action" and appealed for the hostages to be released.[57] Yet the pattern of Palestinian terror

[56] Ibid. For Jacob Doron's description of the attack on Ma'alot see "Letter Dated 24 May 1974 from the Acting Permanent Representative of Israel to the United Nations addressed to the President of the Security Council," UNSC, UN ODS, S/11297; and "Letter Dated 13 June 1974 from the Acting Permanent Representative of Israel to the United Nations addressed to the President of the Security Council," UNSC, UN ODS, S/11319. On the Lebanese response, Edward Ghorra to President of the Security Council, see "Letter Dated 17 May 1974 from the Acting Permanent Representative of Israel to the United Nations addressed to the President of the Security Council," UNSC UN ODS, S/11289.

[57] "Annex I: Statement by Secretary of State Kissinger," "Letter Dated 15 May 1974 from the Permanent Representative of the United States of America to the United Nations

attacks, Israel efforts to destroy terrorist bases, followed by denunciation of Israel's efforts at armed self-defense at the UN, illustrated how the anti-Israeli majority there mobilized international opinion in support of the Arab and Palestinian terrorist campaign against Israel.[58] On May 17, following the Israeli retaliation, the US UN ambassador John Scali sent a second message from Kissinger to Waldheim in which he deplored "the loss of innocent life whenever it occurs in this tragic conflict."[59] Scali added that people needed to learn that "there is nothing in the world that can justify the slaughter of innocents."[60] Scali's reference to "the slaughter of innocents" opened the door to equating the intentional murder of civilians by terrorists with the unintended civilian deaths caused by Israeli retaliatory raids in Lebanon. It was proving impossible for Israel to defend itself against terrorism and at the same time win political victories in the court of "world public opinion" at the United Nations. Fighting terrorism in the Middle East had the price of losing battles in the political warfare in at the UN.

THE EAST GERMANS GREET THE PLO IN EAST BERLIN IN AUGUST 1974

Three months after the attack on Ma'alot, the East Germans welcomed a PLO delegation led by Arafat in East Berlin. From August 6 to 8, 1974, they were again warmly greeted by Gerhard Grüneberg.[61] The other members of the PLO delegation were Khaled Fahumy, president of the Palestinian

Addressed to the Secretary-General," United Nations General Assembly–Security Council, UNGA-SC UN ODS A/9534; S/11287, 2. The American UN Ambassador John Scali was "sickened, outraged and depressed by this barbaric incident."

58 For a resolution by the U.S. Senate denouncing the Ma'alot attack see "Annex III: Resolution Passed by the United States Senate," in "Letter Dated 15 May 1974 from the Permanent Representative of the United States of America to the United Nations Addressed to the Secretary-General," UNGA-SC, UN ODS A/9534; S/11287, 4.

59 "Annex I: Statement by the Secretary of State," in "Letter Dated 17 May 1974 from the Permanent Representative of the United States of America to the United Nations Addressed to the Secretary-General," UNGA-SC, UN ODS A/9535; S/11288, 4.

60 "Annex II: Statement by the Permanent Representative of the United States to the United Nations, Ambassador Scali," in "Letter Dated 17 May 1974 from the Permanent Representative of the United States of America to the United Nations Addressed to the Secretary-General," UNGA-SC, UN ODS A/9535; S/11288, 4.

61 Gerhard Grüneberg, "Information Nr. 74/74 für das Politbüro, Betr.: Bericht über den Aufenthalt einer Delegation des Exekutivkomitee der PLO under Leitung von Yasser Arafat, Vorsitzender der PLO, in der DDR vom 6.-8. August, 1974," BAB DY 30/B2/20/84, Abteilung für Sicherheitsfragen des Zentralkomitee (ZK) der Sozialistische Einheitspartei (SED), 1–8.

National Council; Farouk Kaddoumi, director of the PLO Political Department; Zouheir Mohsen, director of the PLO Military Department; Abdel Mohsen Abou Maizar, official spokesman of the PLO; Yasser Abdel Rabbo, director of the PLO Information Department; Abou Ismail, member of the Jordanian Communist Party; and Nabil Kuleilat, director of the PLO Bureau in East Berlin. The East German officials included Eberhard Heinrich, member of the SED Central Committee; Friedel Trappen, deputy director of the Central Committee's Department of International Relations; Bruno Wansierski, deputy director of the Central Committee's Department of International Relations; Klaus Willerding, deputy minister of foreign affairs; Siegfried Buttner, sector director in the Central Committee's Department of International Relations; Peter Rebenhorst, member of the Department of International Relations; and Kurt Krüger, general secretary of the GDR Solidarity Committee.[62]

Many of these same individuals had met in July and August 1973 when Arafat and Grüneberg signed the first formal agreement between the GDR and the PLO. Grüneberg described the atmosphere of the talks as "warm and open."[63] Arafat voiced the PLO's leadership's "great trust" in the policies of "the socialist community of states," that is, the Soviet bloc and its Communist allies outside Europe. Arafat told the East Germans that the PLO was ready to recognize Israel on the basis of existing UN resolutions. He claimed to "recognize the danger of extremist terrorist actions for the cause of the Arab peoples of Palestine" created by groups such as George Habash's PFLP, Ahmid Jibril's General Command, and the Arab Liberation Front. Despite these reassuring tones, Grüneberg referred to a continuing "underestimation of the political-diplomatic battle," a PLO reluctance to participate in the Soviet-sponsored Geneva peace conference, and an insistence on including "the right of return" in the concluding communiqué, something that the SED delegation would not do at that point. The East Germans were willing to call the PLO "the only legitimate representation of the Arab people of Palestine" and to renew the agreement of 1973. The two sides agreed to continue to exchange information "at a high level." The GDR promised to continue its "material support," that is, to offer weapons and training for the PLO, and would expand reporting about it in the East German mass media.[64] In view of the PLO broadcasts on the *Voice of Palestine* after the attacks in

[62] Ibid.
[63] Ibid., 4.
[64] Ibid., 8.

Kiryat Shmona and Ma'alot, it appears that Arafat, by presenting himself as the realist and moderate in contrast to the extremists, was playing the same charade with his Communist patrons, or at least with Grüneberg and the East German diplomats, as he did with the Western media. Either cynically or as a result of gullibility, Grüneberg and others went along with the pose of Arafat's moderation compared to the extremism of the PFLP and PDFLP.

On August 7, 1974, the East Germans gave Arafat the platform of a national television broadcast. He denounced Israel's "most brutal terror" and its attacks on "innocent women, children and the elderly" with "American bombs and American napalm." Israel rested on ignoring human rights but "today our people firmly stands up against imperialist-Zionist conspiracies" with support of "freedom-loving people of the whole world." An unspecified "conspiracy" was being waged against the Palestinians. The socialist camp with the Soviet Union in the lead "forms the avant garde of these true friends in the world...against the conspiracies and imperialist-Zionist exploitation.... We are not conducting a war against the Jews and we don't want to wage war against them. Rather we fight against Zionism as a racist, colonialist and expansionist movement that dreams of ruling our Arab nation and forming its own empire." The Palestinian "revolution," on the other hand, would form a "democratic Palestinian state in which Muslims, Christians and Jews live alongside one another in peace and prosperity."[65] The Palestinians had risen up after they had given up hope in UN resolutions and made use of their "right to armed struggle as all people who are oppressed or whose country is occupied" had. He expressed thanks to his "comrades and friends in the GDR, its government, party and people."[66] On East German national television, Arafat informed East German viewers that the PLO was engaged in armed attacks on the state of Israel.

Grüneberg and Arafat signed a formal agreement that renewed the previous year's agreement between the SED and the PLO. They were bound together by their "common struggle against imperialism and Zionism and for peace, national independence and social progress." East Germany and the PLO renewed the formal agreements on an annual basis. The agreement for 1976/1977, signed by Grüneberg and Arafat, called for continuing exchange of delegations, for consultation, and for sharing

[65] Yasser Arafat, "Erklärung von Yasser Arafat im DDR-Fernsehen," [East] Berlin (August 7, 1974), BAB DY 30 IV/2/2.023/89.

[66] Ibid., 1–5.

of information. The East Germans offered a modest 5 million marks in financial support for "civilian goods" and an unspecified amount of support in the "noncivilian," that is, military, area. Each year, East Germany agreed to provide free medical care to 50 wounded PLO fighters in East German hospitals. It offered places for 80 Palestinian children to spend summer vacation in East Germany and reserved four vacation spots for PLO leaders.[67] The agreement for 1978/1979, again signed by Grüneberg and Arafat, maintained the terms of the previous years, reduced financial support to 4 million marks, but added paying the costs of the PLO office in East Berlin. It reduced the number of children able to vacation in the GDR to 50. "Solidarity measures," a euphemism for arms shipments, would be handled by the Political Division of the PLO, that is, by Farouk Kaddoumi's office or with "the Office of the Chairman of the Executive Committee and Commander in Chief of the Armed Forces" of the PLO, that is, with Arafat himself. In addition, the GDR would place four office staff at the service of the PLO office in East Berlin. It would offer an appropriate building, find apartments for the Palestinian staff, and place a car at the staff's disposal. It would also cover the costs of rent, utilities, and long-distance calls up to 15,000 marks a year; auto insurance and gasoline for the car up to 17,000 marks a year; medical care for the Palestinian staff; and five round-trip flights from East Berlin to Beirut.[68] The agreement for 1980/1981 added that five leading members of the PLO could have medical treatment in East German hospitals and that the SED and PLO would expand exchanges between the staffs of *Neues Deutschland* and the PLO's official newspaper, *Falistin al-Thaura* (Palestinian Revolution).[69]

Though East Germany formalized its alliance with the PLO while it continued to conduct a terrorist campaign against Israel, Grüneberg reminded Arafat in 1978 that the East Germans "always regard the battle on the political and military level as a unity. It's crucial that the

[67] Gerhard Grüneberg and Yasser Arafat, "Vereinbarung zwischen der Sozialistischen Einheitspartei und der Palästinensischen Befreiungsorganisation für die Jahre 1976/1977," [East] Berlin (December 1, 1975) BAB DY 30 IVB/2/20/309 Abteilung Internationale Verbindungen des Zentralkomitee der SED, 1–3.

[68] Gerhard Grüneberg and Yasser Arafat, "Vereinbarung zwischen der Sozialistischen Einheitspartei und der Palästinensischen Befreiungsorganisation für die Jahre 1978/1979," [East] Berlin (March, 1978) BAB DY 30 IVB/2/20/309 Abteilung Internationale Verbindungen des Zentralkomitee der SED, 4–9.

[69] ZK d. SED und Exekutivkomitee der PLO, "Vereinbarung zwischen der Sozialistischen Einheitspartei Deutschlands und der Palästinensischen Befreiungsorganisation (PLO) für die Jahre 1980/81," [East] Berlin (March, 1978) BAB DY 30 IVB/2/20/309 Abteilung Internationale Verbindungen des Zentralkomitee der SED, 15–18.

initiative must always remain in our hands."[70] The East German message to the PLO was not to stop the terror war against Israel. On the contrary, it praised its "just struggle of the Arab people's against Israeli aggression" but said it was essential to combine the use of force against Israel, that is, in the radical leftist language of the time, "armed struggle," with the political and diplomatic offensive at the UN and elsewhere. The East German leaders recognized that Arafat and Kaddoumi, in contrast to leaders of the PFLP or DPFLP, had a more nuanced understanding of the intersection of force and diplomacy and thus of the connection between the criticism of weapons in the Middle East and the weapons of criticism in the United Nations in New York. The PLO's terrorist war against Israel was a necessary complement to the political warfare that the East Germans, among others, waged at the United Nations. Despite their rhetorical support for "political solutions," the East Germans gave aid to those groups that, as the Godley memos indicated, were trying to sabotage efforts at reaching diplomatic compromises. Arafat's international celebrity and the popularity of the PLO thus grew precisely in the years in which the PLO and its various affiliates were engaged in terrorist attacks on Israeli civilians.

The memos of the Middle East Department in East Germany's Ministry of Foreign Relations conveyed the political strategy to be implemented by Peter Florin and his staff at the UN in New York.[71] In August 1974 it instructed Florin to stress that the GDR, in accord with decisions of the Arab Summit in Algiers in November 1973, the Islamic states in Lahore in February 1974, the Organization of African States (OAU) in June 1974, and the Arab summit in Rabat in 1974, recognized the PLO as "the sole, legitimate representative of the Palestinian people." At that point, no vote of Palestinians had been taken as to whether they viewed the PLO as their representative. East Germany believed that the PLO's "struggle was in complete agreement with the basic principles and goals of the Charter of the United Nations." The achievement of the Palestinians' "right of self-determination" was an "indispensable precondition" for achieving a "just and lasting peace in the Middle East." Israeli withdrawal from "all of the territories occupied since June 5, 1967" was "the fundamental

70 "Vermerk Betr.: Informationsgespräch des Genossen Gerhard Grüneberg Mitglied des Politbüros und Sekretär des ZK der SED mit der Delegation der PLO unter Leitung von Yasser Arafat am 5. Juni 1978," [East] Berlin (June 6, 1978), BAB DY 30 IVB/2/2.023/89 Abteilung Internationale Verbindungen des Zentralkomitee der SED.

71 "Gen. Florin, New York: Beachten Sie in Rede zur Palästinafrage insbesonder folgende Gesichtspunkte," Politisches Archiv des Auswärtiges Amt, PAAA MFAA Abt. Naher- und Mittlerer Osten, Behandlung der Palästinafrage auf UN-Vollversammlungen, C7679, Bd. 1, 1974–1975, 24–25.

precondition" for Palestinian self-determination. Further, a Geneva conference with participation of the PLO as an equal partner with Israel was essential for a solution of the Middle East conflict.[72]

On September 10, 1974, Hildegard Kiermeier (1932–1990), who had directed the East German Foreign Ministry's Department for International Organization since 1960, expressed the Foreign Ministry's support for an Arab proposal to give the PLO observer status in the General Assembly of the United Nations.[73] She argued that East German support for the PLO followed logically from opposition to colonialism and racism and "military occupation by foreign forces." Israel, in her view, was guilty of all three of these evils and thus constituted an "ongoing danger for peace and human rights."[74] On September 26, 1974, Karl Heinz Lugenheim (1928–), director of the Near and Middle East Department in the East German Foreign Ministry and later the East German ambassador to Iraq and Syria, wrote that the PLO should have a representative in UNESCO.[75] He agreed that the PLO was "the sole, legitimate representative of the Palestinian people."[76] He observed that "for years," East Germany had accepted members of the PLO in its universities and technical schools. "In the face of the anti-Arabic campaign in the FRG," that is, the decision to ban GUPS and GUPA after the Munich massacre in 1972, East Germany had given "the Palestinians who had been deported the opportunity to complete their learning in educational institutions in the GDR." He recommended that East Germany, with other representatives of the Soviet bloc together with the Arab states, jointly seek resolutions in the UN General Assembly that "condemn Israel's human rights violations in the occupied territories."[77]

72 "Gen. Florin, New York: Beachten Sie in Rede zur Palästinafrage insbesonder folgende Gesichtspunkte," PAAA MFAA Abt. Naher- und Mittlerer Osten, Behandlung der Palästinafrage auf UN-Vollversammlungen, C7679, Bd. 1, 1974–1975, 24–25.

73 Hildegard Kiermeier, Abteilung UNESCO to Abteilung Naher und Mittlerer Osten (September 10, 1974), PAAA MFAA, Abt. Naher- und Mittlerer Osten, Tätigkeit von UN-Spezialorganisationen und der UNRWA zur Unterstützung des palstinensischen Volkes, C 7682-C7683, Bd. 1, 1975–1976, Bd. 2, 1978–1979, 75–76.

74 Ibid., 77.

75 Karl-Heinz Lugenheim, "Note der Libyschen Arabischen Republik," (September 26, 1974), PAAA MFAA, Abt. Naher- und Mittlerer Osten, Tätigkeit von UN-Spezialorganisationen und der UNRWA zur Unterstützung des palstinensischen Volkes, C 7682-C7683, Bd. 1, 1975–1976, Bd. 2, 1978–1979, 73–74; see also "Lugenheim, Karl-Heinz," in Siegfried Bock, Ingrid Muth and Hermann Schwiesau, eds., *DDR-Außenpolitik, Ein Überblick: Daten, Fakten, Personen (III)* (Berlin: LIT Verlag, 2012), 331.

76 Ibid., 73.

77 Ibid., 74.

On October 14, 1974, the UN General Assembly debated whether to accord the PLO observer status to participate in the workings of the General Assembly. Yosef Tekoah made the following argument against doing so: "The independence and sovereign equality of Member States are the cornerstone of the United Nations. The draft resolution before us proposes to reward a relentless campaign against the very existence of an independent Member State." Granting observer status to the PLO would give "succor to an organization which strives to deny the Jewish people its right to national liberty and self-determination."[78] While the UN had tried to combat international terrorism, "now it is called upon to welcome those who have turned the premeditated murder of innocent children, women and men into a profession."[79] Tekoah then quoted from Articles 19, 20, 22, and 9 of the PLO Charter of 1968. He reminded the members that it called the establishment of Israel "null and void," advocated the liquidation of Zionist presence in Palestine, and asserted that "armed struggle" was the "only way to liberate Palestine." Presumably with reference to the PLO Charter's statements that the Balfour Declaration of 1917 was null and void, Tekoah also asserted that according to the PLO's Covenant, "only Jews who lived in Palestine in 1917 – I repeat, in 1917 – would be allowed to remain" in a state established by the PLO.[80]

Tekoah described the goals of the PLO: "[to] liquidate the Jewish state; to destroy, uproot and scatter its people; to deprive them of their independence, sovereignty, self-determination and equality with other nations." In pursuit of those goals, it employed "the most despicable of methods witnessed by mankind in recent decades – the deliberate murder of guiltless civilians." Their deaths were "not the accidental loss of civilian lives in warfare against military targets, but willful, cold-blooded, carefully prepared, bestial assaults on innocent and defenseless children, women and men."[81] He then recalled the terror attacks of recent years both in Israel, at the Munich Olympics, on civil aviation, and against diplomats in other countries. It was "the criminal responsible for such abominable crimes that the General Assembly is about to invite into its midst."[82] Tekoah said that the proposed resolution's description of the PLO as the representative of the Palestinian people was "ignominious and ludicrous." It had not

78 Yosef Tekoah, "Question of Palestine," UNGA, 29th Session, 2267 Plenary Meeting (October 14, 1974), UN ODS A/PV.2267, 665–668.

79 Ibid., 665.

80 Ibid., 665–667.

81 Ibid., 667.

82 Ibid., 665–668.

been elected by its own people and was instead "a band of international criminals pursued by the police of tens of countries."[83]

East Germany's UN ambassador Peter Florin supported the resolution.[84] It was "perfectly legitimate and natural but also necessary for the sole legitimate representative of the Arab people of Palestine – that is, the Palestine Liberation Organization [PLO] – to participate in the discussion of this agenda item."[85] The GDR had "always been and will continue to be on the side of the Arab peoples in their just struggle against persistent Israeli aggression." He said, "We fully support" the "just struggle to ensure that the people of Palestine exercise their legitimate rights. The slander of the Israeli representatives against the PLO is simply a desperate effort to distract attention from Israel's continuing aggression against neighboring Arab States and shows that Israel is still not inclined to acknowledge the rights of the Arab people of Palestine."[86] Florin neither challenged nor acknowledged the Israelis' factual assertions about the PLO's campaign of terrorism yet referred to Tekoah's characterizations of the PLO as a slander.[87]

On November 14, 1974, Arafat himself, dressed in combat fatigues and with a pistol in a holster, received the honor of speaking to the UN General Assembly. He spoke at noon, the time ordinarily reserved for addresses by heads of state. In a 90-minute address he repeated the PLO's version of the history of Israel expressed in its Charter of 1968. He described Zionism as racist and imperialist. He justified war and violence, that is, "armed struggle," to attain what he called the rights of the Palestinians. At the outset he was greeted with a standing ovation by many delegates. When he finished, "a large part of the Assembly" led by Arab, African, and other third-world countries "gave him a standing ovation that lasted nearly two minutes."[88]

On November 22, 1974, an overwhelming majority in the UN General Assembly passed two resolutions concerning the PLO. Resolution 3236

[83] Ibid., 667.

[84] Peter Florin, "Agenda Item 108: The Question of Palestine," UNGA, 2268 (October 14, 1974), UN ODS, A/PV.2269, 671.

[85] Ibid., 671.

[86] Ibid.

[87] In response to Tekoah's denunciation of the PLO's terrorism, Cuba's UN ambassador said that the UN majority could "not be won over by" what he called "the worn out language of colonialists and imperialists." Ricardo Alcaron, UNGA, 29th Session, 2267 Plenary Meeting, October 14, 1974, UN ODS A/PV.2267, 668–669.

[88] Paul Hofman, "Dramatic Session: P.L.O. Heads Says He Bears Olive Branch and Guerrilla Gun," 1 and 24; and "Transcripts of Addresses to the U.N. Assembly by Arafat and Israeli Delegate," *New York Times* (November 14, 1974), 22–23.

placed "The Question of Palestine" on the agenda of the upcoming 30th Session. Resolution 3237 granted the PLO observer status at the UN, thereby allowing it to participate in the sessions and work of the General Assembly, in "all international conferences convened under the auspices of the General Assembly" and "other organs of the United Nations." Resolution 3236 passed with 89 yes votes to 8 opposed and 37 abstentions. UN 3237, granting observer status, passed with 97 yes, 17 opposed, and 19 abstentions. The East Germans voted in favor of both resolutions. West Germany abstained on the first and voted against according observer status to the PLO.[89]

Resolution 3236 defined the "inalienable rights of the Palestinian people in Palestine" to include the right "to return to their homes and property from which they have been displaced and uprooted." It further recognized "the right of the Palestinian people to regain its rights by all means in accordance with the purposes and principles of the Charter of the United Nations." That is, it supported the PLO's resort to force. It appealed "to all States and international organizations to extend their support to the Palestinian people in its struggle to restore its rights" and requested that the UN secretary general (Kurt Waldheim at the time) "establish contacts with the Palestine Liberation Organization on all matters concerning the question of Palestine."[90] By inserting the "right of return" into Resolution 3236, the General Assembly, in effect, supported the destruction of the state of Israel. By supporting the right to regain rights "by all means in accordance" with the charter, it sanctioned the use of force by the PLO against Israel, and by referring specifically to the PLO, it had the effect of approving the terrorist actions against Israel for which, by 1974, the PLO had become world famous. Resolution 3236 again demonstrated clearly that the anti-Israeli majority in the General Assembly was functioning as the political and diplomatic arm of the PLO's war against Israel.

In response to the votes, Ambassador Tekoah said these "are sad days for the United Nations. These are days of degradation and disgrace, of surrender and humiliation for the international community.... One PLO supporter after another denied the Jewish people's right to

[89] UNGA, 29th Session, 2296 Plenary Meeting, New York (November 22, 1974), "The Question of Palestine," UN ODS A/PV.2296, 1066. Those voting against granting the PLO observer status were Belgium, Bolivia, Canada, Chile, Costa Rica, Denmark, Germany (Federal Republic of), Iceland, Ireland, Israel, Italy, Luxembourg, Netherlands, Nicaragua, Norway, United Kingdom of Great Britain and Northern Ireland, United States of America.

[90] "The Question of Palestine," 106.

life and independence, negated its national identity and its history. One after another disparaged the people of Israel by trying to present it as a stranger in its own homeland."[91] For the PLO and its followers, "savagery is praiseworthy, defense against atrocities condemnable. Terror against civilians is acceptable, but a State's protection of its citizens is terrorism. The murder of Jewish children and the destruction of the Jewish state is called liberation. Zionism, the Jewish people's national liberation movement, is calumnied as evil." All national liberation movements had "at one stage or another resorted to arms. However, the targets have generally been of a military nature. Sometimes there might be incidental civilian casualties."[92]

> Arafat and the PLO, on the other hand, have concentrated mainly on murder for murder's sake. Their targets have never been military targets. They have always planned and carried out attacks on civilians. They have always chosen the most savage method and the most innocent and defenseless target. Massacres of school children have been their specialty; the hijacking and blowing-up of civil airliners their favorite. The killing of helpless persons in their homes, of defenseless passengers at air terminals, of sportsmen in Olympic Games, of diplomats at Embassy receptions have become synonymous with the names of Arafat and the PLO.... Only Arafat's agents cold[ly] slaughter children by shooting them one by one in the head as in Ma'alot. Only one other movement ever practiced such savagery – the Nazis. The PLO murderers are their heirs in method and objective.
>
> Every national liberation movement strives to free its own people from colonial yoke. No liberation movement aims at subjugating another people and depriving it of its national rights. The PLO's avowed goal is, however, to destroy the Jewish State and to wrest from the Jewish people its liberty and its independence. Again, only the Nazis denied to the Jewish people the rights of all nations. Only the Nazis refused to recognize that the Jewish people was equal with others. Arafat and the PLO hold the same view. The only right that the PLO is prepared to grant Jews is to live as an oppressed minority in one more Arab state.[93]

Tekoah referred to an interview that morning in the *Wall Street Journal* with Farouk Al-Kaddoumi, the head of the PLO UN delegation, who articulated a three-stage strategy: First, the PLO would establish authority over the West Bank and Gaza. Then "we would have to see to it that refugees would return to their homes and to their property," after which the PLO would establish "our democratic, secular state" with support from the Soviet Union and China. Tekoah replied that "Israel has no

[91] Yosef Tekoah, UNGA, 29th Session, 2296 Plenary Meeting, New York (November 22, 1974), "The Question of Palestine," UN ODS, A/PV.2296, 1066–1068.

[92] Ibid.

[93] Ibid., 1067–1068.

intention of being replaced by the Nazis of the Middle East. The Jewish people will not be swallowed up by PLO barbarity."[94] By passing these resolutions the UN had "plunged into an abyss from which there is no exit." They encouraged the PLO "to pursue its goals and methods," which were "contrary to international law and morality" and dealt "another grievous blow to peace-making efforts in the Middle East."[95] Israel would "treat the resolutions for what they are and deserve to be: utterly contemptible and devoid of legal and moral worth."[96]

In 1974 and 1975, high-ranking East German officials met with Arafat and other PLO figures in East Berlin and in the Middle East. Arafat met with Horst Sindermann (1915–1990), then the chair of the powerful Council of Ministers, in Damascus in November 1974; with the East German ambassador to Lebanon, Bruno Sedlaczek, in December 1975; and with a range of East German officials on a visit to East Berlin in August 1975.[97] In preparation for a visit with Farouk Kaddoumi using the nom de guerre "Abou Lutf," from November 28 to December 2, 1975, a memo in the Near and Middle East Department denounced Israel's "criminal terror acts against the Palestinian people in Lebanon" and extolled "the great political success of the PLO in its struggle to attain the national rights of the Palestinian people." The diplomats were advised to express "joy and pleasure" about the visit of a PLO delegation led by "Abou Lutf" and the 1975 agreement for SED-PLO cooperation in 1975 and to express readiness to intensify relations; expand "solidarity assistance," that is, weapons; and support the PLO's "political offensive." This support included raising the status of the PLO office in Berlin, that is, the diplomatic privileges and immunities of the director and deputy director, and supporting the PLO's efforts to gain observer status at the UN. East Germany was now prepared to train cadres of the PLO in a special course in the Institute for International Relations and offered to consult in preparation for the Security Council meeting of January 12, 1976 concerning offering the PLO observer status at the United Nations.

The PLO visit to East Berlin in December 1975 went well. Lutf/Kaddoumi said that "the PLO attributed particular importance to the

[94] Ibid.

[95] Ibid., 1068.

[96] Yosef Tekoah, UNGA, 29th Session, 2296 Plenary Meeting (November 22, 1974), "The Question of Palestine," UN ODS A/PV.2296, 1068.

[97] "Hinweis für ein Gespräch mit dem Vorsitzenden des PLO-Exekutivkomitees, Yasser Arafat," [East] Berlin (December 3, 1975), Besuche von Delegationen der PLO in der DDR, 1971, 1973–1979, PAAA MFAA (Ministerium für Auswärtige Angelegenheiten der DDR) Abteilung Naher- und Mittlereer Osten C 7678, 23.

political-diplomatic battle" and placed particular importance on the United Nations decisions of 1974 and 1975 and "the role that the SU/SSG [Soviet Union and the Soviet bloc] played" in helping to pass them.[98] The PLO thought the alliance with the Soviet bloc was of "strategic significance."[99] Kaddoumi assured the East Germans that the PLO "placed great importance on the political-diplomatic battle," on the UN resolutions of 1974, and on the role that the Soviet bloc had played in passing them. Oddly, while praising resolutions that placed the entire blame for the Middle East conflict on Israel, the East German diplomats spoke of the PLO's "realism about a possible recognition of Israel as a state" and a readiness to "cooperate with progressive anti-Zionist forces in Israel," that is, with the Israeli Communist Party. In view of the terrorist attacks of 1974, it was odd that the memo referred to the decline of the "leftist danger for the PLO."[100] The combination of militant anti-imperialist and anti-Israeli ideology with references to an undefined "political solution" had become a distinctive East German and Soviet-bloc stance. While the officials in the Near and Middle East Division spoke vaguely about political solutions, the radicalism of East German Communism was evident in the continuing delivery of weapons to the Palestinian terrorist organizations, in public verbal attacks on Israel, in the refusal to condemn Palestinian terrorism, and in public and private praise for the PLO even in the aftermath of some of the famous terrorist assaults of spring 1974.

THE WEST GERMAN RADICAL LEFT RESPONDS TO THE PLO'S TERRORISM

In 1975, the West German Left comprised a milieu of both New Left and orthodox Marxist-Leninist organizations known as "*K-Gruppen,*" or Communist groups.[101] The West German government's Office for the Protection of the Constitution (Verfassungsschutz) counted 119,000 members in orthodox Communist organizations, who included 15,000

[98] "Information über die Ergebnisse des Besuchs einer Delegation der PLO unter Leitung des Mitglieds des Exekutivkomitees der PLO und Leiters der Politischen Abteilung, Abou Lutf, in der DDR, vom 29.11–2.12.1975," [East] Berlin (December 3, 1975), Besuche von Delegationen der PLO in der DDR, 1971, 1973–1979, PAAA MFAA (Ministerium für Auswärtige Angelegenheiten der DDR) Abteilung Naher- und Mittlereer Osten C 7678, 25.

[99] Ibid.

[100] Ibid.

[101] Gerd Koenen, *Das Rote Jahrzehnt: Unsere kleine deutsche Kulturrevolution 1967–1977* (Frankfurt/Main: Fischer Taschenbuch, 2001).

Maoists, 1,200 Trotskyists, 4,500 in various New Left organizations. The organizations had 140,000 members composed of 105,000 people when multiple memberships were taken into account.[102] In 18 student parliaments at universities, these "left-wing extremist groups" had more than 50 percent of the seats and 37.4 percent of the student government (ASTA) representatives overall.[103] The German Communist Party linked to East Germany, the DKP (Deutsche Kommunistische Partei), had increased its membership to 42,000. It had received more than 50 million marks from East Germany to finance its activities, which included publication of its newspaper *Unsere Zeit* (Our Time) with a daily circulation of 30,000 and a Friday edition of 60,000.[104] "Anti-imperialist solidarity for Africa, Asia and Latin America" was one of its major themes. That included support for the PLO.[105] Like *Neues Deutschland*, it remained silent about Palestinian terrorist attacks on Israel while expressing support for the PLO. The Maoist Kommunistische Bund Westdeutschland (Communist Organization West Germany) had about 2,500 members and 1,000 sympathizers. It could mobilize about 8,000 people for demonstrations and published a newspaper, *Kommunistische Volkszeitung* (Communist People's Newspaper), with a circulation of about 32,000. The Kommunistische Bund (Communist Organization) (KB) now had about 1,700 members and could mobilize 3,000 to 4,000 people at demonstrations, mostly in the Hamburg area. Its newspaper, *Arbeiterkampf* (Worker Struggle), had a circulation of about 24,000.[106]

These were among the organizations that found common cause with Palestinian supporters of the PLO in West Germany. In February 1975, the General Union of Arab Students in the Federal Republic of German and West-Berlin (GUAS) was established as a successor to the GUPS. It had about 1,000 members. It represented the views of the PLO led by Arafat but also had a "strong faction" that supported the PFLP, led by George Habash. It opened an "Information Center" in Bonn.[107] The West German Interior Ministry concluded that Al Fatah and the PLO had "preserved a network of conspiratorially functioning cells and contact in

[102] *Verfassungsschutzbericht* '77, No. 25 (Bonn: Bundesminister des Innern, 1976), 62.

[103] Ibid., 64–65.

[104] Ibid., 71–72.

[105] Ibid., 72.

[106] Ibid., 98–99.

[107] *Verfassungsschutzbericht* '75, No. 25 (Bonn: Bundesminister des Innern, 1976), 135–136. The German title is: *Generalunion Arabischer Studenten in der Bundesrepublik Deutschland und West-Berlin.*

Germany" whose members took weapons training courses in Palestinian camps and then returned to Europe.[108]

Among the Marxist-Leninist organizations that emerged in the aftermath of the 1960s New Left, two Maoist organizations were noteworthy for their propaganda support for Palestinian terrorism. They were the Kommunistische Bund Westdeutschland (Communist Association in West Germany, hence KBW), and the Kommunistische Bund (Communist Association, hence KB). The KBW, with about 2,800 members and 250 cells in factories, schools, and universities, was the strongest Maoist-oriented Marxist-Leninist party in West Germany. Joscha Schmierer, a former leader of SDS from Heidelberg, was its driving spirit and the editor of its journal, *Kommunismus und Klassenkampf* (Communism and Class Struggle). The KB, founded in Hamburg in 1971, had a membership ranging from 800 to 1,500. The pages of its newspaper, *Arbeiterkampf* (Workers Struggle), with a circulation of 17,000 in 1972, edited by Jürgen Reents, included praise for the PLO and especially for the PFLP.[109]

The admiration of the Kommunistische Bund for the PFLP was evident in the May 1, 1974, issue of *Arbeiterkampf*. It ran an ad for a book entitled *Palestine: The Masses are the Driving Forces of the Revolution, The Struggle Continues to Victory, Interviews and Conversations with Fighters from the PLO, Al Fatah, PFLP-General Command and PFLP* (*Palästina: Der Kampf geht weiter bis zum Sieg, Die Massen sind die Triebkraft der Revolution: Interviews und Gespräche mit Kämpfer der PLO, Al Fatah, PFLP-Allgemein Führung und PFLP)*.[110] The KB publishing house Verlag Arbeiterkampf published the work. The text reported on a trip by KB members to PFLP camps.[111] It countered what the authors called the "superficial and nonsolidaristic reactions by some [West German] leftist groups to the action of Black September in Munich," that is, rejection of the attack on the Israeli athletes in Munich in 1972. The

[108] Ibid., 136.

[109] *Verfassungsschutz '72: Öffentlichkeitsarbeit des* Bundesinnenministerium (Bonn: Der Bundesminister des Innern, 1973), 91–92. On the Maoist groups see Andrei S. Markovits with Gregory Wilpert, "Revolutionary Cadre Politics and Terrorism" in Andrei Markovits and Philip S. Gorski, *The German Left: Red, Green and Beyond* (New York: Oxford University Press, 1995), 63–65; and Gerd Koenen, *Das Rote Jahrzehnt: Unsere kleine deutsche Kulturrevolution 1967–1977* (Frankfurt/Main: Fischer Taschenbuch, 2001), 257–316 and 415–468.

[110] *Palästina:, Die Massen sind die Triebkraft der Revolution. Der Kampf geht weiter bis zum Sieg, Interviews und Gespräche mit Kämpfern der PLO, Al Fatah, PFLP-Allgemeine Führung und PFLP* (Hamburg: Verlag Arbeiter Kampf, 1974).

[111] "Anzeige: *Palästina: Der Kampf geht weiter, Die Massen sind die Triebkraft der Revolution*," in *Arbeiterkampf*, Hamburg (May 1, 1974), 4.

book offered hagiographic profiles of leaders of the Palestinian terrorist organizations including George Habash (1926–2008) of the PFLP; Nayef Hawatmeh (1938–) of the PDFLP; Ahmed Jibril (1938–) of the PFLP-General Command; and Arafat as well. It presented the history of Zionism as a "conspiracy against the people of Palestine" that began in 1897 at the first Zionist congress in Basel and continued up to 1974.[112] It was a story that omitted the history of the European and German anti-Semitism and persecution of the Jews that had led Herzl and others to support the Zionist option in the first place and included nothing about the Holocaust. In view of the "Zionist terror," the authors found it "easy to explain" why "the actions of Black September and the PFLP find the broadest support in the Arab and especially among the Palestinian masses."[113] As "the Arab masses" supported actions such as the Lod airport massacre and the Munich Olympics attack, it would be an act of "sheer arrogance and superiority" for the members of the KB to make any judgments about the strategy and tactics of the "Palestinian revolution."[114]

The attacks on Kiryat Shmona and Ma'alot put the willingness of these West German Communist groups to support Palestinian terror to the test. On May 1, 1974, *Arbeiterkampf* ran an article on "The Action of Kiryat Shmona"[115] Rather than address the Zionists' "propaganda lies," the unsigned author "wanted to report things that the Zionists have 'forgotten' without in so doing justifying the whole action."[116] The anonymous author then proceeded to do just that. He claimed that "the action" took place on the one-year anniversary of a "Zionist terror undertaking" that led to the "murders" of three leaders of Palestinian "resistance organizations" in Beirut and on the 26th anniversary of the Israeli attack on the Arab village of Deir Yassin on April 10, 1948. Thus it was presumably an act of justified retaliation. It incorrectly described "Kiryat Shmona" as "not just any Israeli city" but a town that had military importance as "an advanced post towards the Lebanese and Syrian borders." Further, "like most Israeli cities," Kiryat Shmona "was built on the ruins of Arab villages in order to guarantee for all time the expulsion of the Arab

112 PLO Informationsbüro, "Kurzer Rückblick auf die palästinensischen Revolution in den letzten 50 Jahren," *Palästina:, Die Massen sind die Triebkraft der Revolution*, 5.

113 "Solidarität mit dem Kampf des palästinensischen Volkes!," *Palästina:, Die Massen sind die Triebkraft der Revolution*, 10.

114 Ibid., 11.

115 "Die Aktion von Kirjat Schmoneh," *Arbeiterkampf: Arbeiterzeitung des Kommunistischen Bundes* (May 1, 1974), 4. Archiv des Institut für Sozialforschung Hamburg [hereafter AIS Hamburg].

116 Ibid., 4.

inhabitants, the destruction of their property and Zionist occupation."[117] The clear implication of these arguments was that an armed attack on the occupants of Kiryat Shmona was fully justified.[118]

The KBW's Joscha Schmierer had an interesting political career. From 1973 to 1982, he was the secretary of the Central Committee of the KBW and editor of *Kommunismus und Klassenkampf*. In those years, Schmierer and the KBW continued to support the PFLP and the PLO. Later, Schmierer joined the Green Party. In 1998, when the Greens joined a coalition government led by the Social Democrats, Joschka Fischer, a veteran of the leftist milieu in Frankfurt/Main and a leader of the Green Party, became West Germany's foreign minister. In 1999 Fischer appointed Schmierer to serve on the planning staff of the Foreign Ministry of the Federal Republic of Germany. He continued in that position until 2007. Schmierer's astonishing political ascendency from leadership of a Marxist-Leninist Maoist organization to the planning staff of the German Foreign Ministry was not accompanied by any public discussion on his part of his radical anti-Zionist views of the past.[119]

In West Germany, leftists who celebrated the PLO's "armed struggle" against Israel faced criticism that leftist anti-Zionism was a cloak for anti-Semitism.[120] In 1974, Schmierer published a long essay by an unnamed German Jewish leftist who criticized the anti-Zionism of the KBW. In the February 1974 issue of *Kommunismus und Klassenkampf*, Schmierer replied to accusations that leftist anti-Zionists such as he were anti-Semitic. He wrote that the editors had published the previous essay because it made clear how "socialists could become advocates of colonialism and Zionism" and express "contempt (*Verachtung)* towards the right of self-determination of nations and the neglect (*Mißachtung)* of the distinction, so important for imperialism, between oppressed and oppressed nations."[121] Schmierer wrote that he had not written that "the

117 Ibid.

118 Ibid.

119 See "Kleine Anfrage der Abgeordneten Jürgen Koppeli, Jörg van Essen, Dr. Wolfgang Gerhardt und der Fraktion der F.D.P," *Deutscher Bundestag, 14. Wahlperiode* (February 9, 2001), Drucksache 14.5303; and "Antwort der Bundesregierung, *Deutscher Bundestag, 14. Wahlperiode* (March 5, 2001), Drucksache 14/5406.

120 See, for example, Henryk M. Broder, *Vergesst Auschwitz: Der deutsche Erinnerungswahn und die Endlösung der Israel-Frage* (Munich: Albrecht Knaus Verlag, 2012); and *Der ewige Antisemit: Über Sinn und Funktion eine beständigen Gefühls*, 2nd. ed. (Berlin: Berlin Taschenbuch Verlag, 2006).

121 J. S. [Joscha Schmierer], "Vorbermerkung: Der Kolonialcharakter des israelischen Staates," AIS Hamburg, *Kommunismus und Klassenkampft* Hamburg Vol. 2, Nr. 2 (February 1974), 55.

Jews were colonialists and conquerors from the beginning" but instead had referred to "Israelis." He continued that "without doubt, the Israelis were colonialists and conquerors in Palestine." Schmierer described the efforts of his anonymous critic to impute anti-Semitism to him as "an old Zionist trick." One of

> the most important educational experiences of young Germans after World War II was the deepest revulsion with anti-Semitism. For a long time, this deep revulsion stood in the way of recognizing the real character of Zionism and the Israeli state. The trick had the desired effect. Now, however, Israel's deeds and its uninterrupted acts of aggression are opening the eyes of more and more people – not only regarding the Israeli state today but also for its past.
>
> Many now see that just as the destruction of the German Reich was right and just, so the destruction of the Israeli colonial state will also be equally just and right. The establishment of a people's republic of Palestine on its ruins will be the guarantee that a new oppressor and conqueror state will not emerge from these ruins.[122]

While Schmierer referred to "the German Reich" rather than to Nazi Germany, the reader could plausibly conclude that he meant that the destruction of the state of Israel would be as justified as was the destruction of Nazi Germany.[123]

[122] Ibid. The German reads in part: "*Viele sehen: Genauso gerecht wie die Zerschlagung des Deutschen Reiches gewesen ist, genauso recht wird auch die Zerschlagung des israelischen Kolonialstaates sein. Die Errichtung einer Volksrepublik Palästina auf seinen Trümmern wird die Gewähr dafür sein, daß aus diesen Trümmern nicht ein neuer Unterdrücker- und Erobererstaat entstehen wird.*"

[123] Also see Joscha Schmierer, "Imperialistische Interessen und Komplotte im Nahen Osten gegen den Kampf des palästinensischen Volkes," AIS Hamburg, *Kommunismus und Klassenkampft*, Vol. 5, No. 8 (August, 1977), 339–343.

9

The United Nations "Zionism Is Racism" Resolution of November 10, 1975

On November 10, 1975 a large majority of the members of the 30th session of the United Nations General Assembly passed a resolution that denounced Zionism as a form of racism. It was the most important victory to date for the PLO and its Soviet-bloc, Arab, and third-world state supporters. The vote was 72 in favor, 35 opposed, and 32 abstentions.[1] East Germany supported the resolution; West Germany voted against it. Resolution 3379 on the "elimination of all forms of racial discrimination" was the most famous of the many defeats that Israel endured at the UN in these decades. It was also a dramatic demonstration of the interaction between force and political warfare, that is, between the PLO's terrorist campaign waged in the Middle East against Israel and the political and diplomatic offensive that it and its supporters waged at the United Nations in New York. For Israel and its supporters, the resolution meant that the United Nations had become a center of both antagonism to Israel and anti-Semitism in world politics. For the PLO, it meant expansion of political support for its campaign to destroy the state of Israel.

The roll call vote was as follows:

[1] "Resolution Adopted by the General Assembly, 3379 (XXX). Elimination of All Forms of Racial Discrimination," United Nations General Assembly, 30th Session, Agenda Item 68 (November 10, 1975), A/RES/3379; also at unispal.un.org/UNISPAL.NSF/0/761C10635 30766A7052566A2005B74D1.

The resolution was sponsored by the following 24 countries: Afghanistan, Algeria, Bahrain, Cuba, Dahomey, Egypt, Guinea, Iraq, Jordan, Kuwait, Lebanon, Libya, Mauritania, Morocco, Yemen Arab Republic, Oman, Qatar, Saudi Arabia, Somalia, South Yemen, Sudan, Syria, Tunisia, and United Arab Emirates. For the debate on the resolution see United Nations General Assembly, 30th Session, 2400th Plenary Meeting Agenda Item 68 (November 10, 1975), 769–806.

In favor: (72) Afghanistan, Albania, Algeria, Bahrain, Bangladesh, Bangladesh, Brazil, Bulgaria, Burundi, Byelorussian SSR, Cambodia, Cape Verde, Chad, China, Congo, Cuba, Cyprus, Czechoslovakia, Dahomey, Democratic Republic of Yemen, Egypt, Equatorial Guinea, Gambia, **German Democratic Republic**, Grenada, Guinea, Guinea-Bissau, Guyana, Hungary, India, Indonesia, Iran, Iraq, Jordan, Kuwait, Laos, Lebanon, Libyan Arab Republic, Madagascar, Malaysia, Maldives, Mali, Malta, Mauritania, Mexico, Mongolia, Mozambique, Niger, Nigeria, Oman, Pakistan, Poland, Portugal, Qatar, Rwanda, São Tomé and Príncipe, Saudi Arabia, Senegal, Somalia, Sri Lanka, Sudan, Syrian Arab Republic, Tunisia, Turkey, Uganda, Ukrainian SSR, USSR, United Arab Emirates, United Republic of Cameroon, United Republic of Tanzania, Yemen, Yugoslavia.

Against: (35) Australia, Austria, Bahamas, Barbados, Belgium, Canada, Central African Republic, Costa Rica, Denmark, Dominican Republic, El Salvador, Fiji, Finland, France, **Germany, Federal Republic**, Haiti, Honduras, Iceland, Ireland, Israel, Italy, Ivory Coast, Liberia, Luxembourg, Malawi, Netherlands, New Zealand, Nicaragua, Norway, Panama, Swaziland, Sweden, United Kingdom, United States, Uruguay.

Abstaining: (32) Argentina, Bhutan, Bolivia, Botswana, Burma, Chile, Colombia, Ecuador, Ethiopia, Gabon, Ghana, Greece, Guatemala, Jamaica, Japan, Kenya, Lesotho, Mauritius, Nepal, Papua New Guinea, Paraguay, Peru, Philippines, Sierra Leone, Singapore, Thailand, Togo, Trinidad and Tobago, Upper Volta, Venezuela, Yugoslavia, Zaire, Zambia.[2]

Resolution 3379, "Elimination of All Forms of Racial Discrimination," incorporated the arguments of the PLO's Charter of 1968. It read as follows:

The General Assembly:

Recalling its resolution 1904 (XVIII) of 20 November 1963, proclaiming the United Nations Declaration on the Elimination of All Forms of Racial Discrimination, and in particular its affirmation that "any doctrine of racial differentiation or superiority is scientifically false, morally condemnable, socially unjust and dangerous and its expression of alarm at the manifestation of racial discrimination still in evidence in some areas of the world, some of which are imposed by certain Governments by means of legislative, administrative or other measures,"

Recalling also that, in its resolution 3151 G (XXVIII) of 14 December 1973, the General Assembly condemned, *inter alia*, the unholy alliance between South African racism and zionism,

Taking note of the Declaration of Mexico on the Equality of Women and Their Contribution to Development and Peace, proclaimed by the World Conference of the International Women's Year, held at Mexico City from 19 June to 2 July 1975, which promulgated the principle that "international co-operation and peace require the achievement of national liberation and independence, the elimination

[2] "Resolution 3379," *United Nations Yearbook*, 1975 (New York: United Nations, 1978), 599.

of colonialism and neo-colonialism, foreign occupation, zionism, *apartheid* and racial discrimination in all its forms, as well as the recognition of the dignity of peoples and their right to self-determination,"

Taking note also of the Political Declaration and Strategy to Strengthen International Peace and Security and to Intensify Solidarity and Mutual Assistance among Non-Aligned Countries, adopted at the Conference of Ministers for Foreign Affairs of the Non-Aligned Countries held at Lima from 25 to 30 August 1975, which most severely condemned zionism as a threat to world peace and security and called upon all countries to oppose this racist and imperialist ideology,

Determines that zionism is a form of racism and racial discrimination.

2400th plenary meeting, 10 November 1975.[3]

Resolution 3379 represented a 1970s version of the Popular Front mobilizations of the 1930s in which Communists and non-Communists, the Soviet bloc and its front organizations agreed on a common denominator with non-Communist but left-leaning states and organizations. In the 1930s, that common denominator was anti-fascism; in 1975, it was anti-Zionism. As anti-fascism became a famous slogan identifying the meaning of leftism in the 1930s and 1940s, so anti-Zionism became a defining element of the global Left during the Cold War. To most Americans and Western Europeans, East Germany appeared to be an isolated and forlorn prison, known above all for having built the Berlin Wall and fortifying its border with West Germany with mine fields and machine gun guard towers designed to prevent its citizens from leaving. Yet as the vote on Resolution 3379 indicated, at the UN, it was not at all isolated. On the contrary, as had been the case since 1967, the diplomatic recognition breakthrough of 1969, and its admission to the UN in 1973, its antagonism to Israel and support for the Arab states and the PLO had contributed to its relations with a large number of states around the world. Anti-Zionist ideology and the pursuit of national interest in a conventional sense merged in a policy of antagonism to Israel. The attack on Zionism, linked as it was to third-world anti-imperialism, was a reassertion of Leninist orthodoxy and as such fit well with the ideological orthodoxy of the East German Communist leadership.

Also on November 10, 1975, the UN General Assembly, by a vote of 101 in favor, 25 abstentions, and 8 opposed, passed Resolution 3375, an "Invitation to the Palestine Liberation Organization to Participate in the Efforts for Peace in the Middle East."[4] West Germany joined the

[3] "3379. Elimination of All Forms of Racial Discrimination," UNGA (November 10, 1975).

[4] A/RES/3375 (XXX) November 10, 1975, UNGA, "Invitation to the Palestine Liberation Organization to Participate in the Efforts for Peace in the Middle East," unispal.un.org/unispal.nsf/9a798adbf322aff38525617b006d88.

Netherlands, Nicaragua, the United Kingdom, Costa Rica, Honduras, the United States, and Israel in voting no. East Germany supported 3375, which gave the PLO observer status at the UN and anointed it as "the representative of the Palestinian people."[5] It invited the PLO "to participate in all efforts, deliberations and conferences on the Middle East which are held under the auspices of the United Nations on an equal footing with other parties." It bestowed on the organization many of the privileges and resources ordinarily reserved for a member state. Also on November 10, East Germany was a co-sponsor and part of the General Assembly majority that passed Resolution 3376, which created the Committee for the Exercise of the Inalienable Rights of the Palestinian People (CEIRPP) as a UN-related body. The vote was 97 in favor, 18 opposed, and 27 abstentions. East Germany voted in favor; West Germany voted no.[6]

The resolutions of November 10, 1975, made Israel a pariah at the UN. They placed the language of "inalienable rights" and the search for a "just and lasting peace" in the service of the PLO's ongoing terrorist campaign waged against Israel. East Germany's vote in favor of Resolutions 3375, 3376 and 3379 reflected its close relationship with the PLO. In East Berlin, the Middle East Department in the Ministry of Foreign Affairs (MFAA, Ministerium für Auswärtige Angelegenheiten) regarded the General Assembly resolutions as a "great success for the just cause" of the Palestinians and for the PLO, which it also viewed as their "sole legitimate representative."[7] The department concluded that the PLO's success at the UN was due to the "coordinated efforts of the PLO, the progressive Arab states and the states of the socialist community and all anti-imperialist forces."[8] It took pride that East Germany was one of the resolution's twenty co-sponsors. The MFAA officials described the "resolution, above all, as one that continues and intensifies the international isolation of the aggressor Israel." Further, "just as the PLO" did,

[5] Ibid., 2.

[6] A/RES/3376 (XXX) November 10, 1975, UNGA, "Question of Palestine," unispal.un.org/unispal.nsf/0/B5B4720B8192FDE3852560DE004F3C47.

[7] "Konzeption Teil II: Haltung der DDR zur Entwicklung im Nahen Osten," [East] Berlin (December 3, 1975), Besuche von Delegationen der PLO in der DDR, 1971, 1973–1979 (Politisches Archiv des Auswärtige Amt) PAAA MFAA (Ministerium für Auswärtige Angelegenheiten der DDR) Abteilung Naher- und Mittlereer Osten C 7678, 27. "Lugenheim, Karl-Heinz," Siegfried Bock, Ingrid Muth and Hermann Schwiesau, eds., *DDR-Aussenpolitik, Ein Überblick* (Berlin: LIT Verlag, 2010), 331. Among other posts, Lugenheim was East Germany's ambassador to Iraq from 1977 to 1982. Also see "Kiermeier, Hildegard," East Germany's longstanding (1972–1990) ambassador to UNESCO, in Bock, et al., *DDR Aussenpolitik*, 320.

[8] Ibid., 32.

East Germany distinguished "fundamentally between Jews and Zionists, between anti-Semitism and anti-Zionism." It noted that Arafat too denied that the PLO attacked "the Jew as a person" but rather only attacked "racist Zionism and its unconstrained aggression."[9]

The "imperialist states and mass media," it added, including those in West Germany, had launched a "campaign of lies and slander against the advocates of the anti-Zionism resolution." Yet such efforts could not obscure the "the success in establishing the international position of the PLO and the isolation of the aggressor" Israel. Those successes were "important results of the political diplomatic offensive of the PLO with the close coordination of the USSR/SSG [Soviet Union/Socialist Community of States]." They should be used to "continue and strengthen this offensive," especially in view of the "continuously changing international balance of forces in our favor."[10] In fall 1975, this reference to the changing balance in "our favor" was presumably a reference to the victory of the North Vietnamese Communists in summer 1975 and to the growth of the Soviet Union's nuclear and conventional forces.

The Middle East Department memo of December 1975 summarized the East German diplomatic strategy in December 1975 in the following sentence: "Always remain on the political offensive!" East German diplomats should make broad use of the Palestine and anti-Zionist resolutions of the past two UN General Assemblies and "seize all opportunities and possibilities to propagate them." Special importance was to be given to the Committee for the Exercise of the Inalienable Rights of the Palestinian People (CEIRPP).[11] Further, the GDR should advance the Soviet proposal for a Geneva peace conference because in that context "the PLO would have favorable possibilities to go on the offensive. There the aggressor [Israel] will find itself in a weak position." It was crucial to "strengthen the struggle on all fronts."[12] The goal of Palestinian self-determination and a Palestinian state would "not be reached with military means alone. It calls for a long diplomatic confrontation with the enemy."[13] For the Middle East Department, the "long diplomatic confrontation with the

[9] Ibid., 33–34.
[10] Ibid.
[11] Ibid., 38.
[12] Ibid., 38–39.
[13] Ibid., 39. The German reads: "Wie die Erfahrungen lehren, wird diese Ziel mit militärischen Mitteln allein nicht zu erreichen sein. Dazu bedarf es eines langen und [unclear] diplomatischen Ringens mit dem Gegner."

enemy" was not an alternative, but a complement to the struggle on "all fronts," that is, the military front.

In this memo of December 1975, the MFAA's Middle East Department claimed that the PLO leadership had decided to "abandon the method of individual terror and concentrate on actions inside the occupied territories."[14] The assertion that the PLO had abandoned "individual terror" made sense only if one defined Israel proper as an occupied territory. The East German delegation at the United Nations had access to the detailed reports presented by the Israeli delegation, reports that clearly indicated that the PLO had not abandoned terrorism at all. The East Germans ignored or dismissed them. As the PLO Charter and various PLO statements defined all of Israel as occupied territory, the language of the East German Middle East Division memo could justify those attacks on Israelis within Israel itself. The attacks on Kiryat Shmona and Ma'alot were only the most famous of the PLO's attacks on dozens of towns and cities of northern Israel in the course of which they had murdered "the Jew as a person" literally hundreds of times. Yet when the Israelis called the PLO a terrorist organization, the East Germans denounced such assertions as examples of slander and defamation.

On November 3, 1975, speaking at the UN a week before the vote on Resolution 3379, the PLO's representative, Farouk Kaddoumi, rejected the notion that anti-Zionism was a form of anti-Semitism.[15] "The Zionists should be the last to raise the subject of anti-Semitism and anti-Semites. For in essence, Zionism is another face for anti-Semitism. Zionism, like anti-Semitism, alleges that no Jew, irrespective of his country, belongs to the nation in which he lives. It calls on each Jew to leave his country and society in order to colonize the country of another people – the Palestinian people – and replace them by the use of force and terror."[16] Zionism and anti-Semitism shared a "common racist ideology.... [They] were two bodies of the same spirit." Indeed, the Zionists' attempt "to confuse Judaism as a religious faith with Zionism as a backward, racist ideology" was "clear evidence of their manipulation of the Jewish faith, which is, in our view, to be greatly respected and honored."[17] Kaddoumi

[14] Ibid., 35.

[15] The Palestine Liberation Organization, Office of the Permanent Observer to the U.N., "Statement of the Head of the Delegation of the Palestine Liberation Organization to the 30th Session of the General Assembly of the United Nations," United Nations File, Palestine Liberation Organization, 1, Papers of Daniel P. Moynihan, Box 339, Library of Congress, Washington, D.C. (hereafter Moynihan Papers), Box 339, 16–17.

[16] Ibid., 16.

[17] Ibid.

used a classic argument of modern anti-Semitism, namely, that Jews were not loyal citizens of their countries of birth, to claim that Zionism was a form of anti-Semitism. In so doing he sought to deflect the accusation that equating Zionism with racism was a new chapter in the history of anti-Semitism. His expression of respect and honor towards "the Jewish faith" was a remarkable statement for one of the leaders of an organization that was carrying out terrorist attacks on actual Jews living in Israel.

As we have seen, the policy of calculated ambiguity regarding terrorism adopted by Arafat in his appeals to global opinion was not adopted by the Popular Democratic Front for the Liberation of Palestine (PDFLP). Its support for terrorism against Israeli civilians was evident in its previously cited communiqués celebrating the attacks in Kiryat Shmona and other towns of northern Israel. On March 12, 1975, Bruno Sedlaczek, the East German ambassador in Beirut, wrote to Kurt Krüger, chair of the GDR Solidarity Committee (and sent copies to the International Department of the SED Central Committee), about a possible visit to East Berlin by Nayef Hawatmeh and a delegation of the PDFLP. "Close, regular contacts," he wrote, "exist between our Embassy [in Beirut] to the comrades of the PDFLP."[18] Sedlaczek was the East German ambassador to Lebanon from 1973 to 1978 when the PDFLP attacked Ma'alot and other Israeli towns; he noted that in March and April 1976, a delegation led by Hawatmeh would again be "traveling to Moscow" and would then go on to Cuba. The PDFLP also had invitations to Prague, Budapest and Hanoi, as well as to Angola and Somalia. As the PDFLP showed "great interest in conversations in Berlin," he suggested making preparations for inviting Hawatmeh to East Berlin in 1976.[19] By then, Hawatmeh had gained international notoriety for his celebration of terrorist attacks on Israeli civilians. Like Arafat, however, he focused terrorism on Israel rather than on operations in Western Europe or outside the Middle East. He remained a welcome guest in the capitals of the Soviet bloc, including East Berlin, as well as in Angola, Somalia, and Cuba.

[18] See Bruno Sedlaczek, Botschaft ... Beirut to Kurt Krüger, Solidaritätskomitee der DDR, Beirut (March 12, 1975), Besuche von Delegationen der PLO in der DDR, 1971, 1973–1979, PAAA MFAA (Ministerium für Auswärtige Angelegenheiten der DDR) Abteilung Naher- und Mittlereer Osten C 7678, 41–42. See "Sedlaczek, Bruno," in Bock et al., *DDR-Außenpolitik*, 353. PDFLP was the same as DPFLP.

[19] Bruno Sedlaczek, Botschaft ... Beirut to Kurt Krüger, Solidaritätskomitee der DDR, Beirut (March 12, 1975), 41–42.

At the United Nations, the Federal Republic's ambassador, Rüdiger von Wechmar (1923–2007), rose in opposition to Resolution 3379, stating that "the equation of Zionism with racism and racial discrimination is devoid of any foundation and therefore unacceptable" to the government of the Federal Republic. Adoption of the resolution would undermine "prospects for a peaceful settlement in the Middle East by inciting emotions and increasing passions through the introduction of racist notions." The Federal Republic believed that a peaceful settlement "must respect Israel's right to live within secure and recognized boundaries" as well as "the right of the Palestinian people to express its national identity" and a "termination of the territorial occupation" by Israel since 1967.[20] The representatives of Australia, Canada, Kenya, the Netherlands, Finland, Denmark, Norway, Luxembourg, Belgium, the Dominican Republic, and Austria also spoke out against the resolution.[21] The two most important dissents came from Israel's UN ambassador Chaim Herzog and United States UN ambassador Daniel Patrick Moynihan. (See Figure 9.1.) Both delivered long and memorable statements that became famous at the time. The following summary is important for this history of the German dimension because it recalls the historical, moral and political arguments that the East Germans heard but dismissed.

Herzog asserted that the resolution was an expression of anti-Semitism.[22] He said that it was fitting that the vote took place on November 10, the anniversary of Kristallnacht, the Nazi anti-Jewish pogrom of 1938. The UN, which had begun "as an anti-Nazi alliance," had become "the world centre of anti-Semitism. Hitler would have felt at home on a number of occasions during the past year, listening to the proceedings in this forum, and above all, to the proceedings during the debate on Zionism." The resolution was not only an "anti-Semitic attack of the foulest type but also an attack in this world body on the religion of Judaism. ..."[23] "Hatred and ignorance" were "the motivating force behind the proponents of this draft resolution and their supporters."[24] Zionism was "to the Jewish people what the liberation movements of Africa and Asia have

[20] Rüdiger von Wechmar, UNGA, 30th Session, 2400 Plenary Meeting, New York (November 10, 1975), UN ODS documents.un.org/ A/PV.2400; 784.

[21] For the full debate, see UNGA, 30th Session, 2400 Plenary Meeting, New York (November 10, 1975), UN ODS A/PV.2400, 769–806.

[22] Chaim Herzog, UNGA, 30th Session, 2400 Plenary Meeting, New York (November 10, 1975), UN ODS A/PV.2400, 773–776.

[23] Ibid., 773.

[24] Ibid.

FIGURE 9.1. Chaim Herzog, Israel's ambassador to the United Nations, in address to the General Assembly rejects the "Zionism Is Racism" resolution, November 10, 1975.
Source: United Nations Photo Library, 163036.

been to their peoples." It was based on "a unique and unbroken connection, extending some 4,000 years, between the People of the Book and the Land of the Bible." Zionism "was the revolt of an oppressed nation against the depredations and wicked oppression of the countries in which anti-Semitism flourished." It was, he continued, with reference to the Arab states, "no coincidence at all and not surprising that the sponsors and supporters of this draft resolution include countries which are guilty of the horrible crime of anti-Semitism and discrimination to this very day." The establishment of Israel was a "vindication of the fundamental concepts of the equality of nations and of self-determination." To deny the Jewish people that right accorded "to every other people on this globe" was "to deny the central precepts of the United Nations."[25] There were, he noted, 20 Arab states with "a hundred million people in four and a half million square miles, with vast resources." The issue was not when the world would come to terms with Arab nationalism but rather

[25] Ibid., 773–774.

when "Arab nationalism, with its prodigious glut of advantage, wealth and opportunity, will come to terms with the modest but equal rights of another Middle Eastern nation to pursue its life in security and peace."[26] He reminded the delegates of Andrei Gromyko's support in 1947 for the Partition Plan for a Jewish and Arab state.[27]

Herzog also discussed a refugee issue that the UN had neglected, namely, the expulsion of the Jews of North Africa and the Middle East since 1948. What, he asked, "has happened to the 800,000 Jews who lived for over 2,000 years in the Arab lands, who formed some of the most ancient communities long before the advent of Islam?" Where were those people, their property, and their communities? Noting their absence, he said, "Where are they in Arab society today? You dare talk of racism."[28] From 1973 to 1983, a decade the UN devoted to fighting racism and racial discrimination, the expulsion of the Jews from the Arab countries after 1948 was a topic that was of no interest either to the majority of states or to the United Nations. Both the East German regime and the West German and international radical Left were part of this broad consensus of indifference and disinterest.

Herzog criticized the majority for refusing to address "the bitter anti-Semitic, anti-Jewish hatred which animates Arab society." "Who would have believed" that in 1975, "the malicious falsehoods of the Elders of Zion would be distributed officially by Arab governments?" The Israelis were being "attacked by a society which is motivated by the most extreme form of racism known in the world today." Arafat had expressed it at a symposium in Tripoli, Libya, when he said that there would be "no presence in the region except for the Arab presence." For the Arab states and the PLO, from the Atlantic Ocean to the Persian Gulf, "only one presence is allowed, and that is the Arab presence. No other people, regardless of how deep are its roots in the region, is to be permitted to enjoy its right to self-determination."[29] The Jews, however, had a "long and proud history" in the face of oppression and evil. He faced the General Assembly "once again outnumbered, and the would-be victim of hate, ignorance and evil." The issue facing the member states

[26] Ibid., 773.

[27] Cited by Herzog, ibid., 774. For Gromyko's statement see, United Nations General Assembly, 77th Plenary Session (May 14, 1947), UN ODS A/2/PV.775.

[28] Herzog, UNGA (November 10, 1975), UN ODS A/2/PV.7, 775.

[29] Ibid., On the distribution of Arabic editions of *The Protocols of the Elders of Zion*, see Robert Wistrich, *A Lethal Obsession: Antisemitism from Antiquity to the Global Jihad* (New York: Random House, 2010), chs. 18–23.

was not Israel or Zionism. It was "the continued existence" of the United Nations, "which has been dragged to its lowest point of discredit by a coalition of despotisms and racists." Each delegation's vote would record "its country's stand on anti-Semitic racism and anti-Judaism." The Jewish people would not forget how the various countries voted. The resolution was "based on hatred, falsehood and arrogance." It was "devoid of any moral or legal value" and "was no more than a piece of paper."[30] The resolution that denounced Zionism as racism was itself a "racist," that is, anti-Semitic, document, which sought to obscure its hatred of the Jews and Judaism in the secular leftist rhetoric of anti-Zionism.

Moynihan spoke on November 10 after the vote was taken on 3379. He delayed his remarks because the American delegation concluded that the result was a forgone conclusion and thus did not want his opposition to offer a rationale for further support for the resolution.[31] He asserted that, first, "the resolution was a lie." That was so because Zionism was not a form of racism; second, if the UN could lie, a precedent would be established that could be turned against "the small and weak nations that voted for it"; and, third, that if it passed, the UN's Decade for Action against Racism and Racial Discrimination "would be dead."[32] The ambassador said, "The United States rises to declare before the General Assembly and before the world, that it does not acknowledge, it will not abide by, it will never acquiesce in this infamous act."[33] On November 10, "a great evil has been loosed upon the world. The abomination of anti-Semitism – as this year's Nobel Peace Laureate Andrei Sakharov observed in Moscow just a few days ago – has been given the appearance of international sanction." As the UN had declared Zionism to be a form of racism, it was necessary to assert "that is a lie, but it is a lie which the United Nations has now declared to be a truth, and so the actual truth must be restated."[34]

If, he continued, as the Soviet delegate declared, "racism is a form of Nazism, and if, as this resolution declared, Zionism is a form of racism, then we have step by step taken ourselves to the point of proclaiming that Zionism is a form of Nazism." This was a lie "scarcely exceeded" in the twentieth century's "annals of untruth and outrage. The lie is that

30 Herzog, UNGA (November 10, 1975), UN ODS A/PV.2400, 776.

31 Daniel Patrick Moynihan, UNGA, 30th Session, 2400 Plenary Meeting (November 10, 1975), UN ODS A/PV.2400, 795–798.

32 Daniel Patrick Moynihan, *A Dangerous Plans* (Boston: Little, Brown, 1978), 179.

33 Daniel Patrick Moynihan, UNGA (November 10, 1975), 795.

34 Ibid., 796.

Zionism is a form of racism. The overwhelmingly clear truth is that it is not."[35] Racism was commonly understood to mean the belief that there were biological differences among clearly identifiable groups, that such differences reflected different levels of humanity, and that some are inherently superior to others. Such a belief was "always altogether alien to the political and religious movement known as zionism." It was a national liberation movement that emerged in nineteenth-century Europe, a fact recognized by Soviet Foreign Minister Andrei Gromyko when, in 1948 at the UN, he deplored the decision of Israel's neighbors of "sending their troops into Palestine and carrying out military operations aimed" – in Mr. Gromyko's own words – "at the suppression of the national liberation movement in Palestine."[36]

The Zionist movement, in contrast to other national liberation movements then and since, "defined its members not in terms of birth but of belief." They were not members of a genetic pool. Zionism was a movement of Jews "and declared to be Jewish anyone born of a Jewish mother or – and this is the absolutely crucial fact – anyone who converted to Judaism." That is, "anyone – regardless of 'race, colour, descent, or national or ethnic origin'" was welcome. In Israel there were "black Jews, brown Jews, white Jews, Jews from the Orient and Jews from the West"; Jews who converted to Judaism; and large numbers of non-Jews including Arabs of both Muslim and Christian religions and Christians of other national origins. Hence, "whatever else Zionism may be, it is not and cannot be 'a form of racism.' In logic, the State of Israel could be, or could become many things but it could not become racist unless it ceased to be Zionist."[37]

Moynihan warned that there would be "terrible consequences" of the "terrible lie that has been told here today" for the cause of human rights. Indeed, "grave and perhaps irreparable harm will be done to the cause of human rights" because the UN resolution "will strip from racism the precise and abhorrent meaning that it still precariously holds today." What will happen to the need to struggle against racism if people are told that "it is an idea so broad as to include the Jewish national liberation

35 Ibid.

36 Ibid., 797. The Israeli delegation sent Moynihan a paper on past Soviet support for Israel. See "Soviet Zionism," Moynihan Papers, Box 345.

37 Ibid., 797. On the preparation for Moynihan's discussion of Zionism, see Norman Podhoretz to Ambassador Daniel Patrick Moynihan, New York (November 6, 1975), Moynihan Papers, Box 339.

movement?" How would "small nations of the world defend themselves ... when the language of human rights, the only language by which the small can be defended, is no longer believed and no longer has a power of its own."[38] Indeed, the loss could be irreversible. Despite Moynihan's argument, many of the small nations to which he referred voted for the Zionism Is Racism resolution.[39]

Two months later, on January 12, 1976, the UN Security Council took a vote on whether to allow the PLO to participate in its deliberations. Moynihan objected.[40] The PLO, he pointed out, was not a state. The UN was an organization of states. Efforts to allow the PLO to speak to the Security Council disregarded UN procedures and even gave it a role greater than the council had granted to observer states. The invitation "would open a veritable Pandora's box of future difficulties": "groups in all parts of the world [that] could seek to participate in our proceedings as if they were Member States." That would have "pernicious consequences" for existing states. Were the UN to change its rules, it would "look forward to welcoming the dissident factions and nationalities of half the world, for in point of fact roughly half the nations in the world today face serious to extreme problems of internal cohesion owing to internal ethnic conflict. This is true of more than half the present members of the Security Council."[41] Moreover, the PLO "does not recognize the right to exist of the State of Israel, which is a Member State, and whose right to exist is guaranteed by the Charter which the Council is pledged to uphold." Nor, he continued, did the PLO recognize the authority of the Security Council, whose Resolutions 242 (1967) and 338 (1973) upheld the rights of the states of the Middle East, including Israel, and their right to exist. Allowing the PLO to participate would also undermine negotiations with Israel, which the PLO has consistently rejected.[42] Nevertheless, the United States was the only member of the Security Council to vote against allowing the PLO to speak. France, Italy, the United Kingdom,

[38] Ibid.

[39] Several memos from Charles Fairbanks on the negative impact of the resolution on the cause of human rights also played a role in Moynihan's speech. See, Charles H. Fairbanks to Leonard Garment, New Haven (October 26, 1975), and Charles H. Fairbanks to Leonard Garment (October 30, 1976), Moynihan Papers, Box 343, 188–192 and 193–204.

[40] Daniel Patrick Moynihan (United States) United Nations Security Council, 1870th Meeting (January 12, 1976), S/PV.1870, 3–4.

[41] Ibid.

[42] Ibid., 4.

Benin, China, Guyana, Japan, Libyan Arab Republic, Pakistan, Panama, Romania, Sweden, the Soviet Union, and Tanzania voted in favor.[43]

On January 12, 1976, Farouk Kaddoumi delivered a 4,500-word statement to the UN Security Council.[44] He repeated the assertions of the PLO Charter of 1968 and said that the "Question of Palestine" was at the core of wars of 1948, 1967, and 1973. The "sinister design against the land and people of Palestine was formally initiated in 1917 with the issuance of the Balfour Declaration." Then "the tragedy of Palestinian dispersion commenced right here, in the United Nations, in the aftermath of the recommendation to partition Palestine in 1947 which was unjust and infamous."[45] The "Zionist enemy, in collaboration with its imperialist supporters" was betting that the Palestinian people "would capitulate." He accused Israel of practicing genocide. "For half a century various malicious attempts were made to liquidate the people of Palestine and dispose of our land. Acts of extinction, through either genocide or assimilation and emigration, have been attempted; all those attempts failed, and nothing weakened the resolve of our people." In the face of "aggression and treachery" and "despairing of a peaceful solution, we resorted to armed struggle to attain our national rights and to put an end to injustice and aggression." The UN Security Council should, "recognize our people's national inalienable rights and to assist it in realizing its national aspirations."[46]

Kaddoumi thereby objected to Israel's existence, not merely its policies. He made clear that the mainstream of the PLO supported an "armed struggle," whose aim was to destroy the existing state of Israel. He rejected the UN Partition Plan of 1947. Though the Palestinian negotiators in 1947 refused to engage in peace talks, Kaddoumi repeated the falsehood that the UN had not permitted them "to express their will." He did not mention that the Arab states had launched a war against Israel in 1948. Rather, it was "natural for the Zionist movement ... as a colonial racist movement, to undertake all measures designed to expel the Palestinians who came under its military control and to utilize the most vicious forms of terrorism to compel them to depart."[47] In 1965, despairing of a solution through negotiations, "we resumed our armed struggle" and "declared that armed struggle was the only means to

43 United Nations Security Council, 1870th Meeting (January 12, 1976), S/PV.1870, 12–13.
44 Farouk Kaddoumi, UNSC, 1870th Meeting (January 12, 1976), S/PV.1870, 16–21.
45 Ibid., 16.
46 Ibid., 16–17.
47 Ibid., 18.

achieve the liberation of our homeland and to attain our national rights" in the face of Zionist "expansionist objectives," which were "based on its racist, backward ideology." Because Israel had ignored UN resolutions, after 1967 "another war in the Middle East became inevitable to compel Israel to evacuate its occupation forces from Arab lands; hence, the 1973 war."[48] Kaddoumi also rejected UN Resolution 338 (1973), which ended the Yom Kippur War of 1973.

Kaddoumi said that the UN had failed to place the Palestinian issue at the center of its deliberations. He reminded the Security Council "that Egypt, Syria and Jordan were in a state of war with Israel before June 1967 and before October 1973, a state of war which had prevailed since 1948 and which was caused by the serious Zionist-imperialist attempt to liquidate the existence of Palestine and its national inalienable rights to independence and sovereignty."[49] The PLO was now in a state of war with Israel. It viewed the UN resolutions of 1947, 1967, and 1973 to be unjust and to have contributed to the oppression of the Palestinians. Despairing of peaceful options both with Israel and through the UN, "we resumed our revolution. We took up arms and had recourse to force in defence of our very existence, of our right to live in our land, and of our independence and sovereignty. While we carry out our armed struggle, we continue to hope to attain our goals through political options," that is, through its successful efforts with the majorities in the General Assembly.[50]

Kaddoumi pointed with pride to the Resolutions 3376, which created the Committee for the Exercise of the Inalienable Rights of the Palestinian People (CEIRIP), and 3375, which gave the PLO observer status at the UN. Both increased the PLO's hope "of reaching a just solution through the United Nations."[51] He said that the Palestinians' "inalienable rights" included the right to return to the land now illegally occupied by the Israelis and that "armed struggle" was necessary and justified to bring about that goal. The logical implication of his statement was to reaffirm the positions of the PLO Charter of 1968: if the PLO won its war against Israel, the vast majority of Jewish citizens of Israel would be expelled from the state that the PLO would establish. Nevertheless, Kaddoumi claimed that the PLO "rejects the false allegations propagated by Zionist and imperialist circles regarding its intention, or the intention of our

[48] Ibid., 19.
[49] Ibid.
[50] Ibid.
[51] Ibid., 20.

people, concerning the fate of the Jews in Palestine. Our struggle is not against the Jews. No, it is not against the Jews in Palestine, but against the Zionist movement, its racist doctrines, its expansionist practices and its aggressive intentions, which have led, in fact, to the exile and homelessness of our people."[52]

There were good reasons for the Israelis to be skeptical about Kaddoumi's reassurances. If the PLO was victorious, its charter demanded that most of Israel's Jewish citizens would be expelled, a process that would certainly have entailed massive loss of life and property. What would be the fate of the vast majority of Jews in Israel who did not think Zionism was a racist doctrine or that Israel was a colonial state but instead viewed Zionism as an admirable national liberation movement and Israel as a beloved homeland and a functioning liberal democracy? Presumably these "Zionists" would be guilty of association with an evil racist doctrine and even of genocide. Would not citizens of Israel with those views metamorphose from "Jews" to "Zionists" and, as such, become acceptable targets for the PLO's "armed struggle"? Given the PLO's record of terrorist attacks on Israeli civilians, the Israelis had good reason to be skeptical about the distinction Kaddoumi made between attacks on Zionists and on Jews. Yet the distinction between presumably good Jews and evil Zionists remained an effective tool in justifying terrorism against Israelis to foreign audiences who rejected open expressions of Jew hatred. Kaddoumi concluded that "a just and lasting peace" would not prevail in the Middle East "unless and until the historic, inalienable national rights of the Palestinian people are fully realized and Palestine resumes its historic role as a bridge between the Arab States west and east of Suez and between Africa and Asia." Until then, "our people" would "continue its just struggle by all legitimate means to attain its legitimate goals."[53] That is, the existence of the Jewish state was incompatible with a just and lasting peace. For the Israelis, Arafat and Kaddoumi used the language of antiracism to advance bigotry against the Jews. For the majority of member states in the UN General Assembly, anti-Zionism as a form of antiracism became a component of the predominant spirit of the age.

Farouk Kaddoumi's statement to the Security Council accurately conveyed the radicalism of the PLO's founding documents and continuing policies. Those who supported Resolutions 3375, 3376 and 3379 were

[52] Ibid., 21.
[53] Ibid.

supporting the PLO's war, the purpose of which was to destroy the state of Israel by force of arms. Yet the Soviet-bloc and East German diplomats at the UN combined support for these resolutions and the extremism they embodied with rhetorical fog about moderation, realism, and "political solutions."[54] East Germany's UN ambassador Peter Florin spoke to the UN Security Council on January 19, 1976. (See Figure 9.2.) Florin was particularly skillful in making extremism sound reasonable and terror seem justified.[55] He praised the resolutions passed by the 30th session of the General Assembly, which constituted "a further step forward in the history of the struggles of peoples for peace, security, disarmament and social progress against the imperialist policies of aggression, oppression and exploitation."[56] Israel's "continuing aggression," its obstinate refusal to withdraw from territories occupied in 1967, and to "recognize the legitimate rights of the Arab people of Palestine" endangered "world peace."[57] Realism demanded that one acknowledge that the PLO was "the sole legitimate representative of the Arab people of Palestine" and should be involved in the search for a solution to the Middle East conflict "on an equal footing," that is, on an equal footing with Israel.[58] Florin's appeal to realism left some questions unanswered. What was realistic about declaring the PLO, which had never run in a free election, to be the sole legitimate representative of the Palestinian people? How could a small country such as Israel be a danger to "world" peace? Was this exaggeration of the role of Israel's role in world politics not an echo of past anti-Semitic inflations of Jewish power and influence?

[54] It was a continuing theme. For example, on December 9, 1977, Gunter Mauersberger, the first secretary of the East German delegation to the UN, wrote the following assessment of Kaddoumi. The PLO speaker "sought to demonstrate the constructive and flexible role of his organization by pointing to Arafat's statement in 1974 to the UN in favor of a multi-religious state in Palestine and to the decision of the Palestine National Council in 1976 to build an independent Palestinian state on liberated territory." Yet Arafat's statement to the UN had repeated the core of the radicalism of the PLO's 1968 Charter. The Palestine National Council's decision of 1976 also restated that radicalism because its definition of "liberated territory" included all of Israel. Gunter Mauersberger, "Die Behandlung des TOP 'Palästinafrage' in Plenum der Vollversammlung," New York (December 9, 1977), 1–4, in PAAA MFAA, Abt. UNO, ZR 330/82, "Berichte über die Behandlung des Tagesordungspunktes 'Palästinafrage' auf der XXXII.–XXXIV. Tagung der UN-Vollversammlung, 1977–1979." See "Mauersberger, Günter," in Bock et al., *DDR Aussenpolitik*, 332.

[55] Peter Florin (German Democratic Republic), UNSCOR, 1876th Meeting (January 19, 1976), UN ODS S/PV.1876, 14–16.

[56] Ibid., 14

[57] Ibid., 15.

[58] Florin, UNSCOR (January 19, 1976), UN ODS S/PV.1876, 15.

FIGURE 9.2. Peter Florin (left), East German ambassador to the United Nations, offers his credentials to Kurt Waldheim, general secretary of the United Nations, in New York, September 20, 1973.
Source: Bild 183-M0921-014, ADN –ZB, Joachim Spremberg, Bundesarchiv Koblenz, Bildarchiv (German Federal Archive, Koblenz Photo Archiv).

Florin added that it was a "source of honor and pride" for East Germany to support "the people of Palestine struggling for the realization of their inalienable rights just as it also stands side by side with the people of a young African state which is obliged to defend itself against the aggression of South African racists."[59] The comparison of Israel to apartheid South Africa was another repeated theme of the anti-Zionist campaign. The "ruling circles" in Israel had "not yet grasped that an aggressive policy based on the Zionist concept of aggression is doomed to failure." The UN's 30th session had shown that "the aggressor and his accomplices were in a state of international isolation." The Israelis had to realize that "the times have changed." The East German ambassador warned the Israelis that there would not be peace in the Middle East, "nor will there be any security for Israel," if Israel continued an "aggressive and annexationist policy" and pursued "annexationist plans."[60] In

[59] Ibid., 15.
[60] Ibid.,16.

other words, the policies of Israel justified the war being waged against it, a war that East Germany was supporting.

As noted previously, on November 10, 1975, the General Assembly also voted in favor of Resolution 3376, which established the Committee on the Exercise of the Inalienable Rights of the Palestinian People (CEIRPP). The committee served as the political and intellectual center of the assault on Israel and support for the PLO at the United Nations. Of the 147 states that were then members of the United Nations, 20, including East Germany, were founding members of the committee: Afghanistan, Cuba, Cyprus, German Democratic Republic, Guinea, Hungary, India, Indonesia, Laos, Madagascar, Malaysia, Malta, Pakistan, Romania, Senegal, Sierra Leone, Tunisia, Turkey, Ukrainian Soviet Socialist Republic, and Yugoslavia.[61] The presence of the East Germans along with Hungary, Romania, and the Ukrainian SSR and Cuba illustrated the importance that the Soviet Union gave to the formation of the CEIRPP. Chaim Herzog declared that Israel would not cooperate with the proposed committee as it arose out of an "entirely one-sided, biased and partial" resolution and was "irreconcilable with the process of negotiation towards peace in the Middle East."[62] However, the purpose of CEIRPP was not to foster negotiations with Israel but to make the case for its destruction.

On February 24, 1976, CEIRPP held its first meeting at the United Nations in New York. As one of the 20 founding members of the committee, East Germany supported implementation of General Assembly Resolutions 3236, adopted in 1974, that reaffirmed "the inalienable right of the Palestinians to return to their homes and property from which they have been displaced and uprooted" and "calls for their return."[63] The right of return was inseparable from a view that Israel's origins lay in an act or acts of displacement, that this displacement was an injustice, and that therefore the Palestinians had an "inalienable right" to return. On February 26, 1976, Bernhard Neugebauer (1932–), East Germany's deputy permanent representative to the United Nations from 1978 to 1990, reaffirmed the "the right of the Palestinians to return to their homes and

[61] Papa Louis Fall, "Pending Appointments," UNGA, 30th Session, 2443rd Plenary Meeting (December 17, 1975), UN ODS, A/PV.2443, 1357.

[62] Chaim Herzog, "Pending Appointments," UNGA, 30th Session, 2443rd Plenary Meeting (December 17, 1975), UN ODS A/PV.2443, 1357.

[63] "Committee on Exercise of Rights of Palestinian People to Meet," *United Nations Press Release*, New York (February 24, 1976), GA/PAL/1 (1876).

their property from which they have been displaced and uprooted."[64] While Palestinian self-determination and a state could be compatible with a two-state compromise solution, the implementation of a right of return was impossible without the destruction of the state of Israel, its replacement with another political entity, and the expulsion of the vast majority of the Jewish population. That was the program that East Germany and the 19 other founding members of CEIRPP supported.

Support for the Palestinians' right to return was an ironic position for the East German government to adopt. In the last months of World War II and in the first several years after the war, approximately 11 million German-speaking citizens from the countries of Eastern Europe were expelled or fled to Western Europe. Some of the Communist regimes defended the expulsions as "anti-fascist" measures. In West Germany, the refugees formed "expellee" organizations and raised the issue of their right to return to their homes in Eastern Europe. The Communist regimes, including the GDR, denounced a right of these Germans to return to homes in Eastern Europe as "revanchism" and a threat to peace and stability in Europe. They insisted on abandonment of a right of return as a price to be paid for peace and stability in Europe. East Germany thus adopted the position that a right of return of expelled Germans to their former homes in Eastern Europe endangered peace but its implementation for Palestinians in the Middle East was a precondition for peace.[65]

Neugebauer's statement illustrated both the Soviet-bloc use of the UN machinery against Israel as well as Communist optimism that the global

[64] "Statement by the representative of the German Democratic Republic at the first meeting of the Committee on 26 February 1976," UNGA, Committee on the Exercise of the Inalienable Rights of the Palestinian People (hereafter CEIRPP) (March 18, 1976), A/AC.183/L.6/. These and all other documents from CEIRPP are available online at the committee Website, unispal.un.org/unispal.nsf/Web%20Search%20Simple2?OpenForm. Neugebauer was the East German representative at the CEIRPP's first meeting. See Department of Public Information, United Nations New Coverage Service, New York, "Committee on Inalienable Rights of Palestinian People Holds First Meeting, Elects Chairman" (February 26, 1976), unispal.un.org/UNISPAL.NSF/0/C51A9B87B8298 1D705256613006D7F44. Ibid. "Neugebauer, Bernhard, geb. 1932," in Bock et al., *DDR-Außenpolitik*, 338. Neugebauer had served in the East German Foreign Ministry since 1953 and was an assistant to deputy foreign minister Otto Winzer (1958–1961), among other positions, before serving for 14 years at the UN in New York.

[65] On the expellee issue in West German politics see Pertti Ahonen, *After the Expulsion: West Germany and Eastern Europe 1945–1990* (New York: Oxford University Press, 2004). Abandonment of a right to return was seen in West Germany as an indispensable component first of détente and then of the unification of Germany and the end of the Cold War.

balance of forces was tilting in its favor. First, the UN passed one-sided anti-Israeli resolutions. Then Israel rejected them and was criticized, in Neugebauer's words, for ignoring "numerous resolutions of the General Assembly and of the Security Council concerning the relaxation of tensions in the Middle East and the political settlement of the conflict." Did they not yet understand that "a policy based on a Zionist concept of aggression and a false estimate of the international balance of force is doomed to failure?"[66] He added that "everybody" knew that Israel was completely at fault for the absence of peace in the Middle East, and that it was now flouting the opinion of the UN General Assembly. Yet the "international balance of forces" was shifting in favor of the PLO, in part because of "the long-standing and growing alliance with the Arab people of Palestine and its only legitimate representative, the PLO" with the Soviet bloc. It was, he concluded, "appropriate" that CEIRPP "invited the PLO to participate in its proceedings."[67]

On November 19, 1976, Florin addressed the General Assembly about what in those years everyone called "the" Middle East conflict. He stated that the "inalienable rights" of the Palestinians "included Israel's withdrawal from all the Arab territories it occupied in June 1967."[68] Florin's reference to "in" rather than "since" 1967 kept open the possibility that an Israeli withdrawal to the 1967 lines would be only part of a settlement and that "all Arab territories" could, as the PLO insisted, include all of Israel itself. Again, Florin's skill lay in making policies that would lead to the destruction of Israel sound like realistic efforts to produce peace in the Middle East. He found it "regrettable" that one of the participants in the debate, presumably the United States, "followed Israel's example of slanderous attacks directed against the front-line warriors of the Palestinian people." He reiterated East Germany's "determination to give the PLO all possible support."[69] It was essential that the UN not be sidetracked by "secondary questions," presumably questions such as terrorism or anti-Semitism, because the "key problem was and remains Israel's continuing aggression." He placed the entire responsibility for the

[66] "Statement by the representative of the German Democratic Republic at the first meeting of the Committee on 26 February 1976."

[67] Ibid. Also see "Statement by the representative of the German Democratic Republic at the first meeting of the Committee on 11 May," UNGA, CEIRPP (May 14, 1976), A/AC.183/L.27/, unispal.un.org/unispal.nsf/9a798adbf322aff38525617b006d88d7/9d828092b0b7aa7085256e31006d4239?OpenDocument.

[68] Peter Florin, New York (November 19, 1976), UNGA, A/31/PV.72, United Nations Archive, New York.

[69] Ibid.

conflict on Israel, on what he called its aggressive and racist policies, and on its key supporter, the United States.

On November 24, 1976, East Germany joined 27 other states in co-sponsoring UN General Assembly Resolution 31/20, "The Question of Palestine." It was adopted by the General Assembly by a vote of 90 to 16 with 30 abstentions. East Germany voted yes; West Germany voted no.[70] The resolution referred to a CEIRPP report that linked attainment of "a just and lasting peace in the Middle East" to "a just solution of the problem of Palestine on the basis of the attainment of the inalienable rights of the Palestinian people, including the right of return and the right to national independence and sovereignty in Palestine."[71] It further called for circulation of the CEIRPP report to "all the competent bodies of the United Nations" and to non-governmental organizations. It also called on the UN secretary general "to give the widest possible publicity to the Committee's work and to provide the Committee with the necessary facilities for the performance of its tasks, including summary records of its meetings."[72] Resolution 31/20 indicated broad UN support for placing the information dissemination machinery of the UN at the disposal of the Palestine Liberation Organization. Several weeks later, on December 9, 1976, East Germany joined 91 General Assembly members to vote in favor of Resolution 31/61. There were 11 no votes and 29 abstentions. The resolution requested "that all States desist from supplying Israel with military and other forms of aid or any assistance which would enable it to consolidate its occupation or to exploit the nature resources of the occupied territories."[73] Reports on "the living conditions of the Palestinian people" and denunciations of Israeli policies in the occupied territories by various UN special committees in fall and winter 1976 were also passed by similarly lopsided margins. In each instance the East Germans found themselves in the midst of the huge anti-Israeli majority while West Germany either voted no or abstained.[74]

70 "The Question of Palestine, Resolution 31/20," *Yearbook of the United Nations, 1976*, vol. 30 (New York: Office of Public Information, United Nations, 1976), 245–246. The other sponsors were Afghanistan, Bangladesh, Comoros, Congo, Cuba, Cyprus, Guinea, Hungary, India, Indonesia, Lao People's Democratic Republic, Madagascar, Malaysia, Maldives, Mali, Malta, Pakistan, Romania, Senegal, Sierra Leone, Sri Lanka, Tunisia, Turkey, Uganda, Ukrainian SSR, United Republic of Tanzania, and Yugoslavia.

71 Ibid.

72 Ibid.

73 "Resolution 31/61" (December 9, 1976), *Yearbook of the United Nations, 1976*, vol. 30 (New York: Office of Public Information, United Nations, 1976), 246–247.

74 *Yearbook of the United Nations, 1976*, vol. 30 (New York: Office of Public Information, United Nations, 1976), 247–263.

On December 2, 1977, Resolution 32/40 repeated the appeal to place UN resources at the disposal of CEIRPP. It passed by a vote of 110 to 12 with 29 abstentions.[75] The United States and the Federal Republic of Germany were among the 12 nations that joined Israel in opposing this resolution. As CEIRPP defined implementation of the Palestinians' "inalienable rights" to include the right of return, a huge majority of the members of the United Nations General Assembly in 1977 again affirmed that a "just and lasting peace" in the Middle East required the end of the state of Israel. As had been the case since the mid-1960s, East Germany's antagonism to Israel won it friends around the world. Conversely, West Germany's support for Israel at the UN displeased Israel's third-world antagonists.

The Soviet-bloc diplomats at the UN also fought effective battles about the meaning of key words. Two words, "aggression" and "terrorism," were of particular importance. In October 1974, the UN's Sixth Committee issued a report "on the question of Defining Aggression." Gunter Görner, East Germany's representative on the committee from 1972 to 1990, spoke on the issue on October 15.[76]

> Our delegation has noted with particular satisfaction that the definition of aggression reaffirms the right of peoples under colonial and racist rule or under other forms of alien domination to struggle for self-determination, freedom and independence and to seek and receive support to that end. As colonial rule, apartheid and other forms of alien suppression constitute a permanent aggression against the oppressed peoples, resistance against these forms of external use of force and suppression is an act of self-defence. Any assistance in that struggle for independence and self-determination, both in the form of political and material aid, are therefore in conformity with the United Nations Charter and other documents of the United Nations, including the Declaration Granting of Independence to Colonial Countries and peoples of 14 December 1960.[77]

When combined with the UN resolutions of the 1970s on "the question of Palestine," this definition of aggression again meant that Israel's existence, not only its policies, constituted a case of aggression. Therefore, Palestinian terrorism was a justified form of "self-defense." In addition, this definition legitimated Soviet-bloc arms shipments to the Arab states

[75] "Resolution 32/40" (December, 1977), *Yearbook of the United Nations, 1977*, vol. 31 (New York: Office of Public Information, United Nations, 1976), 303–304.

[76] "Statement made by Dr. Gunter Görner in the Sixth Committee on agenda item 86: 'Report of the Special Committee on the Question of Defining Aggression' on October 15, 1974," PAAA MFAA Abt. Recht: Berichte und Positionspapiers zu den 28.-34. UNO-Vollversammlungen, 6. Komitee, C3765-3774, Bd. 1–10, 118–119.

[77] Ibid., 118.

and the PLO and other armed groups as efforts to support battles against colonialism. To deter future aggressors, he added that "any act of aggression is a crime against world peace and gives rise to international responsibility."[78] As the Soviet Union and East Germany had described Israel's wars of 1948, 1967, and 1973 as wars of aggression and thus "an international crime," it followed that "changes of the situation unlawfully brought about by the aggressor are null and void."[79] With these definitions, the results of Israel's these major wars in the Middle East would be declared "null and void."[80]

Also in 1977, the East German delegation participated in debates about the definition of terrorism in a UN Ad Hoc Committee on International Terrorism. Its official position was that it "rejects any act of international terrorism," whether by "individuals, groups of persons or States," because terrorism interfered with "peaceful cooperation among States" and obstructed "the process of international détente." However, it called for further study of "the underlying causes of international terrorism," which it viewed as "the policy of aggression and oppression pursued by some imperialist states.... State terrorism of colonial, racist and other reactionary regimes has an especially pernicious effect."[81] The East Germans stated that certain forms of resort to force were not terrorism. They included "the struggle, including armed struggle, against colonial and racist regimes and against other forms of alien domination which the national liberation movements wage in accordance with the purposes and principles of the United Nations and the relevant resolutions of the United Nations organs." These resorts to force "should not be impaired."[82] As the East Germans defined the activities of the PLO and affiliated organizations as an "armed struggle" of that nature, they rejected the application of the word "terrorism" to describe its armed attacks on Israel. In 1974, when the Egyptian delegate to the UN's Sixth Committee suggested inviting the PLO to a conference on international terrorism, the Israeli delegate objected. The East German diplomat's

[78] Ibid.

[79] Ibid., 119.

[80] "Abschlussbericht über die Ergebnisse der Arbeit des 6. Komitees, XXIX UN-Vollversammlung," New York (December 11, 1974), PAAA MFAA Abt. Recht: Berichte und Positionspapiers zu den 28.-34. UNO-Vollversammlungen, 6. Komitee, C 3765–3774, Bd. 1–10, Bd. 2, 1974 C 3766, 149–152.

[81] "Position of the German Democratic Republic pursuant to General Assembly Resolution 32/147 of 16 December 1977," PAAA MFAA Abt. Recht: Berichte und Positionspapiers zu den 28.-34. UNO-Vollversammlungen, 6. Komitee, Bd. 8 1977, C 3772, 1–3.

[82] Ibid., 2.

report about the objection stated that the Israeli delegate "defamed the PLO as a terrorist organization which murders innocent people.... The defamation by the Israeli representative was rejected by the Egyptian representative in an objective manner."[83] According to these definitions of aggression and terrorism, the PLO, which intentionally attacked Israeli civilians, was not a terrorist organization. Rather, it was Israel, which made extensive efforts to avoid causing civilian casualties, that this Ad Hoc Committee on terrorism described as pursuing policies of terrorism. In so doing, these definitions transformed the Arab states, which had threatened Israel with destruction in 1967, launched a surprise attack in 1973, and, with Egypt's exception, refused to recognize it, into victims of Israeli aggression.

These positions were articulated in an unsigned 10-page "position paper" from the East German UN delegation that reported on the discussions in the "Ad Hoc Committee on International Terrorism."[84] The Soviet-bloc states denounced both international terrorism as well as what they called "the pretext of fighting acts of terror" to act "against the national liberation movements." Such policies rested on an overly "broad definition of international terrorism." Rather it was essential to focus on "the social and political origins of international terrorism" that they saw "especially in the imperialist, colonial and racist forms of the exercise of power." These causes needed to be "set aside."[85] One case of international terrorism was of particular interest for the Ad Hoc Committee. The delegates from Czechoslovakia and East Germany described "the Israeli attack (on the airport in Entebbe Uganda) last year" as "a dangerous action of international terrorism for which there is no justification."[86] Along with Algeria, Egypt, India, Indonesia, Libya, Nigeria, Sri Lanka, Uganda, Yemen, Yugoslavia, and Zaire they supported a resolution that found "the roots of terrorism in colonialism, racism and foreign domination."[87]

[83] "Bericht über die Arbeit im 6. Komitee der XXIX. Vollversammlung in der Zeit vom 23. September bis 3. Okotber 1974," PAAA MFAA Abt. Recht: Berichte und Positionspapiers zu den 28.-34. UNO-Vollversammlungen, 6. Komitee, Bd. 2, 1974 C 3766, 20. Ibid., 149.

[84] "Positionspapier ... Diskussion zu Fragen des internationalen Terrorismus im 6. Komitee der XXXI. Vollversammlung als auch im Ad-hoc-Komitee, das vom 14–25.3. 1977 in New York," PAAA MFAA Abt. Recht: Berichte und Positionspapiers zu den 28.-34. UNO-Vollversammlungen, 6. Komitee, C3765-3774, Bd. 1–10, Bd. 7, 3771, 298–306.

[85] Ibid., 298.

[86] Ibid., 299.

[87] Ibid., 302.

The report noted a shift in the Sixth Committee toward the Soviet-bloc view. "In contrast to the past year [1976], the defense of the right of peoples to self-determination and independence, and the justification for the use of force and violence in all forms by national liberation movements assumed a central place in the various statements." The report drew attention to the disagreement between the "socialist," that is, Communist, regimes and "non-aligned" states with "the imperialist states" about the causes of international terrorism. There were differences as well over the effort to "equate international terrorism with the actions of national liberation movements exercising their right to self-determination."[88] The East German diplomats agreed that "state terrorism" was "the most dangerous and serious form of international terrorism" and was "very often the cause of terrorist attacks by individuals or groups of individuals" who were responding to "massive violations of human rights" by policies of "colonialism, racism and apartheid."[89] Because the UN's Resolution 3379 of November 1975 had declared Zionism to be a form of racism, the consequence of these definitions was again to provide justification for PLO terrorist attacks by describing them as justified resistance to violations of human rights.

After the airplane hijackings of the mid-1970s, especially those in Entebbe and Mogadishu, West Germany took the lead in proposing UN resolutions denouncing hostage-taking and attacks on civilian aviation.[90] The East Germans, on the other hand, viewed the issue of hostage-taking "only as a partial problem," which "cannot be separated from examination and explanation of the question of international terrorism in its totality."[91] The "question of the definition of certain concepts, especially 'hostage taking' and 'hostage' " and of "eliminating the causes leading to hostage taking" had to be "in the center" of discussions. The UN's Ad Hoc Committee on International Terrorism had to ensure that any international convention against hostage-taking did not damage "the right of

88 Ibid., 305.

89 "Entwurf: 32. Tagung der UN-Vollversammlung: Rede eine Vertreters der Deutschen Demokratischen Republik zum TOP auf der XXXII. UN-Vollversammlung," PAAA MFAA Abt. Recht: Berichte und Positionspapiers zu den 28–34. UNO-Vollversammlungen, 6. Komitee, C3765-3774, Bd. 1–10, 307–309.

90 The files of the West German Foreign Ministry on domestic and international terrorism, airplane hijacking, and efforts to persuade the UN to take action against it are extensive. See PAAA, Bestand 83, Referat 511, Strafrecht, Steurer-und Zollercht, 1952–1952, 1973–1994.

91 "Entwurf: 32. Tagung der UN-Vollversammlung: Rede eine Vertreters der Deutschen Demokratischen Republik zum TOP auf der XXXII. UN-Vollversammlung," 309.

peoples to self-determination and independence" and would avoid "every misuse of such a convention to damage the legitimate liberation struggles of oppressed peoples."[92] This verbiage offered justification of hostage-taking so long as it was undertaken in what the Soviet and third-world bloc called a national liberation struggle. Specifically, the preceding arguments could justify hostage-taking by the Palestinians in various airplane hijackings or at the Munich Olympics in 1972. This redefinition of the meaning of "hostage" had added serious implications. For if, as the UN had now declared, Israel was a racist state based on aggression, then all of the citizens of Israel could be said to be engaged in an ongoing violation of the rights of Palestinians. If so, the distinction between soldiers and civilians would vanish, to be replaced by the all-encompassing label "Zionists." These qualifications and redefinitions could thus serve to justify seizing Israeli citizens, none of whom would be considered non-combatants, as hostages. At least such definitions would justify the East German policy of silence in the face of attacks on Israeli civilians.

East Germany's support for radicalism in the Middle East was evident in its opposition to the Camp David Accords of September 1978. They called for Israeli withdrawal from the Sinai and establishment of diplomatic relations with Egypt. In November, Erich Honecker assured Arafat of his opposition to the agreement. In December, Arafat wrote to Honecker to denounce the accords as a "conspiracy" that only "deepened the Zionist occupation of Arab territory."[93] On March 26, 1979, the peace treaty between Egypt and Israel that followed from the Camp David Accords of the previous year was signed in Washington, DC On the same day, Yasser Arafat wrote to Erich Honecker to denounce the "aggressive actions of USA-imperialism" in the Middle East.[94] "Without the realization of the inalienable national rights and goals of our Arab Palestinian people, including the right of return, self-determination and creation of an independent state on national territory, there can be no

[92] Ibid.

[93] Erich Honecker to Yasser Arafat, [East] Berlin (November 24, 1978) and Yasser Arafat to Erich Honecker [Beirut] (December 5, 1978), PAAA MFAA C 7667 Abt. Naher- und Mittlerer Osten, "Noten und Schreiben außenpolitischen Charakters zwischen der DDR und der Palästinensischen Befreiungsbewegung zur Unterstützung der PLO durch die DDR, 1972, 1974, 1978–1979," 33–37.

[94] Yasser Arafat to Erich Honecker, Beirut (March 26, 1979), PAAA MFAA C 7667 Abt. Naher- und Mittlerer Osten, "Noten und Schreiben außenpolitischen Charakters zwischen der DDR und der Palästinensischen Befreiungsbewegung zur Unterstützung der PLO durch die DDR, 1972, 1974, 1978–1979," 15–17.

peace in this region." The Palestinians rejected "this conspiracy" [the Camp David Accords and the Egyptian-Israeli Peace Treaty, JH].[95] Four days later, Honecker assured Arafat that he regarded the "separate peace" as a "serious barrier" to a "just and lasting peace in the Middle East" because it "ignored the will and rights of the Palestinian people and other peoples in the region." Honecker called for Israel's "complete withdrawal" to the 1967 lines and the realization of the Palestinians' right to their own national state. Though he did not add support for the right of return, he wrote that "our common struggle against the conspiracy of imperialism and reaction will lead to the implementation of the legitimate rights of the Palestinian people and to victory for the just struggle of the Arab peoples."[96]

A report by a member of the East German delegation on November 7, 1978, about Israeli participation in a UNRWA (United Nations Relief and Works Agency) committee dealing with Palestinian refugees conveyed the hostility that surrounded Israel at the UN. According to the East German representative, the Israeli representative had "defamed the brotherly assistance of the socialist countries" by claiming that East Germany "delivered weapons" to the PLO. The GDR and the USSR had "rejected these slanders."[97] The Israelis, he continued, "disrupted the work of the committee with presumptuous and arrogant 'commentaries'" about the statements of others. They called for moderation and urged committee members to support the Camp David Accords. At the 1978 UN General Assembly session debates about the Palestinian issue, "the efforts of Israel and its imperialist allies to misuse the forum to propagate their proposals for a separate peace failed as a result of the firm stance of most of the Arab states and their socialist allies. Israel was again pilloried as the aggressor."[98] East German bonds with Israel's enemies were as evident in

95 Ibid., 16.

96 Erich Honecker to Yasser Arafat Yasser [East] Berlin (March 30, 1979), PAAA MFAA C 7667 Abt. Naher- und Mittlerer Osten, Noten und Schreiben außenpolitischen Charakters zwischen der DDR und der Palästinensischen Befreiungsbewegung zur Unterstützung der PLO durch die DDR, 1972, 1974, 1978–1979, 20–21.

97 S. Schade, Abschlussbericht zum TOP 54: UN-Hilfswerk für Palästinaflüchtlinge im Nahen Osten (UNRWA), New York (November 7, 1978), 120123. Politisches Archiv des Auswärtiges Amt, Ministerium für Auswärtige Angelegenheiten der DDR (MFAA) Abt. Naher- und Mittlerer Osten, ZR 2066/2067/81, Tätigkeit von UN-Spezialorganisationen und der UNRWA zur Unterstützung des palstinensischen Volkes, C 7682 Bd. 1 1975–1976, B 7683, Bd. 2 1978–1979.

98 Ibid.

these behind-the-scenes committee meetings as they were in the public debates in the General Assembly and in the pages of *Neues Deutschland*. Behind the scenes and in public discussions at the UN, East Germany played an important role in the distortion of the meaning of key words such as "racism," "aggression," and "terrorism" that was one of the most important products of the United Nations in these years.

10

The Entebbe Hijacking and the West German "Revolutionary Cells"

On June 27, 1976, Wilfried Böse and Brigitte Kuhlmann, members of the West German Revolutionary Cells (*Revolutionäre Zellen* or *RZ*, hence RC), together with comrades from the Popular Front for the Liberation of Palestine (PFLP) hijacked an Air France plane with 248 passengers on board and forced the pilots at gunpoint to land the plane at the airport in Entebbe, Uganda. There the terrorists were warmly greeted by Uganda's president, Idi Amin. The hijackers separated the Israelis and Jews from the larger group of hostages. In the next two days, using passports as identifiers, they released 148 non-Israeli and non-Jewish passengers, keeping more than 100 Israelis, some non-Israeli Jews, and the non-Jewish pilot as hostages. For the government of Israel, the question of whether the hijackers were motivated by anti-Semitism or "merely" by anti-Zionism was irrelevant. As its citizens were now hostage only because they were citizens of the Jewish state, it had a responsibility to do all it could to free them. The RC and PFLP demanded the release of 53 terrorists held in prisons in France, Israel, Switzerland, Kenya, and West Germany and threatened to kill the remaining Israeli hostages unless their demands were met. The prisoners whom the PFLP/RC team sought to have released included six members of the Red Army Faction in West German, Swiss, and French prisons as well as the surviving member of the Japanese Red Army squad that had perpetrated the Lod airport massacre in Tel Aviv in 1972.[1] That same day the office of the PFLP in Aden,

[1] Embassy of Federal Republic of Germany in Yemen to Auswärtiges Amt, Bonn, Referat 511, "Aus: Kampala nr. 161 vom 29.06.1976 an Bonn, betr.: entführung air bus der air france nach kampala, hier: forderungen der entführer)," PAAA B 83, Nr. 1422, 510–530.36 UGA Flugzeugentführung Terrorismus. The names of the RAF prisoners were Werner Hoppe, Jan Carl Raspe, Ingrid Schubert, Ralf Reinders, Inge Vieth, Fritz Teufel, Petra Krause, Impar Sliova Masimia, and Kozo Okamato of the Japanese Red Army.

Yemen, issued a communiqué claiming that it had captured the French aircraft "to declare to the world that the French state is a historical enemy of our Arab nation" and to denounce French assistance to Israel.[2] The PFLP's goals were "the complete liberation of the Palestinian soil, the expulsion of the Zionists and the setting up of a democratic, secular, socialist state in Palestine."[3] "Nazism," the statement asserted, "whether in Germany or in Israel will not be forgiven by history for the crimes it committed against Arab strugglers and their comrades." It advocated that "rifles be raised in the face of the imperialist Zionist enemy, the enemy of mankind, civilization and progress" in order to "free the world of the chains and handcuffs imposed on it by capitalism, imperialism, reaction and Zionism."[4]

On July 4, Israel conducted a military raid that freed the more than 100 hostages held at the airport. In the course of the raid, 3 hostages died, as did all of the hijackers; the commander of the Israel forces, Yoni Netanyahu, and 20 Ugandan soldiers. Dora Block, an elderly Jewish hostage, was then murdered while in a hospital in Kampala. At the Entebbe airport, the West German members of the RC, Böse and Kuhlmann, who were both killed in the gunfight with the Israelis, became the first Germans since the Holocaust to point machine guns at unarmed Jews and, as far as we know, the first Germans to exchange fire with Israeli armed forces. Böse and Kuhlmann's participation in the Entebbe attack was one of the most important and widely publicized examples of the cooperation between the West German terrorist organizations and the PFLP in this era.[5]

In deciding to work with Amin, the RC and the PFLP threw in their lot with a man whose admiration for Hitler and for mass murder of Jews in Europe had been, as noted, on the record since his 1972 public letter to Kurt Waldheim, Yasser Arafat, and Golda Meir. In 1973, Amin again publicly expressed his visceral anti-Semitism. The *New York Times* reported that at a reception for the Soviet ambassador in Uganda's

[2] "Political Statement about the Operation for the Hijacking of the French Aircraft," Aden (June 29, 1976), PAAA B 83, Nr. 1422, 510–530.36 UGA Flugzeugentführung Terrorismus, 1.

[3] Ibid., 2–3.

[4] Ibid., 4.

[5] On the connections of West German leftist terrorist organizations with the PFLP, see Thomas Skelton Robinson, "Im Netz verheddert: Die Beziehungen des bundesdeutschen Linksterrorismus zur Volksfront für die Befreiung Palästina (1969–1980)," in Wolfgang Kraushaar, ed., *Die RAF und der linke Terrorismus* (Hamburg: Hamburger Edition, 2006), 828–904; and Martin Jander, "German Leftist Terrorism and Israel: Ethno-Nationalist, Religious-Fundamentalist, or Social-Revolutionary?," *Studies in Conflict & Terrorism*, Vol. 38, No. 6 (June 2015), 456–477.

capital, Kampala, Amin said that he was convinced he was right when he stated that "if Hitler had not slain the Jews, the present problem in the Middle East would be occurring now in the Soviet Union and the whole of Europe" and that "the people of the world would agree with him that the Israelis were criminals."[6] On October 17, 1973, at a press conference in Damascus, Syria, he said that "the American government is controlled by Jews.... Nixon has to follow the advice given him by the Zionist-like Secretary of State, Henry Kissinger."[7] In response to those comments and to his threats against Americans in Uganda, the United States closed its embassy in Kampala the following month. In working with Amin in Entebbe, the distinction between anti-Zionism and hatred of the Jews – anti-Semitism – vanished. The two hatreds merged into one. In both their collaboration with the PFLP and the actions they took in Entebbe, Böse and Kuhlmann became, along with Dieter Kunzelmann and Ulrike Meinhof, the most consequential West German leftists who had overcome their "Jewish complex."

The United Nations Security Council met from July 4 to 14, 1976, to discuss the events in Entebbe. It did not do so in response to Israel's request to discuss terrorism and hostage-taking. Rather it acted in response to a request from members of the Organization of African Unity "to consider the aggression of Zionist Israel against the sovereignty and territorial integrity of Uganda." The agenda was set by those who denounced Israel's raid that freed the hostages.[8] A joint British and American resolution to "condemn hijacking and all other acts which threatened the lives of passengers and crews" failed to attain a majority.[9] Jogo Ores

[6] "Amin Says War Confirms His View on Hitler and the Jews," *New York Times* (October 11, 1973), 19.

[7] "FM AMEMBASSY KAMPALA TO SECSTATE WASH DC 3182, Subject: General Amin's Travels in the Middle East" (October 17, 1973), NACP AAD, Diplomatic Records, Central Foreign Policy Files, Electronic Telegrams, 1/1/1973–12/31/1973. On threats to Americans see FM AMEMBASSY KAMPALA TO SECSTATE WASH DC 3155: Subject: GOU account of meeting with General Amin, October 11," United States National Archives in College Park (NACP) Access to Archival Databases (AAD), Diplomatic Records, Central Foreign Policy Files, Electronic Telegrams, 1/1/1973–12/31/1973.

[8] Mr. Abdalla (Uganda), United Nations Security Council Official Records, 1939th Meeting: 9 July 1976 (New York), S/PV.1939, documents.un.org/. UN Official Documents System, 3; and "Chapter XV: Other Political and Security Questions, Complaint of Aggression by Israel against Uganda," *United Nations Yearbook, 1976* (New York: United Nations Public Information Service, 1976), 315–320; also see "Benin, Libyan Arab Republic and United Republic of Tanzania draft resolution," UNSCOR, 12 July 1976" (New York), UN ODS, S/12139.

[9] "Chapter XV: Other Political and Security Questions, Complaint of Aggression by Israel against Uganda," *United Nations Yearbook, 1976*, 315–320.

Abdalla, Uganda's UN ambassador, told the Security Council that "the Ugandan Government got involved in this affair accidentally and purely for humanitarian reasons." Israel's response was an "act of naked aggression against Uganda," which "killed Ugandans who were trying to protect the hostages."[10]

Israel's ambassador to the UN, Chaim Herzog, replied that Israel was "in no way sitting in the dock as the accused party."[11] Rather, those sitting in the dock were "the terrorist organizations which are plaguing this world, and whose representatives [i.e., the PLO] have in the past been seated here by the world body with rights equal to those of Member States." Also in the dock were "all those countries which have collaborated with the terrorists and which have aided and abetted them" and "have blocked every international move to deal with this plague of terror which besets this world" and whose representatives "stood and applauded the entry into the hall of the General Assembly of a gun-toting terrorist [i.e., Yasser Arafat] in 1974."[12] Herzog focused on Amin's collaboration with the terrorists. Amin "arrived at the airport shortly before the hijacked plane landed and embraced the hijackers in a gesture of welcome and with a promise of support and assistance." Ugandan soldiers trained their guns "not on the hijackers, but on the innocent civilians – men, women and children." Hostages who were released reported that "Ugandan soldiers, under the orders of President Amin, supervised the separation of Jewish from non-Jewish passengers." With Amin's past statements in mind, it became apparent to the Israeli government that "there was no alternative but to conduct a rescue operation to save the lives of its citizens.[13] Herzog, drawing on accounts by members of the Air France crew and the hostages who had been released, asserted that "the entire story" of the Entebbe hostage seizure "is one of collusion from beginning to end on the part of the Ugandan Government."[14] The plane's captain had stated that "the German hijacker, Wilfred Bose, knew

[10] "Mr. Abdalla (Uganda), UNSCOR, 1939th Meeting: 9 July 1976," UN ODS, S/PV.1939, 5.

[11] "Chaim Herzog (Israel), UNSCOR, 1939th Meeting: 9 July 1976," UN ODS S/PV.1939, 7–8.

[12] Ibid., 8.

[13] Herzog also distributed Israeli Prime Minister Yitzak Rabin's statement to the Knesset of July; Chaim Herzog, "Letter Dated 4 July 1976 From the Permanent Representative of Israel to the United Nations Addressed to the Secretary General," and "Annex: Excerpts from the Statement Delivered by the Prime Minister of Israel, Mr. Yitzak Rabin, on 4 July 1976 in the Knesset," UNGA/SC (July 5, 1976), UN ODS A/31/122-S/12123.

[14] "Chaim Herzog (Israel), UNSCOR, 1939th Meeting: 9 July 1976," 10.

in advance that Entebbe was the plane's destination." When the plane landed, "the German woman hijacker," Brigitte Kuhlmann, said "everything is OK; the army is at the airport." Then, "immediately on arrival" Ugandan soldiers surrounded the plane and "were accompanied by five armed Arab terrorists who embraced and kissed the hijackers on the plane." Ugandan soldiers supplied the hijackers with submachine guns and explosives.[15] Amin could have released the hostages if he wished. The broadcasts of the government radio, monitored by the BBC, revealed "a complete identity of purpose with the hijackers and their demands on the part of the Ugandan authorities."[16] In response to states at the UN that criticized Israel for its raid, Herzog replied that they would have attacked Israel had it been able to rescue Jews from the Holocaust for violating the national sovereignty of the Third Reich. "What," Herzog asked "would have been more important: Hitler's sovereignty or rescuing innocent people from a holocaust?"[17]

Herzog had called Libya a sponsor of international terrorism. Libya's UN ambassador Mansour Rashid Kikhia replied that "the history of the establishment of the Zionist state is a history of terrorism." As East Germany developed extensive links to Libya, Kikhia's response merits our attention:[18]

> The Zionist representative mentioned Auschwitz, he mentioned Dachau, he mentioned Buchenwald. He said that "Auschwitz, Dachau and Buchenwald belonged to the past and would never again return."... I say that Dachau, Auschwitz and Buchenwald are not things of the past; they are still alive, physically and spiritually, only this time the roles are reversed; those who were the victims – or pretend to have been the victims – are now the torturers. The racist and criminal exercises and policies are being executed against the Palestinian people by the Zionist racists and against the African peoples by the other racist regimes of southern Africa.
>
> Certainly, Mr. Herzog, you did not learn the lessons of Dachau, of Auschwitz, of Buchenwald. But you learn through experience. We admit that you were, and you are excellent disciples of the Nazis. You have done even better than your Nazi masters. You have improved their techniques, you have pushed to perfection their style and practice. By your fabrications, Mr. Herzog, and lies, you are merely trying to cover up the wanton crime committed against Uganda.[19]

[15] Ibid.

[16] Ibid., 11–12.

[17] Ibid., 14.

[18] "Mr. Kikhia (Libyan Arab Republic), UNSCOR, 1939 Meeting, 9 July 1976," New York, UN ODS, S/PV.1939, 24–25.

[19] Ibid., 26.

Kikhia then made a striking admission in response to Herzog's assertion that Libya, with its recently acquired oil revenues, had "for years acted as paymaster of international terror movements." He replied that though Libyans were "not paymasters to anybody," they were "trying to do our best to help our brothers, to help liberation movements. We help them, we train them," in their fight against colonialism, imperialism, racism, apartheid and "will continue to do that. If we do not do that, we shall lose our *raison d'etre*."[20]

Because West Germans citizens had participated in the hijacking, Rüdiger von Wechmar, West Germany's UN ambassador, addressed the Security Council for the first time since the Federal Republic was admitted to the UN in 1973.[21] It was, he said "with profound relief that we learned of the failure of the terrorist action and the rescue of the hostages at the very last minute before the announced intention to kill them was carried out." West Germany had been directly affected because the threat to kill the hostages was "intended to compel the Federal Government ... to release criminals who, as is well known, in no sense can be called freedom fighters but are persons convicted of, or under criminal investigation for, the murder of a judge and other capital crimes under penal law."[22] Wechmar expressed regret that German nationals were among the kidnappers. Their plot was "marked by total disregard for the fundamental human rights of innocent persons and was a barbarous assault on the States they tried to blackmail. In view of the kidnappers publicly announced determination to kill the hostages, the rescue operation was undertaken to resolve a situation which must have appeared hopeless."[23] William Scranton, then the US ambassador to the UN, also defended Israel's action in Entebbe, arguing that it was based on "a well-established right to use limited force for the protection of one's own nationals from an imminent threat of injury or death in a situation in which the State in whose territory they are located is either unwilling or unable to protect them."[24] However, the United States and West Germany were unable to induce the UN to adopt resolutions and effective measures to condemn

[20] Ibid., 24–25.

[21] "Mr. [Rüdiger] von Wechmar (Federal Republic of Germany), UNSCOR, 1941st Meeting: 12 July 1976," New York, UN ODS, S/PV.1941, 5.

[22] Ibid., 6.

[23] Ibid.

[24] "Mr. [William] Scranton (United States of America), United Nations Security Council, Official Records, 1941st Meeting: 12 July 1976," New York, United Nations Official Documents System, S/PV.1941, 8.

and eradicate terrorist attacks on civil aviation in order to prevent future hijackings.[25]

Instead the General Assembly majority embraced an interpretation of the events that stood the facts on their heads and turned Israel into the aggressor. Mikhael Kharlamov, then the Soviet Union's deputy ambassador to the UN, told the Security Council that the sole issue to be discussed was Israel's violation of Uganda's sovereignty.[26] Forty-eight African countries had adopted an Organization of African Unity resolution that "roundly condemns Israel's aggression against the sovereignty and territorial integrity of Uganda." It also shared the views of the "non-aligned countries."[27] "Israel's wanton attack" was "fully within" the definition of aggression adopted by the UN. "What more," he asked, "do we need to say?" Hence the Soviet Union supported a resolution condemning "Israeli aggression against the sovereignty and territorial integrity of the Republic of Uganda."[28]

In reply to Kharlamov, Herzog focused on the "the group which organized this hijacking, namely, the PLO." Its denials of involvement were "a lie. The PFLP, to which the hijackers belonged, is a constituent member of the PLO."[29] Herzog's skepticism about Arafat's denial gained credibility in light of a public exchange of letters between Idi Amin and Arafat. On July 17, Amin sent greetings to Arafat, to the Palestinian people, and especially to members of the PFLP, "who shed blood and lost their lives at Entebbe airport at the wicked hands of Zionists and racist Israel."[30] On July 21, the Uganda government press agency published Arafat's reply:

Your excellency and dear brother.... I have received with great pride your graceful telegram, in which you declared in no uncertain terms your support for the Palestinian people and your solidarity with their just struggle against all conspiracies, there in Uganda and here in Lebanon. In the name of the Palestinian revolution and the Palestinian people, I wish to express in this message our admiration and estimation of the noble stand Uganda, in the person of her president, has taken during the barbaric Zionist raid on Uganda soil. We express our deep regret

[25] Ibid., 7–10.

[26] "Mr. [Mikhail] Kharlamov (Union of Soviet Socialist Republics), UNSCOR, 1941st Meeting: 12 July 1976," New York, UN ODS S/PV.1941, 16–19.

[27] Ibid., 18.

[28] Ibid.

[29] "Mr. [Chaim] Herzog, UNSCOR, 1942nd: 13 July 1976," New York, UN ODS, S/PV.1942, 14–15.

[30] "Amin Sends Message to Arafat, Expresses Solidarity," *Kampala Domestic Service*, 1976-07-17, *Foreign Broadcast Information Service (FBIS) Daily Report, Middle East and Africa*, Library of Congress, infoweb.newsbank.com, onsite online access; also *Daily Report: Sub-Saharan Africa, FBIS-SSA-76–139 on 1976-07-19.*

for the Uganda heroes who have fallen victim to the Zionist piracy on Entebbe airport. While you were undertaking [a] humanitarian and positive role in your attempt to remove the hostages without blood being shed, the Zionists launched this vile and sinister operation, thereby shedding innocent Uganda blood, when they [Amin and the Ugandans] were only trying to play the role of mediator, whose aim was to save the lives of all. This was not the first time that Palestinian blood was mixed with Ugandan blood. The brotherly ties and relations of combat between our two peoples are not new.[31]

Arafat promised Amin that "the Palestinian revolution" would put at "the disposal of the Ugandan people all that is within its power, to destroy the imperialist and Zionist conspiracies." He ended with his customary "Revolution until victory," "your brother, Yasser Arafat."[32] The *Guardian* newspaper in London cited an unnamed Israeli intelligence official saying that the connection between the PFLP and the PLO was "so strong that we have reason to believe Arafat had advance information and could have stopped the operation if he wished."[33] Whether or not that was the case, his letter to Amin documented his willingness to praise a leader whose enthusiasm for Hitler and the Holocaust was a matter of public record.

As the Entebbe discussion took place only in the Security Council, East German diplomats at the UN did not have an opportunity to comment publicly. *Neues Deutschland* ran small articles about the hijacking on June 29 and July 1.[34] A third one-paragraph article on July 3 announced that 110 hostages had been freed but did not mention that the Israeli and non-Israeli hostages had been separated.[35] On July 5, *ND* reported on "Israel's Bloody Attack on Airport in Uganda."[36] The next day it ran a headline announcing "Israeli Attack on Uganda Is Sharply Denounced: UN General Secretary Waldheim: Violation of Sovereignty."[37] The following

[31] "Arafat Sends Congratulatory Message to Amin," *Kampala Domestic Service 1976-07-21, FBIS Daily Report, Middle East and Africa,* Library of Congress, infoweb.newsbank.com, onsite online access; also *Daily Report: Sub-Saharan Africa, FBIS-SSA-76–141 on 1976-07-21.*

[32] Ibid.

[33] See "Sources Say Arafat Knew of Hijacking, Name Leader," *Guardian*, London (July 12, 1976), *FBIS Daily Report, Middle East and Africa,* Library of Congress, infoweb.newsbank.com, onsite online access; also *Daily Report: Sub-Saharan Africa, FBIS-MEA-76–135 on 1976-135 on 1976-07-13.*

[34] "Entführtes französisches Flugzeug in Uganda gelandet," *Neues Deutschland* (June 29, 1976), 7; and "Flugzeugentführer in Entebbe ließen 47 Geiseln frei," *ND* (July 1, 1976), 15.

[35] "110 Geiseln weiter in der Gewalt der Luftpiraten," *ND* (July 3–4, 1976), 7.

[36] "Blutiger Überfall Israels auf Flughafen in Uganda," *ND* (July 5, 1976), 6.

[37] "Israelische Überfall Uganda scharf verurteilt: UNO-Generalsekretär Waldheim: Verletzung der Sourveränität," *ND* (July 6, 1976), 7.

day it sharpened its tone with the headline "Tel Aviv's Criminal Attack Is Labeled as Aggression: Governments and Organizations Condemn Attack on Entebbe,"[38] followed by a one-paragraph article headlined "Rabin: Israel Will Ignore World Public Opinion."[39]

A July 10 *ND* article, "Israel's Zionist Policy Again Shows Its Racist Essence: TASS Commentary on the Act of Aggression against the Republic of Uganda," asserted that Israel's raid demonstrated that it viewed Africans as "second-class" countries, a view that stemmed from Israel's "ever closer alliances with South Africa and Rhodesia." Denouncing Israel's act of aggression was not tantamount to protecting terrorists, *ND* said, but would help prevent Israel from carrying out yet further acts of aggression.[40] Two days later, *ND* falsely reported that the Security Council had "condemned Israeli piracy." In fact, a resolution to that effect had been withdrawn.[41] On July 16, under the headline "Majority Condemns Aggression," *ND's* account focused on the condemnations of Israel raised in the Security Council debates.[42] *Neues Deutschland* did not report that the Amin cooperated with the hijackers, that Israelis and non-Israelis and Jews and non-Jews were separated, that Amin was an admirer of Hitler, and that two West German leftists were among the hijackers. By contrast, *Die Welt*, a few miles away on the other side of the Berlin Wall, reported on Amin's involvement, the terror experienced by the hostages, and the separation of Israelis and Jews from the other passengers.[43]

38 "Verbrecherischer Anschlag Tel Avivs wird als Aggression gebrandmarkt: Regierungen und Organisationen verurteilen Überfall auf Entebbe," *ND* (July 8, 1976), 7.

39 "Rabin: Israel Will Ignore World Public Opinion," *ND* (July 8, 1976), 7.

40 "Zionistische Politik Israels zeigt erneut ihr rassistisches Wesen: TASS-Kommentar zu Aggressionsakt gegen die Republik Uganda," *ND* (July 10/11, 1976), 7.

41 "Israelisches Piratum im UNO-Sicherheitsrat verurteilt: Dr, Kurt Waldheim: Ernste Verletzung der Sourveränität Ugandas," *ND* (July 12, 1976), 5.

42 "Mehrheit veruteilte Aggression: UNO-Sicherheitsrat beendet Debatte über israelischen über israelischen fall," *ND* (July 16, 1976), 6.

43 See "Bonn will nicht nachgeben: Terroristen bleiben in Haft," and "Israel soll auch den Mörder von Lod Freilassen," *Die Welt* (July 1, 1976), 1; "Sie kamen buchstäblich von Himmel," *Die Welt* (July 5, 1976), 1; "Idi Amin such Sündenböcke und nennt sich 'Menschenfreund'," *Die Welt* (July 6, 1976), 1; "Idi Amin such Sündenböcke und nennt sich 'Menschenfreund'," *Die Welt* (July 6, 1976), 1; "Beerdigung wird al 'historischer Augenblick' bezeichnet: Idi Amin läßt Entführer mit militärischen Ehren beisetzen," *Die Welt* (July 7, 1976), 1; Erich Weidemann, "Die Verschwörerposse began auf dem Flughafen von Entebbe," *Die Welt* (July 6, 1976), 9; "General Gur: Darum mußten die Terroristen erschossen werden," *Die Welt* (July 10/11, 1976), 1; William Stevenson, "Die Herkules beweist, daß sie ein Akrobat unter Flugzeugriesen ist," *Die Welt* (August 20, 1976), 4; Stevenson, "Die Uhr läuft ab: Hinrichtung der Geiseln wird vorbereitet," *Die Welt* (August 16, 1976), 8; Stevenson, "Gespräch mit einem Mordgehilfen, der sich menschlich gab," *Die Welt* (August, 1976).

The Stasi's Counterterrorism Department XXII produced a detailed report on "the hijacking of an Air France plane by terrorists to Entebbe as well as the Israeli aggressive actions against the Republic of Uganda."[44] It condemned "Israel's aggression" against Uganda.[45] It expressed alarm that the Israeli commandos were presented as heroes "so that similar actions will be encouraged and that sympathy for the aggressor will be won in other parts of the world." Such celebration "obscures the deep causes of this war." It sought "to glorify the actions taken against such terrorist activities that emerge from a feeling of suffering injustice and from [a desire for] revenge for the violent expulsion from one's homeland and in so doing [seeks to] neutralize the right of resistance."[46] As the Entebbe events had "practical significance for *all* operative units of the MfS," the report included a detailed chronology of the hijacking and rescue raid.[47]

THE PATH FROM FRANKFURT/MAIN TO ENTEBBE

Wilfried Ernst Böse (1949–1976) emerged from the radical leftist milieu in Frankfurt/Main in the late 1960s and early 1970s (Figure 10.1). After attending a humanistic *Gymnasium* in Bamberg and then Ansbach in Bavaria, he began studies at the University of Freiburg in fall 1968.[48] After one semester he transferred to a larger mecca of the West German radical Left, the University of Frankfurt/Main, where he studied sociology and psychology. In Frankfurt, he met Karl-Dietrich Wolff, president of West German SDS, and worked with him on a Black Panther Party

44 "Zum Ablauf und den Begleitumständen der Entführung eine Flugzeuges der 'Air France' durch Terroristen nach Entebbe sowie den Israelischen Aggressionshandlungen gegen die Republik Uganda," BStU, Archiv der Zentralstelle (Berlin), MfS-HA XXII, Nr. 105418, Teil 1 von 2, 3–21.

45 Ibid., 5.

46 Ibid.

47 "Chronologischer Ablauf der Ereignisse um die terroristischen Flugzeugentführung bis zum Zeitpunkt des israelischen sogenannten Kommandounternehmens," BStU, Archiv der Zentralstelle (Berlin), MfS-HA XXII, Nr. 105418, Teil 1 von 2, 7–18. On the prisoners whose release was demanded see "Von den in Israel Inhaftierten, deren Freilassung gefordert wurde, sind folgende bekannt," in "Zum Ablauf und den Begleitumständen der Entführung eine Flugzeuges der 'Air France' durch Terroristen nach Entebbe sowie den Israelischen Aggressionshandlungen gegen die Republik Uganda," BStU, Archiv der Zentralstelle (Berlin), MfS-HA XXII, Nr. 105418, Teil 1 von 2, 20–21.

48 From September to October 2013, the Ansbach city library showed an exhibition about Böse, his path to terrorism, and the events in Entebbe. Se Ute Kissling, "Wilfried Böse – der Begründer der terroristischen Revolutionären Zellen: Oder: Sympathie ist kein Delikt," *Bibliotheksforum Bayern* (August, 2014); www.bibliotheksforum-bayern.de/fileadmin/archiv/2014-2/PDF-Einzelbeitraege/BFB_0214_23_Kissling_V03.pdf.

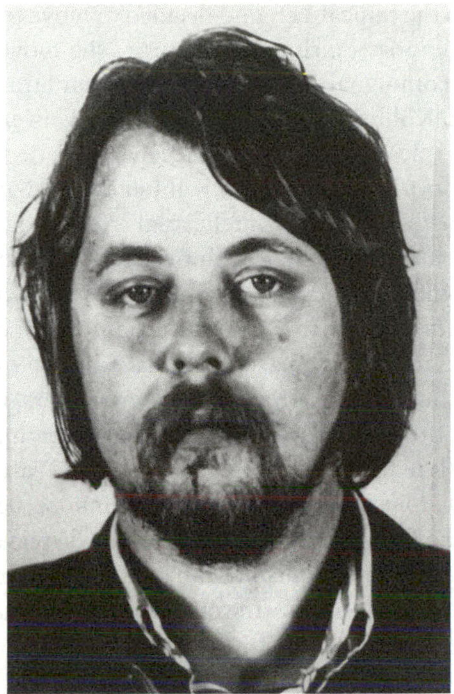

FIGURE 10.1. Wilfried Böse, participant in the Entebbe hijacking of May–June 1976. Undated police photo. Deutsche Presse Agentur DPA/LANDOV.

Solidarity Committee. In 1970 the two traveled to North Korea. Together with Wolff and Johannes Weinrich, another subsequent member of the RC, Böse founded Roter Stern Verlag (Red Star Publishers). Among its early publications was a collection of essays by Kim Il Sung, the dictator of North Korea. By 1973, Böse and Weinrich had developed sharp differences with Wolff about the terrorism of the Red Army Faction. Kurt Rebmann, West Germany's attorney general (*Generalbundesanwalt)*, in a report of March 19, 1980, concluded that from 1973 to 1976, Böse wrote manifestos and statements in *Revolutionäre Zorn* (Revolutionary Rage), a publication of the Revolutionary Cells group.[49] Brigitte Kuhlmann (1949–1976) had attended vocational school and then worked as a legal secretary and appraiser in Hannover. In 1967, she began studying education at the pedagogical university in Hannover. Presumably, it was there

[49] [Kurt] Rebmann to Bundesminister der Justiz, "Ermittlungsverfahren gegen ... Revolutionäre Zellen (RZ)" Karlsruhe (March 19, 1980), Bundesarchiv Koblenz BAK, Bundesministerium des Innern, B106/403104, 75–80.

that she turned to the radical Left and decided to move to Frankfurt/Main, where she became Böse's girlfriend. In 1971, she moved into the Roter Stern office and communal house on Holzhausen Strasse in Frankfurt's Near North End. Kuhlmann also studied at the University of Frankfurt in the 1974–1975 academic year and received her degree in November 1975.[50] In Frankfurt/Main, Böse and Kuhlmann lived and worked in the midst of Frankfurt/Main's leftist intellectual and political milieu.

Between 1973 and 1980, the Revolutionary Cells claimed responsibility for 67 firebombings and explosions in West Germany. The targets included the offices of German businesses, chambers of commerce, public transport offices, automatic metro card machines, US Army bases near Frankfurt/Main, the *Berliner Morgenpost* newspapers, the Springer publishing building, the city hall in Krefeld, the Argentinian Consulate in Munich, and the Italian and Chilean Consulates in West Berlin.[51] As with Kunzelmann's *Shalom and Napalm* and Meinhof's celebration of the Munich attack, the RC's selection of targets also displayed a convergence of anti-Semitism with anti-Zionism. Many of the RC's targets were related to Israel or were Jewish businesses and institutions that were assumed to support Israel. The RC set off a bomb at an Israeli travel bureau in Frankfurt/Main on August 26, 1974. On February 8, 1976, it bombed the office of the "State of Israel Bonds" in Berlin. On December 23, 1976, RC members threw a stink bomb into a movie theater in Berlin during a showing of the film *Operation Entebbe*. On January 3, 1977, its members used firebombs to attack theaters showing the same film in Aachen, and in Dusseldorf and Hannover on the following day. On March 30, 1978, RC members attacked the El-Al office in West Berlin and the Israeli firm Agrexco in Frankfurt/Main on June 20, 1978.[52] Individual members of the RC worked with the Lebanese Michele Wahaeb Moukarbel as well as Ilich Ramirez-Sanchez, known as "Carlos," in terrorist actions carried out in connection with the PFLP, including a missile attack on an El-Al plane at Orly airport in Paris on January 13, 1975, and the attack on and hostage-taking of OPEC oil ministers in Vienna on December 21, 1975.

[50] Ibid., 85–87.

[51] Prof. Dr. [Kurt] Rebmann, [Generalbundesanwalt] Beim Bundesgerichtshof to Bundesminister der Justiz, "Ermittlungsverfahren gegen Johannes Weinrich und andere Mitglieder einer terroristischen Vereinigung Revolutionäre Zellen (RZ)" wegen Verdachts eine Vergehens nach para. 129a StGB und andere Straftaten," Karlsruhe (March 19, 1980), Bundesarchiv Koblenz (BAK) Bundesministerium des Innern, Bundesgerichtshof, B106/403104.

[52] Ibid., 2–8.

The RC's most consequential collaboration with the PFLP was Böse and Kuhlmann's participation in the Entebbe hijacking and hostage seizure.[53]

In interviews and in a memoir, Hans-Joachim Klein, a former member of the Revolutionary Cells, asserted that the fusion of anti-Zionism with anti-Semitism played a major role in his decision to leave the group. Of particular importance were the RC's plans to assassinate Heinz Galinski and Ignatz Lipinski, the leaders, respectively, of the organized Jewish communities in West Berlin and Frankfurt/Main. Klein revealed these plans in a letter he sent to the weekly West German newsmagazine *Der Spiegel*, which it published in its issue of May 9, 1977.[54] He also stressed the links between the RC and the PFLP. He claimed that the RC was financed by Wadid Haddad, the leader of the PFLP, with payments of 3,000 marks a month to each West German member. According to Klein, members of the RC had offered logistical assistance and accommodations to the Black September group during the attack on the Israelis at the Munich Olympics.[55] West German judicial authorities confirmed parts of Klein's story. They concluded that members of the RC had acquired military training in Palestinian training camps "in an Arab country."[56] They met members of the Red Army Faction and the June 2nd movement in training camps of the PFLP in South Yemen. In a 1980 report on the radical Left, Attorney General Rebmann's office counted 15 West Germans who were "strongly suspected" of being members of the group, while another 23 were believed to be members and three more to have supported it.[57]

On March 7, 1973, the District Attorney's office (Staatsanwaltschaft) in Frankfurt/Main opened an investigation of Verlag Roter Stern to find out whether it was supporting the Red Army Faction terrorist campaign.

53 Ibid., 8–9. The monthly *Informationen des Bundesamt für Verfassungsschutz*, offered reports about extremist groups and political violence. See, for example, "Sprengstoffanschlag auf das Staatliche israelische Verkehrsbüro in Frankfurt," *Informationen des Bundesamt für Verfassungsschutz*, Cologne (August 6, 1974), B 443/641, 30.

54 Hans-Joachim Klein, "'Ich habe genug angestellt': Opec-Terrorist Hans-Joachim Klein enthüllt Attentspläne – Sein Brief an den Spiegel," *Der Spiegel*, Nr. 20 (May 9, 1977), 33–34. Also see "Dokumentation, Spiegel Gespräch: Hans-Joachim Klein über Attentats und Entführungspläne im internationalen Terroristen Milieu," in Hans-Joachim Klein, *Rückkehr in die Menschlichkeit: Appel eine ausgestiegenen Terroristen* (Reinbek bei Hamburg: Rowohlt, 1979). By December 1979, Rowohlt had printed 40,000 copies of Klein's memoirs. With a foreword by Daniel Cohn-Bendit it became a widely read work in West Germany.

55 Ibid.

56 Rebmann to Bundesminister der Justiz, "Ermittlungsverfahren gegen ... Revolutionäre Zellen (RZ)" Karlsruhe (March 19, 1980), BAK, B106/403104, 13–14.

57 Ibid., 43–44.

It closed the investigation on February 14, 1974, without filing any indictments.[58] However, the investigation documented Böse's role as co-founder of Roter Stern Verlag and his arrest on June 24, 1975 in France due to his connection with Michel Moukarbel, whom the French police suspected of involvement in terrorist activities.[59] An investigation by the West German Federal Criminal Office (*Bundeskriminalamt*) confirmed that Karl Dietrich Wolff knew people who, unlike him, had decided to engage in terrorist activity. However, having known or knowing people who had joined the Red Army Faction or the Revolutionary Cells was neither illegal nor grounds for indictment in West Germany. In an era that the West German Left frequently described as one of human rights violations, repression, and authoritarianism, Roter Stern Verlag thrived as Wolff turned it away from the Maoist and North Korean pamphlets it had once published toward cultural criticism and a successful edition of the collected works of the German poet Friedrich Hölderlin.[60] That said, the West German attorney general's investigations offered compelling evidence that Böse and Kuhlmann were indeed embedded in the political and ideological world of the New Left in Frankfurt/Main. They leaped over an abyss that others in Frankfurt/Main did not, yet the leap was inspired by ideas about Israel and the Palestinians that had been percolating in the West German New Left since the Six-Day War. One bitter irony of the actions of the West German leftists in Entebbe lay partly in the fact that Böse and Kuhlmann, mouthing the slogans of anti-fascism and anti-racism, collaborated in an attack on Israelis with Idi Amin, an admirer of Hitler and of the Holocaust.[61]

On August 17, 1976, a West German diplomat in Baghdad noticed a remarkable color poster produced by the PFLP showing photos of seven of the Entebbe hijackers, including Wilfried Böse and Brigitte Kuhlmann,

[58] Bundeskriminalamt, "Bericht: Verlag Roter Stern KG," Bonn-Bad Godesberg (November 11, 1975), Bundesarchiv Koblenz, Bundesministerium des Innern, B106/106583. This report was an annex to a close reading of RAF statements, "RAF-Schrift, Guerilla, Widerstand, Antiimperialistische Front," also B106/106583.

[59] Ibid., 18.

[60] See, for example, Klaus Theweleit, *Männerphantasien, Band 1: Frauen, Fluten, Korper, Geschichte* (Frankfurt/Main: Roter Stern Verlag, 1977); and Dietrich E. Sattler, *Friedrich Hölderlin: Sämtliche Werke, Frankfurter Ausgabe* (Frankfurt/Main: Roter Stern Verlag, 1984).

[61] On these issues see Wolfgang Kraushaar, "Antizionismus als Trojanisches Pferd: Zur antisemitischen Dimensionen in den Kooperationen von *Tupamaros West-Berlin*, RAF und RZ mit den Palästinensern," in Wolfgang Kraushaar, ed., *Die RAF und der linke Terrorismus, Bd. 1* (Hamburg: Hamburger Edition, 2006), 676–695; and Hans Kundnani, *Utopia or Auschwitz: Germany's 1968 Generation and the Holocaust* (New York and London: Oxford University Press, 2009).

whom the poster named "Mahmud" and "Hallma," respectively.[62] It called "Hallma," that is, Kuhlmann, a "heroic victim" (*Heldenopfer)* and offered the following praise: "She fought against the new German fascism and racism, for international liberation movements and for Palestine. On July 4, 1976, she fell in battle in Entebbe, Uganda."[63] It described Böse, or "Mahmud," as "a co-founder of the Revolutionary Cells Germany which fought imperialism and Zionism. The organization represented the German armed struggle against Nazism," that is, against the Federal Republic of Germany, not Nazi Germany. "It cooperated with the Popular Front [for the Liberation of Palestine] and had engaged in various actions against the German system and American bases in Germany." Böse "died a hero's death (*Heldentod)* in Uganda." Of "Mahmud," "Hallma," and the other hijackers killed in the Entebbe hijacking, the poster claimed (Figure 10.2): "With their sacred blood, our comrades have written an epic for our great Palestinian people and have opened a new phase in the battle of the revolutionary liberation movements of the world in struggle against imperialism, Zionism and reaction."[64] On September 16, 1981, the German Embassy in Kampala informed the Foreign Ministry in Bonn that a Dutch missionary, apparently at the embassy's request, traveled to Uganda's cemetery for revolutionary heroes in Jinja, about 50 miles east of Kampala. There he saw the gravestones of Wilfried Böse and Brigitte Kuhlmann with the names "Mujnoud" and "Halime" and an inscription: "Country of origin West-Germany."[65]

Though Böse and Kuhlmann died in Entebbe, the Revolutionary Cells continued their terrorist activities in the Federal Republic of Germany and their efforts to suppress the screening of the film *Operation Entebbe*. By January 6, 1977, there had been eight attacks against theaters showing the film, including ones in Rome and Athens as well as in West Germany. In Greece, the violent campaign caused 15 theaters in Athens to cancel the film's showing.[66] Several of the firebombs exploded, causing fires; others were defused before they could inflict great harm. A bomb timed to explode at 9:10 P.M. at the Residenz film center in Düsseldorf was

[62] "Aus: Bagdad nr. 171 vom 17.08.76 an: Bonn, betr.: Geiselbefreiung in Entebbe," PAAA (Politisches Archiv des Auswärtiges Amt) B 83 Referat 511, Strafrecht, Steuer- und Zollrecht, 1952–1972, 1973–1994, 530.36 UGA 1976–1979.

[63] Ibid.

[64] Ibid.

[65] "Menne, Botschaft der Bundesrepublik Deutschland, Bagdad an das Auswärtige Amt: Referat 632, Betr.: 3. Palästina-Filmfestival in Bagdad vom 18. Bis 25.3.1978," PAAA, Referat 511, Einzelfälle 1976.

[66] "Entebbe-Film unter Polizeischutz," *Die Welt I* (January 1977). The film was shown in Freiburg, Bamberg, Stuttgart, Mains, Recklinghausen, Frankfurt (Main), Mülheim/

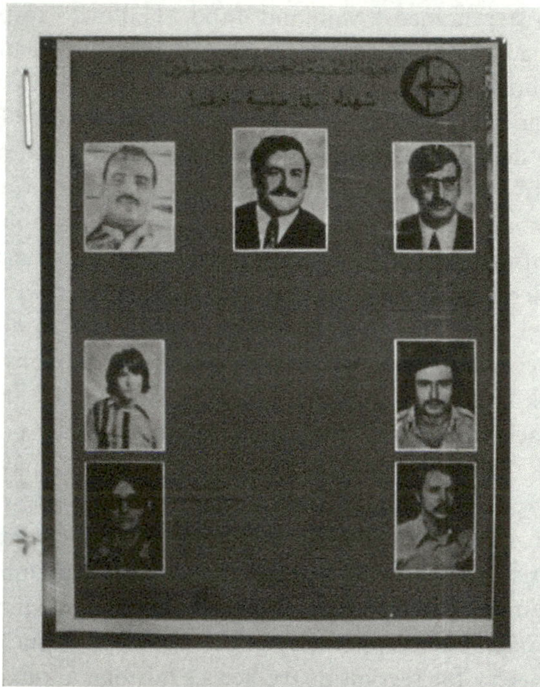

FIGURE 10.2. Popular Front for the Liberation of Palestine poster in Baghdad, Iraq, in August 1976 shows photos of members of PFLP who participated in hijacking of an Air France plane to Entebbe, Uganda. Wilfried Böse (middle right) and Brigitte Kuhlmann (lower left).
The text reads: "With their holy blood, our comrades have written an epic for our great Palestinian people and opened a new phase in the struggle of the revolutionary liberation movement of the world in struggle against imperialism, Zionism and reaction."

defused by police, as were several others. Had they exploded, they would have killed and injured many people.[67] The RC compared the movie to Nazi propaganda films and defended the Entebbe hijacking, which "was not supposed to exterminate life but to save life that is being destroyed in Israeli and European prisons." The "action" in Entebbe was designed "to protect the lives of the hostages and was only endangered by the Israeli

Ruhr, Bielefeld, Münster, Heidelberg, Karlsruhe, Saarbrücken, Heilbronn, Gießen, Aschaffenburg, though it was canceled in Kassel out of fear of harm to the moviegoers. On the attacks and on the RC with roots in leftist ideological assaults on capitalist consumer society see Alexander Sedlmaier, *Consumption and Violence: Radical Protest in Cold-War Germany* (Ann Arbor: University of Michigan Press, 2014), 242–246.

67 "Immer mehr Bomben gegen Film über Entebbe-Befreiung," *Die Welt* (January 6, 1977), BStU.

attack."[68] The "struggle against Zionism has as little to do with racism as was the struggle against fascist Germany," which was waged not against the German people but against fascism as a form of domination.[69] The Revolutionary Cells proudly took credit for the firebombings: "Today we set fires in several West German movie theaters that are showing the film 'Entebbe.' This should be understood as a warning both to the film distributers and theater owners who want to profit from this racist propaganda as well as to those who want to see the film." To prevent future risks, the RC demanded "*the immediate cancellation of the propaganda film Entebbe!* " (emphasis in original) and a "boycott of all following films about Entebbe!" for the sake of "the international struggle against exploitation, racism and political unfreedom!"[70] In, other words, the RC sought to suppress artistic freedom with violence, threats of violence, and calls for boycotts.

In 1978, the RC attacks took an even more sinister dimension as they focused specifically on Jewish institutions in West Germany. On June 20, 1978, the RC bombed the offices of the Israeli importing company Agrexco in Frankfurt/Main, the largest importer of Israeli agricultural produce in Germany. It did so to support Arab workers who allegedly made Israeli oranges inedible by poisoning them with quicksilver poison.[71] In the same communiqué, the RC included the following justification for attacking "Zionist" and "Israeli" institutions in West Germany that supported and gathered funds to send to Israel, which they said were supporting its "campaign of expulsion and extermination" against the Palestinians:

> These institutions have made a principle of placing Jewish cultural and social establishments (homes for the aged, day care centers, etc.) in their immediate vicinity or even in a normal home filled with families. They do this so that if there are attacks on their offices, as many people will be affected and injured so that the affected Jewish institutions can use an age-old and proven Zionist strategy

[68] ID-Archiv im IISG Amsterdam, eds., "Brandanschlag gegen die Vorführung des 'Entebbe' Films," *Die Früchte des Zorns: Texte und Materialien zur Geschichte der Revolutionären Zellen und der Roten Zora, Band I* (Edition ID-Archiv: Berlin, 1993), 129–130.

[69] Ibid., 129–130. The German reads in part: "Die Aktion war so angelegt, daß auch das Leben der Geiseln geschont war und erst durch den israelischen Angriff gefährdet wurde."

[70] Ibid., 130.

[71] ID-Archiv im IISG Amsterdam, eds., "Aktion gegen die Israelische Import-Gesellschaft Agrexco, Frankfurt (June 1978)," *Die Früchte des Zorns: Texte und Materialien zur Geschichte der Revolutionären Zellen und der Roten Zora, Band I* (Edition ID-Archiv: Berlin, 1993), 131–132.

of denouncing such attacks as "anti-Semitic incidents." This form of barricading, the systematic misuse of uninvolved people as a living protective shield who do not know who has placed them in the middle, is one of Zionism's most despicable and inhuman "specialties."[72]

These assertions were a cynical and chilling variation of the policy of PLO and affiliated terrorist organizations of placing their military bases and training camps in Lebanon close to Arab and Palestinian civilian institutions and of using civilian populations as human shields against Israel retaliation for terrorist attacks. The statement indicated that the RC regarded the offices, schools, homes for the aged, and day care centers and synagogues associated with the Jewish community in West Germany – that is, perfectly legal activities having nothing to do with military matters – to be legitimate military targets. Hence, the RC legitimated "attacks of this sort," that is, on the offices of "Zionist" institutions. In view of what it called "the gigantic propaganda apparatus at Israel's disposal" in West Germany, it was "not enough to say" that Israel's policies "correspond to the Nazis' blood and soil policies." Now the RC was going to hold the Jewish institutions in West Germany responsible for those alleged policies.[73] Having publicly justified attacks on Jewish institutions in West Germany, the RC dismissed the idea that such a campaign had anything to do with anti-Semitism. Echoing the arguments made by Farouk Kaddoumi in the United Nations, the RC asserted that "the battle (*Kampf*) against Zionism is the decisive battle against any anti-Semitism. For just as this battle was one fought against fascist crimes, so it is fought against the crimes of the Israeli state against the Palestinians, who are themselves semites."[74] In other words, for the West German Revolutionary Cells organization, killing Jews in West Germany in 1978 was a way to fight anti-Semitism.

[72] Ibid., 132. The German reads: "Diese Institutionen habe es sich zum Prinzip gemacht, in ihrer unmittelbaren Umgebung kulturelle und soziale jüdische Einrichtungen anzusiedeln (Altenfürsorge, Kinderkrippen, etc.) – oder einfach in ein normales Wohnhaus voller Familien zu ziehen, mit der Absicht, daß bei Anschlägen auf ihre Agenturen möglichst viele Menschen getroffen und verletzt werden, um diese dann nach uralter und bewährter zionistischer Strategie als 'antisemitische Ausfälle' denunzieren zu können. Diese Art der Verschanzung, die ganz systematische unbeteiligte Menschen als lebendes Schutzschild mißbraucht, die zumeist gar nicht wissen, wer sich da mitten zwischen sie gestext hat, ist eine der niederträchtigsten und menschenverachtensten 'Spezialitäten' des Zionismus."

[73] Ibid.

[74] Ibid., 132–133. Also see the Revolutionary Cells' arguments for boycotting Israeli goods and defining such efforts as anti-fascist in "Aktion gegen die Import-Firma Hameico" Frankfurt/Main (June 79), 133.

WEST GERMAN JEWISH LEADERS RESPOND TO ENTEBBE

For Jews in West Germany and for some significant part of West German public opinion, the participation of the Revolutionary Cells in the Entebbe hijacking reinforced their by-then decade-long conviction that the West German radical Left had become anti-Semitic. It not only was a political enemy of Israel and its Jewish supporters in West Germany but posed a direct threat of physical harm. For the leaders of West Germany's Jewish community, the hostage-taking in Entebbe and the separation of Israeli and non-Israeli and Jewish and non-Jewish passengers evoked memories of the Holocaust. As a lead essay in the *Allgemeine Jüdische Wochenzeitung* put it, 30 years after "the greatest genocide in history, the Jews again had to experience being 'selected' when the terrorists in Entebbe released the non-Israeli and non-Jewish hostages."[75] After the attacks on the screenings of *Operation Entebbe*, Galinski noted that in the leftist leaflets that accompanied the attacks "there is not a word of regret for the hostages of Entebbe, not a hint of empathy for the innocent people who spent days facing deadly danger." Instead the leaflets purveyed "a bundle of untruths about Israel and a defamatory campaign against Zionism." A leaflet distributed by Joscha Schmierer's Kommunistische Bund Westdeutschland drew their attention. It described Palestinian airplane hijackings as "the answer to Zionist aggression" and said that the "hijackers made just demands" for release of prisoners. Galinski called on judicial and police authorities to defend the ability of theaters to show *Operation Entebbe* and "finally decide to act in the spirit of militant democracy" against those who glorified "criminal acts of violence." Terrorists, he added, must not be given the power to decide which films could be shown in West Germany.[76]

THE IMPORTANCE AND THE LIMITS OF LEFTISTS' CRITICISM OF ENTEBBE

With one exception, the leading personages who emerged from the West German New Left remained silent at the time about the events in Entebbe. The rule-proving exception came from Detlev Claussen, then a doctoral

[75] Thomas Stein, "Das Fanal von Entebbe: Israel setzt Zeichen im Kampf gegen den Terrorismus," *Berliner Allgemeine jüdische Wochenzeitung*, West Berlin (July 9, 1976), 1–2.

[76] Heinz Galinski, "Terror darf nicht hingenommen werden," *Berliner jüdische Allgemeine Wochenzeitung*, Dusseldorf (January 14, 1977).

student in sociology who had studied with Theodor Adorno in Frankfurt/Main. He had been a member of West German SDS in the 1960s and become a professor of sociology at the University of Hannover, where he published works on social theory and on the nature of anti-Semitism.[77] In September 1976, he published "Terror in the Air, Counterrevolution on the Ground," in the pages of *Links* (Left), the monthly journal of the Socialist Bureau, an organization of democratic socialists.[78] He raised the tactical criticism that the use of "terror in the air" to gain public support and attention mirrored "a lack of social revolutionary importance on the ground" in West Germany.[79] The hijacking diverted the attention of the world's media from Israel's military retaliation against Palestinian bases in Lebanon, which Claussen described as "the counter-revolutionary effort to extinguish the existence of the Palestinian people."[80] The attack on the Munich Olympics by Black September had damaged the Palestinian cause. However, in Lebanon the PLO and Lebanese leftists had created the possibility of "social revolutionary change in the Arab region." In Israel, the Palestinians faced a "repressive colonial product." The Entebbe and other airplane hijackings of the Palestinian "fringe organizations" undermined, rather than advanced, "the liberation struggle."[81] Claussen called Idi Amin a "laughable figure" who "did not represent Africa." "National liberation struggles," he wrote, had "nothing to do with terrorism." The error of the Entebbe hijacking was that it was indeed "terroristic." Israel itself had "the most experienced terrorist organizations," for it rested on "a terrorist foundation which can persist only through the oppression of the Palestinian people."[82]

Claussen combined this expression of conventional leftist views of the time with an atypical historical self-awareness of the role of Germans in the attacks. "The practical participation of Germans in the action in Entebbe only handed Israel an argument to strengthen its nationalism."[83] He criticized what he called the "ahistorical" nature of West German leftist anti-Zionism. "Every inhabitant of Israel will find it incomprehensible

[77] See Detlev Claussen, *Vom Judenhass zur Antisemitismus: Materialien einer verleugneten Geschichte* (Darmstadt: Luchterhand, 1987). For his political essays see *Mit steinernem Herzen: Politische Essays, 1969–1989* (Bremen: Verlag Bettina Wassmann, n.d.).

[78] Detlev Claussen, "Terror in der Luft, Konterrevolution auf der Erde," *Links* (September 1976); reprinted in *Mit steinernem Herzen*, 145–155.

[79] Ibid., 146–148.

[80] Ibid., 148.

[81] Ibid., 149–150.

[82] Ibid., 153.

[83] Ibid., 154–155.

that civilians of Jewish belief are made victims of terrorism organized by Germans." It was not a defense of Zionism to "criticize this ahistorical anti-Zionism, one that places any use of violence of Germans against Jewish civilians into the continuity of German anti-Semitism. Palestinian organizations that fail to exclude Germans from armed actions against Israel inflict great damage on the anti-racist character of the Palestinian revolution. We come to the key point: the hijacking to Entebbe was a counter-revolutionary action."[84]

The logical corollary of his argument was that Palestinian terrorist attacks on Israeli civilians that were not carried out by Germans did not "inflict great damage on the anti-racist character of the Palestinian revolution." He continued that "the terror of anti-imperialist revolution always limited itself to legitimate targets, that is, to the occupier and its institutions." Its function lay "in breaking the will of the occupier and fostering its international isolation. The hijacking to Entebbe neither struck the occupier nor did it foster its isolation. One the contrary, it was a contribution to the international isolation of the Palestinian revolution. Legitimate social revolutionary violence is distinguished from that of the counter-revolutionary enemy."[85] So, while criticizing "ahistorical Zionism," Claussen offered a justification for the PLO's attacks on "the occupier" – that is, the citizens of the state of Israel. Though Claussen's essay reflected the anti-Zionist consensus of the West German Left, he voiced a historical self-consciousness about the legacies of anti-Semitism in Germany, one that the members of the Revolutionary Cells and the Red Army Faction (RAF) had suppressed and disparaged.

THE PFLP, THE RAF, AND THE HOT AUTUMN OF 1977

In fall 1977, about 15 months after the Entebbe hijacking, members of the Red Army Faction kidnapped Hans-Martin Schleyer, president of the Confederation of German Employers Association.[86] In exchange for his freedom, they demanded the release of RAF members held in West German prisons. In support of those efforts, members of the PFLP hijacked a Lufthansa flight from Majorca to Somalia and demanded the

84 Ibid.

85 Ibid.

86 The literature the famous events of the hot autumn is extensive. Two standard accounts are Butz Peters, *Tödlicher Irrtum: Die Geschichte der RAF*, 3rd ed. (Frankfurt-Main: Fischer, 2007); and Stefan Aust, *The Inside Story of the R.A.F* (New York: Oxford University Press, 2009).

prisoners' release. The attempt was foiled by a West German government commando operation in Mogadishu that freed the hostages and killed the terrorists. The RAF kidnappers then murdered Schleyer. On October 15, 1977, the left-liberal daily *Frankfurter Rundschau* published the text of a PFLP communiqué. It underscored the importance of shared antagonism to Israel for the alliance between the RAF and the PFLP.[87]

The group called itself the "Commando Martyr Halimeh," using the Islamic name given to Brigitte Kuhlmann. The purpose of the hijacking of the Lufthansa flight was to "free our comrades from the prisons of the imperialist-reactionary-zionist alliance." The communiqué attacked the United States as well as "imperialist subcenters such as Israel and the FRG (Federal Republic of Germany)," which it claimed had the role of suppressing revolutionary movements in their own area. It referred to "Israel's expansionist and racist nature" and attacked West Germany for its "close and special cooperation in military and economic matters" with Israel. West Germany "delivered weapons and military, technical and atomic know-how" to Israel. It sent "mercenaries and offered credit. It opened markets and broke the [Arab League] boycott and the economic siege" of Israel. The PFLP alleged close cooperation between the Mossad and the West German secret services, which "made possible the filthy piracy of the imperialist-reactionary alliance manifest in the invasion of Entebbe."[88] It described both West Germany and Israel as successors to Nazism. "The similar character of neo-Nazism in West Germany and Zionism in Israel becomes ever clearer. A reactionary ideology dominates both countries." They both allegedly passed laws that were "fascist, discriminatory and racist" and engaged in "psychological and physical torture and murder" against "fighters for freedom and national liberation.... While the Zionist regime is a highly original and practical continuation of Nazism, the regime in Bonn and the political parties in its parliament do their best to renew Nazism and expansionist racism in West Germany." Jürgen Ponto, Hans-Martin Schleyer, and Siegfried Buback, all of whom the RAF had murdered, were "merely examples of persons who served the old Nazism well and today implement the goals of neo-Nazis in Bonn and of the Zionists in Tel Aviv."[89] This most famous attack in the 30-year history of the Red Army Faction entailed collaboration with the PFLP.

[87] "Kommunique Kofr Kaddum," *Frankfurter Rundschau* (October 15, 1977). My thanks to Martin Jander for drawing this important document to my attention.

[88] Ibid.

[89] Ibid. On the communiqué also see the short description in Stefan Aust, *Der Baader Meinhof Komplex* (Munich: Wilhelm Goldmann, 1998), 597–599.

The 1977 report of the Federal Office for Protection of the Constitution (Bundesamt für Verfassungsschutz) drew attention to the international contacts of West German terrorists with Palestinians. It asserted that in February 1975, the General Union of Arab Students in the Federal Republic of German and West-Berlin: (GUAS) was established as a successor to the General Union of Palestinian Students (GUPS). With about 1,000 members, it represented the views of the PLO led by Arafat. It also had a "strong faction" that supported the Popular Front for the Liberation of Palestine (PFLP) led by George Habash. It had opened an "Information Center" in Bonn.[90] The Interior Ministry concluded that Al Fatah and the PLO had "preserved a network of conspiratorially functioning cells and contact in Germany" whose members took weapons training courses in Palestinian camps and then returned to Europe.[91] It placed the hijacking of fall 1977 in this context.

> The hijacking of the Lufthansa plane "Landshut" from Majorca to Somalia in connection with the kidnapping of Dr. [Hans-Martin] Schleyer primarily served the interests of German terrorists. It was the first time that a purely Palestinian commando supported such an action by German terrorists. It took place after Germans had previously repeatedly offered personal and material support to Palestinian groups. The obviously coordinated action in this hijacking was, at that time, the highpoint of cooperation of German and Palestinian terrorist organizations.[92]

The report noted that among Palestinians in West Germany in the GUAS, there was increased support for the PFLP and a rapprochement between the PLO and the PFLP and others in "the rejection front," that is, Palestinians who opposed Egyptian President Anwar Sadat's negotiations with Israel. German-language leaflets of Palestinian radical organizations in West Germany asserted that in the "war" against Zionism and imperialism "the imperialist regional centers such as the Zionist community in West Germany had the task of carrying out the oppression and liquidation of every revolutionary movement in a particular area." The "Zionist regime" was the "most genuine and practical continuation of Nazism," which the West German government and the political parties supported and did what they could "to renew expansionist racism in West Germany."[93] For the police and counterterrorism officials of the

90 Verfassungsschutzbericht '75, No. 25 (Bonn: Bundesminister des Innern, 1976), pp. 135–136. The German title is: "Generalunion Arabischer Studenten in der Bundesrepublik Deutschland und West-Berlin."

91 Ibid., p. 136.

92 "3.22. Internationale Verflechtung," *Verfassungsschutzbericht* '77, No. 25, 119.

93 Ibid., 149.

Federal Republic, these statements amounted to threats to attack the Jewish community in West Germany as well as its political leaders.

HANS-JOACHIM KLEIN ON THE REVOLUTIONARY CELLS AND HIS "RETURN TO HUMANITY"

In 1979, Hans-Joachim Klein expanded on his revelations about the Revolutionary Cells in *Rückkehr in die Menschlichkeit: Appell eines ausgestigenen Terroristen* (Return to Humanity: The Appeal of a Terrorist Who Has Abandoned Terrorism). It sold 40,000 copies in a month. Daniel Cohn-Bendit, well known for his role in the leftist revolt of May 1968 in Paris but then living in Frankfurt/Main and editing *Pflasterstrand*, a local magazine, wrote the afterword.[94] Klein reported that according to Waddid Haddad, the leader of the PFLP, Idi Amin strangled Dora Bloch himself. Klein asked his RC comrades what killing "an old woman with heart illness has to do with a peoples' liberation struggle?" Was it "yet another important victory in the struggle against Zionism?" However, both the RC and the June 2nd movement people only found the murder of Dora Bloch to be not "particularly clever." Further, Klein reported that even after Entebbe as well as before, the Red Army Faction, the RC, and June 2nd worked together with the PFLP, which offered them the military supplies they needed.[95] Klein's assertions were in accord with Western intelligence reports that viewed the PFLP as the PLO's key organizational connection to West German and West European leftist terrorists. In Klein's view the PFLP was important for the survival and persistence of the leftist terrorist organizations in West Germany.[96]

In *Return to Humanity* Klein wrote that the plan to assassinate Galinski and Lipinski "was and is fascist, even if the killers call themselves 'revolutionaries.'" Klein's RC comrades told him that though they had no "political interest" in killing Galinski and Lipinski, they had to show their Arab counterparts that they remained an effective force after Entebbe. They needed "countries where they could take hostages, weapons and above all," they "needed money." Carrying out the murders of the two Jewish leaders would satisfy PFLP demands.[97] The alliance was

[94] Hans-Joachim Klein, *Rückkehr in die Menschlichkeit.*

[95] Ibid., 80–81.

[96] See Thomas Skelton Robinson, "Im Netz verheddert: Die Beziehungen des bundesdeutschen Linksterrorismus zur Volksfront für die Befreiung Palästina (1969–1980)"; and Martin Jander, "Deutscher Linksterrorismus und Israel: Ethno-nationalistisch, religiös-fundamentalistisch oder sozialrevolutionär?"

[97] Klein, *Rückkehr in die Menschlichkeit,* 87–88.

one of mutual benefit to the West German and Palestinian terrorist organizations. Klein took pride in helping to prevent the assassinations. No matter what the Jewish leaders' political views were, he viewed these planned "murders in the sequence of the disastrous history of German Nazi-fascism." He also revealed that members of the RC were contemplating murdering Simon Wiesenthal, director of an organization in Vienna that focused on bringing ex-Nazis to trial. Members of the Revolutionary Cells told Klein that Wiesenthal was "just for that reason a swine and ready to be hit." Those views, which he regarded as echoes of "German Nazi-fascism," also led Klein to write the following to his former comrades in the RC:

> You can't deny, it is a bloody fact that this Idi Amin Dada is a fascist and mass murderer. There two of you [Böse and Kuhlmann] participated in the selection of Jews/Israelis and non-Jews. One of your members, Halimeh (The Quiet One) [Kuhlmann], did not refrain from hitting Jews on the head if they were wearing yarmulkes.
>
> You say that this is your form of "love and solidarity."
>
> I'm telling that with your actions about Galinsky, Libinsky [*sic*], Wiesenthal, Entebbe and also new plans that will certainly involve West German guerrillas, you have catapulted yourselves out of any political context. I don't have to betray anything. You are committing suicide. The revolutionary violence you talk about has degenerated into a tool of the murderous business of cynical, neurotic outsiders.[98]

On May 13, the *Jüdische Allgemeine* responded to the Klein revelations. "Leading Jewish personalities" as well as other public figures were fully aware of "the dangers that come with open opposition to murder and deadly attacks, to anarchist bands of murderers and their henchmen, to left-wing and right wing extremists and their press organs which include attacks on Jews, Jewry, democracy and freedom in every issue."[99] As had been the case since the late 1960s, the organized Jewish community viewed the national, state, and local authorities, whom the radical Left had denounced as revivals of Nazism, as vital institutions of liberal democracy, necessary for the fight against terrorism and indispensable protectors of the Jewish communities in West Germany against threats of assassination from the terrorist organizations of the radical Left.

[98] Ibid., 88–89.

[99] Hermann Lewy, "Ein Terrorist gibt auf: Hans-Joachim Klein enthüllt weitere Mordpläne." *Berliner Allgemeine jüdische Wochenzeitung* (Dusseldorf, May 13, 1978), 1.

11

An Alliance Deepens: East Germany, the Arab states, and the PLO: 1978–1982

One of the most striking visual images of the era of East Germany's undeclared war with Israel was captured in a photo of March 11, 1978 in East Berlin. It shows Yasser Arafat accompanied by Gerhard Grüneberg and others walking solemnly into the memorial to "the victims of fascism and militarism" on the famed Unter den Linden Strasse. Soldiers of East Germany's National People's Army stand at attention in the background as Arafat pays his respects to the victims of Nazi Germany's war on the Eastern Front in World War II. (See Figure 11.1). The photo captures the transformation of the meaning of anti-fascism in the Soviet bloc and in East Germany that made it possible for the East Germans to ask Arafat, then at war with the Jewish state, to pay homage to Nazism's victims. Communist anti-fascism had long become compatible with ideological and military anti-Zionism. This transformation of anti-fascism's meaning in public political culture had its counterpart in continuing Soviet-bloc, including East German, military assistance to the PLO.

By the mid-1970s, the West German press reports mentioned East German military assistance to radical movements in Africa, Asia, Latin America, and the Middle East, including the PLO.[1] The archives of the East German regime, especially the files of its Ministries of Defense, Foreign Affairs, State Security, Politburo, and Council of Ministers, offer

[1] See "DDR: Kalschnikows für die Dritte Welt," *Der Spiegel* (August 30, 1975), 60–63; "DDR verteidigt Waffenlieferungen an 'Befreiungsbewegungen'," *Frankfurter Allgemeine Zeitung* (April 1, 1978); "DDR will Arafat Waffen liefern," *Süddeutsche Zeitung* (June 8, 1978); "DDR -Waffen für die PLO," *Frankfurter Rundschau* (June 8, 1978); "Ost-Berlin gibt PLO Waffen," *Berliner Zeitung* (June 8, 1978); "Arafat läßt sich in der 'DDR' feiern," *Die Welt* (June 8, 1978), and "Liefert Ost-Berlin modernste Waffen an Arafat?"

FIGURE 11.1. Yasser Arafat (front, second from right), Gerhard Grüneberg (front, third from right) with PLO delegation on March 11, 1978, prepare to lay a wreath at the memorial to "victims of fascism and militarism" on Unter den Linden in East Berlin. Units of East Germany's National Peoples' Army stand at attention in the background.
Source: German Federal Archive, Koblenz, Photo Archive: Bild 183-T0311-014, ADN-ZB, Manfred Siebahn.

abundant evidence of the intensification and expansion of those activities. What was sometimes called a "second Cold War" erupted in Europe as the Soviet Union expanded intermediate-range nuclear missile forces and conducted a vigorous "peace campaign" intended to block NATO's "double-track decision" of 1979.[2] In the Middle East, the Soviet Union and its Arab allies, stung by Egypt's departure from the Arab "rejection front," also went on the political and military offensive. Yet both in Western Europe and in Israel, Soviet pressure led to a Western reaction. In retrospect, Israel's June 1982 invasion of Lebanon, "Operation Peace for Galilee," and the implementation in fall 1983 of NATO's double-track

[2] On the second Cold War and the euromissiles see Jeffrey Herf, *War by Other Means: Soviet Power, West German Resistance and the Battle of the Euromissiles* (New York: Free Press, 1991). Also see Phillip Gassert, Herman Wentker, and Tim Geiger, eds., *Zweiter Kalter Krieg und Friedensbewegung: Der NATO-Doppelbeschluss in deutsch-deutscher und internationaler Perspektive* (Munich: Oldenbourg Verlag, 2001); and the volumes of *Akten zur Auswärtigen Politik der Bundesrepublik Deutschland* now published up to 1983.

decision of 1979 in Western Europe indicated that the United States and its allies, including Israel, were shifting the "correlation of forces" in world politics against the Soviet bloc and, in the Middle East, against the rejectionist Arab states and the PLO.

THE STASI'S DILEMMA AND ITS EUROCENTRIC DEFINITION OF COUNTERTERRORISM

As noted in previous chapters, Gerhard Neiber, the deputy ministry of East Germany's Ministry of State Security, oversaw its Hauptabteilung XXII, Terrorabwehr, the Main Department XXII for Defense against Terror.[3] Actually this counterterrorism department was responsible for contact with leftist terrorist organizations in the third world and in Western Europe. The Stasi's "Action Friendship" (Aktion Freundschaft) was its key program of support to many leftist third-world states and "national liberation movements." Recipients of East German assistance included the PLO as well as the governments of North Vietnam, Mozambique, Yemen, Ethiopia, Libya, Laos, Zanzibar, Sudan, Congo, Cape Verde; and organizations including SWAPO (Southwest African People's Organization); the Sandinistas in Nicaragua; the Farabundo Marti National Liberation Front, or FMLN, guerrillas in El Salvador; and the ANC (African National Congress) in Angola.[4] In a memo of April 26, 1977, the MfS Finance Office reported that from 1967 to 1977 the MfS spent 104,638,800 marks for travel, training, and equipment in support of "young national states in the non-civilian area."[5]

[3] See "Neiber, Gerhard," in Bernd-Rainer Barth, et al., eds., *Wer war Wer in der DDR: Ein biographisches Handbuch* (Frankfurt/Main: Fischer, 1996), 533.

[4] "Vorschlag zur Verschlüsselung," BStU, Archiv der Zentralstelle, MfS-BCD (Bewaffung und Chemische Dienst), Nr. 2802, 59; and "Zusammenarbeit mit Sicherheitsorganen national befreiter Staaten und Nationaler Befreiungsgewegungen und deren Unterstützung," [East] Berlin (December 7, 1885), BStU, Archiv der Zentralstelle, MfS Abt.X, Nr. 93, 14. Also see for example, "Chekist Development and 'Anti-Imperialist Solidarity,'" in Jens Gieseke, *History of the Stasi* (New York: Berghahn Books, 2014), 180–183.

[5] Abteilung Finanzen, "Übersicht über Ausgaben für durchgeführte Hilfeleistungen gegenüber jungen Nationalstaaten auf nichtzivilen Gebiet von 1967 bis 1976," [East] Berlin (April 26, 1977), BStU, Archiv der Zentralstelle, MfS Abt. Finanzen, Nr. 1393, 152. East Germany's Ministry of Interior (Ministerium des Innern, MdI) also became known for training police forces that were effective in sustaining dictatorships in these countries. In 1978, the GDR Ministry of the Interior spent 10,924,200 marks on support for police training in these countries. See Abteilung Finanzen, "Zusammenstellung der Ausgaben des MfS und des MdI für Hilfeleistungen an junge Nationalstaaten 1978," [East] Berlin (December 15, 1978), 150. In view of the document destruction of fall 1989, figures about spending may not be complete.

As a memo of October 26, 1976, from Department XXII indicated, Israel's successful raid in Entebbe worried the Stasi and the PLO.[6] The officials of Department XXII wanted to assist the PLO in defending it against possible attacks by Israeli's clandestine service, the Mossad.[7] Yet another problem turned out to be an even greater impetus for intensified cooperation between the Stasi and the PLO. The officials of Department XXII knew that terrorists from the Arab states and Palestinian organizations were flying from the Middle East to Berlin-Schönefeld airport in East Berlin and from there were traveling to West Berlin. They also knew that West German leftist terrorists were fleeing from West to East Germany.[8] Stasi surveillance of Mamoud Odeh, alias Abu Daud, illustrated the problem. The ministry recorded his arrival in East Berlin on April 27, 1979, and return to Beirut on May 1. It reported that he had "been held responsible for organizing serious terrorist attacks by the Black September organization (for example, during the Summer Olympics in Munich in 1972)" and played a "key role in coordinating the world wide actions of the Palestinian liberation movement. His arrival [in East Berlin] likely signals imminent actions of considerable dimensions."[9] In West Germany, the Bavarian judicial and police authorities learned of his presence in East Berlin and immediately sought to have him extradited to face charges connected to the attack on the Olympics. The East Germans refused.[10] Soviet-bloc intelligence services had observed him in East Berlin, Budapest, Sofia, Prague, Beirut, and Warsaw in the late 1970s and early 1980s. They knew that he remained in contact with Abu Ayad, director of the PLO intelligence service, as well as with the Carlos group,

6 "Zusammenfassender Bericht," Bundesbeauftragte für die Unterlagen des Staatssicherheitsdienst der ehemaligen Deutschen Demokratischen, BStU, Archiv der Zentralstelle, MfS-HA (Hauptverwaltung Aufklärung) XXII, Nr. 105418, Teil 1 von 2, [East] Berlin (October 23, 1976), 50–56.

7 "Zusammenfassender Bericht," BStU, Archiv der Zentralstelle, MfS-HA XXII, Nr. 105418, Teil 1 von 2, [East] Berlin (October 23, 1976), 50. For a history of the Mossad see Dan Raviv and Yossi Melman and *Every Spy a Prince: The Complete History of the Israeli Intelligence Community* (New York: Houghton Mifflin, 1990).

8 Also see Gieseke, *History of the Stasi*, 183.

9 "Aktivitäten von Vertretern der Palästinensischen Befreiungsbewegung in Verbindung mit internationalen Terroristen zur Einbeziehung der DDR bei der Vorbereitung von Gewaltakten in Ländern Westeuropas," [East] Berlin, May 8, 1979, Z 3021, BStU, Ministerium für Staatssicherheit, [East] Berlin, May 8, 1979, 9. For another report on his participation in the Munich attack also see "Information zur Person, ODEH, Mahmoud," [East] Berlin (October 1982), BStU-AZ, MfS-HA XXII, 1978, 11–12. The German reads: "Unter seiner Leitung wurden mehrere schwerwiegende Terroranschläge, so der Anschlag auf die israelische Olympia-Mannschaft 1972 in München, verübt."

10 Ibid., 10.

with Arab diplomats in the Communist countries, Arabs living in the GDR, and persons living in the GDR, West Berlin, Denmark, Yugoslavia, Romania, Italy, France, and Sweden. They kept a close eye on him. The Stasi reported that he continued "to engage in extensive intimate contacts with women in the GDR."[11] On August 1, 1981, in Warsaw, Daud was shot five times but recovered in a Warsaw hospital. After his recovery, the Stasi learned that he "was again active in the service of Abu Ayad," that is, of the PLO secret intelligence services.[12]

The presence and activities of Abu Daud in Eastern Europe and East Berlin posed the dilemma that the American warnings of 1973 had emphasized. How could East Germany maintain "anti-imperialist solidarity" without antagonizing West Germany and the United States and thereby undermining support for détente in the West? On the one hand, Daud was welcome in the Soviet bloc as an ally in the battle against the West and Israel. On the other hand, he was a wanted man sought by the West German and Israeli governments for his role in the attack on the Munich Olympics. If the East Germans turned him over to the West Germans, they would be denounced for betraying the revolutionary cause. Yet granting him refuge made it possible for him to evade capture and continue his activities, which would reinforce Western suspicions that the East Germans and the Soviet bloc were state sponsors of terrorism.

A November 14, 1979, report from Department XXII offered another example of the Stasi's dilemma. "X," a Palestinian who in 1972 had been indicted by the district attorney in Cologne on five charges of murder (probably stemming from the murders of five Jordanians by PLO operatives), was studying economics at the Martin Luther University in Halle, East Germany. He attracted the Stasi's attention because during a visit on April 3–4, 1979, to East Germany by Abu Hisham, a senior official in the PLO's intelligence service, "X" served as the translator of conversations between Hisham and members of the Carlos group.[13] A subsequent, undated note about "X" asserted that he "participated in the attack on the Israeli Olympic team in Munich" and was a "trusted and close aid to Abu Hisham."[14] Hence both the PLO and the Stasi knew that another participant suspected of participation in the Munich attack was in East

[11] Ibid.

[12] Ibid., 12.

[13] "Auskunftsbericht," [East] Berlin (November 14, 1979), BStU, Zentralstelle, Abteilung XXII/1, 52–53.

[14] "Kurzauskunft," [East] Berlin (November 14, 1979), BStU, Zentralstelle, Abteilung XXII/1, 59.

Germany. Again, the Stasi officials did not turn him over to West German authorities.

As the previously discussed American response to the opening of the PLO office in East Berlin in 1973 illustrated, both the Soviet Union and the East German government had to assume that the United States and the Western allies were aware of the potential threat from Arab terrorists who found a base in the Soviet bloc and in East Germany. The presence of Arab, including Palestinian, terrorists in East Germany and their potential for carrying out terrorist attacks in West Germany and Western Europe compelled Erich Mielke and Gerhard Neiber to ask how East Germany could reconcile "anti-imperialist solidarity" with such organizations and persons with the preservation of détente and improved East German relations with West Germany. How could it prevent their presence from lending credence to the view that East Germany and the Soviet-bloc states were state sponsors of terrorism? The Stasi addressed the issue in May 1979 in a remarkable report ordered by Mielke entitled "Information about Activities of Representatives of the Palestine Liberation Movement in Association with International Terrorists Seeking to Include the GDR in the Preparation of Acts of Violence in the Countries of Western Europe."[15]

Groups within the Palestinian liberation movement in association with anarcho-terrorist groups have intensified their efforts to use the territory of the GDR as a logistical base and starting point for the implementation of acts of violence in Western Europe. The GDR's generous stance of solidarity toward the national liberation movement of the Arab peoples is seen by these groups as offering favorable conditions for the planning and implementation of operations. The communications possibilities of the GDR's capital city [East Berlin, JH] are also taken into account. In particular, after the separate peace [the Camp David Accords] between Egypt and Israel of April 25, 1979 went into effect, the Palestinian Liberation Movement activated the planning and preparation of acts of violence seen as acts of war (*Kriegshandlung)* against Western countries. Such

[15] "Aktivitäten von Vertretern der Palästinensischen Befreiungsbewegung in Verbindung mit internationalen Terroristen zur Einbeziehung der DDR bei der Vorbereitung von Gewaltakten in Ländern Westeuropas." [East] Berlin, May 8, 1979, Z 3021, BStU, Ministerium für Staatssicherheit, [East] Berlin, May 8, 1979, 1–16. The author of the report appeared to be Werner Irmler. See "Irmler, Gerhard" in Barth et al., *Wer war Wer in der DDR*, 330. In his memoirs, Markus Wolf, who oversaw East German espionage operations in West Germany, wrote that "Mielke was terrified that our," that is, the Stasi's, "Palestinian connection would become public," by which he meant not the well-known public connection but that between the Stasi and the PLO intelligence agencies involved in terrorist activities. See Markus Wolf, *Man without a Face: The Autobiography of Communism's Greatest Spymaster* (New York: Times Books/Random House, 1997), 274.

activities that are based in the territory of the GDR create political dangers and damage our national security interests.

According to our internal information, influential forces within the Palestinian liberation movement are strengthening their efforts especially against Israel and Egyptian persons and objects, are preparing terrorist attacks and acts of violence and are operating in part from the territories of the socialist [that is, Communist, JH] countries.[16]

The report concluded that the Stasi's "favorable stance and loyalty ... toward members of extremist groups of the Palestinian liberation movement as well as toward the members of anarcho-terrorist groups allied with them [the Palestinians, JH] has apparently strengthened their view that the GDR can be won over to their strategic concept of 'armed struggle' that includes world-wide acts of violence." Yet infiltration of the Palestinian organization and "the repeated efforts of Western politicians, security officials and journalists to hold the socialist [Communist, JH] states responsible for increasing terror in their countries raise resulting political and security risks related to these matter for our republic."[17] In fact, the Stasi did support "acts of violence" outside Europe.

Nevertheless the Stasi's report of May 1979 indicated that its officials were fully aware of the presence of Arab, Palestinian, and West European terrorists in East Germany and that it had aided them in their efforts, given them safe haven and looked the other way as Arab embassies and perhaps the PLO office in East Berlin gave active support to such efforts as well. Apparently the evidence was now becoming obvious to Western intelligence agencies. Now the East German government was worried that continued toleration toward these actors would undermine support for détente in Western Europe and for continued West German financial

[16] Ibid., 1–2.

[17] Ibid., 16. The Stasi files on Abu Daud are extensive. See a memo of May 23, 1979, from Neiber to Mielke. Gerhard Neiber to Erich Mielke, "Genossen Minister," [East] Berlin (May 23, 1979), VNE 1026/79, Bundesbeauftragte für die Unterlagen des Staatssicherheitsdienst der ehemaligen Deutschen Demokratischen Republik(BStU), Archiv der Zentralstelle, MfS-HA XXII, Nr. 17508, Teil 1 von 2, 59–66; "Zur Einreise des zu extremistischen Flügel der PLO zählenden Palästinensers, Abu DAUD, in die Haupstadt der DDR," [East] Berlin (September 7, 1978), and "Bericht über den Aufenthalt des zu extremistischen Flügel der PLO zählenden Palästinensers, Abu DAUD, in die Haupstadt der DDR," [East] Berlin (September 7, 1978), 52, BStU, Archiv der Zentralstelle, MfS HA II, Nr. 27077, 2 and 52; "Auskunftsbericht über den zum extremistischen Flügel der PLO gehörenden Palästinenser 'Abu Daud,' " [East] Berlin (April 30, 1979) BStU, Archiv der Zentralstelle, Z 3021, 18–31; and "Einschätzung der Ursachen des Verlaufes und der Auswirkunen des Terroranschlages während der MÜNCHENER OLYMPIADE," BStU, Archiv der Zentralstelle, MfS-HA XXII, Nr. 21596, 4–54; "Über Abu Daud, Nr. 1051/78" BStU, Archiv der Zentralstelle, MfS HA II 27075, 69–72.

FIGURE 11.2. On October 19, 1981, members of East Germany's Politburo congratulate graduates of military academies. From left to right, Horst Sindermann, Willi Stoph, Erich Honecker, Heinz Hoffmann, and Erich Mielke, the Minister of the State Security Service (the Stasi) (second from right), minister of state security (Stasi), and Joachim Hermann.
Source: German Federal Archives, Koblenz, Photo Archive: Bild 183-Z1019-025, ADN-ZB, Rainer Mittelstadt.

payments to East Germany. One effective way to counter terrorism in Western Europe that had origins in the Soviet bloc would be to draw on the expertise and information of the PLO. Intensification of contact between the MfS and the PLO intelligence agencies would simultaneously serve to "counter terrorism" in West Germany and Western Europe and offer support to the PLO's terrorist campaign against Israel. Trying to prevent terrorist attacks against Western Europe that were traceable to East Germany while supporting terrorist attacks on Israel emerged as the essence of the Stasi's Eurocentric definition of the "fight against terrorism."

The report noted that Ilich Ramirez, better known as Carlos, was prominent among those who created "political dangers" and could "damage" East German national security interests. Since the beginning of March 1979, the Stasi kept him under close surveillance, as it did Abu Hisham, an aide to Abu Ayad, the head of the PLO's intelligence service.[18]

[18] Ibid., 2 and 7.

The Stasi was aware that the Carlos group had established logistical bases in East Germany, met with citizens of different Arab countries, and had contact with members of the Carlos group in West Germany and other West European countries. The group maintained "close, constant contact to the embassies of the Peoples' Republic of Yemen, Iraq, Libya as well as the PLO representation in East Berlin." It sought to acquire "weapons, explosives, money and information" to be used in "armed struggle" including "assassinations and the like against imperialist policies of the USA, the Zionists and the clique around [Anwar] Sadat." It had "contacts with anarcho-terrorists groups from the Federal Republic of Germany and West Berlin" and was using the Soviet and East German embassies in Damascus to establish an operational basis in Syria.[19]

The Mielke report also examined connections between the "June 2nd Group" and the Communist states in Eastern Europe. Associates of Till Meyer, a leading member of the June 2nd Movement, aided his escape from the West Berlin Moabit prison on May 27, 1978. "The transit routes of the socialist [i.e., Communist, JH] countries were used in the planning and implementation of the liberation action." Meyer was captured in Bulgaria by West German officials of the Bundeskriminalamt (Federal Criminal Office, or BKA, the West German counterpart to the FBI). The capture caused "great political and security problems for Bulgaria" because "the presence of the June 2nd Movement in the Peoples' Republic of Bulgaria made clear that anarcho-terrorist groups from the Federal Republic of Germany and West Berlin believed that they would be relatively safe and could move around freely in the socialist [Communist, JH] countries." Further, the MfS had "operational indications and knowledge about the existence of close ties and increasingly coordinated action of extremist groups of the Palestinian liberation movement and the anarcho-terrorist groups in the FRG and West Berlin." West German members of the June 2nd Movement including Inge Viett, Ingrid Siepmann, and Regine Nicolai had "close cooperation" with Wadid Haddad's PFLP and his successors.[20] On the day that Meyer broke out of West Berlin's Moabit prison, Viett, Siepmann and Nikolai "received permits to travel from West Berlin to Czechoslovakia after they were identified at the border crossing" in East Berlin. "All three had fake passports." On June 27, 1978, the three were arrested by the Czech police and transferred to the MfS. "From June 28 to July 12, 1978 they were in the GDR in a secret safe house. They were then flown while under the control of the MfS to Baghdad, Iraq where

19 Ibid., 8.

20 Ibid., 10–11.

they claimed to have an operational basis."[21] The Stasi had thereby facilitated their escape from West German authorities and had allowed them to use Soviet-bloc and Arab countries for escape.

Another Stasi memo of June 21, 1979, on "Measures for operative control of extremist forces from Arab and other states staying in the GDR," focused on the presence of Carlos, Abu Daud, as well as possible activity by the Japanese Red Army in Europe.[22] In contrast to the language games played by Soviet-bloc diplomats at the United Nations, the Stasi report was strikingly frank about the subjects of terrorism and extremism. The memo noted that in view of the bomb plots recently thwarted by Western intelligence agencies in West Berlin, it was especially important to have information about the possibility that "the GDR and especially the capital Berlin could be used" by the groups and individuals mentioned as "the starting point for preparation and organization of acts of violence in Western states."[23] The MfS offices for domestic surveillance and for counterterrorism were ordered to intensify their surveillance of what the memo called these "extremist forces" as well as of the East Berlin embassies of the Peoples' Republic of Yemen, and of Iraq "in connection with the extremist forces." That surveillance included closer observation of Arab citizens traveling to East Germany; the Arab embassies in East Berlin; "travel activities of the members of Arab Embassies," especially those of Yemen and Iraq; and of "Carlos and his circle of contacts." It also ordered searches for "known terrorists of the 'Red Army Faction' Japan" that is, the Japanese Red Army terrorist organization.[24]

In Arafat and the PLO, East Germany had an ally familiar with Arab and Palestinian persons and organizations engaged in what the Stasi recognized as terrorism directed against Israel, the United States, and Western Europe. Arafat appeared to have concluded that terrorist attacks in Western Europe undermined the PLO's goal of winning political support there in its battle against Israel. Hence, in exchange for the support it was receiving from the Soviet bloc, including from East Germany, the PLO agreed to assist the Stasi in reducing the terrorist threat to West Germany and Western Europe if that threat originated with foreign groups and individuals working in East Germany or other Soviet-bloc states. A joint effort to achieve that goal became grounds for intensified cooperation

[21] Ibid., 12.

[22] Hauptabteilung II, "Maßnahmen zur operative Kontrolle der in der DDR aufhältigen extremistischen Kräfte aus arabischen und anderen Staaten," [East] Berlin (June 21, 1979), BStU, Archiv der Zentralstelle, MfS HA II, Nr. 25009, 58–61.

[23] Ibid., 63.

[24] Ibid., 63–65.

between the Stasi and the PLO. The purpose of the cooperation was not to discourage terrorism directed at Israel or the Egyptian government of Anwar Sadat. On the contrary, the goal was for "the GDR as its ally, to enhance the PLO's ability to carry out actions that it describes as 'acts of war' (*Kriegshandlungen)* against anti-Palestinian, Zionist centers as well as against the traitorous Sadat regime."[25] Especially compared to East Germany's obfuscations in the UN Sixth Committee in New York, there was a refreshing honesty to this Stasi memo about aiding the PLO to carry out "acts of war" against Israel.

In April 1979, in a conversation with the East German ambassador in Beirut, Achim Reichardt (1929–), Arafat requested support in training soldiers, police, and intelligence officers.[26] In that same month, Abu Hisham of the PLO intelligence services also proposed to Reichardt that official discussions begin with the MfS for training in "general security, small weapons, explosives, organization of special actions," and acquisition of unspecified "technical and electronic equipment ... pistols, explosives and assistance in transporting them to Western Europe."[27] Hisham asserted that he was "acting on orders from Abu Ayad, member of the Central Committee of Fatah and in agreement with PLO-Chairman Arafat. On political grounds, Arafat as well as the representative of the PLO in the GDR had to be kept out of this cooperation."[28] In other words, the Stasi was learning that Arafat and the PLO appeared to be playing a double game, denouncing terrorism in Western Europe in public but tolerating it in fact.

THE STASI AND THE PLO INTELLIGENCE SERVICE FORMAL COOPERATION AGREEMENTS OF 1979–1980

In June 1979 the MfS signed a formal agreement of cooperation with the PLO intelligence services based on their shared interest in preventing the use of East Germany as a base for terrorist operations against Western

[25] "Information über Aktivitäten von Vertretern der Palästinensischen Befreiungsbewegung in Verbindung mit internationalen Terroristen zur Einbeziehung der DDR bei der Vorbereitung von Gewaltakten in Ländern Westeuropas," 13. See "Reichardt, Achim," in Siegfried Bock, Ingrid Muth, and Herman Schwiesau, eds., *DDR-Außenpolitik: Ein Überblick* (Berlin: LIT Verlag, 2010), 344.

[26] "Information über Aktivitäten von Vertretern der Palästinensischen Befreiungsbewegung," 13.

[27] Ibid.,14.

[28] Ibid. The German reads: "Abu Hisham erklärte, im Auftrage des Mitgliedes des ZK der FATAH, ABU AYAD, und in Abstimmung mit dem PLO-Vorsitzenden ARAFAT zu handeln. Aus politischen Gründen müßten jedoch sowohl ARAFAT als auch die Vertretung der PLO in der DDR aus dieser Zusammenarbeit herausgehalten werden."

Europe but for retaining it as a base for terrorist operations against Israel.[29] The cooperation was intended to produce "preventive information (*Verbeugende Aufklärung*)" and plans to fight "subversive plans and intentions as well as other activities that harm the state order and security of the GDR"; gather "information about terrorist and extremist forces in the FRG/West Berlin acting against the GDR and other socialist countries"; "gain possibilities to influence Palestinian citizens to participate in implementation of operative missions of the Ministry of State Security"; and acquire "political-operative influence on Palestinian citizens, other Arabs and other foreigners working with them to obey the GDR's laws and state rules (such as passport and visa order, custom and currency laws, orders for registration and drug laws)." Working together, the Stasi and the PLO intelligence service would keep track of Palestinian and Arab terrorists residing in East Germany in order to prevent them from carrying out attacks in West Germany and Western Europe. The contact between the two services would be handled by Neiber's Counterterrorism Department XXII.[30] The Stasi's Eurocentric definition of counterterrorism was now codified in a formal agreement with the PLO.

Around the same time, George Habash, a co-founder of the PFLP, met with the East German Politburo and officials in the Stasi's Counterterrorism Department to discuss "international terrorism."[31] The unnamed Politburo members told Habash that they would "not permit the GDR to be used for terrorist activities aimed at Western Europe or for building logistical centers for that purpose."[32] East Germany had "some peculiarities" of a political, geographical, military, and security-political nature that the PFLP needed to consider. These included its location "between the most powerful military alliances in the world," its ideological confrontation with the West, the possibility that military conflict "between socialism and imperialism could be easily provoked," the need to prevent damage to the GDR's relationship to West Germany, West Berlin's impact on Europe's political climate, and its importance in "the international class struggle," especially in the realm of enemy intelligence

[29] Stellvertreter des Ministers, Genossen Generalmajor Neiber, "Vorlage zum Einsatz eine Vertreters der Vereinigen PLO-Sicherheit in der DDR," Berlin (April 1, 1980), BStU, Archiv der Zentralstelle, Ministerium für Staatssicherheit (MfS) Hauptverwaltung (HA) XXII, Nr. 17508, 70–77.

[30] Ibid.

[31] "Anlage 2: 'Internationale Terrorismus'," BStU Archiv Zentralstelle, MfS-HA XXII 5537/3, 119–125.

[32] Ibid., 119.

agencies. Again they acknowledged that "important forces of international terrorist groups use the territory of the GDR as a logistical base or starting point for their actions."[33] Habash agreed with the Politburo that the focus of "the revolutionary struggle should be exclusively against imperialism, Zionism and Arab reaction above all in the occupied territories," which for the PFLP included all of Israel.[34] An implicit East German definition of moderation and extremism emerged in these conversations. An "extremist" was a terrorist who extended the "international class struggle" to include attacks in Western Europe while a "moderate" was a terrorist from the Arab states or the Palestinian organizations who focused attacks only against Israel, and perhaps "imperialist" targets outside Western Europe.

On February 2, 1980, the MfS and the PLO security services agreed that a permanent representative of the MfS would be assigned to work with Abu Ayad and his staff in Beirut. It also called for "operational cooperation" between the MfS and the PLO intelligence service in East Germany.[35] Contact with Palestinian citizens in the East Germany should aid in efforts to "stop the misuse of transit routes, especially from the Berlin-Schönefeld Airport to West Berlin" and to "stop or hinder the use of fake travel documents for entry, exit or transit through the GDR." Further, the cooperation should provide information and introduce preventive measures about "terrorist and left-wing extremist forces whose plans and intentions, activities, residence and travel activities, contact persons in the GDR and its base of operations and logistical bases" in order to protect the security of East Germany "as well as other socialist states."[36] From 1980 until the collapse of the regime in 1989, Ayad or his second-in-command, Amin al-Hindi, met several times a year with Erich Mielke or with Gerhard Neiber to implement this program.[37]

[33] Ibid.

[34] Ibid.

[35] Stellvertreter des Ministers, Genossen Generalmajor Neiber, "Vorlage zum Einsatz eine Vertreters der Vereinigen PLO-Sicherheit in der DDR," Berlin (April 1, 1980), BStU, Archiv der Zentralstelle, Ministerium für Staatssicherheit (MfS) Hauptverwaltung (HA) XXII, Nr. 17508, 70–77.

[36] Ibid.

[37] Ibid. Amin El-Hindi was a member of the General Union of Palestinian Students (GUPS) in Frankfurt/Main in the late 1960s. See Isabel Kershner, "Amin al-Hindi, Former Palestinian Intelligence Chief, Dies at 70," *New York Times* (August 18, 2010); and Abdallah Frangi, *Der Gesandte: Mein Leben für Palästina: Hinter den Kulissen der Nahost-Politik* (Munich: Wilhelm Heyne Verlag, 2010).

CANDID DISCUSSIONS ABOUT TERRORISM IN EAST BERLIN BETWEEN ABU AYAD AND STASI OFFICIALS

When Abu Ayad spoke with officials in Department XXII, their conversation dispensed with the euphemisms and linguistic contortions favored by Soviet-bloc diplomats at the United Nations. On July 15, 1980, officials in the Counterterrorism Department discussed "terrorist forces and their activities" with Ayad.[38] Before offering a 20-page report about various terrorist organizations, Ayad candidly explained the meaning of some important terms. The PLO, he said, distinguished between "right-wing terrorism," "left-wing adventurers," and "terrorist forces that are active in the interest of the Palestinian resistance movement." While it rejected both "right-wing terrorists" and "left-wing adventurers," the "PLO supported the other terrorist forces and at times worked together with them." The unnamed Stasi counterterrorism official replied that the Stasi "could support a certain toleration of left-oriented terrorist forces so long as they preserve strict secrecy, obey [East German, JH] law, and preclude any kind of political or any other kind of damage for the GDR and its allies." Ayad assured his counterparts that the PLO agreed with the MfS on this matter. He suggested that agreement about these issues was a basis on which "the exchange of information could continue to be improved."[39]

Ayad then offered "details about terrorist groups and forces to which the PLO had contacts and connections."[40] The groups included the Carlos group, Abu Nidal, Saddam Hussein's regime, former members of the Wadi Haddad group, the Armenian Liberation Front, and the Japanese Red Army. Regarding "terrorist groups in the FRG," that is, in West Germany, he said that the PLO had no contact with the June 2nd Movement or the Red Army Faction. It did have contacts with the Revolutionary Cells, the group that participated in the hijacking of the Air France flight to Entebbe. The PLO was working with the Revolutionary Cells and "intended to expand the connections to the so-called 'Revolutionary Cells' in the Federal Republic and eventually to use it to carry out particular armed actions."[41] Three years later, a Department XXII memo indicated that

38 "Bericht über das Gespräch mit dem Leiter der 'Vereinigten PLO-Sicherheit' – ABU AYAD – am 15.7.1980 zu terroristischen Kräften und ihren Aktivitäten," [East] Berlin (June 18, 1980), BStU MfS ZA HA XXII, Nr. 17508, Teil 2, 304–323.

39 Ibid., 304.

40 Ibid., 305.

41 Ibid., 319.

while the PLO adhered to the terms of the agreement, "our experiences in recent years indicated that difficulties are to be expected due to lack of discipline [and] violation of agreements by individual functionaries of the PLO."[42] Implementing the Stasi's Eurocentric counterterrorism policy required continuous surveillance and effort.

"ACTION FRIENDSHIP": WEAPONS DELIVERIES FROM THE STASI AND THE DEFENSE MINISTRY TO THE PLO: 1976–1982

The files of the Stasi's Department of Weapons and Chemical Services (Abteilung Bewaffnung und Chemische Dienst, hence BCD) and of its Finance Department contain detailed records about its weapons deliveries to the PLO and the many other already mentioned third-world armed movements that assisted in "Action Friendship." By "PLO" the MfS meant the main forces of Al Fatah led by Arafat, as well as those whom the East Germans called the "left-wing extremists" in the PFLP and the DPFLP. On October 16, 1976, about three months after the events in Entebbe, Defense Minister Heinz Hoffmann informed Erich Honecker that the Democratic Front for the Liberation of Palestine (DFLP) had requested communications equipment from East Germany. He sent Honecker a list of East German shortwave radio receivers and senders that were available for delivery. On October 18, 1976, Honecker penned his handwritten approval.[43] East Germany's weapons deliveries to Yemen in these years were particularly extensive. Given the presence of a variety of Palestinian guerrilla bases in that country, which in contrast to the PLO had its own airport and a number of ports for deliveries by sea, it is probable that weapon shipments sent there also wound up in the hands of Al Fatah, the PFLP, or the DPFLP. In 1980, it appears that the 5,119,108.98 marks worth of military equipment that the Stasi sent to Yemen was about four times as much assistance as the files indicate were sent directly to the PLO.[44]

42 Abteilung XXII, "Konzeption für die Gespräch mit dem Leiter der 'Vereinigten PLO-Sicherheit' Abu Ayad auf Linie XXII," [East] Berlin (January 3, 1983), BStU ZA HA XXII, Nr. 17508, Teil 1, 178–181.

43 Heinz Hoffmann to Erich Honecker, [East] Berlin, A-249–76 (October 16, 1976), BAMA, DVW 1/114448, 64–65.

44 "Lieferungen 1980 Gesamt," BStU, Archiv der Zentralstelle, MfS-BCD, Nr. 2802, 73. For very extensive data on the significant amounts of weapons delivered to Yemen from 1965 to 1982 see the files of the MfS Abteilung Bewaffnung und Chemische Dienst (Weapons and Chemical Services) BStU, Archiv der Zentralstelle, MfS-BCD, Nr. 2844, 80–228, and in MfS-BCD Nr. 2802.

East Germany did not produce major weapons systems, such as jet planes and tanks. However, by the late 1970s, its modest defense industry was producing versions of weapons needed for guerrilla warfare and terrorist attacks. These domestically produced items included an East German version of the Kalashnikov assault rifle (AK-47), hand grenades, rocket-propelled grenades, anti-tank bazookas, a variety of explosive charges, and different caliber machine-gun cartridges.[45] On August 4, 1980, the MfS delivered the following weapons to the PLO: 2000 MPi, a modernized version of the famous Kalashnikov machine gun; 5,000 hand grenades; 750 explosives of 200 grams each and 372 explosives of 400 grams each together with detonators and wire, with a value of 1,296,000 marks.[46] On April 11, 1980, the MfS sent 5,000 hand grenades, as well as explosives, detonators, wire, and ammunition valued at 114,102.38 marks to the PLO.[47] In February of 1981, the MfS sent 3,500 Kalashnikovs and 350 pallets of ammunition. In 1981, when the PLO was building up its arsenal in Lebanon, the Stasi weapons deliveries were worth 2,269,190 marks.[48] On April 6, 1982, the MfS sent the PLO 564,400 bullets and 1,400 Kalashnikovs. On April 23, 1982, it sent 10 rocket-propelled grenade launchers and 5 heavy machine guns costing 18,905 and 35,225 marks, respectively.[49] On July 1, 1982, shortly after Israel's invasion of Lebanon in June, East Germany sent the PLO the following weapons: 900 Kalashnikovs (MPi KMS-72) worth 583,000 marks; 720 RGD-5 anti-personnel fragmentation hand grenades worth 11,260.80 marks; 297,480 bullets worth 121,907.30 marks; 15 anti-tank rifles (RPG-7) worth 67,410.75 marks; and two light machine guns (lMG RPK Kal. 7.62).[50] On July 7, 1982 it sent 96 HL-grenades, designed for attacking tanks, worth 46,694.40 marks. The cost of weapons deliveries for this one week in July 1982 exceeded 720,000 marks.[51] The MfS sent an additional 300 Kalashnikovs (AK-47), 240 fragmentation hand

45 "Abteilung Bewaffnung und Chemischer Dienst, Versorgungsdienste, Referat 2," "Lt. Schreiben der HVA Forderung vom 4.8.1980 steht zur Abgabe noch bereit: 1982, DDR-Erzeugnisse," [East] Berlin (October 26, 1982), BStU, Archiv der Zentralstelle, MfS-BCD, Nr. 2802, 285.

46 "Lieferungen 1980 gesamt," BStU, AZ, MfS, BCD (Abteilung Bewaffnung und Chemischer Dienst) Nr. 2802, 73–75.

47 Ibid., 76.

48 "Lieferungen 1981 – gesamt", BStU, AZ, MfS, BCD Nr. 2802, 80.

49 "Aufstellung über Abgabe 1982 DDR Erzeugnisse: Beleg-Nr. 18306 v. 23.4. 1982," [East] Berlin (October 21, 1982), BStU, AZ, MfS, BCD Nr. 2802, 97.

50 Ibid., 96 and 98.

51 Ibid., 98.

grenades, and 99,160 "M-43" cartridges for the AK-47 on a special flight on July 7, 1982.[52]

In sum, from 1980 to 1982 in the course of "Action Friendship," the Stasi sent 8,300 Kalashnikovs and 10,896 hand and rifle-mounted grenades to the PLO, presumably as "solidarity goods" and thus cost-free. The MfS files on weapons deliveries to the PLO continued until 1989; the surviving documentation about those deliveries becomes sparse compared with the more detailed information about continuing deliveries of Kalashnikovs, bullets, hand grenades, and explosives to Yemen, some of which may have found its way into PLO affiliates.[53]

EAST GERMAN RELATIONS WITH SADDAM HUSSEIN'S IRAQ

In the 1970s and 1980s, East Germany delivered weapons to and repaired military equipment for Iraq as well as the following other "befriended developing countries": Afghanistan, Angola, Algeria, Benin, Congo, Ethiopia, Guinea, Guinea-Bissau, Guyana, India, Libya, Madagascar, Mozambique, Nigeria, Syria, Tanzania/Zanzibar, and Yemen.[54] Though the heart of the Soviet-bloc and East German alliance in the Middle East lay in Hafez al-Assad's Syria, Saddam Hussein's Iraq also had extensive military as well as cultural and educational cooperation with East Germany. During the 1970s, trade as well as cultural and intellectual exchanges expanded. In January 1973, East Germany and Iraq signed an agreement for ten Iraqi students to do postgraduate work in the GDR universities, five more for postgraduate work in engineering, and 80 to receive fellowships to study in East German universities in 1973 and 1974 for between five and ten months. The two governments signed an agreement to exchange twelve professors each from the Universities of Rostock and Halle with faculty from universities in Baghdad and Basrah. Three junior professors from East Germany were to spend nine months studying at Iraqi universities. Ten Iraqi scholars of German could take summer courses in the GDR. Officials of the respective education ministries would spend 10 days in the other country. Up to 15 faculty members from the

[52] Hauptverwaltung A, Abteilung III, "Freundschaft 'J'," [East] Berlin (July 14, 1982), BStU, Archiv der Zentralstelle, MfS-BCD, Nr. 2844, 232.

[53] See, for example, Hauptverwaltung A, Abteiling III, "Aktion 'Freundschaft'," [East] Berlin (April 10, 1989), BStU Archiv Zentralstelle, MfS-BCD, Nr. 2803, 165–167.

[54] "Verzeichnis der befreundeten Entwicklungsländer, an die auf der Grundlage der bestehenden Weisungen Lieferungen und Leistungen auf dem Gebiet des speziellen Außenhandels in den Jahren 1979 und 1980 erfolgen können," BAB DC 20/12897, 47. On East German military deliveries over the course of the decade see BAB DC 20/12897, 2–196.

universities in Halle and Baghdad, as well as Rostock and Basrah, would teach in their partner university as guest professors. Further exchanges of faculty in technical and vocational schools were planned.[55] A thick web of educational affiliations complemented the political and military dimensions of the Soviet-bloc/East German alliance with Iraq.

In November 1974, Horst Sindermann, then president of East Germany's Council of Ministers, traveled to Baghdad to negotiate agreements about economic and technical cooperation and about purchasing oil from Iraq.[56] Saddam Hussein told Sindermann that as the Palestinians had been driven from their country, Iraq would not accept that "large parts of Palestine still belong to those who stole it." Iraq would not accept the establishment of a Palestinian state "only on a part of Palestinian territory instead of the whole territory.... A small Palestinian state on the small area must pursue the goal of liberating the whole of the territory."[57] For Saddam Hussein, the demand that Israel withdraw to the 1967 lines was insufficient. He thus made clear to Sindermann that the existing state of Israel had to be eliminated. Hussein added that he was particularly impressed with East Germany's security and police forces and also sought exchange of experience in the work of the mass media in East Germany.[58]

Saddam Hussein led an Iraqi delegation to East Berlin in May 1975.[59] In their preparatory notes for the meeting, Sindermann's staff correctly noted that Iraq supported "the path of the military solution. Iraq is oriented to the liquidation of the state of Israel." It rejected the UN Resolutions 242 and 338 that accompanied the end of the wars of 1967 and 1973, both of which acknowledged Israel's right to exist within secure borders. Iraq "categorically was opposed to conversations with Israel."[60] In East Berlin, Hussein met with Honecker. Their photos graced

55 "Bericht über die Verhandlungen und den Abschluß des Arbeitsplanes über die kulturelle und Wissenschaftliche Zusammenarbeit zwischen der DDR und der Republik Irak für die Jahre 1973/1974," BAB DC 20 /10166

56 "Besuch des Vorsitzenden des Ministerrat der Deutschen Demokratschen Republik, Genossen Horst Sindermann, in der Republik Irak vom 18.111974 bis 21.11.1974," BAB DC 20/16841.

57 "Niederschrift über die Ausführungen des Vorsitzende des Ministerrates der DDR, Genossen Sindermann, und des stellvertretenden Vorsitzenden des Revolutionären Kommandorates der Republik Irak, Saddam Hussein, während der offiziellen Verhandlungen, am 19. November 1974," BAB DC 20/16841.

58 "Vertrauliches Gespräch zwischen ... Saddam Hussein und ... Horst Sindermann am 19. November 1974 in Bagdad," BAB DC 20/16841

59 On Saddam Hussein's visit to East Berlin see BAB DC 20/16847, 28–157.

60 "Empfehlungen für die Beratungen des ... Horst Sindermann mit ... Saddam Hussein (9.-11.5.1975)," BAB DC 20 /10166.

the front page of *Neues Deutschland*. The joint statement with Honecker voiced sentiments of mutual admiration, friendship, and agreement on major issues of international affairs including opposition to "imperialism, Zionism, neo-colonialism and reaction." Honecker and Hussein offered "firm solidarity and support" to the PLO.[61]

WEAPONS DELIVERIES AND AGREEMENTS BY THE EAST GERMAN DEFENSE MINISTRY

While the Stasi played an indispensable role in the East German relationship with the PLO, it was the East German Ministry of Defense together with its Warsaw Pact allies that was able to deliver more and larger weapons system to third-world allied states. East Germany began to deliver heavier weapons including tanks, planes, and larger artillery to the armed forces of Egypt and Syria in the 1960s.[62] In the first half of the 1970s, East German assistance consisted primarily of repairing jet engines, delivering machine guns, and training Syrian military officers in the GDR.[63] After Egyptian President Anwar Sadat broke with the Soviet bloc in 1975, Hafez al-Assad's Syria became the lynchpin of Soviet-bloc military and economic assistance in the Middle East. As important as its relationship with the PLO and other guerilla organizations was, the relationships of the East German Ministry of Defense with the militaries of other states were even more extensive in both the types and amount of weapons involved. As Defense Minister Hoffmann's summary of July 6, 1976, of East German weapons for delivery to other states by 1980 indicated, East Germany specialized in the repair and overhaul of larger weapons systems including ships, jet planes, anti-aircraft guns, missiles and helicopters, as well as production of large amounts of small arms

[61] "Die Zusammenarbeit DDR-Irak entwickelt sich in raschen Tempo," *Neues Deutschland* [East] Berlin (May 12, 1975), 1–2.

[62] Heinz Hoffmann, Sekretariat des Ministers UA Militärpolitik, Bundesarchiv-Militärarchiv Freiburg, DVW 1/ 114478 VS-Akte. Hoffmann, the head of the Defense Ministry from to referred to weapons deliveries to Egypt, Syria and Yemen that began in 1965. Also see Storkmann's excellent account in *Geheime Solidarität*, 183–243.

[63] Heinz Hoffmann to Erich Honecker, Tgb. Nr.: A-258/76 [East] Berlin (October 27, 1976), and Honecker's written approval on October 28, 1976, BAMA DVW 1/114448, 84. On training see Heinz Hoffmann to Erich Honecker, GVS-Nr.: A 500 131 [East] Berlin (November 26, 1976), BAMA DVW 1/114448, 120. In August 1976, the Syrians said they would cover the expenses for 20 East Germans to travel to Syria to "spread knowledge about socialism." See Heinz Hoffmann to Erich Honecker, Tgb-Nr.: A-171/76, [East] Berlin (August 11, 1976) with Honecker's written reply of August 13, 1976, BAMA, DVW 1/114448, 10.

TABLE 11.1. *Summary of Selected Deliveries and Overhaul of Military Technology and Equipment from the East German Economy for the National People's Army, other Armed Services, and for Export*

1. Production and overhaul until 1980

Product	Amount/Annual production
Warships	
Landing ships	12 (total)
Overhaul and repair of:	
Missile and torpedo fast boats	19
Minesweeper	12
Antisubmarine ships	3
Planes and missiles	
Airplane equipment (*Fleugzeuganlagen*)	10
Repair and overhaul of	
MiG-21 fighter jets	70
MiG-16 F fighter jets	9
Jet engines	320
Transport planes	12
Polish helicopter Mi-2	11
Anti-aircraft SAM missiles (Wolchow, Dwina)	8
Anti-aircraft missiles	40
Small arms and ammunition	
Kalashnikov AK-47 assault rifle	105,000
Soviet anti-tank rocket-propelled grenade RPG-18	70,000
Hand grenades	700,000
PPM-2 plastic, pressure-operated anti-personnel blast mine	230,000
SM-70 directional anti-personnel mine	24,000
Cartridges for Kalashnikov assault rifle (M-43)	150,000,000

Source: Heinz Hoffmann, "Übersicht zu ausgewählten Lieferungen und Instandsetzungsleistungen der Volkswirtschaft der DDR an militärischer Technik und Ausrüstung," [East] Berlin (July 6, 1979) (Geheime Verschlußsache!) GVS-Nr.: A 507 815, BAMA DVW 1/ 114489, 5–6.

including an East German version of the Kalashnikov assault weapon, hand grenades, and rocket-propelled grenades (RPGs). See Table 11.1.

In July 1979, Hoffmann requested and received Honecker's approval to expand arms production from 1981 to 1985.[64] In the 1950s and 1960s, East German arms production was limited mostly to non-lethal

[64] Heinz Hoffmann to Erich Honecker, and Honecker's written approval, [East] Berlin (July 6, 1979) and (July 7, 1979) (Geheime Verschlußsache!) GVS-Nr.: A 507 815, Bundesarchiv-Militärarchiv, BAMA DVW 1/ 114489.

equipment and to what Hoffmann described as "limited amounts of weapons." Weapons production expanded in the 1970s. From 1971 to 1975, the East German government spent approximately 8.6 billion marks on "the production of weapons and equipment as well as repairs of military technology for the National People's Army and the border troops of the GDR." The amount spent from 1976 to 1980 expanded to 12.6 billion marks. Sixty percent of these goods were from East German factories and 40 percent was imported, presumably from the Soviet Union and other Warsaw Pact states.[65] From 1966 to 1970, a modest 295 million marks worth of weapons and equipment was delivered to "allied armies." The deliveries were due to a combination of East German research and development, production of goods licensed (again presumably from the Soviet Union and Warsaw Pact allies), and repair of military goods. The pace increased by 192 percent between 1971 and 1975 to 567 million marks and again by 264 percent between 1976 and 1980 to 1.5 billion marks. Hoffmann requested and Honecker approved a further expansion of 226 percent to 3.4 billion marks for the period 1981 to 1985.[66]

Hoffmann informed Honecker that in "years past" production based on licenses from the Soviet Union included such "important armaments" as laser sights for the T-72 tank, an infrared optical-imaging system for Soviet K-13 air-to-air target-seeking missiles, and the RPG-18 anti-tank rocket-propelled grenade launcher. In so doing, Hoffmann continued, the East Germans had addressed the Soviet requests that they increase their contribution to military technology.[67] The East Germans also developed and produced warships including mine layers, submarine hunters, and landing ships. Hoffmann agreed with Soviet defense minister Dimitri Ustinov's 1979 request to expand East German production "of weapons and armaments for the National People's Army and for delivery to the Soviet Army and to other allied armies" and to make greater use of East German scientific and technical potential for the development of weapons and military equipment.[68] For the period of 1981 to 1985, Hoffmann suggested and Honecker approved further increases in East German arms production and exports to "progressive national states," a category that included Syria, Iraq, Libya, and Yemen, among others. He advocated concentration on optical and electronic equipment, anti-tank missiles, defensive arms, explosives, communications equipment,

[65] Ibid.
[66] Ibid.
[67] Ibid., 2.
[68] Ibid.

and warships.[69] As a result, in these years, both by transferring Soviet weapons in its arsenals and through its own production facilities, East Germany was able to assist in training and equipping *armies*, not only *terrorist groups*, engaged in armed conflict with Israel. It became a reliable supplier of arms to the armed forces of Syria, Iraq, Libya, and Yemen as well as a reliable and excellent repair shop and mechanic for the air forces of Syria and Iraq, among others. While the East German files offer a wealth of details about the weapons program, reliable figures about the amounts of money involved remain difficult to establish as costs could be hidden in other accounts. Hence the following figures should be treated as minimum amounts.

In 1979, the East Germans continued their role as reliable mechanics for the planes of the Arab air forces. In that year, they repaired for Syria 6 MiG-21 and 23 MiG-21 engines for Syria, 43 R-13–300 and 33 R-11-F2-S-300 MiG engines for Iraq. Also in 1979, East Germany delivered 50,000 AK-47s to Iraq, Angola, and Libya; 20,000 hand grenades to Iraq and Ethiopia; and more unspecified equipment for a "chemical room."[70] In 1979, the East Germans repaired and reconditioned 79 engines for several different types of Soviet MiG fighter planes in the Iraqi air force as well as unspecified chemical equipment.[71] In 1981, East Germany repaired 25 MiG-21 jet engines, but because of its war with Iran, Iraq's need for East German services expanded. In 1981, the East Germans repaired 20 R-13–300 and 10 R-11-F2-S-300 engines for the MiG-21s for Iraq. They sold 20 million 7.62 mm cartridges for the M-43 U and 12.1 million 7.62 mm cartridges for the M-43 P versions of the AK-47 assault rifle and 30,000 units of the AKM-S AK-47 assault rifle as well as air conditioning equipment, radio equipment, camouflage material and tents.[72]

In 1981 and 1982, East Germany's "special foreign trade" program was selling and in fewer cases giving weapons to the following countries and to the PLO: Afghanistan, Algeria, Angola, Benin, Congo, Ethiopia, Guinea, Guinea-Bissau, India, Iraq, Libya, Mexico, Madagascar,

[69] Ibid., 3–4.

[70] Willi Stoph, "Plan der Lieferumöglichkeiten von militär-technischer Ausrüstung für befreundete Entwicklungsländer und progressive nationale Befreiungsbewegungen in den Jahren 1979/80," BAB DC 20/ 12897, 37–40.

[71] "Teil I-spezieller Export, Lieferungen von militär-technischer Ausrüstung an befreundete Entwicklungensländer im Jahre 1979 auf der Grundlage des Exportplanes (kommerziell)," BAB DC 20/12897, 38–40.

[72] Willi Stoph, "Plan der Lieferumöglichkeiten von militär-technischer Ausrüstung für befreundete Entwicklungsländer und progressive nationale Befreiungsbewegungen in den Jahren 1979/80," BAB DC 20/ 12897, 2–6.

Mozambique, Nicaragua, Nigeria, Palestinian Liberation Organization, Syria, Tanzania/Zanzibar, Tunisia, Arab Republic of Yemen, People's Republic of Yemen, Zambia, and Zimbabwe.[73] With this impressive customer base, East Germany concentrated on small arms but also began to deliver larger weapons. In 1981/1982 East Germany could offer varieties of military equipment from the stock of East Germany's National People's Army and from the stocks of the Ministry of the Interior. The items included older Soviet T-35 tanks, varying sizes of hand grenades, cartridges for the AK-47, various models of the AK-47 and ammunition for it, fragmentation grenades, anti-tank grenades, radio and radar equipment, pistols, machine guns, medical technology, and braking parachutes for the MiG-17 and MiG-21. The total cost for these weapons and services was 42,997,720.00 East German marks.[74]

In the mid-1970s, East Germany's Ministry of Defense was also supplying weapons to the PLO during the period of its frequent terrorist attacks on Israel from its bases in southern Lebanon. On March 12, 1975, Hoffmann wrote to the director of the Security Department (then Paul Verner) of the SED Central Committee to recommend sending the PLO 10 7.62 mm sniper rifles with 2,000 cartridges, 1,000 RGD-5 Soviet antipersonnel fragmentation hand grenades, 1,000 RGD-3 Soviet anti-personnel fragmentation hand grenades, 10 pairs of binoculars, 30,000 first aid kits, and 500,000 7.62 cartridges for the M-43 AK-47 assault rifles.[75]

EAST GERMAN RELATIONS WITH THE PLO, PFLP, AND DFLP

On January 19, 1981, East Germany's ambassador to Lebanon, Achim Reichardt, sent a 19-page year-end report from Beirut about the PLO to the Foreign Ministry in East Berlin.[76] He wrote that the PLO opposed the Camp David Accords and engaged in "defense against the escalation of Israel's policy of aggression against the Palestinian presence in Lebanon" and "resistance" to the Israeli "occupation regime in the

[73] "Verzeichnis der befreundeten Entwicklungsländer, an die auf der Grundlage der bestehenden Weisungen Lieferungen und Leistungen auf dem Gebiet des speziellen Außenhandels in den Jahren 1981 und 1982 erfolgen können," BAB DC 20/12897, 12.

[74] "Teil II-Hilfe und Solidaritätslieferungen: Lieferungsmöglichkeiten von Kampftechnik, Bewaffnung und Ausrüstung aus Beständen der NVA und des MdI im Jahre 1981," BAB DC 20/ 12897, 13–23.

[75] Heinz Hoffmann to Zentralkomitee der SED, Leiter der Abteilung Sicherheit, VVS-Nr. A 391 002 [East] Berlin (December 15, 1975), BAMA DVW1/114489.

[76] Achim Reichhardt, "Jahresbericht 1980-PLO," Beirut (January 19, 1981), BAB DY30/13795), 33–51.

FIGURE 11.3. Erich Honecker (third from right) welcomes Yasser Arafat (third from left) and PLO delegation in East Berlin, December 29, 1980. Also see Politburo member Herman Axen (front, second from left), Farouk Khaddoumi (front, second from right), and Gerhard Grüneberg (front right).
Source: German Federal Archive, Koblenz, Photo Archive: Bild 183-W1229-0028, ADN-ZB, Hartmut Reiche.

occupied Palestinian areas."[77] With support "above all from the Soviet Union and the SSG" [socialist state community] as well as progressive Arab states," the "imperialist plans to liquidate the Palestinian problem with the so-called autonomy plan" had been prevented. It had reinforced its status as "the only legitimate representative of the Palestinian people" and destroyed efforts by "imperialism and Arab reaction" to support alternatives.[78] Reichardt pointed to the "continuous, further development of political connections" with the GDR evident in signing of a cultural agreement and a new agreement with the SED Central Committee. These connections were apparent in Honecker's meeting with a PLO delegation led by Arafat in December 1980, Farouk Kaddoumi's official visit with Foreign Minister Oskar Fischer, Gerhard Grüneberg's meeting with Arafat in Damascus, and other meetings of East German politicians with their counterparts in the PLO.[79] (See Figure 11.3.) These political

[77] Ibid., 33.
[78] Ibid., 46–47.
[79] Ibid., 47.

conversations were continued "by contact of the GDR Embassies in Beirut and Damascus with PLO leaders." Those talks with the PLO's political department led by Kaddoumi focused on "the coordination of positions in connection with UN meetings and other international conferences."[80]

Reichardt reported on the "first official visit to the GDR by a delegation of leaders of DFLP led by N. [Nayef] Hawatmeh." The visit led to agreement for "measures of cooperation and solidarity support" and "a new quality and official status of the [GDR's] relations with the DFLP." As a result of a visit to East Germany "by a leadership delegation of the PFLP, there will be an effort to place relations with it on the same level" as that of the mainstream Al Fatah led by Arafat.[81] Reichardt added that the East German Embassy in Beirut was in regular contact "with important leading personalities of the PLO Executive Committee, the (*Teilorganisationen)* associated organizations, Fatah, DFLP, PFLP, the most important departments of the PLO headquarters, above all the Political Department, and the Department of Information and Culture." The Embassy tried to intensify contacts with "right-wing forces, especially those in the Fatah leadership without, in so doing, damage [to] the connections to the leftist forces," such as the DFLP. As a result of the DFLP visit to East Germany and "the resulting signed agreements for measures of support, a qualitatively higher level of cooperation was reached with this progressive organization without, thereby, damaging relations with the PLO central. We should undertake focused efforts to also place cooperation with the PFLP on the same level."[82] In other words, the East German Embassy in Beirut was in regular contact not only with Arafat, Kaddoumi, and the PLO mainstream but also with the PFLP and DFLP, organizations then famous for carrying out terrorist attacks against the citizens of northern Israel from bases in Lebanon, for participation in terrorist attacks against civil aviation, and for collaboration with West German terrorist organizations such as the Revolutionary Cells. Reichardt advocated placing relations with the PFLP on "the same level" as with Arafat and Al Fatah.[83]

80 Ibid.

81 Ibid., 48. DFLP was same organization as DPFLP.

82 Ibid., 50.

83 In an email to the author of January 14, 2015, Reichardt confirmed that while serving as East Germany's ambassador in Lebanon from 1978 to 1981, he "developed a genuinely friendly relationship" with Yasser Arafat and Farouk Khaddoumi. He wrote that East German diplomats urged Palestinian leaders "to recognize Israel's existence and to turn away from every form of terrorist action against the civilian population" and that "it was unquestionably a service of the GDR, above all GDR diplomats in different Arab states, to influence Palestinian leading personalities in a similar manner and thus to contribute

THE PLO AND THE EAST GERMAN DEFENSE MINISTRY, 1980–1982

The depth of East Germany's military alliance with the PLO was evident in a six-day visit to East Berlin in November 1981 when the PLO's top military leaders met the highest-ranking officials in the East German Ministry of Defense.[84] The visit took place as the PLO was expanding its arsenal in Lebanon from that of a guerrilla force to an army fit for a mini-state. It needed the larger weapons and training in military strategy that defense ministries more than secret services such as the Stasi were best able to offer. The top-ranking East German delegation included Fritz Streletz, the deputy minister of defense and chief of the National People's Army General Staff; Wolfgang Reinhold, deputy minister of defense responsible for air defense; and General Werner Fleißner, deputy ministry for technology and weapons; as well as general officers of the air force and army and officers charged with military training.[85] Preparations for the visit were secret. Press reports were issued only after the official departure of the PLO delegation.[86] It was led by Kahlil Al-Wazir (Abu Jihad), commander of Al Fatah's armed forces, as well as representatives from the PLO Politburo, the PFLP, the DFLP, Saika, the Arab Liberation Front (ALF), a military representative of the "Palestinian People's Front" (PPSF), and a representative of the Palestinian military forces in the occupied territories.[87] The meeting drew leaders of the East German armed forces together with the full cross-section of the PLO's Executive Committee.

The PLO delegation was received with full military honors at Berlin-Schönefeld airport on November 15. On November 16 negotiations took place with General Fleißner about the PLO requests, followed by an afternoon laying of a wreath at the Memorial to the Victims of

to negotiations that led to the Oslo agreements." The public record of East German diplomacy does not include such appeals for moderation. I have found no evidence in files of the East German Foreign Ministry to support them.

84 "Organisation, Sicherstellung und Verantwortlichkeiten für den Besuch der Militärdelegation der Palästinensischen Befreiungsorganisation in der Zeit vom 15. Bis 21. November 1981," Bundesarchiv-Militärarchiv, Freiburg, BAMA DVW 1/40833, Nationale Volksarmee, Ministerium für Nationale Verteidigung. Sekretariat des Ministers. Vorbereitung und Durchführung von offiziellen Freundschaftsbesuchen, 1980–1989, Bd. 4.

85 Ibid., 1–2. On Fleißner, Reinhold and Streletz see Barth et al., *Wer war Wer in der DDR*, 116, 368 and 445, respectively. Also see Klaus Froh and Rüdiger Wenzke, *Die Generale und Admirale der NVA – ein biographisches Handbuch* (Berlin: Links Verlag, 2000).

86 "Organisation, Sicherstellung und Verantwortlichkeien ...," 2.

87 Ibid., 2.

Fascism and Militarism in East Berlin. On November 17, the group traveled to Klosterfelde to view an anti-aircraft division of the East German army. Later the delegation met with Honecker.[88] The visitors toured the National People's Army training school for junior officers; had lunch with General Horst Strechbarth, chief of the East German Army; then visited a tank regiment in Spremberg, the Friedrich Engels Military Academy, and the Ernst Thälmann officer school. On November 20, 1981, the delegation had a formal dinner with defense minister Hoffmann "in honor of a military delegation under the leadership of the Deputy Commander of the Armed Forces of the Palestinian Revolution and Member of the Central Committee of Fatah, Comrade KHALIL AL-WAZIR (ABU JIHAD)."[89] The seating arrangements for the formal dinner interspersed the top leadership of the East German armed forces with the PLO delegation. In addition to Hoffmann, the East German dinner guests included Strechbarth; General Heinz Keßler, deputy minister of defense and Hoffmann's successor as the defense minister after Hoffmann's death in 1985; and Streletz, Fleißner, and Reinhold. The seating arrangement for the evening placed Al-Wazir at the head of the table between the defense minister and the deputy foreign minister.[90] Seven months later, on May 5, 1982, Honecker approved Hoffmann's support for a PLO request to raise the status of Major Abdul Menem Al-Amouri, the "representative of the armed forces of the Palestinian Liberation Organization" in East Berlin, to "military attaché." That step followed formal accreditation of the PLO representative in East Berlin as an ambassador in April 1982.[91] The meeting was to

88 "Verpflichtungen des Ministers für Nationale Verteidigung in der Zeit vom 08.11 bis 21.11 1981 im Zusammenhang mit den Militärdelegationen," BAMA DVW 1/40833, Nationale Volksarmee, Ministerium für Nationale Verteidigung. Sekretariat des Ministers. Vorbereitung und Durchführung von offiziellen Freundschaftsbesuchen, 1980–1989, Bd. 4, 177.

89 "Armee General Heinz Hoffmann beehrt sich zu einem ESSEN zu Ehren einer Militärdelegation unter Leitung des Stellvertretenden Oberkommandierenden der Streitkräfte der Palästinensischen Revolution und Mitglieds des Zentralkomitees der FATAH Genossen KHALIL AL-WAZIR (ABU JIHAD) einzuladen." BAMA DVW 1/40833, Nationale Volksarmee, Ministerium für Nationale Verteidigung. Sekretariat des Ministers. Vorbereitung und Durchführung von offiziellen Freundschaftsbesuchen, 1980–1989, Bd. 4, 133–134.

90 Ibid.

91 Heinz Hoffmann to Erich Honecker and Honecker's written approval, [East] Berlin (May 5, 1982), MFNV Sekr. d. Min. Schriftverkehr mit dem Gensekr. Des ZK der SED, 1982, PLO, BAMA DVW 1/ 114495, 139. Also "Anlage 1: Auszug aus einem Artikel der libaneischen Wochenzeitschrfit 'Monday Morning', Woche vom 07.-13.12 1981, der im Ergebnis eines Interviews von Abu Jihad, Leiter der PLO-Militärdelegation in der DDR, veröffentlicht wurde," BAMA DVW 1/ 115628.

be followed by further visits by PLO military delegations to implement the agreements.[92]

On April 13, 1982, Willi Stoph assigned General Helmut Borufka the task of negotiating an agreement for military cooperation with the PLO.[93] On April 19, 1982, Borufka, the inspector general of the East German National People's Army, signed an agreement with Mahmoud Da'as, the "Director of Officer Affairs of the Armed Forces of the Palestinian Revolution," to offer "political, military and military-technical training" with three-year fellowships to 20 "Palestinian military cadres" in the GDR from 1982 to 1985. The recipients were artillery commanders and unspecified weapon technicians.[94] The agreement was animated by a "common interest in the peoples' struggle for national and social liberation and against imperialism, colonialism, neo-colonialism, racism, Zionism and reaction." The contract stipulated that the training would take place in the German language. It thus required a first year of intensive German language study along with "political education." The East German Ministry of Defense paid for the military training, clothing, lodging, medical care, cultural entertainment, and excursions within East Germany. Each cadre would receive 200 marks each month for expense money and an initial 400 marks to purchase clothing for the colder German climate. The PLO would cover the costs of travel to and from East Germany.[95]

On June 6, 1982, following the attempted assassination of Israel's ambassador in London and shelling and attacks on the towns of northern Israel that were launched from PLO bases in Lebanon, Israel began "Operation Peace for Galilee" in an effort to end the terrorist attacks. On June 8, Al-Amouri spoke with Streletz in East Berlin. Hoffmann told Streletz to tell Al-Amouri that "in view of Israel's aggression," he

92 "Anlage 1: Auszug aus einem Artikel der libaneischen Wochenzeitschrfit 'Monday Morning', Woche vom 07.-13.12 1981, der im Ergebnis eines Interviews von Abu Jihad, Leiter der PLO-Militärdelegation in der DDR, veröffentlicht wurde," BAMA DVW 1/115628.

93 Will Stoph, Ministerrat der Deutschen Demokratische Republik, "Vollmacht," [East] Berlin (April 13, 1982), BAMA DVW 1/54345.

94 "Abkommen zwischen der Regierung d. DDR und dem Exekutivkomitee der Palästinensischen Befreiungsorganisation über die Ausbildung von Militärkadern der Streitkräfte der Palästinensischen Revolution in der DDR," and "Anlage 1: Plan der Ausbildung der palästinensischen Militärkader," [East] Berlin (April19, 1982), BAMA DVWI 1/54345.

95 "Abkommen zwischen der Regierung d. DDR und dem Exekutivkomitee der Palästinensischen Befreiungsorganisation über die Ausbildung von Militärkadern der Streitkräfte der Palästinensischen Revolution in der DDR," [East] Berlin (April19, 1982), BAMA DVWI 1/54345.

"assured him of the unlimited solidarity and solidarity of all military and civilian personnel of the National People's Army."[96] Amouri expressed his appreciation for East Germany's solidarity. He noted that East Germany was one of the first states to condemn "the Israeli aggression" and convey its "full solidarity and support." It was "a stance that is known to all of the fighters of the PLO." It was painful to report that the other Arab states, including Syria, did not offer any "active help and support." Hoffmann approved delivery of 10,000 hand grenades, 90,000 14.5 mm machine-gun cartridges, and 46,000 12.7 mm machine-gun cartridges.[97] He also confirmed that Honecker agreed to deliver immediately the items worth 2,171,100 East German marks free of charge to the PLO. Eight hundred Shpagin Soviet submachine guns with 720,000 cartridges, 2,500 blankets, 50,000 packages of bandages, and 300 binoculars would be delivered by air. Six Soviet mobile anti-aircraft guns (S 60 57 mm) and 10,000 grenade shells to be used in them would arrive by ship. A GDR military delegation currently in Syria would handle the delivery of the weapons to the PLO.[98] After the Lebanon War in 1982 and the departure of the PLO from Beirut, Honecker approved Hoffmann's suggestion to continue the military training of PLO "military cadres," in 1982–1983 and 1983–1984.[99]

EAST GERMANY'S SPECIAL RELATIONSHIP WITH SYRIA

Especially after Egypt's President Anwar Sadat expelled Soviet advisers in 1972, Syria had become the lynchpin of the Soviet-bloc efforts in the Middle East. East Germany's relationship with Hafez al-Assad's Baath deserves the adjective "special," one that is often assigned to West Germany's relations with Israel. The alliance of strange bedfellows, of

[96] Heinz Hoffmann to Erich Honecker and Honecker's written approval, [East] Berlin, June 9, 1982, MFNV Sekr. d. Min. Schriftverkehr mit dem Gensekr. Des ZK der SED, 1982, PLO, BAMA DVW 1/ 114495, 144–147.

[97] Heinz Hoffmann to Erich Honecker and Honecker's written approval, [East] Berlin, June 9, 1982, MFNV Sekr. d. Min. Schriftverkehr mit dem Gensekr. Des ZK der SED, 1982, PLO, BAMA DVW 1/ 114495, 145.

[98] "Anlage: Positionen für die vorgesehene unentgeltliche Hilfslieferung and die PLO," Heinz Hoffmann to Erich Honecker and Honecker's written approval, [East] Berlin, June 9, 1982, MFNV Sekr. d. Min. Schriftverkehr mit dem Gensekr. Des ZK der SED, 1982, PLO, BAMA DVW 1/ 114495, 147.

[99] Heinz Hoffmann to Erich Honecker and Honecker's written approval, [East] Berlin, September 6, 1982, MFNV Sekr. d. Min. Schriftverkehr mit dem Gensekr. Des ZK der SED, 1982, PLO, BAMA DVW 1/ 114495, 149–150.

Communists with Baathists, was the closest and most intense of all of East Germany's connections to a Middle Eastern state.

From November 8 to 14, 1981, a Syrian military delegation of 19 people led by General Mustafa Tlass, Syria's defense minister, visited East Berlin.[100] Following a welcome with military honors at Berlin-Schönefeld airport, the delegation spent several hours with defense minister Hoffmann. The Syrian delegation met East Germany's chiefs of the navy, army, and air force and visited the Friedrich Engels and Ernst Thälmann military training schools. The group visited the Erich Habersaath military school, known for its work on missiles, and the officer training school of the East German navy. On November 10 it laid a wreath at the Memorial for Victims of Fascism and Militarism and visited the Brandenburg Gate in East Berlin with party and government leaders. On November 11 the group observed a squadron of jet fighters and met with Honecker.[101] The following day included a visit to the Friedrich Engels military school. On November 13, the Tlass delegation had a second meeting with Hoffmann followed by a formal dinner in Tlass's honor.[102] The leadership of the East German armed forces, Generals Heinz Keßler, Fritz Streletz, Horst Strechbarth, Werner Fleißner, and Wolfgang Reinhold, were in attendance together with Hoffmann and the deputy foreign minister. They were joined on the Syrian side by Tlass, seated next to Hoffmann and Syrian brigadier generals Shafiq Fiyadh,

[100] "Organisation, Sicherstellung und Verantwortlichkeiten für den Besuch der Militärdelegation der Syrischen Arabischen Republik in der Zeit vom 08. bis 14. November 1981," Bundesarchiv-Militärarchiv, Freiburg, BAMA DVW 1/40833, Nationale Volksarmee, Ministerium für Nationale Verteidigung. Sekretariat des Ministers. Vorbereitung und Durchführung von offiziellen Freundschaftsbesuchen, 1980–1989, Bd. 4.

[101] "Verpflichtungen des Ministers für Nationale Verteidigung in der Zeit vom 08.11 bis 21.11 1981 im Zusammenhang mit den Militärdelegationen," BAMA DVW 1/40833, Nationale Volksarmee, Ministerium für Nationale Verteidigung. Sekretariat des Ministers. Vorbereitung und Durchführung von offiziellen Freundschaftsbesuchen, 1980–1989, Bd. 4, 176.

[102] "Armee General Heinz Hoffmann beehrt sich zu einem ESSEN zu Ehren einer Militärdelegation der Syrischen Arabischen Republik under Leitung des Stellvertreters des Oberkommandierenden der Armee und der bewaffneten Kräfte und Minister für Verteidigung Korpsgeneral Dr. Mustafa Abdel Kader TLASS einzuladen," BAMA DVW 1/40833, Nationale Volksarmee, Ministerium für Nationale Verteidigung. Sekretariat des Ministers. Vorbereitung und Durchführung von offiziellen Freundschaftsbesuchen, 1980–1989, Bd. 4, 157–163. Also see "Anlage 1: Artikel aus der Syrischen Armeezeitschrift 'Jaich al-Chaab' vom 15.11.1981 über den Besuch der Syrischen Militärdelegation in der DDR," BAMA DVW 1/ 115628.

Mohammed Khalid Sheikhgal and Heitham Sabouni, and Abadallah Mohammed Abd.[103]

As with relations with Iraq, the alliance with Syria included exchanges between their universities as well. An agreement in 1974 and 1975 called for up to seven year-long stays by East German scholars in Syria; up to three Syrian scholars for up to ten months in East Germany; 60 places for summer study in East Germany; exchanges between the Technical University in Dresden and the University of Damascus as well as between the Technical University in Karl Marx City and the University of Aleppo; ten places for students and ten places for those seeking to become students at East German universities and 15 places for German language training; a professor of German at the University of Damascus; three Syrian professors of German in summer courses at East German universities; two East German students of Arabic to study in Syria; and places for Syrian scholars to study economics, archival methods, education, and information sciences in East Germany.[104] An agreement signed in Damascus on November 12, 1973, for "scientific and technical cooperation" between Syria and the GDR also illustrated the deepening of the relationship. The East Germans agreed to send to Syria 25 experts in the fields of agriculture (8), textile industry (3), transportation (3), energy (2), geology (1), machine tools (2) and chemicals (2), and to reserve 75 places for study in East Germany in the fields of agriculture (35), textiles (5), teacher education (15), and "other areas" (15).[105]

The importance of East Germany's alliance with Syria was on full display when Hafez al-Assad visited East Berlin, October 2–5, 1978. Assad's visit took place soon after the signing of the Camp David Accords, which he had denounced. The Syrian leader sought further support for the Arab rejection front opposed to the Camp David Accords.[106] Assad's visit was front-page news in *Neues Deutschland* for all four days of the visit and was featured on East German television. On October 2, the entire front page of *ND* was devoted to his arrival including photos of Honecker

[103] Ibid.

[104] "Arbeitsplan zwischen der DDR und der SAR u. die. kulturelle und wissenschaftliche Zusammenarbeit ... 1974 und 1975," BAB Ministerrates DC 20/ 11411.

[105] "Protokoll über die wissenschatlich-technische Zusammenarbeit zwischen der Deutschen Demokratischen Republik und der Syrischen Arabischen Republik für die Jahre 1973–1975," BAB Ministerrat der DDR DC20/11418,

[106] On the rejection of the Camp David Accords among Arab intellectuals, see Fouad Ajami, "The Orphaned Peace," in *The Dream Palace of the Arabs* (New York: Vintage, 1998, pb. 1999), 253–312.

and his wife, Margarete, with Assad and his wife, Anisa.[107] In his evening dinner toast, Honecker called the friendship between the GDR and Syria "proven and stable." He referred "especially to the new dangerous conspiracy (*Verschwörung*) of imperialism and reaction organized in Camp David," one that "anti-imperialist forces" needed to oppose.[108] Honecker "wholly and completely" supported the initiative of "the conference of steadfastness" (*Standhaftigkeit*) launched by Assad and its "program against the most recent conspiracy of imperialism and Zionism," that is, the Camp David Accords. This "separate peace" did not address the core issues. Peace required Israeli withdrawal from (unspecified) "all occupied Arab territories," implementation of the rights of the Palestinians to form their own state, and "the guarantee of the security of all states in the Near East." It could only be attained with participation of the PLO. Honecker assured Assad "that in the future we will wholly and thoroughly support the just and courageous struggle of the Syrian people.[109] Conspiracies also played a large role in Assad's reply.[110] Syria faced "imperialist conspiracies." The Camp David Accords created "the most dangerous conspiracy that we [Syria] have faced in our modern history."[111] It was "an effort to force the Arab nations to capitulation" by splitting Egypt off from "the Arab front against occupation and aggression."[112] Assad admired East Germany's "firm and principled stance" in support of the Arabs and observed that "the cooperation between the Syrian Arab Republic and the German Democratic Republic had been beneficial for the peoples of both countries."[113]

For the next three days the editors of *Neues Deutschland* filled the paper with articles about Assad. There were photos of Assad at the memorial to the victims of fascism, overlooking the Berlin Wall at the Brandenburg Gate, driving down a main street in an official motorcade applauded by cheering crowds, and finally together with Honecker, signing a "Common Declaration of Friendship and Cooperation" on

[107] "Hafez al Assad wurde in der DDR herzlich willkommen geheißen," [East] Berlin (October 2, 1978), 1.

[108] Erich Honecker, "Freundschaft DDR-Syrien ist erprobt und stabil," *Neues Deutschland* [East] Berlin (October 2, 1973), 3.

[109] Erich Honecker, "Freundschaft DDR-Syrien ist erprobt und stabil," *ND* (October 2, 1973), 3.

[110] Hafez al-Assad, "Zusammenarbeit nutzt den Völkern beider Länder," *ND* (October 2, 1978), 3.

[111] Ibid., 3.

[112] Ibid.

[113] Hafez al-Assad, "Zusammenarbeit nutzt den Völkern beider Länder," and "Gespräche im Geiste antiimperialistischer Solidarität fortgesetzt," *ND* (October 2, 1978), 1; "Besuch bei den Soldaten an der Staatsgrenze der DDR," and Begegnung mit Diplomaten," 3.

October 4.[114] The final communiqué reaffirmed the "shared conviction that the unity of action of all forces that fight against imperialism, colonialism, racism and Zionism was of great importance for bringing about independence and progress of liberated states."[115] Honecker and Assad agreed on the virtues of détente and blamed "imperialism" for endangering it. They reaffirmed support for the PLO, "the legitimate representative of the Palestinian people," and condemned "continuing Israeli terror, violation of human rights, racial discrimination and oppression in the occupied territories" as well as the "separate peace" of the Camp David Accords. They supported the decisions of conference of the "Arab Front of Steadfastness and Resistance in Tripoli, Algiers and Damascus as an important step in establishing unity of action of all Arab states and forces in battle against the imperialist-Zionist conspiracy." Syria expressed appreciation for East Germany's support for "the Arab peoples and opposition to the imperialist-Zionist conspiracy" (*imperialistisch-zionistischen Verschwörung*). Both supported strengthening the "anti-imperialist solidarity between states of the socialist community of states [that is, the Soviet bloc] and the peoples of Asia, Africa and Latin America."[116] (See Figure 11.4.)

In October 1982, in the wake of Israel's invasion of Lebanon and the PLO's expulsion from Beirut, Honecker traveled to Damascus for a four-day visit. It dominated the pages of *Neues Deutschland*. He was greeted with military honors at the airport. A photo of a smiling Honecker and Assad graced page 1. The leaders stressed the commonality of their opposition to "the aggressor Israel." The visit was a "milestone" in their relationship characterized by "anti-imperialist solidarity and close friendship."[117] Mustafa Tlass accompanied Honecker on a visit to a Syrian air

[114] For example, "Ehrung für die Opfer des Faschismus," *ND* (October 2, 1978), 4; "Erich Honecker und Hafez al Assad bei Ludwigsfelder Automobilbauern," *ND* (October 3, 1978), 1; "Freundschaftliche Begegnungen mit Arbeitern, Bauern und Soldaten," *ND* (October 4, 1978), 1. For the photo of signing the common declaration see "DDR und SAR entwickeln ihre enge Freundschat und Zusammenarbeit," [East] Berlin, *ND* (October 5, 1978), 1.

[115] Erich Honecker and Hafez al-Assad, "Gemeinsame Erklärung über Freundschaft und Zusammenarbeit zwischen der Deutschen Demokratischen Republik und der Syrischen Arabischen Republik," *ND* (October 5, 1978), 1.

[116] Ibid., 4. Also see "Präsident Assad antwortete auf Fragen der Journalisten," *ND* (October 4, 1978), 6.

[117] "Erich Honecker von Präsident Hafez al Assad in Damaskus herzlich willkommen geheißen,"; "Begegnung im Amtssitz des SAR Präsidenten,"; "Neuer Meilenstein in unseren Beziehungen," "Offizielle Gespräche aufgenommen," *ND* (October 12, 1982), 1.

FIGURE 11.4. Syrian President Hafez al Assad (front, fourth from right) sits between Erich Honecker (front, third from right) and East German Defense Minister Heinz Hoffmann (front, second from right) in Cottbus, East Germany, on October 3, 1978, as they observe exercises by East German armed forces and anti-aircraft defenses.
Source: German Federal Archive, Koblenz, Photo Archive: Bild 183-T1003-33, ADN-ZB, Peter Koard.

force base in Demeir.[118] *Neues Deutschland* reported that "the people in Demeir greeted the guest with cheers of friendship between the DDR and SAR [Syrian Arab Republic]." The Syrian youth organization cheered the East German leader. At the gate of the military field, a banner in German read: "We thank the GDR for its just stance on the Palestine Question and for its support in the struggle for justice and peace" and "The fighters of the Syrian air defenses and warmly greet Syria's honored guest, Erich Honecker, President of the GDR!"[119] Honecker observed Syrian pilots flying Soviet MiG jets. "He wished them success in their important and responsible service" and received Syria's "national coat of arms as a gift of honor (*Ehrengeschenk)* from the [Syrian] soldiers and officers."[120]

118 "Erich Honecker besuchte die Kämpfer eine Syrischen Jagdfliegerregiements," *ND* (October 13, 1982), 1.

119 Ibid.

120 "Erich Honecker besuchte die Kämpfer eine Syrischen Jagdfliegerregiements," *ND* (October 13, 1982), 1.

Defense Minister Hoffmann and his wife, along with Generals Keßler, Fleißner and Reinhold, visited Syria from May 7 to 12, 1983. There they met Hafez al-Assad and other high-ranking Syrian and Soviet officials. They discussed agreements to continue training Syrian armed forces in East Germany and weapons sales from East Germany to Syria. Syrian defense minister Tlass bestowed on Hoffmann the "Order for Service to the Syrian Arab Republic."[121] In his report to Honecker about the trip to Syria, Hoffmann informed him that President Assad had described Honecker as "his best friend."[122] Assad thought that cooperation and exchange of experiences by the East German regime, the Communist Party, and the East German armed forces could be particularly helpful in "strengthening political work among the people and the armed forces, especially in the development of an effective counter-propaganda."[123] The East Germans and Syrians concluded an important agreement to train 310 Syrian military personnel from 1983 to 1988 in East Germany. Hoffmann reported that "all of the meetings were characterized by the spirit of true comradeship and political agreement and common purpose (*Zusammengehörigkeit)* in the struggle against Zionism and imperialism and the USA and NATO."[124]

The expressions of affection and mutual admiration went beyond the usual diplomatic niceties.[125] Assad actually did refer to Honecker as his "closest friend" (*engsten Freund),* whose political agreement was so extensive that it "almost amounted to a blood relationship" (*fast eine Blutsverwandschaft verbinde)*. Hoffmann told Assad that he had orders from Honecker to do "everything to deepen bonds between our states and armies" especially regarding the "just struggle of the Syrian people, and to strengthen the certainty that the GDR will always" stand on Syria's

[121] Heinz Hoffmann to Erich Honecker, [East} Berlin, March 11, 1983; and Heinz Hoffmann to Erich Honecker, [East] Berlin, May 13, 1983, MfNV, Sekretariat des Ministers, Schriftwechsel des Ministers für Nationale Verteidigung 1983 mit dem Generalsekretär des Zentralkomitees der SED, mit dem Leiter der Abteilung für Sicherheitsfragen des ZK der SED und dem Vorsitzenden des Ministerrat der DDR, BAMA DVW 1/114496, 24–27.

[122] Heinz Hoffmann, "Bericht über die Reise der Militärdelegation der DDR in der SYRISCHEN ARABISCHEN REPUBLIK IN Mai 1983," [East] Berlin, May 1983, BAMA DVW 1/114496, 28.

[123] Ibid., 29.

[124] Ibid., 31–32.

[125] Heinz Hoffmann, "Anlage I: Wesentlicher Inhalt des Gesprächs während der Visite beim Präsidenten der Syrischen Arabischen Republik, Hafez al-Assad," [East] Berlin, 1983, BAMA DVW 1/114496, 33–36.

side "against imperialism and Zionism." Hoffmann praised the "élan and fighting spirit" of the young commanders of the Syrian Fifth Mechanized Division near the Golan Heights. They not only knew "how to defend themselves against the Israelis but also how to defeat the Israelis in offensive battles."[126] Assad stressed that exchange of experiences between Syria and the DDR was important because both countries were located in "the most forward trenches in the battle against imperialism." East Germany had particular importance in helping the Syrian government deepen the necessary political convictions.[127]

MUSTAFA TLASS'S *THE MATZO OF ZION*

At a reception in the East German Embassy in Damascus in honor of Mustafa Tlass that evening, Hoffmann raised a toast to the friendship between Syria and the GDR and to "the community borne of struggle (*Kampfgemeinschaft*) of soldiers of the Syrian armed forces and of the National People's Army of the GDR, to the health of all members of the Syrian armed forces and to its Minister of Defense, comrade General Mustafa Tlass!"[128] The Hoffmann files offer no evidence that the defense minister was aware of Tlass's literary contribution to Syrian anti-Semitism. In 1983, Tlass published *The Matzo of Zion*, a work that repeated what was known as the Damascus blood libel of 1840. According to that famous case of anti-Semitic paranoia, a group of Jews were accused of murdering a priest named Tomas Al-Kaboushi in order to drain his blood to prepare matzo for the Passover seder.[129] As *The Matzo of Zion* made painfully evident, the man Hoffmann toasted on that May evening in Damascus in 1983 had just published a book that repeated the

126 Ibid., 33.

127 Ibid., 34.

128 Heinz Hoffmann, "Empfang in der Botschaft der DDR," MfNV Sekr. Des Ministers. Militärdelegation der DDR nach Syrien, Ägypten, Irak., BAMA DVW1/115673.

129 General Mustafa Tlass, *The Matzo of Zion* (Damascus: Tlass Publishing House, 1991); also see the report by the Middle East Media Research Institute, MEMRI, "The Damascus Blood Libel (1840) as Told by Syrian Defense Minister Musafa Tlass," *Inquiry and Analysis Series Report* No. 99 (June 27, 2002), www.memri.org/report/en/0/0/0/0/0/0/688.htm. The MEMRI report translates Tlass's introduction written in 1986, one that served as the introduction to the 1991 edition. Earlier, I am quoting the English version published by the Tlass Publishing House in 1991. On the Damascus blood libel, see Jonathan Frankel, *The Damascus Affair: "Ritual Murder," Politics and the Jews in 1840* (New York: Cambridge University Press, 1997); and Ronald Florence, *Blood Libel: The Damascus Affair of 1840* (Madison: University of Wisconsin Press, 2004).

lies of modern European anti-Semitism.[130] In the 1986 introduction to this work, Tlass wrote that "this crime was committed by a group of Jews who wanted to extract his blood to make a matzo."[131] It was, he wrote, "not the first crime of its kind for the West had already experienced many crimes of this sort, not to forget those that found their scene on Czarist Russia. Some crimes were discovered and recorded despite all efforts to cover up or destroy the evidence."[132] Tlass provided footnotes in the second edition. In note 2, which offered no source, he wrote that "a similar crime was committed in Algeria in the middle of the 18th century when Jews kidnapped a Christian boy and drained his blood; but the Jews succeeded in getting this incident dismissed by offering money to the Turkish governor of Algeria."[133] Tlass wrote that the crime in Damascus "is surely not the last of its kind either."[134] The source for that assertion was August Rohling, an anti-Semitic and anti-Catholic German Protestant theologian of the nineteenth century, in his anti-Jewish text *Der Talmudjude*.[135] In that work, Rohling repeated falsehoods that the Talmud declared that it was the duty of Jews to destroy Christian churches, "curse the Christians three times daily, and pray that God may destroy them all." It was, according to Rohling, "the duty of Jews to consider the Christians as beasts and to treat them as such. If a Jew sees a Christian on the edge of a cliff, he should push him or throw him to the bottom."[136] Tlass translated Rohling into Arabic and thus made a contribution to importing European anti-Semitism into the Middle East.[137]

Tlass said of the Jews in Europe in the nineteenth and twentieth centuries that they continued "to commit individual crimes and collective slaughtering. They succeeded in wiping out evidence of their crimes by the virtue of using their financial, political, and propaganda influence in

[130] For a recent discussion of the blood libel in medieval England see Anthony Julius, *Trials of the Diaspora: A History of Modern Anti-Semitism in England* (New York: Oxford University Press, 2010).

[131] Matzo is prepared for the Jewish holiday of Passover, not Yom Kippur.

[132] Tlass, *Matzo of Zion*, 26.

[133] Ibid., 27.

[134] Ibid., 28.

[135] August Rohling, *Der Talmudejude* (Munster, 1871). On Rohling see Richard Levy, *Antisemitism: A Historical Encyclopedia of Prejudice and Persecution, Vol. 1* (ABC-CLIO, 2005), 609.

[136] Tlass, *Matzo of Zion*, 29.

[137] On this importation, see Bernard Lewis, *Semites and Anti-Semites: An Inquiry into Conflict and Prejudice* (New York: W. W. Norton, 1999), 106–107, 199–200; and Robert S. Wistrich, *A Lethal Obsession: Anti-Semitism from Antiquity to the Global Jihad* (New York: Random House, 2010), 791–795, 808.

the ruling circles of Europe and the United States." Yet both "Western and Eastern societies were way ahead of Arab-Islamic countries in discovering the Jewish ideology, and its hidden contents of destructive evil." They had done "research and serious inquiries regarding the self-isolation of the Jews, in their own quarters (the ghettos), and their own insistence upon this isolation, in order to attract and invite hatred, so they will be singled out for their marked character and characteristics." Muslim Arab tolerance toward Jews had unfortunately allowed them to "enjoy the life of complete freedom throughout the Arab-Islamic region," while they benefited "from their private isolation, and shrouded their own world with obscurity" so that the world around them had only meager information about them.[138] Such tolerance had harmed the Muslim-Arab societies. Europe, on the other hand, was composed of a more advanced set of societies than the Arab-Islamic region precisely because it had discovered the danger of "Jewish ideology" and its "destructive evil." Tlass argued that anti-Semitism had contributed to European success while Arab tolerance toward the Jews had contributed to failure. Arabs thus had much to learn from Europe's anti-Semites about how intolerance toward the Jews contributed to political and economic success.

Tlass then drew a direct line from the accusation of the blood libel in nineteenth-century Damascus to his denunciation of "Zionist racism" in the 1980s.

> The alarmed call of the city was expressed by the mothers warning their children: beware of going far from your own house; because the Jews might pass by you, they might put you in their sacks and take you away to slay you and drain your blood to make their bread of Zion. Generation after generation carried this warning of "Jewish betrayal" with them. Then the Jews established a country for themselves in the land of Greater Syria. But did the Jewish hatred of others disappear? Or had the Talmudic teachings, with their crimes and distortions, continue the practice of their hatred against humanity, and the surrounding societies? The observation of the daily events as to what is happening in the occupied land [i.e., Israel, JH] gives daily confirmation beyond the shadow of a doubt that what is described as the Zionist Racism is nothing but an extension and remolding of the Talmudic teachings. And if the Jew refuses to live in the non-Jewish home, this led to the refusal of the enlarged ghetto's society (Israel today) to live in the home of some other societies. My intention in publishing this book was nothing more than the exposure of some secrets of a Jewish religion sect and the practices of its adherents … their hateful, blind solidarity to their beliefs, and the execution of Talmudic teachings which were formulated by their religious beliefs and teachings (The Law of their Prophet Moses).[139]

[138] Tlass, *Matzo of Zion,* 32 and 35.
[139] Ibid., 36.

For Mustafa Tlass, the second most powerful political figure in Baathist Syria and the key contact to the East German – and Soviet-bloc – military leadership, "anti-Zionism" was not only indistinguishable from anti-Semitism, that is, hatred of the Jews as Jews. It was its direct result. The files do not reveal whether he discussed his views of the Jews with Hoffmann. Be that as it may, he was the man whom Hoffmann joined in a "community of struggle" against imperialism and Zionism.

INTERNATIONAL COMMUNISM AND MILITARY TRAINING IN EAST GERMANY

For observers of modern European history, the phrase "international Communism" evokes a Eurocentric story focused on the history of the Comintern and the decades between the First and Second World Wars. Yet the term achieved its full international dimensions during the Cold War as the Soviet Union and its allies sought to gain influence and spread revolutionary Communism in Latin America, Africa, the Middle East, and Asia. The Communists not only traveled to other countries. They also invited thousands of young people from third-world countries to study in the military academies and universities of the Soviet Union and the Warsaw Pact from the 1950s to 1989. The East Germans had active programs that mixed technical and military training with ideological Marxist-Leninist schooling for students and officers from North Vietnam, North Korea, Mozambique, Nicaragua, Libya, Tanzania, Morocco, Egypt, Jordan, the People's Republic of Yemen, the Yemen Arab Republic, Kuwait, Syria, Iraq, Iran, and the PLO. The military cadres received three-year fellowships to study in East Germany. The stipends paid for a year of intensive German language study as well as classes in East Germany's various military academies. These classrooms and the friendships and contacts that emerged from them constituted a still underexamined chapter in the history of international Communism during the Cold War. From 1972 to 1983, 755 students graduated from East Germany's eight military academies.[140] Heinz Hoffmann's "Support Order" (*Untersützungsordnung)*

[140] Handke, "Meldung über die Ausbildung ausländischer Militärkader" (November 17, 1983), BStU, Archiv der Zentralstelle, MfS-HA I, Nr. 13695, 1–3. Also see annual Defense Ministry reports for 1980 to 1985: General Heinz Hoffmann, "Arbeitsgrundlage zur Entwicklung und zum Ausbau der militärpolitischen Auslandsbeziehungen im Ausbildungsjahr 1980/81," [East] Berlin (December 8, 1980), MfNV Sekretariat des Ministers: Plan der Dienstreisen sowie Entwicklungen und Ausbau mit politische Auslandsbeziehungen 1980–1985, BAMA DVW 1/ 115655.

of April 18, 1980, called on the Defense Ministry to "support friendly developing countries and progressive national liberation movements in the area of political work, training of military cadres, delivery of military technology, armament and equipment, military-technical and military-economic cooperation." By 1980, East Germany was training soldiers from Egypt, Iran, Iraq, Jordan, Lebanon, Morocco, the PLO, Syria, Tanzania, the People's Republic (South) Yemen, and the Yemen Arabic Republic (North).[141]

The network of agreements and depth of relations with Syria were the most extensive of those with the Arab allies. They included meetings of a joint working group of military leaders, training of Syrian military personnel, long-term military and economic ties, continuation of sport and vacation exchanges, and cooperation in the field of military medicine. In 1984, the National People's Army representative in the East German Embassy in Damascus was elevated to the level of military attaché. The same status was accorded the East German Embassy to Lebanon, which was located in Damascus.[142] Iraq also had a military attaché in its embassy in East Berlin. In 1985, an Iraqi and East German joint working group met for the third time;[143] in 1986, East Germany was also training military personnel form Libya. In April 1986, a working group from the Defense Ministries in East Germany and Syria met for the fourth time. Military delegations continued to visit each other while training of the Syrian armed forces in East Germany also continued, as did exchanges between the Wilhelm Pieck Military College and the "Political College" of the Syrian armed forces.[144]

As of December 1981, according to a Stasi report, there were 579 "foreign military cadres" in training or educational institutions affiliated with the East German armed forces. The GDR was planning to sign an agreement in January or February 1982 to train 20 cadres from the PLO at its "Otto Winzer" officer training academy in Prora and was negotiating with Syria to train 80 cadres in 1982.[145] In 1983, there were 549

[141] Ibid., 163–182.

[142] Ibid., 178–180.

[143] Ibid., 181.

[144] Bundesarchiv-Militärarchiv, Freiburg, BAMA DVW 1/40833, Nationale Volksarmee, Ministerium für Nationale Verteidigung. Sekretariat des Ministers. Vorbereitung und Durchführung von offiziellen Freundschaftsbesuchen, 1980–1989, Bd. 4, 276–277.

[145] Hauptabteilung I/AKG, "Aktenvermerk über die Absprache mit Gen. Oberst Weidner, Bereich des Hauptinspekteurs des MfNV," [East] Berlin (December 7, 1981), BStU, Archiv der Zentralstelle, MfS HA 1, Nr. 13618, Teil 1 von 2, 33–35. The countries of origin and numbers were USSR, 10; Poland, 16; Vietnam, 66; Laos, 20; Congo, 86;

military personnel from "anti-imperialist states and national liberation movements" studying at training centers of the East German armed forces. Twenty-nine were from the Yemen Arab Republic and 40 from the People's Republic of Yemen. Libya had 117 personnel in the GDR in military training between 1980 and 1984 with a focus on naval officers, including 19 frogmen (*Kampfschwimmern*). Between 1982 and 1985, 30 PLO officers were studying artillery and armor.[146] In 1983 as well, the East German Defense Ministry had signed agreements with the Syrian *Armed Forces* to train 70 officers and 240 junior officers primarily in East German air force training institutions.[147]

The numbers and country of origin at the Otto Winzer Officer School in Prora in 1984 and 1985 convey the international flavor of its student body. In 1984, 618 foreign military personnel were in training in the GDR. The largest contingent, 117 students, were from Syria, followed by Vietnam (81) and Mozambique (78). Thirty-seven PLO officers were in the GDR for training that year, all of them at the Officer School in Prora. At Prora, their fellow students were from Vietnam (20), Cambodia (10), Afghanistan (29), Ethiopia (36), People's Republic of Yemen (38), Syria (10), Mozambique (71), Zambia (15), and Nicaragua (35). Forty-eight Syrians were at the Higher Officer School of the East German *Air Force* and 58 were at the air force Junior Officer School in Bad Düben.[148] In 1985, 335 students were studying in Prora: 32 from Mozambique, 18 from the People's Republic of Yemen, 18 from the PLO, 10 from Zambia, 30 from Vietnam, 134 from Nicaragua, 29 from Tanzania, 48 from Ethiopia, 20 from Syria, 20 from Zimbabwe, and 9

Mozambique, 178; Libya, 155; Peoples' Republic of Yemen, 10; Yemen Arab Republic, 37; Ethiopia, 1. The institutions and number of students were Otto Winzer Officer School in Prora; Military technical school of the air force in Bad Düben; Officer School of the navy in Stralsund; Institute for Foreign Language Training in Naumburg; Officer School of the air force in Kamenz; Friedrich Engels Military Academy in Dresden; Officer School of Border Troops in Suhl; Military Medicine Section in Greifswald; Military Medical Academy in Bad Saarow.

146 Hauptabteilung I/AKG, "Ausbildung von Militärkadern antiimperialistischer Staaten und nationaler Befreiungsbewegungen an Bildungseinrichtenungen der NVA," [East] Berlin (August 1, 1983), 99–101.

147 Hauptabteilung I/AKG, "Anlage: Für den Zeitraum ab 1983 zur Ausbildung an Lehreinrichteungen der NVA vorgesehene Militärkader aus antiimperialistischen Staaten," [East] Berlin (August 1, 1983), BStU, Archiv der Zentralstelle, MfS HA 1, Nr. 13618, Teil 1 von 2.

148 Hauptabteilung I/AKG, "Zahlenmäßige Übersicht über die in der DDR studierenden ausländischen Militärkader, Stand: November 1984," [East] Berlin (November 28, 1984), BStU, Archiv der Zentralstelle, MfS HA 1, Nr. 13618, Teil 1 von 2, 92–93.

from Laos.[149] Eight-hundred forty-one foreign military cadres studied at East Germany's nine military training institutions in 1985/1986, from 14 states of Asia, Africa, the Middle East; from the PLO; and from the Sandinistas in Nicaragua. Three-hundred ninety-seven studied at Prora. In 1986/1987, 942 students were from 18 different countries. Contracts with those countries extended into the 1990s.[150] Between 1983 and 1995, the Defense Ministry intended to train 510 military cadres from Syria in East Germany. In 1986, there were 304 Syrian, 46 Libyan, and eight PLO persons in military training in the GDR.[151]

These military training schools were important institutions of international Communism in these years. They built networks of support and fostered goodwill toward East Germany. For the students, the programs opened educational opportunities, foreign language instruction, military expertise, contacts and friendships around the world, prestige, and thus paths to careers in Communist and radical leftist politics in their home countries. Finally, they contributed to the improvement of the military capabilities of all of these movements and states, including those of the various organizations on the PLO Executive Committee.

East Germany's relationship with the military leadership of the PLO continued into the 1980s. As the Stasi office responsible for liaison with the East German Defense Ministry noted in a memo of September 18, 1985, "Abu Jihad," that is, Ibrahim Al-Wazir, led delegations of the Palestinian National Liberation Army to East Berlin in 1981, 1982, 1984, and 1985.[152] On each of those occasions, Al-Wazir, the co-founder with Arafat of Al Fatah, met with high-ranking East German military and intelligence officials. During the visit in 1985 from August 28 to September 1, he led a PLO delegation that met with Defense Minister Hoffmann, attended the graduation ceremony of the first PLO graduates of the Otto Winzer Officer School in Prora, and signed an agreement to

[149] Hauptabteilung I, Kommando Landstreitkräfte, Potsdam (September 30, 1985), BStU, Archiv der Zentralstelle, MfS HA 1, Nr. 13618, Teil 1 von 2, 312–313.

[150] "Zur politisch-operativen Situation unter den ausländischen Militärkadern im Verantwortungsbereich der Hauptabteilung I," BStU, Archiv der Zentralstelle, MfS HA 1, Nr. 13618, Teil 1 von 2, 48.

[151] "Bericht über die politisch-operative Situation unter den ausländischen Militärkadern im Verantwortungsbereich der Hauptabteilung I," BStU, Archiv der Zentralstelle, MfS HA 1, Nr. 13618, Teil 1 von 2, 56–57.

[152] Hauptabteilung I, Abteilung MfNV, "Information zum Bestand der Delegation der Palästinensischen Nationalen Befreiungsarmee," Strausberg (September 18, 1985), BStU, Archiv der Zentralstelle, MfS-HA1, Nr. 11962, 1.

continue military training of PLO cadres from 1986 to 1989.[153] Wazir/Jihad told Hoffmann that despite being driven out of its bases in Lebanon, the PLO had increased its operations from 390 in 1983 to 460 in the first half of 1985 "in the occupied territories." He expressed gratitude to the GDR for its support for military training, which "we will never forget." Hoffmann assured Wazir/Jihad that "we support all of the actions of the PLO and political and military forces of the Arab world against Zionist attacks." Training and support would continue. The Defense Ministry's report of the meeting noted the "imperialist mass media claim" that Wazir/Jihad was responsible for the attack on an Israeli bus north of Tel Aviv (known as the Coastal Road Massacre in 1978), the attacks on the Munich Olympics in 1972, an attack on the Hotel Savoy in Tel Aviv in 1975, and the assassination of the Israeli ambassador in Bangkok in 1972.[154] The military relationship with the PLO endured into the late 1980s. In 1983 and 1984, the East Germans signed additional agreements to train members of the Libyan and Iraqi armed forces.[155] In 1987, Al Wazir again led a PLO military delegation visit to East Berlin. It followed the script of the previous meetings with the top leadership of the East German armed forces.[156]

[153] "Abschlußbericht über dem Aufenthalt der Delegation der Palästinensischen Nationalen Befreiungsarmee under Leitung des Stellvertreters des Oberkommandierenden der Palästinensischen Revolutionären Streitkräfte Khalil Al-Wazir/Abu Jihad in der DDR in der Zeit vom 28.8. bis 1.9.85," BStU, Archiv der Zentralstelle, MfS-HA 1, Nr. 11862, 4–6.

[154] Ibid., 5–6, 8.

[155] Abu-Baker Ynis Gabir to Heinz Hoffmann, Tripoli (February 27, 1984), NVMfNV, Vorbereitung von Besuchen ausländischer Militärdelegationen, 1983–1983, BAMA DVW 1/ 40841; Heinz Hoffmann, "Befehl Nr. 22/84 über die Vorbereitung und Durchführung des Besuches einer Delegation der Streitkräfte der Sozialistischen Libyschen Arabischen Volksjamahiriya in der Deutschen Demokratischen Republik vom 29.02.1984," NVMfNV, Vorbereitung von Besuchen ausländischer Militärdelegationen, 1983-1983, BAMA DVW 1/ 40841; and Heinz Hoffmann, "Befehl Nr. 70/83 des Ministers für Nationale Verteidigung über die Vorbereitung und Durchführung des Besuches einer Delegation der Irakischen Armee in der Deutschen Demokratischen Republik vom 15.07.1093," NVMfNV, Vorbereitung von Besuchen ausländischer Militärdelegationen, 1983-1983, BAMA DVW 1/ 40841.

[156] See material on PLO visit of November 2–6, 1987, in Nationale Volksarmee. Min für Nationale Verteidigung. Sekr. Des Ministers, "Vorbereitung und Durchführung von offiziellen Freundschaftsbesuchen 1980–1989," Bd. 3, BAMA DVW 1/ 40832; and General Fritz Streletz to Defense Minister Heinz Keßler, "Aktennotiz für den Minister für Nationale Verteideigung," [East] Berlin (date illegible, 1987), in "Nationale Volksarmee. Min für Nationale Verteidigung. Sekr. Des Ministers, Vorbereitung und Durchführung von offiziellen Freundschaftsbesuchen 1980–1989, Bd. 3, BAMA DVW 1/ 40832, 12.

On the eve of Israel's invasion of Lebanon in June 1982, East Germany had close alliances in the Middle East, most importantly with the PLO and Syria. The Stasi had formulated its Eurocentric interpretation of counterterrorism. East German officials especially in the Stasi and the Defense Ministry were involved in supplying and training terrorist organizations at war with Israel. The Defense Ministry had a web of alliances with Arab states, above all, with the Baathist regime in Syria. Away from the political warfare at the United Nations, the East German leaders dispensed with euphemisms about terrorism and spoke frankly of their support for its practitioners in the PLO, PFLP, and DFLP. Publicly in New York their diplomats spoke of realism, political solutions, and fulfilling UN resolutions. Secretly, with delivery of weapons and military training and intelligence cooperation, the East Germans backed up their words with deeds. When Israel's armed forces attacked the PLO bases in Lebanon in 1982, they were in combat with soldiers trained and equipped primarily by the Soviet-bloc countries, including East Germany.

12

Terrorism from Lebanon to Israel's "Operation Peace for Galilee": 1977–1982

In the same years in which the East Germans were expressing their solidarity with the PLO and the Arab states, the various affiliates of the PLO's Executive Committee waged a terrorist campaign from their bases in southern Lebanon against the towns and villages of northern Israel. Volleys of Katyusha rockets, attacks by terrorist squads armed with Kalashnikov assault weapons and hand grenades, as well as artillery barrages aimed specifically at civilian targets, forced the population into bomb shelters and basements for extended periods. The deaths and injuries of these civilians were not collateral damage. They were the intended purpose of the attacks. The PLO, the PFLP, and the PDFLP hoped to make normal life for Israelis so miserable that Israelis would leave and immigrants would decide not to live there. East Germany joined the Soviet Union and the Warsaw Pact states in the military and diplomatic support of the PLO in these years.

As had been the case for many years, the Israeli delegation's reports offered detailed accounts of the terrorist campaign. On March 28, 1977, Israel's UN Ambassador Chaim Herzog, speaking in the UN Security Council, observed that a week earlier the Palestine National Council "by a vote of 194 to 13 – the 13 thought that the resolution was not extreme enough" – voted to continue "the armed struggle" against Israel and rejected recognition of Israel as well as Security Council Resolution 242 of 1967 as a basis for peace and negotiation.[1] Herzog pointed out

[1] Mr. (Chaim) Herzog (Israel), United Nations Security Council Official Records, New York, 1995th Meeting: March 28, 1977, United Nations Official Documents System (UN ODS), S/PV.1995 and Corr.1, documents.un.org/welcome.asp?language=E, 6.

that the PLO Charter still "in effect called for the expulsion of the bulk of the Jewish population ... calls in effect for the destruction of the State of Israel ... makes the preposterous assertion that 'the claim of a historical or spiritual tie between Jews and Palestine does not tally with historical realities.' " Its purpose remained the destruction of Israel, whether immediately or in stages.[2] He derided talk of "moderates" in the PLO as a "popular fallacy." The differences between the moderates and the extremists were only about tactics. "The negation of Israel's right to exist is a principle accepted by all groupings within the PLO."[3] The moderates were willing to adopt a political approach "as a tactic, on condition that such an approach will ultimately lead to the destruction of Israel"; that was why they rejected UN Resolution 242, which affirmed Israel's right to exist. In Herzog's view, the "crux of the problem is the Arab refusal to recognize Israel's right to exist."[4] The Israeli government viewed the terrorist attacks from Lebanon as the logical result of the positions presented in the PLO Charter.

In a letter to UN secretary general Kurt Waldheim of November 11, 1977, Herzog reported that in September and October, the PLO launched eight rocket attacks on civilian targets in the Israeli towns of Safed, Kiryat Shmona, Nahariya, Acre, Metulla and Ramat Alma, causing injuries to several civilians and considerable property damage.[5] The PLO also stepped up its attacks on Lebanese Christians. "Then on 6 November 1977, a Katyusha rocket attack using 12-millimeter rockets with a range of 22 kilometers, was mounted against the town of Nahariya. In this attack, two civilians were killed. On 8 November, a further barrage of 22 Katyusha rockets was launched against Nahariya, with the result that one woman was killed and five were injured."[6] Hence, on November 9, the Israeli Defense Forces attacked "terrorist headquarters" and "terrorist bases" in the Lebanese towns of Ras Al-Bayde, Tel Armis, Al Aziya, and Al Haniya and "ammunition" supplies in Burt Al Shamli and Wadi Al Aswad. In the course of the attacks "the ammunition stores were hit and resulted in extensive chain explosions, thus causing considerable damage and apparently leading to civilian casualties. The fault for this

[2] Ibid.

[3] Ibid.

[4] Ibid.

[5] Chaim Herzog to Kurt Waldheim, "Letter Dated 11 November 1977 from the Permanent Representative of Israel to the United Nations Addressed to the Secretary Genera," UNGA/SC, UN ODS A/32/337; S/12444, documents.un.org/welcome.asp?language=E.

[6] Ibid., 1–2.

lies entirely with the PLO terrorist groups, which as a matter of policy locate their military installations in or near civilian centres in the hope of inhibiting action against them."[7] Herzog cited an address by the Lebanese ambassador to the UN of October 14, 1976, that asserted that the PLO had accumulated arms and placed them in "the vicinity of large civilian conglomerations."[8]

As had become its custom, the General Assembly denounced Israel's retaliation but not the original attacks to which Israel was responding. On November 25, 1977, it passed General Assembly Resolution 33/20 by a vote of 102 to 4 with 29 abstentions, which "condemned Israel's continued occupation of Arab territories in violation of the [UN] Charter, the principles of international law and repeated resolutions of the United Nations" and proposed a peace conference co-chaired by the Soviet Union and the United States "with the participation on an equal footing of all parties concerned, including the PLO." The resolution said nothing about Israel's right to exist or its right to defend itself against attack. It did not specify what it meant by occupied territories and did not condemn Palestinian terrorism. East Germany was part of that huge majority. West Germany, along with the other members of the European Union, as well as Australia, Japan, New Zealand, Ireland, Iceland, Nicaragua, Panama, Paraguay, Uruguay and the United Kingdom, abstained. Just three other countries, Canada, El Salvador, and the United States, joined Israel in opposition.[9] In 1977, the now-automatic majority of the Soviet bloc, China, India, the Arab states and most states in Asia, Africa and Latin America (including the right-wing dictatorships in Chile and Argentina) remained intact.

On March 11, 1978, the PLO carried out what became known as "the Coastal Road Massacre." On March 17, 1978, Herzog requested that the UN Security Council be convened

> to consider the continuous acts of terror and violence against Israeli civilians, together with the frequent shelling, sabotage incursions, bombing and murder being perpetrated from Lebanese territory against Israel, its people and property,

[7] Ibid., 2–3.

[8] Chaim Herzog to Kurt Waldheim, "Letter Dated 11 November 1977 from the Permanent Representative of Israel to the United Nations Address to the Secretary General," UNGA/SC, UN ODS A/32/337; S/12444, 2–3. For a summary of the Security Council and General Assembly statements from various countries, also see *Yearbook of the United Nations 1977*. Vol. 31. "Questions Relating to the Middle East" (New York: Department of Public Information, 1977), 266–278.

[9] "Resolution 32/20," *Yearbook of the United Nations 1977*. Vol. 31. "Questions Relating to the Middle East," 293–294.

in flagrant violation of international law and the Charter of the United Nations, and with the declared intention of throwing into jeopardy the negotiations aimed at achieving a final peace agreement between Israel and its Arab neighbors.[10]

He included a letter from Pinhas Eliav, the chargé d'affaires of the Israel UN delegation, to secretary general Kurt Waldheim that described the attack.[11]

On Saturday, 11 March 1978, a barbaric outrage was committed against innocent Israeli civilians on the Haifa-Tel Aviv highway. The murder squad whose victims now number 37 dead and 76 wounded, some of them critically, was dispatched by the so-called "PLO", which has taken full responsibility for the incident.

The 11 assassins infiltrated the Israeli coastline on Saturday afternoon, having received their order from Halil al-Wazir ("Abu Jihad"), one of the principal aides of Yasser Arafat, who is the head of Fatah, the largest constituent terror group within the PLO. The weapons which they were carrying were mainly Soviet made and Soviet supplied. Their instructions were to take hostages with a view to secure the release of Arab and other terrorists convicted of such atrocities as the Ben Gurion Airport massacre. The murder squad was to kill all the hostages if the Government of Israel did not surrender to its demands.

Having summarily killed a woman after stopping her on the beach near Caesarea, they commandeered a taxi and killed its passengers. They then seized a bus, carrying Israeli civilians, one half of them children, on a day's outing, and ordered the driver to proceed in the direction of Tel Aviv. En route, they overtook a second bus, opened fire on it, and killed and wounded other civilians. The survivors were then herded onto the first bus, which continued southwards towards Tel Aviv, while the terrorists shot indiscriminately at passing traffic, leaving more carnage in their wake.

At the "Country Club" intersection, the bus was stopped by a roadblock, with machine gun and rocket fire blazing from its windows. The terrorists had already bound the hostages to their seats to prevent their escape and had placed explosive charges throughout the bus. In an effort to take cover, the terrorists fled the bus, and in the course of the battle that ensued, they blew up the bus, mercilessly killing many of the hostages who were still trapped inside.[12]

[10] Chaim Herzog, "Letter Dated 17 March 1978 From the Permanent Representative of Israel to the United Nations Addressed to the President of the Security Council," UNSCOR, UN ODS, documents.un.org/welcome.asp?language=E, S/12607. Also see "Prime Minister's Statement: Statement by Prime Minister Menachem Begin at a Press Conference in Jerusalem on 12 March," *Jerusalem Domestic Service* (March 12, 1978), in *Daily Report. Middle East and North Africa*, [*Foreign Broadcast Information Service*] *FBIS-MEA-78-049 on 1978-03-13*, "Israel. Terrorists Arrive by Sea, Stopped Near Tel Aviv, Israel," Access via Library of Congress, infoweb.newsbank.com.

[11] Pinhas Eliav, "Letter Dated 13 March 1978 from the [acting] Chargé D'affaires a.I. of the Permanent Mission of Israel to the United Nations Addressed to the Secretary General," UNGA/SC, UN ODS, A.33/64-S/12598.

[12] Ibid.

Eliav added that in "the last three months," Palestinian groups connected with the PLO had placed bombs on buses in Jerusalem and at the Hebrew University and had assassinated prominent Arabs in the West Bank and an editor of the Cairo newspaper *Al-Ahram*.

In a press conference in Jerusalem on March 12, 1978, Israel's prime minister Menachem Begin reported that the terrorists arrived in two boats made in the Soviet Union and that their rocket-propelled grenades (RPGs), mortars, machine guns, and submachine guns were Soviet-made and-supplied.[13] For years, he said, the Israelis had tried to explain "to free public opinion in the world that this organization called Fatah or PLO is one of the meanest, the basest armed organizations ever in the annals of mankind, since the days of the Nazis. Their purpose is to kill Jews. They never attack military installations. They come to kill our civilians." Begin stressed the role of the Soviet Union in supplying "murderous weapons to wound and to kill the remnants of the Jewish people." He recalled Arafat's enthusiastic reception at the UN but added that "we shall not forget. And I can only call upon other nations not to forget the Nazi atrocity that was perpetrated upon our people yesterday." Begin said that it was Abu Jihad, that is, Khalil al-Wazir, the head of Fatah's military branch, who sent the terrorists on their mission.[14]

On March 12, the clandestine *Voice of Palestine* radio announced that the "General Command of the Palestine Revolution Forces" had "carried out the heroic confrontation with enemy forces" in the past two days in the area between Haifa and Tel Aviv. The unit "engaged in a battle with a military force of the enemy and managed to blow up a big bus after its civilian passengers had been forced to get off. The force returned to base safely."[15] The PLO's representative in Algiers, one Abu Hasan, described the "Kamal Udwan operation" as "the start of a series of such operations to be carried out throughout occupied Palestine." He stated that the purpose of such attacks was "to thwart all the capitulationist designs in the Arab area and frustrate the visit carried by President Sadat to our occupied homeland and his meetings with Zionist leaders" and bring about "the

[13] "Menachem Begin's 12th March Press Conference Statement, Israel Television Service 1130 gmt 12 Mar 78, Text of Prime Minister's Statement at Press Conference in Jerusalem – Live in English," BBC *SWB Summary of World Broadcasts* (March 14, 1978), ME/5763/A/7.

[14] Ibid., A/7–8; also cited in Pinhas Eliav, "Letter Dated 13 March 1978 from the Chargé D'affaires a.i. of the Permanent Mission of Israel to the United Nations Addressed to the Secretary General," 2.

[15] "Palestinian Communiqués, *Voice of Palestine* (Clandestine) (i) 1634, 1628 gmt Mar 78," BBC, *SWB:* (March 14, 1978), ME/5763/A/10.

complete liberation of Palestine." It was an expression of "steadfastness and struggle and supporting armed struggle inside occupied Palestine."[16] Abu Hasan left no doubt that in 1978 the PLO viewed all of Israel as "occupied" territory. The Libyan News Agency, JANA, stated that "the operation by the Palestinian freedom fighters of al-Fatah was brilliantly executed just a few miles north of Tel Aviv." It was a "heroic deed" whose "successful outcome" struck "the Zionist settler state in its heart."[17] The paper of the Baath Party in Damascus wrote that the importance of "the courageous operation carried out by Palestinian revolutionaries inside the occupied territories" was that it "explodes the Zionist claims about the questions of security and defensible borders." In Beirut on March 13 a rally took place to commemorate "one of the Palestine Revolution martyrs," that is, one of the terrorists killed in the attack. George Habash praised the participants in the attack as "heroes."[18]

On March 13, Prime Minister Begin spoke to the Israeli parliament, the Knesset, about the attack.[19] He had seen the "men, women and children who lay dead after an attack by evildoers." From the Arab states "there is no word of sorrow, no participation in the sorrow of the bereaved families. On the contrary, voices of joy and exhilaration are reaching us, boasts and bragging." Then the prime minister turned to Arafat's presence in Moscow:

> Only three days ago the leader of the murderers was in Moscow. He was received with honours. The ruler of the Soviet Union himself had a talk with him. They conducted negotiations. Why did they confer and what did they talk about? To the best of our knowledge, dozens of training courses for Fatah members and for those who are called the PLO have recently been conducted in the Soviet Union and in other communist East European countries, courses in which Soviet experts taught them how to use weapons, how to attack.

While Israel could not "reach the heart of the totalitarian countries to put an end to this shameful situation," he urged "the democratic countries in Europe" to close the PLO offices. How, he asked, could "they

[16] "PLO Official's Warning of Further Operations in Occupied Palestine, Algiers Home Service in Arabic 1200 gmt 12 Mar 78, Excerpts from recorded interview with Abu Hassan, PLO Representative in Algiers," BBC, *SWB:* (March 14, 1978), ME/5763/A/11.

[17] "Reaction to the Incident North of Tel Aviv (e) JANA in English 1545 gmt 12 Mar 78," BBS, *SWB:* (March 14, 1978), ME/5763/A/13.

[18] "Reaction to the Incident North of Tel Aviv (f) Damascus Home Service 0415 gmt 13 Mar 78." BBC, *SWB:* (March 14, 1978), ME/5763/A/13.

[19] "Menachem Begin's 13th March Statement in the Knesset, IDF Radio 1510 gmt 13 Mar 78, Text of Recording of Begin's statement from the Evening Newsreel," BBC, *SWB:* (March 14, 1978), ME/5764/A/6.

continue permitting the existence of such offices in which such murderous schemes are being plotted."[20] As we have seen, the evidence in the East German archives confirms the validity of Begin's comments about the training of the PLO in the countries of the Soviet bloc and of their support for terrorist attacks on Israel.

On March 13, *Neues Deutschland* ran two stories about these events. "Palestinian Military Action in Israel" and "Israeli Armed Forces Provoke in South Lebanon."[21] The East German correspondent in Damascus cited the Palestinian news agency WAFA reporting that a "commando of the resistance organization Al Fatah had carried out a military operation between Haifa and Tel Aviv," one that began with an attack on "two vehicles with Israel soldiers" in them. Despite a strong response by the Israeli military, the "Palestinian commandos escaped in the direction of the Mediterranean."[22] The report was a fabrication. The attack was not "military" in the conventional understanding of that term. It did not begin with an attack on soldiers. It was from beginning to end a terrorist attack on unarmed civilians. Six of the attackers were killed. On March 16, *ND's* front page led with the headline "Israel Unleashes Brutal Aggression against Lebanon."[23]

Soviet media took the lead in accusing Israel of engaging in genocide in Lebanon. On March 22, in an article entitled "Israeli Genocide," V. Kudryavtsev in *Izvestiya* asserted that there was "no justification for the Israeli Zionists' barbaric act. The 11 March incident near Tel Aviv was not the result of anyone's malice."[24] Having driven "the people of Palestine ... from their native land," Israel was now "not only pursuing its policy of genocide in practice" but was "reinforcing it through legislation."[25] On March 20, 1978 East German diplomats participated in a meeting of the Committee for the Exercise of the Inalienable Rights of the Palestinian People (CEIRPP) at the UN in New York. The East German representative stated that the "Israeli aggression against Lebanon was

[20] Ibid.

[21] "Palästinensische Militäraktion in Israel," and "Israelische Streitkräfte provozierten in Südlibanon," *Neues Deutschland* ([East] Berlin [March 13, 1978]), 5.

[22] "Palästinensische Militäraktion in Israel," 5.

[23] "Israel entfesselte brutale Aggression," *ND* [East] Berlin (March 17, 1978), 1. Also see "Israel bereitet Überfall auf den Süden Libanons vor: Tel Aviv plant Großoffensive gegen die palästinensische Resistance," *ND* [East] Berlin (March 16, 1978), 7. *Neues Deutschland* never referred to "Jerusalem," Israel's capital, but only to "Tel Aviv."

[24] "Israeli Genocide," Moscow, Izvestiya (March 22, 1978), *FBIS, Middle East*, infoweb.newsbank.com at Library of Congress online; and *Daily Report: Soviet Union, FBIS-Sov-78-061 on 1978-03-29.*

[25] Ibid.

directed against the people of Lebanon and against the Palestinians living in that country."[26] CEIRPP, *Neues Deutschland*, and *Izvestiya* followed the now-familiar rules of Soviet-bloc and PLO political warfare against Israel: never mention or give accurate details about Arab state or Palestinian terrorist attacks on Israel, in this case, those of the Coastal Road Massacre; then follow that silence with assertions that the Israeli government's retaliation constituted acts of unprovoked aggression and even genocide.[27]

The UN Security Council devoted five sessions from March 17 to 19, 1978, to the coastal road attack and Israel's military response, named "Operation Litani," an air and ground offensive into southern Lebanon.[28] Herzog expressed disgust with the Security Council's treatment of the Middle East conflict. As the Security Council had "failed for 30 years to adopt a single resolution condemning the murder of innocent Israeli civilians," it had "long ago forfeited its right to pass judgment on actions stemming from terrorist outrages."[29] Since the attack on the Munich Olympics, the UN had not agreed on "a single resolution condemning terrorism"; at the same time it had given observer status to the PLO, "an organization which openly and proudly proclaimed its responsibility for the cold-blooded assassinations and meticulously planned murder of small children."[30] Herzog said Israel's Defense Forces had crossed into Lebanon to make it possible for their citizens to "live safe from the fear of indiscriminate attack and murder." Israel's diplomats had gone to the Security Council "to accuse those criminals who slaughtered our citizens and those who were accessories to the crime."[31] Since 1968, more than 1,500 separate acts of international terrorism had taken place throughout the world. "Not once," he said, "has the Security Council been jarred

[26] Mr. Joachimi, "Committee on the Exercise of the Inalienable Rights of the Palestinian People, Summary Record of the 30th Meeting," New York (March 20, 1978), UNGA, A/AC.183.SR.30, 23 March 1978, UN Archive, New York.

[27] As crude as *Izvestiya* was, Georgi Kaloyanov in an article headlined "Is It 'Defense' or 'Genocide'?" on March 19 in *Rabotnichesko Delo*, the newspaper of the Bulgarian Communist Party and Government, made even more blatantly anti-Semitic assertions. Georgi Kaloyanov, "Calls Israeli Action Genocide," Sofia, *Rabotnichesko Delo-1978-03-19, FBIS, Middle East*, infoweb.newsbank.com via Library of Congress onsite online; also *Daily Report: Eastern Europe, FBIS-EEU-78-058 on 1978-03-24*

[28] UNSCOR, 2071-2075th Meeting: March 17–19, 1978, UN ODS S/PV.2071–2075. S/PV.2017–2075.

[29] Mr. [Chaim] Herzog (Israel), New York (March 17. 1978), UNSCOR, 2071st Meeting: March 17, 1978, UN ODS, S/PV.2071, 2.

[30] Ibid., 3.

[31] Ibid.

into response." West Germany's efforts to introduce a convention against taking of hostages had "been allowed to sink into the quicksands of General Assembly committees, from which it has yet to emerge." Israel "long ago" had concluded that the UN was neither able nor inclined to "deal with terror and terrorists, and it is for that reason that we crossed into Lebanon."[32]

He offered the following record of Palestinian terrorist attacks against Israel:

> Since the end of 1973, there have been 1,548 individual acts of aggression arising out of artillery, Katyusha, mortar and terrorist attacks mounted against Israel by those terrorists. In those attacks, 108 Israeli citizens, mostly women and children, were killed and 221 wounded. These figures alone – 1,548 attacks in four years – surely vindicate Israel's action in recent days and testify to the incontrovertible fact that Israel for years exercised a forbearance and patience which, alas, produced no results. Last Saturday's senseless and brutal massacre on the Haifa-Tel Aviv road, which only emphasized in lurid and tragic detail the levels of bestiality to which these murderers have sunk, was but a further savage link in a diabolical chain of carnage and death. The Government of Israel has therefore been faced with the problem of doing its duty, the inherent duty of every Government to exercise its right of self-defense in the protection of the inviolability of its territory and its people.[33]

As the government of Lebanon had lost control over large parts of southern Lebanon and as the UN was unable or unwilling to put an end to the attacks, "the government of Israel was compelled to act."[34]

On March 19, 1978 the Security Council adopted the American-sponsored Resolution 425, which established a United Nations Interim Force for Lebanon (UNIFIL). It called for respect for Lebanon's territorial integrity and demanded that Israel "immediately cease its military action against Lebanese territorial integrity and withdraw forthwith its forces from all Lebanese territory."[35] The "Interim" UN force was still in Lebanon in 2015. Even faced with an atrocity of such vivid dimensions as the coastal road attack, the UN Security Council did not pass a resolution that condemned the PLO's terrorist campaign. Through its choice of condemnation, praise, and selective silences, the anti-Israeli majority in the UN General Assembly continued to function as the diplomatic arm of the PLO's campaign of terrorism against Israel. East Germany continued to

[32] Ibid., 4.

[33] Ibid., 3.

[34] Ibid., 6.

[35] "Resolution 425," *Yearbook of the United Nations 1978* (New York: Department of Public Information), 312.

FIGURE 12.1. Yehuda Blum, Israel's UN ambassador, 1978–1984. Blum's letters to the UN offices offered a detailed record of the Palestinian terrorist campaign waged against northern Israel from PLO bases in southern Lebanon.
Source: Israel National Photo Collection, Government Press Office, D153-055.

be in the midst of this very large majority and to swim with, not against, the current of opinion.

ISRAEL'S UN AMBASSADOR YEHUDA BLUM ON PLO TERRORIST ATTACKS ON ISRAELI CIVILIANS: 1980–1981

On March 10, 1981, Herzog's successor as Israel's UN ambassador, Yehuda Blum (Figure 12.1), provided the following summary of PLO attacks on Israel from Lebanon from May 5, 1980, to March 7, 1981 (Table 12.1).[36]

Also on March 10, 1981 Blum wrote to the president of the UN Security Council to report "indiscriminate shelling of towns and villages in northern Israel carried out on 2 and 3 March, 1981, by PLO terrorists operating from Lebanon." The shelling incidents with Katyusha rockets were connected to an arms build-up of "sizable quantities of armour and artillery of Soviet manufacture." The 26 "acts and attempted acts of terror" carried out by the PLO included shelling or attacks on the following

[36] Yehuda Z. Blum, "Annex: PLO Terrorist Activity Emanating from Lebanon since 7 April 1980," New York (March 10, 1981), S/14398, 1–2.; UN ODS, S/14398.

TABLE 12.1. *PLO attacks on Israel, May 1980–March 1981*

1.	14.5.1980	Three PLO terrorists killed in attempting to cross from Lebanese territory near Kibbutz Habia.
2.	17.5.1980	Katyusha rockets fired from Lebanese territory at civilian centres in the "Galilee Panhandle."
3.	16.6.1980	Israel naval vessel intercepted and destroyed a terrorist vessel opposite the village of Achziv on the Mediterranean coast.
4.	20.7.1980	An abortive attempt made by PLO terrorists to cross from Lebanese territory into Israel by balloon.
5.	14.7.1980	Katyusha rockets fired from Lebanese territory at civilian centres in the "Galilee Panhandle."
6.	20.8.1980	Katyusha rockets fired from Lebanese territory at civilian centres in the "Galilee Panhandle."
7.	23.8.1980	Katyusha rockets fired from Lebanese territory at civilian centres in the "Galilee Panhandle."
8.	17.9.1980	Katyusha rockets fired from Lebanese territory at civilian centres in the "Galilee Panhandle."
9.	6.11.1980	Katyusha rockets fired from Lebanese territory at civilian centres in the "Galilee Panhandle." Five civilians wounded at Kiryat Shmona.
10.	13.11.1980	Two PLO terrorists killed in attempting to cross from Lebanese territory near Kibbutz Misgav Am.
11.	14.12.1980	Unsuccessful attempt by a PLO terror squad to cross from Lebanese territory west of Kibbutz Zar'it.
12.	19.12.1980	Katyusha rockets fired from Lebanese territory at civilian centres in the "Galilee Panhandle."
13.	25.12.1980	Five terrorists killed in attempting to cross from Lebanese territory near Kibbutz Hanita.
14.	28.1.1981	Katyusha rockets fired from Lebanese territory at civilian centres in the "Galilee Panhandle."
15.	28/29.1981	Katyusha rockets fired from Lebanese territory at civilian centres in the "Galilee Panhandle." Seven civilians, including four children, wounded in Kiryat Shmona.
16.	29/30.1981	Katyusha rockets fired from Lebanese territory at civilian centres in the "Galilee Panhandle."
17.	29/30.1981	Two hours later, a second barrage of Katyusha rockets fired from Lebanese territory at civilian centres in the "Galilee Panhandle."
18.	30.1.1981	Katyusha rockets fired from Lebanese territory at Kiryat Shmona. Three civilians wounded.
19.	30.1.1981	Katyusha rockets fired from Lebanese territory at civilian centres in the "Galilee Panhandle."
20.	30.1.1981	A second barrage of Katyusha rockets fired from Lebanese territory at civilian targets in western Galilee.
21.	2.3.1981	Katyusha rockets fired from Lebanese territory at Kiryat Shmona. Four civilians wounded.

TABLE 12.1 (*continued*)

22.	2.3.1981	Katyusha rockets fired from Lebanese territory at civilian centres in the "Galilee Panhandle."
23.	2.3.1981	A second barrage of Katyusha rockets fired from Lebanese territory at civilian targets in western Galilee.
24.	3.3.1981	Katyusha rockets fired from Lebanese territory at civilian centres in the "Galilee Panhandle."
25.	3.3.1981	A second barrage of Katyusha rockets fired from Lebanese territory at civilian targets in western Galilee.
26.	7.3.1981	Two PLO attempts to fly from Lebanese territory into Israel on terrorist missions.

Source: Yehuda Z. Blum, "Annex: PLO Terrorist Activity Emanating from Lebanon since 7 April 1980," New York, UNSC (March 10, 1981), UN ODS S/14398, 1–2.

32 towns in northern Israel: Amir, Auyalon, Beit Hillel, Betzet, Dafna, Even Manachem, Fasuta, Goren, Hule, Idmit, Jurdah, Kfar Blum, Kfar Giladi, Kfar Szold, Kfar yuval, Dan, Kiryat Shmona, Ma'ayan Baruch, Manara, Margaliot, Metulla, Metzuva, Misgav Am, Nahariya, Ne'ot Mordechai, Netu'a, Sasa, She'ar Yashuv, Shlomi, Shnir, Shtula, Ya'ara.[37]

In letters to the secretary general from February to April 1981, Blum described continuing terrorist attacks.[38] Celebrating the "resistance" and fedayeen heroism, the PLO claimed responsibility for the following attacks: hand grenades thrown at cars; a shooting murder (January 10 and 11); Katyusha attacks on Kiryat Shmona (January 28/29 and dawn on January 30); a knife attack on a bus driver (March 11); a hand grenade and machine gun attack on a bus in a Jerusalem suburb (March 14); the explosion of a bomb that injured four people on a bus as it entered the central bus station in Tel Aviv (March 29); an explosive device discovered in the town of Dimona (March 30) and on the same day an explosive device placed on a railway line between the southern towns of Kiryat Gat and Beer Sheba; Katyusha rockets aimed at Kibbutz Maoz Haim; a hand grenade hurled at the participants of a wedding party in Jerusalem (April 8); Katyusha rockets fired from Jordan at several kibbutzim in the Upper Jordan valley; the explosion of a bomb at a bus stop on Bethlehem

[37] Ibid.

[38] Blum, "Letters from the Permanent Representative of Israel to the United Nations Addressed to the Secretary General," of January 15, 1981 (S/14328); March 11, 1981 (S/14403); February 2, 1981 (S/14355); March 8, 1981 (S/14394); March 16, 1981 (S/14409); April 3, 1981 (S/14427); April 10, 1981 (S/14438; April 17, 1981 (S/14448); May 6, 1981 (S/14476); May 28, 1981 (S/14492); all at UN ODS.

Road in Jerusalem (April 13); an explosion outside the municipal building in Jerusalem (April 24); discovery of a bomb in a café in central Jerusalem. A police sapper had to have his hand amputated after being injured while trying to defuse the bomb (May 1); a hand grenade was hurled at a civilian truck outside the town of Gaza (May 26).[39]

Blum reported the following PLO attacks in July and August 1981: an attack on a passenger bus that wounded four passengers, including a young woman seven months pregnant who lost her infant (July 29); placing bombs that were discovered before they exploded in Jerusalem's Old City and in a suburb of Jerusalem (August 8); a bomb explosion at the El Al office at Rome's Fiumicino International Airport injuring two persons and causing heavy damage (August 9); and explosions outside the Israeli Diplomatic Mission in Athens and near the Israeli Embassy in Vienna (August 10). Blum held the PLO responsible for the murder of a young German tourist who was shot in the head in the Old City of Jerusalem (August 23). The PLO claimed credit for a bomb that injured a commuter at the Ra'anna intersection and another at a hitchhiking post near Jerusalem (August 24).[40] On Saturday morning, August 29, two terrorists who identified themselves as belonging to the PLO hurled hand grenades and fired submachine guns at a crowd of worshippers outside a synagogue in Vienna for the Sabbath morning service and a bar mitzvah ceremony with many participating children. A 68-year-old man and a 25-year-old woman (the latter while attempting to protect a child) were killed and 17 other worshippers and passersby, as well as two Austrian policemen, were wounded.[41]

In a letter of October 2, 1981, Blum reported that the PLO claimed responsibility for the following attacks in fall 1981: On September 23, five Cyprus citizens were injured when a hand grenade was thrown at the offices of the Israel shipping companies Zim and Shoham; a booby-trapped car was discovered in the Ramle marketplace and defused.[42] On November 17, Yusus al-Khatib, the head of a village association in the

[39] Ibid.

[40] Yehuda Z. Blum, "Letters from the Permanent Representative of Israel to the United Nations" UNSC July 30, 1981 (S/14622); August 17, 1982 (S/14631); August 28, 1981 (S/14668); New York, UN ODS, S/14398.

[41] Yehuda Z. Blum, "Letter Dated 31 August March 1981 from the Permanent Representative of Israel to the United Nations Addressed to the President of the Security Council," New York, UNSC, UN ODS S/14670.

[42] Yehuda Z. Blum, "Letter Dated 2 October 1981 from the Permanent Representative of Israel to the United Nations Addressed to the Secretary General," New York, UNSC (October 5, 1981), UN ODS S/14714.

Ramallah area, and his son, Katim, were ambushed by PLO gunmen. Katim was killed instantly while his father was severely wounded. The PLO took responsibility for the action on its radio in Lebanon. The PLO radio warned that it would continue its campaign "to intimidate and silence Arab leaders in Judea, Samaria and the Gaza District who oppose terrorism and favor peace with Israel." Blum added that in operating in this manner "the PLO is following the violent tradition of its mentor, the notorious Mufti of Jerusalem, Haj Amin al-Husseini, who, in the 1920s and 1930s, had no compunction about terrorizing and liquidating his political rivals." According to Blum, since 1966, the PLO had killed almost 400 Arabs and wounded almost 2,000 others.[43]

In a letter of November 30, Blum reported that on October 26 schoolchildren discovered a live hand grenade on public school grounds in the Patt residential neighborhood in Jerusalem.[44] On October 17 a hand grenade was hurled at passersby at the Zion gate in Jerusalem, injuring a woman and her two young daughters. On November 13 an explosive device was discovered on a crowded bus near Beit Shemesh. On November 26, a bomb exploded at a kiosk in the Geula residential neighborhood in Jerusalem, and another in a paint store in the center of Jerusalem, injuring an employee. Blum told his fellow UN ambassadors in the letter of November 30, 1981, that such acts revealed the true nature of the PLO. "It is a group of international criminals bent on the indiscriminate murder of civilians while at the same time masquerading under the guise of a 'national liberation movement,' " a masquerade that was "of course facilitated" by the UN's decision to grant it "irregular rights" and observer status.[45] In the course of 1981, Israel sent about 40 letters to the secretary general or to the president of the Security Council about the continuing attacks of Palestinian terrorist organizations on Israel. They were distributed to all the member states of the United Nations. The UN General Assembly majority dismissed them as it continued to pass anti-Israeli resolutions on "the question of Palestine" by large margins.

In spring and summer 1981, the Israeli delegation at the UN also drew attention to the expansion of the size and nature of the PLO arsenal in

43 Yehuda Z. Blum, "Letter Dated 18 November 1981 from the Permanent Representative of Israel to the United Nations Addressed to the Secretary General," New York, UNSC (November 19, 1981), UN ODS S/14760.

44 Yehuda Z. Blum, "Letter Dated 30 November 1981 from the Permanent Representative of Israel to the United Nations Addressed to the Secretary General," New York, UNSC (December 3, 1981), UN ODS, S/14776.

45 Ibid.

Lebanon. On July 17, Blum informed the Security Council of the PLO acquisition of "heavy weapons with far greater fire-power than before and in quantities which they have never had before."[46] He said Libya supplied the PLO "both directly and indirectly through Syria" with SAM-9 surface-to-air missiles. The Soviet Union had been supplying the PLO "with new and sophisticated military material" from both other Soviet-bloc states and Arab countries. In addition to the 130-millimeter and 155-millimeter howitzers and Katuysha rockets and launchers, the PLO was now being "supplied through a Soviet-bloc country with over 50 additional tanks as well as troop carriers." The T-34, T-54, and T-55 tanks were "located in PLO emplacements in Sidon and in Beirut." In the south, the PLO now possessed recoilless rocket launchers up to 122- and 130-millimeter caliber. The military supplies of the recent months represented "a significant escalation in the Soviet Union's arms supply policy to the PLO."[47]

Israel had called "PLO outrages" to the attention of the Security Council and to the secretary general "but to no avail." The UN had refused to condemn "the PLO's criminal activities." All of Israel's numerous communications to the council and secretary general had "gone unheeded." So, given the absence of effective international pressure, it had fallen to the government of Israel "to stand up to the scourge of PLO terror." Israel, he continued, could not be expected "to sit back passively and wait with folded arms for further barbarities to be perpetrated against the civilian population by PLO terrorists." What member of the council "would sit back idly and allow its own women and children to be murdered and maimed by terrorists?"[48] As East Germany was a temporary member of the Security Council, its representative was in the room when Blum asked that question.

Blum described the following targets of Israel's military actions in Lebanon: bases of the PLO, the Democratic Front [DFLP] and the Arab Liberation Front; a Fatah training camp; the Fatah operations center in Beirut and the headquarters of the Democratic Popular Front [DPFLP], also in Beirut. Israel did not intend to harm Lebanese civilians but because the PLO had taken cover in villages and refugee camps, some were caught

[46] Yehuda Z. Blum, UNSCOR, 2292 Meeting: July 17, 1981 (New York), UN ODS, S.PV.2292.

[47] Ibid., 4–5.

[48] Yehuda Z. Blum (Israel), United Nations Security Council Official Records, 2292 Meeting: July 17, 1981 (New York); UN ODS, S.PV.2292 at: documents.un.org/welcome.asp?language=E, 4–5.

in the cross-fire. Israel deeply regretted "any loss of life or injury of civilians" on either side of the border. The key problem facing the council was "how to put an end to international terror in general … and more specifically, how to put an end to PLO terror against Israel." Blum was not optimistic. The council needed to "abandon the blinkered attitude it has so studiously exhibited thus far in the face of the slaughter of tens of thousands of Lebanese civilians by the Syrian army of occupation and by the terrorist PLO over recent years."[49]

EAST GERMAN RESPONSES

Four days later, Siegfried Zachmann, East Germany's ambassador to UN from 1977 to 1983, spoke in the Security Council about the events in Lebanon.[50] The only notable aspect of his remarks was that they were made by a representative of a German government and that, like the vast majority of the contributors to the UN discussions, he ignored every factual assertion that Blum had made about the PLO's terrorist campaign. Zachmann even rejected the notion that Israel was faced with a terrorist campaign at all. He drew on the PLO representative, Zedhi Terzi's, reference to Israel's "acts of terror."[51] Zachmann said that with its "terror raids," Israel was seeking "to destroy their homes and to liquidate their families. The Israeli aggressors, who drove the Palestinians from their homeland more than three decades ago today claim that they feel threatened by the very existence of those Palestinians in Lebanon."[52] In response to Blum's focus on the terrorist organizations in Lebanon, Zachmann asserted that the delegation of the GDR "again strongly opposes any attempt to bring the national liberation movements into discredit by branding them as terrorist. Under the cloak of anti-communism, some seek to disguise the terrorism of dictators against their own people and against other peoples." In other words, according to Zachmann, the PLO, the PFLP, the Popular Front-General Command, and the PDFLP, who had

[49] Yehuda Z. Blum, UNSCOR, 2292 Meeting: July 17, 1981 (New York); UN ODS, S.PV.2292. 4–5.

[50] Siegfried Zachmann (German Democratic Republic), UNSCOR, 2293 Meeting: July 21, 1981 (New York); UN ODS, S.PV.229. See Siegfried Bock, Ingrid Muth, and Hermann Schwiesau, eds, *DDR Aussenpolitik: Ein überblick*, 368.

[51] See Zehdi Terzi (PLO), UNSCOR, 2292 Meeting: July 17, 1981 (New York); UN ODS, S.PV.2292, 4–5

[52] Siegfried Zachmann, UNSCOR, 2293 Meeting: July 21, 1981 (New York), 8–9.

all celebrated the attacks on Israeli civilians and had never denied doing so, were not terrorist organizations.[53]

While East German diplomats in New York indignantly rejected the idea that the Palestinian terrorist organizations were, in fact terrorists, a Stasi memo of June 25, 1981, offered further evidence of East German support for the PFLP.[54] Stasi officials wrote that "in all basic questions of the international class struggle, the PFLP agrees with the socialist community of states [that is, the Soviet bloc, JH] and is interested in close political and ideological cooperation with the USSR, CSSR [Czechoslovakia], VRB [People's Republic of Bulgaria] and the GDR." Within the Palestinian movement, it actively opposed "reactionary, bourgeois, petty-bourgeois nationalist forces" that favored "imperialist versions of solutions to the Middle East conflict."[55] The stance of the PFLP toward the Middle East was "constructive and realistic" because it opposed the policies of the United States, the European Community, and the "reactionary Arab forces." It sought to "overcome the stagnation" that followed the Camp David Accords between Egypt and Israel and the associated effort to exclude the PLO from a solution to the conflict.[56] The PFLP sought "close cooperation with the 'front of steadfastness' (Libya, Algeria, Syria and the People's Republic of Yemen)" opposed to the Camp David accords.[57] Oddly, the Stasi memo incorrectly claimed that the PFLP had abandoned terrorist activities after 1972. PFLP delegations led by George Habash had "repeatedly" visited the Soviet Union in 1978 and 1980, Czechoslovakia and Bulgaria in 1979, Romania in 1980, and Cuba as they "were interested in increasing the number of PFLP members who could study in "the countries of the socialist community."[58]

The Stasi memo of June 25, 1981, about the PFLP can be rephrased as follows. The PFLP's return to the Executive Committee and the close organizational links to Nayef Hawatmeh's DPFLP indicated that the PLO was, as the Israelis were claiming, an umbrella organization with a central leadership represented by Arafat. The East German government regarded rejection of the Camp David Accords as a "realistic" approach

[53] Ibid., 9.

[54] "Information über die Haltung der PFLP zum Nahostproblem und zu anderen internationalen Fragen sowie zu einigen Problemen ihrer inneren Entwicklung," [East] Berlin (June 25, 1981), BStU, MfS Zentralarchiv, Hauptverwaltung Aufklärung, Nr. 7., 124.

[55] Ibid., 124–125.

[56] Ibid., 125.

[57] Ibid., 126–127.

[58] Ibid., 127–128.

to the Middle East conflict. The claim that the PFLP had not carried out any terrorist actions since 1972 (probably referring to the massacre at the Munich Olympics) ignored the PFLP's public claims of involvement in the attack on Kiryat Shmona in April 1974 and the hijacking of the Air France plane to Entebbe in 1976 and a Lufthansa flight to Mogadishu in 1977. The claim was plausible only if one adopted the Communist definition of terrorism in those years, which described attacks on Israeli civilians as justified actions in an "armed struggle" against Zionism, imperialism and racism, and that Israelis – and in Entebbe, Jews as well – were legitimate military targets. As the citizens of Israel were colonial occupiers, none murdered in these attacks were innocent victims. Killing Israelis was thus, by these definitions, not terrorism.

BLUM ON THE PLO ATTACKS AND THE ARMS BUILDUP IN LEBANON, 1981–1982

On July 20, 1981, Blum sent another comprehensive summary of PLO terrorist attacks to the president of the Security Council. Since mid-June 1978, there had been "115 such acts, or attempted acts of, terror which the PLO has perpetrated from Lebanese territory against civilian targets in Israel."[59] He again drew attention to "the steady build-up of arms in PLO hands" and the widening of its infrastructure in Lebanon as a result of a buildup of Soviet-bloc armaments. The equipment included "Soviet-manufactured tanks, mainly T-34s, T-54s and T-55s; armoured troop carriers and other vehicles; large artillery pieces including 40-barrel multiple rocket launchers ('Katyushas'), mounted on heavy trucks; 130 mm and 155 mm Howitzers; recoilless rocket launchers, of up to and including 130 mm caliber; anti-aircraft guns; SAM 7 surface-to-air missiles; and SAM 9 surface-to-air missiles (in this case, together with Libyan crews to man the missile batteries."[60] Blum reported that the frequency of attacks grew along with this weapons accumulation. He included the following list (Table 12.2) of 45 terrorist attacks on Israel emanating from Lebanon from March 7 to July 20, 1981.

Blum's summary of July 20, 1981, indicated the growing frequency of attacks and confirmed Israel's claims regarding the growth of the PLO

[59] Yehuda Z. Blum, "Letter Dated 20 July, 1981 from the Permanent Representative of Israel to the United Nations Addressed to the President of the Security Council," New York, UNSC (July 20, 1981), UN ODS S/14602.

[60] Ibid. The Katyusha rocket launcher became famous in World War II when it was used by the Red Army. It was then known as the "Stalin Organ."

TABLE 12.2. *Annex: PLO terrorist activity emanating from Lebanon since 7 March 1981*

1.	16.4.1981	An abortive attempt by PLO terrorists to cross from Lebanese territory into Israel by balloon.
2.	20.4.1981	At about 16:00 hours, shelling from Lebanese territory of Western Galilee.
3.	20.4.1981	An hour and one-half later, a second shelling from Lebanese territory of Western Galilee.
4.	20.4.1981	At about 22:00 hours, a third shelling from Lebanese territory of Western Galilee.
5.	20.4.1981	Shelling from Lebanese territory of the Galilee Panhandle.
6.	21.4.1981	Shelling from Lebanese territory of the Galilee Panhandle. One civilian was injured.
7.	24.7.1981	Katyusha rockets and artillery shells fired from Lebanese territory at the Galilee Panhandle.
8.	24.7.1981	Shelling from Lebanese territory of the Galilee Panhandle.
9.	24.7.1981	Shelling from Lebanese territory of Western Galilee.
10.	28.4.1981	Katyusha rockets fired from Lebanese territory at the Galilee Panhandle.
11.	29.4.1981	Katyusha rockets fired from Lebanese territory at the Western Galilee.
12.	29.4.1981	Katyusha rockets fired from Lebanese territory at the Galilee Panhandle.
13.	30.4.1981	Katyusha rockets fired from Lebanese territory at the Galilee Panhandle.
14.	30.4.1981	Katyusha rockets fired from Lebanese territory at the Western Galilee.
15	10.7.1981	Katyusha rockets fired from Lebanese territory at the Western Galilee. Six civilians wounded.
16.	15.7.1981	Katyusha rockets fired from Lebanese territory at Upper Galilee.
17.	15.7.1981	Katyusha rockets fired from Lebanese territory at the Western Galilee.
18.	16.7.1981	Katyusha rockets fired from Lebanese territory at Upper Galilee.
19.	16.7.1981	In the afternoon, Katyusha rockets fired from Lebanese territory at Western Galilee. Two civilians were wounded.
20.	16.7.1981	At about 19:00 hours, shelling from Lebanese territory of Western Galilee.
21.	17.7.1981	At 08:30 hours, Katyusha rockets fired from Lebanese territory at the Galilee Panhandle. Two civilians were wounded.
22.	17.7.1981	At about 10:00 hours, Katyusha rockets fired from Lebanese territory at the Galilee Panhandle.

TABLE 12.2 (*continued*)

23.	17.7.1981	At 11:30 hours, Katyusha rockets fired from Lebanese territory at WesternGalilee. A maternity hospital was hit, and two young mothers, as well as three other civilians, were wounded.
24.	17.7.1981	At 20:00 hours, Katyusha rockets fired from Lebanese territory at the Galilee Panhandle.
25.	17.7.1981	At 23.10 hours, Katyusha rockets fired from Lebanese territory at the Galilee Panhandle.
26.	18.7.1981	At 00.25, Katyusha rockets fired from Lebanese territory at the Galilee Panhandle.
27.	18.7.1981	At 02.05 hours, Katyusha rockets fired from Lebanese territory at the Galilee Panhandle.
28	18.7.1981	At 02:30 hours, Katyusha rockets fired from Lebanese territory at the Galilee Panhandle. One civilian wounded in Kiryat Shmona.
29.	18.7.1981	At 04:25 hours, Katyusha rockets fired from Lebanese territory at the Galilee Panhandle.
30.	18.7.1981	At 04:30, Katyusha rockets fired from Lebanon territory at the Galilee Panhandle.
31.	18.7.1981	At 06:10 hours, Katyusha rockets fired from Lebanese territory at the Galilee Panhandle. One civilian was wounded.
32.	18.7.1981	At 09:55 hours, Katyusha rockets fired from Lebanese territory at Western Galilee.
33.	18.7.1981	At 10:10 hours, Katyusha rockets fired from Lebanese territory at the Galilee Panhandle.
34	18.7.1981	At 10:30, Katyusha rockets fired from Lebanese territory at Western Galilee.
35.	18.7.1981	At 21.30, Katyusha rockets fired from Lebanese territory at the Galilee Panhandle.
36.	19.7.1981	At 00:10 hours, Katyusha rockets fired from Lebanese territory at the Galilee Panhandle.
37.	19.7.1981	At 08:30 hours, Katyusha rockets fire from Lebanese territory at the Galilee Panhandle. A 14-year old boy was killed in Kiryat Shmona, and 15 civilians were wounded, 2 of them (including the mother of the dead boy) seriously.
38.	19.7.1981	At 12:00, Katyusha rockets fired from Lebanese territory at Western Galilee.
39.	19.7.1981	At 19:00 hours, Katyusha rockets fired from Lebanese territory at the Galilee Panhandle.
40.	19.7.1981	At 21:00 hours, shelling from Lebanese territory of the Western Galilee. Two persons were injured in Nahariya.
41.	20.7.1981	At midnight, shelling from Lebanese territory at the Galilee Panhandle.

(*continued*)

TABLE 12.2 (*continued*)

42.	20.7.1981	At about 3:30 hours, shelling from Lebanese territory at the Galilee Panhandle.
43.	20.7.1981	At 04:00 hours, shelling from Lebanese territory at the Galilee Panhandle.
44.	20.7.1981	At about 06:30 hours, shelling from Lebanese territory at the Galilee Panhandle. A woman killed at Kibbutz Misgav Am, and another civilian was injured.
45.	20.7.1981	At 20:00 hours, shelling from Lebanese territory of the Galilee Panhandle.[61]

Source: Yehuda Z. Blum, "Annex: PLO Terrorist Activity Emanating from Lebanon since 7 March 1981," New York, UNSC (July 20, 1981), UN ODS S/14602.

arsenal. In the midst of the shelling from the Katyushas, Israel's residents in the north were again forced to spend days, even weeks in bomb shelters. Blum described the "objectives of these bombardments" to be "the indiscriminate murder of civilians." The PLO was aiming directly at civilian centers. From July 15 to 19, 1981, 18 towns and villages in northern Israel were struck. The prime targets were Kiryat Shmona and the vicinity (164 hits), Metullah (100 strikes), and Nahariya (49 strikes).[62] On July 22, Blum reported that between July 15 and 21, there had been 58 Katyusha barrages, consisting of 840 Katyusha rockets and artillery shells, which killed five people and injured 47 civilians.[63] On the same day, he sent a second letter to report of "the vast disruption of normal life and harassment of the civilian population as a result of continued indiscriminate shelling of civilian targets in the north of Israel by PLO terrorists operating in Lebanon." In the past two days alone, there had been 22 additional attacks with Katyusha rockets and artillery shells. On July 21, from 2:30 A.M. to midnight there were 12 different barrages, the last one continuous fire from 10 P.M. to midnight.[64] Neither the UN General Assembly nor the Security Council passed a resolution condemning the terrorism of the Palestinian organizations.

[61] Ibid.

[62] Yehuda Z. Blum, "Letter Dated 19 July, 1981 from the Permanent Representative of Israel to the United Nations Addressed to the President of the Security Council," New York, UNSC (July 20, 1981), UN ODS S/14600.

[63] Yehuda Z. Blum, "Letter Dated 22 July, 1981 from the Permanent Representative of Israel to the United Nations Addressed to the President of the Security Council," New York, UNSC (July 22, 1981), UN ODS S/14605.

[64] Yehuda Z. Blum, "Letter Dated 22 July, 1981 from the Permanent Representative of Israel to the United Nations Addressed to the President of the Security Council," New York, UNSC (July 22, 1981), UN ODS, S/14606.

On January 14, 1982, a bomb exploded in the office of El Al Israel Airlines in Istanbul, Turkey. Though no one was injured, property damage was extensive. Two days after the explosion, the PLO issued a statement to the Kuwaiti press that, in Blum's words, "boasted of its responsibility for this outrage." Blum further reported that on January 11, "two explosive devices placed under a vegetable stand in the crowded market place of the town of Petah-Tikva blew up in rapid succession.... Large quantities of nails contained in them were scattered as lethal projectiles in every direction." Though no shoppers were injured, a policeman was wounded. "As is its wont, the PLO immediately broadcast its responsibility for this criminal act on its radio station in Lebanon."[65] On January 19, Blum informed UN secretary general Perez de Cuellar that "in keeping with its vicious anti-Semitic outlook and with the long series of anti-Semitic outrages perpetrated by it, the PLO, on Friday evening, 15 January 1982, bombed a Jewish-owned restaurant frequented by Jewish patrons in West Berlin. The ensuing explosion killed a fourteen-month-old infant girl and wounded 24 other people."[66] The next day "Reuters reported from Beirut that one of the constituent groups operating under the PLO umbrellas boasted of its responsibility for the attack." Blum added that "these ugly incidents" demonstrated the PLO's "true character" as a terrorist organization. "Under the guise of 'national liberation' and of conducting an 'armed struggle against the Zionist entity,' the PLO not only aims at the destruction of a Member State of the United Nations but is also embarked on a ruthless campaign against Jews and Jewish institutions everywhere."[67]

On February 2, 1982, Blum informed Cuellar that on the night of January 28/29, five or six PLO terrorists infiltrated from Jordan into the Beit Shean valley, south of Tiberias. Israeli security forces captured them before they could attack Israeli villages.[68] On March 15, Blum wrote to Cuellar about "yet another attempt by the terrorist PLO to perpetrate an

[65] Ibid., 1. Also see Yehuda Z. Blum to Javier Perez de Cuellar, "Letter Dated 14 January 1982 from the Permanent Representative of Israel to the United Nations Addressed to the Secretary General," New York, UNSC (January 15, 1982), United Nations General Assembly/Security Council, UN ODS, A/37/65-S/14836.

[66] Yehuda Z. Blum to Javier Perez de Cuellar, "Letter Dated 19 January 1982 from the Permanent Representative of Israel to the United Nations Addressed to the Secretary General," New York, UNGA/SC (January 20, 1982), UN ODS, A/37/71-S14842.

[67] Ibid.

[68] Yehuda Z. Blum to Javier Perez de Cuellar, "Letter Dated 2 February 1982 from the Permanent Representative of Israel to the United Nations Addressed to the Secretary General," New York, UNGA/SC (February 3, 1982), UN ODS, A/37/79-S/14856.

atrocity against Israeli children."[69] "On 11 March 1982, at 11:30 hours (local time), a time bomb exploded outside a crowded nursery school in the Jesse Cohen neighbourhood in the city of Holon. The device contained nails, which scattered as lethal projectiles in every direction. Mercifully, no one was injured in the blast since the children were inside the building at the time of the explosion."[70] Blum referred to previous letters to the secretary general that described terrorist attacks on "Israeli children and Jewish children outside of Israel" since 1970 in Kibbutz Misgav, Bat Yam, Kiryat Shmona, Ma'alot, and Antwerp, Belgium. He wrote that these "these acts of PLO terror serve as further reminders, if such are still needed, of the true nature and objectives of that murder organization, which is a group of international criminals bent on the murder of civilians in general and of children in particular."[71]

On March 31, 1982, Aryeh Levin, the chargé d'affaires in the Israeli UN delegation in New York, wrote to Cuellar about "the intensified PLO campaign of political intimidation, assassination and attempts at assassination against Palestinian Arabs in Judaea, Samaria and the Gaza District who have indicated their desire to live in peace with Israel."[72] On that day, "Mr. Kamal Al-Fatafta, a prominent member of a village association in the Hebron area, was seriously wounded in an explosion when he opened the door of his car, which had been booby-trapped by PLO terrorists." On March 12, 1982, "a barrage of bullets struck the home of Mr. Fahr Issah Ismail, another prominent member of a village association in the Ramallah area." Such acts were "the latest in a long series of assassinations and attempted assassinations carried out by the PLO against leading Palestinian Arab personalities" in an effort "to intimidate those individuals who oppose terrorism and desire to co-operate and co-exist in peace with Israel."[73] In a letter of March 31, Levin reported on machine-gun fire at the Israeli Trade Mission at the Israeli Embassy in Paris. The day before, a hand grenade was thrown by PLO terrorists at

[69] Yehuda Z. Blum to Javier Perez de Cuellar, "Letter Dated 16 March 1982 from the Permanent Representative of Israel to the United Nations Addressed to the Secretary General," New York, UNGA/SC (March 16, 1982), UN ODS, A/37/116-S/14906.

[70] Ibid.

[71] See UN ODS S/14906; S/13767; S/13264; S/11290; S/9810, and S14081.

[72] Aryeh Levin, to the President of the Security Council, "Letter Dated 31 March 1982 from the Chargé D'Affaires A.I. of the Permanent Mission to the United Nations Addressed to the President of the Security Council," New York, UNGA/SC (April 2 1982), UN ODS, S/14938.

[73] Ibid.

a crowded intersection of Ben Jehuda and King George Streets in downtown Jerusalem. On March 28, two "high-powered explosions" were set off outside Jewish-owned stores in downtown Rome, Italy. On March 24 "a band of PLO terrorists" was captured in the Western Galilee equipped with "Soviet-made Kalachnikov [*sic*] rifles, ammunition and explosives." Levin quoted Arafat's calling for a restructuring of "the map of the region" and referred to Kaddoumi's appeal to the Arab states to abandon the political path in favor of "armed struggle."[74] On April 3, 1982, Levin reported that a 20-year-old woman shot and killed Yacov Bar-Somantov, an Israeli diplomat, in Paris as he was leaving his house in the company of his 10-year-old daughter and 17-year-old son.[75] An organization calling itself the "Lebanese Armed Revolutionary Faction" claimed responsibility, though Levin said the responsibility lay "with the PLO perpetrators who have the cowardly habit of hiding behind assumed names." The Israeli government, Levin continued, would "hold the instigators, the perpetrators and the abettors of these crimes responsible and answerable for their deeds."[76]

In letters to the president of the Security Council on April 12 and 13, 1982, Yehuda Blum offered details of more PLO attacks.[77] On May 10 he informed the president of the Security Council that "a bomb exploded in a crowded passenger bus in Jerusalem, injuring two small children and a woman" and that another bomb went off "on the premises of a vocational high school in Ashkelon."[78] On May 7 "several mines" were planted on the main road in the Har Dov region "by PLO terrorist[s] infiltrating from South Lebanon" and on May 4 "an explosive device was planted at the crowded central bus station in Hadera." On April 7 a grenade had been thrown "into the Greek Orthodox Church of Jacob's Well in Nablus, during a peak visiting hour. One nun was seriously wounded and a local resident sustained injuries."

[74] Ibid., 1–2.

[75] Aryeh Levin, to the President of the Security Council, "Letter Dated 3 April 1982 from the Chargé D'Affaires A.I. of the Permanent Mission to the United Nations Addressed to the President of the Security Council," New York, UNGA/SC (April 3 1982), UN ODS, S/14951, 1–2.

[76] Ibid.

[77] Yehuda Z. Blum, to the President of the Security Council, "Letter Dated 12 April 1982 and 13 April 1982), UNSCOR UN ODS /14965 and S/14972.

[78] Yehuda Z. Blum, to the President of the Security Council, "Letter Dated 10 May 1982 from the Permanent Representative of Israel to the United Nations Addressed to the President of the Security Council," UNSCOR UN ODS, S/15066.

Blum concluded that these were "only a small sample of those in the long list of atrocities perpetrated by the PLO" since the governments of Israel and Lebanon had signed a cease-fire agreement in July 1981 ending hostilities. Since then, PLO terror attacks in Israel had caused 17 deaths and 240 injuries in the course of 138 separate attacks, "all of them originating from PLO terrorist bases inside Lebanon." Blum, again, warned the members of the UN Security Council that "the Government of Israel considers itself duty-bound to take all necessary measures to protect the lives and safety of its citizens."[79] On May 24, Blum again wrote to the president of the Security Council to report that on May 9, 13, 14, and 17 three more bombs were set off within Israel and one more was detected before it exploded.[80]

Blum's letter of June 4 to the president of the Security Council drew "most urgent attention to the heinous terrorist outrage perpetrated in London" the previous night against Shlomo Argov, Israel's ambassador to Great Britain. Argov had been shot in the head by an "Arab terrorist" and was in critical condition after undergoing brain surgery. (Argov was paralyzed and in permanent hospital care for the next 21 years and died in 2003.) The assailant and three accomplices had been arrested. Such attacks were not only, as Cuellar had put it, a threat to diplomacy and international relations. Blum wrote that they posed "a grave threat to the very fabric of civilization."[81] It was, Blum wrote, "regrettable" that the UN had "granted rights and privileges – in violation of the Charter – to the PLO," which constituted "one of the foremost exponents and linchpins of international terrorism." Now, "the Government of Israel for its part will take the measures necessary to protect the lives and ensure the safety of its citizens."[82] In other words, because the UN was unable or unwilling to stop a campaign of terror against one of its member states, Israel, as would any other sovereign state, was going to exercise its right to defend itself by using force to put an end to the Palestinian terrorist attacks from bases in Lebanon.

79 Ibid., 1–2.

80 Yehuda Z. Blum, to the President of the Security Council, "Letter Dated 24 May 1982 from the Permanent Representative of Israel to the United Nations Addressed to the President of the Security Council," New York UNSCOR (May 24, 1982), UN ODS, S/15107.

81 Yehuda Z. Blum, to the President of the Security Council, "Letter Dated 4 June 1982 from the Permanent Representative of Israel to the United Nations Addressed to the President of the Security Council," New York UNSCOR (June 4, 1982), UN ODS, S/15158.

82 Ibid., 1–2.

ARAFAT IN EAST BERLIN IN SPRING 1982

During these months of the intensifying PLO terrorist attacks on Israel, Arafat remained a welcome and honored guest in East Berlin. On March 9 and 10, 1982, *Neues Deutschland*'s lead story announced his arrival as head of a PLO delegation "at the invitation" of Erich Honecker. On page 1 in boldface type, Arafat's titles were given as both the chairman of the PLO Executive Committee and "Commander in Chief of the Armed Forces of the Palestinian Revolution." A by-then familiar photo of the bearded Arafat with a keffiyeh appeared on the front page followed by a short summary of his political biography.[83] On March 10, for the first time since the beginning of the East German–PLO alliance, *Neues Deutschland*'s entire front page, including three articles and four photos, was devoted to Arafat's visit. Moreover the whole of page 3 was devoted to the Arafat visit as well. It featured four additional photos of Arafat. Arafat and Honecker were shown greeting one another with smiles at the airport, sitting beside one another in office chairs, taking part in a motorcade accompanied by motorcycles in downtown Berlin, and sitting across from one another with their accompanying high ranking delegations in the offices of the SED Central Committee building. The coverage conveyed the message that Arafat was a highly respected and important political actor on the international stage. The headlines amplified that theme. The PLO delegation was "Greeted with Brotherhood" (*brüderlich begrüßt*). "Official Conversations in Berlin" took place between Honecker and Arafat. There was a "Friendly Meeting with the Guest in the House of the Central Committee." A third front-page headline read: "Bound in Firm Solidarity: Erich Honecker and Yasser Arafat Praise the Continued Deepening and General Strengthening of Cooperation."[84]

The importance that the East Germans attached to Arafat's visit was apparent in the guest list at the evening dinner. In addition to Honecker, key members of the Politburo were in attendance, including Willi

[83] "Yasser Arafat trifft heute in der DDR ein: Offizielle Freunschaftsbesuch in unserer Republik auf Einladung Erich Honeckers," *Neues Deutschland* (March 9, 1982), 1.

[84] "Delegation der Palästineensischen Befreiungsorganisation in DDR brüderlich begrußt: Offizielle Gespräche in Berlin zwischen Erich Honecker und Yasser Arafat aufgenommen," *ND* (March 10, 1982), 1; as well as "Freundschaftlich Begegnung mit dem Gast im Hause des Zentralkomitees: Erste Meinungsaustausch zwischen beiden Staatsmännern über die traditionsreich Beziehungen DDR-PLO und über Grundfragen der gegenwärtigen internationalen Lage," and "In fester Solidarität verbunden: Erich Honecker und Yasser Arafat würdigten kontinuierliche Vertiefung und allseitige Festigung der Zusammenarbeit," *ND* (March 10, 1982).

Stoph, the chairman of the Council of Ministers; Horst Sindermann, president of the Volkskammer; Herman Axen; Defense Minister Heinz Hoffmann; Minister of the Ministry of State Security Erich Mielke; and Foreign Minister Oskar Fischer. The names of the PLO delegation also appeared on page 1 of *Neues Deutschland*. They included PLO Executive Committee members Farouk al-Kaddoumi, director of the PLO Political Department; Abdel Mohsen; Abou Maizar, the PLO spokesman; Abou Maher Al –Yamani; Yasser Abo Rabboh, director of the PLO Information and Culture Office; Ahmed Abdul Rahman, editor-in-chief of *Palastin al-Thawra*; and Dr. Isam Kamel Salem, director of the PLO office in East Berlin.[85]

The editors of *Neues Deutschland* published the full texts of Honecker's and Arafat's formal toasts.[86] Honecker referred to Arafat as "our friend and comrade in struggle." He was the "outstanding leader of Palestinian resistance" and of the PLO, the "legitimate representative of Palestinian people." Honecker looked back on "years of common struggle in which our relations became deeper and more extensive." Arafat, he continued, stood for peace, but "with help of its spearhead Israel, the aggressive circles of imperialism" sought to "strengthen their military-strategic presence" in the Middle East. Israel, however, had refused to learn from history.[87] On page 1, the editors of *Neues Deutschland* excerpted Honecker's comments on the requirements for peace and security in the Middle East. They included "Israel's complete withdrawal from all occupied territories and the realization of the inalienable rights of the Arab people of Palestine, including the right of return to the homeland and the formation of an independent state" to be brought about by an international conference with participation of the PLO as "the legitimate representative of the Palestinian people."[88] The prominent inclusion of the right of return again indicated the East German support for the PLO's radicalism. Honecker toasted his "Dear friend and comrade! We raise our glass and drink to your good health! To the Chairman of the Executive Committee of the Palestinian Liberation

85 "Delegation der Palästineensischen Befreiungsorganisation in DDR brüderlich begrußt: Offizielle Gespräche in Berlin zwischen Erich Honecker und Yasser Arafat aufgenommen," *ND* (March 10, 1982), 1.

86 "DDR unterstützt den Kampf des Volkes von Palästina: Toast von Erich Honecker," *ND* (March 10, 1982), 3.

87 Ibid.

88 "Delegation der Palästineensischen Befreiungsorganisation in DDR brüderlich begrußt: Offizielle Gespräche in Berlin zwischen Erich Honecker und Yasser Arafat aufgenommen," *ND* (March 10, 1982), 1; and "DDR unterstützt den Kampf desVolkes von Palästina: Toast von Erich Honecker," *ND* (March 10, 1982).

Organization and the Commander in Chief of the Armed Forces of the Palestinian Revolution, our friend and comrade in struggle (*Kampfgenosse)*. To the further deepening of the all-around, friendly cooperation between the German Democratic Republic and the Palestinian Liberation Organization in the spirit of anti-imperialist solidarity."[89]

Arafat expressed thanks for the GDR's "stance of unconditional solidarity" with the Palestinians and with people all over the world "fighting for freedom and independence."[90] He extolled the "continuity of our close relationship of many years standing."[91] Arafat denounced Israel's "barbaric attacks on Lebanese and Palestinian civilians," its "terror in occupied territories." The Palestinians, he continued, "felt a deep obligation and commitment (*Verpflichtung)* and trust in the warm relationships born of struggle (*herzliche Kampfbeziehungen)* which bind them to the leadership of the German Democratic Republic."[92] Arafat concluded to his "dear friend," that is, Honecker, and "dear friends," the East German leadership in the room, "Let us raise a glass to the unbreakable friendship between the Palestinian people and the people of the German Democratic Republic, to the friendship of struggle and the friendship of fighters for the good of humanity." He too drank to Honecker's health and expressed confidence that "our revolution will be victorious!"[93] It was an evening to look back on relationships that had developed in the course of many meetings, a good deal of economic assistance, diplomatic support, educational and cultural exchanges, medical assistance, and, as we now know in considerable detail, extensive military training and weapons deliveries in the service of the common struggle by the East Germans and the Palestinians against the Jewish state.

The following day *Neues Deutschland* published a 2,500-word communiqué by Honecker and Arafat.[94] They announced that the status of the PLO in East Berlin would be raised to that of an embassy. They

89 "DDR unterstützt den Kampf des Volkes von Palästina: Toast von Erich Honecker," *ND* (March 10, 1982), 3.

90 "Delegation der Palästineensischen Befreiungsorganisation in DDR brüderlich begrußt: Offizielle Gespräche in Berlin zwischen Erich Honecker und Yasser Arafat aufgenommen," *ND* (March 10, 1982), 1

91 Yasser Arafat, "Sieg unserere gemeinsamen Sache ist unausbleiblich: Toast von Yasser Arafat," ND, March 10, 1982, 3.

92 Yasser Arafat, "Sieg unserere gemeinsamen Sache ist unausbleiblich: Toast von Yasser Arafat," ND, March 10, 1982, 3.

93 Ibid.

94 "Erich Honecker und Yasser Arafat bekräftigten volle Übereinstimmung: DDR und PLO wirken konstruktiv für die Gesundung der Weltlage," *ND* (March 11, 1982),1.

called not only for Israel's "unconditional withdrawal from all occupied Palestinian and Arab territories including Jerusalem," but the formation of a Palestinian state. Honecker again agreed publicly to define "realization of the inalienable rights of the Arab peoples of Palestine" to include "their right to return to the homeland"[95] As Yehuda Blum and his colleagues in the Israeli delegation at the UN had carefully documented, East Germany's decision to elevate the PLO's diplomatic status to embassy level occurred when the PLO was engaged in an intense terrorist campaign against Israel and was also accumulating a more formidable arsenal of larger Soviet-bloc weapons in Lebanon. In March 1982, far from seeking to moderate Arafat and his comrades, Honecker and the East German leadership encouraged them in adopting positions, such as the right of return, that could only be accomplished by destroying the state of Israel by force of arms. A rhetorical fog about peace, justice, political solutions and a Geneva conference only served to obscure the reality of the East German government's emphatic support for the PLO's radicalism and for its ongoing campaign of terrorism against Israel.

[95] "Gemeinsames Communique," *ND* (March 11, 1982), 1 and 3.

13

The Israel-PLO War in Lebanon of 1982

With the "Operation Peace for Galilee," Israel forces crossed into Lebanon on June 6, 1982, to destroy the PLO's military infrastructure and put an end to the terrorist campaign it was waging against northern Israel.[1] East Germany and the West German radical Left claimed that Israel's attack on the PLO was comparable to the Nazi invasion of the Soviet Union in 1941 and that Israel was adopting a policy of genocide and mass murder against Palestinians and Lebanese civilians. The East German regime made these accusations on the front pages of *Neues Deutschland* and at the United Nations. West German leftists repeated the charges in leaflets and at demonstrations. The accusations became standard fare in the entire Soviet bloc and the global Left. They struck a nerve, but they were not true. The television images of a modern army attacking a guerrilla force embedded near or in civilian areas also sent grim images of unintended civilian casualties. Yet the attribution of genocidal policy to the Jewish state conformed to an anti-Zionist ideology that by then had conquered the United Nations and found support in part of the media in the West as well. The murder of innocents was a theme that resonated with older accusations made against the Jews. Yet those accusations were also fueled by rage that was accompanying the collapse of hopes of the PLO

[1] Israel's retaliation against PLO bases was only one episode of a longer war that saw Lebanon's fabric torn to shreds. See, for example, Benny Morris's extended discussion in *Righteous Victims: A History of the Zionist-Arab Conflict, 1881–2001* (New York: Vintage, 2001), 494–560; Fouad Ajami, *The Dream Palace of the Arabs: A Generation's Odyssey* (New York: Vintage, 1999). On the PLO in Lebanon, see Yezik Sayigh, *Armed Struggle and the Search for a State: The Palestinian National Movement, 1949–1993* (Oxford: Clarendon Press, 1997), 319–543.

and its Soviet-bloc patrons of achieving victory in the Middle East by the PLO's terrorist war.[2]

In the pages of *Neues Deutschland*, then edited by the veteran journalist Gunter Schabowski, the East German regime immediately threw its support to the PLO.[3] On June 9, *ND* placed Arafat's "urgent call for help" against "Israeli aggression" on page 1.[4] On the same day, in a statement sent to Secretary General Javier Perez de Cuellar, the SED Central Committee said Israel's "renewed aggression" was "all the more detestable" as it took place when the Soviet Union, East Germany, and "other socialist states" were "insisting on having the Middle East problem solved by negotiation."[5] In view of Honecker's support for the right of return just three months earlier, it was a dubious claim. On June 10, *ND*'s page 1 headline declared that with the "open agreement" of the United States, "Tel Aviv wants to exterminate the Palestinians."[6] It quoted Arafat saying that Israel's "aggression" was "not only a military operation against our armed forces. Rather it is a *(Vernichtungsfeldzug)* a war of annihilation against the Palestinian people in their camps and against the Lebanese people in their cities and villages." Israel was "making no distinctions between civil and military targets, the destruction of homes and the expulsion of their inhabitants, the murder of children, women and the aged" as it continued its "campaign of terror" (*Terrorfeldzug).*[7] On June 15, 1982 *ND*'s lead story claimed that there had been "26,000 victims of Tel Aviv's brutal aggression against Lebanon," including 10,000 dead; 16,000 wounded, mostly civilians; as well as 600,000 refugees.[8]

[2] On this also see Paul Thomas Chamberlin, *The Global Offensive: The United States, the Palestine Liberation Organization and the Making of the Post–Cold War Order* (New York: Oxford University Press, 2012).

[3] "Schabowski, Günter," in Bernd-Rainer Barth et al., eds., *Wer war Wer in der DDR: Ein biographisches Handbuch* (Frankfurt/Main: Fischer, 1996), 626.

[4] "Widerstand gegen Aggression Israels braucht Unterstützung aller Staaten," *Neues Deutschland* (June 9, 1982), 1.

[5] "Annex: Statement of the Central Committee of the Socialist Unity Party of Germany, the Council of State and the Council of Ministers of the German Democratic Republic concerning the Aggression of Israel against Lebanon," UNSC (June 9, 1982) UN ODS, S/15186.

[6] "Aggressoren beschießen jetzt die Vororte Beirut" and "Yasser Arafat richtete Botschaft an die arabischen Staatsoberhäupt: Tel Aviv will das Volk der Palästinenser vernichten," *ND* (June 10, 1982), 1. Though Israel's capital was in Jerusalem, the East Germans, and presumably the Soviet-bloc states as well, always referred to "Tel Aviv" as if it were the city of political decision making.

[7] "Yasser Arafat: Kampf gegen den Aggressor" and "Israel setzt Terrorfeldzug brutal fort," *ND* (June 16, 1982), 1.

[8] "Über 26,000 Opfer der brutalen Aggression Tel Avis gegen Libanon," ND (June 15), 1.

A front-page article appealed for financial donations to be sent to a special bank account for "help for victims of Israeli aggression."[9]

On June 15, *ND* again reported the figure of "over 26,000 victims of Tel Aviv's brutal aggression in Lebanon."[10] In an opinion piece on June 15, the *ND* editorial board member "W. M." wrote that the Israeli aggressor was following "his open, declared goal, that is, the destruction of the Palestinian people. The 'final solution' sought by the Zionist power holders in Tel Aviv is the physical extermination of the Palestinians. Their cynical calculation is that the dead cannot any longer fight for the right of return to their homeland and for the establishment of their own independent, sovereign, national state."[11] On June 18, *ND* claimed that after ten days of war, there were "more than 30,000 dead and injured, over 10,000 people were missing" and "more than 800,000" were homeless.[12]

The headlines of *Neues Deutschland* applied the infamous terms associated with Nazi Germany's race war on the Eastern Front in World War II and the Holocaust to describe Israel's invasion. On June 28, a front page headline referred to a "war of extermination (*Austrottungskrieg)* with poison gas and phosphorus." The East German news service (ADN) in Beirut claimed that "in the barbaric extermination actions (*Vernichtungsaktion)* by Israeli troops in Lebanon, [they] have used poison gas and phosphorus bombs." The article cited reports by the International Red Cross that the war that was then two weeks old had caused 14,000 deaths and 26,000 wounded.[13] On June 29, in a note to the UN's Peres de Cuellar, East German Foreign Minister Oskar Fischer referred to "crimes committed by the aggressor's forces" in its "war of extermination."[14] On June 30, in a page 1

9 "Sonderkonto 555," *ND* (June 15, 1982), 1.

10 Über 26,000 Opfer der brutalen Aggression Tel Avivs gegen Libanon," *ND* (June 15, 1982), 1.

11 "Mehr den je: Feste Solidarität mit Palästinas Volk! Israel eskaliert seinen Ausrottungskrieg," [More than Ever: Firm Solidarity with the Palestinian People: Israel Escalates Its War of Extermination] *ND* (June 15, 1982), 2. The German read: "Denn der Aggressor der mordend und singend in den Libanon eingefallen ist and sie nun in einem Ghetto eingekesselt hat, verfolgt das offen erklärte Ziel, das palästinensische Volk zu vernichten. Die von den zionistischen Machthabern in Tel Aviv angestrebte 'Endlösung' der Palästinafrage ist die physische Ausrottung der Palästinenser. Ihr zynisches Kalkül ist: Tote können nicht mehr für das Recht auf Rückkehr in ihre Heimat, auf Gründung eine unabhängigen, sourveränen, eigenen nationalen Staates kämpfen."

12 "Mehr als 30,000 Tote und Verletzte, mehr als 10,000 Menschen vermißt, über 800,000 sind obdachlos: Arafat informiert UNO-Generalsekretär über Verbrechen der israelischen Invasoren," *ND* (June 18, 1982), 1.

13 "Ausrottungskrieg mit Giftgas und Phospher," *ND*, (June 28, 1982), 1.

14 Oskar Fischer, "Annex: Telegram from the Minister of Foreign Affairs of the German Democratic Republic to the Secretary General," UNSC (June 29, 1982), UN ODS S/15262; and Oskar Fischer to Javier Perez de Cuellar, "Staatstelegram," Bundesarchiv

interview in *ND*, Arafat said that the Palestinians would "never forget" the support they received from the GDR.[15]

On June 15, Israeli prime minister Menachem Begin reported that the Israeli armed forces had captured an "unbelievable" PLO arsenal including "hundreds of tons of explosives.... The terrorists had more than 100 tanks. We destroyed them. We destroyed 250, close to 300 Syrian tanks, but the terrorists had heavy cannons, for example the 130 mm cannon, range 27 km [kilometers]; they have heavy Katyushas with a range of 35 kms, not only the regular ones with a range of 21.6 km [and] unlimited ammunition."[16] The IDF found certificates of officer training in the Soviet Union and an order for PLO units to target "a public place, Kiryat Shemona, [*sic*] She'ar Yashu, Dan, Kfar Yuval, Hagoshrim, Maayan Baruch, Kfar Gildai. All of them settlements with a civilian population." The only way to give "peace to Galilee" was to push the PLO's weapons out of range of the towns and villages of northern Israel. As of June 20 there were no longer Katyushas landing there. He also reported that the Syrian air force met with disaster when it tried to intervene. The Israeli air force shot down 85 Syrian MiGs and destroyed Syria's previously formidable 19 ground-to-air Soviet SAM anti-aircraft weapons and 300 Syrian tanks, including nine Soviet modern T-72 tanks, which NATO thought could not be hit from the front.[17]

On June 29, 1982, Begin and Defense Minister Ariel Sharon addressed the Knesset. Begin responded to criticism of Israel not only from the Soviet bloc but also from Western Europe and the United States.[18] "Over the past three weeks, the world was flooded with the abomination of falsehood. Germans – destroyers and the children of destroyers – are saying that the renewed Jewish army is perpetrating Nazi acts. And nations talk of genocide and slaughter – and by these nations I mean not only the east, but the West also." Begin rejected lectures about morality. The army

Berlin (BAB) DY30 / 13797, Abteilung International Verbindungen, 1946–1990, Palästinensischen Befreiungsorganisation, 1982–1988," 13–14.

[15] "Yasser Arafat: Ich stehe im Kontakt zu den arabischen Staatsoberhäupten," ND (June 30, 1982), 1.

[16] "21. Interview with Prime Minister Begin on Israel Television 15 June 1982," Israel Ministry of Foreign Affairs, Historical Documents. Volume 8. 1982–1984, mfa.gov.il/MFA/ForeignPolicy/MFADocuments/Yearbook6/Pages/21%20Interview%20with%20Prime%20Minister%20Begin%20on%20Israel%20t.aspx.

[17] Ibid.

[18] "36. Address in the Knesset by Prime Minister Begin, 29 June 1982," Israel Ministry of Foreign Affairs, Historical Documents. Volume 8. 1982–1984, 1. mfa.gov.il/MFA/ForeignPolicy/MFADocuments/Yearbook6/Pages/36%20Address%20in%20the%20Knesset%20by%20Prime%20Minister%20Begin-.aspx.

and air force had made intense efforts to prevent civilian casualties at the express orders of the political leadership. Israel was both in a military battle and in a "battle over the truth." Yet in his experience he did "not remember a period when the whole world was overwhelmed with such a lie as it has been in these days, regarding one of the most noble campaigns ever waged in the history of humanity – to ensure peace for citizens, for human beings."[19]

Mario Suarez, the prime minister of Portugal, showed Begin Willy Brandt's declaration in the name of the Socialist International that condemned Israel's invasion. Begin replied to Suarez as follows:

For what are you condemning us? What injustice have we done? What invasion? You invade another country to occupy territory, to subjugate it. We entered Lebanon because from there came those who murdered the bus passengers on the coastal highway – 38 men, women and children, from there came those who took out a father and his little six-year-old daughter, cracked her brain and killed the father; from there came those who made 22 14-year old male and female pupils lie on the floor and opened fire on them from machine guns; from there came the most vicious shelling on 23 settlements in the Galilee – Kiryat Shmona, Nahariyah, Dan Dafna, Metullah, Kfar Giladi, Avivim, Misgav Am and more. They came from there. We went in there to disarm them, to push them away, to remove our settlements from the range of their satanic fire. Why do you condemn us?[20]

Israel was in a "battle over the truth." It "never wanted to harm civilians" and had "never wanted this whole war," but faced with the terrorist campaign of recent years, Israel was not going "to wait for assistance from any state." Further, "we will not let the lie dominate, not in Europe, not in America, neither in the east nor in the west."[21] He attacked the double standards that he felt were being applied to Israel. British prime minister Margaret Thatcher had appealed to Article 51 of the UN Charter when she sent British forces 8,000 miles to fight in the Falkland Islands, "and we go out a few kilometers from our border and we have no right to base ourselves on Article 51 of the United Nations Charter, the inherent right of self-defense?" Soviet Foreign Minister Andrei Gromyko said that the Middle East was near the southern border of the Soviet Union and thus had a right to see that there be peace there. Yet, Begin said, "if the State of Israel is attacked from a distance of 10 kilometers, it is forbidden for a small nation under attack to try and fight and disarm the armed

[19] Ibid., 3.
[20] Ibid.
[21] Ibid., 3–4.

bands" that according to Soviet definitions had been engaged in aggression against Israel for the preceding eight years.[22]

Begin presented the Knesset with preliminary details about the PLO arsenal that the IDF found in Lebanon. An arms depot near Sidon contained so many weapons that 500 trucks traveling for six weeks would be needed to remove them. It included "thousands of R.P.G. shells, thousands of Katyushas, the arms for thousands of soldiers, perhaps hundreds of thousands." The prisoners captured by the Israelis demonstrated the PLO's international connections: "416 from Syria, 30 from Iraq, 55 from Jordan, 62 from Egypt, 4 from Morocco, 5 from Tunis, 5 from Algeria, 3 from Libya, 26 from Turkey, 58 from Pakistan, 9 from Somalia, 380 from Bangladesh, 72 from Yemen, 3 from Niger, 23 from Ceylon Sri Lanka, 1 from Brazil, 1 from Canada, 1 from Nigeria, 45 from India, 8 from Iran, 2 from Saudi Arabia, 1 from Abu Dhabi, 3 from Kuwait, 4 from Mali, 5 from Sudan, 3 from Mauritania."[23] Begin himself was astonished at the amount of arms that the IDF had captured.

On June 28, the *Jerusalem* Post reported that PLO bunkers in Lebanon were filled with "enough light arms and ancillary weapons to equip five infantry brigades." The Israelis showed journalists machine guns, assault rifles, tanks, Katyusha-firing trucks, guns and mortars of different caliber, and rocket launchers. The quantity of arms discovered by then was "ten times larger than the IDF had estimated." The weapons were "predominantly of Russian or East bloc manufacture" with others from North Korea, Vietnam, and China. The weapons were found primarily near mosques, churches, and schools, so that if the IDF bombed them, it could be accused of harming civilians.[24] Begin told the *Los Angeles Times* that the army had captured 4,000 tons of ammunition, 144 armored vehicles including tanks, 12,500 small arms, 515 heavy weapons, 369 sophisticated communications devices, and 708 optical instruments including field glasses and range finders, and night-vision scopes. The army, he said, had found "other arms depots containing fully 10 times as many weapons as we found before, enough to equip not five brigades, but five or six divisions." He was certain the Israelis would find much more.[25]

[22] Ibid., 4.

[23] Ibid., 5.

[24] Ya'acov Friedler, "Arms Booty in Lebanon Could Equip 5 Brigades," *Jerusalem Post* (June 28, 1982), 3.

[25] Frank Gervasi, "Menachem Begin on PLO and Peace," *Los Angeles Times* (July 18, 1982), A1 and A5.

In late June, the Israeli government took journalists to warehouses where "17,000 pieces of artillery, assault rifles and rocket launchers lined the walls."[26] In late July, the Israelis captured records and documents that confirmed PLO forces had been trained in the Soviet Union, East Germany, Hungary, Czechoslovakia, Bulgaria, Romania, China, Vietnam, Pakistan, India, Algeria, Libya, Yemen, South Yemen and Austria. The Israeli military then issued a detailed list of the captured PLO weapons. They included 25,000 submachine guns and other light arms, 19,000 hand grenades, 46,000 mortar rounds, 14,000 artillery shells, 16,000 anti-personnel and anti-vehicle mines, 883 anti-tank weapons, 148 mortars and artillery pieces, almost 80 tanks, about 170 armored personnel carriers, and 95 anti-aircraft guns. Most were produced in the Soviet Union. Of the 25,000 light arms, about 10,000 were top-of-the-line Soviet AK-47 assault rifles.[27] Elahu Ben-Elissar, then chair of the Defense and Foreign Affairs Committee of the Knesset, told the *Los Angeles Times* that while the PLO arsenal did not put it in position to defeat the Israeli army in conventional warfare, if it "opened up with all their artillery and all their tank guns on the Israeli north, they could have caused a few thousand dead."[28]

On July 9, Hirsh Goodman, the *Jerusalem Post*'s military correspondent, described the enormous size of the PLO arsenal as one of "the mysteries of this war."[29] The war had caught the PLO at a "crossroads" at which the PLO appeared to be moving toward a "more formal military framework" evident in the larger weapons it was receiving. Yet, Goodman wrote, it was an "absurdity" to describe the PLO as a serious threat to the Israeli Defense Forces. It did not have a "cohesive, disciplined, formal army." What the Israelis found in Lebanon

> were mainly the weapons of the terrorist. Thousands of Katyusha rockets intended to make life intolerable for Israel's northern settlers. Thousands of tons of TNT and other explosives, meant for supermarkets and buses and Israeli and Jewish objectives wherever they could be found. Hand guns, grenades and other infantry weapons needed in terror operations and clashes with the IDF patrols during infiltration attempts. And basic anti-tank and anti-aircraft equipment, providing a rudimentary defense against Israeli attack. These weapons were

[26] Also see "Israel Shows Vast Stockpile of PLO Arms," *Washington Post* (June 28, 1982), A16

[27] Norman Kempster, "Israel Finds PLO Arms Puzzling: Wonders If Arsenal Was Intended for Some Future War," *Los Angeles Times* (July 25, 1982), 1.

[28] Ibid.

[29] Hirsh Goodman, "A Farewell to Arms," *Jerusalem Post* (July 9, 1982), 14.

sophisticated – some of them the best the Soviets produced. But they were basically the tools of terror – not of an army.[30]

If the 130-mm cannon, mobile multi-rocket Katyusha systems, and SAM-7 shoulder-held anti-aircraft missiles had been combined with Syria's air and ground forces, the PLO could have posed a greater military threat beyond terrorist operations. The Israeli air force ended that threat when it destroyed Syria's anti-aircraft system at the outset of the war. Goodman viewed the PLO arsenal in Lebanon in 1982 as one suitable primarily for terrorist attacks on Israeli civilians.

In the Knesset, Ariel Sharon noted that the entire Israeli cabinet supported the decision on June 5, 1982, to "get all the settlements in the Galilee out of range of fire of the terrorists, who together with their bases and headquarters are concentrated in Lebanon."[31] He told the Knesset that between 1970 and 1981, the Israeli Defense Forces (IDF) "initiated no less than 9,794 operations of daily security along the Lebanese border and inside Lebanon, including patrols, observations and ambushes." In addition, the IDF carried out "605 different operations deep inside Lebanon" and "over 50 operations per year on land, air and sea and combined operations." Nevertheless, southern and central Lebanon "became an expanded arsenal and training site for Palestinian terror." The PLO headquarters in Beirut prepared "an artillery system of hundreds of Katyusha barrels, cannons and mortars against our settlements in the Galilee." When combined with "the support of the armored corps, the artillery and the anti-aircraft missile batteries of Syria," it amounted to a serious military threat. In summer 1982, Israel's "settlements and towns in the Galilee became the indiscriminate targets of the terrorists artillery fire. The orders came straight from Beirut," that is, from the PLO leadership there.[32] When it signed the cease-fire agreement with the PLO on July 24, 1981, the Israeli government stressed that it "would not tolerate acts of terror directed from Beirut against our settlements and citizens in the Galilee and throughout Israel or acts of terror directed against us anywhere else in the world." However, "the Palestinian terrorist organizations in Lebanon thought otherwise." Since the date of the cease-fire in July 1981, "290 acts of terror" had been carried out both in

[30] Ibid.

[31] "Ari'el Sharon Knesset Speech," *Jerusalem DomesticService-1982-06-29, FBIS Middle East*, Library of Congress, inforweb.newsbank.com; also *Daily Report: Middle East and Africa, FBIS-MEA-82–126 on 1982-06-30.*

[32] Ibid.

Israel and overseas, "which caused the death of 29 people and the injury of another 271 persons." Defensive measures had failed to stop Arab terror. The Israelis had urged other countries at the UN and elsewhere to bring political pressure to bear to stop the terrorist campaign. Those efforts had not borne fruit. Sharon rejected what he called the false accusations against Israel regarding civilian casualties. There was, he said, "a basic and substantial difference" that was being overlooked between the deliberate killing of civilians and deaths of civilians that were unintended consequences of war.[33]

On July 6, in remarks at the IDF Command and Staff College, Sharon said the military leadership concluded that "the PLO terror would bring down a general war sooner or later, within a year or two, in a place and time which would not be to our advantage, and in a situation which would cause us great casualties." The PLO arms build-up and plans for war had been drawn up in cooperation with Syria. "The Syrian armed forces were ordered to be ready for war on a certain date this year," as they did not believe that Israel had answers to its more than 700 new T-72 Soviet tanks or to the great number of missiles the Syrians were receiving from the Soviet Union. "The Syrians and the PLO hoped that they then could drag over Arab states into the war against us."[34]

POLITICAL WARFARE AT THE UN AND IN GERMANY OVER ISRAEL'S WAR IN LEBANON

With an overwhelming vote of 127 to 2, the UN General Assembly in New York condemned Israel's non-compliance with UN cease-fire resolutions of June 5 and 6. Only the United States joined Israel in opposition.[35] The list of the resolution's co-sponsors illustrated the broad coalition within which East Germany was active:

Afghanistan, Algeria, Angola, Bahrain, Bangladesh, Benin, Bulgaria, Chad, Congo, Cuba, Cyprus, Czechoslovakia, Democratic Yemen, Djibouti, Ethiopia, Gambia, **German Democratic Republic**, Ghana, Greece, Guinea-Bissau, Guyana,

[33] Ibid.

[34] "41. Remarks by Defense Minister Sharon at the I.D.F. Command and Staff College, 6 July 1982," Israel Ministry of Foreign Affairs, Historical Documents. Volume 8. 1982–1984, 1. mfa.gov.il/MFA/ForeignPolicy/MFADocuments/Yearbook6/Pages/41%20Remarks%20by%20Defense%20Minister%20Sharon%20at%20the%20IDF%20C.aspx.

[35] "General Assembly Action (June), Chapter IX, Middle East," *Yearbook of the United Nations 1982*, Vol. 37 (New York: United Nations, Department of Public Information, 1986), 440–444.

Hungary, India, Indonesia, Iran, Iraq, Jordan, Kenya, Kuwait, Lao People's Democratic Republic, Libyan Arab Jamahiriya, Madagascar, Malaysia, Maldives, Mali, Malta, Mauritania, Morocco, Mozambique, Nicaragua, Niger, Nigeria, Oman, Pakistan, Qatar, Sao Tome and Principe, Saudi Arabia, Senegal, Seychelles, Somalia, Sri Lanka, Sudan, Syrian Arab Republic, Togo, Tunisia, Turkey, Ukrainian SSR, United Arab Emirates, United Republic of Cameroon, United Republic of Tanzania, Viet Nam, Yugoslavia, Zambia.[36]

The resolution called for an "immediate" end to all military activities in Lebanon, that is, before Israel was able to destroy the PLO's military bases. It said nothing about the PLO's terrorist campaign of the previous months and years and made no mention of Israel's right to self-defense. In 1982, Western European countries joined this huge majority.

Israel's UN ambassador Yehuda Blum said that the resolution undermined the goal of restoring sovereignty to Lebanon and ignored the fact that Lebanon had been "the launching pad for hundreds of attacks on Israeli civilians" and that operation "'Peace for Galilee' had been prompted solely by self-preservation and self-defense." Immense quantities of arms at the disposal of terrorists had been found. Reports of thousands of civilian casualties were wildly exaggerated, and the responsibility for them "must be borne by the PLO, which had placed its camps and depots in civilian areas."[37] None of these arguments convinced the majority of members of the UN. Rather, it was the PLO's assertions that the "aim of Israel's aggression was to eliminate the Palestinians and the PLO" that received majority support in the General Assembly.[38]

The UN *Yearbook* summary captured the mood in the General Assembly in June. Indonesia and Iraq charged Israel with trying to annihilate the Palestinian people. Bangladesh, Bulgaria, Hungary, Lebanon, Malaysia, the Syrian Arab Republic, Tunisia, Yemen and others spoke of holocaust, genocide and attempts to create a "final solution" to the Palestine question. Qatar said Israel was trying to exterminate an entire people using internationally prohibited weapons of mass destruction such as cluster and fragmentation bombs, napalm, and other weapons in the American arsenal and that its invasion was an atrocity.[39] East Germany called for cessation of hostilities, Israeli withdrawal, and restoration of

[36] "64 nation draft, Sponsors, General Assembly resolution ES-7/5 (June 26, 1982)," *Yearbook of the United Nations 1982*, Vol. 37 (New York: United Nations, Department of Public Information, 1986), 451.

[37] "General Assembly Action (June)," *Yearbook of the United Nations 1982*, Vol. 37 (New York: United Nations, Department of Public Information, 1986), 440–441.

[38] Ibid., 440.

[39] Ibid., 442.

Lebanon's territorial integrity. So did Belgium, representing the European Community, as well as Bulgaria, Canada, China, Cyprus, Czechoslovakia, Ecuador, Ethiopia, Finland, France, Indonesia, Japan, New Zealand, Norway, Pakistan, Poland, Romania, Tunisia, Turkey, the USSR, Vietnam, Yugoslavia and Zaire. Syria and others held the United States responsible. Tunisia stated that "everything was proceeding as though Israel's genocidal operation against the people of Palestine had United States support." Austria considered measures to impede the flow of military equipment to Israel. Cuba called for sanctions against Israel if it did not comply. The Soviet Union, supported by Bulgaria, Czechoslovakia and East Germany, called on the Security Council to take immediate unspecified measures to halt "the killing and destruction."[40] The UN majority was consistent with its past votes. Having celebrated the PLO, justified or ignored its terrorist campaign and denounced Israel as a racist and oppressive state, its members naturally opposed Israel's efforts to drive the PLO out of Lebanon and deprive it of its ability to attack Israeli citizens.

On July 6, *Neues Deutschland* published a report from Moscow's *Pravda* that asserted that Israel's army was committing "genocide" in Lebanon.[41] According to the Soviet Union's official government paper, "the Zionists solve the 'Palestinian Question' exactly as the Nazis solved the 'Jewish question,' the 'Zigeuner Problem,' 'the problem' of the Slovenes and other 'Non-Aryans' through total extermination and genocide." *Pravda* continued: "The 'Great-Israel' was built with the same methods as was the 'Great-Germany'," that is "by territorial conquest" at "the cost of the blood and bones (*Knochen und Blutes*) of other peoples."[42] In daily page 1 lead stories in July and August, *Neues Deutschland* hammered away at the Israeli "aggressors" and their "criminal" and "murderous" blockade of Beirut, their "barbaric aggression," "bestial bombardment" of civilian apartment areas, "murderous tactics of aggression troops" and "barbaric terror," and referred to their *Sonderkommando* who hunted down Palestinian and Lebanese "patriots." Israel was engaged in a

[40] Ibid., 442–443.

[41] "Prawda zum israelischen Völkermord in Libanon: Aggressor wird politisch und mit Waffen unterstützt," *ND* (July 6, 1982), 5.

[42] "Prawda zum israelischen Völkermord in Libanon," ND (July 7, 1982), 3. "Die Zionisten lösen die 'Palästina-Frage' genauso, wie die Nazis die 'Juden-Frage,' das 'Zigeuner-Problem' und die 'Probleme der Slowen' und anderer 'Nichtarier' gelöst haben – durch totale Vernichtung und Völkermord." Weiter betonte Prawda: 'Das 'Groß-Israel' wird met den gleichen Methoden errichtet, wie audh das 'Groß-Deutschland' des von den Völkern verfluchten 'Dritten Reiches,' und zwar durch Aggression und territorial Eroberung auf Kosten der Knochen und des Blutes andere Völker."

"campaign of murder" (*Mordfeldzug)* that intentionally inflicted terror on Beirut's civilian population and was carrying out a "war of extermination" or a "Zionist war of extermination" (*Ausrottungskrieg)* in Lebanon.[43] On July 21, *ND* ran a front page lead story about an interview Soviet premier Leonid Brezhnev had given to *Pravda* about the war in Lebanon. He stated that "the Israelis' actions can only be described as genocide" (*Völkermord)*, which in turn, was possible only because of the support it received from the United States.[44] On August 6, *ND* reported on its front page that Israel's prime minister Menachem Begin had "again affirmed the policy of the extermination of the Palestinians."[45]

On July 23 Arafat repeated his thanks to East Germans for their support in a conversation with East Germany's ambassador in Beirut, Bruno Sedlaczek.[46] On August 9, *ND* ran Honecker's reply to Arafat on its front page with a three-column heading. It conveyed the now-familiar expressions of support and solidarity, this time combined with praise for the "heroic resistance" of the PLO and condemnation for Israel's "intentional campaign of murder and extermination against the Palestinian people."[47] In an article written by the Palestinian news agency, WAFA, and published in *ND* on August 10, a PLO official offered some preliminary conclusions to be drawn about the war 65 days after it began.[48] "First: No large, expensive and extensive preparations were necessary in order to offer effective resistance to Israel." It referred to "65 days of resistance from a handful of badly armed, but determined Palestinians, Lebanese and Arabs."[49] In fact, as the arsenal that the Israelis captured in

[43] The Israeli government made it plain (1982), 1; "Tel Aviv terrorisiert die Zivilbevölkerung: Pausenlos Tiefflieger über Wohngebieten von Beirut," ND (July 14, 1982), 1; *"Dem Ausrottungskrieg muß ein Ende gesetzt werden!,"* *ND* (July 29), 1; "Dem zionistischen Ausrottungskrieg muß endlich Einhalt geboten werden," *ND* (August 3, 1982), 5; *ND* (August 6, 1982), *ND*, 5; "Gegen die israelische Politik des Völkermordes: Maßnahmen zur Zügelung der Aggressor sind dringlich," *ND* (August 6, 1982), 5; and "Aggressor muß Völkermord bedingungslos einstellen!" *ND* (August 9, 1982), 5.

[44] "Leonid Breshnew zur Situation in Lebanon," *ND* (July 21, 1982), 1.

[45] "Begin droht erneut mit Ausrottung der Palästinenser: Aggressionkurs Israels bekräftigt," *ND* (August 6, 1982), 1.

[46] "Yasser Arafat dankt für breite Solidarität des Volkes der DDR," *ND* (July 23, 1982), 1.

[47] "Botschaft von Erich Honecker an PLO-Vorsitzender Yasser Arafat," *ND* (August 9, 1982), 1.

[48] "Palästinensische Nachrichtenagentur WAFA: Der 65. Tag des palästinensisch-israelischen Krieges," *ND* (August 10, 1982), 2.

[49] Ibid. The German reads: "klingen hohl nach 65 Tagen des Widerstandes einer Handvoll schlecht bewaffneter, aber entschlossener Palästinenser, Libanesen und Araber."

Lebanon indicated, the PLO and its affiliates were very well armed and well trained.

A Stasi report of July 1982 entitled "Slander Campaign against the PLO and the Socialist Countries Supporting It" indicated that the East Germans were worried about the impact of Israel's capture of the PLO arsenal and revelations about the realities of the Soviet-bloc military alliance with the PLO.[50] American and Israeli intelligence agencies were cooperating "to collect information in the occupied territories in Lebanon about the PLO in general and its connections to the Soviet Union and the socialist states. The purpose was to use them in a campaign of slander against the PLO, the Soviet Union and the socialist brother countries due to a supposed 'terrorist conspiracy.'" A member of the American journalist Jack Anderson's staff had asked the East German Embassy in Washington to confirm the validity of names of leading officers of the East German military found in documents captured by Israel in southern Lebanon.[51] The officers named were Werner Fleißner, Helmut Boromache, and Helmut Borowka. The memo confirmed that the first official visit to East Germany by a PLO strictly military delegation led by Khalil al-Wazir (Abu Jihad) took place in November 1981 at the invitation of the Ministry of Defense. As we have seen, on that occasion, Wazir met with Honecker, Hoffmann, and deputy minister of defense Fleißner and signed agreements for weapons deliveries and military training.[52] Israel's capture of the PLO arsenal in Lebanon offered compelling evidence of the extent of Soviet-bloc military support for the PLO.

On August 16, *ND* published "In Hitler's Footsteps" by a "TASS commentator" with the peculiar sounding last name of "Boris Schabajew," an anti-Semitic pun on the phrase Shabbas Jew.[53] Israel's actions in Lebanon, he wrote, recalled "the evil deeds of the Hitler fascists in the years of the Second World War. They recall not only the deeds but also the inhuman (*menschenfeindliche)* ideology of this scum of humanity." Schabajew then claimed to be quoting Menachem Begin saying that the only solution to the Middle East conflict was "a Palestine without Arabs" and that there should not remain "a single village, a single tribe" of Arabs left in the territory of Israel. The quote was pure fiction. "Begin

50 "Verleumdungskampagne gegen die PLO und die sie unterstützenden sozialistischen Länder," BStU, Archiv der Zentralstelle, MfS-HA II, 32887, 20.

51 Ibid., 20–21.

52 Ibid., 21. "Borowka" probably referred to Generla Helmut Borufka.

53 Boris Schabajew, "In Hitlers Fußstapfen: TASS-Kommentar von Boris Schabajew." *ND* (August 16, 1982), 2.

and his clique seek to realize their program of a 'Greater Israel' with the same methods which their ideological relatives the German fascists used." This was how one should understand the "merciless destruction of West Beirut and the extermination (*Ausrottung*) of its inhabitation." Schabajew concluded that "it is clear to everyone who still is able to see things as they really are that Begin and the state he leads walk in Hitler's footsteps."[54]

At the UN, East Germany's Siegfried Zachmann sent a public letter that Honecker sent to Arafat to the UN secretary general to be distributed as an official document of both the Security Council and the General Assembly.[55] Honecker said that the GDR "was following with admiration the heroic struggle of the Palestine Liberation Organization and the Lebanese Patriots for their profoundly just cause." He expressed the GDR's "full solidarity." It condemned "in the strongest terms the murderous extermination war against the Palestinian and Lebanese people which Israel and the most aggressive circles of US imperialism had planned for a long time." East Germany, "as it has done so far," would provide political support at the UN, in other international organizations and bilateral relations, as well as "increased material solidarity." Zachmann assured Arafat that those, that is, the Israelis, "who have been causing that immense suffering to your people and the Lebanese will not be able to escape their responsibility before history."[56] On June 22, the East German representative to the Committee for the Exercise of the Inalienable Rights of the Palestinian People (CEIRPP) referred to "the Israeli commitment to exterminate the Palestinian people."[57]

Wildly inflated numbers of deaths and refugees, some exceeding the population of southern Lebanon, were repeated in the world press. Establishing reliable figures of military and civilian casualties during Operation Peace for Galilee was a difficult task. On July 14, 1982, David Shipler in the *New York Times* wrote that "the chaos of the warfare, the destruction of city neighborhoods and refugee camps, the haste with which bodies were buried in mass graves and the absence of impartial agencies

[54] Ibid., 2.

[55] Erich Honecker to Yasser Arafat, "Annex: Message Dated 6 August 1982" to Siegfried Zachmann, Charge d'Affaires of GDR Mission to the United Nations to the UN Secretary General (August 11, 1982), UNGA/SC, UN ODS A/37/383; S/15352.

[56] Ibid.

[57] Kutschan, Committee on the Exercise of the Inalienable Rights of the Palestinian People (CEIRPP), Summary Record of the81st Meeting, New York (June 22, 1982), UNGA, 25 June 1982. UN ODS A/AC.183/SR.81.

gathering statistics have made a reliable accounting impossible." For anyone who had traveled in southern Lebanon, it was clear "that the original figures of 10,000 dead and 600,000 homeless, reported by correspondents quoting Beirut representatives of the International Committee of the Red Cross during the first week of the war, were extreme exaggerations."[58] The Israeli Foreign Ministry offered a figure of 460 to 470 civilians killed and 1,600 wounded in the fighting. To prevent civilian casualties, the Israeli air force dropped leaflets and broadcast warnings to the civilian populations of Tyre and Sidon to leave before attacks took place. Soldiers were instructed when going into villages not to shoot unless fired upon first, measures that cost the Israeli military some lives.[59]

In early September, the Beirut newspaper *An Nahar*, described by the *Washington Post* as "the most respected in the Arab world," reported that 1,709 civilians and 5,862 troops of the PLO, the Syrian Army, and Lebanese private militias had been killed in southern Lebanon since the Israeli invasion began on June 6. The figure of those killed in Beirut was 5,515, but the paper did not offer a breakdown between military and civilian deaths.[60] Both Shipler's report and the assessment of *An Nahar* indicated that the initial claims of more than 26,000 or 30,000 victims and 10,000 civilian deaths repeated in *Neues Deutschland* were indeed wild exaggerations. It would take time to arrive at reliable statistics. These figures also demonstrated that claims of "mass murder," "murder campaign," "genocide," "war of annihilation," and "war of extermination" made by *Neues Deutschland* had no basis in fact.

The West German radical Left also accepted the factual assertions made by the PLO and repeated the accusation that Israel was engaging in mass murder and genocide in Lebanon. On July 17, 1982, the Lebanon Action Group of the German Peace Society in Kiel distributed a leaflet about "Genocide in Lebanon"[61] referring to "the deaths of 35,000 people" in Lebanon. Rather than "Peace for Galilee," the operation should be called "death for Palestinians." Israel was waging a "war of extermination"

58 David Shipler, "Toll of Lebanon Dead and Injured Is Still Uncertain in Chaos of War," *New York Times* (July 14, 1982), 1.

59 Ibid., A10.

60 Jay Ross, "War Casualties Put at 48,000 in Lebanon," *Washington Post* (September 3, 1982), A22. The headline figure of 48,000 was peculiar as there was no such assertion in the article.

61 Libanon-Aktionsgruppe (Kiel), "Völkermord im Libanon," 82.3, Antiimperialistisches Solidaritätskomittee (Frankfurt/Main) Collection, ASK, Palästina Solidarität BRD J-L, 1977–1988, International Institute for Social History, Amsterdam, Netherlands.

(*Vernichtungskrieg)*.[62] On August 8, 1982, a broad coalition of leftist organizations in Frankfurt/Main animated by a "shared perspective of Jews and Arabs" sponsored a demonstration called to "End the War of Extermination against the Palestinians and Lebanese!"[63] It too described Israel's invasion as a "war of extermination" (*Vernichtungsfeldzug*), which had made a million people refugees and led to "over 40,000 deaths" according to the Palestinian Red Cross. It described Israel's war aims as destruction of the PLO and creation of a "marionette regime" in Lebanon as a precondition for annexation of the West Bank and Gaza Strip. It called for an immediate and unconditional withdrawal of Israeli troops from Lebanon, "the right of self-determination of the Palestinian people, its right of return and its right to establish an independent state" and recognition of the PLO by the West German government."[64] The demonstration had support from a cross-section of the West German Left including several prominent Jewish leftists, the counter-cultural "sponti" scene in Frankfurt/Main, a variety of Marxist-Leninist groups, and "Palestine solidarity" organizations.[65] A similar breadth of support was evident in a demonstration of September 25 in Bonn to protest the Israeli invasion and "mass murder in Beirut."[66] The depth and breadth of leftist sentiment illustrated that anti-Zionism had remained a defining or "wedge" issue in the West German Left.[67]

The Israeli siege of 6,000 to 7,000 PLO armed forces in Beirut continued into August. Cut off from further ammunition resupply, Arafat and the PLO leadership accepted an agreement negotiated by the American diplomat Philip Habib with the Israelis. It allowed Arafat and thousands of PLO fighters to leave Beirut by sea with their small arms. In the last ten days of August, the PLO's main forces left Beirut under the protection of American, British and French forces. The PLO's mini-state, its infrastructure of military bases, as well as its access to logistical resupply via the Beirut airport and the coastal cities in Lebanon were finished. In

[62] Libanon-Aktionsgruppe (Kiel), "Völkermord im Libanon," 82.3, ASK (Frankfurt/Main) Collection, Palästina Solidarität BRD J-L, 1977–1988, IISH Amsterdam.

[63] "Schluß mit dem Vernichtungskrieg gegen Palästinenser und Libanesen!" 82.1, ASK (Frankfurt/Main) Collection, ASK, Palästina Solidarität BRD F, 1977–1988, IISH Amsterdam.

[64] Ibid.

[65] Ibid.

[66] "Bundesweite Demonstration, Bonn, 25.9.1982," 81.6, ASK (Frankfurt/Main) Collection, Palästina Solidarität BRD C-D, 1975–1986, IISH Amsterdam.

[67] For an analysis of anti-Zionism as a "wedge issue" see Andrei Markovits, "Preface," in *Uncouth Nation: Why Europe Dislikes America* (Princeton, NJ: Princeton University Press, 2007), xiv.

the years to come, PLO terrorist attacks on Israel continued but were reduced enough so that life in northern Israel was able to return to a semblance of normality.

The departure of the PLO from Beirut and the loss of its bases in southern Lebanon were historically significant. The defeat ended its hopes of employing a terrorist campaign to destroy the state of Israel by force of arms. Though the Soviet bloc and the Arab states continued to support the PLO until they themselves succumbed to popular revolts in 1989–1991, the war in Lebanon of 1982 represented one of the most significant defeats for Soviet and East German foreign policy in the history of the global Cold War. *Neues Deutschland* sought to put the best face on the outcome by reporting none of its details. Yet Arafat's assertions that the PLO would never be defeated could not obscure the realities. The PLO ceased to be a guerrilla army with thousands of men under arms based within fifteen miles of the Israel's northern border.[68]

From September 16 to 18, 1982, between 762 and 3,500 Palestinians were massacred in the Sabra and Shatilla refugee camp in Lebanon by Christian Falange fighters who sought revenge for the assassination of the newly elected Lebanese president, Bashir Gemayel, and previous Palestinian attacks on Christians. The subsequent Israeli Kahan government report concluded that Ariel Sharon had to accept "personal responsibility" for allowing the Falange soldiers into the camp and for failing to stop the massacre in progress. The PLO made the false claim that Israeli soldiers had stormed the camp. The Arab states repeated the claim that Israel was primarily responsible. At the UN, the East Germans opined that "the mass murder of defenceless Palestinian was irrefutable proof that Israel was trying to solve the Palestinian problem by genocide."[69] On September 20, 1982, on page 1, *Neues Deutschland* quoted the GDR Solidarity Committee's expression of "anger and revulsion" when it learned of "the frightful massacre that Israeli commandos carried out on over 1,000 defenseless Palestinian refugees in West Beirut, mostly women, children, young people and the aged.... The massacre was further evidence that Israel and its supporters were seeking to solve the Palestine question via genocide of the Palestinian people." The Solidarity Committee reaffirmed its "full solidarity with the heroic Palestinian people which is faced with a murder campaign

[68] "PLO-Vorsitzender Arafat in Tunesien herzlich begrüßt," *ND* (September 4/5, 1982), 1.

[69] "Massacre in the Beirut Area," *United Nations Yearbook 1982* (New York: UN Public Information Service, 1986), 481–484.

(*Mordfeldzug*) conducted with fascist methods."[70] On September 22, *ND* ran two page-1 stories repeating the accusation: "Yasser Arafat: 3,300 Defenseless People Were Butchered by Israel's Murder Commandos" and "Horror in the Whole World about Tel Aviv's Policy of Genocide."[71] On September 23, *ND* led with a story about the expression of thanks from the Arab ambassadors of Iraq, Tunisia, and the PLO for East Germany's "condemnation of Israel's bloody deeds" and for its support for the Palestinian struggle.[72]

Harry Ott (1933–2005) was East Germany's UN ambassador from 1982 to 1990.[73] Like Peter Florin, Ott had an impressive Communist political biography. He joined the SED in 1953, worked in the International Relations Department of its Central Committee, and had been East Germany's ambassador to the Soviet Union from 1974 to 1980. On December 1, 2, 6, 7, and 8, the UN General Assembly discussed the war in Lebanon. A long list of states denounced Israel.[74] Ott added his voice to those who argued that the Israelis "backed and supported by the main imperialist Power," that is, the United States, were "trying to solve the question of Palestine according to their concept – that is, by the genocide of the Arab people of Palestine." The recent months had shown "the Israeli rulers do not stop at any crime, however abhorrent, to realize their chauvinistic great-power aspirations." Their policies not only threatened the Arabs but posed "a serious threat to peace and security all over the world."[75]

[70] "Solidaritätskomitee der DDR: Israel betreibt Völkermord," *ND* (September 20, 1982), 1.

[71] "Yasser Arafat: 3300 Wehrlose wurden von Mordkommandos Israels niedergemetzelt" and "Abscheu in aller Welt über Völkermord-Politik Tel Avivs," *ND* (September 22, 1982), 1.

[72] "Botschafter arabischer Staaten: Dank an DDR für Verurteilung der Israelischen Bluttaten, für Solidarität mit der PLO," *ND* (September 23, 1982), 1.

[73] "Ott, Harry," in Barth et al., *Wer war Wer in der DDR*, 551. Ott joined the SED in 1952, studied at the Institute for International Relations in Moscow from 1953 to 1959 and joined the East German Ministry of Foreign Relations in 1959. He rose through various positions in the Central Committee of the SED and served as ambassador to the Soviet Union before his years in New York at the UN.

[74] See summary in "Chapter IX, Middle East," *Yearbook of the United Nations 1982*, Vol. 37 (New York: United Nations, Department of Public Information, 1986), 433–488. Also see "93rd Plenary Meeting" (December 7, 1982), Official Records of the General Assembly, 37th Session, Plenary Meetings. Volume III. 1533–1601.

[75] Harry Ott (German Democratic Republic), *Yearbook of the United Nations,* 37th Session, 93rd Plenary Meeting, New York (December 7, 1982), 1539.

The repeated charges of genocide raised a delicate and rarely posed question. As was clear during the war and became clearer afterward, the accusations were false. Two conclusions could be drawn. The first was that governments knew they were lying but did so in order to weaken Israel and support the PLO. The second was that at least some of the governments actually believed that Israel was, in fact, among the genocidal powers of the twentieth century. If that was their belief, then it was striking that not a single one, with the short-lived and disastrous exception of Syria's aerial debacle, sent significant military forces to Lebanon or used their own military forces to enter the war on the side of the PLO. East Germany had much company in sending public messages of solidarity. Its flow of arms and military training continued, but in the face of what it called genocide against its Palestinian ally it refrained from sending its own soldiers into harm's way. This combination of extreme rhetoric and refusal to place soldiers in harm's way of Israel's armed forces was one of the most telling aspects of this chapter in the history of international antagonism to Israel. During the war in Lebanon a yawning gap opened up between Arab and Communist rhetoric and Arab and Communist actions or, rather, lack thereof. In the crucial moment, the PLO was left on its own and was saved, ironically, by the "American imperialists," whose diplomacy arranged and implemented its exit from Beirut.

On September 15, *Neues Deutschland* featured Soviet general secretary Leonid Brezhnev's expression of "firm solidarity the struggle of the PLO" on page 1.[76] Brezhnev and Honecker were loath to acknowledge that their investment in Arafat and the PLO, as well as the other Palestinian terror organizations such as the PFLP and PDFLP, as a means of defeating Israel and fundamentally changing the correlation of forces in the strategically vital Middle East had been a dismal failure. Their propaganda assault had a longer-lasting impact. The millions of people who read the accusations of "genocide" and "war of extermination" were paying less attention when accurate figures of numbers of dead and wounded soldiers and civilians were published and largely confirmed the factual assertions made at the time by the government of Israel. Israel's military victory in Lebanon coincided with defeats in political warfare that the Soviet bloc, the Arab states, and the non-aligned third-world bloc continued to wage at the United Nations. Parts of the West European Left repeated the false accusations. Israel's invasion of Lebanon was controversial in Israel, but

[76] "Botschaft Leonid Breshnews an Yasser Arafat: Feste Solidarität mit dem Kampf der PLO bekräftigt," *Neues Deutschland* [East] Berlin (September 15, 1982), 1.

the attribution of genocidal intent and policy to the government was not, on the whole, a component of the domestic dissent. Abroad, the association of the Jewish state with mass murder became the most important point of connection between leftist anti-Zionism of that era and the old themes of the murderous Jew found in the traditions of anti-Semitism.

14

Loyal Friends in Defeat: 1983–1989 and After

After the PLO's defeat in Lebanon in 1982, East Germany remained a loyal friend to it and to the Arab states of the rejection front. On May 11, 1983, in Damascus, General Werner Fleißner, the GDR's deputy minister of defense, and General Samil Al-Akel, the director of logistics of the Syrian army, signed an agreement for "cooperation in the military field."[1] Five years later, on April 12, 1988, the two governments renewed the agreement and extended the training of Syrian military forces in East Germany until December 31, 1995.[2] On April 10, 1984, Dr. Klaus Bartsch of the East German Defense Ministry signed a two-year agreement with Abdul Menem Al Amouri, the PLO's military attaché, in its embassy in East Berlin to offer medical care in East Germany to members of "the armed forces of the Palestinian Revolution."[3] The agreement called for treatment of five wounded officers of the PLO in East Germany each year in the military hospitals of the East German armed forces. Beginning in 1984 as well, the East Germans agreed to undertake "research in

1 "Abkommen zwischen der Regierung der Deutschen Demokratischen Republik und der Regierung der Syrischen Arabischen Republik über die Zusammenarbeit auf militärischen Gebiet," Damascus (May 11, 1983), Bundesarchiv Militärarchiv (BAMA), Freiburg, DVW 1/54313.

2 "Protokoll zum Abkommen zwischen der Regierung der Deutschen Demokratischen Republik und der Regierung der Syrischen Arabischen Republik über die Zusammenarbeit auf militärischen Gebiet vom 11.05.1983," Damascus (April 12, 1988), BAMA, DVW 1/54313

3 "Abkommen zwischen der Regierung der Deutschen Demokratischen Republik und dem Exekutivkomitee der Palästinensischen Befreiungsorganisation über die medizinische Behandlung und die flugmedizinische Untersuchung von Angehörigen der Streitkräfte der Palästinensischen Revolution in der Deutschen Demokratischen Republik," PLO Medizinische Behandlung 1984, BAMA DVW 1/ 54346, 1–7.

flight medicine" (*flugmedizinische Untersuchung*) with up to 25 "pilots (*Flugzeugführen*) of the armed forces of the Palestinian Revolution."[4] As the PLO did not have its own air force, the medical treatment of PLO "pilots" raised the question of whose planes they were planning to fly.

On September 25, 1984, the East German Ministry of Foreign Trade signed an agreement with Syria to deliver $50 million of "special equipment" to Syria's Ministry of Defense. Among the items to be delivered were "chemical warfare" equipment including a "vehicle of special treatment ... chemical-radiological reconnaissance apparatus," and "equipment for chemical practice field." The agreement also called for delivery of ammunition for small arms, submachine gun parts, and spare parts for small arms; tools and spare parts for tanks and BMP-1, a Soviet amphibious-tracked infantry-fighting vehicle; spare parts for armored personnel carriers; "tanks of Soviet origin"; and patrol boats. For the Syrian air force, the East Germans agreed to develop radar repair workshops, send a remote control system for signals and navigation equipment, repair aircraft engines, send aircraft spare parts, and deliver technical equipment to maintain and repair runways and aircraft maintenance hangars. Medical services included field hospitals, ambulances, field laboratories, mobile X-ray facilities, and medical instruments and equipment. Finally the agreement also called for sporting equipment, equipment for a sports medical center, and unspecified "articles and equipment for sports."[5] The diversity of such items required the involvement of many different specialists in the East German military, who in turn would be working with an equally diverse and broad group of their Syrian counterparts.

An agreement of August 30, 1985, with the PLO stipulated that East Germany would continue to train 20 military personnel in East Germany until the end of 1989.[6] Each trainee would spend three years in East Germany. The first year included intensive German-language training along with "political education." The East German Defense Ministry

[4] Ibid., 3–4.

[5] "Annex: Abkommen zwischen der Regierung der Deutschen Demokratischen Republik und dem Exekutivkomitee der Palästinensischen Befreiungsorganisation über die medizinische Behandlung und die flugmedizinische Untersuchung von Angehörigen der Streitkräfte der Palästinensischen Revolution in der Deutschen Demokratischen Republik," PLO Medizinische Behandlung 1984, BAMA DVW 1/ 54346, 1–3.

[6] "Abkommen zwischen der Regierung der Deutschen Demokratischen Republik und dem Exekutivkomitee der Palästinensischen Befreiungsorganisation über die Ausbildung von Militärkadern der Streitkräfte der Palästinensischen Revolution in der Deutschen Demokratischen Republik," [East] Berlin (August 30, 1985), BAMA DVW 1 54347, PLO Ausbildung Militärkader 1985.

would cover "the costs for all of the personal, technical and material expenditures for language, political, military and military-technical training, for personal equipment and uniforms, for official travel and excursions in the German Democratic Republic, and for food and lodging as well as medical and cultural care of the military cadres" plus 200 marks a month for spending money and 400 marks for a civilian wardrobe appropriate for the colder East German climate.[7]

From 1983 to 1989, *Neues Deutschland* continued to publish exchanges of anti-imperialist solidarity between Honecker and Arafat on its front pages, but the articles were smaller and the events to which they referred were largely non-events of meetings, conferences, and public rituals of mutual admiration and expressions of solidarity.[8] Arafat reminded readers that he was not only "Chairman of the Executive Committee of the Palestine Liberation Organization" but also "Commander in Chief of the Armed Forces of the Palestinian Revolution."[9] The aftermath of the Lebanon War led to bitter reproaches between Hafez al-Assad and Arafat. On August 1, Honecker sought to use East Germany's good relations with both leaders to heal the rift. "The consolidation of the community of struggle (*Kampfgemeinschaft)* between the SAR (Syrian Arab Republic), the PLO and the patriotic forces in Lebanon" was "an urgent task of the moment."[10] Arafat replied that the Arab League, the Organization of the Islamic Conference, the Organization of African Unity, the Movement of Non-Aligned States, Yuri Andropov in the Soviet Union, and Fidel Castro had all attempted, without success, to reestablish the "fighting alliance" with the Syrian regime.[11] The Syrians and Libyans had "stabbed the PLO in the back." The PLO was "now facing a genuine conspiracy aiming at

[7] Ibid., 2–3.

[8] See, for example: "Glückwunsche Erich Honeckers an Yasser Arafat," *Neues Deutschland* (February 27/28, 1983), 1; "Yasser Arafat würdigt die prinzipielle Haltung der DDR," *ND*(January 6, 1983), 2; "Herzliche Begegnung mit Yasser Arafat," *ND* (February 15, 1984), 2; "Gluckwunsch für Yasser Arafat," *ND* (November 30, 1984), 1; "Yasser Arafat dankt für die Solidarität der DDR," *ND* (November 27, 1985), 2; "Erich Honecker mit Yasser Arafat," *ND* (April 21, 1984), 1; "Botschaft von Yasser Arafat an Erich Honecker übermittelt," *ND* (January 13, 1988), 1; "Schreiben von Yasser Arafat an Erich Honecker," *ND* (December 13, 1988), 1;"Preäsiden Arafat würdigt die Hilfe der DDR," *ND* (April 7, 1989), 1.

[9] Yasser Arafat to Erich Honecker, Beirut (April 1, 1982), BAB DY 30/13797, Abteilung Internationale Verbindungen, 1946–1990, d. ZK d. SED, Palastinensischen Befreiungsorganisation, 1982–1988, 4–6.

[10] Ibid., 19–23.

[11] Yasser Arafat to Erich Honecker, Tunis (August 5, 1983), BAB DY 30/13797, Abt. Int. Verb., 1946–1990, d. ZK d. SED, Palastinensischen Befreiungsorganisation, 1982–1988, 28–33.

splitting the PLO, liquidating its accomplishments and sidelining its role in the struggle." Now, real friends, such as East Germany, needed to use all means to end this "dangerous negative development."[12] East Germany maintained its alliances with both Syria and the PLO, but there were limits to its ability to heal their conflicts.

On April 5, 1986, a bomb exploded in the La Belle Disco in West Berlin. The explosion killed three people and wounded around 230. Two of those killed and 79 of the injured were American soldiers. As the Ministry of State Security files reveal, it was an attack that the Stasi could have prevented but did not, either through incompetence or through intent. A subsequent trial confirmed what Western intelligence agencies learned at the time, namely, that the attack was carried out by members of the Libyan Embassy in East Berlin, which the Libyans called the "Libyan People's Bureau."[13] The attack was an exception that proved the rule of the Stasi's Eurocentric counterterrorism policies.

Beginning at least as early as June 6, 1977, the Stasi had established formal cooperation with Libya's armed forces and intelligence services.[14] The 1977 agreement called for training 700 persons with "special emphasis on development of combat abilities which will enable the trainees to foil the enemy machinations with the use the most modern scientific methods." The Libyans, then flush with oil revenues, would pay $2.5 million for the training.[15] In 1979, the Stasi signed an agreement with the Libyan intelligence services to offer training in developing codes.[16] As a Stasi report of December 1979 indicated, its relations with the Libyan intelligence services began in "March/April 1976 in connection with support for the PFLP." However, relations with Libya's security services had "not gone beyond the basis of buying knowledge and experience, including technology."[17] In the context of "Action Friendship," the training of

[12] Ibid., 32.

[13] After a four-year trial, the state court in West Berlin found four people guilty of participation in the attack, including members of the Libyan People's Bureau in East Berlin. See Steven Erlanger, "4 Guilty in Fatal 1986 Berlin Disco Bombing Linked to Libya," *New York Times* (November 14, 2001).

[14] "Vereinbarung: Lieferungen, Montage, Ausbildung am 02.6.1977 … zwischen Ministerium für Staatssicherheit der Deutschen Demokratischen Republik … und … dem Sekretariat für Öffentliche Verbindungen der Libyschen Arabischen Sozialistischen Volksjamahirija," BStU, Archiv der Zentralstelle, MfS-Abt. X, Nr. 1766, 1–25.

[15] Ibid., 2, 4–5.

[16] Hauptverwaltung A, "Vorlage: Ausbildung in der deutschen Sprache und in Chiffre für das National Sicherheitsorgan der SLAVJ in der DDR," East Berlin (June 21, 1979), BStU, Archiv der Zentralstelle, MfS-Abt. X, 2241, 2–4.

[17] HV a/III/AG/015, Weller, "Bericht: Beziehungen des MfS zu Organen in der SLAVJ," East Berlin (December 3, 1979), BStU, Archiv der Zentralstelle, MfS-Abt. X, 2241, 5 and 9.

Libyan officers in East German military institutions continued into the 1980s. However, unlike the PLO, Libya had oil wealth. Money bought autonomy. As the events of April 1986 indicated, unlike the PLO, the Libyans did not follow the East German counterterrorism rules.

On March 27, 1986, Francis J. Meehan, the US ambassador to East Germany, met with East German deputy foreign minister Bernhard Neugebauer in the East German Foreign Ministry. On the same day, the United States informed Soviet representatives in East Berlin that it had information that "Libyan citizens in East Berlin were planning terrorist actions against American objects in West Berlin."[18] Meehan informed Neugebauer that the United States had "evidence that the Libyan Embassy in the GDR plays an active role in hostile activities against the USA in Western Europe and possibly also in West Berlin." Meehan "wanted to draw the attention of the GDR to these questions" and requested increased security measures around the US Embassy in East Berlin. Neugebauer responded that on "political and humanitarian grounds" the GDR "rejects and condemns any kind of terrorism." The East German government had "no knowledge" of the activities to which Meehan referred.[19]

On the day of the La Belle attack, the US mission in West Berlin wrote to the Soviet Embassy that it possessed "incontrovertible information" that the Libyan People's Bureau in "the Soviet sector" was responsible for the attack. It reminded the Soviet authorities of their responsibility for the security of American institutions and persons against attacks that originated in the Soviet sector. In view of the American warning of March 27, the American mission viewed the attack as "a direct result of the failure of Soviet authorities to undertake effective measures on the basis of the information offered by the US Mission on March 27." The US mission "protested sharply against the indifference of the Soviet Embassy towards its responsibility." It insisted that the Soviet authorities adopt "necessary measures to set aside the terrorist threat to Berlin by expelling the terrorist base known as the Libyan People's Bureau from the Soviet sector."[20]

[18] Herbert Barth, "Vermerk über ein Gespräch des Stellvertreters des minister für Auswärtige Angelegenheiten, Genossen Bernhard Neugebauer, mit dem Botschafter der USA in der DDR, Francis J. Meehan, am 27. März1986 im MfAA," [East] Berlin (March27,1986), BStU, Archiv der Zentralstelle, MfS-HAII, Nr. 32887, 11–12; "Anlage 6," [East] Berlin (March27,1986), BStU, Archiv der Zentralstelle, MfS-HAII, Nr. 32887, 13.

[19] Ibid., 11–12.

[20] "Non-paper an die Botschaft der UdSSR vom 5.4.1986," [West] Berlin (March27, 1986), BStU, Archiv der Zentralstelle, MfS-HAII, Nr. 32887, 22.

On April 7, the United States intercepted a message of congratulations from the Libyan government in Tripoli to the Libyan People's Bureau in East Berlin for the La Belle bombing. On April 9, 1986, Meehan told Herbert Barth, director of the USA Department of the East German Foreign Ministry, that the United States was very disappointed that although it had offered the GDR "clear and timely" warning that the Libyan People's Bureau was "organizing and steering" terrorist attacks against American targets in Berlin, the GDR had failed to "take appropriate measures to prevent the terrorist attack of April 5."[21] Meehan added that it was the East German government's responsibility to prevent people with diplomatic status from engaging in illegal activities. The United States "did not understand why" the GDR "allowed the members of the Libyan People's Bureau to misuse its hospitality" by "using their diplomatic status to carry out terrorist activities." Future relations with the United States would be "decisively" affected by the East German reaction in this matter. Meehan gave Barth the names of four Libyans believed to have terrorist connections in the People's Bureau.[22] Barth denied that the GDR had anything to do with the terrorist attack. He insisted that it had "no information at all in connection with this attack and emphatically rejected any responsibility for it."[23]

Whatever Barth and the Foreign Ministry knew, a Stasi memo of April 10, 1986, indicated that in March 1986, the Stasi learned that members of the Libyan intelligence service in the Libyan Embassy (People's Bureau) in East Berlin were indeed thinking of conducting "terrorist attacks on American institutions in West Berlin."[24] They took advantage of "favorable conditions (short distances, freedom from border controls by GDR organs, personal links) that could be used." In March, the Stasi was aware that the Libyans were observing possible American targets, including the La Belle Disco, in West Berlin.[25] The Stasi report about the La Belle bombing concluded that "there must be a direct or indirect participation of members of the Libyan People's Bureau in the GDR as well as from pro-Libyan as well as hired criminals among Palestinians in West

[21] "Vermerk über ein Gespräch des leiters der Abteilung USA im MfAA Dr. Herbert Barth, mit dem Botschafter der USA, Francis J. Meehan, am 9 April 1986, im MfAA," BStU, Archiv der Zentralstelle, MfS-HA II, Nr. 32887," 125–126.

[22] Ibid., 126.

[23] Ibid.

[24] "Lageentwicklung im Zusammenhang mit dem Anschlag auf eine Diskothek in Westberlin," BStU, Archiv der Zentralstelle, MfS-HAII, Nr. 32887, 156.

[25] Ibid., 156.

Berlin." The MfS had information that two of the Libyan operatives had ten kilos of explosives and two pistols in their West Berlin apartments and were planning further "actions."[26]

The policy conclusions drawn by the Stasi leadership shed light on what I have called the Eurocentric definition of East German counterterrorism.

> The unusually sharp reaction by the United States against East Germany and the Soviet Union immediately before and after the attack in West Berlin leads to the conclusion that the US administration will use these events to reinforce the lie about terrorism (*Terrorismuslüge*). We have to face the possibility that they will use the "evidence" presented here.... The activity of the imperialist mass media toward the Libyan People's Bureau in the GDR (ARD, ZDF, Reuters) aims at a focused and broad campaign aimed at discrediting the GDR and its socialist allies.[27]

The Stasi memo cautioned that it was essential not to give the impression that East Germany's relations with other states were influenced by the United States. Therefore, "necessary steps toward terrorist forces within the Libyan People's Bureau should be implemented only when they no longer convey an impression that they are a reaction to demands by the USA."[28] These steps included "ending the misuse of diplomatic immunity by representatives above all of the Arab Embassies, ... limiting the accreditation of persons from third states in Arab Embassies (especially Palestinians)" and "clearly limiting the presence of shady (*zwielichtiger*) persons especially from the Palestinian scene in East Berlin."[29] Again, the Stasi's lack of euphemism regarding terrorism was in evidence. "The enemy will use the bomb attack in West Berlin to launch a slanderous propaganda campaign against the GDR and other socialist states" and "attempt to torpedo the intensive efforts of the USSR to engage in fruitful conversations with the USA." Hence "conversations at the highest levels with the Libyan side appear useful and necessary."[30] These arguments were identical to those that Mielke and Neiber had formulated in 1979. Unlike the PLO, which was heavily dependent on the Soviet-bloc support, the financially independent Libyans had flouted the rules of East German hospitality and counterterrorism policies. They were willing to use their "People's Bureau" in East Berlin to plan and carry out attacks in West

[26] Ibid., 157.
[27] Ibid., 158.
[28] Ibid.
[29] Ibid.
[30] Ibid., 159.

Berlin, thereby causing serious problems for both the Soviet Union and East Germany.

Without photos on the front page of *Neues Deutschland*, East Germany continued to welcome the leaders of the Popular Front for the Liberation of Palestine (PFLP) and the Popular Democratic Front for the Liberation of Palestine (PDFLP) to East Berlin in the 1980s.[31] On April 26, 1989, George Habash, the general secretary of the PFLP, met in East Berlin with high-ranking officials of the SED Central Committee's Department of International Relations and with the GDR's Solidarity Committee.[32] With the movements for democracy and challenges to the Communist regimes then gathering strength in Eastern Europe, he thought that "the assessment of the past of the USSR" emerging from the reform process there was "partly irresponsible and one-sided. Negative phenomena were so exaggerated that the impression was left that there had been no successes."[33] On October 7, 1989, Nayef Hawatmeh, the "General Secretary of the Central Committee of the Democratic Front for the Liberation of Palestine," the same Hawatmeh who had ordered and then celebrated the attack on Israeli civilians in Kiryat Shmona and other places, wrote to Erich Honecker to send "the warmest best wishes" *(herzlichsten Gluckwunsche)* on East Germany's 40th anniversary. He recalled the "superb *(hervorragende)* role that [you, the GDR have played] with support for the struggle of the Palestinian people for their freedom and national independence."[34] On October 22, 1989, Habash wrote to Egon Krenz to congratulate him on his appointment as head of the SED Central Committee, replacing Honecker, who had been forced to resign in the face of massive street protests against the Communist regime.[35] He was

[31] During the 1980s, two leaders famous for terrorist attacks in the 1970s, George Habash, the leader of the Popular Front for the Liberation of Palestine, and Nayef Hawatmeh, head of the Democratic Popular Front for the Liberation of Palestine, wrote to Honecker. See Naife Hawatmeh to Erich Honecker (April 23, 1984) and (October 4, 1986), 63–66 and 122–124, and George Habash to Erich Honecker (April 19, 1984), 46–49, in BAB DY 30/13797, Abteilung Internationale Verbindungen, 1946–1990, d. ZK d. SED, Palastinensischen Befreiungsorganisation, 1982–1988.

[32] "Vermerk uber ein Gesprach mit George Habbash, Generalsekretar der Volksfront fur die Befreiung Palastina, am 26.4.1989," Abt. Int. Verb. East Berlin (April 27, 1989), Bundesarchiv Berlin BAB DY/13794, 59–62. He met with Peter Bathke, Director of the Department of International Relations, Wolfgang Krause, Deputy Secretary General of the GDR Solidarity Committee, Willi Sommerfeld, Department Director of the Solidarity Committee and Werner Krause, a staff member in the Department of International Relations.

[33] Ibid., 59.

[34] Nayef Hawatmeh to Erich Honecker (October 7, 1989), Bundesarchiv Berlin BAB DY/13794, 45–46.

[35] George Habbash to Egon Krenz, Damascus (October 22, 1989), BAB DY30/13794, 112–113.

"firmly convinced that the German Communists" would "master the tasks facing them and ... strengthen the socialist construction of their country." He again expressed his thanks for "the unbroken and selfless assistance that the GDR has shown and shows to the just cause of our people and to the PLO, its sole legitimate representative."[36]

During the week of November 5–11, 1989, Wolfgang Krause, the deputy secretary of the GDR's Solidarity Committee, led an East German delegation to visit the PLO leadership at its headquarters in Tunis.[37] He learned that the PLO's leaders were deeply worried about events taking place in Eastern Europe and in East Germany. On November 9, the Berlin Wall was opened and forty years of one-party Communist dictatorship was in the process of falling apart. Krause reported the following.

> The deep concern and worry of the PLO representatives about the tempo and the depth of political changes in the GDR was clearly evident. The conversations made apparent the PLO's concern about a possible change in the GDR's position toward the Middle East conflict (emphasis in original, J. H.). This worry was reinforced by developments in Poland, Hungary and especially in the Soviet Union which have already led to a weakening of solidarity for the PLO by these countries. Especially, the appearance of Deputy Foreign Minister Tarassow with the PLO leadership in which he called for more flexibility in the search for peace in the Middle East was a source of disappointment. All of our conversation partners feared that the Soviet Union will leave the main role in the search for a solution to the Middle East conflict to the USA, be satisfied with a secondary role for itself, will leave Europe completely out of the picture and will quickly agree to solutions that come at the expense of the PLO.[38]

Krause reported that Arafat himself expressed "deep concern about the recent developments in the GDR." He assured Arafat and the other PLO leaders that "the friendship and solidarity of the GDR with the Palestinian people and the PLO had a long tradition and deep roots in the GDR. Despite deep domestic changes in the GDR that friendship and solidarity would certainly continue."[39] Krause's reassuring words could not obscure the political realities that were unfolding in East Germany. The files of the East German regime's most sensitive institutions were going to be made public. Sooner or later, the details of weapons deliveries, military training, and the Soviet-bloc and East German alliance with the PLO during the

[36] Ibid.

[37] Wolfgang Krause, "Bericht über die Reise einer Delegation des Solidaritätskomitees der DDR zu einem Arbeitsbesuch beim PLO-Hauptquartier in Tunis vom 5. Bis. 12.11.1989," BAB DY30/13794, 115–117.

[38] Ibid., 115.

[39] Ibid., 116–117.

era of its terrorist campaigns against Israel were going to become public knowledge, and those activities were also going to come to an end.

Following the collapse of the Communist dictatorship in fall 1989, the first free elections to be held in Eastern Germany since 1932 produced a multi-party parliament (Volkskammer). It met from April 5 until October 2, 1990. On April 12, 1990, the Volkskammer voted 379 to 0 with 21 abstentions to approve a resolution that accepted East Germany's joint responsibility for addressing the aftermath of Nazi Germany's crimes.[40] The resolution asked "the people in Israel for forgiveness for the hypocrisy and hostility of official GDR policy toward the state of Israel and for the persecution and humiliation of Jewish fellow citizens in our country."[41] The parliament also looked forward to establishing diplomatic relations with Israel, something the GDR had never done. On July 22, 1990, the Volkskammer passed a second resolution, in which it distanced "itself from all forms of the anti-Israeli and anti-Zionist policies that were practiced in this country [East Germany, JH] for decades and from their domestic and foreign policy consequences. It distances itself in particular from [East Germany's] agreement to Resolution 3379 of the 30th United Nations General Assembly of November 10, 1975" and from the "equation of Zionism with racism" in that resolution.[42]

[40] "Antrag aller Fraktionen der Volkskammer der Deutschen Demokratischen Republik zu einer gemeinsamen Erklärung," Deutscher Bundestag, *Protokolle der Volkskammer der Deutschen Demokratischen Republik 10 Wahlperiode (5. April bis 2. Oktober 1990), Band I, Protokolle der 1. Sitzung bis 9. Sitzung, Nachdruck* (Bonn: Deutscher Bundestag; Leske and Budrich, 2000), 23–24. On the Volkskammer resolution see Jeffrey Herf, *Divided Memory: The Nazi Past in the Two Germanys* (Cambridge, MA: Harvard University Press, 1997), 364–365; also see 366.

[41] Ibid., 23. The second part of the statement expressed similar sentiments toward the peoples of the Soviet Union, the third about East German support for the suppression of the "Prague Spring" in 1968, and the fourth referred to a "special responsibility" to the peoples of Eastern Europe in the course of German unification and affirmed that the German-Polish border lay on the line of the Oder-Neisse rivers, 23–24.

[42] "Antrag von 23 Abgeordneten über die Distanzierung von der Resolution Nr. 3379 der UNO-Vollversammlung vom 10. November 1975 und ihren Aussagen über den Zionismus durch die Deutsche Demokratische Republik," Deutscher Bundestag, *Protokolle der Volkskammer der Deutschen Demokratischen Republik 10 Wahlperiode (5. April bis 2. Oktober 1990), Band 3, Protokolle der 26. Sitzung bis38. Sitzung, Nachdruck* (Bonn: Deutscher Bundestag; Leske and Budrich, 2000), 1280–1283. The 23 signers were Johannes Gerlach (SPD); Jörg Brochnow (CDU/DA); Sabine Bergmann-Pohl (CDU/DA); Harald Ringstorff (SPD); Hans GEisler (CDU/DA); Konrad Weiß (Bundnis 90/Grüne); Werner Schulz (Bundnis 90/Grüne); Wolfgang Ullmann (Bundnis 90/ Grüne); Stefan Gottschall (DSU); Nikolai Tschalamoff (CDU/DA); Bertram Wieczorek (CDU/DA); Boje Schmuhl (CDU/DA); Uwe Grüning (CDU/DA); Hans-Dirk Bierling (CDU/DA); Joachim Steinmann (CDU/DA); Reinhard Höpper (SPD); Eberhard Brecht

Twenty-three members of the parliament spanning the spectrum of all the parties except the successor party to the East German Communists co-sponsored this resolution. The sponsors included Konrad Weiss, its leading proponent; Wolfgang Thierse, a future president of the Bundestag; and Joachim Gauck, a future president of a unified Germany.[43]

On August 31, 1990, the treaty of German unification was signed. On September 24, 1990, the GDR officially left the Warsaw Pact. The treaty dissolved the armed forces of the GDR. On October 3, 1990, the treaty of German unification ended the political and legal existence of the German Democratic Republic and incorporated it into the Federal Republic of Germany. The treaty declared that the bilateral "treaties of friendship and cooperation" that East Germany had signed with its Warsaw Pact allies were no longer valid.[44] It also ended treaties for military cooperation or those concerning armaments with third states, that is, states outside the Warsaw Pact, such as Syria, Libya, and Iraq.[45] In view of the fact that the agreements of "Action Friendship" signed by the Stasi, the Central Committee, the Council of Ministers, and the Defense Ministry with the PLO and other "national liberation movements" were part of Warsaw Pact policy, they too would be null and void. The military cadres in training from third-world countries had to depart. The training institutes were closed. The weapons deliveries to the PLO, among others, ceased. The collapse of Communism in East Germany was an unmitigated disaster for the PLO and its affiliated organizations.

Aside from agreements with the Soviet Union, the East European members of the Warsaw Pact, China, Cuba and Vietnam, the largest number of written agreements between East Germany and other states were those with the Arab states. As of 1996, Germany had conducted negotiations about the following number of treaties with the Arab states: Egypt (42), Iraq (27), Libya (22), Syria (32), and Yemen (54).[46] The large number of treaties still in force with Egypt is surprising in view of its very

(SPD); Joachim Gauck (Bundnis 90/Grüne); Ibrahim Böhme (SPD); Rainer Ortleb (Liberale); Wolfgang Thierse (SPD); Helmut Krause (Liberale); and Lothar Klein (DSU), "Antrag der Abgeordneten," Volkskammer der DDR 10.

43 Ibid.

44 On these issues see Dieter Papenfuß, *Die Behandlung der völkerrechtlichen Verträge der DDR im Zuge der Herstellung der Einheit Deutschlands: ein Beitrag zur Frage der Staatennachfolge in völkerrechtliche Verträge* (Heidelberg: C. F. Müller Verlag, 19970, 204–205 and 209.

45 Ibid., 210.

46 "Anlage 6: Konsultation genaβ Art. 12 Einigungsvertrag (Stand 31.12.1996)," in Papenfuß, *Die Behandlung der völkerrechtlichen Verträge der DDR im Zuge der Herstellung der Einheit Deutschlands*, 259–264.

public exit from the Soviet orbit. The significance of treaty relations with Syria was understandable in light of the evidence of the preceding chapters. The even larger number of treaties with Yemen points to an as-yet unexamined and potentially important chapter in the history of the link between the Soviet bloc and international terrorist organizations of the secular Arab Left, such as the PFLP, PDFLP, and PLO, and perhaps others, from the 1960s to 1990. As all of the military agreements of "Action Friendship" and those with Syria, Iraq, Libya, and Yemen were signed in the common "struggle against imperialism," that is, aimed against the Western democracies, the government of unified Germany would have viewed them as aimed against its own national interests and declared the whole program null and void.

Eight years later, in March 1998, remaining members of the Red Army Faction (RAF) in West Germany issued a 12-page statement announcing that they were formally dissolving the organization.[47] There was only one organization that they praised by name and to which they expressed gratitude: the Popular Front for the Liberation of Palestine. "We will never forget the comrades of the Palestinian liberation front, the PFLP, who died in fall 1977 when they offered international solidarity in the effort to free political prisoners."[48] The reference was to the collaboration of the PFLP with the Red Army Faction's failed effort to force release of RAF members in German prisons by hijacking a Lufthansa plane to Mogadishu. Indicative of the fluid lines between the major leftist terrorist organizations of the 1970s and 1980s, the RAF dissolution text of 1998 included the names of Revolutionary Cell members Wilfried Böse and Brigitte Kuhlmann. It listed them among the 32 members of the "armed struggle" who had died since 1970.[49]

[47] Rote Armee Fraktion, *Die Auflösungserklärung der RAF, März 1988,* www.20min.ch/interaktiv/RAF/dokumente/raf_maerz1998.pdf

[48] Ibid. The German reads: "Wir werden die Genossen der palästinensischen Befreiungsfront, PFLP nie vergessen, die im Herbst 1977 in internationaler Solidarität, beim Versuch, die politischen Gefangenen zu befreien ihr Leben liessen." On this important text see Martin Jander, "German Leftist Terrorism and Israel: Ethno-Nationalist, Religious-Fundamentalist or Social-Revolutionary?," *Studies in Terrorism and Conflict Resolution,* Vol. 38, No. 6 (2015), 456-477.

[49] Rote Armee Fraktion, *Die Auflösungserklärung der RAF, März 1988,* www.20min.ch/interaktiv/RAF/dokumente/raf_maerz1998.pdf.

On the toll of those killed and wounded by the RAF, see Butz Peters, *Tödlicher Irrtum: Die Geschichte der RAF* (Frankfurt/Main: Fischer, 2007); and Jeffrey Herf, "The Age of Murder: Ideology and Terror in West Germany," *Telos* 144 (Fall 2008), www.telospress.com/from-telos-144-fall-2008jeffrey-herf-an-age-of-murder-ideology-and-terror-in-germany/.

The RAF had remained a sect, but the larger radical Left was successfully making the transition from the leftist fringes into mainstream politics. The Green Party was the vehicle of the turn away from terrorism to participation in democratic politics.[50] In 1998, a coalition of Social Democrats and Greens won national elections and assumed power in Berlin, now the capital of a unified Germany.[51] Joschka Fischer, veteran of the leftist scene in Frankfurt/Main and the Greens' most prominent leader, became Germany's foreign minister. Fischer, who knew about the Frankfurt/Main connections of the Entebbe hostage episode, had turned away from the anti-Israeli stance of the radical Left in the 1970s.[52] As previously noted, Fischer appointed Hans-Gerhart Schmierer, better known as "Joscha" Schmierer, the former leader of the Kommunistische Bund West Deutschland (KBW, Communist Organization, West Germany), to be a member of the Policy Planning Staff of the German Foreign Ministry. He remained in that position until 2007. On February 7, 2001, three members of the liberal Free Democratic Party posed questions in the Bundestag regarding Schmierer's past affiliations and political activities related to the KBW, including one about a note he had sent to Cambodia's Pol Pot congratulating him on "his victory over US imperialism."[53] They did not ask him about his past support for "armed struggle" against Israel and his comparison of the end of the destruction of the German Reich to the destruction of Israel. An opportunity for a parliamentary discussion of the radical Left and anti-Zionism in West Germany was missed.

As I have noted at the outset, there are important works that have examined the complex of West German leftist antagonism, terror, and

[50] The literature on the Greens is extensive. See Andrei Markovits and Philip Gorski, *The German Left: Red, Green and Beyond* (New York: Oxford University Press, 1993).

[51] On the move from the margins to the mainstream, see Paul Berman, *Power and the Idealists: Or the Passion of Joschka Fischer and Its Aftermath* (New York: Softskull Press, 2005).

[52] See Wolfgang Kraushaar, *Fischer in Frankfurt: Karriere eines Außenseiters* (Hamburg: Hamburger Edition, 2001), esp. "Fischer in Tel Aviv," 192–223; Hans Kundnani, *Utopia or Auschwitz: Germany's 1968 Generation and the Holocaust* (London: C. Hurst, 2009); Paul Hockonos, *Joschka Fischer and the Making of the Berlin Republic: An Alternative History of Postwar Germany* (New York: Oxford University Press, 2008); and Andrei Markovits, *Uncouth Nation: Why Europe Dislikes America* (Princeton, NJ: Princeton University Press, 2007).

[53] "Kleine Anfrage der Abgeordneten Jürgen Koppelin, Jörg van Essen, Dr. Wolfgang Gerhardt und der Fraktion der F.D.P," Deutscher Bundestag, 14 Wahlperiode, Drucksache 14.5303, 1–3. dipbt.bundestag.de/dip21/btd/14/053/1405303.pdf.

antagonism to Israel from 1967 to the end of the Cold War.[54] However, for the past 25 years, an issue that led the vast majority of the short-lived Volkskammer to reject East Germany's antagonism to Israel in the two resolutions of April and July 1990 has aroused only modest interest among scholars on both sides of the Atlantic working on German history and on the history of East Germany. The preservation of the files of the East German regime has made it possible to write an account of its involvement in the Arab and Palestinian attacks on the state of Israel and its citizens from the 1960s to the collapse of the regime in 1989. The East German Communists indignantly dismissed assertions that the PLO was a terrorist organization and kept the details of their support for those activities secret. Yet, as research in their own files confirms, East German leaders knew they were allies of Palestinian organizations engaged in terrorist attacks on Israel. They supported them knowing full well that the victims of terror were the citizens of the state of Israel.

54 For trenchant observations by a long-term journalistic observer, see Henryk M. Broder, *Vergesst Auschwitz: Der deutsche Erinnerungswahn und die Endlösung der Israel-Frage* (Munich: Albrecht Knaus Verlag, 2012).

15

Conclusion

The preceding chapters confirm that the East German government combined hostile words with secret military assistance to the Arab states and the Palestinian terrorist organizations at war with Israel. In West Germany, the terrorist activities of the Revolutionary Cells, the Red Army Faction, the June 2nd Movement, their collaboration with Palestinian terrorist organizations, as well as the anti-Israeli propaganda of the other radical leftist organizations, were public knowledge at the time. These assaults on Israel were never merely a criticism of Israel's policies. At its core, the Communist regime in East Berlin and the radical Left in West Germany rejected Israel's moral legitimacy and thus its right to exist as an independent state. In contrast to the German tradition of *Vergangenheitsbewältigung*, they tried to do a great deal of harm to the Jews and to Israel. Had their Arab and Palestinian allies been successful, Israel would have been destroyed by force of arms. Though it remained undeclared, East Germany and the West German radical leftists were, in effect also at war with Israel. Without moral qualms, they abetted those who made no secret of their desire to kill, injure, harm, and terrorize Israelis. East German diplomats emitted a rhetorical fog about moderation and negotiated solutions based on United Nations resolutions while placing the entire blame for the Israel-Arab-Palestinian conflict on Israel. Simultaneously, and in secrecy, the flow of weapons, military training, and intelligence cooperation from East Germany solidified alliances with Syria, Iraq, Libya, and the various Palestinian terror organizations represented on the PLO's Executive Committee.

A great and bitter irony of the Communist and leftist war against Israel was that its advocates often presented it as a second war against fascism, this time embodied in the Jewish state. During World War II, the Soviet Union fought against Nazi Germany with the slogans of anti-fascism. While "the Jewish question" had always been a marginal theme for the Communists even during that war, the emergence of Communist and leftist anti-Zionism and anti-Semitism in the postwar decades replaced marginality with open hostility. Both the East German state and the members of the radical Left in West Germany seemed not to have known that the Nazi regime had been an emphatic enemy of Zionism and that it too hoped that its hatred of Zionism would gain it friends among the Arabs. The photo of Yasser Arafat as honored guest in East Berlin paying his respects at the memorial to victims of fascism in East Berlin captured this irony in the 1970s. Through the magic of radical dialectics, the description of the Jewish state as the successor to Nazi Germany neatly assimilated the attack on Israel into the traditions of anti-fascism. In so doing the advocates of such views wrote one of the most disgraceful chapters in German history since World War II and the Holocaust.

But they were not alone. For the global Left from the 1960s to the 1990s, anti-Israeli passion became one of its defining, and enduring features. The majority of the states in the United Nations General Assembly also described Zionism as a form of racism, turned a blind eye to Palestinian terrorism, and denounced Israel's efforts at self-defense as forms of aggression. Yet, in contrast to their comrades around the world, the German actors stood in the continuities of German history after Nazism and the Holocaust. In announcing their enmity to Israel, they were, in effect, seeking to escape the unique moral and political burdens that emerged from that past. The East Germans expressed contempt for West Germany's policies of diplomatic relations with Israel and financial restitution to Jewish survivors of the Holocaust. The West Germans in SDS disdained their government's policies as a form of philosemitism that somehow amounted to anti-Semitism. In different ways, Walter Ulbricht, Erich Honecker, Heinz Hoffmann and others in the East, and Ulrike Meinhof, Dieter Kunzelmann and Wilfried Böse and others in the West, imagined that the Holocaust did not create any responsibilities for Germany's successor regimes, even one that described itself as antifascist. Their leap into the ideological embrace of global anti-imperialism became a form of national liberation from those bothersome details of recent German history. They were not only indifferent to the Jews in Israel who were killed and wounded in the terror attacks and wars; when they denounced as slander the description of the Palestinians armed organizations as terrorist, they were implicitly saying that the targets of the terror deserved what was inflicted on them.

The leaders of East Germany angrily rejected the very idea that their policies had any relation to anti-Semitism. On the contrary, they claimed that it was West Germany that was swarming with Nazis and anti-Semites. Yet the East German Communists who survived or carried out the anti-cosmopolitan purges never really understood the nature and sources of Jew-hatred. Moreover, their long antagonism to Israel was filled with the clichés and stereotypes about Israel's malevolence, deceit and vast conspiratorial power that were familiar themes in the traditions of anti-Semitism. Marxism nurtured their suspicions about a pejorative connection between the Jews and capitalism. Leninism deepened them by linking Israel to the archenemy American imperialism. East German antagonism included not only the public spectacle of support for the Palestine Liberation Organization, but also secret support for what the Stasi officials called the "extremists" of the Popular Front for the Liberation of Palestine and the Popular Democratic Front for the Liberation of Palestine. These were the organizations whose leaders dispensed with Yasser Arafat's clever ambiguities and publicly celebrated their terrorist attacks on Israeli civilians. East Germany consistently supported the Arab states, Syria most importantly, who were implacable in their hatred of Israel. Despite the fog of Soviet-bloc diplomatic rhetoric about "political solutions" and Geneva conferences, the East Germans and the Soviet Union supported those forces who opposed moderation and compromise in the Middle East. Their ambassadors in the Arab capitals were aware of the celebration of terrorist attacks against the Israelis yet left no public or archival record of denouncing terror aimed at Israeli civilians. As the 1969 breakthrough of diplomatic recognition from the Arab states first made clear, taking a stance against Israel was a matter of both ideological conviction and national self-interest. While support for Israel and counterterrorism policies in the aftermath of the Munich Olympics placed West Germany on the defensive in some Arab capitals, East Germany played the anti-Zionist card with great success in seeking and gaining friends and allies around the world. Ideology and self-interest were also important for the West German leftist terrorists that collaborated with the PFLP. Their ideological passion became interwoven with a need for escape routes, weapons and money.

The leaders of West Germany's Jewish community such as Heinz Galinski argued that in a society only decades away from Nazism, the anti-Zionist Left was playing with fire. In response, their leftist antagonists dismissed concerns about anti-Semitism as a familiar "Zionist trick." Yet Galinski and his colleagues were correct that by 1967 the anti-Israeli passion had become a defining feature not only of world Communism but also of the Western or at least parts of the 1960s New Left as well. The West German radical Left threatened not only Israel but Jews in West Germany in the form of a bomb placed in the Jewish Community Center in West Berlin on November 10, 1969; numerous letter bombs sent to Jewish institutions; a bombing campaign by the Revolutionary Cells in the 1970s; and credible death threats. While the West German New Left and its successors described the Federal Republic of Germany as an authoritarian or even fascist state, the Jewish community looked to its police and judicial authorities at the federal, state, and local levels for protection from neo-Nazis, but in these years even moreso from Palestinian terrorist organizations and their West German supporters and collaborators. Despite rhetoric about the outsized power of the Jews, the members the Central Council of Jews in Germany were aware of their small numbers, limited powers, and inability to influence West German government policy. They were not able to convince Willy Brandt to abandon neutrality and support Israel during the Yom Kippur War, nor were they successful in their efforts to get the West German government to make a major issue of East German support for the Arab states and Palestinian terror in the era of détente.

The evidence in this book indicates that while the West German terrorists had a significant impact on the history of their own country, their impact on the Middle East was in inverse proportion to the amount of media attention they received. Conversely, East Germany was able to use the institutions of dictatorship and complete control over the press and other media to keep secret its agreements for weapons deliveries and military training to the Palestinian organizations and the Arab states. The arms shipments, mechanical repairs and military training East Germany offered to the Arab states and the PLO did far more to shape the course of events in the Middle East than the assassinations, explosions, and bank robberies that captured the headlines in the West German and then the global media. Research in the East German archives has confirmed the importance of the much greater but far less publicized capacities of the East German state. When West German authorities raided terrorist safe houses, they found arsenals well-suited to carry out assassinations that included assault rifles, high-powered pistols, sniper rifles, and hand grenades. As deadly as they were, these arms caches were but a tiny fraction of the weapons that East Germany – and even more the Soviet Union and the other Warsaw Pact countries – were sending to Palestinian terrorist organizations and to the Arab states before, during and after the major wars and terrorist campaigns of this period.

Given the secrecy that surrounded the East German weapons programs, it is possible that additional shipments were recorded in files under code names or were in files that were destroyed as the regime was collapsing in fall 1989. As weapons in the "Action Friendship" program went to many armed leftist movements in the third world, especially to Yemen, where Palestinian terror organizations had bases, weapons shipped to those other destinations may have found their way into the arsenals of Al Fatah, the PFLP, PDFLP, and other Palestinian armed organizations. As we have seen, the larger weapons systems such as tanks, MiG fighter jets, Katuysha rocket launchers, and artillery that East Germany shipped to the armed forces of Egypt, Syria, Iraq, and Libya were produced in the Soviet Union. With the decision of 1969 to expand military support to states and movements around the world, however, East Germany began to manufacture its own version of the Kalashnikov assault weapon, hand grenades, cartridges, and land mines.

The following is an approximation based on the now-available East German archives of the total amount and kinds of weapons that East Germany gave as "solidarity" goods free of charge or sold to the Arab states and the Palestinian armed organizations at war with Israel from 1967 to 1989: 750,000 Kalashinikov assault weapons; 120 MiG Fighter jets; 180,000 anti-personnel land mines; 235,000 grenades; 25,000 rocket-propelled grenade (RPG) launchers; and 25 million cartridges of various sizes. In addition, during these years, East German technicians repaired and serviced 350 MiG fighter jets for the air forces of Iraq and Syria. From 1972 to 1989, more than 3,000 foreign military personal received training in East Germany military institutes, including several hundred from Syria, Iraq, Libya, and the PLO. A long list of other equipment with military purposes included binoculars, tents, parachutes, radios, field hospitals, unspecified equipment for chemical warfare, sniper rifles, carbines, fuses, and explosives.

The Yom Kippur War of 1973 brought into sharp relief the clear contrast between East Germany's explicit partisanship for the Arab states and the policy of neutrality adopted by the Brandt government. In the same weeks that the East Germans secretly sent their own ships full of weapons to Syria, West Germany publicly insisted that Israel's ships leave its harbors and that American planes not be allowed to land and refuel at bases in West Germany. In the most dangerous moments of Israel's history since 1948, the unity of the Warsaw Pact during the Yom Kippur War stood in striking contrast to the deep transatlantic tensions that emerged during Operation Nickel Grass and Nixon's and Kissinger's decisions to resupply Israel. The crisis of fall 1973 illustrated the limits of both the tradition of *Vergangenheitsbewältigung* and the "special relationship" between West Germany and Israel, as well as the centrality of US–Israeli alliance for Israel's survival.

In an era when "totalitarianism" fell out of favor in some Western intellectual circles, the anti-Zionist alliance demonstrated the continuing applicability of the term as its members distorted the meaning of words. The Arab states waged wars of aggression against Israel, yet when Israel defended itself, they called Israel the aggressor. In the 1970s, the Palestine Liberation Organization carried out more than 1,500 attacks aimed at Israeli civilians, then publicly insisted that calling the PLO a terrorist organization was a form of defamation and slander. The PLO Charter of 1968 implicitly called for the expulsion of the vast majority of Israel's Jewish population – an action that, if successful, would have been tantamount to what would later be called ethnic cleansing. Yet seven years later, the PLO succeeded in getting the United Nations to declare Zionism, rather than its own charter, to be a form of racism. As US ambassador to the UN Daniel Moynihan pointed out when he rejected the "Zionism Is Racism" resolution, the racism and anti-Semitism of those decades were all the more dangerous because they draped themselves in the language of national liberation and inalienable rights.

In both East and West, hostility to Israel brought these Germans membership in a global club. Indeed, for the radical Arab states and the Palestinian terror organizations, East Germany became "the good Germans" – the ones who despised Israel. As noted, West German leftists gained valuable support from Palestinian organizations including escape routes, military training, weapons, collaboration in terrorist attacks, and money. For East Germany, antagonism to Israel yielded the enormous international political benefits of diplomatic recognition and popularity on full display at the United Nations in New York, where it helped build huge majorities in the UN General Assembly denouncing Israel's sins. Ironically in view of its firm opposition to a "right of return" for the 11 million Germans who fled or were expelled from Eastern Europe during and after World War II, East Germany came to adopt a right of return for the Palestinians. It never acknowledged its own inconsistency in insisting that abandonment of the right of return in Europe and its implementation in the Middle East were both preconditions of peace.

The East German government and West German leftist organizations adopted the following policies for reporting and narrating the events of the Middle East conflict. The first and most important was that in every instance of disputed factual claims, it took the view that the government of Israel was lying and that the Arab states and PLO and affiliated organizations were speaking the truth. Second, East German Communists and West German radical leftists repeated the claim of the PLO that Zionism was a form of racism and was to be associated with colonialism and imperialism, and Israel was to be described as a state bereft of moral legitimacy. Third, the press and other media omitted or failed to report attacks by Arab states or terrorist attacks by the Palestinian organizations in Israel or, if they published them, did not offer accurate details about dead and injured Jews. If attacks were aimed specifically at Israeli civilians, they were to be presented instead as part of a justified "armed struggle" against Israeli armed forces and thus never described as terrorism. Fourth, at the same time, Communist and leftist propagandists insisted that Israel did not face any serious military threats. They described all of its efforts at self-defense as acts of unprovoked aggression. Fifth, they did not publish reports about Arab and Palestinian celebrations of terrorist attacks on Israeli civilians, even if the celebrations were published in Arab and Palestinian newspapers or broadcast on radio. The Arab and Palestinian political culture praising "martyrdom" and support for terror was not a subject for discussion. Sixth, if Arab and Palestinian civilians were killed or wounded in the course of Israel's counterterrorism operations, the numbers provided by the PLO and the Arab states were to be taken as reliable. If there were deaths and injuries to civilians, they were described as the result of intentional Israeli policy, not unintended collateral damage. Seventh, the East Germans in particular denounced assertions that the PLO and its affiliated organizations were engaged in terrorism as forms of slander and defamation. Eighth, they denied assertions that Communist policy amounted to support for a war to destroy the state of Israel and thus they themselves posed a threat to peace. The Communists and radical Left merely wanted to see the realization of Palestinians' "inalienable rights" in a "political solution" of the Middle East conflict. Finally, they claimed that the policies of the Soviet bloc, the West German Left, and the Arab states at war with Israel had nothing to do with anti-Semitism, that is, hatred of Jews or Judaism. Accusations of anti-Semitism were, they claimed, an instrument of imperialist propaganda intended to discredit wrongly those struggling against colonialism, racism and imperialism and for human rights, peace and justice.

The decade of the 1970s up to the Israeli invasion of Lebanon was a particularly dark chapter in the history of East German and West German leftist engagement in the Middle East conflict. The preceding chapters draw on the astonishingly detailed reports about the Palestinian terrorist attacks of those years written by Israel's ambassadors to the UN, Yosef Tekoah, Chaim Herzog, and Yehuda Blum. These reports made clear that the purpose of the attacks was to kill and wound Israeli civilians, seize them as hostages to compel release of terrorists held in Israeli prisons, and in general make life in Israel dangerous and intolerable. East Germany joined the majority of members of the General Assembly in responding to these reports with indifference. In neither the public nor archival records of the East German regime did I find expressions of concern, not to mention revulsion, over the stories of Israeli civilians murdered in cold blood, children thrown to their deaths from upper floors of apartment buildings, passengers tied to their seats in buses that were then blown up, or Katyusha rocket attacks on towns and villages at all hours of the night and day. East German diplomats in Beirut and Damascus could hear the same celebrations of these attacks that so appalled the American ambassador to Lebanon, G. McMurtrie Godley. If the German representatives found them repellent, they did not record their sentiments in their memos to the East German Foreign Ministry. Indeed, in the same months in which the PLO was killing and wounding Israeli civilians in Israel, the East German government accorded Arafat the honors usually given to a respected head of state.

It was precisely in the midst of the PLO's campaign against the towns and villages of northern Israel from 1970 to 1982 that the Soviet bloc, including East Germany, intensified deliveries of weapons and military training to the terrorists, who were using Lebanon as a base for their attacks. East German weapons flowed as well to the PFLP and PDFLP, organizations that boasted of their participation in gruesome actions against Israeli civilians. Israel's capture of the PLO arsenal and then the expulsion of Arafat and the PLO leadership from Beirut in 1982 represented a significant defeat for Soviet and East German policy in the Middle East. It eliminated the most proximate military threat to Israel from the forces of primarily secular Arab radicalism that had emerged in the 1960s. By fall of 1982, it was clear that the Soviets and East Germans had lost their bet on the PLO. After that war, Israel would face many challenges, but, barring a shattering of its alliance with the United States, the prospect of a military defeat inflicted by the PLO or the PLO in collaboration with one or more of the secular nationalist Arab states ceased to be realistic.

Unlike East Germany, whose policies toward the Middle East were, as discussed previously, determined at least to some extent by its membership in the Soviet bloc, the West German leftist turn against Israel was the result of autonomous and voluntary decisions based on ideological conviction. As with the radical Left around the world, opposition to the American war in Vietnam was a central cause for the West German New Left and its successors. Because of its connection to the consequences of Nazism and the Holocaust, the conflict between Israel, the Arabs and the Palestinians struck a nerve in parts of the West German Left in ways that the wars in Southeast Asia could not. Dieter Kunzelmann's pleas in 1969 for his comrades to overcome their "Jewish complex" and support "the fighting Fedayeen" against Israel were pioneering texts of West German radical leftist anti-Semitism and hatred of Israel. So too was Ulrike Meinhof's 1972 essay celebrating the Black September attack on the Israeli athletes at the Munich Olympics as an "anti-imperialist, anti-fascist and internationalist" deed. In the process, she became the most famous person in postwar West German history to openly celebrate the killing of Jews. West German government investigations after the Munich attack disclosed the role of the General Union of Palestinian Students (GUPS) and the General Union of Palestinian Workers (GUPA) in offering political support for the terrorist war on Israel. Subsequent West German government investigations revealed GUPS's presence in many West German universities and its advocacy of terrorism in the Middle East. In his order banning both organizations in September 1972, then–Interior Minister Hans Dietrich Genscher and the West German judicial investigating judges concluded that both organizations were working to open a "front" for the PLO in West Germany and supporting the use of violence to achieve their political goals. Genscher was emphatic that the West German government would not allow front organizations of the PLO to use its territory to support a terrorist campaign against Israel or against Jews and Israel's supporters living in West Germany.

Walter Ulbricht and Erich Honecker's East Germany adopted precisely the opposite policy. In the aftermath of the Munich attack and the ban on GUPS and GUPA, they tolerated and encouraged the use of East Germany as a base for operations against Israel and welcomed Palestinian members of GUPS who had been expelled from West Germany to study in East Germany. East Germany benefited from the West German ban of GUPS and GUPS in several ways. First, the Arab states portrayed Genscher's decision as an "anti-Arab" measure, that is, as a manifestation of prejudice rather than counterterrorism. It was, they said, indicative of West Germany's support for Israel, support that angered the Arab leaders. East Germany gained favor as the German state that, in contrast to the government in Bonn, was an enemy of Israel and a supporter of the Arab states and Palestinian organizations. Second, because the East Germans welcomed some of the Palestinians who had been expelled from the Federal Republic, they earned more goodwill from the PLO and the Arab states. Though East Germany's leaders were aware of West German revelations of the links among Black September, the PLO and Arafat, they accepted the public fiction that the PLO had no connection to Black September. It was in the months following the Black September attack that East Germany's relations with the PLO gained so much momentum that a year later East Germany became the first state in the Soviet bloc to agree to open a PLO office in its capital city.

The historic importance of the Entebbe hijacking in 1976 was threefold. First, so far as we know, it was the first and only time after 1945 that Germans, East or West, pointed machine guns at unarmed Jews and threatened to kill them. Wilfried Böse and Brigitte Kuhlmann, both members of the West German Revolutionary Cells group, participated in separating Jewish and non-Jewish, and Israeli and non-Israeli hostages from one another, an act that obliterated the distinction between anti-Zionism and anti-Semitism. Second, Böse, though not one of the leading theorists for which the New Left was well-known, was not a marginal figure in the West German, especially the Frankfurt/Main, radical Left. Third, the Entebbe operation was made possible by collaboration between West German radical leftists and the government of Uganda's president, Idi Amin, whose admiration for Hitler and approval of the Holocaust and of the attack on the Israelis in Munich in 1972 were matters of public record.

Following the opening of the PLO office in East Berlin in 1973, American officials, including secretary of state Kissinger and David Klein at the US mission in West Berlin, told Soviet officials in East Berlin that the United States would hold the Soviet Union responsible for preventing terrorist attacks in West Berlin and West Germany that originated in East Germany. American and West Berlin officials were aware of the ease with which Arabs, including Palestinians, could travel from the Middle East to Berlin-Schönefeld airport in East Berlin and from there to West Berlin and West Germany. By 1979, the East German minister of state security Erich Mielke, and deputy minister Gerhard Neiber, as well as other high-ranking Stasi officials, formulated what I have called East Germany's Eurocentric definition of counterterrorism. The policy was to accomplish three goals: preserve the credibility of East Germany's public declarations of opposition to terrorism; ward off the dangers to détente in Europe posed by terrorist attacks in Western Europe that could be traced back to the Soviet bloc; and continue the Soviet bloc's and East Germany's undeclared war against Israel and support for other Communist and radical leftist movements in the third world.

In 1980, the Stasi signed formal agreements of cooperation with Abu Ayad, the head of the PLO intelligence service, to implement these policies. Speaking with his Stasi counterparts, Ayad dispensed with the euphemisms and apologia offered by Soviet-bloc diplomats at the United Nations. He said that the PLO supported "terrorist forces that are active in the interest of the Palestinian resistance movement" and even supported other terrorist forces, at times working together with them. Ayad understood terrorism to be the intentional targeting of civilians – something distinct from acts of war carried out against military forces. In relevant United Nations committees, the PLO, East Germany and the Soviet bloc as a whole dismissed Western attacks on "international terrorism" as imperialist propaganda. When speaking frankly to one another, however, Stasi officials used refreshing candor, acknowledging the nature of terrorism and their willingness to support it, provided that doing so did not damage East Germany's national interests.

The cooperation of the Stasi with the PLO was beneficial to both parties. First, military training would aid the PLO and organizations such as the PFLP in their terrorist campaign against Israel and help protect the PLO from attacks by Israel's secret service, the Mossad. Second, by giving the Stasi information about other Arab and Palestinian terrorist organizations, the PLO would aid the East Germans in preventing them from using East German territory as a base from which to launch attacks in West Germany and Western Europe. The resulting Eurocentric definition of East German counterterrorism meant that the Stasi would assist the Palestinian terrorist organizations in continuing their war against Israel and other "imperialist" targets in the developing world. At the same time it would benefit from the PLO's deeper knowledge of the world of international terrorism to prevent attacks in West Berlin, West Germany, and Western Europe that could be traced back to the Soviet bloc in general or East Germany in particular. Counterterrorism in East Berlin meant diverting terrorist attacks that had any connection to East Germany away from Europe and toward Israel or to other targets in the third world. The attack on the La Belle disco in West Berlin in 1986 by agents of the Libyan "People's Bureau" in East Berlin was an exception that proved the rule. The Libyans did not play by the Soviet-bloc rules, and the Stasi, either through incompetence or intention, failed to prevent the attack. If the Stasi, over the years, had wanted to prevent the PLO and its affiliates from using East Germany as a base from which to attack Israel, it could have done so. As its training and weapons programs indicated, it did just the reverse.

The East German Politburo was the central decision-making institution in East Germany, yet the Defense Ministry and Council of Ministers were central for the delivery of the largest number of weapons to the Arab states. The files of the offices of Heinz Hoffmann, Willi Stoph, and Gerhard Weiss contain details of the emerging alliance between East Germany and the Arab states, an alliance manifest in weapons deliveries and military training programs. They also complement the Stasi files to offer details of "Action Friendship," the program in which the Defense Ministry joined the Stasi to offer military assistance to non-state armed leftist guerrilla movements around the world. The information in these East German files confirms the broad outlines of CIA analyses written at the time about the strategic priority that the Soviet Union and its allies assigned to the Middle Eastern theater of the Cold War.

The collapse of the Communist regimes in Eastern Europe, including East Germany, in 1989, followed by the demise of the Soviet Union in 1991, was a catastrophe for secular Arab radicalism. With the disappearance of the Soviet bloc went its military, political, diplomatic and economic support for the Arab states and for the PLO and its Executive Committee affiliates, the PFLP and PDFLP. These events may have been one of the factors behind Arafat's turn to the Oslo peace process, a hypothesis that will await further research. It seems plausible, however, that as Arafat no longer had a realistic possibility of destroying Israel by force of arms, the diplomatic route became unavoidable. The UN continued to be, in Daniel Moynihan's phrase, "a dangerous place" for Israel. Yet in 1991, the General Assembly voted 111 to 25, with 13 abstentions, to revoke the "Zionism Is Racism" resolution of 1975. That would most probably not have happened if the Soviet bloc had been intact.

For the Israelis who were killed or wounded, either as civilians or in the armed forces in these years, it made no difference whether their enemies were motivated by the atavism of anti-Semitism or the more fashionable anti-Zionism of the global Left. The idea that seeking the destruction of the Jewish state had nothing to do with hatred of the Jews was one of the central leftist illusions of this era. However, whether or not they were motivated by hatred of the Jews, one consequence of the secular radical leftist attack on Israel in Germany and elsewhere was opposition to examination of anti-Semitism in the Arab or leftist context. The East German anti-Israeli passion shared this stance with its West German counterpart: for both what Heinz Hoffmann called "the community of struggle" against the common Israeli enemy displaced concerns about the existence of anti-Semitism among their Arab and Palestinian Arab allies. The centrality of the Soviet and East German alliance with Baathist Syria was a key example of such indifference. The East German dictatorship was a different kind of dictatorship from its Nazi predecessor but, albeit for different reasons, it became the second German dictatorship to regard Zionism as an enemy.

In defining the traditions of leftist anti-fascism to justify the attack on Israel, the global secular Left – the Communists in the Soviet bloc as well as the third-world Western radical Left – developed dangerous political habits. They lent respectability to hatreds of the Jewish state, of Zionism, and, yes, at times Jews as well, which they had lost so long as they were associated with the defeated and disgraced Nazi regime and the movements of European fascism. From the late 1960s to the mid-1980s, in the era of détente in the 1970s and of the tensions of the second Cold War of the 1980s, the Communists and radical leftists did more than launch ideological offensives at the state of Israel. They took the leap from ideology to acts of war and terrorism.

In 2008, Germany's chancellor Angela Merkel, who came of age in East Germany, addressed the Israeli parliament, the Knesset. She reaffirmed Germany's traditions of *Vergangenheitsbewältigung*, coming to terms with the Nazi past, and declared that Israel's survival was part of Germany's reason of state. Merkel's bold and welcome words were a rebuke to the ideas and policies examined in this book. Nevertheless, though defeated, the Communists and radical leftists of the last decades of the Cold War left behind a toxic ideological brew. Their distortions about the history of the state of Israel, their extensive use of terrorism, and their justifications for it have cast a long and destructive shadow over politics and political culture in the Middle East, in Germany, and around the world.

Bibliography

Primary Sources

Bundesarchiv Berlin (BAB), Berlin Lichterfelde, Stiftung Archiv der Parteien und Massenorganisationen der DDR im Bundesarchive (SAPMO)
(German Federal Archive, Berlin Lichterfelde, Foundation Archives of Parties and Mass Organisations of the GDR in the Federal Archives)

DY 30 DY 30/J IV 2/2/	Büro des Politburo des Zentralkomittee (ZK) der Sozialistische Einheitspartei (SED).
DY 30 IVB/2/20/	Abteilung Internationale Verbindungen des ZK der SED, 1946–1989
DY 30/B2/20/	Abteilung für Sicherheitsfragen des ZK d. SED, 1972–1980
DY/30	ZK der SED, Büro Honecker
DY/30	ZK der SED, Büro Ulbricht
DY 30/B2/2.023/89	ZK der SED, Büro Gerhard Grüneberg
NL/182	Nachlass Walter Ulbricht
DC 20	Ministerrat der DDR Regierungen bis November 1989. – Teil 1: Ministerpräsident/Vorsitzende des Ministerrates (1949–1989), Außenpolitische Angelegenheiten, Außenhandel

Bundesarchiv-Koblenz (BAK) (German Federal Archive, Koblenz)

Bundesministerium des Innern B106, Terroranschlag auf die Israelische Olympiamannschaft und seine Folgen (8 folders)

Bundesministerium des Innern, B 106 (Extensive files on terrorism in 1970s and 1980s)

Bundesminiseterium für Justiz, B 141, Generalbundesanwalt beim Bundesgerichtshof

Bundesministerium des Innern, B 443, Bundesamt für Verfassungsschutz

Informationen des Bundesamtes für Verfassungsschutz
Bundespräsident, B 122
Bundeskanzleramt, B 136
Die Kabinettsprotokolle der Bundesregierung
Referat B 6: Bilder, Karte, Plakate, Tonträger

Bundesarchiv-Militärarchiv (BA-MA), Freiburg (German Federal Archive, Military Archive, Freiburg)

AZN	Ministerium für Nationale Verteidigung (MfNV)
DVWI	MfNV, Sekretariat des Ministers (Heinz Hoffmann)

Bundesbeauftragte für die Unterlagen des Staatssicherheitsdienstes der ehemaligen Deutschen Demokratischen Republik (BStU) (Federal Commissioner for the Records of the State Security Services of the Former German Democratic Republic, Berlin)

MfS	Ministerium für Staatssicherheit
BCD	Bewaffnung und Chemischer Dienst
HA I	Hauptabteilung I Abwehrarbeit in NVA und Grenztruppen
HA II	Hauptabteilung II Spionageabwehr
HA VII	Hauptabteilung VII Beobachtung/Ermittlung
HA X	Hauptabteilung X Internationale Verbindungen
HA XII	Hauptabteilung XII: Auskunft, Speicher, Archiv
HA XX ZMA	Hauptabteilung XX ZMA
HA XXII	Hauptabteilung XXII Terrorabwehr
HA A	Hauptabteilung Aufklärung
ZAIG	Zentrale Auswertungs- und Informationsgruppe
ZKG	Zentrale Koordinierungsgruppe (ZKG): Flucht, Übersiedlung
ZMA	Zentrale Materialablage
Finanzen	Abteilung Finanzen
Sekr. Neiber	Sekretariat Gerhard Neiber
Sekr. d. Min	Sekretariat des Ministers (Erich Mielke)
AOP	Archivierter operative Vorgang

Freie Universität, APO-Archiv (Ausserparlementarischen Organizationen Archive) (Archive of Extra-Parliamentary Organizations, Free University of Berlin)

SDS-Archiv (u.a. Archiv des Bundesvorstandes des Sozialistischen Deutschen Studentenbundes)

National Consortium for the Study of Terrorism and Responses to Terrorism (START) University of Maryland, College Park (2013). Global Terrorism Database. Retrieved from www.start.umd.edu/gtd

Israel, 1970–1990

Institut für Sozialforschung Hamburg, Archiv, Sondersammlung, Protestbewegungen (Archive of the Hamburg Institute for Social Research, Special Collection, Protest Movements)

Zeitschriften/Broschuren Palästina, Al Tahrir: Zeitschrift des Komitee zur Unterstützung der Kämpfenden Völker im Nahen und Mittleren Osten, (Cologne, 1973)

Agit 883: Revolte, Underground in West Berlin, 1969–1972

Al-Thaura: Zeitschrift des Palästina Kommittee Bonn

Arbeiterkampf: Arbeiterzeitung des kommunistischen Bundes

Internationale Solidarität

Kommunismus und Klassenkampf

Kommunistische Volkszeitung

Palästina Blatt (Heidelberg)

Palästinensische Revolution, 1969–1971

Tahrir. Befreiung Zeitschrift des Komitees zur Unterstützung der Kämpfenden Völker im Nahen und Mittleren Osten

SDS 130	Bundeskonferenzen, Delegiertenkonferenzen
SDS 140	Diskussionspapiere, Organisationsdebatte, Politische Initiativen
SDS	Blattsammlung, Presse, Flugblatter, Entwicklung des SDS im Jahr 1967

Heidelberg, Zentralarchiv zur Erforschung der Geschichte der Juden in Deutschland (Heidelberg, Central Archive for Research on the History of the Jews in Germany)

B.8 Zentralrat 1	Jüdischer Presse Dienst, 1965–1974 Sonderinformation
B.8 Bonn Zentralrat	Jüdischer Presse Dienst
B.8 Berlin 1	*Für unsere Mitglieder*
B.8. Frankfurt 3	*Frankfurter Jüdisches Gemeindeblatt 1968–1986*
B.1/7. 516	POV b-C 1952-
B.1/7 K	Ginsburg, Alexander, Generalsekretär des Zentralrat der Juden in Deutschland bis 1988
	Allgemeine Jüdische Wochenzeitung
	Berliner Allgemeine Jüdische Wochenzeitung
B.8 Frankfurt 7	[Frankfurter] *Jüdische Nachrichten 1960–1980*
B.8 München 6	*Münchener Jüdische Nachrichten*
B.1/7	Nah Ost

International Institute of Social History, Amsterdam (IISH)

Antiimperialistisches Solidaritätskomittee (ASK) (Frankfurt/Main) Collection, ASK, Palästina Solidarität BRD F, 1977–1988

Library of Congress, Washington, D.C.

British Broadcasting Corporation (BBC) Summary of World Broadcasts, Part 4, The Middle East and Africa Library of Congress, (microfiche)

The Papers of Daniel Patrick Moynihan (Manuscript Reading Room)

Militärhistorisches Museum der Bundeswehr, Berlin, Flugplatz Berlin-Gatow
(Military history Museum of the Bundeswehr, Berlin, Berlin-Gatow Airport)

National Archives and Records Administration of the United States, College Park, Maryland (NACP)

General Records of the Department of State, Record Group (RG) 59
Central Foreign Policy Files, Diplomatic Records, Electronic Telegrams, 1/1/1973–12/31/1973
Central Foreign Policy Files, Diplomatic Records, Electronic Telegrams, 1/11974–12/31/1974
CIA Records Search Tool CREST (CIA database of declassified intelligence documents)

National Archives and Records Administration, Washington, D.C. (NARA)

Hearings, Committee on Foreign Affairs of the House of Representatives, Emergency Security Assistance Act of 1973, 93rd Congress (November 30 and December 3, 1973)

Politisches Archiv des Auswärtiges Amt (PAAA), Berlin
(Political Archive of the German Foreign Office)

Ministerium für Auswärtige Angelegenheiten (MFAA), Deutschen Demokratische Republik, DDR

(Ministry of Foreign Relations, German Democratic Republic)
Außereuropäische Abteilung
Abteilung Arabische Staaten Gesamtarabische Fragen
Abt. Naher- und Mittlereer Osten
Abteilung UNO. [United Nations]
Aktivitäten der Ständigen Vertretung der DDR bei den Vereinten Nationen, 1974–1975
Abteilung Recht
Berichte und Positionspapiere zu den 28.-34. UNO-Vollversammlungen, 6. Kommitte, 1973–1979

Auswärtiges Amt, Bundesrepublik Deutschland

(Foreign Office, Federal Republic of Germany)

Bestand 83, Referat 511, Strafrecht, Steurer-und Zollercht, 1952–1972, 1973–1994
Bestand 530: Terrorismus
Bestand 36, Naher Osten und Nordafrika
Bestand 38, Referat 210, Außenpolitische Fragen, die Berlin und Deutschland als Ganzes betreffen, Beziehungen DDR zu 3. Staaten / Länder
Bestand 130, Referat IB4 92.-82.00 SB
Bestand 2, Büro Staatssekretäre (014), 1949–1998
Bestand 1, Büro Bundesminister (010)

Staatsanwaltschaft bei dem Landgericht Frankfurt am Main (Office of the District Attorney, Frankfurt/Main)

Ermittlungsverfarhen gegen Sufian Radi Kaddoumi und Musa Badawi Jawher, Ersaztakten, Hauptakten, Bd II, III, IV, 61/51/22/ Js 2/76

United Nations Archive, New York

General Assembly, Official Records (some online, some on microfiche at UN Archive, New York, or at United Nations depositories)

Records of the Security Council sessions are online; many but not all records of General Assembly Sessions are also available in the online Official Documents System

Committee for the Exercise of the Inalienable Rights of the Palestinian People, unispal.un.org/unispal.nsf/Web%20Search%20Simple2?OpenForm

Letters to the Secretary General and to the President of the Security Council by Member States UN Official Documents System (online)

United Nations, online Official Documents System (ODS): /documents.un.org/

Also see *UN Yearbook* for citations to documents in ODS system

Newspapers, Journals, Radio Stations

Al Ahram
Al-Thaura
Allgemeine unabhängige jüdische Wochenzeitung
Arbeiterkampf
Aus Politik und Zeitgeschichte
Berliner Allgemeine jüdische Wochenzeitung
Die Welt
Die Zeit
Deutschland Archiv
Frankfurter Allgemeine Zeitung
Frankfurter Rundschau
Haaretz
Jerusalem Post
Jüdische Allgemeine Wochenzeitung
Jüdischer Presse Dienst, Informationen des Zentralrats der Juden in Deutschland
Kommunismus und Klassenkampf
Links
Los Angeles Times
New York Times
Neues Deutschland
Palastina Blatt
Pflasterstrand
Quick
Der Spiegel

Süddeutsche Zeitung
Voice of Palestine (Cairo, Damascus, Beirut and clandestine broadcasts).
Washington Post

Published Documents and Memoirs

Akten zur Auswärtigen Politik der Bundesrepublik Deutschland, Bde. 5–25, (Munich: Oldenbourg, 1965–1984)

Allertz, Robert with Gerhard Neiber, Die RAF und das MfS (Berlin: Edition Ost, 2008)

Axen, Hermann, *Ich war ein Diener der Partei: Autobiographische Gespräche mit Harald Neubert* (Berlin: Edition Ost, 1996)

Bator, Wolfgang and Angelika Bator, eds., *Die DDR und die arabischen Staaten Dokumente 1956–1982* ([East] Berlin: Staatsverlag der Deutschen Demokratischen Republik, 1984)

Ben-Natan, Asher, *Die Chutzpe zu Leben: Stationen meines Lebens* (Dusseldorf: Droste, 2003)

Der Blues: Gesammelte Texte der Bewegung 2. Juni ([West] Berlin: 1982

Biographical Register, Department of State, United States of America

Dokumente zur Außenpolitik der Deutschen Demokratischen Republik ([East] Berlin: Staatsverlag der Deutschen Demokratischen Republik)

Der Einigungsvertrag: Vertrag zwischen der Bundesrepublik Deutschland und der Deutschen Demokratische Republik über die Herstellung der Einheit Deutschlands (Munich: Goldmann Verlag, 1991)

Foreign Broadcast Information Service (FBIS), United States Government, *FBIS Daily Reports, Eastern Europe; Middle East; Africa; Sub-Saharan Africa,* Library of Congress, infoweb.newsbank.com, onsite online access

Foreign Relations of the United States (FRUS), 1969–1976, Volume XXV, Arab-Israeli Crisis and War, 1973, Nina Howland and Craig Daigle, eds., (Washington, D.C.: United States Government Printing Office, 2011)

Frangi, Abdallah, *Der Gesandte: Mein Leben für Palästina: Hinter den Kulissen der Nahost-Politik* (Munich: Wilhelm Heyne Verlag, 2010)

Die Früchte des Zorns: Texte und Materialien zur Geschichte der Revolutionären Zellen und der Roten Zora, Band I, (Edition ID-Archiv: Berlin, 1993)

International Institute for Strategic Studies, London, *The Military Balance,* 1967–1980

Israel Ministry of Foreign Affairs, Historical Documents: mfa.gov.il/MFA/ForeignPolicy/MFADocuments/Pages/Documents_Foreign_Policy_Israel.aspx

Klein, Hans-Joachim, *Rückkehr in die Menschlichkeit: Appell eines ausgestiegenen Terroristen* (Reinbek bei Hamburg: Rowohlt, 1979)

Kraushaar, Wolfgang, ed. *Frankfurter Schule und Studentenbewegung: Von der Flaschenpost zum Molotowcocktail 1946 bis 1995: Chronik,* 2 vols. (Hamburg: Rogner & and Bernhard, 1998)

Middle East Media Research Institute, MEMRI (website)

Protokolle der Volkskammer der Deutschen Demokratischen Republik 10 Wahlperiode (5. April bis 2. Oktober 1990), Band I–III, Nachdruck (Bonn: Deutscher Bundestag; Leske and Budrich, 2000)

Quellen zur Geschichte des Parlamentarismus und der Politischen Parteien, Vierte Reihe 13/VI, Der Auswärtige Ausschuß des Deutschen Bundestages, Sitzungsprotokolle, 1969–1972, Erster und Zweiter Halbband, Wolfgang Hölscher, et al., eds., (Dusseldorf: Droste Verlag, 2007)

Rote Armee Fraktion: Texte und Materialien: Texte und Materialien zur Geschichte der RAF (Berlin: ID Verlag, 1997)

Sindermann, Horst, *Alles für das Volk – alles mit dem Volk: Ausgewählte Reden und Aufsätze* (Berlin: Dietz Verlag, 1985)

Stoph, Willi, *Zur weitern Entwicklung der Sozialistischen Gesellschaft in der DDR: Reden und Aufsätze* (Berlin: Dietz Verlag, 1974)

Tlass, Mustafa Tlass, *The Matzo of Zion* (Damascus: Tlass Publishing House, 1991)

Verfassungsschutzbericht, (Bonn: Bundesinnenministerium, 1968–1980)

Verhandlungen des deutschen Bundestages (1965–1989)

Wolf, Markus, *Man without a Face: The Autobiography of Communism's Greatest Spymaster* (New York: Times Books/Random House, 1997)

Yearbook of the United Nations, 1967–1990

Index